The Main Event

Readings for Writing and Critical Thinking

Catherine A. Hoffman
San Diego State University

Andrew J. Hoffman
San Diego Mesa College

PEARSON

Prentice
Hall

Upper Saddle River, New Jersey 07458

Library of Congress Cataloging-in-Publication Data

Hoffman, Catherine A.
  The main event : readings for writing and critical thinking / by Catherine A. Hoffman, Andrew J. Hoffman.
    p. cm.
  Includes index.
  ISBN 0-13-048658-2
  1. College readers.   2. English language—Rhetoric—Problems, exercises, etc.   3. Critical thinking—Problems, exercises, etc.   4. Report writing—Problems, exercises, etc   I. Hoffman, Andrew J.   II. Title.

  PE1417.H59 2005
  808'.0427—dc22

                                                                    2004014879

Editorial Director: Leah Jewell
Senior Acquisitions Editor: Brad Potthoff
Assistant Editor: Jennifer Conklin
Editorial Assistant: Steve Kyritz
Executive Marketing Manager: Brandy Dawson
Marketing Assistant: Allison Peck
Production Liaison: Fran Russello
Manufacturing Buyer: Mary Ann Gloriande
Cover Design: Kiwi Design
Cover Image: Wayne J. Hoffman, "Catalina Sunset", oil on canvas, 24 × 30.

Permissions Specialist: The Permissions Group
Manager, Cover Visual Research and Permissions: Karen Sanatar
Project Management: Karen Berry/ Pine Tree Composition, Inc.
Composition: Pine Tree Composition, Inc.
Printer/Binder: Phoenix Book Technology Park
Cover Printer: Phoenix Book Technology Park

Credits and acknowledgments borrowed from other sources and reproduced, with permission, in this textbook appear on pages 761–767.

Pearson Education LTD., London
Pearson Education Singapore, Pte. Ltd
Pearson Education Canada, Ltd.
Pearson Education–Japan
Pearson Education Australia PTY, Limited

Pearson Education North Asia Ltd
Pearson Educación de Mexico, S.A. de C.V.
Pearson Education Malaysia, Pte. Ltd
Pearson Education, Upper Saddle River, New Jersey

10 9 8 7 6 5 4 3 2 1
ISBN 0-13-048658-2

This book is dedicated to my father, with all my love, whose intelligence, common sense, and creativity have inspired me always

— C. A. H.

Contents

Chapter 1　Film and Television　15

Chapter 2　Democracy in the Classroom　76

Chapter 3　Dreams　149

Chapter 4   Marriage and Divorce   197

Chapter 5   American Cities and Towns   255

Chapter 6   Technology and Society   309

Chapter 7   Your Body   353

Chapter 8   Youth Culture   425

Chapter 9   Biographies   486

Chapter 10   Fairy Tales   530

Chapter 11   The Justice System   592

Chapter 12   Jobs in the 21st Century   673

Preface

In today's classroom, students are looking for relevance in the curriculum. They want to know that what they are learning has practical applications, both in their future studies and in the world beyond schooling. Facing this is the composition instructor. One tool for the instructor is a reading text that provides articles and essays that are interesting, challenging, and relevant. A composition instructor needs a text that provides practical advice and solid examples of composition. Of course, instruction on critical thinking skills is an important facet of many composition courses, so the selected text must help students learn this vital skill, too. In short, teaching composition involves the teaching of reading, writing, and critical thinking. An instructor needs a text designed for that task.

The Main Event: Readings for Writing and Critical Thinking is a thematic reader that meets the needs of freshman English and composition courses in which reading, writing, and critical thinking form the core of the instruction. The reader allows instructors to explore a particular subject of relevance to today's students. In each chapter, there is a featured essay, called the Main Event Reading. The Main Event Reading is the work on which that chapter's instruction on reading, writing, and critical thinking is based, giving all lessons a common ground. The Main Event Reading is followed by the writing assignment. The writing assignment in each chapter covers a different type of writing, both academic and practical. In this way, instructors can build a course with confidence, knowing their students will gain experience writing for a variety of situations.

Building a course with *The Main Event* is easy. An advantage of the Main Event format is that instructors can choose which types of writing assignments they wish to cover and feel comfortable that the pedagogy in each chapter is tailored to suit the needs of each writing situation. The writing lessons are practical, and each chapter presents a sample essay written for each particular type of writing situation. The themes in this text meet both the academic requirements of freshman English and composition courses and the interests of many college students.

Instructors have a choice of twelve thematic chapters, with twelve different types of writing assignments. The chapters are essentially self-contained, so instructors can teach any selection of the chapters. To design a course, instructors can choose the themes they want to teach, confident that the writing lessons, assignments, and readings will provide good opportunities for learning. Because the instruction is based on the Main Event Reading, instructors and students are provided with a context for each writing lesson. Beyond each Main Event Reading, there are six to eight additional readings in each chapter. The text provides many opportunities to provide students with good reading, writing, and critical thinking instruction.

Critical thinking skills are an increasingly vital aspect of all college classrooms, and in college writing classes, these skills may be used to analyze readings and to produce written materials, such as essays and term papers. Consequently, *The Main Event* helps with this process by not only providing critical thinking questions for each reading in the text, but also by integrating critical thinking skills into the writing lessons. Critical thinking is not separate from but an essential element of good writing.

FEATURES OF *THE MAIN EVENT*

The Main Event begins with an Introduction to Reading that covers the basics of reading college-level material. Included in the introduction is instruction on reading for meaning, highlighting, separating facts and inferences, and analyzing the credibility of an author. The Introduction to Reading provides students with the thinking tools needed to succeed in critically analyzing the readings. We highly recommend instructors assign the Introduction to Reading early in the semester, if not at the very start.

Following the introduction are twelve chapters, each on a different theme. Each chapter contains the following features:

The Main Event Reading

Each chapter begins with a Main Event Reading that serves as the *context* for the lessons. It is also the principal reading for most of the critical thinking questions, and the sample paper is based on a response to this reading. The reading is marked with handwritten margin notes, serving as a model for students to see how to mark up a text themselves. The margin notes encourage students to consider the important questions that each Main Event Reading presents. In other words, as students are reading the text, they are thinking critically.

Preceding each reading is a list of vocabulary words with definitions. Following the reading are three sets of questions. The first questions are "What Did You Read?" questions that encourage students to read for comprehension. Questions labeled "What Do You Think?" provoke inquiry and discussion about each reading that can also provide alternative writing contexts to the Main Event Writing Assignment questions. Lastly, "How Was It Done?" questions explore the rhetorical strategies embedded in each essay, helping students examine how professional writers choose to organize and develop their essays.

The Main Event Writing Assignment

Each chapter introduces a new writing assignment. Each assignment provides four to five different questions as options for the assignment. The questions are not only based on the issues raised directly by the Main Event Reading, but also by the theme of the chapter itself. Students do not have to be limited by the Main Event Reading if they wish to investigate other areas related to the theme. Each Main Event Writing Assignment requires a different approach and form from those found in other chapters, giving students more variety and practical experience in confronting different writing situations.

Preparation Punch List

This is a suggested list of questions that instructors and students can consider *before* beginning the drafting process. The Preparation Punch List guides students in thinking about their writing options, and the types of reading and research they might need to do *before* composing their essays. The list can also provide instructors with questions to stimulate in-class discussions. Of course, the list is only a starting point. As a prewriting exercise, the punch list can help students brainstorm their own ideas.

The Main Event Writing Lesson

Each chapter has a writing lesson that describes the tasks for the Main Event Writing Assignment, so students have an understanding of what each assignment requires. Emphasis is on practical considerations, including preparation for writing, form, audience, content, and presentation. Instruction is provided for the following aspects of writing:

- Basic essay form
- Definition
- Using summary in an analysis
- Conducting an interview
- Audience, tone, purpose
- Critique
- Causal analysis
- Critical analysis
- Historical analysis
- Literary analysis
- Policy report
- Research-based paper

Main Event Sample Essay

Each chapter includes a model paper, done on a question from the Main Event Writing Assignment, and which applies the Writing Lesson. Key parts of each sample paper are highlighted with margin notes. Each paper provides students not only with a good example of what a successful final product looks like, but, as the chapters proceed, each essay demonstrates increasing sophistication with incorporating research and documenting those materials in Modern Language Association (MLA) format.

Additional Readings

In addition to the Main Event Reading, each thematic section features six or seven more readings. These readings range from classic to contemporary. The additional readings also have vocabulary lists and sets of questions called "What Did You Read?", "What Do You Think?", and "How Was It Done?".

Appendices

After the last thematic chapter, there are two appendices. Appendix I presents the basics of the MLA documentation system, based on *The MLA Handbook for Writers of Research Papers*, 6th edition, and Appendix

II does the same for the American Psychological Association (APA) documentation system, based on the *Publication Manual of the American Psychological Association,* 5th edition. Examples of both in-text documentation and bibliographic entries are included in both appendices.

ACKNOWLEDGMENTS

We would like to acknowledge with sincere gratitude the efforts of those who helped to make this textbook possible. At Prentice Hall, our sponsoring editor, Corey Good, showed a strong commitment to *The Main Event* even when the textbook was in its initial rough form. For his help, his patience, and his belief in our concepts and our abilities, we are truly thankful. We would also like to thank Steve Kyritz for his helpful assistance. We wish to extend our appreciation to the marketing efforts of Brandy Dawson and Allison Peck, who let everyone know that this new book is out there, ready to be used. We would also like to thank those involved in the production of the book's final form, including Fran Russello at Prentice Hall and Karen Berry at Pine Tree Composition.

The Main Event has taken its final shape after careful review and criticism from professional educators. We gratefully offer our thanks to them. Among those who contributed to this book are Angie Pratt, Montgomery College; Chere Berman, College of the Canyons; Paul Northam, Johnson County Community College; Jennifer Vanags, Johnson County Community College; CC Ryder, West L.A. College; John Lucarelli, Community College of Allegheny County; Linda A. Archer, Green River Community College; Stephen H. Wells, Community College of Allegheny County; Terry Jolliffe, Midland College; Anthony Armstrong, Richland College; Dimitri Keriotis, Modesto Junior College; Robert G. Ford, Houston Community College; Carla L. Dando, Idaho State University; Lori Ann Stephens, Richland College; Debra Shein, Idaho State University; Cara Unger, Portland Community College; Dr. Emily Dial-Driver, Rogers State University; Jesse T. Airaudi, Baylor University; Camilla Mortensen, University of Oregon; Kathryn Neal, York Technical College; K. Siobhan Wright, Carroll Community College; Rosemary Day, Ph.D., Albuquerque Community College; Jacob Agatucci, Central Oregon Community College; Peggy Cole, Ph.D., Arapahoe Community College; and James Jenkins, Mt. San Antonio College.

Finally, we would like to extend our thanks to our students at San Diego State University and San Diego Mesa College. The prevailing wisdom is that teachers shape students; however, our interaction with many students has in fact shaped us into who we are and what we do in the classroom. It was because of these students, and for the many to come in the future, that this book was conceived and written. Of special consideration are those students who used early drafts of this book and provided helpful comments. Their classroom experiences and feedback were invaluable in molding *The Main Event* into its final form. We owe them much.

C.A.H.
A.J.H.

Introduction
Reading Critically

You might imagine that reading skills hardly need to be taught—after all, haven't you been reading since you were a child? For some, reading has been a fun activity all their lives, something they have done for pleasure. Stories of romance, ghosts, cowboys, princesses, detectives, adventurers—tales, read by a child or to a child, can fill their imagination.

However, reading in college is different, and not simply because the topics are not likely to be the same as in a child's nighttime reading. Reading is a fundamental aspect of the academic process. Much university and college curriculum requires students to read, no matter what the specific subject area may be. As a result, students who fail to read effectively will struggle with their studies. One practice that can get many college students into trouble is reading assignments without being fully engaged in the material. College students must approach reading in a way that is productive and effective.

Reading for academic purposes involves four critical components:

- Comprehension
- Demonstration
- Stimulation
- Connection

Comprehension

Reading for comprehension involves understanding the material that you have read. This might sound relatively obvious, but the ability of the reader to understand the material is fundamental to the learning process. Comprehension means that the reader knows the vocabulary of a piece, and understands the main idea and supporting ideas within a piece of writing. This means also suggests that the reader must be involved in analysis—looking at the parts of a text to see how those parts work together to form the whole. A casual or cursory reading of a text will not do; rereading a text is a powerful way to increase your comprehension. Also, using a dictionary, taking notes, and asking questions of the material can potentially help in improving your understanding of a text.

Demonstration

Much college reading serves as models to student writers of how to handle a particular writing situation. You can see how a work has been put together. Using margin notes to mark your way, you can ask important questions about the rhetorical strategies behind a text. In other words, you can follow the challenges a writer has faced throughout the writing process and the decisions that were made about what to say, where to say it, and how to say it. For example, one writer may begin an article with the definition of a key term, and another writer may choose to begin with a brief anecdote. The results of such choices shape the final work. It can be enlightening to try to examine the choices made by others and to see how that may influence the decisions you make as you write your own works.

Stimulation

A good piece of writing will stimulate your own imagination, and move you to explore ideas of your own. Much of what makes a piece of writing good is its ability to generate ideas within readers. Creativity often comes not from a vacuum but from ideas already out there. For centuries, writers have been inspired by earlier writers, creating new works that were sparked to life by the works of others before them. As student writers, you can find many ideas in the writings of others to explore and develop from your own perspective.

Connections

Texts do not exist in a void. All written works exist within the larger world—a world with many other means of artistic expression and communication. An idea from a text can make a connection to something else in your own experience or areas of interest. Ideas cross genres of expression as well, such as when a novel is made into a movie. A lesson in history class can connect with something learned in political science, and math problems cross with computer programming concerns. Things learned from reading in an academic environment also connect with the world outside of school. In fact, lessons that are not related to something within a person's realm of experience or interest often are not remembered for that very reason—there seems little point to them outside of their own context. However, reading can help you find connections. Once that connection occurs, learning becomes more meaningful.

Understanding that reading in college is a central, vital aspect of the educational process is the first part. The next step is learning how to read critically. This term can be contrasted with "casual" reading, which is reading often characterized as reading for pleasure, with less emphasis on comprehension and analysis. Casual reading has a light touch, like glancing through a newspaper while waiting for a bus. Critical reading is different, and knowing how to do it is essential for your success in the college classroom.

THE BASICS OF READING CRITICALLY

What is critical reading? The word "critical" in our everyday use has come to mean "assessing negatively," but in an academic setting, the word has a more neutral meaning. A reader must assess the material, but the assessment is not always negative. More than deciding whether you like or dislike a work, critical reading asks you to understand the work fully. You must see how it is put together logically to uncover the underpinnings of the author's presentation.

The following steps will help you to read critically. However, before you examine the list, keep one general piece of advice in mind: read with a pen or pencil in your hand. You need to learn to mark up texts in order to get the most meaning out of them. Seldom will you uncover or retain as much information if you do not.

To read critically you should:

- **Read about the author.** If a brief biography of the author is presented with the reading, check to see if the author is an expert in his or her subject, or if the author is a professional journalist. If no biography of the author is available, you can try to find the author's name in a library (by doing an "author" search) or by looking at other materials in the same subject area and finding other articles by that same author.

- **Think about the title.** Although authors do not always get to choose the titles of their own works (particularly when writing for magazines and newspapers), the title will give you a sense of the subject of the work, and perhaps even the attitude the author will take toward it.

- **Find the thesis.** The thesis is the main point or idea of the article. Sometimes the thesis is located in a single sentence, sometimes it is extended over several sentences, and sometimes the thesis is implied. By the end of the essay, you should be able to identify the thesis by answering the question, "What's the point of this essay?" Once you have found the thesis, you will be in a better position to evaluate whether or not the author has supported that thesis well. Be sure to mark the thesis!

- **Look for topic sentences.** Topic sentences are to paragraphs what the thesis is to the essay: the main point or idea. By finding the topic sentence of a paragraph, you can begin to trace the logical steps the author is making toward supporting the thesis. Topic sentences are usually found at the start of paragraphs, but not always. As with the essay, some paragraphs have no explicit topic sentence. When that happens, the relationship between the point of the paragraph and the thesis is implied.

- **Evaluate the support.** No author can expect a reader to accept a thesis without evidence to support the thesis. You should note significant pieces of evidence, and also any evidence you find suspect or illogical. Be aware of a writer's attempts to manipulate you with overly emotional appeals or unsubstantiated claims.

- **Understand what you have read.** This advice is so simple, yet so often ignored. If you come across a word you do not know, and you cannot tell its meaning from the context, look the word up. If there is a reference to a person, place, or event that you are not familiar with, find out about it. Don't just pass over something you don't understand in the hope that it "doesn't really matter."

- **Read the material more than once.** Almost all works will yield more meaning to the reader upon a second or even third reading. Seldom will you understand everything the first time through. In fact, one good strategy is to read a work the first time without marking it, and then mark it on the second read. Budget your homework time so you have enough time to do this!

In the end, none of this will work if you fail to mark the text. Use a highlighter or pen to underline significant sentences, especially the thesis and topic sentences. Use a pen or pencil to make notes in the margins. Use Post-It notes to tab important sections, particularly if you are reading a book. Remember, the key to reading critically is to keep your brain involved!

The following passage, taken from "The Stoned Screen" by Brian D. Johnson, is an example of how a passage could be marked by a critical reader:

The (Stoned) Screen   *A play on "silver screen" Why?*

Famous director Director <u>Martin Scorsese</u> once said that movies are "really a kind of dream state, like taking dope." But a lot of movies these days are not just like taking dope; they're about taking dope. Just look at   *Assumes the audience knows this?*

Greek myth — refers to a handsome young man

Means "female slave or concubine"

some of the recent Oscar nominees. In *Traffic,* a 16-year-old white girl lying in bed—an (odalisque) with baby fat—watches in a stoned reverie as a naked black man shoots heroin into her ankle. In *Requiem for a Dream,* a junkie (Adonis) probes for a vein in a black-and-blue forearm, while his mother is strung out on diet pills and TV game shows. In *Almost Famous,* a rocker on acid proclaims he's God and jumps off a roof into a pool. And now comes *Blow,* a drug-culture version of the American Dream—starring Johnny Depp as George Jung, the entrepreneur who unleashed cocaine on North America in the 1970s.

DETERMINING MAIN IDEAS AND SUBORDINATE IDEAS

An important part of reading critically is determining the main ideas and subordinate ideas in any piece of writing. Too often readers can get bogged down in details and minutia, so they miss the bigger picture as a result. Details can be important, but they need to be seen in light of main ideas.

When you are reading, you should mark the text by highlighting, underlining, or jotting notes in the margins; as you do this, you should get a good sense of what the most important ideas are. You want to be able to find the thesis of an essay. However, supporting the thesis are usually other important ideas, and supporting those ideas are the details.

One way to locate these other important ideas is to look for the topic sentences. These sentences usually present the rational basis—that is, the reasons why the author believes the thesis is true. You should find the topic sentences and evaluate them. Are they all equal in importance to the thesis? Probably not. You will want to determine which ones are more important and which are of lesser importance.

After you find the topic sentences, then you can assess the strength of the support given to each of the topic sentences. This includes looking at any quotations, paraphrases, statistics, examples, or specific personal experiences that may be used. These details support the topic sentences, and therefore they are of lesser importance. Do remember, though, that an essay built on weak support is a weak essay overall, no matter how much you may agree with the thesis.

Examine the following passage, from "Crossing Boundaries" by Mike Rose, in which the reader has marked the text to determine the difference between main ideas and subordinate ideas.

There is a strong impulse in American education—curious in   *Topic*
                                                                sentence
a country with such an ornery streak of antitraditionalism—to de-

fine achievement and excellence in terms of the acquisition of a

historically validated body of knowledge, an authoritative list of   *2nd*

books and allusions, a canon. We seek a certification of our na-   *sentence*
                                                                   continuing
tional intelligence, indeed, our national virtue, in how diligently   *the idea*

our children can display this central corpus of information. This

need for certification tends to emerge most dramatically in our   *Consequence*

educational policy debates during times of real or imagined threat:

economic hard times, political crises, sudden increases in immigra-

tion. Now is such a time, and it is reflected in a number of influen-

tial books and commission reports. E. D. Hirsch argues that a core   *Expert*
                                                                     example
national vocabulary, one oriented toward the English literate tradi-

tion—Alice in Wonderland to zeitgeist—will build a knowledge

base that will foster the literacy of all Americans. Diane Ravitch   *Another*
                                                                     example
and Chester Finn call for a return to a traditional historical and lit-   *from*
                                                                          experts
erary curriculum: the valorous historical figures and the classical

literature of the once-elite course of study. Allan Bloom, Secretary

of Education William Bennett, Mortimer Adler and the Paideia

Group, and a number of others have affirmed, each in their very   *Particular*

different ways, the necessity of the Great Books: Plato and Aristotle   *works in*
                                                                       the canon
and Sophocles, Dante and Shakespeare and Locke, Dickens and

Mann and Faulkner. We can call this orientation to educational   *Concluding*
                                                                 idea
achievement the <u>canonical orientation</u>.

From Rose's paragraph, we can learn several things.

- His main point is expressed in the first sentence, which is the topic sentence of the paragraph. He speaks of excellence in education as connected to the acquisition of a set body of knowledge, which he refers to as a "canon."

- He continues this point by saying in his second sentence that we define our students' success in terms of how well they know the canon.

- His calls for educational reform are connected to the perceived inability of students to know the canon.
- He then gives a series of specific authorities that have tried to advance a return to canonical teaching. The names of the authorities are not as important as understanding that there is a strong movement in this direction.
- He also includes names of the authors and philosophers who figure prominently in the canon. The names of these particular individuals are not as important as understanding what they represent: traditional, historical, and classical texts. A critical reader should note that current writers, including women and minorities, are not included.

SUMMARIZING THE READING

Writing a summary of a work you have read is one way to ensure that you understand the reading. After all, if you cannot write a summary of a reading, you have not fully understood it. Because a summary is a restatement of the reading in your own words, by writing one you see exactly how an article, essay, or even a book has been put together logically. Writing a summary can be an important study tool, too. Summarizing a work will help you remember it later. A summary does not include analysis or criticisms of the reading because those ideas are not part of the reading itself. (In some writing situations, you may present a summary of the reading first and then give the analysis or critique.) A summary can be as short as a single sentence, but usually several sentences or a paragraph will be required. For long works, such as a book or novel, a summary may require several paragraphs. The writing of summaries is discussed in greater detail in the Writing Lesson in Chapter Three.

ANALYZING THE EVIDENCE

Sometimes an article, essay, or book is based solely on a writer's personal ideas and experience. More often, however, writers must rely on the facts, experiences, and opinions of others to help support a particular position or view. Writers for nationally prominent publications, such as newsmagazines (like *Time* or *Newsweek*), celebrity-focused magazines (such as *Vanity Fair* or *Entertainment Weekly*), and essay-oriented magazines (including *The New Yorker* and *The Atlantic*) are usually professional writers and journalists. While they may specialize in certain subject areas, often they are not subject matter experts themselves. Instead, these writers must investigate their subject to supply the information for their articles. This may mean interviewing experts, traveling, and researching what others have learned. For that reason, it is important to separate the author, who is the organizer of the material, from the experts.

A writer's use of reliable authorities is crucial to maintaining credibility with the reader. When you read an article, pay attention to what sources the writer uses. Assessing the credibility of the source—and the validity of the material gathered from the source—goes a long way toward establishing the strength or weakness of an article or essay.

Keep in mind that writers of articles that appear in newspapers and magazines do not always cite where their evidence came from. Readers must rely on the credibility of author and publication in deciding whether or not to accept this evidence. If a magazine or newspaper publishes essays or articles with faulty or incorrect evidence, that publication's reputation might suffer. For example, in 2003, the *New York Times* was hit by a scandal when it was discovered that one of its reporters had been falsifying stories. Not only was the reporter fired, but also several prominent editors were dismissed. This demonstrates why editors have a stake in making sure that no faulty or incorrect statements are published. However, a publication's concern for integrity may be a reader's only protection against sloppy research.

Academic journals have more stringent requirements about the documentation of evidence. These journals, written by experts for experts, publish original research; therefore, they put a premium on proper documentation. Articles in academic journals usually adhere to a documentation standard and frequently include bibliographic information about their sources.

ESTABLISHING THE CREDIBILITY OF THE AUTHOR

Can you trust what you read? It's not a simple question to answer. Part of answering that question must involve a second question: "Can you trust the author?"

You are likely to be unfamiliar with most of the authors whom you will read. Occasionally you may come across a familiar or famous author, but more often, the author's name is likely to mean nothing to you. You should establish the credibility of the author. After all, the author is asking you to accept whatever he or she is saying. You want to be sure you have good grounds for accepting the author's words.

There are different points that can help establish an author's credibility:

- currency or timeliness
- journalist versus researcher
- education
- affiliation
- type of publication
- other published works

Currency or Timeliness

How recent is the source? If the material is too old, the question of the author's credibility may be irrelevant. An important question may be "How old is too old?" No single answer to that question can be given, of course. Some subjects, particularly in the sciences, can be very time sensitive. For example, what is known today about the human body is much more than was known twenty or even ten years ago. Thus, a ten-year-old article about cancer research would be useful only for historical purposes. You would want to find out what is known today.

Journalist versus Researcher

Knowing whether the author is a journalist—meaning a professional writer who publishes in magazines or newspapers—or a researcher, who is likely to publish primarily in academic journals, is an important step in establishing credibility. Professional journalists write most articles that you read in magazines and newspapers. These journalists are usually not subject matter experts themselves. Most rely on interviews with subject matter experts in order to supply information for their articles. Thus, journalists are generally at least one step removed from the actual source of information. Researchers are the subject matter experts themselves, so they can supply the information directly to the readers. However, most research is published only in academic journals, and since the readership of those journals is primarily made up of other experts, articles in those journals are often quite difficult for the average reader to follow.

Education

In some publications, an author's educational background, including his or her highest degree, is sometimes included. This usually occurs in publications or subject areas in which advanced degrees are considered crucial. For instance, in an article discussing the problems related to eating disorders, knowing if the author holds an MD (a medical degree) or PhD (a doctorate in an academic subject) may be important in assessing that person's credibility.

Affiliation

As with education, sometimes an article may include an author's affiliation—where they work. That can be important, especially if the author is not a journalist. Researchers are usually connected either with educational institutions, such as universities or colleges, or with research foundations. Typically, research done in educational institutions is done in an atmosphere of academic freedom, so researchers have broader latitude in terms of how they conduct their research and what subjects they wish to explore. Universities also compete with each other for research dollars, so there is pressure on researchers to do good research. The prestige that follows helps to generate more dollars. Universities are ranked against each other in all subject areas every year; you may wish to check such lists to see how well recognized an author's particular institution is.

On the other hand, research foundations tend to be more biased in their orientation than most educational institutions. This is because research foundations often get their funding from private groups or industries. Some foundations, in fact, exist entirely to do research that promotes the interests of a particular group or industry. Thus, the research these foundations produce must be examined in that light. This does not mean these groups do not conduct valid research—if they did not, their purpose for existing would quickly disappear—but they do not always approach all issues fairly or with an open mind. You will want to familiarize yourself with the positions and orientations of any research foundations whose authors' works you are using.

Type of Publication

When you see a screaming banner headline on a supermarket tabloid that reads "Alien Invasion Due Soon—Elvis Returns to Fight It," do you take that headline seriously? This is unlikely because you know that such publications are inherently untrustworthy. The tabloids may doctor photographs and invent imaginative stories to grab a shopper's attention. On the other hand, when a national newspaper runs an article, you are more likely to accept what the article says because you know they probably have checked their stories for accuracy. Understanding how periodicals and books are published is vitally important in assessing the credibility of an author.

Periodicals

Periodicals generally take three forms: newspapers, magazines, and academic journals. Newspapers are usually published daily, with some big city newspapers publishing several different editions during the course of a day. Newspapers feature hard news stories, feature articles, editorials, and opinion (or "op-ed") pieces. A real strength of newspapers is they provide the most comprehensive coverage of local issues that are unlikely to be discussed anywhere else. Newspapers are run by an editorial staff, which determines what is published. This editorial staff often determines the quality and character of a newspaper. The trustworthiness of articles written by journalists working for a newspaper is a reflection of this. Some of the better newspapers in the United States include the *New York Times*, the *Washington Post*, and the *Los Angeles Times*.

Magazines, like newspapers, are written for a general readership. Even those that focus on hobbies or areas of specialization, such as sports, music, automotive, or fashion, are written so that the widest possible audience can read them. Magazines, like newspapers, have editorial staffs that determine which articles are printed, and as with newspapers, the reputation of the magazine has much to do with determining the credibility of its material. Some of the more credible magazines for news include *Time, U.S. News & World Report*, and *Newsweek*. Some of the better magazines for in-depth feature articles covering a variety of subjects include *The Atlantic, Forbes*, and *The Economist*.

Academic journals are different because they are written by experts for experts, and most importantly, they are "peer reviewed." This means that a group of experts has looked at each article and determined that its scholarship and value meets the highest standards. Articles in academic journals frequently include documentation for the research—you do not simply rely on the reputation of the author or publication. Because experts write the articles in academic journals, they are not always easy for the average reader to understand. The payoff, however, is the information is unfiltered, unlike in newspapers and magazines. The author is the source for most of the information. Academic journals are seldom found in supermarket checkout lines—they are to be found in the holdings of university and college libraries. Academic journals include publications such as *Nature, Science*, and the *Journal of the American Medical Association*.

Books

The nature of book publishing, particularly the expenses involved, means that most publishers are only willing to publish books that sell. While this might suggest publishers will not publish books by authors who lack credibility, the truth is a bit murkier. Most reputable publishing houses will not publish books that are poorly written or researched, but many do publish books that may have a strong "fad" appeal, such as books that promote a new form of dieting or promise ways to improve one's love life. Therefore, do not assume that simply because an author was able to publish a book that that author has the highest credibility.

In contrast to commercial publishers are university or college presses. They serve the same role in books that academic journals do in periodicals. This type of publishing house is interested in publishing books that meet the highest standards of credibility and scholarship. Because of their affiliation with a university or college, profit is not the publisher's leading motive. Books published by university or college presses have the highest level of credibility. Highly regarded university presses include the Oxford University Press, the University of Michigan Press, and the Harvard University Press.

Be especially aware of self-published books and books published by small presses. Self-published books are books that the author him- or herself has paid to have published. For this reason, companies that provide this service are called "vanity presses." They appeal to the vanity of a writer who cannot otherwise get published. This is usually because the quality of the book, either in terms of the writing or the scholarship, is too low for any legitimate publisher to accept. The problem with small presses, on the other hand, is that they often have a social or political agenda. Look at a list of books they publish. A small press might well only publish books that promote a certain ideology, political perspective, or social position. Books from vanity presses and small, agenda-oriented presses tend to have the lowest level of credibility.

Other Published Works

Check the author's other publications, if any are listed. See if they are in the same subject area, or if the author moves from subject to subject. If the latter is true, then the author is not a specialist, but a professional writer who moves from one topic to another. This is not necessarily bad, but it does mean the author's credibility will be determined by his or her research.

If no other publications are listed, you may wish to do some research of your own. You can check the *Library of Congress Books in Print* and look up the author's name to find other books written by him or her. Again, see if those books are in the same subject area or not. You may also wish to do an author search in a periodical database to see if the author's name appears. See if the articles the author writes are in the same subject area. If the periodical database does not have the capability of searching by author, do a subject search and see if the author's name appears. (Unfortunately, this method is less exact than doing an author search.)

Of course, no author is going to be right 100% of the time. Honest mistakes may happen, and honest disagreements exist as well. However, you can protect yourself best, as a critical reader, by knowing as much about the authors that you read as you can. Make sure also that you read a variety of sources from more than one author on the subject. This will give you a much better perspective about the credibility of the material you encounter.

READING YOURSELF INTO AN EXPERT

In order to write intelligent, well-reasoned papers, you may find your-self moving out of your own areas of knowledge and experience. You will have to do research in order to learn more about the topic of your paper. We call this "reading yourself into an expert" because by the time you finish your research, you should be an "expert" at your new topic.

Where do you go to do research and how do you do it?

- **The library.** Your local community or college library is an excel-lent place to begin your research. In order to make effective use of the library, you should know whether it is arranged according to the Dewey Decimal system (as many public libraries are) or the Li-brary of Congress system (as many college and university libraries are). Once you know how the library has organized its holdings, use its catalogue to do a subject search. Begin your search with the broadest terms. While that will give you more sources than you are likely to want, and many sources will be inappropriate for you to use, you will also get some "hits"—texts you want to use. Then, examine what subject headings and subheadings that text was cat-alogued under, and narrow your search accordingly.

  Libraries also have periodical holdings. Ask a librarian how to search the periodicals for your subject. For generations of students, *The Reader's Guide to Periodical Literature,* in its distinctive green binding, was the best source for finding articles by subject in peri-odicals. Copies of the *Reader's Guide* are still likely to be in your li-brary and may be helpful for finding older articles; however, in today's age of computers, many libraries have computerized data-bases that can track down articles in periodicals by subject almost instantaneously. Find out what method is used in your local library.

  In addition to the actual periodical holdings in your library, many libraries have computer databases that include articles and essays that are "clipped" from magazines and newspapers from around the country or the world. Older versions of these data-bases were kept on microfilm or microfiche. Today, these data-bases are available through computers. To use these databases, you may need to be in the library itself, but some libraries offer off-campus access to these databases through the Internet. These computerized databases are called "subscription services."

  The use of subscription services is popular in many college and university libraries because these services make it possible for students to get articles from hundreds or even thousands of peri-odicals, all organized by subject. (These services are much less ex-pensive for libraries than actually subscribing to each periodical separately.) The services may offer different databases, each one specializing in a different subject area or different type of periodical. Before using a database from a subscription service, know what types of periodicals are in the database, and what subject areas are more likely to be covered.

Of course, the best resource in a library is likely to be the librarians themselves. First, see if your library has a reference desk or a specific reference librarian. That person can give you valuable information about where sources for your subject area are to be found. They might help you with searches, and even suggest alternative sources that are available. Do not hesitate to ask librarians for help—that's why they're there.

- **Bookstores.** While libraries allow you to borrow books at no cost, bookstores do have one advantage over libraries: they have more current books. Go to your local bookstore, find your subject area, and simply scan the stacks. A good bookstore will offer a range of authors and titles within any given subject area, with some classic or best-selling texts, but with new ones as well. The new books will give you an excellent idea of what is being written about your subject *now*.

- **Home.** Check out the books, magazines, and newspapers you already have at home. You might be surprised at what you find. There may be an excellent source already in your personal library!

- **The Internet.** Since the rise in popularity of the Internet in the 1990s, many students have taken to the practice of turning to the Internet first to do research. The Internet can be a valuable resource, but it should be consulted only after other forms of research have already been used. One reason for this is that the nature of the Internet itself—a veritable Wild West of ideas—means that some, perhaps much, of what is on the Internet is not reliable. Chapter 12 discusses the use of the Internet in research in greater detail, but keep one thing in mind: Virtually anyone can publish on the Internet, and what gets written is neither strictly regulated nor checked for accuracy. In short, anyone can say practically whatever he or she wishes. Thus, the phrase from Latin *caveat emptor* ("buyer beware") is especially appropriate for materials taken from the Internet. Before you use material, make sure you know the source of the information, check the credibility of the website, and double-check statistical information with reliable print sources.

Reading well ultimately is just one part of the educational process. Fundamentally, reading well is connected to thinking well, and those thoughts can then be expressed well in writing. *The Main Event: Readings for Writing and Critical Thinking* seeks to help you develop reading, writing, and critical thinking skills that will apply far beyond the classroom, into your work world and personal life. It is for this purpose that *The Main Event* has been written.

1

Film and Television

Films are watched by hundreds of thousands of people every week; millions watch television every day. The size of the audience and the regularity with which the audience views these forms of entertainment mean their influence is strong. Indeed, much debate has centered on whether films and television programs do cause people to copy the things they see on the screen—for instance, commit acts of violence, try drugs, or engage in dangerous sexual behavior. Many argue that because of this influence, we need varying degrees of censorship and restraint. Others argue the causes of antisocial behavior go much deeper than simply responding to an image on the screen. There are other issues concerning film and television as well, including discussions about artistic value and commercial exploitation. The fact is, nearly everyone watches at least some television, and most people go to see films at least once in a while. That alone makes them worthy of our investigation.

In this chapter's Writing Lesson, we discuss the basic form of the essay. Essay writing begins with the development of a thesis sentence—the main point or argument of the essay. The lesson explains the idea of a thesis, the basic structure of an essay, and the development of the body paragraphs. The writing assignment in this chapter gives you an opportunity to put those ideas to work while writing about film and television. The objective in this chapter is to present you with a few important keys to essay writing that will provide a solid foundation for future writing situations.

THE MAIN EVENT READING

The Stoned Screen

Brian D. Johnson

Brian D. Johnson argues that Hollywood glorifies illegal drugs even in movies that have drug-using characters who come to some disastrous end. He announces the emergence of the "Drug Movie" as a new formula film—a film in which actions and characters follow a predictable pattern. In the "Drug Movie," drug users are almost always punished in the end, but these films also provide a way for the audience to have a "high," having fun watching other people having fun. Johnson includes a list of films dating back to 1936 that have prominently featured drug use.

Key Words

odalisque	a female slave; a concubine in a harem
Adonis	a handsome young man; a figure from Greek mythology
burlesque	humorous in a mocking way
bohemian	a writer or artist living an unconventional lifestyle
homage	expression of respect or regard
vicarious	living through others
counterculture	a culture whose values and morals are different from those of the established culture

 quote

he assumes the audience knows this?

Director Martin Scorsese once said that movies are "really a kind of dream state, like taking dope." But a lot of movies these days are not just like taking dope; they're about taking dope. Just look at some of the recent Oscar nominees. In *Traffic,* a 16-year-old white girl lying in bed—an odalisque with baby fat—watches in a stoned reverie as a naked black man shoots heroin into her ankle. In *Requiem for a Dream,* a junkie Adonis probes for a vein in a black-and-blue forearm, while his mother is strung out on diet pills and TV game shows. In *Almost Famous,* a rocker on acid proclaims he's God and jumps off a roof into a pool. And now comes *Blow,* a drug-culture version of the American Dream—starring Johnny Depp as George Jung, the entrepreneur who unleashed cocaine on North America in the 1970s.   *sarcasm*

exp's

why "adorable" for a drug dealer?
why is marijuana good and cocaine bad?

Depp is adorable. Who else could make a big-time drug dealer seem so sweetly naive? He comes across as the Johnny Appleseed of cocaine. But *Blow*'s nostalgia trip through the drug culture's coming of age—from the innocence of weed to the corruption of coke—follows a familiar arc. And by the end of it, the kicks have been cut with so much baby-powder sentiment, it makes you wonder if the Drug

Movie, once at the experimental edge of cinema, is now being peddled as just another recreational formula.

The genre has been with us for a while, at least since 1969's *Easy Rider*. And let's be specific. By Drug Movie, we don't mean crime flicks like *The French Connection* that focus on catching drug dealers. Or rehab movies like *Clean and Sober* that are about getting off drugs. The Drug Movie is about getting off, period. Which is not to say the euphoria goes unpunished. Those who get off rarely get off scot-free: the high is usually followed by a sobering crash.

contrasting detail

In fact, the Drug Movie has a hyperbolic sense of morality that's at once biblical and burlesque. From the martyred bikers of *Easy Rider* to the tortured souls of *Requiem for a Dream*, its heroes are typically outlaw pilgrims on a quest for altered consciousness. And the drug itself is an ingestible *Treasure of the Sierra Madre*. It's taboo crystallized, the ultimate fetish commodity. Cocaine is powdered greed; heroin is the slow ink of the devil; hallucinogens are a ticket to madness. Only marijuana gets off lightly, blowing smoke in the face of banal rectitude, although let's not forget that in *American Beauty* the suburban dad who develops a taste for killer weed ends up dead. Not from the weed, of course, but from the marine next door—not unlike the redneck shotgun blast that blew away Dennis Hopper and Peter Fonda at the end of *Easy Rider*.

More often than not, the Drug Movie is a doomed romance, the last stand of the stoned against the system. But it has also been synonymous with a revolution in filmmaking, a desire to disrupt straight narrative with visual delirium. It's no coincidence that *Easy Rider*, which erupted from the counterculture and served as its eulogy, became the first independent film of the American New Wave to challenge Hollywood. As amateurish as it was, it ushered in the idea of the movie-as-drug-trip. (Of course, some might argue that the previous year's *2001: A Space Odyssey* was the first trip flick, even if the only drugs involved were those ingested by the audience.)

5 Key idea

contrast to society and everyday living

Over the past three decades, the Drug Movie, like the drug trade, has expanded its arsenal. Attempts to synthesize mind-altering experience on-screen have become more authentic and non-judgmental. Gus Van Sant captured the snowy cocoon of pharmaceuticals in *Drugstore Cowboy*—the unrepentant memoir of a jailed dope fiend who describes the rush "as a warm itch that surged along until the brain consumed it in a general explosion." Oliver Stone (*The Doors*) and Canada's Bruce McDonald (*Hard Core Logo*) have both scaled the Everest of drug re-enactment: the acid trip. *Trainspotting* rolled back new frontiers of junkie heaven, and hell, by plunging the camera into the eye of the needle, and down the toilet. And you can almost hear the brain cells popping in *Human Traffic*, an exhilarating ode to ecstasy: a movie that wants to be a drug.

Simulating substance abuse has become a kind of pornography. And in the repertoire of drug porn, shooting up is still the most cinematic fetish—the equivalent to the money shot in a sex scene. David Cronenberg once told me that needles are the one thing that makes him squeamish in movies. Well, he must have squirmed like a creature from *Shivers* when he saw *Pulp Fiction*'s scene of an overdosed Uma Thurman being stabbed in the heart with a giant syringe of adrenaline. Like addicts constantly upping their dose, filmmakers keep devising ever more graphic fix scenes. Melanie Griffith jams a needle into her neck in *Another Day in Paradise*, as does Ben Stiller in *Permanent Midnight*. *Requiem for a Dream* takes drug porn to new heights with a techno-pulse montage of microscopic close-ups: smack bubbling under a flame, a needle snorkelling it up, a pupil dilating like a spring-loaded parasol.

Shoving cocaine up your nose, on the other hand, is not very sexy to watch. While heroin in movies has come to signify bohemian squalor—and tragic wisdom—cocaine almost always represents corruption and the wrong kind of wealth. It's the New Money drug. That was its role in Scorsese's *Goodfellas*, about a New Jersey kid who makes it as a gangster, then gets lost in a blizzard of coke. P.T. Anderson took a similar tack with *Boogie Nights*, about a porn star whose career nose-dives.

Both are stories of Seventies excess, about the rise and fall of blue-collar boys who make it in the underworld. And so is *Blow*, a movie transparently modelled on *Goodfellas*. Like the Scorsese film, it's based on the biography of a man behind bars (*Blow*, Bruce Porter's compelling 1993 biography of George Jung). Director Ted Demme mimics the *Goodfellas* style of voice-over narration. And to drive home the homage, he even casts *Goodfellas* star Ray Liotta as George's father.

Here the author begins plot summary

The movie starts well, with "Can't You Hear Me Knocking" by the 10 Rolling Stones scorching through a fast-cut odyssey of cocaine production, from a vat of paste in the Colombian jungle to bundles of white bricks on a California airstrip. Then we flash back to a blue-collar household near Boston, where George is being raised by a broken-down father (Ray Liotta) and a mean-spirited mother (Rachel Griffiths). With a friend, George drives out to California in 1965, and ends up in Manhattan Beach, where the streets are paved with Acapulco gold and the girl next door is a stewardess in a bikini.

Our hero hooks up with a pot-dealing hairdresser (a flaming Paul Reubens), and before long George is flying in bales of marijuana from Mexico. When he gets caught with 660 lb. of the stuff, he tells the court that he just "crossed an imaginary line with a bunch of plants." In jail, George meets the high-level Colombian contact who guides him to the next level. Prison, says George, "was a crime school—I went in with a bachelor of marijuana and graduated with a doctorate of cocaine."

use of analogy

All this is heady stuff, and as George brazenly sets himself up as the American point man for Pablo Escobar's Medellin cocaine cartel, the film skips along with the energy of a good success story. But as George's world unravels, the movie stalls, like a drug wearing off. *Is the author suggesting drugs are more interesting than personal relationships?* Penelope Cruz shows up in a shallow role as his Colombian wife, Mirtha, who turns into a fiery nag. (Between his wife and mother, George is beset by shrewish women.) The chemistry between Cruz and Depp never materializes. And as the movie drifts to a melancholy fade—George bonding with his dad and missing his daughter—you're really starting to miss the cocaine.

Blow lacks the intricate detail and propulsive rhythm that made *Goodfellas* so satisfying. It's a substance-abuse flick that lacks substance. But it does touch on quite a phenomenon. As George observes: "Cocaine exploded on American culture like an atomic bomb. It started in Hollywood and spread." Once it was accepted by actors and musicians, he adds, everyone else followed. *Critical comparison* *glorifying drugs in a*

Show business has always been the motor force of the drug culture. And drug movies are a form of Hollywood self-portraiture. Depp, who played gonzo acidhead Hunter S. Thompson in *Fear and Loathing in Las Vegas,* has his own history of heavy drug use. As for Demme (nephew of director Jonathan), in a phone interview from New York City last week, he declined to talk about his personal habits. "But obviously being in the entertainment biz, you see a lot," he said. "I've been around people who have been in the game. And recently, I've run into a few people who have been affected pretty badly by the game. And that has affected my life." Demme, 36, certainly knows that any drug movie, pro or con, has to provide a vicarious high. "A lot of people will tell you that drugs are really fun," he says, "particularly people who were partying a lot in the '70s. If the whole movie is no, no, no, then who would want to go to that party?" *Thesis statement* *counter culture fantasy world* *only available to a when small community*

Even Steven Soderbergh, whose *Traffic* paints a dark picture of drugs, appreciates the importance of making them seductive. The drug-taking scenes are the movie's most erotic moments—its only erotic moments. Over lunch in Toronto last year, Soderbergh said that when he shot the scene of teenagers cooking up free-base cocaine, he had no shortage of volunteers from the crew offering to demonstrate exactly how it was done. But then, Hollywood has a firsthand appreciation of the art of getting high, and the price of coming down. It is, after all, in the business of trafficking dreams. *15 Connects drugs and sex*

movies like drug stints end and must end in the same fashion

Cool Movies on Drugs: A User's Guide

Reefer Madness 1936 (Marijuana)

The anti-pot propaganda film (aka *Tell Your Children*) is reborn as a high-camp comedy for the children of the Sixties.

Valley of the Dolls 1967 (Prescription drugs)

Showbiz melodrama, with Patty Duke as an actress on uppers ("Sure I take dolls! I got to get up at five in the morning and sparkle, sparkle, sparkle!")

Easy Rider 1969 (Marijuana, Psychedelics, Cocaine)

A movie about the stoned, by the stoned, for the stoned. The screen's first "you had to be there" acid trip is improvised in a New Orleans cemetery. Far out.

Gimme Shelter 1970 (Marijuana, Psychedelics)

The Rolling Stones and the Hells Angels bring music, drugs and murder to Altamont, Calif. A gloriously bad trip.

Performance 1970 (Psychedelics, Marijuana)

Mick Jagger does some bisexual shape-shifting with a gangster, two girls and some psychedelics in a London flat.

The Panic in Needle Park 1971 (Heroin)

Junk verite, with Al Pacino cruising Manhattan's mean streets: when an extra shoots up, it looks very unsimulated.

Up in Smoke 1978 (Marijuana)

Cheech and Chong target an audience highly prone to laughter.

Altered States 1980 (Psychedelics, Marijuana)

William Hurt looks for enlightenment in LSD and sensory deprivation tanks. Problem is, he keeps having religious hallucinations during sex.

Sid & Nancy 1986 (Heroin)

As junkie Sex Pistol Sid Vicious, Gary Oldman is a human train wreck.

Blue Velvet 1986

Dennis Hopper, who has tried everything, plays a psycho sucking on nitrous oxide.

Dead Ringers 1988 (Prescription drugs)

David Cronenberg directs Jeremy Irons as self-medicating twin gynecologists.

(continued)

Cool Movies on Drugs: A User's Guide (continued)

Drugstore Cowboy 1989 (Heroin, Prescription drugs)

As a defrocked junkie priest, William Burroughs gives Matt Dillon his Beat blessing. Director Gus Van Sant's finest hour.

Goodfellas 1990 (Cocaine)

The ultimate cocaine jag: Ray Liotta races around like a man on fire, trying to deal coke, and fix his life, while making tomato sauce.

Naked Lunch 1991

A writer cuts "the black meat of the giant aquatic Brazilian centipede" with insecticide ("It's a Kafka high. You feel like a bug.")

Rush 1991 (Heroin, Cocaine)

Jason Patric and Jennifer Jason Leigh are narcs who get hooked on hard evidence.

The Basketball Diaries 1995 (Heroin)

A pre-*Titanic* Leonardo DiCaprio rolls up his sleeves to play junkie poet Jim Carroll.

Hard Core Logo 1996 (Psychedelics, Marijuana)

Canada's Bruce McDonald whips up a goat's head soup of an acid trip.

Trainspotting 1996 (Heroin)

Heroin, pro and con. Pro: "Take the best orgasm you've ever had and multiply it by a thousand." Con: a mother ignores her dead baby to look for another fix.

Fear and Loathing in Las Vegas 1998 (Marijuana, Psychedelics, Cocaine)

Slapstick psychedelia. Johnny Depp dresses up as Hunter S. Thompson, for whom ether is the drug of last resort. A movie that must have seemed like a good idea at the time.

Go 1999 (Designer drugs)

Sarah Polley deals ecstasy. Look for the stoned subtitled conversation with a cat.

Grass 1999 (Marijuana)

Ron Mann compiles the greatest hits of pot prohibition. Woody Harrelson narrates.

(continued)

Cool Movies on Drugs: A User's Guide (continued)

Human Traffic **1999 (Designer drugs, Cocaine, Marijuana)**

Trainspotting without the violence or the hassle. A bunch of kids from Cardiff, Wales, go to a rave and live to tell about it.

Requiem for a Dream **2000 (Heroin, Prescription drugs)**

Hair-raising drug porn, making the equation between legal and illegal addictions.

Traffic **2000 (Heroin, Cocaine, Marijuana)**

It covers all the bases: gangsters, cops, pimps, kids, parents. Its mantra: the war on drugs can't be won, let the healing begin.

What Did You Read?

1. Although most people condemn drug use, why is it that many people tend to enjoy films in which selling and doing drugs are at the core of the film?

2. Is there a historical precedent for the current drug film genre? Explain.

3. Does the author feel the movie *Blow* belongs to the experimental counterculture, or does he dismiss it as a glossy, big-budget Hollywood production (in other words, a safe, mainstream film)?

What Do You Think?

1. Johnson states that show business has been the "motor force of the drug culture"? Do you agree? Why?

2. What are some of your favorite films of the last five years? Did any involve undesirable elements such as drug abuse? Was that integral to the film? Why was the movie such good entertainment?

3. Do audiences consider films that are set in the past that depict drug use safer and more artistic than films that depict drug use in the world today? Why or why not?

How Was It Done?

1. Is the article crafted around different types of movies, or around a key idea with examples from movies?

2. What is the point of having fifteen small paragraphs as opposed to fewer, larger ones?

3. Does the article revolve too much around the author's personal selection of films—in other words, could a different viewer look at a
   different list of films and come to a different conclusion?
4. Does the author overly depend on the reader's knowledge of particular films?

THE MAIN EVENT WRITING ASSIGNMENT

Write an essay in which you respond to one of the following questions:

1. Is it necessary for artistic endeavors, including film, to depict socially unacceptable behavior in order to have artistic integrity?
2. Are films more interesting when they are based on true events?
3. Should we be critical of the fact that films largely cater to a youth-
   oriented audience?
4. Are roles and characters for minorities in film still limited?
5. Is feminism in the movies alive or dead?

PREPARATION PUNCH LIST

Before you begin writing the essay, you need to prepare yourself to
write. One way to prepare is to work through the following strategies.

Consider films of merit that depict "disturbing"
or unacceptable behavior.

These films might include behavior such as illegal drug use, violence, alcoholism, sexual abuse, sexually irresponsible behavior, bad
language, or exploitation of women. Many famous and critically acclaimed films have depicted these types of behavior, including *Saving
Private Ryan* (intense graphic violence), *Requiem for a Dream* (drug
use—both legal and illegal), and *Pretty Woman* (prostitution). On your
own, make a list of films you have seen and describe the "disturbing"
or unacceptable behavior in each.

Answer questions such as "What makes good art?"
or "What makes a good artistic film?"

In answer to these questions, you might consider that a good work
of art may have the following qualities:

- A good story creatively told
- Something that causes an authentic emotional reaction

- Memorable imagery
- Vehicle that allows you to experience something that you cannot or will not
- Something human that shows how people master the challenges of life
- Something that presents the human condition
- Something that is intellectually stimulating
- Of underexposed but real issues

Then ask, "What makes a bad film?"

- Cheap manipulation, such as the use of familiar music, nonorganic plot lines, two-dimensional characters.
- Repetition
- Predictability
- Simplistic
- Vehicle for simply sex (e.g., *College Co-eds on Spring Break)*, moralizing (e.g., *Johnny Q.*), or promoting a celebrity (e.g., *Glitter*, starring Mariah Carey).

Ask, why are so many films about undesirable behavior?

- Experimental or cutting edge moves away from the mainstream
- Reflects a counterculture desire to stand against the system
- The behavior creates a source of conflict
- The behavior is based on real-life events
- The behavior is erotic and seductive—appeals to the audience
- Provides an intersection for politics, criminals, youth, elderly, rich, poor, among others.

Discuss films, current and older. Talk about which were good and which were not, and why.

THE MAIN EVENT WRITING LESSON: BASIC ESSAY FORM

Learning about writing an essay may seem a mysterious process, especially if you do not know what the word "essay" means. In all likelihood, you have already read many essays in school if not on your own. However, writing an essay can seem a difficult task, if for nothing more than the simple reason that no one has ever explained to you exactly what an essay is. In simple terms, an essay is a short written work on a single subject. This definition alone may not tell you much, however. How is it constructed? What are its parts? What brings the essay together and makes it different from other forms of writing?

Without a doubt, the most important aspect of an essay is the thesis. The thesis is the main point or argument of the essay; everything else in the essay revolves around it. The thesis is what the author has to say about his or her subject, and the essay exists to prove to the reader that the thesis is true.

When you read, you look for the author's thesis in order to understand what his or her main point is. The same applies when you are the one writing the essay. Your thesis communicates your central idea to a reader, and in order for a reader to understand your essay, that reader must be able to identify your thesis.

Thesis

Definition of thesis: A thesis is an argument or statement of what you intend to convince the reader, crystallized into one sentence.

- The thesis appears at the beginning section of a piece of writing. In an essay it is often best placed at the end of the Introduction.
- The thesis should be only one sentence long because it is one complete thought.
- The thesis has three parts: the subject, the argumentative edge, and the rational basis with (often) three controlling ideas.

Example:

Corporal punishment is wrong because it teaches that violence is an appropriate way to resolve conflicts, it damages self-esteem and promotes dependence, and it can be physically hurtful.
- Subject = Corporal punishment
- Argumentative edge = is wrong
- Rational basis = controlling idea 1 (because it teaches that violence is an appropriate way to resolve conflicts), controlling idea 2 (it damages self-esteem and promotes dependence), and controlling idea 3 (it can be physically hurtful).

This format compels you to think through *why* you believe what you believe. It permits you to organize and blueprint your material or research more efficiently. (When you read professionally written essays, the thesis may not appear in this form, but professional writers have a strong sense of all the thesis parts—subject, argumentative edge, and rational basis. In particular, some authors might not include the rational basis in the thesis; however, the author must have a rational basis in mind. If not, the thesis cannot be supported.)

In the Main Event Reading, "The Stoned Screen," the thesis can be found near the end of the essay. The sentence "Show business has always been the motor force of the drug culture" best sums up the point of Brian D. Johnson's essay because he examines the role the drugs have played in the movies for decades.

In the Main Event writing sample, "Disturbing Films," which responds to the first question of the Main Event Writing Assignment, the thesis is "Artistic endeavors, especially in film, need to portray socially unacceptable behavior because it gives a gritty and unabridged view of life as it actually is, provides impetus for catharsis and change, and presents a philosophical view of the human condition." The sentence contains the subject ("artistic endeavors"), the argumentative edge ("need to portray socially unacceptable behavior"), and the rational basis ("because it gives a gritty and unabridged view of life as it actually is, provides impetus for catharsis and change, and presents a philosophical view of the human condition").

Here are some examples of thesis sentences with all three parts expressed:

- Television provides an incomplete view of life because of time constraints, sensationalism, and slanted viewpoints.
- Movies cater to a youngish audience as evidenced by the ages of the actors, the musical soundtrack, and the content matter.
- America's fascination with Hollywood celebrities is destructive to itself and the celebrities because many people get a false sense of the reality of celebrities' lives, the materialism of many celebrities is glamorized, and the intense scrutiny of the media and public can cause celebrities to turn to drugs and alcohol to relieve stress.

The Essay

A thesis is the main point or idea of an essay, but what constitutes an essay? An essay is a short piece of prose writing, ranging from a few paragraphs to several pages, on a single subject in which the author attempts to prove a thesis. You might begin writing essays that have as few as five paragraphs, which is useful for learning the various tasks that you are faced with in the writing of an essay. After you master this relatively short essay, you can expand your essays rather easily into essays of six, seven, eight, or more paragraphs. The principles remain the same, no matter what the essay's ultimate length.

Structure of the Essay: The Funnel System

You can see the shape of the paragraphs of the essay as forming a series of "funnels" in the sense of how the ideas in each paragraph are developed.

Introduction

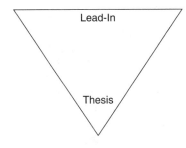

The funnel system works in the **introduction** in that the sentences **leading in** are more general and sweeping about the subject. This does not mean, however, that specific details should not be included. Strategies for a lead-in might include a three- or four-sentence definition, an anecdote (a short story with a point), an interesting quotation, or some detailed background information about your subject. Near the end of the lead-in, you need to narrow your introductory material to provide a bridge to your **thesis,** which includes the argument pertaining to the subject. You move from more general information (the lead-in) to the most specific statement, your thesis statement.

Main Body Paragraphs

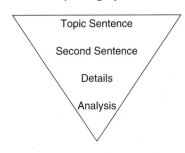

The body of the essay is composed of **main body paragraphs.** Again, the funnel system works in that each middle paragraph will begin with a **topic sentence,** a sentence that is the most general sentence in the paragraph that also connects to some aspect of the thesis. Likewise, the **second sentence,** although a bit more specific, is preparing the reader for **details,** such as data, examples, or citations from expert sources. Middle paragraphs will all end with some kind of specific, narrowed-in **analysis** of how these details support your topic sentence, and by extension, your thesis.

Conclusion

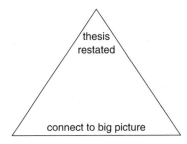

The **conclusion** is different from other paragraphs in the funnel system in that it is an inverted funnel, meaning it begins very specifically with a **restatement of the thesis** and then moves on to broader, more general statements that put your specific argument into a larger context. You are trying to show how your thesis is **relevant to the "big picture."**

Body Paragraph Development

Each part of the essay—the introduction, the main body, and the conclusion—has certain tasks to perform, so the paragraphs that you write for those parts will be different. The Main Body paragraphs are special because they are the bulk of the essay; they carry most of the substance of the essay. It is important, therefore, to have fully developed main body paragraphs. All too often, students have a tendency to write body paragraphs that are too short. As demonstrated, the body paragraph can be thought of as a funnel—in which you move from more general ideas to increasingly more specific ideas.

A body paragraph has four parts:

- **Topic Sentence**—A topic sentence needs to be the most general sentence in the paragraph. (Never use a quotation or paraphrase as a topic sentence.) It also must relate the topic of the paragraph to the thesis sentence. The topic sentence will be a more specific sentence than the thesis.

- **Second Sentence**—This sentence follows the topic sentence and provides more details, but still remains relatively general. The second sentence has more concrete words, meaning words that refer to things rather than ideas. The second sentence helps provide a transition between the topic sentence and the details, which are introduced to the rest of the paragraph.

- **Details**—Details include direct quotations, paraphrased material, examples, case studies, statistics, and references to expert opinions.

- **Analysis**—The analysis needs to make sense of the details and relate the details in the paragraph back to the topic sentence. Analysis makes clear how the details support the topic sentence, and by extension, the thesis.

Body paragraphs need to be developed. That is the point of an essay: to develop and illustrate ideas. Any paragraph that is obviously short is usually not as developed as it could be. Make sure not to use a quotation or other specific piece of evidence as a topic sentence. To do so is like putting the cart before the horse—getting too specific before the general point has been laid out.

Of course, avoid making paragraphs too long. Material in a paragraph is unified by a topic sentence. The most common reason for a paragraph to be too long is when it includes ideas not related to the topic sentence. Such unrelated ideas should be placed into a separate paragraph, under a different topic sentence, or removed entirely.

Refer to the Main Event Writing Sample to see how these principles have been applied.

THE MAIN EVENT WRITING SAMPLE

The following is an essay written for this text in response to the Main Event Writing Assignment, Question #1.

Disturbing Films

Arguably one of the greatest paintings of all time is Pablo Picasso's *Guernica,* which depicts scenes of graphic violence and mutilation. D.H. Lawrence's novel *Women in Love* depicts lovers who by society's standards should never have gotten together. *Last Tango in Paris,* starring Marlon Brando, is considered by many film critics as one of the best movies ever made, yet it received an "X" rating when it was first released for its graphic sex scenes. *Who's Afraid of Virginia Woolf,* a Pulitzer-prize winning play by Edward Albee, brought to the screen by Richard Burton and Elizabeth Taylor, is about a dysfunctional couple whose marriage is characterized by abuse, adultery, and alcoholism. These great works from decades past all portray socially unacceptable and undesirable behavior; they are great in part because they do so. Artistic endeavors, especially in film, need to portray socially unacceptable behavior because it gives a gritty and unabridged view of life as it actually is, provides impetus for catharsis and change, and presents a philosophical view of the human condition.

Lead-In (presents examples of different types of art that depict socially undesirable behavior)

thesis

rational basis

Many exceptional films have delved into the margins of life, where people reside who do not live in mainstream culture. The characters make choices that appear to the audience as potentially immoral, uneducated, dangerous, or foolish, but these choices spring from their character and circumstances. For example, the movie *Boogie Nights,* a film that depicts the porn-movie industry in the late 1970s and early 1980s, shows the rise and fall of a young man who wants money, fame, and acceptance—things that most of

Topic Sentence

Second Sentence

Details: Example 1

Analysis us want—and he does it within the arena of pornography. With humor and emotional intensity, the film shows the consequences of Dirk Diggler's choices—choices that nearly cost him his life. For the audience, the film provided a voyeuristic journey into a

Example 2 marginalized lifestyle. The film *American History X* explores the life of a young white racist who commits a grotesque, vicious murder of a black man. The movie examines the seeds of racism planted at the family dinner table, and how that murder (as well as a subse-

Analysis quent murder) grows from such feelings. The marginalized white racists are not so much accepted as understood. Films can give us a sense of the human, in both its good and evil aspects.

Topic Sentence   Artistic endeavors, particularly in film, can inspire in the audience a sense of catharsis and change. Since the time of the ancient

Second Sentence Greeks, critics have commented upon the emotional power of drama to create a sense of release in the audience when presented

Details with the experience of great tragedy and loss. War films, such as

Examples 1 & 2 *Apocalypse Now* and *The Deer Hunter,* take the audience through the possibilities of what can happen to people when they go through a process of intense distress. The characters experience vi-

Analysis olence, torture, sadism, and senseless death. In *The Falcon and the Snowman,* a disillusioned ex-priest teams up with a drug dealer to betray America for power, money, and a vague sense of justice. The audience realizes how easy it can be to succumb to temptation

Example 4 when one's values are being questioned. A newer movie, *American Beauty,* uses violence in the forms of suicide, murder, and abuse to show how rigid control of self and others can lead to catastrophic

Analysis consequences. While intensely disturbing images are integrated into these films, the images are necessary to break down the audience's resistance to being moved by these films. This movement is what catharsis is all about.

Unpleasant themes and images are also needed to present a *Topic Sentence* philosophical view of the human condition. Often that view is a dark, unsettling image that does not support the surface images *Second sentence* that we are asked to accept. For example, in *Chinatown,* starring Jack Nicholson, characters and their relationships are not what *Details: Example 1* they seem. Eventually, the detective played by Nicholson unravels not just the mystery of a murder, but an incestuous, corrupt relationship in which a father—a rich, powerful man—has a child by his own daughter. Thus, the public actions of this man are ultimately rooted in private evil. In *Boyz N the Hood,* three young *Analysis* black men in Los Angeles are faced with the troubles of growing *Example 2* up in a neighborhood where gangs rule. The relentless violence *Analysis* produces a strong sense of anxiety and despair that seems inescapable. In *Affliction,* Nick Nolte's character is a neglectful father, *Example 3* an intimidated son, and an angry man whose life spins out of control. The vision of the peaceful countryside and small towns is ultimately disrupted by the sight of the burning barn in which Nolte's character has left his father's corpse. These films, and others like *Analysis* them, are powerful visions of how life can be different from how the audience imagines it.

Films need to be able to present an artistic vision that is at *restate thesis* odds with mainstream values. We need to depend on art to present an artistic vision that does not necessarily mirror back ourselves, but presents alternatives that allow us in our imaginations to learn about and escape into other worlds. Art sometimes shakes us out of *connect to the big picture* our complacency and jolts our lives into new awareness and new consciousness. This can be entertaining, this can be educational, but it can also be disturbing and frightening. Art can provide impetus for change.

Works Cited

Affliction. Dir. Paul Schrader. Perf. Nick Nolte, James Coburn, and Sissy Spacek. MCA, 1997.

American Beauty. Dir. Sam Mendes. Perf. Kevin Spacey, Annette Benning, Scott Bakula, Wes Bentley, and Mena Suvari. Dreamworks, 1999.

American History X. Dir. Tony Kaye. Perf. Edward Norton, Avery Brooks, Beverly D'Angelo, and Stacy Keach. New Line, 1998.

Apocalypse Now. Dir. Francis Ford Coppola. Perf. Marlon Brando, Martin Sheen, Sam Bottoms, and Robert Duvall. Paramount, 1979.

Boogie Nights. Dir. Paul Thomas Anderson. Perf. Burt Reynolds, Mark Wahlberg, Don Cheadle, Heather Graham, William H. Macy, and Julianne Moore. Warner, 1997.

Boyz N the Hood. Dir. John Singleton. Perf. Cuba Gooding, Ice Cube, and Laurence Fishburne. Columbia-Tristar, 1991.

Chinatown. Dir. Roman Polanski. Perf. Jack Nicholson, Faye Dunaway, John Huston, and Diane Ladd. Paramount, 1974.

The Deer Hunter. Dir. Michael Cimino. Perf. Robert DeNiro, Christopher Walken, Meryl Streep, and John Savage. MCA, 1978.

The Falcon and the Snowman. Dir. John Schlesinger. Perf. Sean Penn and Timothy Hutton. MGM, 1985.

Last Tango in Paris. Dir. Bernardo Bertolucci. Perf. Marlon Brando and Maria Schneider. MGM, 1973.

Lawrence, D.H. *Women in Love.* 1921. New York: Knopf, 1992.

Picasso, Pablo. *Guernica.* Museum of Modern Art, New York.

Who's Afraid of Virginia Woolf? Dir. Mike Nichols. Perf. Richard Burton, Elizabeth Taylor, George Segal, and Sandy Dennis. Warner, 1966.

ADDITIONAL READINGS

Go Ahead, Make Her Day

Richard Corliss and Jeanne McDowell

Richard Corliss and Jeanne McDowell examine the female action hero in film and television. Examining heroines such as the cartoon Powerpuff Girls *and the cartoonish* Charlie's Angels, *they argue that the nature of the female heroine is now consciously "girlish," combining crime-fighting prowess with pouting and prowling for men. Whether this represents a step forward or backward is, in the authors' words, up to the reader.*

Key Words

willful	obstinate; done intentionally
suavely	doing something smoothly; graciously

levitation	the rising or lifting of something
connotes	conveys ideas in addition to the exact meaning of something
poignancy	deeply affected or touched, often with painful feelings
juxtaposition	two things placed side by side
protagonist	the main character in a literary work

It used to be the heroine's job to get in trouble and the hero's job to get her out of it. How many films ended with the good guy and the bad guy battling it out while the sweet young thing shivered to one side, never thinking to pick up a plank and help out?

You've come a long way, baby. Flick on the TV, and see women—young women, almost always—kicking and thinking and winking at both the old notion of femininity and the aging precepts of feminism. *Buffy the Vampire Slayer* (in her fifth season on the WB) saves her classmates from Evil, when she's not cracking a book or a joke. The Cartoon Network's *Powerpuff Girls,* "the most elite kindergarten crime-fighting force ever assembled," protect Townsville with their magical powers. Max, the bionic babe on Fox's *Dark Angel,* occasionally lets a mere man help her save the world, after which she suavely extracts herself from his adoration. "What's the plan?" asks her enraptured swain of the moment, who doesn't deserve to be in her car pool, let alone her gene pool. Max's blunt reply: "I'm the plan."

Fact is, TV has long been a woman's medium. Movies are guy space. So consider the release next month of *Josie and the Pussycats,* a live-action version of the comic book and '70s TV cartoon series, and this summer's *Tomb Raider,* with Angelina Jolie as supervixen Lara Croft. Consider, and savor, the success of *Crouching Tiger, Hidden Dragon,* the all-time top-grossing foreign-language film that was set to hit the $100 million mark at the North American box office last weekend. Ang Lee's martial arts fantasy features two strong women, a 30ish warrior (Michelle Yeoh) and a willful teen (Zhang Ziyi) just discovering to what uses, good or ill, she may put her powers of physical levitation and female cunning.

"It's mythic epic narrative which has as its center a female consciousness," says James Schamus, one of the film's writers and producers. "In all the great epics, from the Iliad on, the protagonists have been masculine, their destinies a masculine destiny. Now a real shift is taking place, in which some collective identities—those created for the whole culture regardless of gender—are female."

The women of the *Charlie's Angels* movie, which has earned $125 5 million since its November debut, might not seem to have kinship with *Crouching Tiger*'s stately stunners. This colorful jape propels Cameron Diaz, Drew Barrymore and Lucy Liu through its empty-calorie plot with the force of a hurricane blow-dryer. The stars giggle, wear swank togs, toss their coiffures in luxurious slo-mo. Diaz shakes her booty a lot. And skeptics may laugh their booty off when told that the Angels are icons of empowerment.

Yet they do fly through the air, giving the bad guys foot-facials (*Charlie*'s stunt maven, Yuen Cheung-yan, is the brother of Yuen Wo-ping, who choreographed *Tiger*). And to Barrymore, who produced it, *Charlie*'s is a tribute to today's woman: able, independent and cute—not so much femi-nist as femi-nice. "We wanted the Angels to be strong, but not masculine," says scriptwriter John August. "They aren't afraid of their sexuality, but they don't use it as power. Drew and I agreed they should be recognizable 'girls.' And she doesn't mind the word girls."

Didn't "girls" used to be a dirty word? To today's in-charge Holly-wood woman, it's le mot du jour. "We're very girlie," says Nancy Juvenon, Barrymore's partner in Flower Films, which will produce a remake of the Jane Fonda sex sci-fi spoof *Barbarella*, with Barrymore in the title role. (Flower has three projects in the works; that makes Barry-more, 26, a baby mogul, or mo-girl.) Now the un-chic phrase, the F word, is feminism, because it connotes a starchy righteousness. "A bad thing about old-style feminism," says Amy Pascal, the Columbia Pictures chairman who greenlighted *Charlie*'s, "was that you could be a brain surgeon but you couldn't be a sexy brain surgeon. Finally some woman said, 'I want to be both.' Men get to be sexy and successful. Feminism should include sexuality."

It surely does for Max (played by Jessica Alba, a kind of Angelina Jolie Jr.); she sizes up a man by scanning him from head to crotch. Other Max attributes were once the prerogative of heroic males: a gravity, a radiating inner ache; a past and a quest. She's lonely on top, flirting with potential mates but searching for a mother. In this sense she is a big sullen sister to Blossom, Bubbles and Buttercup, the Powerpuff Girls. They too are the spawn of a biological experiment. (They also levitate, like the Tiger women.) And though the show is perky, and its pace frenetic, the Girls carry the burden of others' expec-tation. When things go wrong, the Townsville adults chant, "Your fault! Your fault!" There is a poignancy to the Girls' perfection.

"I wanted the heroes to be strong, tough and cool," says Craig McCracken, the show's creator. "The juxtaposition of their being really cute and really strong seemed more interesting than if they had been muscley guys. People are starting to accept that girls are cool, and girlie things are cool." Schamus, who has daughters ages 4 and 8, thinks the *Powerpuff Girls* offer positive action role models: "My daughters are provided with more tools to gain confidence in the mas-tery of their own lives."

We will let others decide if this new trend is progressive or helpful 10 to female viewers—let alone to unenlightened males, who have long appreciated the spectacle of women fighting (it used to be called mud wrestling). But the action woman is certainly a corrective to a zillion idiot action films and XFL games and episodes of *Jackass*. Women of any age hardly get a break in pop culture. So you go, girlie.

What Did You Read?

1. According to the authors, what is the difference between feminist and feminine?
2. What is the authors' view of feminism today?
3. Do the authors feel that the current pop culture female role models are positive? Explain.

What Do You Think?

1. Do you think that films like *Charlie's Angels* and *Tomb Raider* are progressive and helpful to female viewers or not? Explain.
2. What films have you seen in which women are smart, sexy, and empowered?
3. Are films that embrace the image of "action-heroine" showing us a new female role model or just a newer version of the old-fashioned sex kitten?

How Was It Done?

1. How does definition of terms play in a role in this article?
2. What evidence do the authors supply to support their contention that TV has long been a woman's medium?
3. How many examples of films are used to support the idea that female heroines are "tough, strong, cool"?

You've Come Which Way, Baby?

Elayne Rapping

Elayne Rapping, examining the role of women as portrayed in television, argues that images on television have an influence on the general public. In this time, which she refers to as "postfeminism," many destructive stereotypical images of women dominate television. Rapping sees television has having taken a virtual U-turn in its presentation of women, threatening to head back to the days of June Cleaver and 1950's-style restrictions on women.

Key Words

staggering	moving unsteadily; rocking violently
engendered	started or given birth to something
metaphorically	showing a likeness between two different things or ideas; not to be taken literally
indispensable	necessary; not able to be done without
obsequious	marked by fawning attentiveness; subservient
clemency	an act of leniency or mercy
catty	malicious; slyly spiteful
reactionary	ultraconservative
devoid	lacking an expected attribute
predator	one that preys, destroys, or devours

In an undergraduate course a friend of mine teaches, she asked the class what, if any, newspapers they read regularly. A young man raised his hand and said, "I don't read the paper but I watch *Law and Order* every week, and they take their story lines from the headlines, so that's how I keep up with what's going on in the world."

Is this story hilarious or alarming? Should we laugh or cry? I suppose we might say "all of the above." But to me—someone who's been studying, teaching and writing about television for what some might consider too long for my own mental health—the story had a deeper meaning.

First a word about the power and importance of television as a social force, the dimensions of which are staggering enough to bear repeating, even to those familiar with them. Television is on, and so consumed in some sense, an average of seven and three-quarter hours a day in the average American home. This average home contains more television sets than bathrooms or household members. One need not be of school age or even literate to understand television's messages. And those messages, repeated in one form or another 24 hours a day, on an average of sixty to seventy channels, are planted in our brains, whether or not we are paying attention. In fact, the power of television is greater when one is not paying attention, and so not thinking critically. Television is, quite simply, the most powerful cultural form in history. What it tells us about the world is, for most people, what is taken for reality.

But what is even more interesting—and my friend's story brings this home—is that what most people are watching for all those hours, and taking for political and social reality, is not the news. In fact, news programming runs at a financial loss because so few people watch it—unless there's a war, a scandal or a particularly shocking murder. What people do watch is fictional programming, from crime series to sit-coms to soap operas. And it is from that cultural material that they get their ideas about "what's going on in the world" and what they should think and feel about it.

So what does this have to do with feminism? Quite a lot. For one thing, it suggests, more strongly than most of us might realize, that television's reflections of and about gender issues—especially in fictional programming—have an enormous influence on the way the general public thinks and feels about these matters. But more important, from a feminist perspective, is the way these images have changed over the years, and how the presence (or absence) of mass social movements have played a role in those changes. It's a long line, after all, from Mrs. Cleaver and her clones—in their shirtwaists and pearls, nailed to their kitchen floors, endlessly tearing iceberg lettuce into Pyrex bowls—to the tough, feminist-inspired heroines of Cagney and Lacey, Murphy Brown and Roseanne. And that line runs parallel to the history of the women's movement. For second-wave feminism—a truth that bears remembering in these less happy times—did in fact change the world. And one of the most dramatic changes it engendered can be seen in the changing images of women and men on television, from the 1950s to the early 1980s.

I grew up watching Mrs. Cleaver tearing away at that lettuce. And like most of my friends (as I later learned in my consciousness-raising groups), I thought that everyone but me actually had mothers and fathers and siblings and kitchens like the ones on TV. That's what we were supposed to think, of course. Because television itself was—and is still—in the business of shoring up, as forcefully as possible, traditional family and corporate values.

But as the fifties turned to the sixties this job became trickier to manage. For the first generation to be raised on those images turned out to be an unexpectedly rebellious one on many levels. And among the first targets of rebellion, for women, was the very media which had so foolishly taken us for granted. Feminists' attacks on the male-run media—as those old enough to have been there remember—literally shook the foundations of the entire industry. Women sat in at magazine offices, defiled sexist billboards, protested beauty pageants and other symbols of sexist popular culture, and metaphorically and actually tossed and burned the painful pastel uniforms of femininity that popular culture, especially television, had so heavy-handedly thrust upon us.

Unfortunately for the media moguls, they relied on women viewers and readers to buy the products their corporate sponsors were selling.

In the postwar, consumer-based economy, women—as viewers and consumers—were the indispensable target audience for all commercial-based media, especially television. We still are. Sixty per cent of the television audience is female, because television—unlike movies, which are geared to an 18- to 24-year-old male audience—has always played to a female audience of family shoppers and socializers.

So the coming of the women's movement—and its enormous impact upon women generally—caused more than a bit of anguish in the Mahogany Row offices of the major networks. Try as they might, the executives could come up with no option except to respond in some way to women's new demands, or lose viewers and revenues. Their response, when it finally came, was dramatic and gratifying. By the late sixties and early seventies, it was good-bye to Mrs. Cleaver and company, hello to a new crop of television heroines whose lives and attitudes were at least a bit more like the ones we wanted for ourselves. Mary Richards of the *Mary Tyler Moore* show, obsequious and maternal as she was, was nonetheless a victory symbol for feminists who had demanded—and gotten—a heroine who was single, successful and independent. She even had relationships which didn't end in marriage (although they didn't end in bed either). Along with Diahann Carroll's *Julia,* a sixties show featuring an African American professional single mother, Mary Richards signaled a new trend in gender imagery which went on to spawn even more gratifying heroines and more politically charged story lines.

Remember *Maude* and *One Day at a Time?* Remember *All in the* 10 *Family's* Gloria and Edith Bunker, who began as ditzy "dingbats," but over the years grew into tough, independent-minded spokeswomen for gender justice? We did that. Gloria and Edith were shadow images of the changes that women all over America were going through. And Norman Lear gradually got the message that feminism, like the other hot button issues his series tackled, was a force to be reckoned with and acknowledged.

Television—unlike the still male-run, male-oriented film industry—was always more open to allowing women into positions of power, as producers as well as executives. For it's another little discussed or acknowledged fact that the lower on the ladder of artistic respectability a cultural form is deemed, the more open it is likely to be to women, racial minorities and gays. Soap operas, for example, are largely written, directed and produced by women. As an actress and sometime-director of *The Bold and the Beautiful* once told me, there are many days when the only men on the entire set of the series are the actors; everyone else—from camera women to prop women to script writers to producers to directors—is a woman. And as those of us who are willing to admit to watching them know, these shows have always been way ahead of prime time—and certainly movies—in addressing issues of gender, race and sexuality from a progressive standpoint.

Women have been allowed more power on television than else-where in the arts, and they have tended until recently to make good use of it. It might surprise readers to learn that as early as the late 1960s, soap operas and daytime talk shows—the most reviled of cultural forms—were already portraying and discussing such topics as rape, domestic violence and sexual harassment seriously, and from a feminist perspective. *All My Children* even had a lesbian story line in the seventies, which, although it allowed for no physical contact, certainly presented the issue sympathetically.

Feminists' influence on prime time programs in the seventies and early eighties began to feed back into the larger political sphere, making them, indirectly, progressive forces in struggles for gender justice. Made-for-TV movies based on "straight from the headlines" stories about gender issues—abortion, incest, sexual violence, employment discrimination and more—drew huge audiences, and played significant roles in changing social, political and legal policies. *The Burning Bed,* for example, about the precedent-setting case of Francine Hughes (played by Farrah Fawcett), who, after years of physical abuse, set her husband's bed on fire and was acquitted, made the "battered woman syndrome" a household term. But it also helped women's groups in their demands for more shelters and for changes in police behavior when called to intervene in what were then considered mere "domestic squabbles." It even influenced the governor of Ohio to grant clemency to nineteen women incarcerated for murdering abusive partners.

Of course the women's movement had been pushing for these things for years. But there is no question that this movie—viewed by 75 million people in its first run—had a massive impact on a public far removed from the grass roots efforts of feminist activists. And so— with all its compromises and flaws (and all television shows have them)—it became a significant player in the struggle for gender justice.

One could make a similar argument about the major media event 15 that the Anita Hill/Clarence Thomas hearings became. Like *The Burning Bed,* this event drew vast audiences. And while Thomas was confirmed and Hill largely defiled at the time, within a year or two—once the event engendered massive, continuing debate about the issue— public views about sexual harassment had shifted to the point where Hill had become a national heroine in the eyes of most women, and laws and codes addressing the issue changed dramatically in workplaces, academia and government agencies.

But once television executives were convinced that they could make more money and good will by producing movies and sitcoms and dramatic series in which subjects like sexual harassment and domestic violence—two terms literally invented by feminists—were treated seriously, there were more and more programs in which feminist issues were not only raised, but treated sympathetically. *Designing Women* even ran a segment in which its heroines ranted angrily about the Hill/Thomas affair, using actual footage from the hearings as the target of their rage. Feminist agitation in the public sphere, and its influence on fictional entertainment programming, helped spread feminist demands and attitudes to an audience even larger than the original audience for the political event itself.

By now, no doubt, some of you are thinking "How far is this woman going to push this argument about how great television has been for women?" Don't worry, I'm finished. And what's sad about that, from my perspective, is that I could only get to the mid-eighties before even I, formerly known to my friends as the Pollyanna of feminist television theorists, had to give up the argument and admit that our glory days of pushing the media envelope were over.

But in fact, my argument has never been that television has been great, or even particularly good, to women (or anyone else except straight, rich white men). On the contrary, what I've been arguing is that feminism has—or had—been great; so great that even that money-grubbing, woman-hating monster, television, was forced—by us—to pay some respect if it wanted to stay in business.

What's happened in the last decade or so makes for a far different and more depressing story; and that story says more about what's happening (or not happening) with feminism than with television. For if we had the power to change media images as much as we once did, we have certainly given up, or lost, that power in recent years. Anyone who teaches, or raises, adolescent girls these days knows what I mean. My own daughter told me—quite wisely as it turned out—that if I wanted my last book to be read by her generation of women I had better remove the F-word from the title and "just say women." For feminism has become at best a confusing and at worst a damning term these days, and television reflects this fact. Young women in particular—like my students and my daughter's friends—are at best confused and at worst horrified by the term.

For one thing, of course, there's the curse of postfeminism: the "be 20 careful what you wish for" effect. Young women today seem to believe that all battles are won and they can pretty much "be and do whatever they want" without any political effort at all. That's why they are so uncritical of the increasingly woman-centered, but far from feminist, television series they watch, and so oblivious to the contradictions and misogynies that infect these shows.

When I showed a segment of *Ally McBeal* to a "Gender and Media" class recently it was, remarkably, the male students (forced to deal with these issues for the first time) who were most likely to be shocked at the negative stereotypes. "I thought this class was supposed to teach us to recognize race and gender stereotypes," said one confused young man. "Yeah," said another, "these women are so competitive and catty, and so man-crazy." And so it went, as these puzzled young men's remarks were met (to my dismay) with utter contempt by some of the brightest and most outspoken of my women students. (If nothing else, feminism has certainly empowered women to speak out in classrooms these days.) "But that's how women really are," they insisted, or, "That's what you have to do to be successful."

Undeniably there's much truth in these attitudes. Postfeminism has created some very poor role models for women in real life and on television, and *Ally McBeal* is certainly one of them. I realize that I may be in a minority here, since many of my feminist friends seem, like my students, to love the show. But these older women have the advantage of having lived through, and been changed by, second-wave feminism; they can enjoy the show without taking it at face value as a feminist treatise. Not so my students. To them, it's very much about female "liberation" because it gives them permission to retreat to the worst pre-sixties attitudes and behaviors and still "succeed" financially and romantically. No shirtwaists and iceberg lettuce for them. They are planning to enter courtrooms and corporate office buildings, anorectic bodies clothed in mini-skirts, minds filled with sexual daydreams, and pockets full of money, just like Ally.

And in some sense I suppose that's progress. Sex, money, the right to dress as you please (at least on television); that's a lot more than Donna Reed could have hoped for. But what about the really important issues we used to talk about; the ones that weren't personal and self-serving? The ones that spoke to every woman—not just the ones who lived on *Melrose Place* or in *Dawson's Creek*. The demands that society—global society—be radically restructured so that women everywhere, no matter their race, class or sexual orientation, might have freedom, opportunity and the ability to fulfill their dreams and desires. Norman Lear seemed to understand at least some of this, and he was, even back in the seventies, a very old white man. So how far have we really come, baby? And why are we still—on television—so happy to be called babes?

I don't want to single out poor Ally here. (She has enough to be neurotically obsessed about.) Television in general has been giving a lot of air time and a lot of bad advice to women—and men—lately. For one thing, the studios that produced the old TV movies that presented politically sophisticated analyses of gender issues are now devoting most of their budgets to movies about sacrificing mothers, battered husbands, father's rights and—my all-time favorite—psychopathically murderous female predators. And then there are the new, terminally soppy, "professional woman" shows like *Providence* and *Judging Amy*, in which successful professional women leave the big city to return to their small town homes and move back in with Mum and Dad to live very rose-tinted, nostalgic versions of 1950s lives. Or the teen series like *Felicity* and *Dawson's Creek* in which girls and boys are on the same fast track, and never a political issue or thought crosses their paths or minds. And we can't overlook *Touched by an Angel*, surely the sappiest of the new woman-centered series. Or the bizarre transformation of Oprah Winfrey, who once led the pack in treating serious issues of race, class and gender in a relatively progressive way, but has suddenly transformed herself into an almost equally sappy purveyor of fashion make-overs and—do we really need more of this?—celebrity puff piece interviews.

I could go on but I might weep. Women, strong, successful women, are everywhere on television today. But their lives are so devoid of any meaning or purpose, except the most reactionary desires for traditional relationships and families and/or lots of money, that it is as though we have won the battle but lost the war.

What to do? To answer that question we need to face the challenging truth which my brief history demonstrates: there is no way to understand what's going on in the world of ideas and policies affecting women today without understanding the enormous give and take, back and forth, symbiotic relationship between social movements and popular culture. When feminism was a powerful, radical and visible force, then television was forced to reflect—at least in part, and within strict ideological limits—its concerns and demands. And if that is no longer the case, it is at least in part because we have stopped mattering to television executives. They have us—and our students and daughters—by the short hairs, and they are not about to let go without a fight. But where is that fight going to come from? Not, it would seem, from the burgeoning lists of new, female "public intellectuals" which the rise of cable and the Internet have made room for. For all the female voices being heard these days, few are daring to say the really radical, angry things that need to be said if we are ever to revive the noble tradition of speaking truth to power.

How can they, you may well ask? They have no armies of women standing behind them, as we did in the sixties and seventies, ready to back up their demands for the kind of radical social restructuring we used to insist upon. Well, yes, that's true. But I guess I would answer, as another (once) young man once said, "When you ain't got nothin', you've got nothin' to lose." And while it's true that we have no radical mass movement to back up our demands these days, I don't see how we ever will build one again, if we are all too timid and intimidated by the gains of the Right to say anything more radical than the Diane Feinsteins, Donna Shalalas, Hillary Clintons or Madeleine Albrights of the world are willing to say, or ask for more than they are willing to ask for, in women's names.

Let me end with a story from the Talmud about a man who spent his life trying to change the world. As he got older and the world resisted his demands for change, he would walk the streets each day; shouting his demands in ever louder tones. One day a youth approached him and said, "Old man, you have spent your life trying to change the world and you have failed. Why, then, do you continue to shout your demands for change?" To which the old man answered, "I know that my attempts to change the world have failed. But I must continue to shout them out in ever louder tones each day, because I fear that if I stop, the world will change me."

I am afraid the world has already changed us. For when no one is willing to shout loudly enough for the television audiences and those who depend upon their dollars to hear and be moved by their words, then television itself—the loudest of all voices in history—is accountable to no one except American Express, Proctor and Gamble and Victoria's Secret. And theirs have indeed become the only messages our students, daughters and sons seem to be hearing these days.

What Did You Read?

1. Why do advertisers for television target a female audience?
2. What images on television still hearken back to female stereotyping?
3. What does the author say about the relationship between social movements and pop culture?

What Do You Think?

1. What role does television play in America? How prominent is it in your own life?
2. Do you believe television is a positive forum for examining social issues? Explain and provide specific examples.
3. Agree or disagree: Television provides the kind of programming that most women can relate to. Be specific.

How Was It Done?

1. How much of the article is based on the personal experience of the author? Is that a weakness or strength?
2. Is a chronological overview of feminism necessary to understand the changing images of women on TV today?
3. Show how the article connects real-world politics with the images on TV.

Working Women

Tess Wilkinson-Ryan

Tess Wilkinson-Ryan goes to the other side of the camera to see how women fare as commercial film directors. She points out the sexism that women face in directing, including finding clients willing to work with a female. She also presents the concept of the "Lucite Ceiling"—stronger than glass because it cannot be broken.

Key Words

quirky	peculiar
breadth	the width of something
zenith	the highest point
stereotype	conforming to a fixed pattern, especially of members of a social group
circuitous	having a circular or winding path
propaganda	the spreading of ideas, information, or rumors for a political or social purpose
antagonism	actively expressed opposition or hostility
stigma	a mark of shame or discredit
condescending	assuming an attitude of superiority

Until recently, women directors were almost invisible in the commercials world. Now, they're getting work from the hot agencies—and not just on diaper and makeup accounts.

It used to be easy to peg commercials directed by women. They featured flowers, meadows, babies, and Muzak. They cut to long product shots of super-absorbent maxi-pads or scenes of attractive women sharing secrets over herbal tea.

Look all you want at recent campaigns for Snapple, Target, Ikea, and Coors Light, but you won't catch sight of a single cooing infant or a stained fine fabric. As a matter of fact, aside from their quality creative content, there isn't much about these spots that's similar at all. Some are stylish and sleek, like Floria Sigismondi's Target work, while others, like Cheryl van Ooyen's Ikea and Snapple spots, employ quirky humor. "It's taken women 10 to 20 years to get to this point," says Pam Maythenyi of online database The Source. "It used to be all feminine hygiene. It's taken the Pam Thomases and Paula Walkers of the world to change it." In the last 15 years, women like Elma Garcia, Paula Walker, Peggy Sirota, and Pam Thomas have cracked the glass ceiling of commercials directing, climbing their way to the A-list spot by spot. In the meantime, they've made room for a whole new class of incoming stars from Yuki to Nzingha Stewart to Lisa Rubisch. Of course, even as the body of work by female directors grows in breadth and depth, women directors on set still get mistaken for makeup assistants, and they have yet to see the critical acclaim that Tarsem, Kinka Usher, and even Bryan Buckley take as their due.

Although Revlon and Tampax commercials are no longer the zenith of a woman's directing career, these kinds of clients are often ground zero; they are the proving ground for the skills and techniques that win other opportunities. Strato Films' Paula Walker's classic Lubriderm spot, "Later Gator," is simple and straightforward: against a white background, a woman sits on a chair as an alligator creeps behind her and looms over her chair. Walker's recent work for Opel, in which dancers mime a trip in a minivan past a white CG city, is much more complex, but has the same serene visual sense. Souzan Alavi, a young director working out of her own production company, Manpower Films in New Orleans, finds that the old stereotypes are helpful when you're trying to break in. "There've been a couple of subjects that have given me an advantage," she says. "I did a commercial for Partners for Healthy Babies, a non-profit that teaches young women about prenatal care. It helped that I could connect with the female cast. They might have been uncomfortable if I'd been a man talking to them about pregnancy." Women also direct spots in which the action is all about style; they've directed for the Gap, Dayton Hudson and Eaton's department stores, and of course cosmetics spots including Anita Madeira's Avon work with the Williams sisters and Fatima's luscious feathery-eyelashes mascara commercial for Maybelline.

Girls Aren't Funny?

The areas that appear harder to break into are also, predictably, those that receive more money and more critical praise. Maggie Zackheim, a Satellite newcomer with experience directing comedy shorts for Comedy Central and VH1, is mystified by the lack of women who direct humor. "I know a lot of really funny women; maybe they don't want to be directors," she shrugs, then reconsiders. "In comedy, there are certain production companies that are very male, lots of SNL alums, and they don't think about hiring women; they want to hire their friends. They don't think that women are going to get a fart joke." Zackheim herself has proven that myth wrong with her Coors Light campaign, which includes a spot featuring, yes indeed, a whoopie cushion and a frantic rush to open some windows. It has also been hard for women to break into the highly lucrative business of car commercials, with a few notable exceptions. Dayton/Faris, the Bob Industries directing team that includes Valerie Faris, directed the hugely popular VW "Milky Way" spot, and of course Paula Walker directed for the Opel minivan. Aside from these unusual spots (and they are unusual—neither shows gleaming sheet metal and curvy roads), the most successful woman directing car commercials today clearly is Peggy Sirota, who's shot for Volvo, BMW, Mercedes, Buick, and Toyota. Not only does she have an impressive array of auto clients, but her stellar reel can stand up against any of the gleaming-chrome work of her male colleagues.

Getting a Break

In some cases, it's not just a genre that opens the door for women; it's a specific client or agency. One of the most impressive clients in this respect is Target. Peterson Milla Hooks CD Dave Peterson has hired many directors for the long-running campaign, and he estimates that over half have been women. Though he is hesitant to generalize about gender matters, he says that "Target is about fashion and trend stuff; we're looking to be a step ahead and there are a lot of strong women that are really great at that." (Case in point is Believe Media's Floria Sigismondi, whose own bold wardrobe is testament to her sense of style.) Peterson also speculates that women seem to come to directing via more circuitous routes than their male counterparts. The old-fashioned way was to begin as a grip and climb the hierarchy to DP and ultimately director. Peterson finds that many women directors come from design or photography backgrounds; Elaine Cantwell, one of Target's directors, had an entire reel of broadcast design work from her career with 3 Ring Circus. In the case of a client like Target, evidence of a well-developed visual sense may ultimately be more important than a demonstration of narrative ability. "Sometimes, women's heightened ability to connect emotionally makes them better able to deliver emotionally charged imagery," says Peterson.

Cheryl van Ooyen didn't have to look far for the client that would give her the break she needed; van Ooyen, a CD at Deutsch, convinced longtime creative clients Snapple and Ikea to give her a shot behind the camera. Van Ooyen has been the lead creative on the Snapple and Ikea accounts since she joined the company over four years ago. In that time, she and her clients grew close enough that they were happy to let her try her hand at directing. "There was enough trust there that they became very excited about me making the leap," Van Ooyen explains. Not only did she break into directing, but she managed to compile a big reel of comedy spots for Snapple and Ikea. Her Snapple work includes sex ed for fruit preparing to merge for mixed juices, and "Where the Bad Fruit Go" with scenes of a rotten fruit jailyard. Ikea features eccentric uses for household products, including a mother who needs a bowl to give her young son a haircut. Van Ooyen also feels she owes some of her on-the-set confidence to Valerie Faris, half of the Bob Industries Dayton/Faris duo with husband Jonathan Dayton, who directed some Ikea work with van Ooyen as CD. "Watching

Valerie gave me an extra boost," she says. "You can just be a person. You're not a girl director; you're a director. Watching her handle herself with the crew and take charge was just really cool."

Training Grounds

Though, like van Ooyen, many women directors arrive at commercials directing via unconventional paths, most begin the road to directing with film experience. Fatima, Yuki, and Liz Friedlander went to film school to learn their craft. Lili Zanuck, producer of *Driving Miss Daisy,* is one of many producers-turned-directors, a category that includes Francine McDougall and Maggie Zackheim. And then there are music videos. For all her artwork and spot success, Floria Sigismondi is probably still best known for her explosive arrival on the scene as a director of Marilyn Manson videos. Propaganda newcomer Nzingha Stewart was signed after proving herself with videos for Rah Digga and Ol' Dirty Bastard, just as Crossroads saw Nancy Bardawil's talent in her Goo Goo Dolls, Veruca Salt, and Hole videos. It's remarkable how many women get their start at MTV shooting shorts or promos. Barbara McDonough, Maggie Zackheim, Lisa Rubisch, Caitlin Felton, and Melissa Bolton have all found a voice behind the camera there. Bolton, now signed with Shelter Films, has directed some run-of-the mill work for Kraft salad dressing and Sarafem, the PMDD medication, but it is her pre-Shelter work for MTV that shows her style. In one spot, a jailed teen gets a quarter to make his one phone call; he shuffles desultorily toward the payphone and dials TRL, requesting a Kid Rock song. "It was one of the best experiences I could have had," says Bolton of MTV. "It's a place you learn and build a reel. I figured out who I was as a director; it allowed me to focus on my voice. I think I've got a slightly sarcastic view of the world. Now I've gotten pegged for the packaged goods. If you look at the MTV stuff, it's really different from the commercials."

The Lucite Ceiling

Given the successes, at first it seems hard to imagine that there are still barriers for women directors. On the other hand, it is also remarkable that for all the great work, there is no female equivalent of Pytka. As Pam Maythenyi notes, directing is like every other business: it's harder for women to succeed than men. "Is it still difficult to become a woman director? Yes. It's still difficult for women in all businesses to rise to the top. I read somewhere recently that the glass ceiling has become the lucite ceiling; it's impenetrable." Maythenyi points out that among the 5,000 or so directors she has cataloged, only 261 are women. Yuki, a rising director with DNA who graduated from Art Center in 2000, noticed that the dearth of women begins early, in film school. "At school our film department was like 85 percent male," she recalls. "I remember being in class and there would be 20 guys and maybe two women. We used to get comments like 'Why are we reading this article? It's written by a chick.'" After film school, the next challenge is to prove your technical skills, which may also be difficult. "A lot of the women were not really getting asked to work on the set, and if they did, it was craft service or maybe wardrobe or makeup," she says. "It was assumed that you wouldn't know the technical stuff." In response, Yuki decided to educate herself in film tech by hanging out in a local Claremont Camera rental house; once she could prove her expertise with the camera, she began getting offers to be camera assistant.

Almost every female director is so adamant to deny that gender is 10 a restricting factor in career success that it's hard to tell if they're trying to convince the interviewer or themselves. Maggie Zackheim is one of many to posit that gender bias is almost a state of mind. "If I give it that kind of power, it will wear me down," she explains. Nonetheless, most women have encountered antagonism that made them wonder if men face the same obstacles. "I've been asked questions that I know guys would not be asked," says Francine McDougall, Production League of America director of Sugar and Spice (with New Line Productions) as well as spots for Kellogg's, Mother's Taffy cookies, and PlayStation. "I was doing a comedy with special effects and they were giving me the third degree on how, exactly, I was going to do it. It just made me think." Unfortunately, this kind of conflict doesn't end once the project is won. "If a woman is fighting for her vision, she's seen as difficult," McDougall insists. "If a man is fighting for his vision, he's artistic. You've really got to be careful how you play the game, and men don't have to be careful." Yuki concurs. "You don't want to be seen as weak or submissive; but then some people just get really tough and they kind of overdo it, to the point where it's unpleasant for everyone."

In some cases, there just isn't a way to be accepted by everyone. Sigismondi remembers a time early in her career when she was shushed by a camera assistant. "I think sometimes it's hard for them to take direction from a young person or a woman," she says philosophically. Souzan Alavi recalls, "On my first commercial, the female talent asked if I was the makeup artist, and then the video assistant guy thought I was the production coordinator." Another female director says that yes, it is different for girls. "I've had to throw producers off my set because they're so condescending and rude. If you call them on it, they get ruder. They don't do that to the Marcus Nispels." Fatima is more blunt: "It's all about how much money they'll trust you with," she says. "I mean, if I looked at work and didn't know who the director was, could I tell if it was a woman? I could tell by the budget or company. You might see a beautiful car commercial, but would they entrust a woman with that budget?" While clients and agencies seem to have endless faith in a woman's organizational capabilities—note the plethora of female producers commanding large budgets—they seem less willing to stake money in her artistic vision.

Luckily for the spot world, neither the up-and-comers nor the A-listers seem daunted by the challenges of the business. "It was not as difficult as I thought it was going to be," says Yuki of launching her still-fledgling career. "In the end it comes down to your work." Observes Shelter's Melissa Bolton, "People will say that one agency or another is a boy's club, but what does that mean now? It's not 1986 anymore. I like golf, I like beer. The same stigmas don't necessarily apply."

What Did You Read?

1. Why do women seem very apt at directing advertising campaigns?
2. Where do most women commercial directors begin their careers?
3. What do men assume about most women in film school? On an expensive product's commercial set?
4. What is the Lucite ceiling?

What Do You Think?

1. In your opinion, what gender do most commercials appeal to most? Why?
2. Have the types of products most frequently advertised changed over time? If so, why might that be?
3. Has the audience for television (and television commercials) changed over time? If so, what effect might that have on what is shown on the screen?

How Was It Done?

1. How does classification form an integral part of this article?
2. What advantage is there for the author to provide a contrast between what men have done and what women have done? Is the article centered on men's ability to advance over women's ability?
3. The author cites specific examples of individual directors and specific products promoted. How effective is this strategy in proving her argument?

Fade to Black

George Alexander

George Alexander examines the difficulties black directors still face in Hollywood in order to make movies. He names specific movies and directors and their difficulties in finding studios interested in making a black director's film and getting budgets large enough to actually make their films the way they want. Alexander also compares the costs and earnings of some black directors' films and the costs and earnings of big-budget mainstream films from the same years. The message is clear: There are profits to be made if black directors are allowed to make more movies.

Key Words

marketability	the ability of something to be sold
notoriety	the quality of being generally known and talked about, especially in an unfavorable way
mainstream	the prevailing current of activity or thought
commensurate	equal in measure or extent
skittish	nervous or uncertain
risk-averse	unwilling to leave something to chance
crossover	a broadening of the popular appeal of an artist or artist's work

At first glance, the summer of 2000 could easily be remembered as a sizzling period for the "black" Hollywood blockbuster film. Temperatures reached record highs and moviegoers flocked to multiplexes to see films directed by or starring African Americans. Heading the list were Keenen Ivory Wayans' *Scary Movie; The Nutty Professor II*, starring Eddie Murphy; and *Big Momma's House*, with Martin Lawrence. Each film cleared the $100 million mark in domestic gross revenues. And director John Singleton's update of the classic, *Shaft*, garnered more than $70 million. While not a blockbuster, Spike Lee's *The Original Kings of Comedy* laughed past $30 million domestically and earned the director his highest opening weekend box office ever.

But even with this success, black film directors still have to fight for big budgets.

Budgets for some mainstream studio fare have reached the $100 million mark, with the average film costing around $50 million, while movies targeted to blacks usually have budgets averaging in the $13 million range. Typically made with no big-name stars, yet armed with marketable sound tracks, "black" films have proven to be moneymakers for studios.

Based on history, it appears the rule is to keep "black" film budgets low and to look to peak domestic gross revenues of between $25 million and $40 million.

Look at *House Party*, which hit the big screen in 1990. It cost $2.5 5 million to make and grossed about $25 million domestically. *Friday* cost about $3.5 million and made about $27 million domestically.

Conversely, big studio event films such as *Mission: Impossible 2* cost $100 million and grossed more than $200 million domestically. *The Adventures of Rocky & Bullwinkle*, however, cost Universal Pictures $76 million but was a major disappointment, grossing only $26 million.

Breaking the Barriers

Unquestionably, Wayans' triumph as the highest-grossing black director of all time with *Scary Movie* (the film has grossed more than $150 million domestically to date)—surpassing Sidney Poitier's *Stir Crazy* (1980), which grossed $101.1 million—is worthy of industry recognition. It demonstrates a black director's ability to succeed in the mainstream. *Scary Movie* is the highest-grossing film in Miramax's history, and Wayans has already agreed to do the sequel.

Scary Movie was marketed to the mainstream as a horror movie spoof, and the producers don't consider it a "black" movie. But the black director still only received a "black" film's budget. Says Jeff Friday, the executive producer and producer of the Acapulco Black Film Festival and president of UniWorld Films, "*Scary Movie* was never intended to be positioned as a black movie. It was a multiracial teen comedy and satire of mainstream horror flicks." The movie spoofs Miramax's *Scream* franchise films, which are targeted to teenagers of all ethnic groups.

Paramount saw *Shaft*'s broad market appeal, a perspective that ultimately allowed Singleton to make the movie he wanted to make. "MGM did not want to spend $25 million on the film. They only saw it as a niche film," he says. Singleton took it to Paramount, and they spent $46 million on it. In addition, *Shaft* had an historical advantage and the marketability of Samuel L. Jackson, he says.

"*Shaft* was a marketing dream. It has been a part of the lexicon of 10 our culture. Its brand is attractive to all audiences," says *Shaft* producer Paul E. Hall.

Studios view films like Universal's *The Nutty Professor II* as star-driven, summer vehicles not solely reliant on black theater attendance. Roz Stevenson, a former publicist for Universal Pictures who now runs her own Los Angeles-based public relations firm with Universal as a client, says, "Eddie Murphy is considered mainstream, not black, and has been marketed as mainstream since the mid-'80s." It was during that time that Murphy emerged as a movie star in *48 Hours*. Murphy's marketability now earns him a whopping $20 million per film.

On the flip side, based on the definition of Stacey Spikes, a former marketing executive at Miramax and October Films (see the sidebar,

"Black Films: The Definition Depends on Who's Talking"), Paramount's *The Original Kings of Comedy*—starring African American comedians Steve Harvey, Bernie Mac, D.L. Hughley, and Cedric the Entertainer—would perhaps be the only film to meet the criteria of a purely "black" film. It is based on the concert tour of the comedians who, while famous in the African American community, do not have the broad market notoriety of Murphy, Lawrence, and Chris Tucker. Shot on digital video as opposed to 35 millimeter film, the movie cost only $3 million to make but has grossed 10 times that already.

It's Not All Laughs

"When there are no models for certain black films, like romantic dramas, there is a tendency on the part of studios to lowball projected grosses," says Spike Lee.

Spike says all the studios have mathematical formulas for estimating gross revenues for each film they produce and what the commensurate budget should be. Such formulas include variables for star marketability, the director's reputation, and how an actor might be received in a foreign territory. Much of the studios' risk analysis is based on precedent, and historically films with all-black casts or dramatic African American themes have not performed strongly overseas, resulting in lower budgets in contrast to comparable white films.

So it would follow that black directors still lament the lack of diversity in films depicting blacks and the difficulty in securing financing for more serious representations of African Americans.   15

"There are lots of comedies, but the battle continues in getting dramas made. We have to look to alternative methods of financing and making films," says Lee.

To circumvent the challenges dramas face, Lee has looked outside the studio system in the past to bring his vision to the silver screen. For example, when Warner Bros financed *Malcolm X*, albeit at a budget lower than what the filmmaker felt necessary to make the epic, Lee raised additional funds from wealthy celebrities, including Michael Jordan and Magic Johnson, to complete the film.

His 1996 film about the Million Man March, *Get On the Bus*, which cost under $3 million, was funded by a group of African American businessmen. And when Lee first brought *Bamboozled*, his controversial fall 2000 release, to New Line Cinema, it was going to cost $23 million. Lee's decision to shoot the film on digital video brought the cost down to $11 million. Digital video is much cheaper than film.

Love & Basketball writer-director Gina Prince-Bythewood faced major hurdles bringing her romantic drama about two aspiring pro basketball players to the big screen. "Every studio in town passed on the script before New Line made the film," she says.

The challenge of pushing dramas through the system is occurring 20 in a climate in which studios are skittish about making dramas of any kind. It doesn't help that recent dramas featuring blacks, such as *Rosewood* and *Beloved,* were box office disappointments.

"It's not just a black thing. It's a Hollywood thing. Black comedies are doing well. People find what works, and they look to repeat it. Studios also look for franchises like *Friday, X-Men,* and *Austin Powers,*" says *Bamboozled* associate producer and New Line executive story analyst Kisha Imani Cameron.

The angst surrounding making "black" dramas is evident in 20th Century Fox's treatment of *Soul Food* writer and director George Tillman Jr.'s fall 2000 film, *Men of Honor,* starring Cuba Gooding Jr. and Robert De Niro. Based on the true story of Carl Brashear, the first African American master diver for the U.S. Navy, the film cost $32 million. It tested well with domestic audiences and international distributors largely due to the positioning of the film as a man's triumph over obstacles, and a race movie. Further, De Niro's character was a compilation of two influential teachers in Brashear's diving school—a rival and a mentor. De Niro enhanced the movie's crossover appeal. "It took me two and a half years to get *Men of Honor* done. De Niro was a key factor in considering overseas markets," says Tillman.

Even with headliners like De Niro and Gooding, Tillman could not get the $50 million budget reserved for mainstream projects.

On the Horizon

African Americans comprise more than 20% of the moviegoing public. However, in 1999, African American directors made up a meager 2.4% (out of a total of 6,564) of the membership of the Directors Guild of America.

Considering there are no African American studio executives with 25 the authority to green-light films, it is not surprising that black films face enormous challenges in advancing through the studio system.

In discussing the issue of real change for African Americans in the current Hollywood system—in the form of diverse stories, more black filmmakers, writers, etc.—director Reginald Hudlin (*House Party, Boomerang, Ladies Man*) asserts, "We need more black executives, and I mean more than one token. Unfortunately, most studios don't even have that. The only way we'll see meaningful change is when blacks have their own studios, or [when] studios create black divisions."

It ultimately means managing risk in a risk-averse environment. And many doubt if budgets for "black" films will increase going forward. "At a time when there is pressure to bring budgets for all films down, I think it is hard to say that budgets for 'black' films will increase based on this past summer," says Jay Stern, executive vice president of production at New Line Cinema, a studio responsible for a number of hit films directed by or starring African Americans, including *House Party, Friday, Next Friday,* and *Love & Basketball.*

Black Films: The Definition Depends Upon Who's Talking

In examining what constitutes "black" cinema, what is most clear is that no one definition exists. Industry experts acknowledge studios' hesitancy at labeling certain films "black" when the prospects for crossover to broader audiences are great. Perhaps director Reginald Hudlin said it best in his recent *L.A. Times* essay, "In Hollywood, 'black' is code for 'limited appeal.'" We asked other major players in the industry to weigh in on what makes a film "black."

Jay Stern, executive vice president of production at New Line Cinema, says that his studio has no written definition of the term "black" movie. "I can only speak for myself. I see a black film as one with a predominantly black cast, and one that is targeted to only a black audience."

Stacy Spikes, a founder of New York's Urban World Film Festival and CEO of the newly formed Urbanworld Group, an independent film distributor, suggests, "If a picture only targets African Americans in its media, then it's a black film. If its media is targeted to a wider audience, then it's considered a film with crossover potential."

The Acapulco Black Film Festival, sponsored by the Black Filmmaker Foundation and UniWorld Films, requires that a film be directed or written and produced by a person of African descend to gain entry to the festival. Others would include in the definition any movie that depicts the African American experience, whether by an African American or not. Here, 1998's *Beloved*, directed by Jonathan Demme, starring Oprah Winfrey, and based on the Toni Morrison best-selling novel would meet the definition. Some would even count films like Forest Whitaker's *Hope Floats* as black, despite the fact it is not about the black experience.

The Patriot

    Executive Producer Dean Devlin
    Producer Dean Devlin
    Director Roland Emmerich
    Lead Actor Mel Gibson
    Lead Actress Mira Sorvino

(continued)

Expenses:

A	B
Film Negative	$110
Worldwide Prints & Advertising	70
Worldwide Home Video	30
Interest & Overhead	17
Profit Participation & Residuals	10
Total Expenses	$237

Legend for Chart:
A - Category
B - Expenses (In Millions)

Net Revenues:

A	B
Domestic Box Office Gross	$60
International Box Office Gross	50
Worldwide Home Video	65
Domestic Pay, Cable, Network TV	42
International Pay, Cable, Network TV	30
Airplane Viewing	3
Total Revenues	$250
NET PROFIT	$13

Legend for Chart:
A - Category
B - Revenues (in Millions)

Source: Coker, Cheo Hodari, "Hollywood Blackout," *Premiere* (October 2000), p. 30.

Scary Movie

Executive Producer Keenen Ivory Wayans
Producer Keenen Ivory Wayans
Director Keenen Ivory Wayans
Lead Actor Ensemble Cast
Lead Actress Ensemble Cast

(continued)

Expenses:

A	B
Film Negative	$19
Worldwide Prints & Advertising	65
Worldwide Home Video	30
Interest & Overhead	5
Profit Participation & Residuals	15
Total Expenses	$134

Legend for Chart:
A - Category
B - Expenses (In Millions)

Net Revenues:

A	B
Domestic Box Office Gross	$70
International Box Office Gross	35
Worldwide Home Video	65
Domestic Pay, Cable, Network TV	40
International Pay, Cable, Network TV	20
Total Revenues	$230
NET PROFIT	96

Legend for Chart:
A - Category
B - Revenues (In Millions)

Source: Coker, Cheo Hodari, "Hollywood Blackout," *Premiere* (October 2000), p. 30.

Big Budget vs. Big Return

A	B		D
		C	E
1986			
SHE'S GOTTA HAVE IT (ISLAND)			
	SPIKE LEE		$120,000
	TRACEY CAMILLA JOHNS, SPIKE LEE		$7.5 MILLION
SHANGHAI SURPRISE (HANDMADE FILMS/MGM)			
	JIM GODDARD		$ Unavailable
	SEAN PENN, MADONNA		$2.3 million
1991			
BOYZ 'N THE HOOD (COLUMBIA)			
	JOHN SINGLETON		$6 MILLION
	LAURENCE FISHBURNE, CUBA GOODING JR., ICE CUBE		$57.5 MILLION

HARLEY DAVIDSON AND THE MARLBORO
  MAN (MGM)
    SIMON WINCER $Unavailable
    MICKEY ROURKE, DON JOHNSON $7 MILLION

1992
MALCOLM X (WARNER BROS.)
    SPIKE LEE $35 MILLION
    DENZEL WASHINGTON $48 MILLION

STOP! OR MY MOM WILL SHOOT (UNIVERSAL)
    ROGER SPOTTISWOODE $ Unavailable
    SYLVESTER STALLONE, ESTELLE GETTY $26.3 MILLION

1995
WAITING TO EXHALE
    FOREST WHITAKER $15 MILLION
    WHITNEY HOUSTON, ANGELA BASSETT $67 MILLION

WATERWORLD (UNIVERSAL)
    DEVIN REYNOLDS (AND KEVIN COSTNER) $175 MILLION
    KEVIN COSTNER $88.2 MILLION

1997
SOUL FOOD (FOX)
    GEORGE TILLMAN JR. $7.2 MILLION
    VANESSA L. WILLIAMS, NIA LONG, $42.7 MILLION
    VIVICA A. FOX

THE PEACEMAKER (DREAMWORKS SKG)
    MIMI LEDER $50 MILLION
    GEORGE CLOONEY, NICOLE KIDMAN $41.3 MILLION

2000
LOVE & BASKETBALL (NEW LINE)
    GINA PRINCE-BYTHEWOOD $13 MILLION
    OMAR EPPS, SANAA LATHAN $28 MILLION

THE ADVENTURES OF ROCKY & BULLWINKLE
  (UNIVERSAL)
    DES McANUFF $76 MILLION
    KEITH SCOTT, MARK SILVERMAN, $6.8 MILLION (OPENING)
    RENE RUSSO

The Original Kings of Comedy
Budget: $3 million
Gross: $30 million +

(continued)

Next Friday
Budget: $10 million
Gross: $57 million

Shaft
Budget: $48 million
Gross: $70 million +

Legend for Chart:
A - film
B - director
C - stars
D - BUDGET
E - DOMESTIC GROSS

What Did You Read?

1. What are some of the reasons it is difficult to secure financing for dramas involving African Americans?
2. What is the biggest stumbling block to getting "black" films made?
3. What does the author mean by "black film"?

What Do You Think?

2. What black films have been received extremely well? Why?
3. In your opinion, do black films themselves fall into the stereotyping of minorities? Why or why not?
4. Of all the minority groups, which one is best represented in films? Which one is represented the least well? Why do you think this is?

How Was It Done?

1. How important are the charts and tables to the article? Do they make it more engaging?
2. How important is the definition of "black film" to the article?
3. Are statistics important to support the proposition that African American directors are becoming a much bigger presence in Hollywood? Explain.

Call It "Kid-Fluence"

Marci McDonald and Marianne Lavelle

Marci McDonald and Marianne Lavelle argue that today's advertisers focus television commercials toward children, and not just the usual array of ads selling toys, games, and junk food. They examine how children exert pressure on their parents (the "nag factor") over large-scale purchases such as cars and family vacations. Cable channels that specialize in children's programming are looking to nontraditional advertisers for revenue, and advertisers are responding. The effects on parental spending patterns are clear, but also advertisers are betting that in the long haul, those young TV viewers will be older viewers who buy the brand names they learned as children.

Key Words

rambunctious	having uncontrollable exuberance
laconic	using a minimum of words
lyricizes	has an intense, personal, emotional quality
clambering	climbing awkwardly
ventured	explored; investigated
testimonial	expression of appreciation or esteem
clout	power or influence
wield	to manage; to deal successfully
icon	a symbol or idol

It's commercial-break time on Nick Jr., the Nickelodeon network's morning programming block for the preschool set. An unaccustomed adult viewer braces for the usual: rambunctious pitches for impossibly adorable dolls and improbably colored food—green ketchup, blue applesauce, and Rugrats-shaped macaroni. But the commercials unfolding on the TV screen aren't for the kinds of kid fare that routinely turn a trip to the mall or grocery store into a whining, tear-stained bargaining process. No, these ads look more like they might have mistakenly strayed onto Nick Jr. from the nightly news or business report.

One laconic spot for Ford's Windstar shows a band of youngsters playing hide-and-seek around a minivan. Another lyricizes over the virtues of Huggies diapers, and a third is a lilting invitation to a family getaway in the Bahamas. This is the new world of children's television, where the shows may still be aimed at the under-5 crowd, but the ads increasingly target the adults curled up on the couch beside them. "A couple of years ago, you would only have seen advertising directed at kids—toys, games, and cereals," says James Perry Nickelodeon's vice president of sales. "But in the 9 A.M.-to-2 P.M. block for preschoolers, we found it's one of the purest places on television for advertisers to reach moms, too."

"Nag Factor"

One result is that everybody from carmakers to corporate healthcare providers is clambering aboard the kids-marketing bandwagon. And why not? According to James McNeal, a retired professor from Texas A&M University who is considered the godfather of kids marketing, children ages 4 to 12 last year spent $29 billion of their own money—from allowances, baby-sitting fees, and handouts their parents doled out on trips to the mall. But McNeal argues that those youngsters also had a direct influence on an estimated $290 billion in family spending in 2000. "That's kids actually pointing fingers and making demands," McNeal notes. Playing on what psychologists call "the nag factor," 2-to-12-year-olds had an indirect impact on another $320 billion of household purchases, he says. "The real story of kids' market power," agrees John Geraci, vice president of youth research at Harris Interactive, "is not their spending. It's their influence on the household."

In response, companies that have never given the slightest thought to an audience they once scorned as ankle biters are retailoring their messages for the kindergarten crowd and their adult "co-viewers," be they parents or nannies. In the past year and a half, Nickelodeon has struck deals with such first-time advertisers as Gateway—which now turns out *Rugrats* and *Blue's Clues* editions of its Astro computer—and Ford Windstar, whose official spokespuppy is the popular, azure-colored, canine star of *Blue's Clues*. And in May, as part of a three-year, $20 million pact, Embassy Suites Hotels began offering every family that checks in this summer a "Nick Trip Pack" with a disposable camera, travel journal, and a *Rugrats* "Tommy" doll. In the month and a half since that Nickelodeon promotion began, visits directly tied to the ads have boosted weekend bookings by 34 percent over last year.

Armed with statistics like that, Perry is crisscrossing the country, trying to sign up other nontraditional advertisers for Nickelodeon's fall lineup. And the network now boasts a separate marketing division devoted to clients who've never ventured into the kinder market. "This is a huge development," he says, "and people are only beginning to grasp the concept."

Nickelodeon is not the only network promoting the notion of what some researchers term "generationally convergent marketing"—better known as using kids to win the hearts and wallets of adults. Three years ago, PBS approached CIGNA, one of the country's largest employee-benefit providers, to sponsor *The Adventures From the Book of Virtues*, an animated series based on the bestseller by former Education Secretary William Bennett. The proposal stunned executives who had spent years marketing directly to their clients: the corporate decision makers who choose among insurers. "At first, our CEO said,

'What? A cartoon show?' " recalled Ed Faruolo, CIGNA's vice president of corporate marketing, at a conference last fall. But three seasons and hundreds of thank-you notes from parents later, internal studies showed that adults who'd watched the series had a more favorable view of CIGNA than those who had not.

For critics of the mushrooming children's marketing industry, the rush of new advertisers into traditional kidspace is hardly good news. Last year, the Kaiser Family Foundation estimated that the average American child is exposed to 40 hours a week of commercial messages on everything from computer screens to roadside billboards—as much time as many of their parents spend on the job.

Some activists, like Eric Brown of the Maryland-based Center for a New American Dream, have long counseled parents to watch TV with their youngest kids as a safety check. But now they see the networks' attempt to cash in on that "co-viewing" as an exercise in cynicism: Parents' efforts to protect their offspring from premature consumerism have become yet another sales opportunity.

Other critics such as Alvin Poussaint, a professor of psychiatry at Harvard Medical School, are calling on Congress to explore the possibility of adopting laws like those in Sweden and the Canadian province of Quebec, which ban advertising to children under 12. But a handful of U.S. media conglomerates, including Disney, have dispatched lobbyists to make sure Sweden's example doesn't spread in Europe. Marketers on this side of the Atlantic seem unfazed by the prospect of such legislative threats. "It doesn't seem to be on the landscape in this country at all," says Mike Burns, who oversees Saatchi & Saatchi's Kid Connection, the world's largest ad agency devoted to children.

Burns and other kids marketers view the explosion in their industry as a testimonial to the phenomenon of "kid-fluence"—the growing clout that children wield in deciding household purchases. "Over the last five years, there's been a substantial increase in the amount of influence kids have on durable goods—cars, boats, big-ticket items," Texas A&M's McNeal says. "The power in the household is being ceded to the children." 10

One reason is the time pressures on single parents or two-career couples. "It's the guilt factor," says Karen Olshan, director of strategic operations for BBDO New York. "With many split families in this country, kids really become partners with adults in making decisions." Agrees Nickelodeon's Perry: "It's a sad but true reality—for working parents, a lot of quality time with the kids means going shopping."

In Search of Cool

Others blame kids' mounting influence on the fact that their baby boomer parents refuse to become the kind of stick-in-the-muds they feel their own parents were. Decked out in the same Gap duds as their offspring, many confer regularly with the younger set on how to stay cool. "The generation gap doesn't exist anymore," says J. Walker Smith, president of Yankelovich Partners. "Nowadays, mothers consult their daughters on what cosmetics to buy. And if you want to sell a car to a dad, you advertise to his teenage son."

In today's families, many kids also serve as chief technology officers. When it comes to computers and other electronic purchases, even 7-year-olds may boast more expertise than Mom or Pop. A 1999 survey by Yankelovich found that 60 percent of parents don't shop for technology without consulting their kids. "Kids tend to be information gateways," says Olshan. "And parents can't help but listen when the kids know more than you do."

In families of recent immigrants, grade schoolers often find themselves playing an even more essential role: cultural interpreter and all-around consumer guide. Isabel Valdes, a top researcher on Hispanic marketing who has lived in California for some two decades, admits that she owes many of her early insights to her own toddlers. "When I immigrated here from Chile, my kids pushed us to have cereal for breakfast," she says. "At home, nobody had ever heard of cereal."

But even a kid-savvy expert like Nickelodeon's Perry was stunned 15 by two studies that documented the full extent of kids' consumer clout. One showed that 65 percent of kids ages 9 to 11 had specific likes and dislikes in hotels, and 56 percent believed their families paid attention to their vacation wish list.

The other report, by automotive researchers J. D. Power & Associates, found that 54 percent to 63 percent of parents acknowledged their kids had been actively involved in shopping for a sport utility vehicle or minivan—and the greatest input appeared to come from 6-to-8-year-olds. Perry promptly called Jim Townsend, brand manager for Ford's Windstar, and proposed targeting an audience well below carmakers' radar—the preschoolers most frequently found in a minivan's back rows. "The question," Townsend says, "was how young do you go?" Late last year, Windstar became the exclusive sponsor of *Blue's Clues* as part of a multimillion-dollar promotional and safety campaign, which includes interactive Web games and Blue's paw prints plastered at strategic kid-friendly locations in the van. "In a showroom, kids will run to the vehicle they like," Townsend says. "And if they run to your vehicle, you know you'll be sitting down to close the deal."

For researchers like McNeal, the Ford campaign to preschoolers represents a triple-barreled play: Not only are the ads reaching both kids and parents but they're also imprinting the Ford brand on young psyches before they get their driver's licenses. Townsend says it's too early to measure the impact of the Nickelodeon deal on sales. But he has seen the branding process in the flesh. In one focus group, he watched a 5-year-old pick out all the pictures on a display that were icons from the *Blue's Clues* show. Then, unprompted, she picked up the blue oval Ford logo and added it to the mix.

What Did You Read?

1. What is the "nag factor"?
2. What is "generationally convergent marketing"?
3. According to the author, why do parents conform to their child's wishes so readily today? Be specific.

What Do You Think?

1. In your opinion, are kids much more powerful than they were when you were growing up? Explain.
2. Should we adopt laws like Sweden did to bar advertising to children under age 12? Why or why not?
3. Do you believe that television has a more positive or negative influence on children? Explain.

How Was It Done?

1. How is the article centered on the concept of the "nag factor" in purchasing?
2. What kinds of strategies do the authors use to support the proposition that children are driving advertising?
3. Who are the experts in this article? How do the authors establish their credibility?

The Market for Television Violence

James T. Hamilton

James T. Hamilton examines the issue of television violence, presenting the TV industry's arguments in favor of violence and why it is not a problem, and responding critically to those arguments. He argues that violence on TV is, in fact, a form of cultural pollution. Hamilton presents ideas on how to combat the effect of violence on TV, especially its effects on children.

Key Words

commodities	goods or products for sale
gratuitous	excessive; overdone; not called for by the circumstances
deflect	to turn aside

demographic	relating to the population, especially the profile based on age, race, class, or gender
perpetrator	one who carries out a crime
desensitization	no longer sensitive or able to respond
noxious	physically harmful or destructive to living beings
ascertaining	being able to determine or conclude something
reluctant	showing hesitation or unwillingness to do something

Fights. Shootings. Killings. If you surf across channels during a normal weekday evening, you are likely to find violent stories unfolding. The violence may seem senseless or aimless, even gratuitous. But the use of violent images is not a random event on television. Violent images are commodities whose quantity and quality are driven by market forces. In a sense, violence on television gives some viewers what they want. Yet because the consumption of these images can lead to harm down the road, the market for television violence can generate costs that do not show up on company balance sheets.

Television violence is at its core a problem of pollution. Programmers and advertisers use violent content to target television's most valuable demographic segment, viewers aged eighteen to thirty-four. The executives who schedule violence to garner ratings and profits do not take into account the full impact of their actions on society. Research shows that television violence increases levels of aggression, fear, and desensitization among some who consume it. The strongest effects are on the youngest viewers. Children are not the target of advertisers on most violent programs, but their exposure to violent images can lead to social damages not factored into decisions about when to air programs and where to draw the line on content.

Responses to Criticism of TV Violence

In writing a book called *Channeling Violence* on the market for violent programming, I (understandably) found few people in the entertainment industry willing to agree that their products generate cultural pollution. Media officials often deflect criticisms of their programs with a standard set of responses, which I came to view as the "Top Five Reasons Why TV Violence is Not a Problem."

1. We Use Violence on Television to Tell, not Sell, Stories

Television executives link the use of violence to narrative needs. In hearings before Congress, network executives have denied that they use violence to earn ratings. Yet I found in my research on programming strategies that every channel type uses violence to gain viewers:

- During the sweeps periods, the four major broadcast networks were much more likely to air movies that deal with murder, focus on tales of family crime, and feature family crime or murder stories based on real-life incidents. Nearly a third of network movies during sweeps periods dealt with murder. The Fox Network, which often aired movies starting at 8 P.M., increased its use of violent movies from 42 percent to 84 percent during sweeps.

- When ABC aired *Monday Night Football,* the basic cable channel TBS dropped its use of violent movies on Monday nights. The percentage of violent movies declined on this channel from 92 percent to 65 percent of the films shown. When football season ended and male viewers were up for grabs, the violent movies returned.

- When Seinfeld dominated ratings on Thursday evenings, HBO had a strategy known internally as "Testosterone Thursday," in which it programmed low-quality violent films at 9 P.M. to attract male viewers uninterested in Seinfeld. These strategic uses of violent programs all contradict the frequent claims that violence is not used to attract viewers.

2. Violence on Television Is a Reflection of Violence in Society

Analyzing data across the country on local news content, I found that the percentage of stories devoted to crime and the percentage of lead stories dealing with crime were not related to the crime rate in a city. Rather, it was audience interest in crime, reflected by ratings for shows such as *Cops* in the market, that predicted the degree to which local news directors focused on crime in their newscasts. The stronger the audience interest in reality police-show programming, the more likely newscasts in an area were to focus on crime.

3. Images on Television Do Not Influence Behavior

Social science research indicates that violent images are more likely to be imitated if they go unpunished, show little pain or suffering, and involve attractive perpetrators. This describes the types of violence often used on television. (For statistical evidence on the context of violence in television, see the work by the National Television Violence Study researchers in Television Violence and Public Policy, James T. Hamilton, editor.)

4. Television Is Less Violent Today

It is true that on prime-time network-broadcast television, the percentage of programs in violent genres dropped in the 1990s. In 1984, 51 percent of prime-time network series were in violent genres, a figure that declined to 23 percent in 1993. But violence has simply migrated to basic and premium cable channels. Nearly two thirds of all basic cable movies on at 8 P.M. on weekdays are violent. Of the top five programs viewed each week on premium channels, more than half are violent movies.

5. *What about* Schindler's List?

Violence is used in high-quality films. Yet these types of movies are only a small percentage of those shown on television. In a sample of five thousand violent movies on broadcast, basic cable, and premium cable channels, I found that only 3 percent were given four stars (the highest rating) by critics.

Unintended Audiences

In opinion surveys about television, the majority of adult respondents indicates that there is too much violence in entertainment programming. Yet there are segments of viewers who enjoy and consume violent shows. Males aged eighteen to thirty-four are the top consumers of violent entertainment fare, followed by females aged eighteen to thirty-four. These viewers are particularly prized by advertisers, in part because their purchase decisions can be more easily influenced than those of older consumers. As a result, programmers often target these young adults and use violent shows to attract them.

These same violent programs also might attract an unintended au- 10 dience, children two to eleven and teens twelve to seventeen. Prime-time shows do not get higher ad rates for attracting child viewers because the products on these programs are aimed at adults. Yet because the programs are on when children are in the viewing audience (nearly one out of three children and teens are watching television at 8 P.M. on weekdays), children see violent shows aimed at adults.

This exposure of children to violent programs generates a pollution problem. Research indicates that some children who consume violent programming are more likely to become aggressive, to feel desensitized to violence, or to experience fear upon viewing. While the market for violence works well in delivering a segment of adult viewers what they want, the market fails with respect to shielding children from harmful effects. Neither advertisers nor programmers are led to consider the full costs to society of using violence to attract viewers because they are not led by the market to internalize in their decision-making the negative effects these programs have on children. The result is too much violence consumed by too many children.

Broadcasters correctly stress that their business is selling audiences to advertisers, not raising or educating children. When they make programming choices, they focus on the number of viewers, the value of these viewers to advertisers, the cost of programs, and the number of competitors offering different types of fare. Multiple incentives favor the provision of violent programming by some channels. Violent shows are cheaper for networks to purchase. Violent programs are twice as likely to be exported, which increases the returns to producers. As the number of viewing options increases, channels serving particular niches continue to grow, including those that specialize in developing a brand name for violence. The proliferation of channels will involve an increase in the number of violent viewing options and the intensity of violence on some channels.

Dealing with Violence as Pollution

If violence on television is a pollution problem, what is to be done? In dealing with everyday pollutants such as toxic chemicals released into the air, the government has a wide array of policy tools to reduce the harm created: zoning of noxious facilities, the direct control of the release of chemicals, the use of liability laws to change behavior, and the taxing of polluting activities. In the media realm, the First Amendment rightfully restricts the policy options available to deal with television violence. However, I do believe that industry, encouraged by government, can take at least three steps to lower children's exposure to violence: provide accurate content information, consider the likely number of children in the audience when scheduling, and take responsibility for the potential harm that may arise from some types of programs.

Information Provision

Parents make the ultimate decisions about whether their children will consume violent content. Yet even for the parents most concerned about shielding their children, the costs in terms of time of finding out what programs contain potentially objectionable content, ascertaining when particular programs are on, and monitoring the viewing of their children are extensive. The V-chip and program ratings provided by the television industry offer the potential to reduce the costs to parents of being responsible. The V-chip and ratings system will work, however, only if parents believe the system is credible, informative, and effective. In my research I found that parents do act if they are provided with program-content information. On prime-time broadcast network movies, the Nielsen rating for children ages two to eleven dropped by about 14 percent on movies that carried a viewer-discretion warning. Because these movies were averaging 1.6 million children aged two to eleven in their audiences, the drop in viewing translated into approximately 220,000 fewer children in the audience for a movie carrying a warning. The warnings had no effect on ratings for teens or adults.

However, the warnings did change the willingness of some adver- 15
tisers to sponsor a program. Once a warning was placed on a violent theatrical film shown on network movies, products likely to experience harm to their brand images by being associated with violence

were less likely to advertise on the movie. In particular, products consumed by women, by older viewers, and by families with children were less likely to advertise on a movie that carried a viewer-discretion warning. The number of general product ads on a movie also dropped slightly when the warning was placed. Products aimed at men and younger adults were actually more willing to advertise on these movies with warnings because their consumers report that they are less likely to see television violence as a problem. The companies advertising on movies with warnings were those at less risk for brand-name damage.

Controversy about content can have a large effect on advertisers. I found that in its first season, ads on *NYPD Blue* sold at a 45 percent discount because of the initial unwillingness of advertisers to be associated with the program. Broadcasters are reluctant to provide viewers with content information in part because of the fear that this information will generate controversy and change the willingness of advertisers to support a particular program. Cable channels have historically provided much more detailed content descriptors for their programs, in part because they are less dependent on advertiser reactions. During the early implementation of the television rating system, I found evidence that continued concern for advertiser reactions kept the broadcast networks from providing accurate program indicators on more controversial programs. Comparing the ratings provided by the networks with program evaluations from the Parents' Television Council, I found that the networks frequently "underlabeled" programs, such as giving a program found by the parents' viewing group to contain "gratuitous sex, explicit dialogue, violent content, or obscene language" a TV-PG rating rather than a TV-14 rating. The networks were more likely to underlabel the programs with higher ad rates. Among the networks, NBC had the highest ad rates on under-labeled programs.

More recent research by Dale Kunkel and colleagues (An Assessment of the Television Industry's Use of V-chip Ratings) indicates that more than three-fourths of programs with violence did not carry a violence indicator. An obvious first step that industry officials can take to reduce the exposure of children to violent content is to label such content more frequently, though they may be reluctant to do this because of fears of advertiser backlash. The effect of improved labeling will take time to develop because the current rating system is akin to providing software without hardware. As sets with V-chips arrive in the market, parents will be able to use the content-rating systems more easily.

Scheduling

A second measure that industry officials could take would be to shift violent programming to times when children are less likely to be in the audience. This shift would require a substantial change in behavior by some programmers because the times when children and teens are in the audience are often the same times when viewers eighteen to thirty-four are also in the audience. At 8 P.M. on weekdays, for example, nearly one out of three children and teens is watching television. At this time, nearly two-thirds of all movies on basic cable are violent. Fox, which broadcast the highest percentage of violent films among the major networks, often began its movies at 8 P.M. Early-evening and daytime hours on weekends are also frequent times for the programming of syndicated violent shows. Half of the weekly exposures of children ages two to eleven to syndicated action-adventure/crime series occurs on weekends during the day or early evening before 8 P.M. If programmers were to shift violent content to hours when viewing by children was less likely to arise, this would reduce the probability that those most susceptible to harm were exposed to violent content.

Responsibility

A final measure that industry officials could adopt would be to admit that some programs may be damaging for some children to watch. In debates about television violence, executives often deny the potential for harm to arise from programming. Parents will be more likely to act to shield their children from violent programming if there is a more consistent message about likely dangers. I found that parents who were personally bothered by television violence were much more likely to intervene and switch channels when objectionable content came on while children were viewing. Parent groups, educators, pediatricians, and foundations all have a role in alerting parents to the need to shield children from violent content and in providing information on how to use options such as the ratings system and the V-chip. Entertainment officials also have a role to play in this education process. The targeting and repetition of messages to change consumer decisions are the economic foundation of television programming. If the industry could add an additional message to the information that it conveys, namely that violent content might be harmful and that parents should shield their children from it, there might be a high payoff to society from this type of advertising.

What Did You Read?

1. Explain the statement "Violent images are commodities whose quantity and quality are driven by market forces."
2. Why do some people think that violence should be eliminated from young viewers' programming?
3. According to the book *Channeling Violence*, what are the five primary reasons why violence is not a problem on TV?

What Do You Think?

1. What is the relationship between violent programming and consumerism?

2. What are some measures that industry officials can take to reduce the exposure of children to violent TV content?

3. Is violence on television entertainment programs more violent than real-life violence reported on in the television news? Explain.

How Was It Done?

1. How is classification used in this article?

2. In the article, the author argues in the following format: he presents a statement from the opposing side, and follows that with his rebuttal of their argument. What is the strength of using this technique of argument?

3. The author uses opinion surveys. How credible are such surveys? Does the author present enough information about the surveys for a reader to accept their results?

4. How important are the concluding paragraphs to the overall effectiveness of the article?

We Are Training Our Kids to Kill

Dave Grossman

Dave Grossman argues that children learn how to aim, shoot, and commit acts of violence through watching television. He cites examples of real-life shootings by children, and the role that TV has played in teaching children to be violent. Grossman urges that children, at a minimum, need to be exposed only to age-appropriate programming.

Key Words

personifies	embodies in a person abstract concepts or ideas
emulate	to imitate; to strive to equal or excel
glorify	to bestow with honor, praise, or admiration
perpetuate	to cause to last indefinitely
carcinogen	a substance that causes cancer
gruesome	inspiring horror and revulsion
mentoring	acting as a counselor or guide

In the military, you are immediately confronted with a role model: your drill sergeant. He personifies violence and aggression. Along with military heroes, violent role models have always been used to influence young, impressionable recruits.

Today, the media are providing our children with many, perhaps most, of their role models. Kids like to emulate their role models. Tragically, media-inspired copycat crimes are now a fact of life. This is the part of juvenile crime reporting that the TV networks would rather not talk about.

Research in the 1970s demonstrated the existence of "cluster suicides" in which the local TV reporting of teen suicides directly caused numerous copycat suicides by impressionable teenagers. Somewhere in every population there are potentially suicidal kids who will say to themselves, "Well, I'll show all those people who have been mean to me. Then I'll get my picture on TV, too."

Because of this research, television stations today generally do not cover suicides. But when the pictures of teenage killers appear on TV, the effect is the same. Somewhere there is a potentially violent boy who says to himself, "Well, I'll shoot all those people who have been mean to me. Then I'll get my picture on TV, too." Thus we get copycat cluster murders that work their way across America like a virus spread by the six o'clock news. No matter what someone has done, if you put his picture on TV, you have made him a celebrity, and someone somewhere will want to emulate him.

The lineage of the Jonesboro shootings began at Pearl, Mississippi, 　5 fewer than four months before. In Pearl, a 16-year-old boy was accused of killing his mother and then going to his school and shooting nine students, two of whom died, including his ex-girlfriend. Two months later, this virus spread to Paducah, Kentucky, where a 14-year-old boy was arrested for killing three students and wounding five others.

A very important step in the spread of this copycat crime virus occurred in Stamps, Arkansas, 15 days after Pearl and just a little over 90 days before Jonesboro. In Stamps, a 14-year-old boy who was angry with his schoolmates hid in the woods and fired at children as they came out of school. Sound familiar? Only two children were injured in this crime, so most of the world didn't hear about it, but it got great regional coverage on TV, and two little boys in Jonesboro, Arkansas, probably did hear about it.

And then there was Springfield, Oregon, and so many others. Is this a reasonable price to pay for the TV networks' "right" to turn juvenile defendants into celebrities and role models by playing up their pictures on TV?

Our society needs to be informed about these crimes, but when the images of the young killers are broadcast on television, they become role models. The average preschooler in America watches 27 hours of television a week. The average child gets more one-on-one communication from TV than from all her parents and teachers combined. The ultimate achievement for our children is to get their picture on TV. The solution is simple, and it comes straight out of the sociology literature: The media have every right and responsibility to tell the story, but they must be persuaded not to glorify the killers by presenting their images on TV.

Unlearning Violence

What is the road home from the dark and lonely place to which we have traveled? One route infringes on civil liberties. The city of New York has made remarkable progress in recent years in bringing down crime rates, but they may have done so at the expense of some civil liberties. People who are fearful say that is a price they are willing to pay.

Another route would be to "just turn it off." If you don't like what 10 is on television, use the "off" button. Yet, if all the parents of the 15 shooting victims in Jonesboro had protected their children from TV violence, it wouldn't have done a bit of good because somewhere there were two little boys whose parents didn't "just turn it off."

Another route to reduced violence is gun control. I don't want to downplay that option, but America is trapped in a vicious cycle when we talk about gun control. Americans don't trust the government. Most believe that each of us should be responsible for taking care of our families and ourselves. That's one of our great strengths—but it is also a great weakness. When the media foster fear and perpetuate a milieu of violence, Americans arm themselves in order to deal with that violence. And the more guns there are out there, the more violence there is. And the more violence there is, the greater the desire for guns.

We are trapped in this spiral of self-reliance and lack of trust. Real progress will never be made until we reduce this level of fear. As a historian, I tell you it will take decades—maybe even a century—before we wean Americans off their guns. Until we reduce the fear of violent crime, many Americans would sooner "die" than give up their guns.

Fighting Back

We need to make progress in the fight against child abuse, racism, and poverty, and in rebuilding our families. No one is denying that the breakdown of the family is a factor. But nations without our divorce rate are also having increases in violence. Research demonstrates that one major source of harm associated with single-parent families occurs when the TV becomes both the nanny and the second parent.

Work is needed in all these areas, but there is a new front—taking on the producers and purveyors of media violence. Simply put, we ought to work toward legislation that outlaws violent video games for children. There is no constitutional right for a child to play an interactive video game that teaches him weapons-handling skills or that simulates destruction of God's creatures.

The day may also be coming when we are able to seat juries in 15 America who are willing to sock it to the networks and video game promoters in the only place they'll really feel it—their wallets. After the Jonesboro shootings, *Time* magazine said, "As for media violence, the debate there is fast approaching the same point that discussions about the health impact of tobacco reached some time ago—it's over. Few researchers bother any longer to dispute that bloodshed on TV and in the movies has an effect on kids who witness it" (April 6, 1998).

Most of all, the American people need to learn the lesson of Jonesboro. Violence is not a game; it's not fun; it's not something that we do for entertainment. Violence kills and maims.

Every parent in America needs to be warned of the impact that TV and other forms of violent media have on their children, just as we would warn them of some widespread carcinogen. The problem is that the TV networks, which use the public airwaves we have licensed to them, are our key means of public education in America. And they are stonewalling.

In the days after the Jonesboro shootings, I was interviewed on Canadian national TV, the British Broadcasting Company, and many U.S. and international radio shows and newspapers. But the American television networks simply would not touch this aspect of the story. Never in my experience as a historian and a psychologist have I seen any institution in America so clearly responsible for so very many deaths and so clearly abusing their publicly licensed and power to cover up their guilt.

Time after time, idealistic young network producers, fascinated by the irony that an expert in the field of violence and aggression was living in Jonesboro and was at the school almost from the beginning, contacted me from one of the networks. But unlike all the other media, these network news stories always died a sudden, silent death when the networks' powers-that-be said, "Yeah, we need this story like we need a hole in the head."

Many times since the shooting I have been asked, "Why weren't 20 you on TV talking about the stuff in your book?" And every time my answer had to be, "The TV networks are burying this story. They know they are guilty, and they want to delay the retribution as long as they can."

A CBS executive once told me his child-rearing plan. He knows all about the link between television and violence. His own in-house people have advised him to protect his child from the poison his industry is bringing to America's children. He is not going to expose his child to TV until she's old enough to learn how to read. And then he will select very carefully what she sees. He and his wife plan to send her to a day-care center that has no television, and he plans to show her only age-appropriate videos.

That should be the bare minimum with children. Show them only age-appropriate videos and think hard about what is age appropriate.

One TV commentator told me, "Well, we only have one really violent show on our network, and that is 'NYPD Blue.' I'll admit that is bad, but it is only one night a week."

I wondered at the time how she would feel if someone said, "Well, I only beat my wife in front of the kids one night a week."

"You're not supposed to know who I am!" said "NYPD Blue" 25 star Kim Delaney, in response to young children who recognized her from her role on that show. According to *USA Weekend,* she was shocked that so many underage viewers watch her show, which is rated TV-14 for gruesome crimes, raw language, and explicit sex scenes. But they do watch.

There are many other things that we can do to help change our culture. Youth activities can provide alternatives to television, and churches can lead the way in providing alternative locations for latchkey children. Fellowship groups can provide guidance and support to young parents as they strive to raise their children without the destructive influences of the media. Mentoring programs can pair mature, educated adults with young parents to help them through the preschool ages without using the TV as a baby-sitter. And most of all, the churches can provide the clarion call of decency and love and peace as an alternative to death and destruction—not just for the sake of the church, but for the transformation of our culture.

What Did You Read?

1. How is it that young killers become role models?
2. What does the author mean by "we are trapped in this spiral of self-reliance and lack of trust"?
3. What does the author think parents can do as an antidote to violence on television?

What Do You Think?

1. Does the reporting of violent crimes inspire violent behavior or copy-cat crimes in others? Explain.
2. Is presenting an image on TV the same as glorifying that image?
3. Is it your opinion that controlling children's access to guns would help control juvenile crime? Why or why not?
4. As a potential or actual parent, how would you control the relationship between your child and the TV?

How Was It Done?

1. The author begins by comparing today's media with real military warfare. How do the opening paragraphs establish the overall tone of the article?

2. How does the author use his own personal experience to support his thesis? Is there any problem with doing this?

3. Can the cause/effect connection established by the author be trusted? In other words, is the use of a few examples of copy-cat crimes enough to establish the principle that media violence causes real-life violence?

4. How does the author craft his conclusion? What call to action does he make?

2

Democracy in the Classroom

Referring to students as the leaders of tomorrow has become a cliché, used by educators, politicians, and commencement speakers. Behind the cliché, however, is a simple truth: the educational experiences of students will shape their personal futures, and those collective futures shape our society, our nation, and our world. So, what happens in a classroom does matter. However, sometimes what goes on in the classroom seems to conflict with the democratic principles of power on which the United States was formed.

First of all, there has been great debate about the curriculum. Is our educational system sensitive to the language barriers of those who speak English as a learned language? Is it wrong of our schools to concentrate on books that represent the white, Protestant, Western heritage and not those of other cultures? Do we encourage all our students to participate?

Second, controversy rages about assessing our students. Are standardized tests such as the SAT exam biased and skewed in favor of whites? Or is our educational system asking less and less of our students so that virtually all students are able to pass classes and earn diplomas or degrees without having learned the material?

Lastly, does the education system as it is conceived truly prepare our students for jobs in this highly technological society? Does, for example, a liberal arts education in which Marx, Freud, and Hegel are studied do much in the way of preparing students for the 21st century? These issues and others can have importance both to the educational world and to the very concepts of democratic government.

In this chapter, the Writing Lesson focuses on the definition of terms. Definition of important terms is frequently a key aspect of writing an essay, and sometimes the entire point of a work. Many words resist simple definitions because they describe ideas and concepts about which people disagree. Thus, the disagreement centers on the ability to control the definition of terms as a way to control an argument. The Writing Lesson shows how to move beyond a simple dictionary definition to develop more complicated, extended definitions in order to explain a term fully. Then, in the Writing Assignment, you can use the extended definition as a key to develop your essay. Convincing your reader that your definition is valid is a good way, in many cases, to convince the reader that your thesis is valid and true.

THE MAIN EVENT READING

Crossing Boundaries
Mike Rose

In this excerpt from his book Lives on the Border, *Mike Rose addresses the importance of the canon in education. He sees it as ironic that in a country that values individualism and scorns traditionalism, the use of a canon—a set body of knowledge to learn—seems at odds with our nation's democratic foundation. That is, the concept of a canon is inherently elitist, including certain voices but excluding many more. Rose argues, on the one hand, that keeping the canon from students is one way to ensure they remain culturally isolated: the knowledge of the canon is one calling card of an educated person. But he also argues that the canon needs to be explored and changed, and perhaps ultimately the concept of a canon itself should be questioned because of its ability to prevent new thinking and lessen tensions that ought to be explored.*

Key Words

validated	made official or sanctioned
allusions	references to other texts or artistic works
canon	an accepted or sanctioned body of works, especially of literature
corpus	a collection or body of knowledge; all the writings on a particular subject or by a particular author
zeitgeist	the spirit of the times; the general intellectual, moral, and cultural climate of an era
valorous	with strength of mind or spirit
elitist	belonging to a group who through position or education exerts strong power or influence
cognitive	based on the ability to be reduced to factual knowledge; related to the ability to think with reason and judgment

linguistic	relating to the study of language or human speech
discordance	lack of agreement; inconsistency between beliefs, or between one's beliefs and one's actions
fragmentation	the breaking up into parts

proposition

With the lives of Mario and Caroline and Chin and Frank Marell as a backdrop, I want to consider a current, very powerful set of proposals about literacy and culture.

topic sen-
tence
is this true?

There is a strong impulse in American education—curious in a country with such an ornery streak of antitraditionalism—to define achievement and excellence in terms of the acquisition of a historically validated body of knowledge, an authoritative list of books and allusions, a canon. We seek a certification of our national intelligence, indeed, our national virtue, in how diligently our children can display this central corpus of information. This need for certification tends to emerge most dramatically in our educational policy debates during times of real or imagined threat: economic hard times, political crises, sudden increases in immigration. Now is such a time, and it is re-

refers to
experts

flected in a number of influential books and commission reports. E. D. Hirsch argues that a core national vocabulary, one oriented toward the English literate tradition—Alice in Wonderland to zeitgeist—will build a knowledge base that will foster the literacy of all Americans. Diane Ravitch and Chester Finn call for a return to a traditional historical and literary curriculum: the valorous historical figures and the classical literature of the once-elite course of study. Allan Bloom, Secretary of Education William Bennett, Mortimer Adler and the Paideia Group, and a number of others have affirmed, each in their very different ways, the necessity of the Great Books: Plato and Aristotle and Sophocles, Dante and Shakespeare and Locke, Dickens and Mann and

Rose's
definition

Faulkner. We can call this orientation to educational achievement the canonical orientation.

compare
and con-
trast strat-
egy

other peo-
ple's sug-
gestions

At times in our past, the call for a shoring up of or return to a canonical curriculum was explicitly elitist, was driven by a fear that the education of the select was being compromised. Today, though, the majority of the calls are provocatively framed in the language of democracy. They assail the mediocre and grinding curriculum frequently found in remedial and vocational education. They are disdainful of the patronizing perceptions of student ability that further restrict the already restricted academic life of disadvantaged youngsters. They point out that the canon—its language, conventions, and allusions—is central to the discourse of power, and to keep it from poor kids is to assure their disenfranchisement all the more. The books of the canon, claim the proposals, the Great Books, are a window onto a common core of experience and civic ideals. There is, then, a spiritual, civic, and cognitive heritage here, and *all* our children should receive it. If we are sincere in our desire to bring Mario, Chin, the younger versions of Caroline, current incarnations of Frank Marell, and so many others who populate this book—if we truly want to bring them into our society—then we should provide them with this stable and common core. This is a forceful call. It promises a still center in a turning world.

I see great value in being challenged to think of the curriculum of the many in the terms we have traditionally reserved for the few; it is refreshing to have common assumptions about the capacities of underprepared students so boldly challenged. Many of the people we have encountered in these pages have displayed the ability to engage books and ideas thought to be beyond their grasp. There were the veterans: Willie Oates writing, in prison, ornate sentences drawn from *The Mill on the Floss*. Sergeant Gonzalez coming to understand poetic ambiguity in "Butch Weldy." There was the parole aide Olga who no longer felt walled off from *Macbeth*. There were the EOP students at UCLA, like Lucia who unpackaged *The Myth of Mental Illness* once she had an orientation and overview. And there was Frank Marell who, later in his life, would be talking excitedly to his nephew about this guy Edgar Allan Poe. Too many people are kept from the books of the canon, the Great Books, because of misjudgments about their potential. Those books eventually proved important to me, and, as best I know how, I invite my students to engage them. But once we grant the desirability of equal curricular treatment and begin to consider what this equally distributed curriculum would contain, problems arise: If the canon itself is the answer to our educational inequities, why has it historically invited few and denied many? Would the canonical orientation provide adequate guidance as to how a democratic curriculum should be constructed and how it should be taught? Would it guide us in opening up to Olga that "fancy talk" that so alienated her?

Those who study the way literature becomes canonized, how linguistic creations are included or excluded from a tradition, claim that the canonical curriculum students would most likely receive would not, as is claimed, offer a common core of American experience. Caroline would not find her life represented in it, nor would Mario. The canon has tended to push to the margin much of the literature of our nation: from American Indian songs and chants to immigrant fiction to working-class narratives. The institutional messages that students receive in the books they're issued and the classes they take are powerful and, as I've witnessed since my Voc. Ed. days, quickly internalized. And to revise these messages and redress past wrongs would involve more than adding some new books to the existing canon—the very reasons for linguistic and cultural exclusion would have to become a

Rose's perspective

thinking about the canon

5

where would this discussion lead?

focus of study in order to make the canon act as a democratizing force. Unless this happens, the democratic intent of the reformers will be undercut by the content of the curriculum they propose.

And if we move beyond content to consider basic assumptions about teaching and learning, a further problem arises, one that involves the very nature of the canonical orientation itself. The canonical orientation encourages a narrowing of focus from learning to that which must be learned: It simplifies the dynamic tension between student and text and reduces the psychological and social dimensions of instruction. The student's personal history recedes as the what of the classroom is valorized over the how. Thus it is that the encounter of student and text is often portrayed by canonists as a transmission. Information, wisdom, virtue will pass from the book to the student if the student gives the book the time it merits, carefully traces its argument or narrative or lyrical progression. Intellectual, even spiritual, growth will *necessarily* result from an encounter with Roman mythology, *Othello,* and "I heard a Fly buzz—when I died—," with biographies and historical sagas and patriotic lore. Learning is stripped of confusion and discord. It is stripped, as well, of strong human connection. My own initiators to the canon—Jack MacFarland, Dr. Carothers, and the rest—knew there was more to their work than their mastery of a tradition. What mattered most, I see now, were the relationships they established with me, the guidance they provided when I felt inadequate or threatened. This mentoring was part of my entry into that solemn library of Western thought—and even with such support, there were still times of confusion, anger, and fear. It is telling, I think, that once that rich social network slid away, once I was in graduate school in intense, solitary encounter with that tradition, I abandoned it for other sources of nurturance and knowledge.

The model of learning implicit in the canonical orientation seems, at times, more religious than cognitive or social: Truth resides in the printed texts, and if they are presented by someone who knows them well and respects them, that truth will be revealed. Of all the advocates of the canon, Mortimer Adler has given most attention to pedagogy—and his Paideia books contain valuable discussions of instruction, coaching, and questioning. But even here, and this is doubly true in the other manifestos, there is little acknowledgment that the material in the canon can be not only difficult but foreign, alienating, overwhelming.

We need an orientation to instruction that provides guidance on how to determine and honor the beliefs and stories, enthusiasms, and apprehensions that students reveal. How to build on them, and when they clash with our curriculum—as I saw so often in the Tutorial Center at UCLA—when they clash, how to encourage a discussion that will lead to reflection on what students bring and what they're cur-

(margin notes)
importance of networks and mentors

examines an assumption

proposal

rently confronting. Canonical lists imply canonical answers, but the manifestos offer little discussion of what to do when students fail. If students have been exposed to at least some elements of the canon before—as many have—why didn't it take? If they're encountering it for the first time and they're lost, how can we determine where they're located—and what do we do then?

Each member of a teacher's class, poor *or* advantaged, gives rise to endless decisions, day-to-day determinations about a child's reading and writing: decisions on how to tap strength, plumb confusion, foster growth. The richer your conception of learning and your understanding of its social and psychological dimensions, the more insightful and effective your judgments will be. Consider the sources of literacy we saw among the children in El Monte: shopkeepers' signs, song lyrics, auto manuals, the conventions of the Western, family stories and tales, and more. Consider Chin's sources—television and *People* magazine—and Caroline's oddly generative mix of the Bible and an American media illusion. Then there's the jarring confluence of personal horror and pop cultural flotsam that surfaces in Mario's drawings, drawings that would be a rich, if volatile, point of departure for language instruction. How would these myriad sources and manifestations be perceived and evaluated if viewed within the framework of a canonical tradition, and what guidance would the tradition provide on how to understand and develop them? The great books and central texts of the canon could quickly become a benchmark against which the expressions of student literacy would be negatively measured, a limiting band of excellence that, ironically, could have a dispiriting effect on the very thing the current proposals intend: the fostering of mass literacy.

connecting to real world examples

To understand the nature and development of literacy we need to consider the social context in which it occurs—the political, economic, and cultural forces that encourage or inhibit it. The canonical orientation discourages deep analysis of the way these forces may be affecting performance. The canonists ask that schools transmit a coherent traditional knowledge to an ever-changing, frequently uprooted community. This discordance between message and audience is seldom examined. Although a ghetto child can rise on the lilt of a Homeric line—books *can* spark dreams—appeals to elevated texts can also divert attention from the conditions that keep a population from realizing its dreams. The literacy curriculum is being asked to do what our politics and our economics have failed to do: diminish differences in achievement, narrow our gaps, bring us together. Instead of analysis of the complex web of causes of poor performance, we are offered a faith in the unifying power of a body of knowledge, whose infusion will bring the rich and the poor, the longtime disaffected and the uprooted newcomers into cultural unanimity. If this vision is

10 relationship between literature and society

democratic, it is simplistically so, reductive, not an invitation for people truly to engage each other at the point where cultures and classes intersect.

I worry about the effects a canonical approach to education could have on cultural dialogue and transaction—on the involvement of an abandoned underclass and on the movement of immigrants like Mario and Chin into our nation. A canonical uniformity promotes rigor and quality control; it can also squelch new thinking, diffuse the generative tension between the old and the new. It is significant that the canonical orientation is voiced with most force during times of challenge and uncertainty, for it promises the authority of tradition, the seeming stability of the past. But the authority is fictive, gained from a misreading of American cultural history. No period of that history was harmoniously stable; the invocation of a golden age is a mythologizing act. Democratic culture is, by definition, vibrant and dynamic, discomforting and unpredictable. It gives rise to apprehension; freedom is not always calming. And, yes, it can yield fragmentation, though often as not the source of fragmentation is intolerant misunderstanding of diverse traditions rather than the desire of members of those traditions to remain hermetically separate. A truly democratic vision of knowledge and social structure would honor this complexity. The vision might not be soothing, but it would provide guidance as to how to live and teach in a country made up of many cultural traditions.

summation   We are in the middle of an extraordinary social experiment: the attempt to provide education for all members of a vast pluralistic democracy. To have any prayer of success, we'll need many conceptual blessings: A philosophy of language and literacy that affirms the diverse sources of linguistic competence and deepens our understanding of the ways class and culture blind us to the richness of those sources. A perspective on failure that lays open the logic of error. An orientation toward the interaction of poverty and ability that undercuts simple polarities, that enables us to see simultaneously the constraints poverty places on the play of mind and the actual mind at play within those constraints. We'll need a pedagogy that encourages us to step back and consider the threat of the standard classroom and that shows us, having stepped back, how to step forward to invite a student across the boundaries of that powerful room. Finally, we'll need a revised store of images of educational excellence, ones closer to egalitarian ideals—ones that embody the reward and turmoil of education in a democracy, that celebrate the plural, messy human reality of it. At heart, we'll need a guiding set of principles that do not encourage us to retreat from, but move us closer to, an understanding of the rich mix of speech and ritual and story that is America.

What Did You Read?

1. What does Mike Rose mean by the canon? Provide some examples of it you have studied.

2. According to Rose, what is wrong in assuming that, if everyone has access to canonical learning, everyone is involved in the learning process? Do you agree or disagree? Why?

3. What does Rose feel is absolutely necessary to take place in a college classroom outside the particular curriculum?

4. Why is Rose critical of the canon?

What Do You Think?

1. What value is there in reading the canon? What are the drawbacks?

2. Do you feel there is a relationship between the reading of the "Great Books" and your ability to have greater insights into life?

3. What does it mean to get a traditional education today?

How Was It Done?

1. The opening paragraph of Rose's article is centered on a discussion of what tradition or concept?

2. What type of evidence does Rose use to challenge the virtue and worthiness of this tradition?

3. Does Rose appeal to his audience by using facts or emotions? How?

4. Does he balance the use of ideology and abstract concepts well with concrete examples? How?

5. How important are Rose's credentials to the credibility of this article?

THE MAIN EVENT WRITING ASSIGNMENT

Write an essay in which you respond to one of the following questions:

1. Do principles of democracy enhance success in the classroom or not? In order to successfully complete this assignment, you will need to define democracy in the classroom.

2. Should values clarification be taught in the lower grades to ensure that students grow up to be responsible citizens?

3. Should we change how we enroll students into colleges? Should standardized test scores be thrown out? How important should grade point averages be? Should greater emphasis be placed on work experience or extracurricular activities? In other words, what signifies a student's potential to do well in college?

4. Do you advocate home schooling? Why or why not?

5. Is the traditional concept of a four-year, text-based education outdated? Why or why not?

PREPARATION PUNCH LIST

Before you begin writing the essay, you need to prepare yourself to write. One way to prepare is to brainstorm a series of questions. The following are examples of important questions you might wish to consider.

1. What are the current issues surrounding education? In other words, what do we read about concerning education?

For instance:

- Do SAT scores accurately reflect one's potential? Or are they racially biased?
- Are grades inflated? How can one tell?
- Are minorities getting the same quality of education as whites?

2. What does democracy in education mean?

- Does it mean equal opportunity? What does the phrase "equal opportunity" mean?
- Is everyone participating?
- Is there equal opportunity for each student to learn?

3. What does success in the classroom mean?

(This is a tricky question depending on your definition of success. For example, from a teacher's perspective, success may mean that all students are doing well. From a student's perspective, success may mean just that he or she is doing well. Success may go beyond simply getting a certain grade.)

- Are you stimulated, or are you encouraged to be passive?
- Are you getting preferential treatment, or are you being discriminated against, even in subtle ways?
- Does the curriculum relate to your culture and your experience?
- Are you encouraged to think in new ways about new things?

4. What are the benefits of democracy working in the classroom?

(In other words, examine the benefit of having the curriculum represent many cultures and races.)

- What is the benefit of having every student in the educational process?
- What is the benefit of having mechanisms built into the education system that mainstream physically, mentally, and financially handicapped students?

5. How does democracy in the classroom hurt a certain kind of student?

- Has education become therapy?
- Has self-esteem earned through hard work and perseverance been replaced with social promotion and watered-down standards?
- Do educational systems now cater to the "average" rather than push students to excel?
- Have we stifled excellence?

THE MAIN EVENT WRITING LESSON: USING DEFINITION IN AN ESSAY

Have you ever had a disagreement with someone, only to realize that the basis of that disagreement was a dispute over the definition of a key term? Definition of terms is often an important issue in writing essays because there are many words over which people can disagree. For example, when people talk about "justice," "fairness," "equality," "freedom," and "success," there can be serious and complex arguments about what those terms mean.

At first this might strike you as nonsensical: after all, a dictionary can define a word. Many words, called **concrete** words, are relatively easy to define because they refer to things that have a material reality. A Corinthian column, for example, can be described in a dictionary, and a drawing of the column can be included to help a reader understand what a Corinthian column looks like. A dictionary, however, cannot adequately define many words because they are **abstract** words. Abstract words define ideas, concepts, emotions, or philosophies. There often is no material reality to the word. Think of the word "fear," for example. There is nothing you can touch, see, feel, or hear that is fear—you can only talk about people's physical reactions to fear, such as screaming at the sight of a monster on a movie screen.

In order to define an abstract term, you can use one or more of the following approaches:

- **Dictionary definition.** While a dictionary is unlikely to provide a complete definition for your needs, it is usually a good place to start. You want to have a strong sense of what the accepted meaning is, even if the dictionary relies on other abstract words in its definition. Ultimately, using an abstract term to define another abstract term sheds little light on the concept, so you will have to employ other approaches as well.

- **Synonyms.** Using words that mean the same thing can be a helpful way to define an abstract term, but keep in mind two things: (1) there are very few exact synonyms in English, so you need to know the different flavors or textures of the words, and (2) the synonyms are likely to be abstract words themselves, and so can be limited. For instance, if you were to define the word "happiness," you might use synonyms such as "joy" or "contentment," but you could also try to indicate how those words differ from "happiness" as well.

- **Stipulation.** This means you present your own definition of the term. Many times, arguments over definition revolve around stipulated meanings. For example, defining the term "poor" can involve disputes over income levels, costs of living, government subsidies, and so forth. Thus, what one person considers "poor" and another person considers "poor" can be debated. To stipulate the meaning of "poor" that you favor, you have to show why the reader should support your view.

- **Examples.** A common method for defining an abstract term is to point to examples and illustrations that demonstrate the term. So, if you wanted to define the term "courage," you might wish to give real-life examples of people who demonstrated the kinds of qualities you believe make up courage.

- **Comparisons.** You can define one thing by comparing it to something else that is similar, but also pointing out the ways in which they are different. For example, you could compare the idea of "democracy" as practiced in ancient Greece with "democracy" as practiced in the United States. You could point out how they are similar (e.g., voting) and how they are different (e.g., strict limits on voting rights in ancient Greece versus universal suffrage in the United States).

- **Analogies.** An analogy is a comparison between two unlike things. Therefore, analogies serve primarily descriptive purposes. For example, in the definition of "animal rights" some observers have used the language of human rights and simply extended them to animals. Thus, animal rights are largely defined through the definition of human rights. Whether animals and humans are enough alike to merit this connection is often the crucial point of debate.

- **Negation.** This effective definition technique addresses what something is not. This technique is particularly useful when you are trying to separate a word from certain commonly held meanings or associations. Negation can seldom be used alone to define a term—after you have discussed what it is not, you must then decide what it is. For instance, if you wanted to define "freedom," you might begin by saying, "Freedom does not mean the ability to act on any impulse or desire without legal consequences; that is anarchy." You would then have to argue what in fact freedom is.

- **Extended definitions.** Often in writing a definition, you will find yourself relying on more than one technique. An extended definition is a definition that uses two or more techniques to define something. An extended definition may last a paragraph; there are essays that consist almost entirely of definition. Ralph Waldo Emerson's "The American Scholar" stands as an example of an essay whose purpose is to define the term in the title. In Emerson's essay, he develops what it means to be an American scholar, and separates it from other (European) types.

In the Main Event Writing Sample, the second paragraph of the essay develops a definition of the term "democracy" as it applies to the classroom. Examine how the author uses different definition techniques:

First, a definition of "democracy" as it applies to the classroom *Topic Sentence* must be established. It does not necessarily mean that all roles are *Negation* equal: teachers by virtue of their position are in a role that involves *Stipulation* mentoring as well as evaluating. Within this, students are those who are mentored and evaluated. This also does not mean that one *Negation* simply votes on everything—voting is a mechanism for ensuring *Stipulation* democracy, not the principle of democracy itself. One principle of democracy is to ensure that everyone is included and participates in the process. Everyone should have an opportunity to receive an *Stipulation* education and to achieve in that educational system. This means that preferential treatment and discrimination have no place in the classroom. This also means that it is the responsibility of the school to do whatever it can to ensure that no one is left out because of cultural, linguistic, racial, or gender barriers. Second, representation *Stipulation* is very important. This means that all cultures and experiences are documented in the curriculum fairly and honestly; for instance,

Example   literature courses should include material from all races. Faculty should be hired in proportion to the population. To argue that minority literature is not excellent, or that there are no minorities

Comparison qualified to teach, is hogwash. In a democratic classroom, everyone is not rewarded equally—there is a difference between equality of opportunity and equality of results. One must remember the roots of our American democracy: hard work, discipline, and perseverance can never be replaced with social promotion, inflated grades, and watered-down standards.

THE MAIN EVENT WRITING SAMPLE

The following is an essay, which incorporates the use of definition, that was written for this text in response to the Main Event Writing Assignment, Question #1.

Democracy Promotes Success

The school system does not appear to be a place where Johnny can feel he's going to get a good education and enjoy positive, social interaction. Quite the contrary, test scores all over the country are down, we are second to last in student test scores in the industrial world (ahead of only Mexico), and violence seems to erupt in reaction to students feeling disenfranchised from school and not being accepted by their peers. Leadership for reform is manifesting itself in the name of charter schools, home schooling, school uniforms, and more centralized and standardized tests. We also believe that throwing a lot of money, particularly to buy computers, will make schools better. It will not. In a democratic society, one of the main aims is to encourage a cooperative and supportive environment where each individual is respected and where common goals can be achieved through this respect and mutual cooperation. We need to ask ourselves how these principles can be applied to our educational process. These principles can enhance success in a classroom because interaction between students and teacher is es- *thesis* sential, respect for diversity in classroom can only improve our un- *rational basis* derstanding of the world, and the trend toward standardized testing must be stopped and replaced with evaluation methods that promote true thinking.

First, a definition of "democracy" as it applies to the classroom *definition* must be established. It does not necessarily mean that all roles are *paragraph* equal: teachers by virtue of their position are in a role that involves mentoring as well as evaluating. Within this, students are those who are mentored and evaluated. This also does not mean that one simply votes on everything—voting is a mechanism for ensuring democracy, not the principle of democracy itself. One principle of democracy is to ensure that everyone is included and participates in the process. Everyone should have an opportunity to receive an education and to achieve in that educational system. This means that preferential treatment and discrimination have no place in the classroom. This also means that it is the responsibility of the school to do whatever it can to ensure that no one is left out because of cultural, linguistic, racial, or gender barriers. Second, representation is very important. This means that all cultures and experiences are documented in the curriculum fairly and honestly; for instance, literature courses should include material from all races. Faculty should be hired in proportion to the population. To argue that minority literature is not excellent, or that there are no minorities qualified to teach, is hogwash. In a democratic classroom, everyone is not rewarded equally—there is a difference between equality of opportunity and equality of results. One must remember the roots of our American democracy: hard work, discipline, and perseverance can never be replaced with social promotion, inflated grades, and watered-down standards.

It is impossible for any individual truly to succeed without some support and cooperation and interaction between students and teachers and students and students. This is fundamental. Whether that means a teacher allays anxiety and fear by sharing experiences of his or her own fears, or whether that means explaining vocabulary words in a Shakespearean sonnet, there needs to be a relationship between the teacher and student that fosters empowerment and a can-do attitude. Mike Rose revealed that when the social context was stripped away from his education, he dropped out of school for a while (236). Only within a supportive environment can inquiry and dialogue occur. Also, students amongst themselves need to be able to mentor one another and form study groups in order to deepen their understanding of the material. Challenging ideas and bringing related experiences to the forum is a process that hopefully will include all students. No one should be left out.

Without having all segments of society represented and respected honestly in a college classroom, there is no democracy and there is no fairness. First, faculty need to represent the student body, proportionately. It is supportive for black, Asian, and Hispanic students to have role models of their race. It is also helpful for white students to hear lectures and participate in discussions that come from a different cultural perspective. Only this kind of tension—between the known and the unknown—can provide truthful learning. Second, the curriculum needs to reflect the achievements and accomplishments of all races. The classics are fine; Plato and Shakespeare certainly have well-earned places in school, but so have Confucius and Toni Morrison. We can study *The Odyssey*, but we should also know *The Epic of Gilgamesh*. Our educational curriculum has long been skewed to the experiences of Western European white males; therefore, our systems of thought have been distorted and limited. Finally, the student body and its ethnic and social diversity provide the richest tradition we have. Teachers need to mine the students for their stories and their experiences to enrich classroom learning.

Unfortunately, politicians and administrators, in efforts to im- *topic sentence*
prove education in this country, have ironically chosen to central-
ize and standardize education. This response is undemocratic in theory and in practice. Centralized control of education works against a 200-year tradition of local control. The best teachers are adaptive and responsive to individual students. They do not rely on one method. By mandating a standard curriculum, politicians take away the power of the teacher to respond to their students. Also, mandates do not operate in the abstract; critical thinking cannot be evaluated from a bubble sheet. Higher-level thinking will be shunned, and teachers will teach the standardized test their students face next. Less attention will be spent on those in greatest need. All the resources will be put toward accomplishing the goals of scoring high on one test, rather than spending more time with special-needs students. Teaching will become a technical activity, not a creative one. All the autonomy and spontaneity of the classroom will be gone. When teachers do not respond to students on an individual basis, those students lose. The best teachers will leave because teaching will no longer be a rewarding experience; the ones who stay will simply be picking up paychecks. At-risk students will be the hardest hit. Apathy will grow, and true learning will disappear.

What we cherish most in a democracy is the freedom to choose. Freedom of choice in education manifests itself in many

examples of freedom in education ways. The student chooses which college to attend, which classes to take, what goals to pursue, and how involved he or she will become. Much of this is rooted in personal responsibility and accountability. However, the environment these freedoms are exercised in must be one that is responsive, supportive, safe, and fair. It is imperative that students with extra needs, be they physical or intellectual, from wheelchair ramps to developmental classrooms, be funded in order to help all students reach a level playing field where access to opportunity exists for all.

Works Cited

Gilgamesh. Trans. David Ferry. New York: Farrar, 1992.

Homer. *The Odyssey of Homer.* Trans. Richard Lattimore. New York: Harper, 1967.

Rose, Mike. "Crossing Boundaries." *Lives on the Border: A Moving Account of the Struggles and Achievements of America's Educational Underclass.* 1989. New York: Penguin, 1990. 233–38.

ADDITIONAL READINGS

Excerpt from *Democracy in America*

Alexis de Tocqueville

Almost two hundred years ago, Alexis de Tocqueville was a keen observer of how democracy operated to embrace some people and isolate others. In a passage from Democracy in America, *Tocqueville, a Frenchman, comments that the United States gives almost absolute power to the will of the majority. While this avoids the problem of relying on a corrupt or incompetent aristocracy, such as the French had experienced, the danger is the majority can itself become a "tyrant." It acts as it wishes, and it has no moral barometer to guide it other than that it is the majority. In other words, the majority can impose its will on a minority, even if what it does is inherently unjust or immoral. Thus, democracy does not always provide freedom, especially for those in the minority.*

Key Words

sovereignty	freedom from external control; self-rule
constituents	people served by a legislative body; the people served by a particular legislator
caprices	sudden, impulsive actions
tumult	commotion or riot
predominant	having superior strength, influence, or authority
maxim	a general truth or fundamental principle
irreconcilable	impossible to bring into agreement
antagonism	actively expressed opposition or hostility
aristocracy	an upper class usually made up of hereditary nobility; rule by such a class
inherent	involved in the essential character of something
vested	fully and unconditionally guaranteed

The natural strength of the majority in democracies. Most of the American constitutions have artificially increased this natural strength. How? Pledged delegates. Moral power of the majority. View of its infallibility. Respects for its rights. What increases it in the United States.

The absolute sovereignty of the will of the majority is the essence of democratic government, for in democracies there is nothing outside the majority capable of resisting it.

Most American constitutions have sought further artificially to increase this natural strength of the majority.[1]

Of all political powers, the legislature is the one most ready to obey the wishes of the majority. The Americans wanted the members of the legislatures to be appointed *directly* by the people and for a *very short* term of office so that they should be obliged to submit not only to the general views but also to the passing passions of their constituents.

The members of both houses have been chosen from the same class and appointed in the same way, so that the activity of the legislative body is almost as quick and just as irresistible as that of a single assembly.

Having constituted the legislature in this way, almost all the powers of government were concentrated in its hands.   5

---

[1]In examining the federal Constitution we have seen that the lawgivers of the Union strove in the opposite direction. The result of their efforts has been to make the federal government more independent in its sphere than are the states in theirs. But the federal government is hardly concerned with anything except foreign affairs; it is the state governments which really control American society.

At the same time as the law increased the strength of naturally powerful authorities, it increasingly weakened those that were by nature feeble. It gave the representatives of the executive neither stability nor independence, and by subjecting them completely to the caprices of the legislature, deprived them of what little influence the nature of democratic government might have allowed them to enjoy.

In several states the majority elected the judges, and in all they depended in a way on the legislature, whose members had the right annually to fix their salaries.

Custom has gone even beyond the laws.

A custom is spreading more and more in the United States which will end by making the guarantees of representative government vain; it frequently happens that the electors, when they nominate a deputy, lay down a plan of conduct for him and impose some positive obligations on him which he cannot avoid. It is as if, with tumult threatening, the majority were deliberating in the market-place.

In America several particular circumstances also tend to make the power of the majority not only predominant but irresistible.   10

The moral authority of the majority is partly based on the notion that there is more enlightenment and wisdom in a numerous assembly than in a single man, and the number of the legislators is more important than how they are chosen. It is the theory of equality applied to brains. This doctrine attacks the last asylum of human pride; for that reason the minority is reluctant in admitting it and takes a long time to get used to it. Like all powers, and perhaps more than any other of them, the power of the majority needs to have proved lasting to appear legitimate. When it is beginning to establish itself, it enforces obedience by constraint; it is only when men have long lived under its laws that they begin to respect it.

The idea that the majority has a right based on enlightenment to govern society was brought to the United States by its first inhabitants; and this idea, which would of itself be enough to create a free nation, has by now passed into mores and affects even the smallest habits of life.

Under the old monarchy the French took it as a maxim that the king could do no wrong, and when he did do wrong, they thought the fault lay with his advisers. This made obedience wonderfully much easier. One could grumble against the law without ceasing to love and respect the lawgiver. The Americans take the same view of the majority.

The moral authority of the majority is also founded on the principle that the interest of the greatest number should be preferred to that of those who are fewer. Now, it is easy to understand that the respect professed for this right of the greatest number naturally grows or shrinks according to the state of the parties. When a nation is divided between several great irreconcilable interests, the privilege of the majority is often disregarded, for it would be too unpleasant to submit to it.

If there existed in America one class of citizens whom the legisla- 15 tors were trying to deprive of certain exclusive privileges possessed for centuries and wanted to force them down from a high station to join the ranks of the crowd, it is probable that that minority would not easily submit to its laws.

But as men equal among themselves came to people the United States, there is as yet no natural or permanent antagonism between the interests of the various inhabitants.

There are states of society in which those who are in the minority cannot hope to win the majority over, for to do so would involve abandoning the very aim of the struggle in which they are engaged against it. An aristocracy, for instance, could not become a majority without giving up its exclusive privileges, and if it did let them go, it would no longer be an aristocracy.

In the United States, political questions cannot arise in such general and absolute fashion, and all the parties are ready to recognize the rights of the majority because they all hope one day to profit themselves by them.

Hence the majority in the United States has immense actual power and a power of opinion which is almost as great. When once its mind is made up on any question, there are, so to say, no obstacles which can retard, much less halt, its progress and give it time to hear the wails of those it crushes as it passes.

The consequences of this state of affairs are fate-laden and danger- 20 ous for the future.

How in America the Omnipotence of the Majority Increases the Legislative and Administrative Instability Natural to Democracies

How the Americans increase the legislative instability natural to democracies by changing their legislators every year and by giving them almost limitless power. The same effect on the administration. In America the drive toward social improvements is infinitely greater but less continuous than in Europe.

I have spoken before of the vices natural to democratic government, and every single one of them increases with the growing power of the majority.

To begin with the most obvious of all:

Legislative instability is an ill inherent in democratic government because it is the nature of democracies to bring new men to power. But this ill is greater or less according to the power and means of action accorded to the legislator.

In America the lawmaking authority has been given sovereign power. This authority can carry out anything it desires quickly and irresistibly, and its representatives change annually. That it is to say, just that combination has been chosen which most encourages democratic instability and allows the changing wishes of democracy to be applied to the most important matters.

Thus American laws have a shorter duration than those of any 25 other country in the world today. Almost all American constitutions have been amended within the last thirty years, and so there is no American state which has not modified the basis of its laws within that period.

As for the laws themselves, it is enough to glance at the archives of the various states of the Union to realize that in America the legislator's activity never slows down. Not that American democracy is by nature more unstable than any other, but it has been given the means to carry the natural instability of its inclinations into the making of laws.[2]

The omnipotence of the majority and the rapid as well as absolute manner in which its decisions are executed in the United States not only make the law unstable but have a like effect on the execution of the law and on public administrative activity.

As the majority is the only power whom it is important to please, all its projects are taken up with great ardor; but as soon as its attention is turned elsewhere, all these efforts cease; whereas in free European states, where the administrative authority has an independent existence and an assured position, the legislator's wishes continue to be executed even when he is occupied by other matters.

Much more zeal and energy are brought to bear in America on certain improvements than anywhere else.

In Europe an infinitely smaller social force is employed, but more 30 continuously.

A few years ago some pious people undertook to make the state of the prisons better. The public was roused by their exhortations, and the reform of criminals became a popular cause.

New prisons were then built. For the first time the idea of reforming offenders as well as punishing them penetrated into the prisons. But that happy revolution in which the public cooperated with such eagerness and which the simultaneous efforts of the citizens, rendered irresistible could not be accomplished in a moment.

---

[2]The legislative acts promulgated by the state of Massachusetts alone between 1780 and the present day already fill three large volumes. Moreover, one must note that the collection to which I refer was revised in 1823, and that many outdated laws and those that had become irrelevant were omitted. Now, the state of Massachusetts, which has a population no greater than one of our departments, might be taken as the most stable in the whole Union and the one which shows most continuity and wisdom in its undertakings.

Alongside the new penitentiaries, built quickly in response to the public's desire, the old prisons remained and housed a great number of the guilty. These seemed to become more unhealthy and more corrupting at the same rate as the new ones became healthy and devoted to reform. This double effect is easily understood: the majority, preoccupied with the idea of founding a new establishment, had forgotten the already existing ones. Everybody's attention was turned away from the matter that no longer held their master's, and supervision ceased. The salutary bonds of discipline were first stretched and then soon broken. And beside some prison that stood as a durable monument to the gentleness and enlightenment of our age, there was a dungeon recalling the barbarities of the Middle Ages.

Tyranny of the Majority

How the principle of the sovereignty of the people should be understood. Impossibility of conceiving a mixed government. Sovereign power must be placed somewhere. Precautions which one should take to moderate its action. These precautions have not been taken in the United States. Result thereof.

I regard it as an impious and detestable maxim that in matters of government the majority of a people has the right to do everything, and nevertheless I place the origin of all powers in the will of the majority. Am I in contradiction with myself?

There is one law which has been made, or at least adopted, not by 35 the majority of this or that people, but by the majority of all men. That law is justice.

Justice therefore forms the boundary to each people's right.

A nation is like a jury entrusted to represent universal society and to apply the justice which is its law. Should the jury representing society have greater power than that very society whose laws it applies?

Consequently, when I refuse to obey an unjust law, I by no means deny the majority's right to give orders; I only appeal from the sovereignty of the people to the sovereignty of the human race.

There are those not afraid to say that in matters which only concern itself a nation cannot go completely beyond the bounds of justice and reason and that there is therefore no need to fear giving total power to the majority representing it. But that is the language of a slave.

What is a majority, in its collective capacity, if not an individual 40 with opinions, and usually with interests, contrary to those of another individual, called the minority? Now, if you admit that a man vested with omnipotence can abuse it against his adversaries, why not admit the same concerning a majority? Have men, by joining together, changed their character? By becoming stronger, have they become more patient of obstacles?[3] For my part, I cannot believe that, and I will never grant to several that power to do everything which I refuse to a single man.

It is not that I think that in order to preserve liberty one can mix several principles within the same government in such a way that they will be really opposed to one another.

I have always considered what is called a mixed government to be a chimera. There is in truth no such thing as a mixed government (in the sense usually given to the words), since in any society one finds in the end some principle of action that dominates all the others.

Eighteenth-century England, which has been especially cited as an example of this type of government, was an essentially aristocratic state, although it contained within itself great elements of democracy, for laws and mores were so designed that the aristocracy could always prevail in the long run and manage public affairs as it wished.

The mistake is due to those who, constantly seeing the interests of the great in conflict with those of the people, have thought only about the struggle and have not paid attention to the result thereof, which was more important. When a society really does have a mixed government, that is to say, one equally shared between contrary principles, either a revolution breaks out or that society breaks up.

I therefore think it always necessary to place somewhere one social 45 power superior to all others, but I believe that freedom is in danger when that power finds no obstacle that can restrain its course and give it time to moderate itself.

Omnipotence in itself seems a bad and dangerous thing. I think that its exercise is beyond man's strength, whoever he be, and that only God can be omnipotent without danger because His wisdom and justice are always equal to His power. So there is no power on earth in itself so worthy of respect or vested with such a sacred right that I would wish to let it act without control and dominate without obstacles. So when I see the right and capacity to do all given to any authority whatsoever, whether it be called people or king, democracy or aristocracy, and whether the scene of action is a monarchy or a republic, I say: the germ of tyranny is there, and I will go look for other laws under which to live.

My greatest complaint against democratic government as organized in the United States is not, as many Europeans make out, its weakness, but rather its irresistible strength. What I find most repul-

---

[3]No one would wish to maintain that a nation cannot abuse its power against another nation. But parties form something like little nations within the nation, and the relations between them are like those of strangers.

If it is agreed that a nation can be tyrannical toward another nation, how can one deny that a party can be so toward another party?

sive in America is not the extreme freedom reigning there but the shortage of guarantees against tyranny.

When a man or a party suffers an injustice in the United States, to whom can he turn? To public opinion? That is what forms the majority. To the legislative body? It represents the majority and obeys it blindly. To the executive power? It is appointed by the majority and serves as its passive instrument. To the police? They are nothing but the majority under arms. A jury? The jury is the majority vested with the right to pronounce judgment; even the judges in certain states are elected by the majority. So, however iniquitous or unreasonable the measure which hurts you, you must submit.[4]

But suppose you were to have a legislative body so composed that it represented the majority without being necessarily the slave of its passions, an executive power having a strength of its own, and a judicial power independent of the other two authorities; then you would still have a democratic government, but there would be hardly any remaining risk of tyranny.

I am not asserting that at the present time in America there are fre- 50 quent acts of tyranny. I do say that one can find no guarantee against it there and that the reasons for the government's gentleness must be sought in circumstances and in mores rather than in the laws.

What Did You Read?

1. What is the absolute essence of democratic government?
2. What does Tocqueville mean by the "moral authority of the majority"?
3. Why is legislative instability inherent in a democratic government?
4. What does Tocqueville mean by the "Tyranny of the Majority"?

---

[4]At Baltimore during the War of 1812 there was a striking example of the excesses to which despotism of the majority may lead. At that time the war was very popular at Baltimore. A newspaper which came out in strong opposition to it aroused the indignation of the inhabitants. The people assembled, broke the presses, and attacked the house of the editors. An attempt was made to summon the militia, but it did not answer the appeal. Finally, to save the lives of these wretched men threatened by the fury of the public, they were taken to prison like criminals. This precaution was useless. During the night the people assembled again; the magistrates having failed to bring up the militia, the prison was broken open; one of the journalists was killed on the spot and the others left for dead; the guilty were brought before a jury and acquitted.

I once said to a Pennsylvanian: "Please explain to me why in a state founded by Quakers and renowned for its tolerance, freed Negroes are not allowed to use their rights as citizens? They pay taxes; is it not right that they should vote?"

"Do not insult us," he replied, "by supposing that our legislators would commit an act of such gross injustice and intolerance."

What Do You Think?

1. Do you feel that education should cater to the majority population?

2. Has education been "dumbed down" to meet the needs of the average student? If so, how does this relate to the "Tyranny of the Majority"?

3. Can you think of particular instances in which the majority of the population acted as a tyrant over a minority? Be specific.

How Was It Done?

1. What single word best describes the main idea of this section of *Democracy in America*?

2. How important are subtitles and footnotes to this work?

3. Is logic the primary tool used to support his claim?

4. Why are definitions of certain terms such as "justice," "majority," and "tyranny" so important to the building of his argument?

5. How do rhetorical questions help drive the argument, such as when he asks to whom can one turn when one suffers an injustice—to public opinion? To the legislative body? To the police? (Note especially the third to last paragraph.)

Tocqueville on Democratic Intellectual Life

Allan Bloom

In this passage from The Closing of the American Mind, *Allan Bloom comments directly on Tocqueville's observations, especially as they relate to the life of the intellect. Bloom recalls Tocqueville's comment that the actions of the majority in a democracy are capable of enslaving a nation, not just freeing it. Thus, it becomes highly important to educate citizens, especially in the promotion of reason. Rational thought is necessary for a democracy to flourish. From that point, Bloom argues what the university (as a general institution, not just one particular school) should do in order to promote the spirit of democracy. He argues that a successful university can "be devoted to the well-being of all, without stunting human potential or imprisoning the mind to the goals of the regime."*

Key Words

inchoate	formless; being only partly in existence
bastion	a fortified area or position
impediment	a hindrance
petrified	something changed into stone; confounded with fear and amazement

ephemeral	lasting a very short time; something without lasting significance
paradox	a statement that is seemingly contradictory or opposed to common sense yet it appears to be true
consensus	agreement by a large body of people
ecclesiastical	of or relating to a church, especially as an institution
repugnance	a strong dislike, distaste, or antagonism
bourgeois	relating to the social middle class; marked by concern for material goods and respectability
Marxism	reflecting the doctrines of Karl Marx; especially the theories of socialism and the classless society; state ownership of the means of production
simulacra	insubstantial form; a trace of something
Hobbes	Thomas Hobbes; 18th-century British philosopher who believed that people had a right to self-preservation and to pursue selfish aims, but people would give up those individual rights to an absolute monarchy in order to preserve the safety and happiness of the many

Tocqueville taught me the importance of the university to democratic society. His noble book, *Democracy in America,* gave voice to my inchoate sentiments. His portrait of the "Intellectual Life of the Americans" is the mirror in which we can see ourselves. But, because the broader perspective he brings is alien, we do not immediately recognize ourselves. In my experience, students at first are bored by Tocqueville's account of the American mind, but, if they are really made to pay attention, they are finally riveted and alarmed by it. No one likes to believe that what he can see is limited by circumstances, no matter how easily he recognizes this fact in others. Tocqueville shows how a democratic regime causes a particular intellectual bent which, if not actively corrected, distorts the mind's vision.

The great democratic danger, according to Tocqueville, is enslavement to public opinion. The claim of democracy is that every man decides for himself. The use of one's natural faculties to determine for oneself what is true and false and good and bad is the American philosophic method. Democracy liberates from tradition, which in other kinds of regimes determines the judgment. Prejudices of religion, class and family are leveled, not only in principle but also in fact, because none of their representatives has an intellectual authority. Equal political right makes it impossible for church or aristocracy to establish the bastions from which they can affect men's opinions. Churchmen, for whom divine revelation is the standard, aristocrats in whom the reverences for antiquity are powerful, fathers who always tend to prefer the rights of the ancestral to those of reason, are all displaced in favor of the equal individual. Even if men seek authority, they cannot find it where they used to find it in other regimes. Thus the external impediments to the free exercise of reason have been removed in democracy. Men are actually on their own in comparison to what they were in other regimes and with respect to the usual sources of opinion. This promotes a measure of reason. However, since very few people school themselves in the use of reason beyond the calculation of self-interest encouraged by the regime, they need help on a vast number of issues—in fact, all issues, inasmuch as everything is opened up to fresh and independent judgment—for the consideration of which they have neither time nor capacity. Even the self-interest about which they calculate—the ends—may become doubtful. Some kind of authority is often necessary for most men and is necessary, at least sometimes, for all men. In the absence of anything else to which to turn, the common beliefs of most men are almost always what will determine judgment. This is just where tradition used to be most valuable. Without being seduced by its undemocratic and antirational mystique, tradition does provide a counterpoise to and a repair from the merely current, and contains the petrified remains of old wisdom (along with much that is not wisdom). The active presence of a tradition in a man's soul gives him a resource against the ephemeral, the kind of resource that only the wise can find simply within themselves. The paradoxical result of the liberation of reason is greater reliance on public opinion for guidance, a weakening of independence.

Altogether, reason is exposed at the center of the stage. Although every man in democracy thinks himself individually the equal of every other man, this makes it difficult to resist the collectivity of equal men. If all opinions are equal, then the majority of opinions, on the psychological analogy of politics, should hold sway. It is very well to say that each should follow his own opinion, but since consensus is required for social and political life, accommodation is necessary. So, unless there is some strong ground for opposition to majority opinion, it inevitably prevails. This is the really dangerous form of the tyranny of the majority, not the kind that actively persecutes minorities but the kind that breaks the inner will to resist because there is no qualified source of nonconforming principles and no sense of superior right. The majority is all there is. What the majority decides is the only tribunal. It is not so much its power that intimidates but its semblance of justice. Tocqueville found that Americans talked very much about individual right but that there was a real monotony of thought and that vigorous independence of mind was rare. Even those who appear to be free-thinkers really look to a constituency and expect one day to be part of a majority. They are creatures of public opinion as much as are conformists—actors of nonconformism in the theater of the conformists who admire and applaud nonconformity of certain kinds, the kinds that radicalize the already dominant opinions.

Reason's exposedness in the rational regime is exacerbated by the absence of class in the old sense, based on principles or convictions of right. There is a general agreement about the most fundamental political principles, and therefore doubts about them have no status. In aristocracies there was also the party of the people, but in democracy there is no aristocratic party. This means that there is no protection for the opponents of the governing principles as well as no respectability for them. There were in the past also parties representing ecclesiastical interests against those of monarchs or aristocrats. These too provided a place for dissenting opinions to flourish. In the heat of our political squabbles we tend to lose sight of the fact that our differences of principle are very small, compared to those over which men used to fight. The only quarrel in our history that really involved fundamental differences about fundamental principles was over slavery. But even the proponents of slavery hardly dared assert that some human beings are made by nature to serve other human beings, as did Aristotle; they had to deny the humanity of the blacks. Besides, that question was really already settled with the Declaration of Independence. Black slavery was an aberration that had to be extinguished, not a permanent feature of our national life. Not only slavery, but aristocracy, monarchy and theocracy were laid to rest by the Declaration and the Constitution. This was very good for our domestic tranquility, but not very encouraging for theoretical doubts about triumphant equality. Not only were the old questions of political theorizing held to have been definitively answered, but the resources that nourished diversity concerning them were removed. Democratic conscience and the simple need to survive combine to suppress doubt. The kinds of questions that Tocqueville put to America—the answers to which allowed him to affirm the justice of equality more reasonably and more positively than most of us can do—came out of an experience that we cannot have: his direct experience of an alternative regime and temper of soul—aristocracy. If we cannot in any way have access to something like that experience, our understanding of the range of human possibilities is impoverished, and our capacity to assess our strengths and weaknesses is diminished.

To make that range of possibilities accessible, to overcome the regime's tendency to discourage appreciation of important alternatives, the university must come to the aid of unprotected and timid reason. The university is the place where inquiry and philosophic openness come into their own. It is intended to encourage the noninstrumental use of reason for its own sake, to provide the atmosphere where the moral and physical superiority of the dominant will not intimidate philosophic doubt. And it preserves the treasury of great deeds, great men and great thoughts required to nourish that doubt.

Freedom of the mind requires not only, or not even especially, the absence of legal constraints but the presence of alternative thoughts.

The most successful tyranny is not the one that uses force to assure uniformity but the one that removes the awareness of other possibilities, that makes it seem inconceivable that other ways are viable, that removes the sense that there is an outside. It is not feelings or commitments that will render a man free, but thoughts, reasoned thoughts. Feelings are largely formed and informed by convention. Real differences come from difference in thought and fundamental principle. Much in democracy conduces to the assault on awareness of difference.

In the first place, as with all regimes, there is what might be called an official interpretation of the past that makes it appear defective or just a step on the way to the present regime. An example of this is the interpretation of Rome and the Roman empire in Augustine's *City of God*. Rome is not forgotten, but it is remembered only through the lens of victorious Christianity and therefore poses no challenge to it.

Second, sycophancy toward those who hold power is a fact in every regime, and especially in a democracy, where, unlike tyranny, there is an accepted principle of legitimacy that breaks the inner will to resist, and where, as I have said, there is no legitimate power other than the people to which a man can turn. Repugnance at the power of the people, at the fact that the popular taste should rule in all arenas of life, is very rare in a modern democracy. One of the intellectual charms of Marxism is that it explains the injustice or philistinism of the people in such a way as to exculpate the people, who are said to be manipulated by corrupt elites. Thus a Marxist is able to criticize the present without isolating himself from present and future. Almost no one wants to face the possibility that "bourgeois vulgarity" might really be the nature of the people, always and everywhere. Flattery of the people and incapacity to resist public opinion are the democratic vices, particularly among writers, artists, journalists and anyone else who is dependent on an audience. Hostility and excessive contempt for the people is the vice of aristocracies, and is hardly our problem. Aristocracies hate and fear demagogues most of all, while democracies in their pure form hate and fear "elitists" most of all, because they are unjust, i.e., they do not accept the leading principle of justice in those regimes. Hence each regime discounts those who are most likely to recognize and compensate for its political and intellectual propensities, while it admires those who encourage them. But, to repeat, this tendency is more acute in democracy because of the absence of a nondemocratic class. In every regime there is a people; there is not necessarily any other class.

Third, the democratic concentration on the useful, on the solution of what are believed by the populace at large to be the most pressing problems, makes theoretical distance seem not only useless but immoral. When there is poverty, disease and war, who can claim the right to idle in Epicurean gardens, asking questions that have already been answered and keeping a distance where commitment is demanded? The for-its-own-sake is alien to the modern democratic spirit, particularly in matters intellectual. Whenever there is a crunch, democratic men devoted to thought have a crisis of conscience, have to find a way to interpret their endeavors by the standard of utility, or otherwise tend to abandon or deform them. This tendency is enhanced by the fact that in egalitarian society practically nobody has a really grand opinion of himself, or has been nurtured in a sense of special right and a proud contempt for the merely necessary. Aristotle's great-souled man, who loves beautiful and useless things, is not a democratic type. Such a man loves honor but despises it because he knows he deserves better, whereas democratic vanity defines itself by the honors it seeks and can get. The lover of beautiful and useless things is far from being a philosopher—at least as far as is the lover of the useful, who is likely to be more reasonable—but he has the advantage of despising many of the same things the philosopher does and is likely to admire the philosopher for his very uselessness, as an adornment. Great and unusual undertakings are more natural to him than to the lover of the useful, and he believes in and reveres motives that are denied existence by utilitarian psychology. He can take for granted the things that are the ends of most men's strivings—money and status. He is free, and must look for other fulfillments, unless he spends, as in the democratic view he should do, his life helping others to get what he already has. Knowing as fulfillment in itself rather than as task required for other fulfillments is immediately intelligible to him. Finality as opposed to instrumentality, and happiness as opposed to the pursuit of happiness, appeal to the aristocratic temperament. All of this is salutary for the intellectual life, and none of it is endemic to democracy.

Thus the mere announcement of the rule of reason does not create the conditions for the full exercise of rationality, and in removing the impediments to it some of its supports are also dismantled. Reason is only one part of the soul's economy and requires a balance of the other parts in order to function properly. The issue is whether the passions are its servitors, or whether it is the handmaiden of the passions. The latter interpretation, which is Hobbes's, plays an important role in the development of modern democracy and is a depreciation as well as an appreciation of reason. Older, more traditional orders that do not encourage the free play of reason contain elements reminiscent of the nobler, philosophic interpretation of reason and help to prevent its degradation. Those elements are connected with the piety that prevails in such orders. They convey a certain reverence for the higher, a respect for the contemplative life, understood as contemplation of God and the peak of devotion, and a cleaving to eternal beings that mitigates absorption in the merely pressing or current. These are images of philosophic magnificence—which, it must be stressed, are distortions of the original, and can be its bitterest enemies, but which preserve the order of the cosmos and of the soul from which philosophy begins. Tocqueville describes this marvelously well in his moving account of Pascal, whom he evidently regards as the most perfect of men. The possibility of such a human type, the theoretical type, is, according to Tocqueville, most threatened in democracy, and it must be vigorously defended if humanity is not to be grievously impoverished. Much of the theoretical reflection that flourishes in modern democracy could be interpreted as egalitarian resentment against the higher type represented by Pascal, denigrating it, deforming it and interpreting it out of existence. Marxism and Freudianism reduce his motives to those all men have. Historicism denies him access to eternity. Value theory makes his reasoning irrelevant. If he were to appear, our eyes would be blind to his superiority, and we would be spared the discomfort it would cause us.

It is to prevent or cure this peculiar democratic blindness that the university may be said to exist in a democracy, not for the sake of establishing an aristocracy but for the sake of democracy and for the sake of preserving the freedom of the mind—certainly one of the most important freedoms—for some individuals within it. The successful university is the proof that a society can be devoted to the well-being of all, without stunting human potential or imprisoning the mind to the goals of the regime. The deepest intellectual weakness of democracy is its lack of taste or gift for the theoretical life. All our Nobel prizes and the like do nothing to gainsay Tocqueville's appraisal in this regard. The issue is not whether we possess intelligence but whether we are adept at reflection of the broadest and deepest kind. We need constant reminders of our deficiency, now more than in the past. The great European universities used to act as our intellectual conscience, but with their decline, we are on our own. Nothing prevents us from thinking too well of ourselves. It is necessary that there be an unpopular institution in our midst that sets clarity above well-being or compassion, that resists our powerful urges and temptations, that is free of all snobbism but has standards. Those standards are in the first place accessible to us from the best of the past, although they must be such as to admit of the new, if it actually meets those standards. If nothing new does meet them, it is not a disaster. The ages of great spiritual fertility are rare and provide nourishment for other less fertile ones. What would be a disaster would be to lose the inspiration of those ages and have nothing to replace it with. This would make it even more unlikely that the rarest talents could find expression among us. The Bible and Homer exercised their influence for thousands of years, preserved in the mainstream or in backwaters, hardly ever being surpassed in power, without becoming irrelevant because they did not suit the temper of the times or the spirit of a regime. They provided the way out as well as the model for reform.

The university's task is thus well defined, if not easy to carry out or even keep in mind. It is, in the first place, always to maintain the permanent questions front and center. This it does primarily by preserving—by keeping alive—the works of those who best addressed these questions. In the Middle Ages, Aristotle was very much present in the minds of the leading elements of society. He was used as an authority almost on a level with the Church Fathers and was assimilated to them. This was, of course, an abuse of Aristotle, who thought that authority is the contrary of philosophy. His own teaching ought always to be approached with questions and doubts, not faith. The essence of philosophy is the abandonment of all authority in favor of individual human reason. Nevertheless, Aristotle was there, his moderate and sensible views had an effect on the world, and he could be a guide to those who came to have philosophic doubt. In our time, freedom from authority and the independence of reason are commonplaces. Aristotle, however, instead of being properly used—now that we have the proper disposition—has to all intents and purposes disappeared. We would hardly be able to use Aristotle, as did Hegel, to grasp the character of modernity. Instead we are more and more restricted to the narrow experience of the here and now, with a consequent loss of perspective. The disappearance of Aristotle has much less to do with his intrinsic qualities than with a political distaste for him, joined with the lack of intellectual discipline that results from a sense of self-sufficiency. Reason has become a prejudice for us. Rousseau noted that in his time many men were liberals who a century earlier would have been religious fanatics. He concluded that they were not really reasonable, but, rather, conformists. Reason transformed into prejudice is the worst form of prejudice, because reason is the only instrument for liberation from prejudice. The most important function of the university in an age of reason is to protect reason from itself, by being the model of true openness.

Hence, without having the answers, the university knows what openness is and knows the questions. It also knows the regime within which it lives, and the kinds of threats this regime poses to its activity. In a democracy it risks less by opposing the emergent, the changing and the ephemeral than by embracing them, because the society is already open to them, without monitoring what it accepts or sufficiently respecting the old. There the university risks less by having intransigently high standards than by trying to be too inclusive, because the society tends to blur standards in the name of equality. It also risks less by concentrating on the heroic than by looking to the commonplace, because the society levels. In an aristocracy the university would probably have to go in a direction opposite to the one taken in a democracy in order to liberate reason. But in an aristocracy the university is a less important institution than in a democratic society, because there are other centers for the life of the mind, whereas in a democracy there is practically no other center, practically no way of life, calling or profession, that requires or encourages or even permits cultivation. This is increasingly the case in the late twentieth century. The university as an institution must compensate for what individuals lack in a democracy and must encourage its members to participate in its spirit. As the repository of the regime's own highest faculty and principle, it must have a strong sense of its importance outside the system of equal individuality. It must be contemptuous of public opinion because it has within it the source of autonomy—the quest for and even discovery of the truth according to nature. It must concentrate on philosophy, theology, the literary classics, and on those scientists like Newton, Descartes, and Leibniz who have the most comprehensive scientific vision and a sense of the relation of what they do to the order of the whole of things. These must help preserve what is most likely to be neglected in a democracy. They are not dogmatisms but precisely the opposite: what is necessary to fight dogmatism. The university must resist the temptation to try to do everything for society. The university is only one interest among many and must always keep its eye on that interest for fear of compromising it in the desire to be more useful, more relevant, more popular.

The university's task is illustrated by two tendencies of the democratic mind to which Tocqueville points. One is abstractness. Because there is no tradition and men need guidance, general theories that are produced in a day and not properly grounded in experience, but seem to explain things and are useful crutches for finding one's way in a complicated world, have currency. Marxism, Freudianism, economism, behavioralism, etc., are examples of this tendency, and there are great rewards for those who purvey them. The very universality of democracy and the sameness of man presupposed by it encourage this tendency and make the mind's eye less sensitive to differences. All the terms discussed in Part Two are evidences of this abstractness, simulacra of thought and experience, hardly better than slogans, which take the place of reflection. In aristocracies men take the experiences of their nations as unique and superior and tend not to generalize, but rather to forget the natural community of men and the universality of thought. But they do really pay attention to their experiences, to the diversity of phenomena that is homogenized by abstract "mind-sets." This is another thing the democratic university must learn from aristocracies. Our temptation is to prefer the shiny new theory to the fully cognized experience. Even our famous empiricism is more of a theory than an openness to experience. Producing theories is not theorizing, or a sign of the theoretical life. Concreteness, not abstractness, is the hallmark of philosophy. All interesting generalization must proceed from the richest awareness of what is to be explained, but the tendency to abstractness leads to simplifying the phenomena in order more easily to deal with them.

If, for example, one sees only gain as a motive in men's actions, then it is easy to explain them. One simply abstracts from what is really there. After a while one notices nothing other than the postulated motives. To the extent that men begin to believe in the theory, they no longer believe that there are other motives in themselves. And when social policy is based on such a theory, finally one succeeds in producing men who fit the theory. When this is occurring or has occurred, what is most needed is the capacity to recover the original nature of man and his motives, to see what does not fit the theory. Hobbes's mercenary account of the virtues, which won out in psychology, needs to be contrasted with Aristotle's account, which preserves the independent nobility of the virtues. Hobbes was thinking of Aristotle, which we never do, when he developed his teaching. In order to restore what was really a debate, and thereby restore the phenomenon *man*, one must read Aristotle and Hobbes together and look at what each saw in man. Then one has the material on which to reflect. For modern men who live in a world transformed by abstractions and who have themselves been transformed by abstractions, the only way to experience man again is by thinking these abstractions through with the help of thinkers who did not share them and who can lead us to experiences that are difficult or impossible to have without their help.

What Did You Read?

1. According to Bloom, why is tradition valuable in a democracy in which every man decides for himself?

2. What is meant by saying that in America "there was a real monotony of thought and that vigorous independence of mind was rare"?

3. Why is the intellectual past so vital to a democracy?

4. Why is the university so important to fight dogmatism?

What Do You Think?

1. Do you think it is important that students be interested in what they are learning? If so, should the university adapt its curriculum to be more popular with students? Why or why not?

2. Are democracy and higher education compatible? Explain.

3. Is the educational system rigorous enough in its demands on students to learn theory and memorize information? Explain your answer.

4. What does an intellectual life mean?

How Was It Done?

1. How important is prior knowledge of *Democracy in America* to the understanding of Bloom's piece?

2. How do transitional words such as "First," "Second," and "Third" help to organize the structure of the article that promotes the ideas, like Tocqueville's, that democracy can sometimes promote comfort and monopoly of thought?

3. Does Bloom succeed in defining and explaining what he means by "democracy"?

4. How does Bloom give the reader a sense of what values he hold dear and which ones he abhors?

5. Where in the article does he define the task of the university?

The De-Democratization of Schools and Literacy in America

James V. Hoffman

James V. Hoffman argues that in the past decade the educational system has moved away from promoting democratic values and ways of thinking. He notes the language of business is being used in schools, promoting a one-size-fits-all attitude. Instead of teaching students to be independent thinkers and learners, our schools, under the pressure from politicians and others, are becoming increasingly centralized and standardized. The effect is to alienate students—not just from boring curriculum but also from their own democratic traditions. Fortunately, working against this tendency are classroom teachers, whom Hoffman sees as grassroots fighters for keeping democracy in schools.

Key Words

mediocre	average; of moderate quality
tracking	the placing of students into classes in which all students have similar academic abilities
de-democratizing	the lessening of the appeal or value to all members of a society
conjoint	united; made up of two or more joined parts
mandate	an authoritative command

imperative	not to be avoided; necessary
partisans	firm believers in a party, faction, or person
centralization	the moving of all important functions to a center point or location
resiliency	the ability to recover or adjust easily
pedagogically	relating to a teacher or education
autonomy	self-rule; the ability to do for one's self

> Certainly, there will be no liberty, no equality, no social justice without democracy, and there will be no democracy without citizens and the schools that forge civic identity and democratic responsibility. (Barber, 1993, p. 46)

Schools are institutions that serve multiple functions but a singular goal: to prepare the young to assume a contributing place in society. Schools are not neutral in their stance toward the nature of that society. Indeed, schools are remarkably self-serving. They enculturate the young toward the values, beliefs, skills, and understandings that will preserve existing structures. But schools can also, under the best of circumstances, challenge us to examine our own society, reflect on its strengths and weaknesses, and set our sights on improvements. This is what a democracy demands if it is to thrive, not just survive.

Educated citizens are a requirement for a democracy to flourish—perhaps more so than in any other form of government (Kane, 1984). The delicate balance between individual freedoms and collective responsibilities are grounded in a collective social capital that is loosely defined around a set of abstract democratic principles. How schools induct the young into this world is a remarkable challenge, but one that we in the United States have lived up to for generations. Educators, and classroom teachers in particular, have a fundamental role to play in the preservation of our democratic way of life. Schools in the U.S. have served our society well because they have embraced democratic values—flawed in execution certainly, but at least valuing democratic ideals. This position regarding democracy and educational goals can be traced throughout the history of educational philosophy in the U.S.

Although publicly embraced, the fusion of democracy and schooling is not easily achieved. John Dewey (1916), the most passionate and articulate spokesperson for education in democracy, argued for the deep complexity of democracy in education:

> The devotion of democracy to education is a familiar fact. The superficial explanation is that a government resting on popular suffrage cannot be successful unless those who elect and who obey their government are educated. . . . But there is a deeper explanation. A democracy is more than a

form of government; it is primarily a mode of associated living, of conjoint communicated experience. (p. 87)

Freedom of speech and freedom of the press have been cornerstones in the evolution, articulation, and protection of democracy in the U.S. A critical reading of the texts that surround us is essential to the foundations of a democratic life (Heath, 1991). Critical and democratic readings of texts might even be considered synonymous. As reading and literacy educators we bear an enormous responsibility for educating citizens. I will argue here that U.S. schools are in danger of failing in their goal to promote democratic values and democratic modes of thinking. I will argue that critical reading of texts has taken a backseat to "teaching the basics" in the reform movement of the past decade. Finally, I will argue that texts themselves have become a primary control mechanism in the de-democratization of schools, teaching, and learning.

Crisis and Reform

The primary purpose of education in a democratic society is democracy. This essential truth has been lost in much of the contemporary educational debates. (Fraser, 1997)

The publication of *A Nation at Risk* by the members of the National Commission on Excellence in Education (1983) stands out as a watershed point in the evolution of education in the U.S. The authors of this report lamented that "the educational foundations of our society are presently being eroded by a rising tide of mediocrity that threatens our very future as a Nation and a people" (p. 5). They went on to warn that "If an unfriendly foreign power had attempted to impose on America the mediocre educational performance that exists today, we might well have viewed it as an act of war." In many ways, this kind of crisis/reform rhetoric was similar to that used 25 years earlier to link the nation's shortcomings in the space race and the Cold War with the failure of the public school system. The rhetoric was where the similarities ended. The public and political responses to the attacks were not at all the same.

The post-Sputnik era response took the form of an enormous investment of resources in education by the federal government. This was an investment unparalleled in U.S. history. Among the targeted points for investment were curriculum development initiatives (e.g., Science Curriculum Improvement Study projects in science, 1970; "Man, a Course of Study" in social studies, Cort, 1971); research initiatives (e.g., the cooperative first-grade studies project in reading, Bond & Dykstra, 1967); and investments in teacher education (e.g., National Defense Education Act seminars and institutes). Leadership for the reform movement came from within the profession. President Lyndon Johnson built on these initiatives to promote educational opportunity for a diverse society through sponsorship of the Elementary and Secondary Education Act in the early 1960s. This act provided the first significant, direct investment in public education on the part of the federal government. Substantial funding for compensatory education programs, for library materials, and for the modernization of school facilities was funneled through this program.

In contrast, the response to the *Nation at Risk* crisis of the 1980s was set in terms of "fiscal conservatism" (read: "Throwing more money at education is not going to solve the problem!"). Although the report offers very specific recommendations for reform, the recommendations can be summarized in terms of three basic themes: raise standards, measure results, and hold people accountable for their performance. The voice of educators as a nurturing and caring profession is absent from this document. Economic discourse and business metaphors abound. Underlying all of the arguments is the belief that for the reform to succeed, policy makers must wrestle control of education from educators.

They have. Centralization and control are the reality in education as we enter the 21st century. Two hundred years of democratic and grass-roots traditions in educational decision making have been abandoned in just a decade. Is there a threat to American society from its schools? Yes, there is. The real threat comes from the de-democratization of our educational system. As a literacy educator, I see this threat represented in the proliferation of reductionist curricula for reading, in the silencing of professional dialogue and debate, in the marginalizing of minority positions and people, in a muting of the voices in the texts our students are expected to read, and in a stern control over the "correct" interpretations of these already bland texts.

The authors of *A Nation at Risk* admonished us to consider that "Children born today can expect to graduate from high school in the year 2000" (p. 36). Here we are in the year 2000, and what do we know about these students? We know they are bored. Studies of secondary teachers reveal that the number one problem they encounter in schools is not violence or disruption—it is the tremendous sense of apathy toward learning (e.g., Sizer, 1984; U.S. Department of Education, 1991). A second reality for students and teachers is high-stakes testing. For those students who cannot pass them, these tests offer one more experience with a lackluster curriculum. For those students who cannot pass them, they are one more instance of schools telling them that they don't have what it takes to make it. A wildly disproportionate number of minority students complete high school requirements but, because they fail the high-stakes test, never graduate. A third reality is tracking. There are gates to accessing certain parts of the curriculum.

Students learn early in their schooling careers which paths are open to them and which are not. The bottom line is that success breeds success and failure breeds failure. Opportunity and choice are not distributed equitably for students in schools (see Oakes, 1985).

What kind of society are we preparing these students for? What kind of society will they be capable of sustaining? These are the issues that should trouble our profession and provoke our conversations. It's our turn to sound the alarm to a society that genuinely believes educational reforms are in our students' and nation's best interests.

The "Business" Metaphor

John Goodlad (1996) noted that the 1986 slogan of the National Governors' Association, "better schools mean better jobs"—repeated over and over again in the 1990s—sells better politically than "education for democracy" (p. 94). We have swallowed the "business" metaphor for schools totally. Social norms are passé. Indeed, any references to a consideration of social factors in schooling (e.g., social promotion) are regarded with skepticism. We are comfortable in the language of productivity, inputs, outputs, standards, and quality control. After all, these are all measurable outcomes where resource management and efficiency are what count. Can democratic outcomes even be measured, let alone taught? Perhaps we have lost sight of what democracy means in our society, and therefore find it difficult to regard it as a priority in our schools. The supply function is easier to deal with and manage. Schools must serve the interests of the society first. If the interests of individual students or entire segments of our society are not met, so be it.

Paulo Freire (1989) reminded us of the undemocratic nature of much current educational practice. He warned of the danger of a curriculum in which, "Instead of communicating, the teacher issues communiqués and makes deposits which the students patiently receive, embrace and repeat" (p. 58). Besides being ineffective most of the time—with the students not being very interested in the teacher's communiqués—this sort of education teaches the opposite set of values from those needed in a democratic society. In a truly liberating education "knowledge emerges only through invention and re-invention, through the restless, impatient, continuing helpful inquiry people pursue in the world, with the world, and with each other" (p. 58).

In Search of Democracy

Most of us can recite the critical features of the institution of U.S. democracy. We can talk about the system of checks and balances, we can describe the division of state and federal responsibilities, and we might even be able to describe some specific abuses of a democracy such as how redistricting was used to promote racism. But our true knowledge of democracy is limited, in some sense, by our lack of perspective. Most of us live in a democracy like fish who live only in water and are therefore blinded to many of its qualities. Often, it takes the outsider to reveal important qualities lived but not noticed. Democracy is not revealed so much in the textbooks as it is in daily living. It took a foreigner to reveal as much to the world—and to Americans.

Alexis de Tocqueville, and his associate Gustave Beaumont, traveled extensively in the United States from May 1831 through February 1832. De Tocqueville's homeland, France, was torn at the time between democratic impulses and the traditions of aristocracy. De Tocqueville was determined to study democracy in America to gain insight into its potential for his own country. He petitioned for an 18-month leave of absence from the Ministry of Justice to study the prison system in America. Prison reform was a heated topic of debate in France at this time, and the Americans had some interesting ideas that appeared worthy of study. The mission was eventually approved by the ministry although the funding for the trip ended up being entirely personal.

De Tocqueville and Beaumont visited all of the major prisons in the U.S. and conducted extensive interviews with both administrators and prisoners. They wrote a comprehensive report that was enormously influential on prison reform in France. Having completed this task, they moved on to their more important effort—the study of democracy in America. They read, traveled, observed, and interviewed people everywhere they went. After returning to France, de Tocqueville and Beaumont divided their writing tasks, with Beaumont focusing on the conditions of Indians and Negroes in America. De Tocqueville wrote more generally regarding democracy and daily life. The *Democracy*, written and published in two parts, explored the nature of democracy in America ranging from political structures to social relations (Pierson, 1938).

The immense popularity of the book among both academics and the general public is indicative of its significance. De Tocqueville not only is recognized for his remarkable insights into the nature of American democracy, but also commonly regarded as one of the pioneers in sociological research. *Democracy* is revealed through the careful inspection of an outsider. De Tocqueville captured in his narrative what was for those "inside" American life hidden in experience. The power of de Tocqueville's writing comes not so much in the points he made as in the narrative he wrapped around them. He has written the story of a lived democracy from the perspective of one who has known only the life of aristocracy in Europe.

There are at least four broad insights from de Tocqueville's writings that I feel can enlighten our understanding of education, literacy, and democracy. First, power and authority reside within the individual citizen in a democracy. No act of the state can take away from individuals their opportunity to act in their interests. Laws of the state protect the individual. They are not designed to control the individual. Second, democracy is highly active but not very efficient in the short term. It may even look like it's not working when it really is. De Tocqueville described town meetings he observed in New England and commented on the slow deliberative processes involved. Despite its short-term uncertainty, in the long run democracy is enormously productive. The best ideas eventually will flourish and take hold. Third, de Tocqueville recognized the critical role that freedom of speech and freedom of the press play as a context for change in a democratic society. Open and protected dialogue is the key. Fourth, leadership in a democracy is not the same as leadership in a more authoritarian or totalitarian system. The strong leader is not the person who forces others down a path he or she has chosen. The strong leader in a democracy is one who recognizes opportunity and is appropriately responsive to the moment.

What would a school system designed to mirror such a society look like? What would a school system designed to prepare the young to become caretakers and contributors to such a society look like? At a minimum, we would expect substantial degrees of autonomy in decision making and respect for individual rights (of both students and teachers). We would expect open dialogue that would be open to all voices and perspectives. We might expect the appearance of chaos or disorganization at times, recognizing that order and direction must emerge and cannot be imposed. Not all schools, curricula, or instruction would be exactly the same. Finally, we would expect leaders who are skilled at nurturing dialogue, at creating synthesis, and at using the school context as a catalyst for change.

What would de Tocqueville see today if he focused on everyday life in the U.S. and life in schools? Are the features of respect for individual rights, dialogue, short-term inefficacy complemented by long-term productivity, and responsive leadership features he would notice? I don't think so. Ironically, his observations might lead de Tocqueville to assume the topic for discussion was prison reform, not school reform.

Does it take an outsider to reveal ourselves to us? Not always. 20 Sometimes the insider can move out and look back. Over the past several years, the International Reading Association has become involved in a professional development effort in Eastern Europe with former Soviet bloc countries. The project, entitled Reading and Writing for Critical Thinking, has involved a collaboration with the Soros Foundation. The Soros Foundation is dedicated to assisting societies in the transformation from authoritarian to democratic ways of living. Education is only one point of intervention, but it is the point of collaboration with the Association. Over 60 volunteers, the majority being faculty from institutions in higher education in the United States, have been working with educators in eastern Europe to transform schools into institutions that prepare young people for living in a democratic society. Teacher education and professional development are key points of entry. Strategies for helping teachers in schools help students engage critically with the texts they read have been the focal point. This is a revolutionary concept in most of the schools where the norm has been on controlled texts and controlled interpretations.

The transformation of schools and the transformation into a democratic society must go hand in hand. There is another message as well. The volunteers who return to the U.S. after their work in these countries almost unanimously report that this has been a transformative experience for them in understanding how democracy must be represented and reflected in all aspects of our schooling—from the critical reading of texts to the nature of leadership in schools.

Policy Mandates and the Erosion of Democracy

> We hear a great deal about readying the next generation of workers for global competition, about being first in the world in such high status subjects as math and science, and about having world class standards for what is learned in school. We hear almost nothing about civic participation or building and maintaining democratic communities, whether these be neighborhoods or governments at the local, state or federal level. Not only does the current national reform movement in the United States pay too little attention to the ideas and ideals of democracy, it pays far too little attention to the ideas and ideals of education. (Fenstermacher, 1994, p. 4)

Recent attempts to reform schools in the U.S. have been decidedly undemocratic in nature and spirit. The reform movement is being led by politicians who are using their positions of authority and power to control the actions of educators. Policy mandates that directly or indirectly control the actions of educators have proliferated over the past decade. Consider the following:

- Practically every state now has in place some form of mandated standardized testing plan. While these assessments are rationalized in terms of accountability, they are in fact being used to control the curriculum. Stakes are being raised for students (e.g., promotion, graduation), for teachers (e.g., merit pay), and for administrators (e.g., pay bonuses, transfers).
- State curriculum frameworks for reading and language arts proliferate and are being mandated. These are not statements of general educational aims or goals, these are detailed scripts and specifications for what is taught, how it is taught, and when it is taught.

- State mandates for helping struggling readers are leading to a wave of labeling, sorting, and prescriptions for treatment of these students.

- The content of commercial materials is being shaped by state mandates and requirements. The marketplace is no longer free to respond to the market forces that have worked in the past. Several states dominate, but the effects are felt nationally.

- Specific methods of instruction are being mandated by state legislation. Over 40 states are considering legislation that would require a phonics-first curriculum for beginning reading.

- The content of teacher preparation programs is being mandated to include preparation and training in specific techniques and over specific content.

- What counts as research has now been defined through federal legislative initiatives. Much of the money targeted for initiatives in education must be used with programs that have been "proven" effective by this research.

- Teacher tests that focus on particular perspectives and particular kinds of knowledge are being developed and used to control entry and advancement within the teaching profession. Much like the mandated testing programs for students, these programs are having a direct impact on the curriculum for teacher education.

All of these initiatives are in the control of politicians. Ironically, democracy is often used as the banner for such reforms. "Broad public and professional participation" (in forums and conferences) does not take away from the fact that each of these is fundamentally undemocratic in character. Reform efforts that rely on mandates developed over time and with "input" may create the illusion of democracy, but they are not democratic.

The real effects of these mandates will be the following:

- Less learning and less high-quality teaching. If we have learned anything from the body of research into effective teaching it is that the best teachers are adaptive and responsive to the needs of the students they teach. They don't rely on one method. They are pedagogically responsive. By mandating methods and curriculum we take away the power to respond.

- A trivialized curriculum. Mandates do not operate in the abstract. They require specificity at a behavioral level that can be observed and documented. Higher level thinking and more abstract learning goals will be shunned.

- Less attention to those in greatest need. We will continue to focus our resources on sorting rather than serving special-needs students.

- Teaching will become a technical activity. The best teachers value autonomy, spontaneity, and the immediacy of the classroom. As these norms are violated, the best teachers will leave and the field will become less attractive to professionals.

- Research as inquiry will be lost. Research in literacy has exploded over the past 2 decades. We have learned that research and practice are close partners in the development of scientific knowledge. If the current conditions prevail, research will be relegated to a position of informing mandates that control practice.

- Students will drop out from school—both literally and figuratively. The dropouts will be seen in the increasing numbers of minorities who simply give up and stop attending, but there will be more. The wave of student apathy toward schools will continue to grow.

- Democracy in schools will die. There will be no space for it to survive.

These will be the real effects of the mindless reform frenzy we 25 are experiencing. The short-term effects may create the illusion of progress: Scores on state-mandated tests will rise because teachers will teach to the test; the numbers seeking to enter teaching as a job will increase as it becomes a more technical profession and a more 8:00-4:00, 5-days-per-week, 9-months-a-year responsibility; and claims for "research verified" practices will become commonplace as the profit principle plays out. But these are illusions of positive impact, not the real points of impact. The negative effects may be masked for the present, but will appear in the long run. De Tocqueville (1945) was right when he observed that

> The partisans of centralization . . . are wont to maintain that the government can administer the affairs of each locality better than the citizens could do it for themselves; this may be true when the central power is enlightened and the local authorities are ignorant; when it is alert and they are slow; when it is accustomed to act and they to obey. Indeed, it is evident that this double tendency must augment with the increase of centralization, and that the readiness of the one and the incapacity of the others must become more and more prominent. But I deny that it is so when the people are as enlightened, as awake to their interests, and as accustomed to reflect on them as the Americans are. I am persuaded, on the contrary, that in this case the collective strength of the citizens will always conduce more efficaciously to the public welfare than the authority of government . . . whenever a central administration affects completely to supersede the persons most interested, I believe that it is either misled or desirous to mislead. . . . These are not the conditions on which the alliance of the human will is to be obtained; it must be free in its gait and responsible for its acts, or (such is the constitution of man) the citizen had rather remain a passive spectator than a dependent actor in schemes with which he is

unacquainted. . . . It is not the administrative, but the political effects of the decentralization that I admire most in America. (pp. 89–91)

Gloom and Doom

I have painted a fairly pessimistic, almost Orwellian, picture of the present and an even darker picture for the future. Sadly, this is what I see when I step back and look at the big picture. But there is another side of my professional life that gives me considerable hope for the future. Every time I go to the classroom in the public school where I teach my undergraduate methods courses, every time I visit the classrooms of teachers who work closely with our program, and every time I work with classroom teachers in inservice settings or graduate classes I am struck with their remarkable enthusiasm and resiliency. Most teachers, despite the conditions I have just described, find a way to teach well. This gives me hope, and it frames the principal message in this essay. The fight for democracy in schools will be won or lost in the classrooms across the U.S. at the most basic grass-roots level, not in the halls of state legislatures. This is not to say that we should not engage at the political level, but our first responsibility is to take care of business at home and not allow, by erosion or coercion, our teaching to be compromised.

And why is this a reading problem and not a science problem, or a mathematics problem? Clearly, the situation is threatening to all who value and have an investment in education, but the situation is particularly crucial to those of us in reading education. Texts in a democracy and the reading of these texts are the lifeblood of a democracy.

> The more I consider the independence of the press in its principal consequences, the more I am convinced that in the modern world it is the chief and, so to speak, the constitutive element of liberty. A nation that is determined to remain free is therefore right in demanding, at any price, the exercise of this independence. (de Tocqueville, 1945, p. 200)

Texts in schools are being controlled and being used to control (Apple, 1993). We are quickly approaching a state, as Dominique Macedo (1994) referred to it, of literacy for "stupidification" (p. 9). It is imperative that those of us who claim reading as our profession act and adopt, as Maxine Greene (1978) suggested, a stance of "wide-awakeness."

> [F]or too many individuals in modern society, there is a feeling of being dominated and that feelings of powerlessness are almost inescapable. . . . I am also suggesting that such feelings can to a large degree be overcome through conscious endeavor on the part of individuals to keep themselves awake, to think about their condition in the world, to inquire into forces that appear to dominate them, to interpret the experiences they are having day by day. (pp. 43–44)

And so I have devised a fairly simple set of principles for literacy educators. There is no revolution here, just good practice and professional responsibility.

- Teach. Immerse your students in texts that make them cry, laugh, scream, puzzle, blabber, or frown. Demand a critical reading of these texts. Teach skills and strategies in a context that nurtures a value for reading.
- Resist. Do not do anything you are asked or told to do that will compromise your responsibility to teach your students in a way your professional knowledge dictates. This is a moral imperative. It cannot be set aside for any reason. This does not always translate to an "in your face" kind of stance. Ayers (1993) reminded us of the many ways in which teachers can be creatively noncompliant.
- Inquire. Don't say you know it all—you don't. Don't say you don't know anything—you do. Reveal what you know through the questions that are important to you. Read widely and deeply.
- Connect. You must not be silenced as an individual or as a professional. A professional voice must be present in the debates over the future of schooling. Your professional organizations must be politically active and effective for you at the local, state, and national levels.

And what about the politicians? What role do they have in education and a democracy? My answer is that they should play a role in education similar to that they play in business and the economy. They must ensure that the market forces are working well and that no groups (e.g., professional organizations, businesses, government bureaucracies) are allowed to take advantage of the system. Further, if they want to assume an active role in promoting quality schools, they should make every effort to increase the supply of quality teachers in the profession (e.g., by supporting teacher education, by enhancing the conditions of teaching as a profession). Following this path, we would soon find ourselves as allies and not adversaries with a common goal.

If we as a teaching profession can persevere in this cause, the public will join with us—because, after all, we aspire to the same goals. Deborah Meier (1982) captured this sentiment well:

> If America can commit itself to this next task—educating all children well—the historic promise of free public schooling will be fulfilled. It doesn't require a nationalized curriculum backed by a high-stakes testing program that falsely promises order and control: for a privatized market-driven system offering the illusion of freedom and individuality. What it

requires is tough but doable: generous resources, thoughtful and steady work, respect for the diverse perspectives of people who work in and attend our schools and, finally, sustained public interest in and tolerance for the process of re-invention. Nothing else will do it. (p. 272)

What Did You Read?

1. What does Freire mean when he says, "Knowledge emerges only through the invention and reinvention, through the restless, impatient, continuing helpful inquiry people pursue in the world, with the world, and with each other"?

2. Who was one of *Democracy in America*'s biggest critics? Explain what he wrote.

3. According to Hoffman, what are Tocqueville's four main points in *Democracy in America?*

What Do You Think?

1. What are some of the problems with our schools today?

2. Can Tocqueville's four principles be applied to education?

3. Do you agree with Hoffman that "mandates" such as the ones listed to reform schools will not work? Why or why not?

How Was It Done?

1. What kind of organized strategies does Hoffman use to streamline the article?

2. How much authoritative evidence is used to support his claim that schools are in danger of failing to promote democratic values?

3. Which two publications does much of this article center on?

4. Why is the conclusion of the article about particular effects in connecting intellectual ideology to the practical realm?

Renewing Democracy in Schools

Nel Noddings

In "Renewing Democracy in Schools," Nel Noddings argues that the movement toward standardizing the curriculum is in fact anti-democratic. She points out that the use of uniform standards almost certainly means limiting or eliminating choices in schools. The rights and privileges of individuals, their freedom and equality, are all dependent on the maintenance of an informed citizenry. Noddings argues that this must be reflected in our educational system. She argues that open discussions will promote inquiry, critical thinking, reflection, and independence.

Key Words

John Dewey	19th- and 20th-century American educational reformer and philosopher; he believed in the importance of a liberal arts education and political liberalism
discourse	capacity for orderly thought and ideas; formal and orderly expression of thought on a subject
parlance	a manner of speech
totalitarian	a form of government in which total control rests with one body, often a single dictator; individual rights are subordinate to the right of the state.
John Stuart Mill	19th-century British philosopher; placed an emphasis on reason and rational inquiry while rejecting spiritual or nonrational explanations to problems
coercion	the use of force or the threat of force to achieve a desired end
heterogeneous	mixed; made up of different elements or parts
judicious	discreet; wise
pernicious	highly destructive; deadly
interdisciplinary	connecting or joining two different academic subject areas
reactionary	ultraconservative

Today's school reform efforts aim almost exclusively at increasing the academic achievement of students. Despite their narrow focus, reform efforts are usually "systemic" in that they address the whole complex—uniform and precise standards, governance, and mechanisms of accountability. But they often fall short in promoting the discourse that lies at the heart of education in a liberal democracy: What experience do students need in order to become engaged participants in democratic life? How can education develop the capacity for making well-informed choices? If liberal public discussion is a foundation for democracy, how can schools promote such discussion?[1] What pedagogical methods are compatible with the aims of democratic education?

In contrast to systemic reform efforts, programs aimed at renewal identify the central purposes and processes of democratic education, attempt to interpret them in contemporary terms, and seek to

---

[1]See Fareed Zakaria, "The Rise of Illiberal Democracy," *Foreign Affairs,* November/December 1997, pp. 22–43; see also Robert D. Kaplan, "Was Democracy Just a Moment?," *Atlantic Monthly,* December 1997, pp. 55–80.

strengthen them.[2] I do not mean to contrast programs of reform and
renewal too sharply. Many in both camps are fine programs. But the
idea of renewal is different. It attends to the underlying ideals and
purposes of democratic education. It takes seriously the judgment of
John Dewey that a democratic society "must have a type of education
which gives individuals a personal interest in social relationships and
control, and the habits of mind which secure social changes without
introducing disorder."[3]

In this article, I will address just two problems that we face in trying to renew democratic education. I will argue that the movement for
uniform standards may actually handicap efforts to renew democracy
in the schools 1) by eliminating many of the legitimate choices that
students should be guided in making and 2) by failing to encourage
the sort of rational political discussion that provides the very foundation of liberal democracy.

Making Choices

Choice figures prominently in liberal/democratic theories.

Some political theorists make it absolutely central to liberalism.[4] 5
Others name a different theme (e.g., preserving diversity) as primary,
but no liberal theorist can deny the importance of choice in liberal
democracies. "Liberal," as I am using it here, is not to be understood
as, in common parlance, the opposite of "conservative" but rather as
reference to a philosophical/political heritage shared by both present-
day liberals and conservatives. In liberal/democratic societies, the
rights and privileges of individuals are taken seriously; freedom and
equality are the watchwords.

It is not simply that citizens of such democracies are expected to
make intelligent choices in voting; more important, they are left to
their own guidance on a wide range of life choices. Educational theories that put great emphasis on preparation for voting miss the very
point of that ritual.[5] Most of us do not care terribly whether those who
represent us in government are (temporarily) Republicans or Democrats, although we may work toward the election of one party or the
other. What rightly concerns us is the maintenance of a form of government under which our right to make choices is held sacred. The
choice of where to live, with whom to associate, what sort of work to

---

[2]See Roger Soder, ed., *Democracy, Education, and the Schools* (San Francisco: Jossey-Bass,
1996).
[3]John Dewey, *Democracy and Education* (1916; New York: Macmillan, 1944), p. 99.
[4]The best-known example is John Rawls, *A Theory of Justice* (Cambridge, Mass.: Harvard University Press, 1971); see also idem, *Political Liberalism* (New York: Columbia University Press,
1993).
[5]For one who puts too much emphasis on voting, see Mortimer J. Adler, *The Paideia Proposal*
(New York: Macmillan, 1982).

do, which professionals to consult, which merchants to patronize, how to spend our leisure time, how to worship, what to read . . . these are choices we cherish. Voting is often little more than a powerful sign that we do cherish these choices.

Because we live in a liberal/democratic society (albeit an imperfect one), political education is a necessity. Amy Gutmann puts it this way: "We can conclude that 'political education'—the cultivation of the virtues, knowledge, and skills necessary for political participation—has moral primacy over other purposes of public education in a democratic society."[6]

Most of us can give assent to this statement even though we might disagree on exactly what is meant by "political" or "democratic." Without attempting a precise definition of either term (a task far too large for this space), I want to make it clear that I am using "political education" in a very broad sense. I do not mean by it simply participation in public life, however important such activity may be. Rather, I mean an education that enhances the likelihood that students will have both richly satisfying personal lives and the willingness to promote such lives for others. It is precisely because we live in a democratic society that such a description of political education is essential. We need to have not only the knowledge and skills for public participation but also those for how to "get about" in an environment of political freedom.

Oddly, liberal theorists often have less to say about education than theorists from other perspectives. Totalitarian thinkers, for example, have usually put great and consistent emphasis on education. One reason for this neglect by liberal theorists may be that systematic education seems to require coercion, and coercion is incompatible with the liberal/democratic spirit. John Stuart Mill, for example, excluded children, dependent young, and "barbarians" from the basic liberal principle of noninterference.[7] He seemed to believe that all those people who had not yet reached a mature rationality might reasonably be coerced for their own good.

In contrast with Mill, Dewey wrote extensively on liberalism and   10
the need for an education consistent with liberalism—one that would provide students with the kinds of experience that would contribute to the personal interests and habits of mind needed for democratic life. A main point of contention between Dewey and traditional educators, such as Robert Maynard Hutchins, centered on exactly this issue: Are students best prepared for democratic life by absorbing a rigorous body of carefully prescribed material, or must they have actual experience with democratic processes? The issue generates a whole set of problems ranging over cognitive, affective, and social domains.

---

[6]Amy Gutmann, *Democratic Education* (Princeton, N.J.: Princeton University Press, 1987), p. 287.
[7]See John Stuart Mill, *On Liberty and Utilitarianism* (1859; New York: Bantam Books, 1993).

Arguments of this sort have raged in the U.S. for more than 100 years.[8] The faculty psychology (or mental discipline) school that was so popular in the 19th century held that the mind had to be exercised vigorously and that the best materials to provide this exercise were the standard disciplines. An interesting variation on mental discipline was suggested by Charles William Eliot, the Harvard president who presided over the Committee of Ten. Eliot defended electives for students on the ground that sustained study—not prolonged study of particular subjects—is what produces the appropriate mental exercise. This theme is echoed in much of Dewey's work. He, too, believed that engaged, sustained study of almost any topic would produce the growth and discipline we seek in education. Further, Dewey held that students' involvement in the choice of topics, projects, and objectives for their own learning was an essential part of what I am calling political education.

The difference of opinion persists today, but the establishment of national standards threatens to suppress discussion. No responsible educator advocates a hodgepodge of unconnected topics as a curriculum, but many of us agree with Dewey that there should be a way to avoid coercion and still provide a rich curriculum that can be varied according to the needs and interests of individual students. Continuity is clearly important, but it can be secured by guidance and discussion; it need not be a product of coercion.[9]

If Eliot was right in his early defense of electives (he seems to have changed his mind later), there is no sensible reason for eliminating them and moving to a "one size fits all" curriculum. However, it has been argued that allowing students to choose their own courses will encourage some to downgrade their own education. The answer to this objection is not to resort to coercion "for their own good" but to ensure that every course offered is worthwhile. An open and rigorous discussion of national standards could be very useful here. Such discussion could encourage educators to think along the following lines: What goals should all courses further? Which of many desirable goals does this particular course promote? If its content is highly constrained (e.g., jewelry making, introductory algebra), is there a way that it can be expanded to include some history, aesthetics, reading, writing, or other material deemed important? How will the methods of teaching and learning contribute to the growth of democratic character?

If every course the high school offers were to be worthwhile in the sense just described, we would not have to worry about students' making choices that would downgrade their education. We would still face

---

[8]See Herbert Kliebard, *The Struggle for the American Curriculum* (New York: Routledge, 1995).
[9]For some ideas on how to accomplish this, see Nel Noddings, *The Challenge to Care in Schools* (New York: Teachers College Press, 1992).

the problem of continuity, however, and we would be required to supply much more information about our courses than we usually do at the high school level. An adequate political education should help students to make well-informed choices. I am not suggesting that students be allowed to exercise blind desire. Indeed, it is because a free society makes it possible for people to follow their blind desires (within their means) that education in a democracy must prepare students to make sound choices. To choose wisely among even fine possibilities requires information. In addition, it requires a relationship between teachers and students that will make it possible for teachers to guide each student responsibly. The flow of information is bi-directional. The student needs information about what the school offers; the teacher needs information about the student in order to guide him or her effectively.

Another argument against a curriculum rich in electives is that 15 students may change their minds by the end of high school and regret that they are not better prepared for college. This worry cannot be brushed aside, but it can be answered thoughtfully. Because we live in a credentialed society, students who have chosen nontraditional courses may find themselves "unprepared" for immediate entry into college, but the power they have acquired in controlling their own studies should make it relatively easy for them to gain the further preparation required. Many such students are better prepared for the actual work of college than the sizable number of youngsters who graduate now with "approved" courses that have, in fact, left them totally unprepared for the rigors of college. If we are looking for a national disgrace, it is not to be found in the fact that too few students take "rigorous" courses but rather in the fact that so many take them and learn so little from them. Responsible educators cannot simply declare credentials unimportant, and we have to be sure that students understand the likely consequences of their choices. But we can also launch a campaign to get colleges to experiment a bit by admitting students with nontraditional preparation. Democratic societies have long professed faith in sound scientific practices, and yet our educational efforts are obstinately conservative. Changing one's mind, one's occupation, one's way of life is enormously attractive in a liberal democracy. Schooling should reflect this cherished privilege.

High school students should be encouraged to make well-informed choices not only of the courses they will take but also of the standards they will attempt to meet within each course. Again, teachers should not turn over the entire matter of standards to students, but it is entirely reasonable to establish several sets of standards for a given course, each carefully constructed to match the purposes of the students who choose to take the course. The provision of variable standards does not necessitate tracking; it can be done within heterogeneous classes. The important point, from the perspective of political education, is that students understand how the standards they are working toward fit their own purposes. To urge all students to do equally well in all subjects is foolish. In addition to being impractical, it is an invitation to mediocrity.

A program of the sort I am suggesting here—one in which students get equal credit for well-done work in art, photography, or algebra—is sometimes criticized as anti-intellectual. This criticism, too, has to be taken seriously. Too often the accusation serves as a conversation stopper. Anti-intellectual? Horrors! But what do we mean by "intellectual"? If we mean that creditable school work should invite critical thought, proficient use of language, and an increase in cultural literacy, then, as I argued above, every course should be "intellectual." But if we mean that an accredited course of study must comprise a specified body of content in order to be intellectual, then what I am advocating is clearly anti-intellectual. This too is an old debate—one that may also be foreclosed by the standards movement. Instead of closing down debate with prescribed objectives for all students, a democratic society would do better to make responsible choice available within its public school system.[10]

Liberal Political Discussion

Several writers have recently noted that democracies seem to maintain themselves and thrive in societies marked by a tradition of liberal public discourse.[11] If this is true, democratic education should give students appropriate practice in such discourse. There is a language to be learned, a form, a whole practice. It could be argued—and has been, at least implicitly—that with sufficient knowledge, the only practice needed is that involved in debating academic questions. Examples of such questions might be: Was Jefferson a liberal? To what extent were the Framers of the U.S. Constitution influenced by economic factors? These questions are interesting to some students, and they certainly can be engaged in a way that introduces students to the forms of public discourse. But they may not matter to many students, and a mark of public discourse is that it arises around issues, things that matter to those speaking.

It would seem, then, that the best practice would invite students to discuss issues of current importance—importance to them, if possible. No one can guarantee that any particular issue will be important to every student in a given class, but educators can make an effort to share questions that are relevant both to the general public and to students.

---

[10]Howard Gardner seems to be suggesting something along these lines in his letter to the editor, *Education Week,* 5 August 1998, pp. 45, 53.
[11]See Zakaria, op. cit.; and Kaplan, op. cit.

Consider, for example, what might be done with the question of 20 whether both evolution and creationism should be taught in public schools.[12] This is a question that is debated by some school boards, but only the decision, in the form of a specified curriculum, is conveyed to students. Why not encourage students to investigate all sides of the question? Are there scientifically defensible objections to evolution? Is there more than one version of evolution theory? What are the issues that separate versions?

Students should also have an opportunity to learn something about the history of evolutionary theory, about the great debates—including the fiery exchange between Bishop Wilberforce and Thomas Henry Huxley, in which Huxley suggested strongly that he would rather share ancestry with apes than with Wilberforce. If students are then convinced that Wilberforce was a dimwitted reactionary, they should be encouraged to learn something about his enlightened social views and his father's fight against slavery. Similarly, when students study the Scopes trial, they should be invited to find out more about both William Jennings Bryan and Clarence Darrow. The biographies of both men are fascinating. Reading about Darrow, for example, students may become interested in the question of determinism versus free will.

The subtopics that arise in a free and full discussion of evolution are almost endless. For example, does human language represent a limitation on the continuity hypothesis? That is, can human language be shown to be continuous with animal communication, or is it what some scholars have called a "true emergent"? Students who are interested in animal behavior might choose to study this topic in considerable depth.

When creationism is discussed, students should be encouraged to examine the two creation stories that appear in Genesis. In one (1:27), God creates "man in his own image . . . male and female created he them." In the second (2:7–23), God first creates Adam and then makes Eve from Adam's rib. Why has this second version been so popular among preachers and storytellers? Why have feminists objected so strongly to it? Does the first version suggest, as Elizabeth Cady Stanton insisted, that God is both female and male? Does the second lead ineluctably to a Judeo-Christian endorsement of the ancient myths that equated the creation of woman with the advent of evil in the world? High school girls often need a special intellectual interest, and this set of topics may thrill many of them. It provides a stimulating introduction to feminist thought.

In addition to the Judeo-Christian creation stories, other such stories should be told. There are wonderful African, Chinese, and Native

---

[12]See Nel Noddings, *Educating for Intelligent Belief or Unbelief* (New York: Teachers College Press, 1993).

American creation stories, and these too would provide excellent centers for further study.

Many students will also be attracted to the study of social Darwin- 25 ism and its pernicious effects on women and non-Europeans. The doctrines of Herbert Spencer, Carl Vogt, Paul Mobius, Edward Clarke, and Darwin himself perpetuated the notions that females are inferior to males, that non-Europeans are inferior to Europeans (northern Europeans), and that most of the poor deserve their misery because of deficient character or constitution. The damage done by these doctrines is incalculable. Again, the number of subtopics that arise from the stem of social Darwinism is impressive.

Instead of battling behind closed doors over whether to teach evolution or creationism, we should bring the debate into the classroom. In doing so, we might begin to see the foolishness of separating school subjects as sharply as we do. Why fight over whether creationism should be mentioned in science class? The topics mentioned above are of great human interest. They create an opportunity for interdisciplinary study and team-teaching. But they can and should be discussed in science classes as well. Willingness to do so signals to students that science is a significant part of liberal studies—studies that initiate students into the practices of a democratic society.

Imagine how much "cultural literacy" students might gain in a unit of study such as this. Working on their own projects, listening to others, trying to fit whatever direct instruction they receive with the material they are learning on their own, they will come across names, events, and concepts that will add immeasurably to their store of knowledge. I am not suggesting that we depend on "incidental learning" for the entire curriculum, but I do think we underestimate the power and scope of such learning. Material that we "pick up" while fully engaged in inquiry is likely to remain with us longer than that which we learn for the purpose of passing a test.

The main point to be made from this example is that the practice in liberal public discourse needed for the maintenance of a successful democracy can be provided in such a way that the questions to be debated are relevant, exciting, intellectually challenging, and culturally rich. Judiciously selected topics also offer the kind of choice that students need to become self-reliant learners.

In addition to a host of questions that are current on the public agenda, students should discuss those that are directly relevant to their own condition.[13] Why, for example, are they required to study al-

---

[13]See Nel Noddings, "Politicizing the Mathematics Classroom," in Sal Restivo, Jean Paul Van Bendegem, and Roland Fischer, eds., *Math Worlds: Philosophical and Social Studies of Mathematics and Mathematics Education* (Albany: State University of New York Press, 1993), pp. 150–61.

gebra and geometry? What arguments are offered and how valid are they? Is it true that most occupations today require the use of algebra? Is it true that people who are competent in algebra and geometry make higher salaries than those who are not? If this is true, is it because mathematical skills are actually in demand or is it largely a result of a credentialing system? On a question such as this last, students should be encouraged to recognize and talk about partial truths.

If it is argued that academic mathematics should be studied be- 30 cause it is a great cultural achievement and might even be regarded as one of the foundations on which great modern civilizations have been built, then what about other institutions and practices that have made significant contributions? What role has been played by the development of the home as a private place? By the modern family? By changing conceptions of child rearing? Why are these topics not part of the standard curriculum? And if mathematics is so vital to cultural development, why do we not study its history, its uses in warfare and politics, its aesthetics, its appearances in literature, the biographies of mathematicians, the historical exclusion of women from its study, and a host of other topics usually identified with culturally rich material?

We have to be careful when we engage in this kind of political education. We want to encourage free and honest discussion, but we should avoid messages that destroy hope and induce cynicism. Some forms of radical pedagogy are too one-sided and leave students with the notion that everything good about their nation and their schooling is but a myth. Further, radical pedagogies sometimes assume that it is legitimate to enlist students in particular campaigns for social transformation, and some teachers become angry and resentful when students resist their revolutionary messages. In political education for democratic living, students should have the right to resist such pressure. We should want them to know that there are groups working hard for (and against) various changes in our society, and we should share with them the strongest arguments on all sides. Such pedagogical generosity should be characteristic of democratic education. It does not require us to be completely neutral. Sometimes, teachers should state frankly where they stand and why, but they should not silence voices that disagree.

Another word of caution is well taken here. Often students who have not yet mastered the standard forms of language and whose cultural practices differ from the rational discussions described here are silenced automatically. Their participation should be strongly encouraged, and classroom conversation should be extended to include this set of problems too. When students use emotional forms of rhetoric, their contributions should be accepted, but further inquiry should be prompted. Who else takes this point of view? What is the logic of the argument? What conditions induce it? What can be said in opposition? If we traded cultural positions, might you react as emotionally as I do?

To accept the contributions of marginalized students does not require teachers to abdicate their responsibility for helping these students to learn standard forms. To reject some arguments as unfounded does not require us to reject the students who make them. Political education in a free society must be designed to help students achieve freedom in both their public and private lives.

When liberal discussion is used to promote inquiry, critical thinking, reflective commitment, and personal autonomy, students are likely to feel more in control of their own schooling. It won't hurt them to hear that much of what they are taught in schools will be useless in everyday life. They need to know that they are living in a highly credentialed society and that the tie between credential and competence is thought by many to be weak. In an adequately politicized classroom, students may begin to experience school as a place to which they can bring some meaning. School will no longer be experienced as a compulsory act in a theater of the absurd.

What Did You Read?

1. What does John Dewey think education must do in a democratic society?
2. What does Noddings mean by a liberal "political education"? Why is it so vital to our society? Do you agree? Why?
3. According to Noddings, what is the mainstay of a totalitarian education?
4. Does Noddings feel that students are best prepared for democratic life by absorbing material or having experience with democratic processes?
5. What does Noddings mean by "incidental learning"?

What Do You Think?

1. Do you personally believe that "national standards" threaten to suppress discussion?
2. Do you feel that most students are underprepared for college?
3. Should students have a choice in the topics they learn and the assignments they do? Explain.

How Was It Done?

1. In the introductory paragraph, what rhetorical device does Noddings use to engage the reader?
2. What central theme is Noddings's article structured around?

3. What two problems facing the renewal of democracy in schools does Noddings classify in her article?

4. How effectively does Noddings contrast her view with other traditional theorists in her development of her explanations?

5. What kind of values does Noddings offer to substantiate her beliefs?

Tests That Fail Democracy
Gregory Shafer

Gregory Shafer argues that using standardized achievement tests works against providing a democratic education. He argues that these tests are not measurements of performance, but are used rather as ways to justify abandoning students in lower socioeconomic areas. Politicians can use test results to justify taking control of education away from teachers and professional educators. The result is poor students are unable to master the test, while students from already privileged backgrounds excel. Shafer also argues that "teaching to the test" is the next step to education reform; however, this sort of teaching provides a limited education—one that improves test scores without enhancing complex learning. Thus, their schools, despite apparent "reforms," do not serve students who are already at risk for educational failure.

Key Words

affluent	wealthy
indolence	laziness; sloth
assiduously	marked by careful attention
disenfranchised	deprived of the right to vote; removed or separated from power
inclusiveness	incorporating a broad range of ideas, cultures, or philosophies
subvert	to overturn; to ruin
deleterious	harmful in often subtle or unexpected ways
truncated	cut short; curtailed
stultifying	appearing stupid, foolish, or illogical
erudite	learned; well-educated
holistic	relating to the whole or complete systems

The language of standardization appears to denote equity, of assuring that all children receive the same education. Behind the usages of these terror in educational policy, however, is a far different political and pedagogical reality.

—Linda McNeil, *Contradictions of School Reform*

It's Tuesday and the hum around the high school is squarely focused on the latest test scores and the windfall they have produced for schools in the more affluent parts of town. To nobody's surprise, generous scholarships are being doled out in droves to the most wealthy districts. In Okemos, Michigan—where the newly constructed senior high has the extravagant look of a five-star hotel—the district has garnered thousands of dollars for its elevated exam scores. No surprise here, since the schools are populated by the sons and daughters of professors from nearby Michigan State University. These are kids who grow up around this kind of academic knowledge. This is part of their world.

Indeed, in the new political game to hold kids and schools accountable through standardized tests, the clear winners are emerging from the privileged class—from those who most eloquently manipulate Standard English and are most assiduously versed in the official language of academia. Few winners, in contrast, come from districts that reside in the inner city, where tests seem like official ways to expose indolence. And while many politicians have suggested that tests act only to expose inferior teaching and initiative, those inside the schools know better. Tests aren't about measuring performance. Rather, they are governmental strategies to abandon children from lower socioeconomic areas while controlling schools and teachers. Instead of broadening the curriculum to make it more accessible to nontraditional pupils—and rather than offering students innovative assessment alternatives—the standardized test policy represents a way to legitimize the status quo while proving the inferiority of the disenfranchised student.

Endemic in this plan is the conspicuous absence of democracy and inclusiveness. Minority students tend not to do as well because they aren't given the time they need to process information, write essays, and unravel the foreign culture they are being asked to identify. Teachers, on the other hand, are relegated to the periphery, distributing exams that have nothing to do with their classrooms, students, or lesson plans. The entire process has become centralized, standardized, and monolithic. While democracy seeks active involvement from various perspectives, tests encourage fealty toward a single organ of truth. Teachers, then, follow dictates from the state, while students equate success with unearthing the questions created on the latest state exam.

In Michigan, the process has become analogous to a Camus novel. Poor students from the most gritty and neglected parts of the state are routinely denied scholarships because they haven't learned to master a test that was supposedly designed to even the playing field. Well-off students, on the other hand, win thousands of scholarship dollars, despite their financial readiness to attend the most prestigious colleges and universities. Indeed, in awarding the affluent these scholarships of $2,500, the Michigan Assessment of Educational Progress (MEAP) has exacerbated the chasm between rich and poor. In Michigan, as with most states that administer standardized assessments, the vast majority of scholarship winners come from the ranks of the college-bound—from the carefully manicured suburbs and prep schools. Statistics from the 2000 testing year show that 80 percent of the students in the wealthy district of Bloomfield Hills garnered scholarships, while a paltry 6 percent earned them from the Detroit area. For a nation that aspires to fairness, it is a paradoxical and troubling way to "leave no child behind."

In her book *Contradictions of School Reform*, Linda McNeil chronicles the way standardized tests subvert the complex, student-based education that transpires in quality institutions. In its place, writes McNeil, is a watered down version that is more congruent with the simplified demands of a standardized test. "This fragmentation of course content," adds McNeil, "tended to disembody the curriculum, divorcing it from the teachers' knowledge of the subject, and from the epistemologies, the ways of knowing, within the subject itself." 5

McNeil's book, it is instructive to note, was written about the standardized testing system in George W. Bush's Texas and the deleterious effects it had on that state's education. Throughout her study, McNeil reveals a series of inconsistencies in the lofty claims made by the test designers and the later reported results. From the start, for example, it was clear that the exams were undermining the education of poor students by reducing their class work to the most simplistic memorization. The overall conflation of content and the lack of choice—as well as the virtual abandonment of creative excursions away from test material—reduced the curriculum to a dumbed-down, truncated education. Students were denied the basic right to learn in personally relevant ways because the road to success was so closely aligned to the results of a single exam. Indeed, how could one justify doing anything that wasn't on the test? And why would teachers try innovative alternatives if the results wouldn't show up on the exam? "In reality these policies of standardization are decreasing the quality of teaching and learning in our schools, especially in the schools of poor and minority children," McNeil suggests.

Thus, students who are more likely to perform poorly on the exam are the first to become part of intensive, all-consuming programs of teaching to the test. In her study of Texas, McNeil found teachers who were abandoning time-honored assignments so as to spend more hours on test preparation. Again, the results of this monomania can only be appreciated with a certain amount of probing and analysis. As a rule, standardized tests measure subjects and disciplines in simplistic, multiple-choice formats. Replacing the essay question, which liberates the writer to incorporate a succession of theories and statistics—and become a better writer through writing—the typical standardized exam reduces the assessment process to multiple guess and stunts development of comprehension skills. For minority students, then, the goal is not more writing and reading but more memorization—more of the stultifying games that work auspiciously for test scores but serve students poorly in a complex world.

The result? Instead of exploring the themes in Conrad's *Heart of Darkness* or another canonical classic, students are limited to questions that can fit neatly on a bubble sheet. This often means relegating participants to a game-show education: naming authors and dates without ever penetrating their significance or demonstrating the more complex thinking skills that accompany their evaluation. In a world that is becoming more reliant on higher level thinking skills and the ability to craft new ideas and solve problems, how does one rationalize the standardized test?

Throughout her study, McNeil tries to answer such vexing questions. The Texas standardized exam has little to do with the poetic, the dramatic, or the innovative. In many instances, McNeil found teachers forsaking elaborate research projects and cultural studies in an attempt to prepare for the test. Supplanting the most progressive and provocative lessons were test-prep packets designed specifically to teach kids how to raise their scores. "The decision to use such materials," McNeil laments, "forces teachers to set aside their own best knowledge of their subject in order to drill their students on information whose primary (and often sole) usefulness is its likely inclusion on the test."

Such revelations also help to expose the anti-democratic, despotic 10 character of standardized testing. Rather than assisting schools to assess more accurately and effectively, these tests tend to subvert the desire to treat kids as individuals and tend to discourage teacher autonomy in choosing what is best for their students. Most vexing, though, are the dictatorial aspects of the exam. While the United States has evolved into a mosaic of various cultures and icons, the test conflates and often negates the diversity that should be studied and celebrated. Because it is standardized, it is monolithic and unresponsive to the voices of others. Only those people and movements which are tested are fair game for study. Why read *Malcolm X* if he is not on the exam? In predominantly Hispanic areas of the nation, cultural pantheons are neglected simply because the test is unresponsive to the diversity of its constituents.

Again, one can see the insidious way such exams affect poor and traditionally disaffected populations. With test selections typically constructed by those who approach knowledge and education from their own cultural and historical values, it is virtually impossible to design an exam that touches the many colors of our national tapestry. Suddenly, the melting pot has become a place where certain ingredients are effaced, where the recipe values some flavors over others.

The Texas plan, chronicled by McNeil, is disquieting not only in what it tells us about Texas but also in what it reveals about George W. Bush and his national plan for educational accountability. First, it is instructive to note that Bush chose Rod Paige, a Houston superintendent and test advocate, as his Secretary of Education. Paige is one of Bush's most vocal proponents and is perhaps most remembered for his appearance on *60 Minutes,* when he derided teachers who complained about the testing mania in Texas, implying that dissenters were afraid of hard work and accountability.

Under the Bush plan, then, one can expect more of the oppressive standardized testing system that was so dehumanizing in Texas during his tenure as governor. While McNeil's book captures the zeal with which Bush tested kids in his home state—and the inimical effects it had on minorities—reports out of Washington, D.C., suggest that much of the same is planned nationally. Indeed, the centerpiece of the Bush educational initiative is predicated upon the efficacy of standardized, systematic testing. And when kids don't measure up, the Bush agenda calls for vouchers and the concomitant withdrawal of public dollars from the "failing school."

Not surprisingly, teachers in the United States' poorest districts are wary. "When I hear the word vouchers," said a teacher from one of Kansas' poorest schools, "I get scared and wonder how much they're going to take away from us." Indeed, with standardized tests at their acme, many are wondering how unfair and ineffective the system can get.

In Michigan, where the affluent continue to garner awards that 15 clearly aren't needed, the cities of Detroit and Benton Harbor—where the neighborhoods are decidedly more black and brown—find that there is precious little to be gained from the MEAP scholarship awards. Perhaps this is why the Michigan branch of the American Civil Liberties Union has filed suit against the exam, asserting that the test is an "unconscionable use of public funds."

More troubling is the conclusions of a six-month study reported by Heather Newman in the January 21, 1998, *Detroit Free Press.* In "Fair Assessment of Students a Thorny Issue," Newman shows that more than half of the differences between the district's scores can be predicted by students' troubles at home. "It is no surprise," she writes, "that districts with less educated parents, high turnover rates, or low per-pupil state aid tended to do worse than those [which] had more educational advantages."

In short, Michigan's standardized test has become a pretext for rewarding prosperity while punishing poverty. Instead of championing innovation, tenacity, and resilience, it is a windfall for rich kids who have no need of scholarships from the state. "What do taxpayers gain by helping to finance the college education of students who were college-bound in any event?" asks *Detroit Free Press* columnist Brian Dickerson in the April 5, 2000, issue. Indeed, when the canard of accountability is exposed, who is really served by standardized tests?

State exams, like those in Michigan and Texas, are bad but certainly not the end of our nation's appetite for simplistic assessment. For decades, the Scholastic Aptitude Test, otherwise known as the SAT, has towered over students and served as a political cudgel against poorly funded schools. Like the state exams, which are designed to make governors look educationally responsive, the SAT has been used historically to undermine democracy by creating specious ways to avoid adequate and equal funding. Want to find an easy excuse for not funding poorer kids? Simply cite the lower SAT scores and demand improvement before funding is renewed.

This, we remember, was the strategy during the Reagan era, when Education Secretary William Bennett used SAT scores as a whip against schools—usually urban—that failed to raise scores. As with state tests, the big losers in this scenario are minority-populated schools, where nontraditional students grapple to unravel a test that was designed to predict the success of students in college. "SAT scores were never intended to be aggregated for evaluating the achievements of teachers, schools, school districts, or states, and such scores have no validity when used for such evaluations," writes David C. Berliner and Bruce J. Biddle in their 1995 book, *The Manufactured Crisis: Myths, Fraud, and the Attack on America's Public Schools.*

So when the media and politicians unite to indict schools for lower 20 SAT scores, the sure loser is the minority system—those institutions that have fewer experienced test takers, those who have fewer resources for exam improvement. Thus it is not surprising to find that SAT scores, like their state counterparts, are easily aligned with socioeconomic background. "The average SAT score earned by students goes down by fifteen points for each decrease of $10,000 in family income," adds Berliner and Biddle. This means that, whenever colleges make decisions about students based on the SAT, they are again subverting democracy by failing to extend equal opportunity to indigent students.

Perhaps this is why Richard Atkinson, president of the University of California, has suggested that the California system stop using SATs as a measure for student applications. "I want examinations that are directly tied to the curriculum, not examinations like the SAT that are really very vague, and it's almost impossible to determine what they indeed are measuring," said Atkinson in a February 17, 2001, *ABC News* report.

Throughout the nation, the testing craze has resulted in a series of responses from scholars and politicians, who are uniting to demand better, more just assessment procedures. The National Council of Teachers of English has spoken out against high stakes testing and the antithetical qualities it brings to the learning context. Democratic Senator Paul Wellstone of Minnesota has labeled the standardized testing craze a "straightjacket" that is "channeling teaching to the kind of rote memorization drill that isn't education." Long-time educator and writer Frank Smith perhaps best captures the essential problem with testing when he contends that "there is one reason only for the insistent control of programmatic instruction and tests in classrooms. That reason is lack of trust."

What, then, is the answer? How do we hold schools accountable without testing?

First, it is time that we learn to trust educators and purge the classroom of the political wrangling that has spawned these ineffective and simplistic tests. If one wonders about accountability, there should be a way to examine entire programs rather than simply looking at a single test score, which invariably will abbreviate any performance. In this spirit, then, we must recognize the fact that assessments of our schools don't have to come in the form of tests. In a nation as diverse as the United States, it is time to develop evaluative programs that respect the many competencies that exist in its myriad cultures.

Despite what many would have us believe, there is no such thing 25 as an objective, all-encompassing test. There are no tests that prove anything beyond their own narrow boundaries and even fewer that have any congruency with local schools. How many of us have walked away from an exam with the disquieting realization that our true potential was clearly not demonstrated? Wouldn't it be wiser to come to terms with the fact that assessment is complicated, sophisticated—that it can never be effectively reduced to a single test?

Today, it makes sense to seek more holistic assessment instruments, using portfolios and presentations that demonstrate the totality of a student's knowledge and growth. In the same spirit of the doctoral dissertation, we can evaluate students for complex learning and erudite analysis by asking them to engage in high-level projects and presentations, which can later be showcased to the public through fairs and public forums. In short, we can demand sophisticated, cerebral education and still maintain local control. This all begins, however, when we transcend the easy simplicity of standardized evaluations and the political agenda they represent.

What Did You Read?

1. What does it mean to say, "the standardized test policy represents a way to legitimize the status quo while proving the inferiority of the disenfranchised students"?

2. What does Linda McNeil mean by saying that "students were denied the basic right to learn in personally relevant ways"?

3. What is undemocratic about the results of standardized tests in Michigan?

What Do You Think?

1. Do you agree with Shafer that standardized tests are not democratic? Why or why not?

2. Do you feel that the typical standardized "bubble sheet" exams subvert the desire to treat students as individuals and discourage teachers from choosing what is best for their students? Why or why not?

3. Is it possible to design an exam that is rigorous in content and not socially biased? Explain.

How Was It Done?

1. What pedagogical device is the article centered on?

2. How does the introductory quote present the essence of this article? Does it establish focus for the article or not?

3. In establishing the gulf that separates the "elite" student and the disenfranchised student, what evidence is provided that supports standardized testing as one of the culprits?

4. How does Shafer craft and manipulate his argument with language? For example, what kinds of words does he use to describe standardized tests?

4. How does Shafer craft and manipulate his argument with language? For example, what kinds of words does he use to describe standardized tests?

5. Why do you suppose much of the evidence is centered on schools in Michigan?

The Good Old Golden Rule Days
William A. Henry III

William A. Henry III, in his book In Defense of Elitism, *claims that schools have lost the standards and values of the past, and instead have replaced them with concerns about meeting students' needs for self-esteem, self-expression, and self-assertion. The worst development was social promotion, a practice in which all students are passed on to the next grade level no matter what their achievement. While social promotion had its roots in the Vietnam War (helping young men avoid the draft), its practice has continued to this day. Part of the problem has been the growth of an entitlement mentality in which the students' wants and desires are most important, and standards are weakened or simply dropped.*

Key Words

egalitarianism	the belief in human equality, especially with respect to social and political rights
metaphysics	a study of what is outside objective experience
erstwhile	in the past; formerly
concomitant	something that accompanies or is connected to something else
venal	open to corruption, especially bribery
perspicacity	keen; shrewd
anecdotally	based on the telling of stories
intransigent	uncompromising; unwilling to abandon an extreme position
vignette	a brief incident or scene

In a combined second- and third-grade class conducted in rural Johnson City, New York, in the spring of 1993, pupils who were engaged in a study of the concept of perimeters tried to find a way to involve a classmate who is mentally retarded and unable to speak. Their solution: to turn her into a giant ruler. They coaxed her to lie on a pad and used her to do their measuring. This incident, reported in *The New York Times,* was neither a scandal nor, alas, an anomaly. In many school districts these days, ordinary classrooms are encumbered with formerly sequestered "special education" students who are ill equipped to learn and who impede the progress of those who can. The same quixotic liberalism that led to the "deinstitutionalization" of genuine lunatics, who now stand on street corners swaying and talking to themselves, has taken hold of public education. Egalitarians have proclaimed that the self-esteem and limited learning opportunities of the disabled are more important than the advancement of the fit, let alone the gifted. Parents of the mentally handicapped, wishing to sustain the illusion that their children are normal, and educators committed to tolerance more than to education have joined forces to compel schools to integrate even the most different children into the ordinary classroom. Where a generation ago parents demanded—rightly—that communities bear the cost of providing specialized education for their offspring, they now want the further equality of having it provided within the mainstream. Children doubtless can accommodate themselves to the disruption; witness the rough and ready way that the retarded girl's classmates perceived exactly what contribution she could make to their learning. But teachers feel compelled as well to honor the egalitarian distortion that every child ought to be judged against his or her potential rather than against absolute standards. In Johnson City and elsewhere, as the *Times* noted, "Teachers set different goals for different students; some might get top grades if they learn part of the material." Consider for a moment the lesson that teaches the rest of the class. Accomplishment is not objective and standards are not fixed. The governing principles are ideology and sentiment.

If one wishes to foretell the future of a society, one should visit its public school classrooms to see what is happening now. This, more than any love of pedagogy for its own sake, has prompted me to write frequent articles for *Time*, including cover stories, about the evolving curriculum and values. Education is both the mirror and maker of modernity, reflecting the values of contemporary culture and instilling them in the succeeding generation. Schools prepare the next entrants into the work force, and the skills and attitudes those pupils absorb will determine the fate of American industry's attempts to compete in a global marketplace. Schools perpetuate the social contract, exposing children to ethnicities, priorities, beliefs, and metaphysics not found at home. Ideally, this leads them to be tolerant and comprehending toward fellow citizens, so that they can join in common cause. Schools promulgate and, in so doing, often redefine the national myth, interpreting the meaning of America's past in the light of its evolving present. Above all, schools take children at an impressionable age and teach them what to expect, or in some cases demand, from life. From what I have seen, they are learning the wrong beliefs.

There was a time, not so very long ago and still fondly remembered by most who lived through it, when schools taught discipline, self-denial, deference to one's betters, and other elitist values. Teachers had little time for encouraging students' self-expression and consumerist self-assertion because it was understood that schools were preparation for life and that very few jobs indeed offered much scope for self-expression or self-assertion. School was boot camp, not therapy. Educators tried to be aware of social problems but had no illusions of being able to solve them immediately; moreover, parents and students did not expect that. Learning was considered a social good because it would improve matters over the course of generations, not necessarily within a single lifetime. The world was bluntly realistic about this. I remember vividly from my fifties childhood a slogan that appeared on innumerable New York City bus and subway advertising cards. "Drop out of school," it read, "and they'll call you 'boy' all your life." This advice appeared without overt protest from minority leaders whose heirs would be howling if it were to be proffered now. The leaders of that era apparently understood the pedagogical values of shame and fear; uproar about individual rights and dignity would ac-

complish nothing of value if it effectively resulted in condoning ignorance and accelerating the dropout rate. By and large, moreover, those
minority leaders recognized that people of whatever social or personal
handicaps had to take responsibility for their own destinies. While
awaiting a better and fairer world, we were obliged to make the most
of the world we lived in.

At about the time I was passing through the schools, the educational establishment started replacing shame and fear with the cotton
candy of the "social promotion"—promoting and even graduating students who had not done the necessary work and achieved the necessary proficiency because it would be too stigmatizing to leave them
back or let them drop out sans diploma. One impetus for the change
was the temporary but pervasive phenomenon of the Vietnam War
draft. Teachers knew that flunking young men, or even giving them
low grades, might literally condemn them to death. At my somewhat
above average suburban high school, from which in previous years no
more than sixty percent of the graduates had gone on to further education (including junior college, electricians' academy, beauty school,
and the like), in my departing year of 1967 some ninety percent continued their schooling, including virtually all the boys—and I know of
only one classmate who died in Vietnam.

The war ended a few years later, but the corrupting policies con-   5
tinued. It has been widely documented that many of our inner-city
high school graduates (particularly those who can dextrously wield a
basketball, football, or baseball) are unleashed upon the world barely
able to read. Or spell. Or count. Or, obviously, fill out a job application,
comprehend the government coverage in a worthwhile newspaper, or
avert exploitation by flimflam artists. If students cannot meet the erst-
while standards of attainment, schools find it easier to lower the standards than to raise the performance.

Teachers and administrators are guided to this misplaced indul-
gence by at least five factors. One is the new place of schools as social
worker and national nanny, providing everything from free hot
lunches for the indigent to counseling and physical protection for the
abused. This breeds in teachers a sense that their primary mission is to
succor the young rather than instruct and assess them. Second is the
increased ideological scrutiny of schools by organized minority
groups, with the concomitant assumption that higher failure rates for
blacks and Hispanics than for whites is a reflection of failure by the
schools rather than by the students, their homes, and their communities. Third is the acceleration in the depth and scope of citizens' feelings of "entitlement," the bane of competition in so many arenas.
Where a generation ago people felt entitled to a chance at education,
they now feel entitled to the credential affirming that they have completed a course of study regardless of their actual mastery.

Fourth, and closely allied, is a widespread erosion in students' regard for authority and willingness to learn. George Cohen, a human-relations specialist in the White Plains, New York, school district, calls this the "Bart Simpson syndrome." As quoted in *The New York Times,* he says of high schoolers given an assignment: "There's a disbelief that somehow they're going to be held accountable for getting it in on time. It's that attitude that drives a lot of us nuts." The *Times* adds: "The change that teachers and administrators talk about is, fairly recent, and noted not just by the middle-aged but by those who are too young themselves to remember dress codes and silence-in-the-halls edicts. 'It's absolutely incredible,' said Carol Gordon Horner, an eighth-grade language arts teacher in Charlotte, North Carolina, who returned to the classroom in 1991 after a thirteen-year absence. 'Kids have a real sense of entitlement now that you didn't see before. It's almost like a make-me attitude—it's not that they won't respect you, but they won't respect you just because you're an adult. It used to be automatic. Now there's a testing mechanism that goes on constantly.'" Lillian Katz, professor of early childhood education at the University of Illinois, sees potential roots of this in a pervasive narcissism and self-congratulation urged upon children at the elementary level. In the summer 1993 issue of *American Educator,* she remarks:

> A project by a first grade class in an affluent Middle Western suburb that I recently observed showed how self-esteem and narcissism can be confused. Working from copied pages prepared by the teacher, each student produced a booklet called "All About Me." The first page asked for basic information about the child's home and family. The second page was titled "what I like to eat," the third was "what I like to watch on TV," the next was "what I want for a present" and another was "where I want to go on vacation."
>
> The booklet, like thousands of others I have encountered around the country, had no page headings such as "what I want to know more about," "what I am curious about," "what I want to solve" or even "to make."
>
> Each page was directed toward the child's basest inner gratifications. Each topic put the child in the role of consumer—of food, entertainment, gifts, and recreation. Not once was the child asked to play the role of producer, investigator, initiator, explorer, experimenter or problem-solver.
>
> It is perhaps this kind of literature that accounts for a poster I saw in a school entrance hall. Pictures of clapping hands surround the title "We Applaud Ourselves." While the sign's probable purpose was to help children feel good about themselves, it did so by directing their attention inward. The poster urged self-congratulation; it made no reference to possible ways of earning applause—by considering the feelings or needs of others.

Fifth and by no means least among these dispiriting trends is the careerist consideration that poor test results and high failure rates can lead to the ouster of administrators and a loss of public support for raises in teachers' salaries. It is in almost everyone's venal interest to make things look better than they are. In truth, of course, they are worse.

Even among the quasi-elite subset of high school students who go on to college, Scholastic Aptitude Test scores have been more or less steadily declining, albeit with a recent minor uptick. The average verbal score was 422 in 1992, versus 478 in 1963—even though many scholars contend that today's test is easier, having been deliberately "dumbed down." The SAT may, as alleged, have a cultural bias. It asks about things that a mainstream person ought to know but that the underclass may not yet have learned. Further, the SAT may not be the ideal test of intelligence or preparation or ability to handle college courses. Yet it *does* measure some things: vocabulary, problem-solving, reading comprehension, ability to draw logical inferences. These skills are undeniably important for college and for further life. The customary explanation for the decline in scores—the increase in numbers of deprived minority students taking the test—does not begin to account for all the difference. Granted that the low-end group might, in a more inclusive admissions era, rank rather lower than before. Why has the statistical performance of the upper-end students, the sort who go to the best colleges, also declined (albeit with a partial rebound in mathematics)? Affirmative action alone won't explain it. Indeed, at most prestigious colleges, affirmative action programs are having trouble meeting their quotas. At my alma mater, Yale, where I served on an alumni board committee concerned with admissions (which meant, for ninety percent of the discussion time, minority recruiting), I learned that as of the late 1980s, black male "yield" had fallen by half compared to the preceding decade, not only at Yale but at many of its competitors. No one was quite sure why, although explanations ranged from drugs to despair. One black Yale classmate of mine assured me, in all seriousness, that it was the result of a conscious decision by the powers that be to "throw away a whole generation of black men." Oddly, black women continued to qualify and enroll, suggesting that the problem lay within the black community rather than in white society. Hispanic students from the Southwest and California were similarly difficult to recruit, I was told, because families were reluctant to send them so far away and because, in a society that no longer encourages elitism, parents were reluctant to see one of their children get a better education and broader opportunities than the others, for fear of breaking up family unity.

Whatever the role minorities play in affecting scores—and that impact should have been fully reflected more than a decade ago, when affirmative action took sway—clearly SAT scores have declined (despite some softening of the test) because student knowledge and perspicacity have declined. Moreover, rather than face up to this decline, 10 lobbying groups assert that the SAT discriminates against the handicapped and that the PSAT, used by the National Merit Scholarships, discriminates against women. The "proof," according to Cinthia Schuman of the National Center for Fair and Open Testing: boys get higher scores. In fairness, girls do get higher grades. But that does not necessarily mean they are smarter. They may just be better behaved and more apt to win teachers over.

It is fashionable to blame television as the primary culprit for the overall decline in student performance, but this assertion is antichronological. Television played at least as pervasive a role in the childhood and adolescence of my contemporaries as it does in our children's generation (as witness the boundless popular taste for fifties and sixties TV nostalgia). Debate continues to rage about why the decline has happened (and, in some quarters where the fact is politically inconvenient, about *if* it has happened), but some of the reasons are obvious. Parents no longer teach reverence for authority and learning. Many of them arrive at teacher conferences loaded for bear, prepared to treat any shortcoming of their child's as exclusively the fault of the school—if they come at all, which is anecdotally reported to be less and less likely, as more mothers work outside the home. Students reared on *Sesame Street* expect learning to be chirpy, funny, swift-paced, and full of entertainment. They have far less patience than their forebears with such wearisome but necessary tasks as memorization. Teachers, who once viewed their work as akin to a religious vocation, are increasingly unionized and intransigent toward extra work. Too often they convey no sense to their students of school as a spiritual place, of learning as holy. School administrators and counselors now see their institutions (or are forced by community pressures to see them) as rehabilitation centers obliged to make up for the social and psychological deficiencies of some parents, the ignorance and bone idleness of others, the economic privations of others still, and the myriad unkindnesses of nature. Where schools of the fifties, particularly post-*Sputnik,* focused on stimulating the brightest, schools of today focus on bringing the backward up to speed. Often, as a matter of policy, they hinder or at least do not help the brightest to become the best they can be. In fifties educational parlance, a "special" child meant a gifted one. Now it usually means one who is severely handicapped.

Last and far from least, authors and publishers have turned the textbook business into a grand truckling to political correctness at the expense of accuracy, of perspective, and above all of challenge. As retired Cornell professor Donald Hayes has demonstrated using a computer analysis, the language difficulty of textbooks has dropped by about twenty percent during the past couple of generations. Having sampled 788 texts used between 1860 and 1992, he says, "Honors high school texts are no more difficult than an eighth grade reader was before World War II."

Perhaps the best measure of what has gone wrong is the fact, attested to by textbook authors and editors, that publishers now employ more people to censor books for content that might offend any organized lobbying group than they do to check the correctness of facts. From a business point of view, that makes sense. A book is far more apt to be struck off a purchase order because it contains terminology or vignettes that irritate the hypersensitive than because it is erroneous.

The results are chilling. When it came time to vote on new textbooks for use in Texas schools during the 1992–93 academic year, one member of the state Board of Education wondered aloud whether the planned $20.2 million expenditure was really quite wise. One of the books scheduled for adoption, she pointed out, informed children that the United States had settled its conflict in Korea by "using the bomb." This apparent reference to nonexistent nuclear warfare was just one of 231 factual errors cited by conservative critics whose deeper objections are to galloping feminism and multiculturalism but who are given ammunition against such volumes by their cheerful disregard for precise fact. Among other prominent errors in the texts were assertions that Robert Francis Kennedy and Martin Luther King, Jr., were assassinated during the Republican presidency of Richard Nixon rather than the Democratic regime of his predecessor, Lyndon Johnson, and that George Bush defeated Michael Dukakis in the election of 1989 rather than 1988—a calendar howler that ought to have jumped out at any author, editor, copy editor, or fact checker who ever took an elementary school civics course about our quadrennial system. For pointing this out, the school board member was criticized by some of her colleagues for allegedly playing politics and by others, including some scholars, for trivializing the more important quest for a politically correct view of the sins of conquest with a "nit-picking" emphasis on fact.

What Did You Read?

1. What is "social promotion"?
2. What does Henry mean by this: "Kids have a real sense of entitlement now that you didn't see before"?
3. What does Henry mean when he says "School was boot camp, not therapy."

What Do You Think?

1. Do you see a classroom as a place where it is the teacher's responsibility that you learn the material or your responsibility? Explain.

2. Do you believe that teachers, when evaluating a student's school-work, should consider the student's personal situation as well? Why or why not?

3. To what extent is television a reason for the decline in students' academic performance?

How Was It Done?

1. How is the article structured around ideology?

2. Henry structures most of his article around what factors that he sees as misplaced by teachers and administrators?

3. Henry bases most of his claim on what? Where do most of his facts come from?

4. How important to the crafting of his argument is Henry's use of contrasting educations in the 1950s and 1960s to the present?

3

Dreams

Dreams have long been a source of interest for people. As far back as the time of the Book of Genesis, people felt that dreams were important and meaningful, perhaps messages from the spiritual realm or predictors of future events. However, when Sigmund Freud published *The Interpretation of Dreams* in 1900, he opened a whole new avenue of investigation—that dreams were messages from our unconscious. Since that time, much debate has focused on whether Freud was right or wrong. If Freud was wrong, then what are dreams? It's a topic investigated in both popular literature and serious academic journals. Dreams are such a part of human experience that they frequently appear in art, literature, movies, and even television soap operas. Dreams and our reactions to them can be frustrating, enlightening, and even fun.

In this chapter, the Writing Lesson focuses on the writing of summaries. The ability to write a summary can be useful for writers as a way to present information, material from another source, or the record of a sequence of events. Writers often use brief summaries within a larger essay. To write a summary, you must be able to distinguish between important ideas and less important details. You need to write with clarity and brevity. Thus, the writing of summaries utilizes important critical thinking and writing skills. In the Writing Assignment, the use of summaries is employed as part of the process of dream analysis. The summary presents a dream that can then be interpreted as you see fit.

THE MAIN EVENT READING

"Distortion in Dreams"

Sigmund Freud

The Main Event reading is an excerpt from Freud's The Interpretation of Dreams, *initially published in 1913. The passage argues that dreams, even those that appear to be disagreeable, are expressions of wish fulfillment. Freud presents a dream, one that appears to be full of frustration, and analyzes how it indeed expresses wish fulfillment. He does so by connecting the dream to other details in the patient's life. Freud's dream interpretations mark a beginning point in taking dreams seriously.*

Key Words

psychoneurotic	someone who suffers an emotional conflict in which an impulse is blocked and finds expression in a disguised response or symbol
subsidiary	providing aid or supporting; of secondary importance
adduced	offered as an example, reason, or proof
reconcile	settle; resolve
psychopathological	of or relating to behavioral dysfunction in a mental disorder or in social organization
elucidate	to make clear, especially by analysis
evasion	a means of evading, dodging
jestingly	in a joking or ludicrous manner

That the dream actually has a secret meaning, which proves to be a wish-fulfilment, must be proved afresh in every case by analysis. I will therefore select a few dreams which have painful contents, and endeavour to analyse them. Some of them are dreams of hysterical subjects, which therefore call for a long preliminary statement, and in some passages an examination of the psychic processes occurring in hysteria. This, though it will complicate the presentation, is unavoidable. *[main idea]* *[present examples as proof]*

When I treat a psychoneurotic patient analytically, his dreams regularly, as I have said, become a theme of our conversations. I must therefore give him all the psychological explanations with whose aid I myself have succeeded in understanding his symptoms. And here I encounter unsparing criticism, which is perhaps no less shrewd than that which I have to expect from my colleagues. With perfect uniformity my patients contradict the doctrine that dreams are the fulfilments of wishes. Here are several examples of the sort of dream-material which is adduced in refutation of my theory.

"You are always saying that a dream is a wish fulfilled," begins an intelligent lady patient. "Now I shall tell you a dream in which the content is quite the opposite, in which a wish of mine is not fulfilled. How do you reconcile that with your theory? The dream was as follows: *I want to give a supper, but I have nothing available except some smoked salmon. I think I will go shopping, but I remember that it is Sunday afternoon, when all the shops are closed. I then try to ring up a few caterers, but the telephone is out of order. Accordingly I have to renounce my desire to give a supper.*" first example

I reply, of course, that only the analysis can decide the meaning of this dream, although I admit that at first sight it seems sensible and coherent and looks like the opposite of a wish-fulfilment. "But what occurrence gave rise to this dream?" I ask. "You know that the stimulus of a dream always lies among the experiences of the preceding day."

Analysis.—The patient's husband, an honest and capable meat salesman, had told her the day before that he was growing too fat, and that he meant to undergo treatment for obesity. He would rise early, take physical exercise, keep to a strict diet, and above all accept no more invitations to supper.—She proceeds jestingly to relate how her husband, at a *table d' hôte*, had made the acquaintance of an artist, who insisted upon painting his portrait, because he, the painter, had never seen such an expressive head. But her husband had answered in his downright fashion, that while he was much obliged, he would rather not be painted; and he was quite convinced that a bit of a pretty young girl's posterior would please the artist better than his whole face.[6]— She is very much in love with her husband, and teases him a good deal. She has asked him not to give her any caviar. What can that mean? 5 Freud's analysis

As a matter of fact, she had wanted for a long time to eat a caviar sandwich every morning, but had grudged the expense. Of course she could get the caviar from her husband at once if she asked for it. But she has, on the contrary, begged him not to give her any caviar, so that she might tease him about it a little longer.

(To me this explanation seems thin. Unconfessed motives are wont to conceal themselves behind just such unsatisfying explanations. We are reminded of the subjects hypnotized by Bernheim, who carried out why this parenthetical paragraph?

---

[6]To sit for the painter.
> Goethe: "And if he has no backside,
> How can the nobleman sit?"

a post-hypnotic order, and who, on being questioned as to their motives, instead of answering: "I do not know why I did that," had to invent a reason that was obviously inadequate. There is probably something similar to this in the case of my patient's caviar. I see that in waking life she is compelled to invent an unfulfilled wish. Her dream also shows her the non-fulfilment of her wish. But why does she need an unfulfilled wish?)

The ideas elicited so far are insufficient for the interpretation of the dream. I press for more. After a short pause, which corresponds to the overcoming of a resistance, she reports that the day before she had paid a visit to a friend of whom she is really jealous because her husband is always praising this lady so highly. Fortunately this friend is very thin and lanky, and her husband likes full figures. Now of what did this thin friend speak? Of course, of her wish to become rather plumper. She also asked my patient: "When are you going to invite us again? You always have such good food." what is important about resistance

Now the meaning of the dream is clear. I am able to tell the patient: "It is just as though you had thought at the moment of her asking you that: 'Of course, I'm to invite you so that you can eat at my house and get fat and become still more pleasing to my husband! I would rather give no more suppers!' The dream then tells you that you cannot give a supper, thereby fulfilling your wish not to contribute anything to the rounding out of your friend's figure. Your husband's resolution to accept no more invitations to supper in order that he may grow thin teaches you that one grows fat on food eaten at other people's tables." Nothing is lacking now but some sort of coincidence which will confirm the solution. The smoked salmon in the dream has not yet been traced.—"How did you come to think of salmon in your dream?"—"Smoked salmon is my friend's favorite dish," she replied. It happens that I know the lady, and am able to affirm that she grudges herself salmon just as my patient grudges herself caviar. first meaning

This dream admits of yet another and more exact interpretation—one which is actually necessitated only by a subsidiary circumstance. The two interpretations do not contradict one another, but rather dovetail into one another, and furnish an excellent example of the usual ambiguity of dreams, as of all other psychopathological formations. We have heard that at the time of her dream of a denied wish the patient was impelled to deny herself a real wish (the wish to eat caviar sandwiches). Her friend, too, had expressed a wish, namely, to get fatter, and it would not surprise us if our patient had dreamt that this wish of her friend's—the wish to increase in weight—was not to be fulfilled. Instead of this, however, she dreamt that one of her own wishes was not fulfilled. The dream becomes capable of a new inter- 10
second meaning pretation if in the dream she does not mean herself, but her friend, if she has put herself in the place of her friend, or, as we may say, has *identified* herself with her friend.

I think she has actually done this, and as a sign of this identification she has created for herself in real life an unfulfilled wish. But what is the meaning of this hysterical identification? To elucidate this a more exhaustive exposition is necessary. Identification is a highly important motive in the mechanism of hysterical symptoms; by this means patients are enabled to express in their symptoms not merely their own experiences, but the experiences of quite a number of other persons; they can suffer, as it were, for a whole mass of people, and fill all the parts of a drama with their own personalities. It will here be objected that this is the well-known hysterical imitation, the ability of hysterical subjects to imitate all the symptoms which impress them when they occur in others, as though pity were aroused to the point of reproduction. This, however, only indicates the path which the psychic process follows in hysterical imitation. But the path itself and the psychic act which follows this path are two different matters. The act itself is slightly more complicated than we are prone to believe the imitation of the hysterical to be; it corresponds to an unconscious end-process, as an example will show. The physician who has, in the same ward with other patients, a female patient suffering from a particular kind of twitching, is not surprised if one morning he learns that this peculiar hysterical affection has found imitators. He merely tells himself: The others have seen her, and have imitated her; this is psychic infection.— Yes, but psychic infection occurs somewhat in the following manner: As a rule, patients know more about one another than the physician knows about any one of them, and they are concerned about one another when the doctor's visit is over. One of them has an attack to-day: at once it is known to the rest that a letter from home, a recrudescence of lovesickness, or the like, is the cause. Their sympathy is aroused, and although it does not emerge into consciousness they form the following conclusion: "If it is possible to suffer such an attack from such a cause, I too may suffer this sort of an attack, for I have the same occasion for it." If this were a conclusion capable of becoming conscious, it would perhaps express itself in *dread* of suffering a like attack; but it is formed in another psychic region, and consequently ends in the realization of the dreaded symptoms. Thus identification is not mere imitation, but an assimilation based upon the same etiological claim, it expresses a "just like," and refers to some common condition which has remained in the unconscious.

In hysteria identification is most frequently employed to express a sexual community. The hysterical woman identifies herself by her symptoms most readily—though not exclusively—with persons with

Margin notes:
concept of identification

deductive logic

why should this be?

whom she had had sexual relations, or who have had sexual inter-course with the same persons as herself. Language takes cognizance of this tendency: two lovers are said to be "one." In hysterical phantasy, as well as in dreams, identification may ensue if one simply thinks of sexual relations; they need not necessarily become actual. The patient is merely following the rules of the hysterical processes of thought when she expresses her jealousy of her friend (which, for that matter, she herself admits to be unjustified) by putting herself in her friend's place in her dream, and identifying herself with her by fabricating a symptom (the denied wish). One might further elucidate the process by saying: In the dream she puts herself in the place of her friend, be-cause her friend has taken her own place in relation to her husband, and because she would like to take her friend's place in her husband's esteem.[7]

The contradiction of my theory of dreams on the part of another female patient, the most intelligent of all my dreamers, was solved in a simpler fashion, though still in accordance with the principle that the non-fulfilment of one wish signified the fulfilment of another. I had one day explained to her that a dream is a wish-fulfilment. On the fol-lowing day she related a dream to the effect that she was travelling with her mother-in-law to the place in which they were both to spend the summer. Now I knew that she had violently protested against spending the summer in the neighbourhood of her mother-in-law. I also knew that she had fortunately been able to avoid doing so, since she had recently succeeded in renting a house in a place quite remote from that to which her mother-in-law was going. And now the dream reversed this desired solution. Was not this a flat contradiction of my theory of wish-fulfilment? One had only to draw the inferences from this dream in order to arrive at its interpretation. According to this dream, I was wrong; *but it was her wish that I should be wrong, and this wish the dream showed her as fulfilled.* But the wish that I should be wrong, which was fulfilled in the theme of the country house, referred in reality to another and more serious matter. At that time I had in-ferred, from the material furnished by her analysis, that something of significance in respect to her illness must have occurred at a certain time in her life. She had denied this, because it was not present in her memory. We soon came to see that I was right. Thus her wish that I should prove to be wrong, which was transformed into the dream that

second example

---

[7]I myself regret the inclusion of such passages from the psychopathology of hysteria, which, because of their fragmentary presentation, and because they are torn out of their context, can-not prove to be very illuminating. If these passages are capable of throwing any light upon the intimate relations between dreams and the psychoneuroses, they have served the intention with which I have included them.

she was going into the country with her mother-in-law, corresponded with the justifiable wish that those things which were then only suspected had never occurred.

Without an analysis, and merely by means of an assumption, I took the liberty of interpreting a little incident in the life of a friend, who had been my companion through eight classes at school. He once heard a lecture of mine, delivered to a small audience, on the novel idea that dreams are wish-fulfilments. He went home, dreamt *that he had lost all his lawsuits*—he was a lawyer—and then complained to me about it. I took refuge in the evasion: "One can't win all one's cases"; but I thought to myself: "If, for eight years, I sat as *primus* on the first bench, while he moved up and down somewhere in the middle of the class, may he not naturally have had the wish, ever since his boyhood, that I too might for once make a fool of myself?"

Is this a fair assumption?

third example

What Did You Read?

1. What does Freud mean by the statement: "You know that the stimulus of a dream always lies among the experiences of the preceding day"? Do you agree with this? Why?

2. What does Freud mean by "hysterical identification"?

3. How does Freud's relationship with his patients get "expressed" in this passage?

What Do You Think?

1. Have you had dreams that at first glance look like the opposite of wish fulfillment but on further investigation do appear to be more consistent with Freud's theory of wish fulfillment? Explain.

2. Do you believe, like Freud, that through analysis of a dream, sensible and coherent meaning of the dream can be derived? Explain.

3. Do you believe that many of your underlying motives for doing things are concealed in your waking life but revealed in your dream life? Explain.

How Was It Done?

1. What is Freud's piece structured around? Be specific.
2. What constitutes the majority of this passage?
3. How does the use of italics and parentheses help to organize Freud's work?
4. What does Freud assume in the development of his argument?
5. How does certain vocabulary (and the understanding of those terms) contribute to the substance of his explanations? Provide examples.

THE MAIN EVENT WRITING ASSIGNMENT

Write an essay in response to one of the following assignments:

1. Choose a recent dream of your own that you can recount in fairly vivid detail. This dream may involve one primary scene, or it may involve different scenes or fragments. Choose a dream in which images and emotions are pronounced. Apply a psychological theory (such as from one of the readings) to the dream for the purpose of analyzing the dream so that you can apply its meaning to your waking life. Two summaries will be involved in the successful completion of the assignment—a summary of your dream and a summary of the basic theory that you apply to your dream.

2. How does Freud's theory of dream interpretation work with his theories of how the mind works? In order to answer this question you must summarize both Freud's theory of dream interpretation and his theories of the mind.

3. Do you believe all dreams are based on wish fulfillment? Summarize some of your own dreams to show how they are not based on wish fulfillment.

4. Argue that there is no inherent purpose or meaning in dreams. Summarize the established scientific view that supports this position.

PREPARATION PUNCH LIST

Before you begin writing the essay, you need to prepare yourself to write. Jot down some notes on what you know in general.

1. What is the first thing you think about when you think of dreams or dreaming?

- Historically, dreams have been considered prophetic (e.g., Joseph in the Book of Genesis). Dreams are also simply a biological function that everyone experiences in different periods of the sleep cycle. Dreams can conjure up images of horror or images of fantasy. Do you think your dreams have meaning?

2. What do you know about Freud, in particular, his thoughts about dreaming?

- He believes in the three-faceted psyche—id, ego, superego. He believes that two-thirds of the psyche is submerged in the subconscious. He believes that hypnosis and dream interpretation can unlock the subconscious. He believes dreams are wish fulfillment. He believes repressed motives are exposed in dreams.

3. What you know about Jung?

- Jung does not believe all dreams are wish fulfillment. He believes that objects in a dream have particular meaning to the dreamer.

4. How does one describe a dream?

- It has always been tricky to verbalize one's dream. It is important first to think about dreams in terms of fragments or scenes. It's important to be aware of color, or the absence of color. Pay particular attention to objects that reveal themselves in a pronounced way. Who are the players in a dream (the main characters)? Are you watching or are you participating? How do you feel in your dream? Are you lonely, do you feel rejected or sad, or do you feel a great sense of happiness or discovery?

- Locales are important. Where are you? Are you in movement? Are you descending or ascending?

- Does your past intersect with the present? Does the dream reoccur?

5. How would you deconstruct or break down your dream using Freudian terminology?

- For example, where is there nakedness (connected to nostalgia for a prelingual state of innocence) in your dream?

- Where is there anxiety? Where is there wish fulfillment? Where is there anger or hostility?

THE MAIN EVENT WRITING LESSON: USING SUMMARY IN AN ESSAY

In order to complete the Chapter Writing Assignment, you will need to write a summary. A summary is a short statement that repeats the main points or ideas of something. You can write a summary of a written work, or you can summarize events, such as in life, in a film, or in a dream. A summary does not include analysis or criticisms because those ideas are not part of the material itself. (In some writing situations, you may present a summary of the reading first and then give the analysis or critique.) A summary can be as short as a single sentence, but usually several sentences or a paragraph will be required. For long works, such as a book or novel, a summary may require several paragraphs.

Follow these steps to write a successful summary of a written work:

1. **Find the thesis of the reading.** If there is no explicit thesis sentence, you will need to determine the thesis by understanding the author's main ideas.

2. **Determine the supporting ideas.** Check the topic sentences of the paragraphs; usually they indicate important supporting points. Also, look for key transitional words or phrases. Words that show sequences, such as "first," "second," or "finally," may also point to important supporting ideas.

3. **Don't get bogged down in the details.** Remember that a summary gives a broad overview of a work. Leave the details for the actual work itself.

4. **Don't comment or add your own opinions.** A summary is about the work, not about your response to the work.

5. **Make sure your summary flows smoothly.** Your summary of a work should be a readable work of its own, too. Do not just string together random ideas from the reading. Be aware of your use of language and the logical development of the summary. Your summary should have a sense of beginning, middle, and end, reflecting the same structure of the material being summarized. Don't forget to use transitions to smooth the reader's path from one idea to the next.

Here is a summary of the excerpt from Freud's *Interpretation of Dreams:*

In a passage from "Distortion in Dreams," a chapter from Sigmund Freud's *The Interpretation of Dreams,* Freud argues that all dreams involve wish fulfillment, even dreams which are painful and frustrating to the dreamer. He cites as an example the dream of a young woman who dreams of not being able to prepare a supper. In her waking-life, the woman's husband is trying to lose weight. Further, she is jealous of a female friend, who is thin; she knows her husband likes full-figured women. This friend has asked for a dinner invitation. Freud interprets the dream to mean that the dreamer would rather not give any supper parties so that her friend cannot get heavier and become more appealing to her husband. He then argues that the dream can be interpreted also as an example of "hysterical identification" in which the dreamer is actually placing herself in the position of her friend. He states that hysterical identification is used to express sexual community, whether real or imagined—in this case, her identification with a woman her husband admires. In other words, Freud argues that the non-fulfillment of one wish may in fact mean the fulfillment of another.

Being able to summarize material is an important step in completing the Chapter Writing Assignment. However, in order to successfully complete this assignment, you need to blueprint each paragraph to determine what should fit into it. The important issue is being able to integrate a summary into your essay in a meaningful way, so that you successfully respond to the question. Here is a suggested, logically coherent pattern for responding to Question #1, using two summaries—of Freud and of your own dream. You can devise your own, similar pattern for responding to the other questions.

Paragraph 1:

- In the introductory remarks of this paragraph (the Introduction), it may be helpful to discuss dreams in a general/informative way. For example, you could include a biological analysis of REM sleep or a look at dream analysis in the centuries before Freud.

- Present your thesis statement. This announces that your particular dream lends itself to a Freudian interpretation and why it does. (For instance, does it include anxiety? Wish fulfillment? Identification? Frustration?)

Paragraph 2:

- Summarize Freudian theory, concentrating on highlighting those aspects that apply to the analysis of your dream. This will start with general information and conclude with the more specific and particular information. It may be helpful to quote directly from your primary source.

Paragraph 3:

- Summarize your dream. This may be a little tricky because often people, places, colors, and events tend to lack coherent shape or order; time sequences are illogical or blurred. When you summarize, concentrate on location, people in the dream, the emotions experienced, particular themes or motifs, and thwarted desire.

Paragraph 4:

- This paragraph will apply Freudian theory to your dream without any knowledge of the dreamer's waking life. In other words, examine the dream complete on its own, without any external, personal contexts of the dreamer (you).

- Often a particular theory (e.g., Freudian, Jungian) can be helpful in assisting you to see symbols or metaphors or even single out particular emotions in order to clarify one's own thinking process.

Paragraph 5:

- This is the second paragraph of analysis, only in this paragraph the analysis includes the Freudian theory applied with knowledge of the dreamer's waking life. (Only in this final step can the true meaning of the dream be found, according to Freud.)

Paragraph 6:

- Begin your conclusion with a restatement of your thesis.
- Based on your newfound understanding of the dream, suggest how you might apply this insight to your waking life.

THE MAIN EVENT WRITING SAMPLE

The following is an essay, which incorporates a summary, that was written for this text in response to the Main Event Writing Assignment, Question #1.

Wish Fulfillment: A Dream of My Mother

A trip to the local bookstore proved that interest in dreams is still alive and well. The shelves are stocked with books, not just older ones by Freud and Jung, but newer ones as well. Literally dozens of books can be found on dream interpretation. Some of these books read like encyclopedias of dream symbols, others claim dreams have prophetic powers, and still others regard dreams as useful psychological tools to understand our waking state. Sigmund Freud, the father of dream analysis, believed that dreams were an effective tool for understanding hidden, unconscious desires and motives. *Thesis statement* Recently, I experienced a dream that lends itself to a Freudian interpretation based on the presence of repressed anger, wish fulfillment, and a sense of hidden motives.

In Freud's book, *The Interpretation of Dreams,* he argues that all dreams are a form of wish fulfillment. Many of his critics contested *Summary of Freud* this assertion; therefore, he presented case studies of dreams that on first glance did not appear to involve wish fulfillment because they featured frustration and other unpleasant experiences for the dreamer. However, Freud believed that repressed feelings, such as anger, were often disguised in waking life, but they were deeply felt within the subconscious. The dream reveals these feelings through actions, symbolism, and what he called identification— that is, a process by which the dreamer identifies with (or symbolically takes the place of) another person.

My particular dream begins with me sitting on a couch facing my mother, who is also sitting. I am feeling extremely angry with such force that I begin to throw stones at my mother's forehead. Finally, I hit her and she falls over. At this point, the tone of the dream changes. I hear a hushed and exotic voice behind me and to the left. This voice is hypnotic, and as it speaks, a fluorescent green light appears. Then, to my amazement, I hear this voice coming from the light that says I have three wishes. It seems very important that I choose carefully. Finally, I choose a job that I want, a million dollars, and perfect protection for my two children.

Summary of my dream

Freud would immediately focus on the hostility between the dreamer and the dreamer's mother. Freud would perhaps say that in order for the child to live, the parent must die, metaphorically. Perhaps it is a rite of passage, or an Electra complex (expressed hostility of a daughter to her mother). He would also comment that it was a wish fulfilled: to kill the mother in order to reap the benefits of a full life. This is confirmed in the second half of the dream in which, like a genie from a bottle, three wishes are granted. There is a fairy tale–like quality that Freud would say shares the same kind of wishes that human beings suppress because they're not socially acceptable (such as hostility toward one's own mother).

Applying Freud's ideas to my dream

When I apply the actual contexts of my waking life, the Freudian analysis is confirmed. While difficult to admit, I had in fact been experiencing a great deal of conflict with my mother. However, because of feelings of guilt and obligation, I had been

Include
contexts
of my
waking
life to
interpret
the
dream

unable to admit to myself that I was angry with her. The genie-like green light perhaps represents what I feel is possible in my life without my mother's interference. The specific wishes connect to my feelings of wanting professional success (the job), seeking financial security (represented by the million dollars), and expressing my love for my children (wanting them to be protected). The wish fulfillment is clear, and the dream suggests that I feel my mother is standing in the way of the fulfillment of my wishes.

Applying
a new
under-
standing
in my
waking
life

My dream was able to be analyzed using Freud's interpretation techniques because it employed frustration, hidden motives, and wish fulfillment. Based on my insight, I was able to fully come to terms with how I was feeling about my mother at that time, and what I perceived as her interference in my life and my children's lives. I was able to accept that I thought her influence was not positive, but destructive. Because of this, I decided in my waking life to change just how much influence I allowed my mother to have. In a sense, my dream gave me permission to feel things I didn't think I really should feel, and to take actions that would ultimately improve my life.

Works Cited

Freud, Sigmund. *The Interpretation of Dreams.* 1900. Trans. Joyce Crick. Oxford: Oxford UP, 1999.

ADDITIONAL READINGS

On the Nature of Dreams
Carl Jung

Another early explorer of dreams was Carl Jung. In this passage, Jung explores the topic of recurring symbols and how objects can mean different things to different dreamers. This idea argues against set "dream symbols" (for example, that a table in a dream means the same thing to everyone) and instead claims that the context of the dream determines the meaning of the dream. Thus, the dreamer and the psychoanalyst must work together to understand the meaning of the dream.

Key Words

involuntary	done contrary to one's will
psychic	relating to the mind
coherence	united in principles, relationships, or interests
aesthetically	of or relating to the concepts of beauty
disconcerting	throwing into confusion
motif	a recurring thematic element
plausible	superficially fair, reasonable
mortifying	subduing or deadening
salient	prominent; standing out in importance
superfluous	extra; not needed; marked by wastefulness

The dream is a fragment of involuntary psychic activity, just conscious enough to be reproducible in the waking state. Of all psychic phenomena the dream presents perhaps the largest number of "irrational" factors. It seems to possess a minimum of that logical coherence and that hierarchy of values shown by the other contents of consciousness, and is therefore less transparent and understandable. Dreams that form logically, morally, or aesthetically satisfying wholes are exceptional. Usually a dream is a strange and disconcerting product distinguished by many "bad qualities," such as lack of logic, questionable morality, uncouth form, and apparent absurdity or nonsense. People are therefore only too glad to dismiss it as stupid, meaningless, and worthless.

Every interpretation of a dream is a psychological statement about certain of its contents. This is not without danger, as the dreamer, like most people, usually displays an astonishing sensitiveness to critical remarks, not only if they are wrong, but even more if they are right. Since it is not possible, except under very special conditions, to work out the meaning of a dream without the collaboration of the dreamer, an extraordinary amount of tact is required not to violate his self-respect unnecessarily. For instance, what is one to say when a patient tells a number of indecent dreams and then asks: "Why should *I* have such disgusting dreams?" To this sort of question it is better to give no answer, since an answer is difficult for several reasons, especially for the beginner, and one is very apt under such circumstances to say something clumsy, above all when one thinks one knows what the answer is. It is so difficult to understand a dream that for a long time I have made it a rule, when someone tells me a dream and asks for my opinion, to say first of all to myself: "I have no idea what this dream means." After that I can begin to examine the dream.

Here the reader will certainly ask: "Is it worth while in any individual case to look for the meaning of a dream—supposing that dreams
have any meaning at all and that this meaning can be proved?"

It is easy to prove that an animal is a vertebrate by laying bare the
spine. But how does one proceed to lay bare the inner, meaningful
structure of a dream? Apparently the dream follows no clearly determined patterns or regular modes of behavior, apart from the well-
known "typical" dreams, such as nightmares. Anxiety dreams are not
unusual but they are by no means the rule. Also, there are typical
dream-motifs known to the layman, such as of flying, climbing stairs
or mountains, going about with insufficient clothing, losing your
teeth, crowds of people, hotels, railway stations, trains, airplanes, au-
tomobiles, frightening animals (snakes), etc. These motifs are very
common but by no means sufficient to confirm the existence of any
regularity in the structure of a dream.

Some people have recurrent dreams. This happens particularly in   5
youth, but the recurrence may continue over several decades. These are
often very impressive dreams which convince one that they "must
surely have a meaning." This feeling is justified in so far as one cannot,
even taking the most cautious view, avoid the assumption that a definite
psychic situation does arise from time to time which causes the dream.
But a "psychic situation" is something that, if it can be formulated, is
identical with a definite *meaning*—provided, of course, that one does not
stubbornly hold to the hypothesis (certainly not proven) that all dreams
can be traced back to stomach trouble or sleeping on one's back or the
like. Such dreams do indeed suggest that their contents have a causal
meaning. The same is true of so-called typical motifs which repeat themselves frequently in longer series of dreams. Here again it is hard to escape the impression that they mean something.

But how do we arrive at a plausible meaning and how can we confirm the rightness of the interpretation? One method—which, however, is not scientific—would be to predict future happenings from the
dreams by means of a dream-book and to verify the interpretation by
subsequent events, assuming of course that the meaning of dreams lies
in their anticipation of the future.

Another way to get at the meaning of the dream directly might be
to turn to the past and reconstruct former experiences from the occurrence of certain motifs in the dreams. While this is possible to a limited
extent, it would have a decisive value only if we could discover in this
way something which, though it had actually taken place, had remained unconscious to the dreamer, or at any rate something he
would not like to divulge under any circumstances. If neither is the
case, then we are dealing simply with memory-images whose appearance in the dream is (a) not denied by anyone, and (b) completely irrelevant so far as a meaningful dream function is concerned, since the

dreamer could just as well have supplied the information consciously. This unfortunately exhausts the possible ways of proving the meaning of a dream directly.

It is Freud's great achievement to have put dream-interpretation on the right track. Above all, he recognized that no interpretation can be undertaken without the dreamer. The words composing a dream narrative have not just *one* meaning, but many meanings. If, for instance, someone dreams of a table, we are still far from knowing what the "table" of the dreamer signifies, although the word "table" sounds unambiguous enough. For the thing we do not know is that this "table" is the very one at which his father sat when he refused the dreamer all further financial help and threw him out of the house as a good-for-nothing. The polished surface of this table stares at him as a symbol of his catastrophic worthlessness in his daytime consciousness as well as in his dreams at night. This is what our dreamer understands by "table." Therefore we need the dreamer's help in order to limit the multiple meanings of words to those that are essential and convincing. That the "table" stands as a mortifying landmark in the dreamer's life may be doubted by anyone who was not present. But the dreamer does not doubt it, nor do I. Clearly, dream-interpretation is in the first place an experience which has immediate validity for only two persons.

If, therefore, we establish that the "table" in the dream means just that fatal table, with all that this implies, then, although we have not explained the dream, we have at least interpreted one important motif of it; that is, we have recognized the subjective context in which the word "table" is embedded.

We arrived at this conclusion by a methodical questioning of the dreamer's own associations. The further procedures to which Freud subjects the dream-contents I have had to reject, for they are too much influenced by the preconceived opinion that dreams are the fulfillment of "repressed wishes." Although there are such dreams, this is far from proving that all dreams are wish-fulfillments, any more than are the thoughts of our conscious psychic life. There is no ground for the assumption that the unconscious processes underlying the dream are more limited and one-sided, in form and content, than conscious processes. One would rather expect that the latter could be limited to known categories, since they usually reflect the regularity or even monotony of the conscious way of life.

On the basis of these conclusions and for the purpose of ascertaining the meaning of the dream, I have developed a procedure which I call "taking up the context." This consists in making sure that every shade of meaning which each salient feature of the dream has for the dreamer is determined by the associations of the dreamer himself. I therefore proceed in the same way as I would in deciphering a difficult text. This method does not always produce an immediately understandable result; often the only thing that emerges, at first, is a hint that looks significant. To give an example: I was working once with a young man who mentioned in his anamnesis that he was happily engaged, and to a girl of "good" family. In his dreams she frequently appeared in very unflattering guise. The context showed that the dreamer's unconscious connected the figure of his bride with all kinds of scandalous stories from quite other sources—which was incomprehensible to him and naturally also to me. But, from the constant repetition of such combinations, I had to conclude that, despite his conscious resistance, there existed in him an unconscious tendency to show his bride in this ambiguous light. He told me that if such a thing were true it would be a catastrophe. His acute neurosis had set in a short time after his engagement. Although it was something he could not bear to think about, this suspicion of his bride seemed to me a point of such capital importance that I advised him to instigate some inquiries. These showed the suspicion to be well founded, and the shock of the unpleasant discovery did not kill the patient but, on the contrary, cured him of his neurosis and also of his bride. Thus, although the taking up of the context resulted in an "unthinkable" meaning and hence in an apparently nonsensical interpretation, it proved correct in the light of facts which were subsequently disclosed. This case is of exemplary simplicity, and it is superfluous to point out that only rarely do dreams have so simple a solution.

What Did You Read?

1. Does Jung believe there is any regularity to the structure of a dream? Explain.
2. How does Jung describe recurrent dreams?
3. What does Jung mean by the statement "no interpretation [of a dream] can be undertaken without the dreamer"?
4. What is a dream "motif"?

What Do You Think?

1. How does Jung disagree with Freud?
2. Have you discovered objects in your dreams that have personal meaning? Explain.
3. Have you found dream motifs in your dreams, such as losing your teeth, encountering scary animals, or climbing stairs? What do you make of this?

How Was It Done?

1. How does the opening of the first paragraph contribute to the development of this work?

2. What expert does Jung defer to in the development of his argument?

3. What artifact or object does Jung center much of his analysis on?

The Nature of Dreaming

James A. Hall

In this excerpt from James A. Hall's Jungian Dream Interpretation, *Hall not only supports Jung's ideas but argues the benefits of dreaming as a part of maintaining a healthy, waking state.*

Key Words

phenomenological	of or relating to the study of human consciousness or self-awareness; the study of how humans know things
verisimilitude	having the appearance of truth; depicting something real
omniscient	all-knowing; infinite awareness, insight, and knowledge
repressed	put down or subdued
assimilation	to take in; to absorb into a system; to make similar
compensatory	to counterbalance; to offset an error or undesired effect
distortion	twisted out of its true nature; to pervert
archetypal	reflecting an original pattern or model of something; an inherited idea, mode of thought, or symbol
residue	remnant, remainder
individuation	the act or process of making something individual

Dreaming is a universal human experience. In a phenomenological sense, a dream is an experience of life that is recognized, in retrospect, to have taken place in the mind while asleep, although at the time it was experienced it carried the same sense of verisimilitude that we associate with waking experiences; that is, it seemed to happen in a "real" world that was only in retrospect acknowledged to be a "dream" world.

The phenomenology of dreams involves events that are not experienced in the waking world: sudden shifts of time and place, changes in age, the presence of persons known to be deceased or of fantastic persons and animals that never existed. Perhaps the most radical shift experienced in a dream is the shift of the ego-identity itself from one character to another, or perhaps to no character at all, the dream-ego seeming to observe events as if from an omniscient floating position.

During the last several decades, an immense amount of work has been done on neurophysiological states associated with dreaming. Thus far such studies have allowed investigators to define with some precision when a sleeping subject is in a REM state, a state of ascending Stage 1 sleep with rapid eye movements. When awakened in such a REM state there is a high probability (but no certainty) that the subject will report having been dreaming just prior to awakening. There are some dream reports, however, from non-REM stages of sleep. Although there were early intriguing studies that seemed to link the direction of eye movements to the content of experienced-dreams, that observation still lacks sufficient confirmation to be generally accepted.

Since the REM state occupies a majority of the time of premature infants, and decreases steadily during the aging process, it would seem to be a biologically determined state rather than one simply serving the psychological needs of the subject. REM sleep is found also throughout most animal species, where psychological factors are not a major consideration. It may initially represent a processing of information related to binocular vision, or may serve the purpose of periodically alerting the central nervous system during the night.

Whatever the biological basis of dreaming, it seems in the human   5
to serve some process necessary to healthy psychological functioning. Freud assigned to the dream the role of guarding sleep from the irruption of repressed impulses, a position not generally thought to be in accord with more modern dream research. In contrast, Jung's position was that the dream compensated the limited views of the waking ego, a purpose in harmony with the information-processing hypothesis of dreaming, but expanding far beyond mere assimilation of new data.

Dreams as Compensation

The dream in Jungian psychology is seen as a natural, regulatory psychic process, analogous to compensatory mechanisms of bodily functioning. The conscious awareness by which the ego guides itself is inevitably only a partial view, for much remains always outside the sphere of the ego. The unconscious contains forgotten material as well as material such as the archetypes that cannot in principle be conscious, although changes in consciousness can point toward their existence. Even within the field of consciousness some contents are in focus while others, although indispensable to the maintenance of the focal awareness, are not.

There are three ways in which the dream may be seen as compensatory, and all are important in understanding the clinical use of dreams. First, the dream may compensate temporary distortions in ego structure, directing one to a more comprehensive understanding of attitudes and actions. For example, someone who is angry at a friend but finds the anger quickly waning may dream of being furious at the friend. The remembered dream brings back for further attention a quantity of anger that had been suppressed, perhaps for neurotic reasons. It may also be important for the dreamer to realize which complex was constellated (activated) in the situation.

A second and more profound mode of compensation is the way in which the dream as a self-representation of the psyche may face a functioning ego structure with the need for a closer adaptation to the individuation process. This generally occurs when one is deviating from the personally right and true path. The goal of individuation is never simply adjustment to existing conditions; however adequate such adjustment seems, a further task is always waiting (ultimately the task of facing death as an individual event). An example of this second type of compensation is the dream of a person who was quite well adapted socially, in the community, family and work areas of life. He dreamed that an impressive voice said, "You are not leading your true life!" The force of that statement, which awoke the dreamer with a start, lasted for many years and influenced a movement toward horizons that were not clear at the time of the dream.

These two forms of compensation—the dream as a "message" to the ego and as a self-representation of the psyche—comprise the classical Jungian idea of the compensatory function of dreams, substantially different from the traditional Freudian view of dreams as wish-fulfillment or protectors of sleep.

It is becoming increasingly clear to me, however, that there is a 10 more mysterious and more subtle third process by which dreams are compensatory. The archetypal core of the ego is the enduring basis of "I" but can be identified with many personae or ego-identities. The dream may be seen as an attempt to directly alter the structure of complexes upon which the archetypal ego is relying for identity at more conscious levels. For instance, many dreams seem to challenge the dream-ego with various tasks, the achievement of which may alter the structure of the waking-ego, since the identity of the dream-ego is most often a partial identity of the waking-ego. Events are experienced by the dream-ego as interactions with "outer" situations within the structure of the dream; but the outer events of the dream may directly reflect complexes that are involved in the day-to-day functioning and structure of the waking-ego. Changes in the relationship with these dream situations can be experienced by the waking-ego as a change in its own attitude or mood. Marie-Louise von Franz gives a particularly clear example of this type of compensation from one of her own dreams. After a day of feeling the nearness of death she dreamed that a romantic young boy—an animus figure—had died.

In the usual course of Jungian analysis dreams are often used as a point of reference for the interaction of the analytic process. Analyst and analysand are allies in attempting to understand the "message" of the dream in relation to the ego of the analysand. At times dreams indicate that attention should be directed to the transference-counter-transference, the particular constellation of interaction in the analytic situation. Since there is no privileged position from which one can know the "truth" of another person's psyche, analyst analysand are engaged in an exploratory venture that involves basic trust between them. If the dream focuses on that relationship, the relationship must be examined analytically.

In interpreting dreams, it is important never to feel that the dream has been exhausted. At best one can find a useful, current meaning to the dream, but even this may be modified in the light of subsequent dreams, for dream interpretation involves a continuing dialogue between the ego and the unconscious, a dialogue that extends indefinitely and whose subject matter may shift both in focus and in level of reference.

Even when dreams are not interpreted they seem at times to have a profound effect upon waking consciousness. From observation of the impact of unanalyzed dreams, it is possible to infer that even when not remembered dreams are a vital part of the total life of the psyche. In the Jungian view, dreams are continually functioning to compensate and complement (a milder form of compensation) the ego's waking view of reality. The interpretation of a dream permits some conscious attention to be paid to the direction in which the process of individuation is already moving, albeit unconsciously. When successful, such a teaming of conscious will and unconscious dynamism furthers the process of individuation more rapidly than is possible when dreams are left unexamined.

An additional benefit from the interpretation of dreams is that the ego retains in conscious memory a residue of the dream, allowing the person to identify similar motifs in everyday life and take the appropriate attitude or action, resulting in less need for unconscious compensation of that particular problem area.

What Did You Read?

1. List some "events" in the phenomenology of a dream.

2. According to Hall, what did Freud think the role of the dream was?

3. What are the three ways in which dreams can be seen as compensatory?

What Do You Think?

1. How does Jung's idea of the compensatory function of dreams differ from Freud's view of dreams?

2. Have you ever had a dream that had a profound effect on your "waking consciousness"? Explain.

3. Do you believe that the dynamic relationship between the dream state and the waking state influence each other? Explain.

How Was It Done?

1. How much of the article is devoted to an identification/definition of the biological basis of dreaming?

2. How does classification act as a primary method of development in this short work? Explain.

3. What logical leap does the author make near the end that contributes to the overall development of his thesis?

The Meaning of Dreams

Peter and Elizabeth Fenwick

Peter and Elizabeth Fenwick, in a passage taken from The Hidden Door, *encourage people to analyze their dreams along the lines of dream symbols. They argue that two important aspects of a dream—dream emotion and dream symbolism—are keys to unlocking a dream's meaning.*

Key Words

precognition	awareness of an event that has not yet occurred; clairvoyance
obscurely	shrouded in darkness; faintly; mysteriously
sloth	laziness
cathartic	purifying or purging of emotions
salutary	promoting health
optimism	an inclination to look at events and people in the most favorable light
allotted	assigned as a share or portion
lorry	a truck
encompass	to go completely around; enclose
quintessential	the essence of something in its purest form; the most typical example

Analysing the Dream

When you come to analyse your dreams in more detail, remember that they are primarily about you—what is happening in your mental, physical and emotional life, your relationships with people around you. Even when a dream seems to tell you something very clearly about somebody else—a precognition of someone else's death, or a disaster, for example—there is almost certainly a link with your own thoughts or feelings. Try to find these dream associations if you can. If in your dream you felt insecure, or jealous, or frustrated, try to identify relationships or situations in your life in which you've felt the same way. They may not be the same situations—in fact it's very likely that they won't be, because your dream mind likes to communicate obscurely. The imagery in our dreams is often symbolic.

Soon after her husband had left, at a time when she was still trying to come to terms with the end of a marriage she had greatly valued and a husband she had loved, a friend had the following dream.

> I dreamed that in my garden was a pure white marble statue. It was a figure, quite beautiful, and I loved it. Then I saw that dark green ivy was growing from its side, twisting around the body of the statue, gradually covering it. Friends kept telling me I had to get rid of the ivy but I didn't want to—I felt it would spoil the statue. But finally I did, stripping the ivy from it. And where the ivy had sprouted there was a wound, a scar in the side of the statue. But even so I realised in my dream that the ivy had to go, that otherwise it would gradually have destroyed the statue. When I woke I realised for the first time that even though I still grieved for our marriage, it had been the right decision for my husband to leave. It had the most powerful effect on me, that dream, and I can still remember it so well, all these years later.

Sometimes a dream can help us see ourselves as others see us, tell us things about ourselves that we find it hard to acknowledge and would rather not know. One man described a particularly vivid dream in which he was in a cave and saw, sitting on a high ledge, "an 'Alice in Wonderland'-type slothful creature. Its face had human characteristics. It disgusted me to the core . . . I had awoken thinking of it . . . I am convinced that I was shown 'sloth personified' as a warning to me of what I was in grave danger of becoming."

Monica Jackson described two profound and rather frightening experiences which were each triggered by powerful, and very negative, emotions.

> The first occurred at a time when I had been very angry, for some time, over family matters. I woke up one night coughing and choking and sat up in bed feeling as if something like hot smoke was coming out of my throat. It came to me that this was anger, and shortly after I felt spent and empty but aware that there was a huge cloud of undirected anger at the foot of my bed. I was frightened but because the anger *was* undirected,

not very frightened. I seized a rosary I kept on my bedside table, put it under my pillow, pulled the bedclothes over my head and promptly went to sleep. In the morning my throat still felt faintly scorched and I felt totally exhausted all day, but all my anger had disappeared and I was at peace with the world, a state which lasted about a month.

On the second occasion, I woke from a nightmare in which I had killed my beloved old dog who had recently been put down on compassionate grounds. I was sitting up in bed crying, "I've killed her," when suddenly I was caught up in what seemed just like the "review" some respondents report in their NDEs [Near Death Experiences]. That is, I went through, very fast, all the wrongs I had done to others in the past, feeling all their pain—it was terrible. I was arched backward in physical as well as mental agony, and thought it would kill me, until the words came into my head. "I accept." I said it aloud—screamed it—and the experience stopped. I was exhausted, tearful and deeply depressed for about three weeks. Very salutary.

It is interesting to compare these experiences, which seem to have had quite different, though in each case very powerful, effects. In the first case the experience was cathartic and healing. It enabled Monica to get rid of her anger, which was made concrete, no longer inside her but at the foot of her bed, and left her feeling at peace. The second experience was a nightmare which triggered guilt feelings which persisted when Monica woke, reminding her of all the wrongs she had ever done in the past, and leaving her exhausted and depressed. However, she described this as "very salutary," so perhaps for her it was a useful, if not a happy experience.

We can look at and learn from a dream in two ways. One way is to see how the emotions and difficulties we have in our lives may be translated into dream language. The other is to look at the dream images and symbols themselves, and see how far we can use these to explain what is going on in our lives.

It is usually easiest to start with the first kind of dream analysis, 5 because there is usually no mistaking the emotional quality of a dream. Anxiety is probably the most common emotion expressed in dreams, and anxiety dreams are troubled, unsettled dreams filled with uneasiness. If too much is going on in our lives, and we're finding it impossible to meet deadlines or fulfil obligations, our dreams will reflect this. We'll be faced with impossible tasks to carry out, we'll be late for a train or an appointment, and events at every turn will transpire to make us even later; although mentally urging ourselves on we can move only in slow motion. If shyness or social inadequacy are making us anxious, our dream situations may involve embarrassment or social humiliation. If you are anxious about failure in real life, you will probably fail in your dreams too. The dream of having to take an examination for which you are unprepared, perhaps even in a subject you have never studied, is a classic failure dream which haunts many people long after they have taken their final examinations in real life.

The following dream shows very well how these two aspects—the dream emotions and the dream symbolism—blended in a dream which had a very clear message for the dreamer. For two years Mary and her husband had belonged to a semi-religious organisation, which they had originally joined out of interest and to make friends. But gradually Mary had come to feel that it was demanding more of her than she wanted to give, and that she was being sucked in far deeper than she wanted to be. One night she had this dream.

> I dreamed I was on a square platform, raised up, rather like a boxing ring, in the middle of a forest, except that there were no ropes around it. There were a lot of other people around and we were all wearing the same uniform, like a school uniform. I hated being there and I wanted desperately to get away. But although there were no ropes around the platform, nothing to keep me there, somehow I couldn't get off.
>
> This dream didn't tell me anything I didn't consciously know. I knew that I disliked the rigidity of the organisation we were in, that it felt like a school, beset with rules and demanding uniformity even if it didn't go so far as to make us wear uniforms, and that I resented having to conform. But it did bring my feelings to the fore and make me realise how strong they were, what a disproportionate part they were playing in my life. It also made me see very clearly that I wasn't actually trapped at all— maybe I felt that way, but in fact, there were no ropes around the ring, nothing to stop me getting off if I really wanted to. The day after my dream we made the decision to leave the organisation.

Is there a dream language, common to everyone? In a very general sense, there probably is. Dreams of being trapped or in captivity, like Mary's dream, for example, may mean that you are unable to express something that is important to you, or that there is something you want to be free of, a relationship perhaps, or a work or social commitment.

If we feel that our lives lack direction, we may feel lost or disorientated in our dreams. Loss of a sense of personal identity may mean that in our dreams we are wandering in a strange town unable to find where we live. The classic identity-crisis dream is of looking into a mirror and seeing someone else's face reflected there.

In dream analysis, symbols that often appear in dreams are sometimes allotted standard meanings. These can be useful as a starting point when you are trying to analyse your own dreams, so long as you remember that your own dreaming mind may not be using this particular symbol in this particular way. It can be interesting to use these as guidelines, to see if this particular meaning seems to be relevant to you, but they are not to be taken too seriously.

Fire, for example, is said to symbolise anger. Climbing dreams are said to symbolise ambition (or, to Freud, a desire for sexual fulfilment). Dreams of falling from a great height may signify failure, or that the dreamer has lost control, that he has reached a position in his professional or personal life that he cannot maintain—that he is, in fact, heading for a fall. Drowning suggests a fear of being engulfed by some unexpressed subconscious need. But, equally, if you have a phobia about fire, a fear of heights, a terror of deep water, whatever anxiety you have may well be expressed by this particular dream metaphor.

Dreams may express a need for change (redecorating or moving house, for example), or a fear of it (finding oneself lost and bewildered in unfamiliar surroundings). A bridge in a dream is a classic symbol of change, but the dreamer may feel dread and apprehension when he approaches, or excitement and optimism at the possibilities of what lies on the other side. Dreaming of a church symbolises the spiritual nature of the dreamer.

In classical dream analysis, the dreamer himself is often represented by a house. The front of the house may represent the face the dreamer presents to the world, the back his more hidden or guarded aspects. When the dreamer comes across a hidden or secret room it may signify some aspect of himself that he has ignored, or needs to explore or develop. These hidden rooms are usually "special" places, and there is usually a feeling of excitement about discovering them. One woman described her room as "full of bits and pieces. I get very excited about it and keep discovering things and thinking, I can use this for something and that for something else."

Another said,

> When I find my room it's always a very exciting discovery. It's always a room I need for something, it's hidden away but just off another room, or up a little staircase that I know and recognise because I've been there often in my dream. When I find it I'm always pleased and think it is just what I was looking for.

Masks are symbols of the image we present to the outside world. A mask that can't be removed or that the dreamer is forced to wear may indicate that the dreamer feels his "real" self is being eroded or obscured.

Animals are common dream symbols, especially in the dreams of children, but whether they are fierce or frightening or playful and friendly will depend on the dreamer's state of mind. Birds are said to symbolise the higher self; the lion is a symbol of power. In Freudian terms, the lion may represent the powerful, benevolent aspects of the father, a wild horse his frightening threatening aspect. Fish, usually considered a lowly form of life, are high in the hierarchy of dream significance, used to symbolise divinity, spiritual abundance and insights into the unconscious.

Dreams of travel are often rich with symbols. For Freud *any* travel dream involved a suppressed desire for sexual intercourse, the quintessential Freudian travel dream, of course, being the train going into a tunnel. Flying dreams are nearly always pleasant, and often exhilarating, with a wonderful sensation of freedom. Dreamers seldom fall out of the air, but float gently to earth. Sometimes the dreamer's bed may take off, or he may take flight in an armchair; this may well suggest a longing for adventure, combined with a reluctance to take too many risks.

Dreams which are concerned with religion or spirituality often contain light—usually a white or golden light, bright, but not dazzling to the eyes. Light in a dream, according to Jung, always refers to consciousness. The being of light is an image that symbolises a universal spiritual principle, common to all cultures and religions. Dreams in which the dreamer goes towards a light, or meets the being of light, have a special mystical or religious quality and are discussed in more detail in chapter 15. The Virgin Mary is a symbol of purity, of selfless love and compassion.

A recurrent dream may be showing us that some problem or conflict is unresolved—when we resolve the problem, the dream may disappear. Children's recurrent dreams are often frightening or disturbing, embodying some nameless undefinable childish fear. One little girl dreamed several times a year, from the age of about four, of a vast room, quite empty except for a raised throne, behind which hung purple curtains. On the throne sat a large wolf. The wolf never moved, she said, never even bared its teeth, and yet it filled her with terror. As often happens, the dream recurred over a period of several years, and then finally vanished, never to trouble her again.

Recurrent dreams can often show us something about our emotional or spiritual life. They don't always recur in exactly the same way, and the way the dream changes may reflect changes in our emotional state. Averil Meallen, a physiotherapist, has two recurrent dreams which have changed in quality over the years in a way which she feels reflects changes in her own life. In the first a tidal wave would sweep over her, and the dream was very frightening. But now she says she is often able to get on top of the wave and ride it. The dream is no longer frightening, in fact she now quite enjoys it. And her mastery of the wave, her ability to ride it, she feels reflects the degree of mastery she has managed to achieve in her own life.

Averil also has a recurrent flying dream. This she has always enjoyed, but when she first had it she had to make a huge effort to get off the ground. Now she can do it easily—she just flaps her arms and off she goes. For Averil, the dream seems to mirror her personal quest for self-realisation. She meditates, and says she can relive the dream when she does so.

Dreams often show us our emotional needs. But sometimes they fulfil them too. MW describes a dream which he had a few nights after the death of his father.

> I went to bed that night, and as far as I know went to sleep. All of a sudden I found myself in the air and floating above Wordsley Church which is about a mile and a half from the house where we lived. I floated down and ended up somehow inside the church. At this point I must say that to my knowledge I had not been inside that church since I was very small.

I was aware of the church organ on the left-hand side of the aisle. As I looked down the aisle of the church, what I can only describe as a panel slid open behind the organ and my father appeared. He was wearing the clothes that he had worn in his occupation as a top-class mechanic and lorry driver. My father saw me and spoke to me and said that he was all right and very happy, and told me not to worry. He then went back inside the organ panel and it slid shut again.

Wordsley Church is the church where my mother and father were married in 1937. Could it be that my father's spirit had returned to the place where he experienced one of the happiest days of his life, and why was I there? Was I privileged on that night? I wish there was a logical explanation.

Such dreams are common after a bereavement, and they can have a cathartic, healing quality. This dream meeting with his father was clearly enormously important to MW, reassuring him that his father was happy, and that he had no need to worry. The dream gave him permission to move on in his own life. If he had any sense of unfinished business with his father, the dream would almost certainly have helped him resolve this too. In that sense, he surely was privileged on that night.

MW himself feels that he did truly meet his father at the church, 20 and rejects the explanation that it was "just a dream" precipitated by his father's death. The fact that he recognised the church even though he hadn't been there since he was a child is easily explained: even childhood experiences are retained in memory and may be re-created long after they have been consciously forgotten. If MW really *did* meet his father on that night, then there *is* no logical explanation: we would have to accept that our current scientific concept of consciousness is too narrow to encompass this kind of experience. In practical terms it really matters very little. Marta Elian too had a dream in which she "met" her father (see p. 75). She has no doubt that it *was* just a dream. But this did not lessen its impact, or the positive and very timely purpose it served. She was "released" by her father just as effectively as if he *had* appeared to her in person. The dream simply displays the power we exercise over ourselves, and our ability to free ourselves from imaginary shackles.

What Did You Read?

1. What is the purpose of keeping a dream diary?
2. What two different ways can we look at and learn from a dream?
3. What are anxiety dreams?

What Do You Think?

1. Do you agree with the Fenwicks' interpretation of common dream symbols, based on your own dream experience?

2. Have you ever had a dream that was cathartic and healing, meaning negative emotions were released?

3. In your dreams, have you met people who have died in waking life who then helped you work through some unfinished business, such as grieving?

How Was It Done?

1. What do the authors center much of the article on?
2. How is classification used to develop this article?
3. What "expertise" provides a scholarly foundation for the article? Is its presence or lack thereof important to the credibility of the article?

People in Dreams

Gayle Delaney

Gayle Delaney, from her book In Your Dreams, *discusses certain common types of dreams—in this case, dreams about family members—and how they can be interpreted.*

Key Words

hindering	making slow or difficult the progress of something
psychotherapist	someone who treats patients with mental or emotional disorders by psychological means
Gestalt	using the study of the perception of things that create a whole unit that is greater than the sum of its parts; tends to reject the analysis of things into distinct, separate parts or events
dictum	a noteworthy statement
ludicrous	amusing or laughable
eliciting	calling forth or drawing out
metaphor	a figure of speech in which one object or idea is used to suggest a likeness to another, unrelated one; not literal
cosmopolitan	worldly; having worldwide rather than provincial or limited scope

Variations

So many of our dreams are peopled by those we grew up with or are currently living with that it's hard to imagine a dream in which family members could not make an appearance. The things to look out for are the following: What roles do your family members play? Are these roles positive or negative? Are they helping or hindering you? How frequently do particular family members recur in your dreams?

In some dreams we want to kill someone in our family; in others we grieve over a dream death that has not occurred in waking reality. Sometimes we tell off our parents or mate in ways we never had the courage to do while awake. Sometimes we discover new depths of tender and loving feelings for a brother or an aunt to whom we are not very close in waking life. These dreams can be terrifying when a family member tries to do us great harm in a dream. Dreams of physical or sexual abuse by family members are important warning signs of serious trouble either in that particular relationship or in one that is similar to it. If you have dreams like this, I encourage you to read chapter 8 of my book *Sensual Dreaming* and to consider consulting a psychotherapist for at least a few sessions to see where such painful images come from in your life. These dreams do not necessarily mean that you have been sexually abused; they do, however, express deep pain and a sense of helplessness in that relationship. Left untended, these feelings could lead you to repeat similar relationships in your adult life, which would bring you only more pain and suffering.

What Others Have Said

Gestalt therapists tend to follow the rigid dictum that every image in your dream represents a part of the dreamer. Thus any family member in your dream would be a caricature or representation of aspects of your personality or feelings that you have projected upon the image of the family member. While almost all contemporary analysts agree that sometimes your family members represent parts of your own personality, this is not generally accepted for many, and perhaps the majority of, such dreams. For example, consider the dream of a woman who has been sexually abused and dreams of being sexually abused by her father. To ask her to interpret her father as her own aggressiveness would be ludicrous. Carl Jung had this rule of thumb: when we dream of people with whom we are not in regular contact, these people tend to represent some aspect of the dreamer's personality or someone in the dreamer's life who is like the dream figure. However, when we dream about people with whom we have regular contact, it is likely such images represent some aspect of the person pictured in the dream image. Thus the woman dreaming of her abusive father is dreaming about her relationship to this man. This dream might also come at a time in her adult life in which she is currently involved in another abusive relationship. The dream then can serve to express similar feelings triggered in the current but repetitive situation.

At our dream center we ask people first to describe the person in the dream (see the first entry in this section) and then to describe the action that occurs between the family member and other people in the dream. After eliciting from the dreamer a good description of the family member and of his or her actions, we can then find out how this particular dream is a metaphor for something going on in the dreamer's current life, either in relation to this family member or to someone who is like the family member. At times we find that when an individual dreams of a mother or a sister the dream may be more about issues around motherhood and sisterhood than about a particular sister or a particular person in the dreamer's life. Again, it all depends upon the individual dream and the feelings it evokes at a particular time.

So many of us dream so frequently about our mothers and fathers   5
that a special word is in order. If you are asked to describe your mother or your father, you could be talking for five or six hours. For the purposes of interpreting this particular dream, it's important to make your description fit the way your mother or father appeared in that dream. Are we talking about the generous or playful part of your mom, or are we talking about the more critical part of her? Your mother or father in a dream could represent issues in your relationship with that person or attitudes that you have incorporated from that person, such as things that you believe about yourself or the world simply because you were taught to believe them by your mother or your father. Or you might use your mother or father to represent certain traits in your current friends or lovers. Again, describe very carefully your mother and your father as he or she appears in the dream, and see how you can relate those traits to some part of yourself, to some situation in your life, or to someone else in your life.

Sample Dreams

Sis Is Gone

Theresa dreamt: "I was leaving my home in Boston to go to San Francisco and live with my sister, but when I arrived at the apartment my sister wasn't there. There was no sign of her, no trace, and I felt so lonely."

Theresa described her sister who, in fact, lives in New Mexico, as a very artistic woman who had enough courage to leave her East Coast academic world and become an artist in Santa Fe. Following her own drummer, her sister became a much happier person whom the dreamer admired. Theresa described San Francisco as a town perhaps less artsy than Santa Fe but nevertheless far more cosmopolitan and exciting, more international in flavor, and very progressive in politics. She thought it was probably the best place to live in the United States. When I asked her if she had any desire to move to a place that was more artistic, more sophisticated, more cosmopolitan, politically liberal, and exciting, she said yes indeed. Although she wasn't actually moving to San Francisco, she had begun to move in social circles that were much more like San Francisco than the traditional Boston cohorts she had known since college. In saying this, she suddenly realized the meaning of her dream. She said, "I've wanted to make a change the way my sister made a change. My goals are different from hers. I've tried to make this change, and I've tried to move into different circles; however, I'm not close to anyone there yet. It's as if I've moved closer to a sister or closer to sisterhood and female friendships, but I'm not really settled there yet."

Trouble

Edgar dreamt: "My brother is very angry at me. He is criticizing me and telling me I'm a selfish son of a bitch. Next scene: I see my mother in a coffin, and I wake up with a start."

Edgar had no trouble understanding his dream. He said that in waking life his brother had indeed called him a selfish son of a bitch for the last twenty years or so, but at the moment his brother was especially angry at him for not coming to visit his mother, who was in the hospital for eye surgery. Edgar thought phone contact was adequate and relied upon his brother to do the in-person attending to his mother since the brother lived near her. However, the coffin scene reminded him of how he would feel if his mother died and he had not gone back to see her. Instead of being his usual defensive self, saying, "Well, I can't come back because I'm so busy in my work," Edgar called his brother, told him he had been right, and announced he would be out to visit his mother within two weeks.

What Do You Say?

1. Describe the family member(s) in your dream. (See the people questions at the beginning of this section.)
2. How do you feel about this family member in waking life?
3. How do you feel about this family member in the dream?
4. Is there anyone in your life, other than this family member, or any part of yourself that is like your description?
5. Describe the dream action.
6. Describe your feelings in the dream.
7. Is the situation, including the people, the actions, and the feelings, similar to any situation in your waking life, now or in your childhood?
8. How so? Elaborate.
9. If the family member in the dream represents himself or herself, how does the dream comment on your relationship?

10. If the family member in the dream represents someone else in your life or some part of yourself, what new insights does this dream figure offer you?

What Did You Read?

1. What do Gestalt therapists say about the relationships between the dream image and the dreamer?

2. In trying to figure out why people with whom you have regular contact are in your dreams and what it means, you need to evaluate what first?

3. Explain how Delaney thinks the appearance of family members can refer to either the actual family member, or be a symbol for someone or something else.

What Do You Think?

1. Is it important to relate situations in your dreams, people, and feelings to situations in your waking life, present or past?

2. In this excerpt, Delaney uses dreams as a means of sorting out relationships among family members. Are there any dangers in using dreams for such a purpose?

3. Have you ever experienced a kind of intersection of past and present in the dreaming state toward family members or friends? Explain what happened and how you responded to it.

How Was It Done?

1. How does the mention of Gestalt theory contribute to the author's thesis?

2. How do subtitles help to organize and streamline the material in this piece?

3. How are the ten questions the author lists at the end of the article a useful mechanism in the interpretation of dreams?

Scientific Debate over Dreams Takes a New Twist

Brigid Schulte

Brigid Schulte reports on scientists who have taken a more biological approach to the study of dreams by studying the brain and neuroscience. Her article, "Scientific Debate over Dreams Takes a New Twist," examines some of the physical causes of dream-

ing. Still, even some scientists are starting to believe that there may be connections between the physical aspects of dreaming and people's emotional states.

Key Words

neuroscience	a branch of life sciences that studies the anatomy, physiology, and biochemistry of the nervous system, especially with relation to behavior and learning
premonition	forewarning; anticipation of an event without conscious reason
random	lacking a definite plan or purpose
ephemeral	lasting a very short time
confabulate	to chat; to hold a discussion
galled	irritated; vexed; annoyed
amnesia	loss of memory, usually due to injury or trauma
florid	marked by emotional or sexual fervor
convoluted	twisted; coiled

For centuries, dreams were the medium of angels. Prophets saw sacred visions. Ancient Greek doctors diagnosed illnesses from dream messages. Dream premonitions forced Hannibal, Ghengis Khan and Xerxes to change battle plans.

Freud and Jung were convinced the bizarre, disturbing realm of dreams held the key to unlocking the mysteries of the self.

But modern neuroscience and its study of the brain have been chipping away at those mystical views. For many scientists, dreams are nonsensical, if entertaining, byproducts of chemical changes—a conclusion that draws howls of protest from the other side of the entrenched dream wars, the psychoanalysts and dream weavers.

Now, even neuroscientists are beginning to disagree.

Researchers at the National Institutes of Health and Walter Reed 5 Army Institute of Research are supporting the mainstream scientific view with the first detailed studies on what parts of the brain are activated while dreaming during rapid eye movement, or REM sleep, the time when most dreams occur. They found the emotional center runs wild while the rational brain snoozes.

But Dr. Mark Solms, a neuroscientist in London, studied people with damage to specific portions to their brains and how that affects dreaming. He found blind people have vivid, visual dreams. And those with damage to either the area of the brain that controls symbolic thinking or the brain's seat of curiosity and interest in the world do not dream at all.

Solms, who has undergone psychotherapy and says he learns from his own dreams, insists both studies show scientifically that dreams can be meaningful.

But the NIH researchers stick to the established neuroscientific view, dating to the 1950s, that dreams are random. They say dreams are merely incidental to the brain machine's running a check on its different parts to see if they're ready to wake up. Like a computer running through a virus scan.

Freud, they say, is completely wrong, and psychoanalytic dream interpretation is of questionable merit. If ephemeral dreams mean anything at all, it's only because we read significance into them once we awaken.

"We may not, in a Freudian sense, need REM sleep to work 10 through unresolved psychological conflicts. Dreams may occur in a post-hoc fashion, as the brain tries to activate itself, and we confabulate a story to fit what's going on after the fact," said Dr. Tom Balkin, a psychologist and sleep researcher at Walter Reed, who claims not to remember nor be interested in dreams. "Like an inkblot. It's not the inkblot that matters. It's what you make of it."

This traditional view has always galled psychoanalysts who believe, as the Talmud says, that a dream uninterpreted is like a letter unopened.

In studying dreams, they've found that two-thirds are unpleasant. That pregnant women who have more terrifying dreams have easier labors, as if they've already worked through their fears. And that dreams can work as "emotional barometers" to help sort out festering problems, regulate mood or consolidate memories.

"If a dream is an inkblot, you have to ask, why were those images there and why were they activated at that particular moment?" said Dr. Morton Reiser, a psychoanalyst at Yale and author of "Memory in Mind and Brain: What Dream Imagery Reveals." "How do you explain that so many scientific breakthrough ideas have been portrayed in a dream image?"

If dreams are random scraps, how does one account for recurring dreams? Premonitions? Or insights? Lincoln dreamed of his death just days before he was assassinated. Composer Igor Stravinsky heard his "Rite of Spring" in a dream.

No one denies the scientific importance of the new NIH research.   15

For the first time, Balkin, Dr. Allen Braun, a neuroscientist at NIH, and others took exacting readings of what parts of the brain are actively working during REM sleep. Balkin and Braun recruited 37 male volunteers, strapped them into a sleep lab and injected them with a solution that enabled them to follow the blood flow in the brain with a positron emission tomography, or PET scan.

They took readings, the most precise to date, at four-minute intervals while the volunteers slept. Previous PET scans may have been too general and included more than one sleep phase.

When the brain is awake, the prefrontal cortex just behind the forehead is most active. This is the most highly evolved part of the brain, the seat of intelligence, reasoning, short-term memory and self-reflection. During REM sleep it is completely shut off.

Instead, what is most active is the limbic system, the portion of the brain that controls emotions, the senses and long-term memory.

"This might account for the heightened emotional tone during 20 REM dreaming, the sexual, aggressive, anxious affects, as well as the retrieval of long-term memories," Braun said. "And the fact that short-term memory is deactivated may account for the bizarre content of dreams, the place changes, the plot lines that don't follow, the peoples' identities that morph into one another. It also might account for the typical amnesia for dreams. They're not properly encoded because working memory is not active."

Likewise, the PET study showed that during sleep the primary visual cortex, what we use to see when awake, is inactive. Instead, what is operating is the extrastriate, the visual area that processes complex objects like faces and emotions. This may explain dreams' "florid visual imagery," Braun said. It also may account for Solms' findings with blind and visually impaired patients.

In Freud's theory, dreams are unfulfilled wishes that are so bizarre and easily forgotten because our conscious mind "censored" and repressed them. To express the perhaps unacceptable wish, Freud said, the dream becomes convoluted and symbolic in order to get around the censor without waking the body up.

Braun and Balkin dispute the theory, saying since the prefrontal cortex, the only area they say could act as a censor, is completely deactivated during sleep. Dreams are not remembered, they say, simply because they're not processed.

"This new research forces us to scrap all the penny-scale old wives' tales and start asking some scientifically intelligent questions about REM dreaming. Is emotional stability enhanced? Is learning enhanced?" said J. Allan Hobson, a Harvard psychiatrist and author of "The Dreaming Brain." "The interpretation of dreams should be outlawed."

Solms, however, begs to differ. Three parts of the brain that his 25 studies showed were critical for dreaming may actually support some of Freud's psychological views, he said.

Patients with damage to the inferior parietal lobes, which govern spatial and symbolic thinking, did not dream. Thus, Solms' reasoned, dream images may very well be symbolic. Further, both he and the NIH study showed the anterior cingulate, a highly evolved part of the mid-frontal brain that governs motivations, is active during dreaming. That fits with Freud's idea that motivations, or wishes, set the tone of dreams, Solms argued.

Solms also found that people with injury to the orbital deep white matter, the area around the eyes that controls curiosity and interest in the world, also provides the inhibition from acting in socially unacceptable ways: Freud's censor.

And so the debate rages on and the reason why we spend one-third of our lives sleeping and dreaming remains a mystery.

"We don't really know what the function of dreams are. We don't know the mechanism that makes us dream like we do," Solms said. "But my research shows psychological mechanisms are essentially involved in the construction and form of dreams. I think we're on the threshold of a very exciting era of dream science."

Rita Dwyer is a scientist who says she owes her life to a dream. 30 When she was working as a chemist in an aerospace lab, a colleague had a recurring nightmare: the lab exploded and he saw himself drag Dwyer from the flames night after night.

Then the lab did explode. And exactly as he saw in his dream, he pulled the badly burned Dwyer to safety. Dwyer, scarred from the burns, now runs the Association for the Study of Dreaming in Virginia, a group of 800 professionals and dream enthusiasts.

"We were scientists, we didn't believe in stuff like that. But it happened. I don't know how to explain it," she said. Now she is a firm believer in the power of dreams: "Dreams come in service of wholeness and healing to move us forward in our lives to help us live better. Scientists would find it ridiculous that I'm saying these things, but as a person trodding the spiritual path, I believe we get messages that reflect who we are in ways that we are not just physical bodies."

What Did You Read?

1. How can dreams be "emotional barometers"?

2. According to the NIH, what part of the brain is the most active during REM (dream state) sleep? What do you make of this?

3. How does Solms's theory of dreaming support Freud's psychological view of dreaming?

What Do You Think?

1. Do you believe, as some scientists do, that dreams are random and incidental to the brain running a check on its different parts?

2. Do you believe that dreaming is an important clue into your psyche? Why or why not?

3. How do the new scientific findings of the NIH explain certain dreams, especially those that involve intense emotions?

How Was It Done?

1. What experts does the author use to provide substance to her explanations? List some.

2. Besides experts in the field, what other kinds of support does the author use to develop the article?
3. Is the article, in its crafting, biased for one position, or is the debate evenly presented?

The Nature and Uses of Dreaming

Ernest Hartmann

Ernest Hartmann reports on his experience as a professor of psychiatry and discusses some of the important connections that are made in dreams and dream interpretation.

Key Words

collaborator	someone who works jointly with someone else
irrational	lacking in usual or normal mental capacity or reason
prominently	standing out; conspicuously
traumatic	an injury to living tissue or to one's emotional state
contextualize	to put something into its environment; interrelated conditions in which something exists
barren	empty; meaningless; not capable of reproduction
continuum	a coherent whole characterized by a sequence or progression of events, values, or conditions
speculative	theoretical rather than demonstrative; marked by questioning curiosity
methodology	a body of rules or procedures employed by a discipline

A 20-year-old college student barely escaped with his life from a fire that killed several members of his family. A few nights later, he had a vivid dream: "I was on a beach when a huge tidal wave came along and engulfed me. I was flipped over and over, there was nothing I could do. I was just about to drown when I woke up." On another night, he also dreamt: "I was swept away in a whirlwind. I was helpless, just blown away." These dreams clearly do not picture the details of what happened to him—the fire. Rather, they picture his emotional state—his feeling of fear, terror, and helplessness.

I have collected and studied many series of dreams after major trauma and repeatedly have come across such dreams as tidal waves, whirlwinds, or being chased by gangs of thugs. I am convinced that these dreams are a sort of paradigm, a place where we can see most clearly what is happening in all dreams. Such dreams are by no means nonsense. They picture the emotional state of our minds.

My collaborators and I have been developing a view of dreams which differs considerably from accepted wisdom on the subject. Nevertheless, it turns out to be very compatible with the commonsense experience of those who remember their dreams and have developed an interest in them.

Over all, dreams have not gotten much respect in the past few decades. There have been two dominant schools of thought. One view championed by some biologists is that dreams basically are random nonsense, the products of a poorly functioning brain during sleep. If there is any meaning to dreams, it is "added on later" as our brains try to "make the best of a bad job." A related view proposed by other biologists is that dreaming may function as an "unlearning" procedure: a dream is garbage being thrown out by a computer to keep itself from being clogged up. In this view, we dream specifically about what we do not need to remember.

The other view of dreams, more common among psychoanalysts   5 and therapists, derives broadly from the work of pioneering psychoanalyst Sigmund Freud. He did take dreams seriously in one sense, calling them the "royal road" to the workings of the unconscious. However, Freud felt that his main contribution—his discovery of the secret of dreams—was his finding that, when properly analyzed, every dream turns out to be a fulfillment of a wish. Further, although Freud appears to take dreams much more seriously than the biologists do, he does not place much value on the dream itself, which he calls the "manifest dream." He repeatedly refers to the dream as an irrational mental product, whose value emerges only when one subjects it to a process of free association leading eventually to an underlying "latent dream" containing the underlying wish.

After having spent many years conducting research on the biology of dreaming, I disagree with both these broad views. Indeed, there now is available a tremendous amount of information about the biology of sleep and specifically the biology of REM (rapid eye movement) sleep, the part of sleep in which most of our memorable dreams occur. However, this knowledge of the underlying biology of dreaming does not tell us the true nature or functions of dreaming, and it certainly is not a reason for dismissing the psychological meaning of dreams. Why should the developing understanding of the biology underlying it make dreaming meaningless, any more than the developing understanding of the biology underlying thought makes thought meaningless?

I have spent many years analyzing my own and my patients' dreams in my clinical practice, using Freud's technique of free association as well as somewhat different techniques developed by psychologist Carl Jung and others. There is no question in my mind that dreams are meaningful and can lead us to useful knowledge about ourselves. However, there are many places where I disagree with

Freud, most prominently in his thesis that every dream, when properly understood, is the fulfillment of a wish. For instance, the hundreds of dreams I have collected of the tidal wave type cannot in any way, with or without free association, be interpreted as fulfillment of wishes. Rather, they are providing a context for an emotional concern.

Work on dreams after trauma as well as in stressful occurrences, pregnancy, and many other defined situations has led gradually to the following view of dreams, which merely can be sketched briefly here. First of all, dreaming makes connections in the nets of the mind more broadly and loosely than waking does. I believe we have no choice but to consider the mind to be based on the functioning of the human cerebral cortex, made up of billions of somewhat similar units (neurons), with some assistance from subcortical parts of the brain. All that can happen in these nets, awake or asleep, is that patterns of units are activated or deactivated in various ways and connections are made and unmade.

When dreaming, we make connections more broadly and loosely than when awake. Although the connection sometimes may seem farfetched or bizarre, they often make obvious sense. Four different women, two patients and two friends, have told me something close to this: "I dreamt of Jim—my boyfriend—but he looked very much like my father (or he changed into someone like my father). Upon waking, I realized, 'Yes, of course, Jim is like my father in a lot of ways. It's strange I never noticed that before.'" These dreams simply have put together things in their minds which they have not quite put together in waking. While awake, "father" and "Jim" occupied different channels, or trains of thought. Only in the broadly connected state of dreaming were the two brought together. The connection is meaningful and can be useful.

The connections made in dreaming are not random. They are 10 guided by the dominant emotions of the dreamer. This is where my work in dreams after trauma begins. I believe that, if we want to understand what is going on in dreams, we should not start with a group of random dreams of students, where we don't know much of what is going on. Rather, we should begin when we know clearly what must be going on emotional in someone's mind.

One such situation occurs in someone who has just been through a traumatic event—a fire or other catastrophe, rape, or attack. This is where we find dreams portraying terror and helplessness: "I was overwhelmed by a tidal wave"; "I was swept away in a whirlwind", "I was chased off a cliff by a gang"; etc. There clearly is a feeling of fear or terror at those times, and these dreams picture or provide a context for this. We speak of dreams "contextualizing the emotion."

Terror and helplessness are not the only emotions pictured in this way. Any emotion that dominates a person's life is pictured likewise in dreams. I had one patient who was functioning very well except for terrible guilt that she was not a good mother to her children. Over and over, she reported dreams such as this: "I let my son play in the yard and a huge cat grabbed him"; "My children were in the woods and a bear was chasing them"; "I left my children in a hotel room and I couldn't find them." Over all, the more powerful and clear-cut the emotional concern, the more clearly the dreams portray this. These dreams in no way can be considered random or nonsense.

We have developed a scoring system for such contextualing images in dreams and have shown in over 500 dreams scored on a blind basis that these images appear to be more frequent and more intense in traumatic and stressful situations than at other times. Here are some of the clear-cut contextualizing images we have found at times of intense emotion:

> **Fear, terror.** "A huge tidal wave is coming at me." "A house is burning and no one can get out." "A gang of evil men, Nazis maybe, are chasing me. I can't get away."
>
> **Helplessness, vulnerability.** "I dreamt about children, dolls— dolls and babies all drowning." "He skinned me and threw me in a heap with my sisters. I could feel the pain. I could feel everything." "There was a small wounded animal lying in the road."
>
> **Guilt.** "My father (whom I'm caring for) is swept away in a flood." "I let my children play by themselves and they get run over by a car."
>
> **Grief.** "A large round hill or mountain has split in two pieces, and there are arrangements I have to make to take care of it." "A huge tree has fallen down in front of my house." "I'm in this vast barren empty space. There are ashes strewn all about."

Connections

Our conclusion based on a great deal of such work is that dreams make connections broadly, but by no means randomly, in the nets of the mind. The connections are guided by the emotional concern of the dreamer. The dreams contextualize or picture the emotional concern. Furthermore, dreams have their own language for doing this. Dreams obviously do not deal in words or mathematical symbols, but, rather, in pictures—in what we might call picture metaphor. There is a whole continuum in our mental functioning, running from focused waking thought at one end (doing an arithmetic problem, for instance), through looser thought, reverie, daydreaming, and finally dreaming at the other end. As we move from the left-hand end to the right-hand end, we think more in pictures and specifically in picture metaphor.

Thus, dreams contextualize emotional concerns, using the language of picture metaphor. For instance, in our culture, a trip in a car often is a metaphor for the course of lives or relationships. I've heard a 15 large number of dreams something like, "I am in a car going downhill and the brakes don't seem to be working," dreamt when a relationship was in difficulty or seemed to be out of control. I discuss all this in far more detail in my book, *Dreams and Nightmares: The New Theory on the Nature and Functions of Dreaming.*

There is another important question to consider: Does dreaming have a function or use? Is all this broad making of connections guided by emotions in metaphoric form simply something that happens every night and is of no further significance, or does it have a function in our lives and can we make use of dreaming? Here, I must be a bit speculative, but my collaborators and I agree with workers from a number of different directions that dreaming probably does have a function.

Roughly, the most basic function can be called reweaving or interconnecting. Returning to one of the many series of dreams after trauma, we have found that the person first dreams about tidal waves and gangs, then gradually more and more about other related material from his or her life. The dream is making connections and tying things together. It starts with a new piece of distressing information—in an extreme case, trauma—and ties it in, connects it with other images of trauma, other memories related to the same feelings, etc. This process interconnects and cross-connects the material so that next time something similar happens it will not be quite so frightening since it will be part of a woven pattern in the mind. The dream reweaves a torn net or redistributes excitation, to use two very different images. Overall, we can talk about the dream as calming by cross-connecting.

What dreams appear to do after a traumatic or disturbing event is similar to what a good therapist does. First a safe place is established. In therapy, this does not mean supplying a nice room with comfortable furniture. The therapist must be someone the patient gradually can learn to trust; safety comes from a sense of alliance between patient and therapist. The patient is allowed to tell his or her story about the trauma or new event over and over again, making connections to other material, gradually seeing it in a new light. I believe this happens in dreaming as well. The safe place is provided by a bed and the muscular inhibition of REM-sleep, which assures that the sleeper will lie quietly in bed, rather than running around acting out the dream. Once safety is established, the broad connections gradually are made.

Finally, in addition to the basic function of dreaming, which I believe probably helps us even when we do no remember dreams, there are many ways in which dreams can be useful to us when we do remember them. For example, the women who dreamt some version of "Jim turned into my father" generally found this a useful insight, a new way of looking at things that helped in their relationship. Sometimes, the new and broader connections made by dreaming can be helpful in our work and in artistic and scientific discovery.

A number of creative people have made use of dreams in their dis- 20 coveries. Some of the best known examples are the French chemist Auguste Kekule, who saw snakes biting their tails in a dream, which led him to the correct ring structure for the benzene molecule. Inventor Elias Howe attributed the discovery of the sewing machine to a dream in which he was captured by cannibals. He noticed as they danced around him that there were holes at the tips of spears, and he realized this was the design feature he needed to solve his problem. Vladimir Horowitz and several other well-known pianists have described playing piano pieces in their dreams and discovering a new fingering they had not tried previously and which turned out to work perfectly. Robert Louis Stevenson said that his book, *The Strange Case of Dr Jekyll and Mr. Hyde,* came to him in a dream.

In these cases, I am not saying that all the hard work of discovery happened in the dream. Generally, the artist or scientist made one new connection in a dream and then developed the work in the waking state. Stevenson probably saw a respectable doctor turning into a monster—this is, in fact, quite a typical nightmare image—and then his waking writing skills took over from there. In each case, the dreamers were well-versed in their fields and were worrying hard about a particular problem, which thus had become an emotional concern and was pictured in a dream.

I believe that, by its broader connective features, dreaming has obvious uses of this kind and we probably can make a good deal more of our dreams than we do. For instance, many Native American and South American cultures have adopted a methodology for career choice. In puberty, a young man—or, in some cases, young woman—is sent out into the desert to have a dream or a vision. Often, the young person will return with a powerful dream which, with or without help from the elders, leads to a decision about a future life course.

We might tend to dismiss this as superstition having no relevance to our lives. However, I suggest that we can benefit from the techniques of these cultures. I believe they are making good use of the broader connective powers of dreaming. The young person, who clearly has his future role or "career" in mind as an emotional concern, goes out and has a dream that makes connections more broadly than he does in waking life, which pictures something for him based on his concerns, wishes, or fears, and this often turns out to be very useful to him.

I have known a few people who informally have made use of such a technique. In our culture, we generally ask a young person to consider carefully his or her possible choices for a career, make a list *of* pros and cons, and so on. There is nothing wrong with this, but I have known several cases in which the decision truly came together or felt right only after a dream.

Sometimes, dreams can be extremely useful in our personal lives, 25 scientific or artistic work, or even something as basic as career choice. I certainly am not suggesting substituting the dream for waking thought, but why leave it out entirely? Dreaming is one end of the continuum, a way of making connections more broadly than our focused waking thought, but guided by what is important to us. Why should we not use everything we have and allow ourselves to notice and employ this additional connecting power?

What Did You Read?

1. What does the author say a dream is?
2. What are the two basic schools of thought on dreaming?
3. What process does the author say Freud uses with the dream to understand underlying meaning?
4. According to the author, when we are dreaming, how are the connections in the brain different from when we are awake? What guides the connection?
5. What does it mean to "contextualize the emotions"? What is a "picture metaphor"?

What Do You Think?

1. What kinds of paradigms or symbols relate themselves to fear and terror in your dreams?
2. Do you believe that dreams are primarily guided by the dominant emotions of the dream? Explain.
3. Explain the connection between dreaming and creativity.

How Was It Done?

1. What does the introductory anecdote accomplish? What key point does it illustrate?
2. Part of the article is structured around two dominant schools of thought concerning dreams. Where in the article is the author's view presented?
3. How is classification of emotions/images and dreams/connections helpful to the overall development of the author's thesis?

I Have a Dream

Roger L. Welsch

*Roger L. Welsch takes a light-hearted look at dreams and how a folklorist's interpreta-
tion may be just as useful as Sigmund Freud's.*

Key Words

inventory	an itemized list of goods; a list of traits, preferences, atti-tudes, or characteristics
transparencies	a picture on a clear sheet of plastic viewed through a pro-jected light
hangar	an enclosed area for storing and repairing aircraft
brash	done in haste without regard for consequences
extragalactic	from outside of the Milky Way galaxy
primal	primitive; of first importance
emanating	coming from a source
tantalizing	teasing or tormenting by presenting something desirable yet keeping it out of reach

Psychologists say we all dream and that we all dream every night. No
doubt they're right, although I rarely recall my dreams—but then, I
can hardly manage to recall why Linda sent me to the grocery store
only moments after she's sent me. What's curious about the dreams I
do remember the next morning is that the inventory is remarkably
thin—a total of maybe three. And they are all bad. Just my luck.

Roger Dream Number 1: I open my mail to find that someone has finally discovered that I served only six years and seven months of my
seven-year military obligation back in the bad old days. I show up at my
base and am standing there in the ranks but I cannot find my cap. So,
there I am, at attention without my cap, knowing that Sergeant Ericson
is going to ream me but good, just as he always did. (I often wonder if
Sergeant Ericson maybe has the same dream but smiles in his sleep.)

Roger Dream Number 2: I suddenly remember that school is about
to start—although in real life I haven't taught in a classroom for more
than seven years. Sometimes I am allowed a couple of days before I
step into the class, but other times I am in my office and the bell is
about to ring. I realize that not only have I not prepared my lesson
plans but that I also don't know where I've put my transparencies—a
professional nightmare indeed.

Roger Dream Number 3: I am about to return home from Europe
from a field trip for the Smithsonian Institution (I frequently went on
these trips twenty years ago). The train is leaving in a matter of minutes for the city where I am to catch my plane, but I have lost my room

key and forgotten my room number. I will never get everything thrown together in time. Sometimes I eventually find my key, remember my room number, and make it to the airport all right, but as I stand there watching my luggage go up a carousel ramp, I realize that I have packed my ticket and passport in the luggage, which is about to go onto the plane—and home—without me.

What's uncanny about these dreams is that I am always in the exact same room, hangar, hotel, or airport. I don't know if these places really exist, but I know them like the back of my hand after years of sweating out the complications of my dreams in these settings. My dreams never contain any surprises.

The real mystery to me, however, is the contrast between my dreams and my wife's. I am big, loud, brash, opinionated, independent, and blunt; I dream about losing my cap, hotel key, or passport. Linda is shy, quiet, gentle, uncertain, and subtle; she dreams about distant planets where fire-breathing gorgons with coppery teeth fight wars, tearing great hunks of flesh from their extragalactic enemies and throwing the pieces they do not eat themselves down long Martian cliffs to packs of green, screeching centaurs who pound the still quivering flesh into the pink soil.

When Linda struggles and groans in her sleep and I wake her up, she tells me about horrors that only special-effects experts can dream up. I, noting that such scenes are clearly outside any conceivable realm of possibility, say, "There, there" and go back to sleep.

On the other hand, when I wake up screaming and kicking the finials off the footboard of our bed and explain to Linda that I had this terrible experience of thinking I packed my passport in my suitcase and checked it in prematurely, Linda says, "Poor baby. At least the airport was in this solar system," laughs out loud, and goes back to sleep.

What would Freud have said about my dilemma? "Forbidden desires cloaked in symbolism"? Maybe in Sergeant Ericson's dream, but not in mine (Sarge always seemed to take special delight in calling attention to my shortcomings). "Resolution or relief of fear and anxiety"? When I wake up moaning and yelling because of a dream, our dog Lucky runs out of his sleeping porch, barking at the primal sounds emanating from the house above, and I spend a good part of the rest of the night calming him down and persuading Linda not to start him up again by laughing too loud. I suspect that even Freud wouldn't find many tantalizing secrets buried in my unconscious. "Herr Velsch," he would say, "my analyziz zuggests, take it a liddle easier on de barbecue zauce next time you pig out on ribs."

One of the first books I remember encountering in my parents' home was *The Gypsy Witch Dream Book: New and Revised, Complete and Up-to-Date*, by the Queen of the Romanies (which beats the living heck out of "Sigmund Freud, M.D."). Whenever I consulted the book fifty years ago to interpret the hidden meanings of my own dreams, I was impressed by how goofy the Gypsy interpretations seemed to be—as I was to learn later, right up there with Freud's. Since I've never thrown the book away (I've never thrown anything away), in desperation I decided to turn to it once again for some idea of what is going on in my tortured nocturnal psyche.

I dug out *The Gypsy Witch Dream Book,* still mysterious in its plain black binding after all these years. It had "reindeer" and "rhinoceros," "stovepipe" and "lemona de," but nothing under "passport," "lesson plans," "airport," or "Sergeant Ericson." But whoops, what was this? "Lose: to dream of losing anything foretells sorrow and remorse." Yep, that was it, all right. When I dream about losing my cap, passport, or lesson plan, everyone from Lucky to Linda is filled with sorrow and remorse.

Eagerly, I read on: "To lose your hat or cap can be an unpleasant experience . . . but you'll have to admit, it beats fire-breathing gorgons and green, screeching centaurs. And, by the way, next time you dig into the ribs, take it easy on the barbecue sauce."

What Did You Read?

1. What is the author's tone? How does he feel about dreaming?
2. What does the author say about the difference between his dreams and his wife's?
3. How does the author feel about scientific explanations versus explanations based on folklore?

What Do You Think?

1. How is it possible to dream about things unknown to us in our waking state?
2. Why do you suppose so many of us have what most would label as "bad" dreams?
3. Do you have any books on the interpretation of dreams that you have consulted? Explain.

How Was It Done?

1. How is the title effective in establishing the overall tone of the article?
2. How do Dream #1, Dream #2, and Dream #3 help the author to make his point about dreams and their content?
3. Explain how the following line contributes to the tone and seriousness of the author's purpose: "Herr Velsch," he [Freud] would say, "my analyziz zuggests, take it a liddle easier on de barbeque zauce next time you pig out on ribs."

4

Marriage and Divorce

Marriage is both a personal experience and a social institution. Most adults marry at some point in their lives, and even today, when both cohabitation and divorce have gained much greater social acceptance, the number of people living in a marriage is still considered an important indicator of society's health overall. Indeed, over half of all households in the United States still consist of married-couple households, although this percentage is in decline. An entire cottage industry has developed around marriage—commentary by doctors, psychologists, and counselors who purport to know what it takes to make and sustain a good marriage.

On the reverse side of the coin is divorce. While rates of divorce in the United States have fallen slowly since the early 1980s, they are still high by historic standards. Since the advent of no-fault divorce laws in 1969, divorce rates have consistently been much higher than before no-fault laws. Some states have attacked the problem by passing new laws creating "covenant marriage," which make divorce more difficult for those couples that marry under such laws. Others have argued that couples should be counseled more before marriage as a way to ward off trouble after the wedding. Still others have argued that adults should have the freedom to choose to be married or not married. In fact, for some, divorce may be a path to freedom from an abusive, cruel, or even dangerous marriage, and any restrictions on the ability to get a divorce could be an injustice.

Of course, children factor into discussions of marriage and divorce as well. The effect of divorce on children—and the effect of a bad marriage on children—is of concern for many observers. Underpinning many approaches to both marriage and divorce is the assumption that the individual partners, their children, and society overall benefit when good marriages can be made and sustained.

In this chapter, the Writing Lesson discusses how to conduct a personal interview. Interviewing someone as a means of gathering information, particularly information based on personal experience, is an important skill. The lesson emphasizes practical aspects of conducting an interview, including what to do before the interview, during the interview, and afterwards. The results of the interview are then integrated into the Writing Assignment, in which the interview can provide perspectives on marriage and/or divorce that derive from direct personal experience.

THE MAIN EVENT READING

Patterns in Marriage

Judith S. Wallerstein and Sandra Blakeslee

In this excerpt from their book, The Good Marriage, *Wallerstein and Blakeslee argue that there are definable categories of marriages. Through the use of interviews with many married couples, the authors settle on four types of marriages: the romantic marriage, the rescue marriage, the companionate marriage, and the traditional marriage. Each type of marriage has both positive aspects and potential drawbacks. No matter what type of marriage one is in, the authors argue, partners need to continually work on the marriage as life brings the inevitable: change.*

Key Words

paraphernalia	personal belongings; various pieces of equipment
infidelity	having sex outside of a marriage
casement	a window sash that opens on hinges at the side
immaculate	containing no flaw or error; spotlessly clean
chateau	a large country house; mansion
sovereign	independent; self-ruled
archetype	the original pattern of all things that are of the same type
typology	classification based on types or categories
hybrids	something made from blends of different types
collusive	done by secret agreement
milieu	the physical or social setting in which something occurs

The first interview I conducted for this study was full of surprises. I interview material #1 met the husband of one of my couples, a fifty-two-year-old engineer, outside a conference room at his main office in San Jose. As he left the meeting for our interview, he told me, his colleagues had ribbed him about participating in a project on happy marriage. He turned and said, "Look, you bastards, you wouldn't qualify."

After leading me to his office, he sat down behind a desk cluttered with charts, reports, and computer paraphernalia. He began with a warning. "I hope it won't offend you if I use strong words." I assured him that it would be hard to offend me. "When I married my wife, at age thirty," he announced, "I liked her. I had been a bachelor in the fast lane and had had plenty of sex with beautiful women. But what I wanted from her was different. I didn't love her when I married her. But somehow, two to three years into the marriage, I realized she was the first woman I had ever really loved."

"What did you love about her?"

"She's beautiful through and through. She's a no-bullshit lady with a set of moral values that are visible, and she doesn't wear them like a badge. She stands for certain things and makes no bones about it." These were not the words that readers of *Cosmopolitan* ever hear about how to catch and keep your man.

Later I asked, "How faithful have you been?"   5

"I've strayed."

"How much?"

"Two times," he said. "Briefly, when I was on the road." He guffawed. "Judy, if this is what infidelity is about, they can keep it."

Several days later I conducted my second interview. The wife I interview #2 was visiting set out a sterling silver coffee service and the most beautiful strawberries I had ever seen. It was nine o'clock in the morning; shafts of sunlight fell through a casement window, accentuating the high polish of this woman's immaculate furniture. I began, "What's happy about your marriage?"

"What's wonderful about my marriage," she said, pouring coffee 10 an elegant manner, "is that I have chosen a very supportive man who's allowed me to grow up within the marriage. I live a very full life. I've changed careers a number of times, and he's supported that. I've raised three men I'm very proud of. And he's had a big input as a father."

Later I asked her, "What do you think he would say about the marriage?"

She laughed. "He would say that I bewitched him thirty years ago so that he hasn't noticed a lot of my faults. He would say that I make him very happy and that we both have kept our sense of humor."

"And humor is important?"

"Yes," she said, "because life is so serious."

interview
#3
The next day I drove up and down hills looking for the house of 15 my third family. At last I found it, set back from the street behind a wild tangle of honeysuckle, ivy, sword ferns, and bamboo. On the path to the front door, I stepped over a bicycle, a washtub, and a truck tire. The wife opened the door, smiled broadly, pushed a large dog out of the way, and greeted me graciously in a finishing-school accent. "Dr. Wallerstein, please come in, we're so happy to meet you." I noticed the portraits of four young children on the piano, a cage full of fluttery finches, and two cats. The house looked as if it had been hit by a hurricane, with stuffing coming out of the sofa, papers strewn on every table, and toys lying about, yet the wife greeted me as if I were being ushered into a chateau. I had entered a hideaway.

start of
analysis
I realized then that each of these marriages was a different world, a sovereign country unto itself. Rather than a single archetype of happy marriage, I found many different kinds. Like a richly detailed tapestry, each relationship was woven from the strands of love, friendship, sexual fulfillment, nurture, protection, emotional security, economic responsibility, and coparenting. But the patterns in the marital weave varied, and gradually I began to see several distinct types.

I learned that at the heart of any good marriage is a core relationship created out of the conscious and unconscious fit of the partners' needs and wishes. This core reflects what each partner wants and expects from the other—expectations influenced by relationships that begin in infancy, childhood, and adolescence but that are ultimately shaped within the marriage. It also reflects what each person considers undesirable or unacceptable. The core relationship includes each person's perceptions of the other: "She is so gentle," "He is so exciting"; and what each values in the other: "She is entirely honest," "He will be a wonderful father." The marital core represents a shared vision of what brought these two people together and what they see for their future as a couple and as a family—Me and You and Us through time.

generaliz-
ing & cat-
egorizing
As my study proceeded, I began to see that these good marriages naturally sorted themselves into distinguishable types. Once the study was completed, I decided to propose a typology that consists of four marriage forms, which I have labeled romantic, rescue, companionate, and traditional. Although a relationship rarely falls neatly into a single category, the couples in this study were largely captured by this typology. Some of the marriages clearly belonged to one type or another, while others were hybrids. Undoubtedly other types of marriage exist. In many cultures throughout the world, marriages are more embedded in the extended family than they are in America. Some long-lasting homosexual relationships would fall into these categories, while others would require an extension of my typology.

Although the types overlap, they are unquestionably distinct forms. Each gives priority to some needs and relegates others to second place. It is inevitable that in weaving one pattern, we exclude others. Every marriage has roads not taken. Each offers a different menu of possibilities and limitations.

Thus each type of marriage provides a different degree and kind of closeness between husband and wife. The views of the roles of the man and the woman vary among the different types; so do the views of the appropriate division of labor and responsibility for child care. For some couples a single pattern of connectedness remains constant throughout the marriage. In others the core relationship may shift gradually or change radically at a critical developmental transition, such as the birth of the first child, the time when the children leave home, the arrival of midlife, or retirement. ^{20 determin-ing charac-teristics}

Sometimes the man and woman are in accord from courtship on. More often they come to agree about fundamental issues during the early years of the marriage. The core relationship emerges gradually as the partners weave the tapestry of their relationship. If the fit is right, the marriage itself helps shape the closeness in values and shared expectations. A marriage in which two people have incompatible expectations or unmodifiable demands is likely to fail.

The first of my proposed types is the romantic marriage, which has at its core a lasting, passionately sexual relationship. A couple in a romantic marriage often shares the sense that they were destined to be together. Exciting, sensual memories of their first meeting and courtship retain a glow over the years and are a continuing part of the bond between them. ^{1st type of marriage}

The second type I identified is the rescue marriage. Although every good marriage provides comfort and healing for past unhappiness, in a successful rescue marriage the partners' early experiences have been traumatic. They are "walking wounded" as they begin their lives together. The healing that takes place during the course of the marriage is the central theme. ^{2nd type}

I call the third type companionate, and this may be the most common form of marriage among younger couples, as it reflects the social changes of the last two decades. At its core is friendship, equality, and the value system of the women's movement, with its corollary that the male role, too, needs to change. A major factor in the companionate marriage is the attempt to balance the partners' serious emotional investment in the workplace with their emotional investment in the relationship and the children. ^{3rd type}

The fourth type is the traditional marriage, which has at its core a clear division of roles and responsibilities. The woman takes charge of home and family while the man is the primary wage earner. Today women in this form of marriage define their lives in terms of chapters: ^{25 4th type}

the time before marriage and children, the chapter when children are young, and a later chapter that may include a return to work or a new undertaking.

second marriages

All marriages need to be renegotiated as they mature, but renegotiation is especially important in second marriages. Although they come in every form—they can be romantic, traditional, companionate, or rescue—second marriages carry a particular set of challenges. They are accompanied by a host of characters from the past: the ex-wife, the ex-husband, children from the first marriage. As I learned from my study, people who enter a second marriage have a specific agenda: to undo the trauma they experienced and prevent its recurrence.

retirement marriage

Also worthy of special mention is the retirement marriage. While there were only a few retired couples in this study, they shared many characteristics, providing insight on happy marriage in older age. The most notable feature is that the couple spends more time together than they have at any earlier time. This togetherness enriches, challenges, and surely changes their relationship.

"anti-marriage" dangers

Each of the four marriage types has a dangerous hidden potential within its design that I call the "antimarriage." The antimarriage emerges when the negative aspects that exist in every marriage begin to dominate. At that point the relationship can become a lifeless shell or a collusive arrangement in which the neurotic symptoms of the partners mesh so well that the marriage endures indefinitely. Thus the romantic marriage has the tragic potential for freezing husband and wife into a self-absorbed, childlike preoccupation with each other, turning its back on the rest of the world, including the children. The rescue marriage can provide, instead of healing, a new forum for replaying earlier traumas. Spouses have the capacity to wound and abuse each other, and one may suffer the abuse without leaving or protesting—mistakenly concluding that this is what life is about. The hopes for rescue and comfort that led to the marriage are buried and forgotten.

The danger in a companionate marriage is that it may degenerate into a brother-and-sister relationship. Invested primarily in their respective careers, husband and wife see each other only fleetingly, sharing a bed with little or no sex or emotional intimacy. And a traditional marriage may focus so narrowly on bringing up the children that the partners view each other only as parents; they dread the time when the children will leave home, knowing they will be left with little in common.

A second marriage also contains the potential for antimarriage. 30 The marriage may be so preoccupied with the earlier failures that it is unable to take off on its own. Sometimes, in their zeal to avoid repeating the earlier suffering, the man and the woman unite as allies in battle, projecting all their current difficulties onto the prior partners. The fighting fueled by shared hostility can absorb energy and large sums of money when it involves children. This form of antimarriage cements the relationship but falls far short of a good marriage.

Marriage today provides a wider range of choices than ever before. Each kind of marriage has its strengths, its limitations, and its hazards. Understanding what each choice entails would enable a couple in the early years of marriage to get their bearings quickly and plan ahead. For example, a companionate marriage requires the couple to make careful decisions about when to have children and how they will be cared for. It also requires them to take special precautions against becoming too separate. Similarly, a traditional marriage depends on having a single sufficient income so that one parent can stay home with the children. It, too, requires particular nourishments in order to flourish.

The choice of a type of marriage is of course not entirely conscious. At its best the choice reflects the partners' unique conscious and unconscious fit. But it is within the couple's power to nurture the marriage and prevent its deterioration.

A good marriage is a process of continual change as it reflects new issues, deals with problems that arise, and uses the resources available at each stage of life. All long-lasting marriages change, if simply because we all change as we grow older. People's needs, expectations, and wishes change during the life cycle; biological aging is intertwined with psychological change in every domain, including work, health, sex, parenting, and friends. The social milieu and external circumstances change as well. Thus the individuals change, the marriage changes, and the world outside changes—and not necessarily in sync with one another. As one woman said, "John and I have had at least six different marriages." *[defining a characteristic of a good marriage]*

Many men and women are still becoming adults as they work on the first chapter of their lives together—getting to know each other sexually, emotionally, and psychologically. This time of absorbing exploration is critically important for defining the couple's core relationship. Sadly, many couples find they cannot navigate this difficult first leg of the course. But if they do succeed, they will have a sturdy foundation for the structure of their marriage.

The birth of a child entirely revamps the internal landscape of marriage. Becoming a father or mother is a major step in the life course, a step that requires inner psychological growth as well as changes in every part of the marital relationship and in the extended family. It is also usually a time when one or both partners have made career commitments; the tough road of the workplace stretches ahead, and its stresses are high. *[35 children & marriage]*

For many people the years when the children are growing up is the busiest time of their lives. A central issue is balancing the demands of work and of home. Children's needs for parental time and attention multiply along with the continuing demands of the workplace and often of school. Many couples cannot find enough time to be together even to exchange greetings, let alone make love.

changes
in life &
marriage
  The course of marriage changes again when children become adolescents, when parents dealing with midlife issues and presentiments of aging are suddenly faced with sexually active youngsters. The growing dependency, illness, or death of the spouses' own aging parents adds further turbulence to this period. When the children leave home, the couple must find each other again and rebuild their relationship. This new stage provides an opportunity to re-create the marriage in a different mold, perhaps with time to travel and play together. If a husband and wife have not succeeded in building a good marriage by now, they may find themselves merely sharing a household.

  A later part of the journey is retirement, when issues of dependency and illness, as well as the opportunity to pursue new hobbies and interests and the continuing need for sexuality, take center stage. Once again the marriage is redefined, as the couple face life's final chapters and inevitably consider the loss of the partner and their own deaths.

  All through adulthood our internal lives change as we create new images of ourselves and call up old images from the past. At each stage we draw on different memories and wishes, pulling them out like cards from a deck held close to the heart. The birth of a child draws on the memories and unconscious images of each parent's own infancy and childhood. That child's adolescence evokes the memories and conflicts of one's own teen years. Parents, watching their teenagers assert their independence, remember their own risk-taking behavior and realize that they were often saved from disaster by the skin of their teeth. And as old age approaches, every person draws on the experiences of prior losses in the family.

  We have for many years told our children that marriage requires hard 40 and continuing work, but since we could not tell them where or how to begin this work, we soon lost their attention. How could we tell them what we did not know?

what
makes for
a good
marriage
  I believe that the happy marriages I explore in this book can tell us a great deal about the kind of hard work that is required. I propose that a good marriage is built on a series of sequential psychological tasks that the man and the woman address together. I am convinced that the achievement of these goals is central to the success of the marriage.

  The concept of psychological tasks is drawn from psychoanalyst Erik Erikson's blueprint of the life cycle. Erikson explains that at each stage, from infancy to advanced old age, the individual confronts specific challenges. If these are not dealt with, psychological development stops dead in its tracks. For example, the task of the child during the elementary school years is to acquire the capacity to learn in the classroom and to get along with peers in play and friendship. If the child fails to master these tasks, she is handicapped in her future development. The psychological task of the adolescent, the best known of Erikson's formulations, is to establish a secure base of identity—who she is and what she expects to be in the future, separate from her family.

As a result of this study, I have extended Erikson's classical concept of tasks that the individual must master. I suggest that the young married couple faces nine life challenges or psychological tasks, which I discuss and illustrate throughout this book. These tasks are not a set of instructions for achieving success, not a checklist to be tacked up on the kitchen wall and marked off as each is completed. I have lifted these tasks out of the living experience of all marriages, including my own, and given them names and shapes. They are not imposed on the couple from the outside, to be accepted or rejected as they wish; they are inherent in the nature of marriage. They represent the essence of living together as man and wife and making it work.

9 challenges in life for a married couple

Whether the couple is aware of it or not, they are necessarily engaged in these tasks if the marriage is on track. And indeed, in many of the divorced families I have studied, these tasks were hardly begun, or their resolution was so brittle that it broke apart at a time of crisis. My goal is to describe the tasks so that people building a marriage can proceed with greater sophistication and confidence.

Folk wisdom captures some of these issues in the story of the three little pigs. Although this is a parable about leaving home, it is also a story about building one's house—an excellent metaphor for marriage. When the first little pig builds a house of straw, the wolf comes along and blows the house down instantly. The second little pig, a bit older and wiser, builds a stronger house of twigs, but it cannot withstand the wolf's onslaught either. The third little pig (who may really be the same pig at a later stage of development) builds a solid house of bricks, which the wolf cannot destroy. The wily wolf then slides down the chimney, but the third little pig has put a pot of boiling water into the fireplace and thus defeats the enemy inside the house. A house built of bricks by a wise pig will withstand not only the wolves outside the door but also those on the inside.

45 analogy to folk story

The metaphor of building a strong house applies to every marriage; when children arrive, the "walls" are extended to accommodate the needs, wishes, and emotional growth of the whole family and to withstand the wolves outside the door and those that lurk within. Because crises are inevitable, a marriage is never out of danger. Threats from without include such unpredictable events as the loss of a job, a

marriage as a house

forced move to a new area, a natural disaster. The stresses on a marriage inside its walls include the maturational changes associated with parenthood, midlife, retirement, and aging, and tragedies such as illness and death. The threat of divorce lurks both outside and inside the house. All major changes—accidental or developmental—have the potential for either weakening the walls of the marriage or leading to their reinforcement, depending on whether the couple blame each other or work together to deal with the threat and move on.

Many of the divorcing families that I have observed failed to construct a marriage strong enough to withstand the inevitable, acute, and ongoing stresses of life. By comparison, the good marriages examined here have maintained their integrity and staying power because they were built of sturdier materials and were reinforced over the years as the menacing wolves appeared. It is the lifetime process of building that distinguishes good marriages and the people in them.

The 9 tasks The nine tasks I have identified are as follows:

- To separate emotionally from the family of one's childhood so as to invest fully in the marriage and, at the same time, to redefine the lines of connection with both families of origin.

- To build togetherness by creating the intimacy that supports it while carving out each partner's autonomy. These issues are central throughout the marriage but loom especially large at the outset, at midlife, and at retirement.

- To embrace the daunting roles of parents and to absorb the impact of Her Majesty the Baby's dramatic entrance. At the same time the couple must work to protect their own privacy.

- To confront and master the inevitable crises of life, maintaining the strength of the bond in the face of adversity.

- To create a safe haven for the expression of differences, anger, and conflict.

- To establish a rich and pleasurable sexual relationship and protect it from the incursions of the workplace and family obligations.

- To use laughter and humor to keep things in perspective and to avoid boredom by sharing fun, interests, and friends.

- To provide nurturance and comfort to each other, satisfying each partner's needs for dependency and offering continuing encouragement and support.

- To keep alive the early romantic, idealized images of falling in love while facing the sober realities of the changes wrought by time.

The first two tasks require psychological growth and subtle accommodation to the other person. Moreover, each requires giving up the independence and freedom of the single life for the satisfactions of being husband and wife. When the task of becoming a parent is added, the baby has the power to throw the relationship out of balance. This strain can break a marriage that is too fragile to contain a child.

The early years of marriage can be difficult because the first several tasks do not come single file. Usually they have to be addressed simultaneously and at least partially resolved to create a firm foundation for the marriage. On the other hand, many of the tasks coincide with the individual psychological tasks of adulthood. Building a marriage profoundly changes and strengthens both people. And as they build the marriage and protect it, they continue to change and grow as individuals.

One of the many pleasures of writing this book has been that it enabled me to reflect on my own marriage. As I retraced the steps my husband and I took together, it was clear to me that no one executes the nine tasks with ease. No amount of communication can eliminate the inherent conflict as two people try to live together and make decisions that will simultaneously further their individual interests while protecting the partner and the marriage itself. Nevertheless, although the tasks are serious, accomplishing them is a richly rewarding process.

50

author connects to herself

What Did You Read?

1. What is the "core" relationship that Wallerstein and Blakeslee talk about?

2. What are the four types of marriages the author identifies? How are they characterized?

3. What is the "antimarriage"?

What Do You Think?

1. Do you think that women in a marriage with children essentially have to make a choice between the husband and the children?

2. Of the four types of marriage, which one would suit you best? Why?

3. What tasks (the authors have nine) do you feel are necessary to build a "good" marriage? Explain the tasks.

How Was It Done?

1. The article is structured around marriage and its forms. How does the article categorize them?

2. How do the authors substantiate their claim about marriage? Besides their own expertise, what else do they offer for support?

3. How does classification dominate and become the central mode for structuring this article?

4. In giving substance to their explanations, do the authors rely most heavily on research and facts or personal values?

THE MAIN EVENT WRITING ASSIGNMENT: USING AN INTERVIEW IN AN ESSAY

Write an essay in response to one of the following assignments:

1. Find a married family member or close friend. Write an interview-based essay describing the type of marriage, as described in the Main Event Reading, and analyze it. Use material from both the Main Event Reading and from your interview.

2. Why do you feel that most people choose to center their lives around marriage? Do interviews with married people.

3. Do you believe that divorce can be a healthy, life-enhancing experience? Explain. Use interviews.

4. Is it your finding, based on interviews, that marriage as an institution is still desired and respected, or does marriage seem more like an optional living arrangement?

PREPARATION PUNCH LIST

Before you begin writing the essay, you need to prepare yourself to write. One way to prepare is to work through the following strategies.

1. The first thing is to determine the point of the analysis.

- Is there benefit in identifying a particular type of marriage and the people who are in it?

- If so, how can that aid in rebuilding a troubled marriage? Is there a benefit to identifying the person/marriage? Can we learn something by investigating these things together?

2. The second thing is to find out about who the person you are interviewing is.

- Is the person an achiever? Aggressive? Or more passive?

- Does the person feel that balance in his or her life has been achieved?

- What are the goals in that person's marriage?

2. *Next, describe the marriage.*

- Based on one of the articles or excerpts, "Marriage and Divorce American Style" or *The Good Marriage,* how would you identify the relationship?

3. *Analyze the marriage.*

- What's good and what's bad about the marriage? What's right? What's wrong?

4. *Now, write a prescription for the marriage.*

- This may mean for the couple to keep doing as they are doing. Or, perhaps the couple needs to change some actions, behaviors, or attitudes? In extreme cases, this may mean divorce.

THE MAIN EVENT WRITING LESSON: AN INTERVIEW

In order to successfully complete the Main Event Writing Assignment, you will need to conduct at least one interview. This should be with someone who is married. The purpose of the interview is to describe the person and his or her marriage.

In order to prepare for the interview, you need to write a list of questions ahead of time. Questions for the interview might include the following:

Identity Questions:

1. What do you like most about your life?
2. What do you hate most about your life?
3. Do you like or fear change?
4. Do you like your job? If you're working in the home full time, do you enjoy that?
5. Are you a patient person?
6. Are you a take-charge type?
7. How do you deal with confrontation?
8. Are you a healer?

Marriage Questions:

1. Does the interviewee feel that he or she can discuss and confront problems and feelings with the other? Or not?
2. Do they share friends, interests, and activities? Do they go to church together? Go to the movies together? Exercise together?

3. Is there physical attraction in the marriage?

4. Who makes the most money? Is that a problem?

5. Do they share household/domestic chores? Equally? (This question is especially important if both partners work full time outside of the home.)

6. Has there been an extramarital affair? How did that affect the marriage?

7. What do you like most about your spouse?

8. What do you dislike most about your spouse?

How to Conduct the Interview

Prepare yourself ahead of time before conducting an interview. There are several steps to take before, during, and after the interview that will help you conduct a more effective and successful interview.

1. Ask for permission to conduct the interview. Do not assume that just because someone is a close friend or relative that he or she will be willing to talk about his or her marriage with you. If you have access to a tape recorder, ask for permission to tape the interview. Plan to take handwritten notes whether or not permission is granted.

2. Even though the person you are going to interview may be a close friend or family member, set up a day and time for the interview well in advance. Be sure to tell the person how much time you will need (for this assignment, you may want a half-hour or even an hour).

3. Conduct the interview in a quiet, relaxing atmosphere: no loud music, no young children running about, no television distracting you or the person you are interviewing. Both of you want to be relaxed and focused during the interview.

4. Have your questions written down ahead of time. Phrase the questions in a neutral, objective manner. Avoid using negative words that might imply you are looking for a certain type of response. (For example, do not ask, "Does your partner drink too much?" Instead, ask, "Is drinking an issue in your marriage?")

5. Be a good listener during the interview. Ask follow-up questions when appropriate. If an interviewee does not respond to your question, ask the question again, phrased slightly differently. Remember, the point of the interview is to get the information you need.

6. After the interview, be sure to thank the person for their time.

If the person is too uncomfortable, or if the person is out of town and cannot sit down one-on-one, you can conduct the interview over the phone or via a chat room or email on the Internet.

Soon after the interview is over, look at your notes. Fill out your notes with more details while your memory of the interview is still fresh. The longer you wait to do this, the less you will remember. If you have taped the interview, listen to the tape and take note of particularly important spots in the interview.

When you write your essay, you will need to incorporate parts of the interview into your own writing. Rarely will you need to present a full question-and-answer format; instead, interviews become a source of information, such as in the Main Event Reading. Ultimately, what you use from an interview is dependent on the points you are trying to make in your own writing.

THE MAIN EVENT WRITING SAMPLE

The following is an essay, which incorporates an interview, written for this text in response to the Main Event Writing Assignment, Question #1.

The Marriage of Serena and Vince

On average, recent studies show that parents and children in married *Determin-* families are happier, healthier, wealthier, and better adjusted than *ing the point of* those in single-parent households (Hetherington). Marriage is a *analysis* good thing, but any reasonable person knows that there are good marriages and bad marriages, that there are common problems in marriages and perhaps even some common types of marriages. The purpose of this assignment is to explore one individual marriage for purposes of analysis, to categorize it according to patterns established by Judith S. Wallerstein and Sandra Blakeslee in their book *The Good Marriage,* to examine what problems are in the relationship, and to prescribe some fresh, exciting, and creative ways of guiding the relationship to better health. The marriage of Serena and Vince Morrow *Thesis* is one with a lot of material signs of success, but upon further investigation, there seem to be a lot of repressed problems.

Serena Morrow, the subject of the interview, has been married *Determin-* *ing who* for almost twenty years. She has two high-school-aged children, *the per-* *son is* both boys, of whom she is very proud. She and her husband own a ranch-style home in Southern California. Both work. In interviewing her, I found Serena to be an attractive, bright woman, but with an edge. Problems with her mother and brother abound. Her mother is critical, and her brother is needy. She had been married before, very briefly, to a man who cheated on her early in their marriage. Needless to say, there is some anger in Serena. However, she has filled her life with friends, her children's lives (sports, school, activities), and her job as a real estate broker. She has a stock portfolio that has grown over the years, so that she has financial security of her own. She derives great satisfaction from this, as well as having something of her own: a job, even if it requires her to work weekends. Her husband, on the other hand, works during the week. This led me to ask some obvious questions about the quality of the marriage these two have if they seldom see each other.

Describing the marriage

Serena and Vince's marriage is not all that it might be. When asked if she is still in love with her husband, Serena replied, "Of course not. I'm sure I was madly in love with him many years ago, but my children have become my priority." She also declares that they share very little in common. Even though Dr. Phillip McGraw, in his book *Relationship Rescue,* says that it is a myth that a great relationship requires a common interest (55), it does appear from my conversation with Morrow that she and Vince do not share many interests, and when they are sharing activities with their children, they do not feel a bond with each other. They are merely friends. We can identify this as a companionate marriage according to Wallerstein and Blakeslee. Some companionate marriages are successful, but Serena's may not be. She says her husband drinks too much. She dislikes this, and she tells him so, but he does not want to stop. She also suspects him of having an affair, having found a champagne cork in his car for no explainable reason. He has also suddenly lost a lot of weight and had his teeth bleached. I jokingly asked Serena if she herself was "on the prowl." She said two things: "I love my husband, but I'm not in love with him. And I'm always a little bit on the prowl." I asked how her husband views her. She answered, "Like a good horse. Good teeth, nice cheekbones, shiny hair."

Identifying problems in this marriage is relatively easy. *Analyzing the* E. Mavis Hetherington says that problems often come when one *ing the marriage* spouse, usually the wife, wants to confront problems and feelings, and the other doesn't want to and withdraws. However, in this marriage, it may be true that neither partner wants to rock the boat. Both have a nice home, stable jobs, shared friends, and two children they both love dearly. In other words, they appear to have a full and balanced life. There is no amount of extreme emotional arousal, but there is no frequent fighting either. It is not a traditional marriage because both partners are working at roughly equally-paying jobs; the couple is not particularly religious either. Michael G. Lawler and Gayle S. Risch reported that women do twice the amount of housework as men, and this holds true for Serena and Vince. Lawler and Risch also say that after balancing job and family, which Serena and Vince have done fairly well, the second great area of concern is frequency of sexual relations. Here, Serena spoke of her lack of desire, attributed partly to the fact that her husband drinks too much. Interestingly enough, Serena is committed to this marriage, at the present.

Bluntly put, Serena and Vince's marriage appears to be in *Prescription for* trouble. Like an iceberg, on the surface their problems appear *tion for the mar-* small, but there are a number of things that they need to address. *riage* Fortunately, they do not have some problems that many marriages do face—they do not have job or financial instability. They also have no health problems. What seems to be the biggest gap, to an outsider, is simply the lack of focusing on one another. Their family duties have been given attention, but not their relationship as husband and wife. Serena needs to communicate with Vince, to share her feelings, even if they are not all necessarily positive, to learn again that she can trust him. She needs to talk and know that he will respond in a supportive manner. Vince needs to stop taking his wife for granted. His life has been consumed with sports, children, and his buddies. Serena says she feels sometimes like she's fallen into a fraternity party. He needs to treat her not like a fraternity brother, but like a valued wife and partner. A romantic candlelight dinner, a weekend getaway for two, or some other activity for Serena and Vince might help put back some of their original feelings. As "The Marriage Rehearsal" states, "If a couple doesn't compromise . . . they're doomed." Perhaps Serena should not work every weekend. Perhaps Vince should cut back on his drinking. They both have a lot invested in this marriage, and they need to do more to make it work better.

Works Cited

Hetherington, E. Mavis. "Marriage and Divorce American Style." *American Prospect* 8 Apr. 2002: 62–63. ProQuest. San Diego Mesa Coll. Lib. 29 Aug. 2002.

Lawler, Michael G., and Gail S. Risch. "Time, Sex, and Money." *America* 14 May 2001: 20–22. ProQuest. San Diego Mesa Coll. Lib. 29 Aug. 2002.

"The Marriage Rehearsal." *Chatelaine* Sept. 2002: 51+ *MasterFile Premiere.* EBSCOHost. San Diego Mesa Coll. Lib. 29 Aug. 2002.

McGraw, Phillip C. *Relationship Rescue.* New York: Hyperion, 2000.

Morrow, Serena. Personal interview. 1 Sept. 2002.

Wallerstein, Judith S., and Sandra Blakeslee. *The Good Marriage.* Boston: Warner-Houghton, 1996.

ADDITIONAL READINGS

Blowing Up the Myths:
Myth #4 and Myth #5

Phillip C. McGraw

In his book Relationship Rescue, *McGraw, known on daytime television as "Dr. Phil," identifies ten myths about marriage. In this excerpt, he talks about two of those ten: the myth that a good relationship requires partners to have a lot in common and the myth that couples in a good relationship do not have arguments. Instead, McGraw points out how relationships do not require couples to be constantly involved in a joint activity. After all, daily life already provides many joint activities, just small, everyday ones that often go unnoticed. McGraw also argues that arguments can be beneficial, especially if how couples argue is healthy. Failure to argue means denial of conflict, but unhealthy forms of arguments can also be destructive.*

Key Words

avid	enthusiastic; urgently eager
camaraderie	a spirit of friendly good-fellowship
lob	to hit a tennis ball easily with a high arc
idiosyncrasies	peculiar characteristics
volatility	a tendency to erupt in violence; explosive
accordance	agreement; in harmony with
cumulative	increasing by successive additions
dogmatic	dictatorial

Myth #4: A Great Relationship Requires Common Interests That Bond You Together Forever

Here we come to a myth that sends people down the road into astonishingly ridiculous situations in which they often return bewildered or unhappy or even hostile. I know the "hostile" part all too well—for I too at one point believed in the myth that my relationship would be better if Robin and I did some activity together, if we developed a common interest.

I wasn't satisfied with the fact that we had all sorts of smaller common experiences that interested us. I thought we needed one big thing to do together. So I came up with the idea: Tennis! I probably play tennis three hundred days a year. My wife, while not nearly as avid a tennis player as I, is an accomplished player who enjoys the game and appreciates the camaraderie. Frankly, I don't play for camaraderie. I play to compete, and everyone I play with plays to compete. The group of guys that I regularly play with would just as soon hit you right between the eyes with a short lob as look at you. My wife, on the other hand, gets a different kind of reward from the game. She loves the exercise, the time that she spends with friends, and the challenge of learning to hit the ball better and better each time she plays.

About ten years ago, based on this very myth, we signed up as a team in a mixed-doubles league. Common interest, right? Shared quality time, right? Good for the relationship, right? As I said, that was ten years ago, and I am not sure we are over it yet. She made me so mad I could have killed her. I made her so mad I think she did try to kill me. By the end of the first set of the first match on the first night, we were not even speaking. She could not believe I was being so mean. I apparently slammed the ball too close to the lady on the other side. I wasn't friendly when we changed sides of the court (they all wanted to have a tea party). I allegedly rolled my eyes and sighed when she missed a ball.

She, on the other hand, wanted to chat during points. Not just with me, but with the people on the other side. If the ball wasn't hit right to her, she wasn't about to run for it, I assume because she didn't want to mess up her hair.

You've no doubt attempted some major project with your partner   5
as well, thinking it would make the two of you closer. I'll never forget a woman friend of mine who tried fly fishing one morning with her husband. After an hour of listening to him complain to her about how she wasn't standing in the right place or casting to the correct part of the river, she dropped her rod and said, "It's six a.m., it's cold, you're rude, and I'm going home. In case you haven't heard, you can buy fish at the supermarket in the middle of the afternoon."

Perhaps you and your partner have a great common interest that makes the two of you happy. That's fine. All power to you. But the greater myth is that if you don't have one, you must find one in order to make the relationship more fulfilling. That's just not true—not true at all. I have encountered thousands of older couples who have been married happily for years and years. They love their time together, they love being great companions, but they also respect each other's idiosyncrasies and don't feel they have to engage in lots of activities together.

It's not what you do, it's how you do it. If forcing yourselves into common activities creates stress, tension, and conflict, then don't do it. Simply don't do it. It's wrong to think that there is something amiss in your relationship if you don't have common interests and activities. I promise, you have a number of significant commonalities that you may not think about. You live together, you sleep together, you eat together, and if you're married with children, you parent together. You may worship together, spend holidays together, and even ride to work together. If it doesn't work for you to take a ceramics class together, just don't do it. The important thing is that you not label yourself as deficient or having a less committed love because you don't share common activities.

Myth #5: A Great Relationship Is a Peaceful One

Once again, wrong! So many people are terrified of volatility because they think arguing is a sign of weakness or relationship breakdown. The reality is that arguing in a relationship is neither good nor bad. Indeed, let me turn this myth on its head. If arguing is done in accordance with some very simple rules of engagement, it can actually help the quality and longevity of the relationship in a number of ways. For some couples, such fighting provides a much needed release of tension. For others, it brings about a certain peace and trust because they know they can release their thoughts and feelings without being abandoned or rejected or humiliated.

I am not saying that arguments are something that you should strive for, but research simply does not support the notion that couples who fight fail in their relationships. In fact, there are as many relationship failures associated with the suppression of conflict and the denial associated with it as there are failures associated with volatile and vocal confrontations.

As children we learned early about the importance of being considerate of another person. We were taught lessons in manners and self-restraint. Oh, God, you're probably thinking, Dr. Phil is about to tell me that politeness is a myth. Wrong again. I reserve a special respect for partners who are polite and full of goodwill toward each other. But think about it. After all we've already discussed about the vast physiological and psychological differences between two people, is it really natural for a couple always to be marvelously thoughtful of each other, never disagree, show little impatience, and rarely get peeved? Is it really natural to avoid getting nose-to-nose on occasion with the one you love the most? Is it a sign of strength if you don't get flat-out pissed off once in a while?

Don't worry about how many times you argue: that's not the determining factor in your relationship stability and quality. Instead, it is determined by the nature of the way you argue, and by how you deal with the argument once it has run its course.

If, for example, you are the type of combatant in a relationship who quickly abandons issues of disagreement and instead attacks the worth of the person with whom you are arguing, you are being a destructive force in your relationship. If you are the type who gets into arguments with your partner because the arguments are, in effect, more stimulating than the day-to-day life of being together, you are being equally destructive. And if your rage and impulses are so unchecked that you pursue a scorched-earth, take-no-prisoners approach, then you are taking on the quality of viciousness, which is an absolute killer in a relationship.

Similarly, if you are the type of combatant who never achieves emotional closure at the end of an argument and instead "gunny sacks" your emotions, only to have them come bubbling out later, this is equally destructive. You must get emotional closure at the end of your arguments; otherwise, you are very likely to react in some cumulative fashion the next time there is a confrontation and create a huge disruption in the relationship.

Don't confuse cumulative reaction with overreaction. Both are destructive interactions and are often mislabeled. Overreaction refers to a disproportionate reaction to an isolated event. It's analogous to the old expression of killing a mosquito with a shotgun. It just seems all out of proportion or scale, particularly from the mosquito's point of view.

Cumulative reaction, while just as explosive, is actually the exact opposite of overreaction. Cumulative reaction occurs when you have failed to get closure in prior confrontations, related or unrelated, because you denied yourself the right to participate healthfully in a confrontation with your partner. If in ten previous situations you have bitten your tongue rather than making an appropriately assertive response, you have stored all of that emotional energy inside. You are now like a pressure cooker with the vent valve closed up. This energy—whether anger, resentment, bitterness, or some other painful feeling—eventually has to go somewhere. In the cumulative reaction, it finally comes bubbling to the top, and the energy from all ten situations comes flooding forth, overwhelming your partner and making you sound like someone who has gone insane over the most trite and insignificant point.

We will have a detailed discussion about how to fight and argue without being destructive, and how to keep from making it a personal attack (or taking it as a personal attack) in later chapters. You must also learn how to properly put your relationship back together after a confrontation and how to let your partner off the hook rather than browbeating them into submission. Similarly, you will need to learn how to make your escape with your ego and feelings intact if you are the one that was wrong, or are the object of dogmatic browbeating by your partner.

Again, let me be very clear about what I mean when I say "emotional closure." I do not mean that you solve the problem. I mean that you get your mind and heart in balance and allow your partner to do the same. That will never happen if you buy into the next myth. Take a look.

What Did You Read?

1. How can fighting be good for a marriage?
2. What type of combatant is a destructive force in a marriage?
3. What is the difference between overreaction and cumulative reaction?
4. What does the author mean by "emotional closure"?

What Do You Think?

1. What rules or myths about marriage would you like to "blow the whistle" on?
2. Do you think hearing about other relationships can help you in yours? Why or why not?
3. How often have you blamed a relationship problem on another person? Explain.

How Was It Done?

1. What does McGraw structure this article around?
2. Is Dr. Phil McGraw's reputation, much of it gained from television appearances, central to the credibility of this piece?
3. Is McGraw, in his development of this passage, appealing most to your knowledge, your understanding of psychology, or common sense? Does this work or not?

Love Lessons from a Divorce Lawyer

Robert Stephan Cohen

Cohen asks couples to pose five questions to determine if there is a problem in their marriage. The questions are intended to point to issues that have the potential to erupt into marriage-threatening problems. Cohen points out that divorce should only be a last resort for couples. By identifying fundamental conflicts early, married couples can hopefully work through problems instead of getting a divorce.

Key Words

matrimonial	relating to a marriage or the married state
incessantly	constantly; continuously
insight	seeing into a situation; understanding

intimacy	familiarity; of a private or personal nature
assets	an item of value; property; resources
mending	fixing or repairing
turbulent	troubled; causing disturbance

If someone had told me 30 years ago that I would someday be giving advice about relationships, I would have laughed. After all, what could a divorce attorney know about keeping couples together? But I'll tell you, in three decades of practicing matrimonial law, I've learned a lot about why some marriages break up—and, more importantly, why some stay strong.

Clients pay me to get them the best possible financial and custody terms, but I do more. I listen. A good divorce lawyer becomes a one-stop emotional support system: confidant, psychiatrist, and clergyman. And as a result, my personal views have changed. I now see divorce not as a solution for troubled couples, but as a last resort. When I meet a new client, I ask myself What went so wrong in her marriage that she is seeking a divorce? And how can other couples avoid ending up in the same unhappy spot?

Here is the answer I've come up with: At the heart of every divorce lies one of a handful of basic marital conflicts. While couples may express their differences in different ways, I guarantee that if a marriage is in trouble, one of these issues is in play. So why not learn to identify the flash points now, while your relationship is still going well? If you and your mate sit down tonight and answer these five questions together, you'll keep your marriage on track for years to come.

1 Does Your Relationship Feel Like a Predictable Routine? YES [ ] NO [ ]

Linda, a nurse, had been married to Phil, a retail manager, for ten years when she came to me for a consultation. Her chief complaint? Life with Phil had become downright boring. "He doesn't want to do anything," Linda said. "When he gets home from work, he just reads a magazine or stares at the television. I've tried talking to him about it, but then he asks me what I want to do, and I really don't have any idea. My friends' husbands are always coming up with fun trips and outings, and all Phil can do is sit around and watch life pass us by."

Let's face it: Most marriages don't end with a resounding thump. 5 There's no bolt of lightning or sudden collision, just a slow leak of air from the tires. Trust me, I've seen it happen enough times to know that the difference between those who stay wed and those who join my client list is that the still-marrieds were smart enough to see the "flat tire" warning signs and quick enough to take action, before it was too late.

Like Linda and Phil, many of us make the mistake of believing love will always be magical and spontaneous. The idea of planning moments together feels unromantic, so we wait for them to happen on their own—and after 15 years of marriage, we're still waiting.

The truth is, shaking up the marriage routine requires an effort on both your parts. The key is to start small—it's amazing the impact simple gestures can have. To illustrate this, I often tell my clients a story: A few years back, I found myself working on a settlement with an especially fierce opposing counsel. Be reasonable? Make compromises? Ha! She actually seemed to want to go to court. Things were looking grim when an assistant stepped in to tell this lawyer that her husband was on the phone. I waited for her to snap at the assistant the same way she'd been snapping at me. Instead, her whole face lit up as she took the call, agreeing to meet at a restaurant for dinner that night and telling him she loved him.

"Oh," I thought, "newlyweds." It turned out, however, they had been married 25 years. Her husband's surprise call transformed her. The rest of our meeting was a breeze.

Bottom line? Keeping things fresh does not take mountains of creativity, just an awareness. The more familiar we are with our partner's routines, the easier it is for our lives to slip onto parallel tracks instead of intersecting. The grooves of Linda's and Phil's side-by-side daily cycles were worn so deep, they had started to live like roommates instead of soul mates. Moments of "planned spontaneity"—as simple as an unexpected phone call or spur-of-the-moment movie tickets—help keep those lines crisscrossing.

2 How Often Do Small Arguments Escalate Into Big Fights? FREQUENTLY [ ] RARELY [ ]

When two people share one roof, one bathroom, and one closet for an   10 extended period of time, it's inevitable that occasional quarrels will arise. To a certain degree, that can be good for a marriage. Impassioned arguments spice things up and help you retain independence within a tight-knit relationship.

The real problem occurs when there are more fights than good times, when shouting matches are so routine, couples forget what a relaxing dinner conversation sounds like. How do you know if your arguments are normal or destructive? Content is key: Do you debate world events and which candidate should be elected president? Or do you argue about who should do the dishes and pick the kids up from school? The first is a sign that you view each other as playful competitors; these debates are energizing, not exhausting. But frequent bickering about the details of everyday life is a red flag signaling general dissatisfaction with the marriage. These arguments are almost never about the official subject (doing the dishes or walking the dog); they're about who has control and who gets to be right.

Three years ago, I represented Susan, an accountant, who confessed to me that she and her husband argued incessantly—so often, in fact, that she couldn't remember an entire day of peace and quiet in the house. When I asked why, she was silent for a minute as she considered the question. Then, in a flash of insight, she confessed, "Well, I guess sometimes I care more about being right than I do about him." In that moment, something clicked: Susan realized that needing to win every argument was the surest way to wind up alone. After our meeting, she decided to go back to her husband and give her marriage another try.

It's the daily arguments, blown out of proportion, that stand in the way of true intimacy. We all want to live with someone who understands and supports us, not someone whose top priority is getting the last word. Next time you sense an argument escalating, step back for a second and focus on connecting with the point your spouse is making, rather than looking for flaws in his reasoning. Constructive arguments—and their successful resolutions—are hallmarks of a healthy marriage.

3 How Comfortable Do You Feel Talking to Your Spouse About Your Financial Situation?
VERY [ ] SOMEWHAT [ ] NOT AT ALL [ ]

If you're like most people, personal questions concerning money often feel, well, personal. Quick, imagine a stranger demanding to know how much you made last year. What did it cost for the kitchen renovation? What about loans for the new car? And while you're at it, how much did you pay for your last vacation? Money is a subject no one wants to think or talk about—but it's one that couples definitely have to address.

Every client who comes into my office has a unique relationship 15 with money. Some are born savers, others boarders, and still others are committed spendthrifts. Depending on the person, money can be a path to freedom or status or self-preservation. Some people see managing their finances as a way of managing their spouses. Just as there are no two people alike, there are no two people whose relationship to money is the same. So, it's natural that when previously independent individuals unite in marriage, they struggle for consensus on how to handle their newly joint finances.

In the long run, couples who are the best money mergers are those who remain open about their finances. Believe it or not, I know many instances in which one spouse hides money from the other, even if the other person earns just as much or more. In my book, concealing assets is one of the fastest ways to end a marriage. In one move, you destroy your partner's trust and cause suspicion to escalate on both sides.

At the end of the day, fighting over finances is rarely just about the money. If you have trouble being forthcoming on this subject, ask yourself what you're really hiding: Are you insecure about your job? Afraid of losing control? Coming clean now can help you confront these issues before they lead to a marital disaster.

4 Have You Ever Suspected Your Partner of Cheating?
YES [ ] NO [ ]

How, I hear you asking, can considering this question possibly help my marriage? The answer (though you may choose to disagree) is that facing the possibility of infidelity forces you to take a closer look at marital problems that might otherwise go ignored. For that reason, I believe confronting an unfaithful spouse can either destroy a relationship or be the first step toward mending one.

As a society, we blame the affair on the cheater—and rightly so. It's one thing to have marital problems, but an entirely different matter to use that as an excuse for cheating. Still, infidelity is often a sign that one spouse is frustrated but can't talk about it, so the affair does the job of signaling a problem. That's why it's important to let your partner explain his actions. Even if you place 100 percent of the blame on him, you will probably learn something about yourself in the process.

I remember one client who was going through a terrible divorce, a [20] split that hurt his children and his career. His wife had been unfaithful, but he still loved her dearly. Obviously struggling, he looked at me during one meeting and asked, "What could be worse than having your wife cheat on you?" The answer, for him, was suddenly quite clear: Divorce was worse.

For two people who love each other and are willing to do what it takes to make the relationship work, an affair does not have to signal the end. In fact, it could be the beginning of something much better.

5 Do You Thrive on Change—or Fear It? THRIVE [ ] FEAR [ ]

Staying married for 20 or 30 years might not be so difficult if it weren't for crises. Somewhere, perhaps, there's a lucky couple that has never had to deal with the stresses of a death in the family, or a home renovation, or unemployment, or empty-nest syndrome, or a midlife meltdown. But I doubt it. Life has a way of wreaking havoc on just about everybody.

From what I've seen, most marriages eventually come face-to-face with a major shake-up. It's a couple's ability to cope during these difficult times that ultimately determines the strength and duration of the union.

One thing that's tough about crises is that they often produce unpredictable behavior, even in people we think we know well. When Sarah's father was diagnosed with lung cancer and told he had one month to live, she flew home to be with him in Ohio. She asked her husband, Ronald, not to come, because the two men had never gotten along. Ronald understood, but after a few weeks, he thought she could use some support, so he flew out to surprise her. Instead of welcoming him, Sarah was furious and asked him to leave. Once home, Ronald expected his wife would phone to thank him for his good intentions. She didn't call for weeks. When she did, it was to say her father had passed away and she would be staying longer to handle family matters. Again, she asked Ronald to keep his distance.

Six weeks later, Ronald still hadn't heard from his wife. He flew 25 back to Ohio and demanded that she come home; she told him she hated him. He came to me for a divorce.

From where I sat, it was clear Ronald still loved Sarah—his threat of divorce was just a last-ditch effort to get her back. In the wake of a tragedy, people often feel detached from their mate, I reminded him— and that's exacerbated if you've lost a parent, because your spouse's presence serves as a constant reminder that he isn't experiencing the same pain as you. Although Ronald felt—not unreasonably—that Sarah had abandoned him, I suggested that he hold off on divorce, leaving open the possibility of her return. Several months later, he called to say Sarah was finally home.

How will your marriage withstand a crisis? Ask yourself: Do you have difficulty changing your mind once it's made up? Do you have trouble letting go of control? Are you uneasy around new people? A yes to any of these questions means you need to work on dealing with change.

There are times when, like Ronald, we have to put aside our usual values and routines in order to save the relationship. And never is that more true than during a time of crisis. Change makes all of us feel vulnerable about the future. The marriage that pulls through in turbulent times is the one that finds ways to remain stable while charting new ground.

What Did You Read?

1. In Cohen's opinion, what does a divorce lawyer need to offer besides legal advice?

2. What five "flash points" does he identify as major conflict sources?

3. What type of support does the author offer besides his own opinions?

What Do You Think?

1. Of the five flash points of conflict, which do you find you most relate to? Why?
2. Are there "flash points" that the author failed to mention that you find common and significant?
3. How would a divorce attorney's perspective be different from that of a counselor or member of the clergy?

How Was It Done?

1. Cohen structures his article about marriage around common flashpoints. How many does he cite and what are they?
2. Cohen's support is based on what?
3. How important are Cohen's credentials to the authority of what he claims in his article?

Marriage and Divorce American Style

E. Mavis Hetherington

Arguing that people are better off married than not, Hetherington addresses the issue of how marriages can be sustained. She questions whether government programs intended to promote marriage and discourage divorce will work. Hetherington creates five categories of marriages: pursuer–distancer, disengaged, operatic, cohesive–individuated, and traditional. She argues that the type of marriage one has can be a predictor of divorce. Ultimately, Hetherington argues that American marriage is so diverse that no single policy to sustain marriage is likely to be helpful or effective.

Key Words

salutary	producing a beneficial effect; promoting health
endemic	characteristic or prevalent in a particular area or environment
belligerence	having an aggressive attitude; hostility
dysfunctional	impaired or abnormal functioning
contentious	having a tendency to argue
efficacy	having the power to produce an effect
exacerbated	made more violent, bitter, or severe
definitive	serving to define; serving as a perfect example
laudable	worthy of praise

On average, recent studies show, parents and children in married families are happier, healthier, wealthier, and better adjusted than those in single-parent households. But these averages conceal wide variations. Before betting the farm on marriage with a host of new government programs aimed at promoting traditional two-parent families and discouraging divorce, policy makers should take another look at the research. It reveals that there are many kinds of marriage and not all are salutary. Nor are all divorces and single-parent experiences associated with lasting distress. It is not the inevitability of positive or negative responses to marriage or divorce that is striking, but the diversity of them.

Men do seem to benefit simply from the state of being married. Married men enjoy better health and longevity and fewer psychological and behavioral problems than single men. But women, studies repeatedly have found, are more sensitive to the emotional quality of the marriage. They benefit from being in a well-functioning marriage, but in troubled marriages they are likely to experience depression, immune-system breakdowns, and other health-related problems.

We saw the same thing in the project I directed at the Hetherington Laboratory at the University of Virginia, which followed 1,400 divorced families, including 2,500 kids—some for as long as 30 years—interviewing them, testing them, and observing them at home, at school, and in the community. This was the most comprehensive study of divorce and remarriage ever undertaken; for policy makers, the complexity of the findings is perhaps its most important revelation.

Good Marriages, Bad Marriages

By statistical analysis, we identified five broad types of marriage— ranging from "pursuer-distances" marriages (which we found were the most likely to end in divorce), to disengaged marriages, to operatic marriages, to "cohesive-individuated" marriages, and, finally, to traditional marriages (which had the least risk of instability).

To describe them briefly: 5

- Pursuer–distancer marriages are those mismatches in which one spouse, usually the wife, wants to confront and discuss problems and feelings and the other, usually the husband, wants to avoid confrontations and either denies problems or withdraws.

- Disengaged marriages are ones where couples share few interests, activities, or friends. Conflict is low, but so is affection and sexual satisfaction.

- Operatic marriages involve couples who like to function at a level of extreme emotional arousal. They are intensely attracted, attached, and volatile, given both to frequent fighting and to passionate lovemaking.

- Cohesive–individuated marriages are the yuppie and feminist ideal, characterized by equity, respect, warmth, and mutual support, but also by both partners retaining the autonomy to pursue their own goals and to have their own friends.

- Traditional marriages are those in which the husband is the main income producer and the wife's role is one of nurturance, support, and home and child care. These marriages work well as long as both partners continue to share a traditional view of gender roles.

We found that not just the risk of divorce but also the extent of women's psychological and health troubles varies according to marriage type—with wives in pursuer–distancer and disengaged marriages experiencing the most problems, those in operatic marriages significantly having fewer, and those in cohesive–individuated and traditional marriages the fewest. Like so many other studies, we found that men's responses are less nuanced; the only differentiation among them was that men in pursuer–distancer marriages have more problems than those in the other four types.

The issue is not simply the amount of disagreement in the marriage; disagreements, after all, are endemic in close personal relations. It is how people disagree and solve problems—how they interact—that turns out to be closely associated with both the duration of their marriages and the well-being of wives and, to a lesser extent, husbands. Contempt, hostile criticism, belligerence, denial, and withdrawal erode a marriage. Affection, respect, trust, support, and making the partner feel valued and worthwhile strengthen the relationship.

Good Divorces, Bad Divorces

Divorce experiences also are varied. Initially, especially in marriages involving children, divorce is miserable for most couples. In the early years, ex-spouses typically must cope with lingering attachments; with resentment and anger, self-doubts, guilt, depression, and loneliness; with the stress of separation from children or of raising them alone; and with the loss of social networks and, for women, of economic security. Nonetheless, we found that a gradual recovery usually begins by the end of the second year. And by six years after divorce, 80 percent of both men and women have moved on to build reasonably or exceptionally fulfilling lives.

Indeed, about 20 percent of the women we observed eventually emerged from divorce enhanced and exhibiting competencies they never would have developed in an unhappy or constraining marriage. They had gone back to school or work to ensure the economic stability of their families, they had built new social networks, and they had become involved and effective parents and socially responsible citizens.

Often they had happy second marriages. Divorce had offered them an opportunity to build new and more satisfying relationships and the freedom they needed for personal growth. This was especially true for women moving from a pursuer–distancer or disengaged marriage, or from one in which a contemptuous or belligerent husband undermined their self-esteem and child-rearing practices. Divorced men, we found, are less likely to undergo such remarkable personal growth; still, the vast majority of the men in our study did construct reasonably happy new lives for themselves.

As those pressing for government programs to promote marriage 10 will no doubt note, we found that the single most important predictor of a divorced parent's subsequent adjustment is whether he or she has formed a new and mutually supportive intimate relationship. But what should also be noticed is that successful repartnering takes many forms. We found that about 75 percent of men and 60 percent of women eventually remarry, but an increasing number of adults are opting to cohabit instead—or to remain single and meet their need for intimacy with a dating arrangement, a friendship, or a network of friends or family.

There is general agreement among researchers that parents' repartnering does not do as much for their children. Both young children and adolescents in divorced and remarried families have been found to have, on average, more social, emotional, academic, and behavioral problems than kids in two-parent, non-divorced families. My own research, and that of many other investigators, finds twice as many serious psychological disorders and behavioral problems—such as teenage pregnancy, dropping out of school, substance abuse, unemployment, and marital breakups—among the offspring of divorced parents as among the children of nondivorced families. This is a closer association than between smoking and cancer.

However, the troubled youngsters remain a relatively small proportion of the total. In our study, we found that after a period of initial disruption 75 percent to 80 percent of children and adolescents from divorced families are able to cope with the divorce and their new life situation and develop into reasonably or exceptionally well-adjusted individuals. In fact, as we saw with women, some girls eventually emerge from their parents' divorces remarkably competent and responsible. They also learn from the divorce experience how to handle later stresses in their lives.

Without ignoring the serious pain and distress experienced by many divorced parents and children, it is important to underscore that substantial research findings confirm the ability of the vast majority to move on successfully.

It is also important to recognize that many of the adjustment problems in parents and children and much of the inept parenting and destructive family relations that policy makers attribute to divorce actually are present before divorce. Being in a dysfunctional family has taken its toll before the breakup occurs.

Predicting the aftermath of divorce is complex, and the truth is obscured if one looks only at averages. Differences in experience or personality account for more variation than the averages would suggest. A number of studies have found, for instance, that adults and children who perceived their predivorce life as happy and satisfying tend to be more upset by a marital breakup than those who viewed the marriage as contentious, threatening, or unfulfilling. Other studies show that adults and children who are mature, stable, self-regulated, and adaptable are more likely able to cope with the challenges of divorce. Those who are neurotic, antisocial, and impulsive—and who lack a sense of their own efficacy—are likely to have these characteristics exacerbated by the breakup. In other words, the psychologically poor get poorer after a divorce while the rich often get richer.

The diversity of American marriages makes it unlikely that any one-size-fits-all policy to promote marriage and prevent divorce will be beneficial. Policy makers are now talking about offering people very brief, untested education and counseling programs, but such approaches rarely have long-lasting effects. And they are generally least successful with the very groups that policy makers are most eager to marry off—single mothers and the poor.

In their recent definitive review of the research on family interventions, Phil Cowan, Douglas Powell, and Carolyn Pape Cowan find that the most effective approaches are the most comprehensive ones—those that deal with both parents and children, with family dynamics, and with a family's needs for jobs, education, day care, and health care. Beyond that, which interventions work best seems to vary, depending on people's stage of life, their ethnic group or the kind of family they are in, and the specific challenges before them.

Strengthening and promoting positive family relationships and improving the many settings in which children develop is a laudable goal. However, policies that constrain or encourage people to remain in destructive marriages—or that push uncommitted couples to marry—are likely to do more harm than good. The same is true of marriage incentives and rewards designed to create traditional families with the husband as the economic provider and the wife as homemaker. If our social policies do not recognize the diversity and varied needs of American families, we easily could end up undermining them.

What Did You Read?

1. What is it that statistics show about the status and health of parent and children in married families?
2. Who tend to benefit from marriage most, men or women?
3. Identify the author's five distinct marriage types. Which one does she think will be most likely to end in divorce?

What Do You Think?

1. If it is men who benefit most from marriage, why do you think that is? If it is women, why do you think that is?
2. If you are in a relationship, or have been, which type would you describe it as?
3. Do you believe that how people solve problems in a relationship is due more to the kind of relationship one is in, or due more to personality type?
4. Do you believe most relationships suffer because of social problems, such as health care, day care, or education, or from personality conflicts?

How Was It Done?

1. What five types of marriage does Hetherington classify?
2. Where does the research come from that the author uses to support her explanations?
3. What primary effects on the female does a bad marriage have?

Fault or No Fault?

Muller Davis

Davis, a family law attorney, takes a look at divorce. He argues that laws need to be made to support marriage better. Davis takes a look at the history of divorce in the United States, especially at the effect of divorce laws before the advent of no-fault divorce. He argues that those fault-based divorce laws created inequities; thus, we should not simply roll back no-fault laws and see the return of these old problems. Additionally, more than laws have to change: attitudes must change. After all, legislation not supported by the public will not work. As a lawyer, Davis argues that, instead of making the quick buck on a divorce, lawyers should be working harder to save more marriages.

Key Words

preclude	to make impossible; rule out in advance
rancorous	marked by deep-seated ill will
proliferated	having grown rapidly
resilient	tending to recover easily from misfortune or change
matriculate	to enroll, especially in a college or university
exacerbated	made more violent, bitter, or severe
concomitant	something that accompanies
mores	moral attitudes
accrue	to accumulate or have added to periodically
inundated	overwhelmed; overflowing with something

Divorce is a disruption of the collective interests of the family by the self-interest of one or both of the spouses. Divorce is selfish. In 35 years of practicing family law, I have seldom encountered a spouse who obtained a divorce out of concern for his or her partner or for the sake of their children.

Lawyers have not contributed much to the support of marriage and the family, even though the need for shoring up such support is quite apparent. Most of the best law schools have not given a high priority to family law. The family law courses that do exist have concentrated narrowly on the substantive law and the mechanics of getting people divorced. Lawyers' role in supporting marriage may not have even been considered relevant. Their focus remains on who gets what, be it income, property or children.

Lawyers can use their offices to support marriage. But this opportunity will be missed if the lawyer does not ask appropriate questions and listen, if he (or she) does not consider the support of marriage a part of his job description, if he takes the position that a client seeking to keep her marriage together is in the wrong place, if he believes that lawyers who encourage reconciliation appear weak, or if he tries to shunt the whole problem off to the mental health professionals. One cannot overlook the role of money in all this. Lawyers are paid more for divorces than for reconciliations.

Prior to 1969, marriage was generally regarded in most states as a contract between two parties that could be dissolved only if one of the spouses committed an act legally recognized as incompatible with the continuation of the marriage. The incompatible action was called a "fault ground" for divorce. Divorce was granted by courts only upon proof of a fault ground, such as adultery, extreme and repeated cruelty or desertion for an entire year. At the granting of a couple's divorce, one person was found guilty and one innocent.

These laws were satisfying to those who for religious or other rea- 5
sons believed that marriage is a union or a contract for life that cannot
be dissolved except in the most exceptional circumstances. But the
fault laws did not necessarily preclude divorce, at least for those who
could afford the process.

There were many avenues open to obtaining a divorce. The most
common method was by agreement. But reaching an agreement almost invariably involved money. If the spouse who sought the divorce
was guilty of adultery, for example, he (or she) could not obtain a divorce in a fault state, because he was guilty of a ground for divorce. He
therefore usually had to satisfy his spouse financially before she
would agree to proceed against him to obtain the divorce. If the nego-
tiations failed, a trial could result in denial of the divorce, even under
circumstances in which each spouse proved the other guilty of a
ground for divorce. Then the spouses, if they did not reach an agreement, were consigned to continue their marriage after a prolonged,
rancorous session in the courthouse.

Fault divorce laws did not readily produce equitable results and
often favored the wealthy. Despite their inadequacies, however, such
laws led to fewer divorces. A partial reason for this is that the less
well-off had less access to the system. A more complete reason is that
the restrictive divorce laws were part of the values of a society that dis-
approved of divorce and favored the preservation of marriage. Marriage therefore had a framework of support in place, not only from the
legal system but also from families, churches, friends, children,
schools, workplaces, media from almost all of society. Marriages in
need of repair had institutional resources from which to seek help. It
was considered right to be married and wrong to be divorced.

No-fault divorce laws were enacted beginning in 1969. Every state
now has no-fault grounds for divorce, permitting a spouse who is dissatisfied with the marriage to obtain a divorce simply on that ground.
The theory is that a marriage in which one or both spouses no longer
wish to participate is irretrievably broken down.

Divorce proliferated under the no-fault divorce laws in numbers
never seen before. Coincidentally, a body of research evolved that gave
divorce a respectable sociological and theoretical foundation. The research concluded that spouses in unhappy marriages are better off obtaining divorces and pursuing their individual lives. Children are
resilient and can recover from being part of a broken family, according to
these findings. Psychological therapy and drugs can repair people
under most circumstances, so any damage that results from divorce can
be fixed. The earlier concern for children of divorce and for the spouse
who wanted to keep the marriage together was seen as misplaced.

It is no surprise that a crumbling of the institutional support for 10
marriage accompanied society's change of attitude about divorce. For

example, families, clergy, psychologists and magazine columnists who formerly supported lifetime marriage now give counsel on how to get through a divorce and live one's life afterwards. William J. Doherty reports that over 60 percent of marriage and family therapists are "neutral" on the subject of marriage or divorce in providing therapy. It does not matter whether they help create a good marriage or a good divorce.

Recently, however, there has been a reaction against the prevailing view of divorce. It began with some disquieting research in 1985 conducted by Lenore J. Weitzman in California. She concluded that, contrary to expectations, women were not able after divorce to achieve the same standard of living they had enjoyed during their marriages. Even worse, after a divorce men's economic circumstances dramatically improved, while women's economic positions and those of the children living with them deteriorated. Weitzman's *The Divorce Revolution* led the proponents of no-fault divorce and women's independence to relinquish one of their fundamental beliefs: that the majority of women could sustain themselves financially after a divorce without help. Most states responded by amending the spousal and children's support laws to provide for more and longer support for dependent women.

Recent research has also emphasized the costs of divorce to children. A child of divorce is commonly subjected to abrupt and traumatic changes: loss of father on a regular and consistent basis, his replacement by a stepfather or the mother's live-in boyfriend, and so on. Most divorces entail the absence of a father. An absent father is likely to spend less money on his children's education and support than does a present, involved father. The absent father leaves his children less protected and more vulnerable to abuse, and his daughters are more likely to become pregnant as teenagers. Children of divorce perform less well in school, are less likely to graduate and less likely to matriculate into college. The prevalence of delinquency in broken homes is 10 to 15 percent higher than in intact homes.

Current findings indicate that children may suffer long-term negative effects from divorce. For example, significant numbers experience moderate to severe depression and difficulty in establishing love relationships. Children of divorced parents are two to three times more likely to dissolve their own marriages than are children of intact marriages. The divorce process itself has a decidedly adverse effect on children. Almost no child wants his parents to divorce. The situation can easily be exacerbated when the children are drawn into the divorce process. It does not take much effort to imagine the damage to a child whose parents are publicly struggling over her. The child herself may have to state a preference in a choice she does not want to make. Since divorce affects close to 1 million children annually, the damage created is enormous.

Not only are children disadvantaged by divorce, but the marriage partner who was supposed to benefit also suffers, according to recent reports. Both sexes have increased health hazards as a consequence of divorce. Depression is relatively well recognized as a possible result, but less obvious are the physical hazards. They range from loss of weight to increased cigarette and alcohol consumption, lower immune function and a higher risk of dying.

This research has at least corrected the assumption that divorce is 15 cost-free to all concerned. The cost is more than individual: when multiplied by the over 1.1 million divorces per year—which affect almost 1 million children annually—an enormous cost is piled on society every year.

In view of these concerns, some have advocated resurrecting the fault laws, or at least enacting more restrictive laws to replace the no-fault laws. Louisiana in 1997 adopted a provision for "covenant marriage" that parties may select as an alternative to ordinary marriage. Louisiana's ordinary marriage law permits no-fault divorce after six months' separation; convenant marriage requires either the proof of a fault ground to obtain a divorce or the couple's living apart for a substantial period of time. Arizona followed suit the next year by enacting a covenant marriage alternative in which proof of one of the fault grounds or living apart for a period of time is required unless both parties agree to the divorce.

The theory behind this partial resumption of fault divorce is that if it becomes more difficult to divorce, there will be fewer divorces. But there is no reason to believe that the widespread reenactment of fault or more restrictive divorce laws by itself would produce beneficial results. There is no easy answer or quick fix to the phenomenon of a deluge of divorces that began in 1969 and has persisted for more than 30 years. Divorce has become ingrained in our culture. It is not even clear that the majority of Americans are interested in such a change.

Besides, the reformers face substantial unanswered questions. For example, if society gives marriage greater protection, what is to be done in cases of adultery? Adultery will not go away. What would be the mechanism to allow the dissolution of verifiably destructive marriages? The trapped and endangered spouse must be allowed to escape.

Nor can we expect research results on divorce to deter husbands and wives from divorce. To change the divorce equation, which now favors the spouse who wants to leave the marriage, requires a change in cultural values. Marriage and the collective interests of the family must be invested with at least as much value as the right of the dissatisfied spouse to abandon the marriage.

Such changes cannot just be legislated, they cannot be accomplished 20 by cost–benefit research, and they cannot be accomplished by one of the professions acting alone. Because these changes deal with a variety of intangibles, it is difficult even to know where to start. A promising place to begin is found in two sentences in a report by the Rutgers National Marriage Project: "Most Americans continue to prize and value marriage as an important life goal, and the vast majority of us will marry at least once in a lifetime. . . . Most couples enter marriage with a strong desire and determination for a lifelong, loving partnership." The separation between the ideal and the reality is wide. But because the ideal of a loving, lifetime marriage exists in the imaginations of so many Americans, it is a starting point from which individuals may be persuaded to give up a portion of their self-absorption in favor of the collective interests of the family.

A practical argument for a stable marriage is that an intact family is the best milieu in which to raise children. A concomitant of increasing the value of marriage in society is enhancing the worth of children. Children are entitled to at least as much attention as is paid to commerce. As children are more prized, the family will be more honored and there will be more of an effort to keep families together.

Marriage needs reinforcement from every aspect of society in order to survive. Legislation without shared social mores will be no more successful than was the prohibition of alcohol. However, this does not mean that legislation has no part in a cultural campaign to change American marriage values. Legislation, rather than facilitating divorce, can support marriage. For example, legislation could give a voice to the spouse who does not want her marriage to fail—as well as to a spokesperson for the children—in deciding whether there should be a divorce. Legislation can be shaped to add balance—not favoring the spouse who wants to terminate the marriage but ensuring more protection to the other spouse and the children.

A proposal has recently been made to have engaged couples commit to mechanisms that would impose penalties or delay on divorce—a way of discouraging divorce by making it a costly and less impulsive procedure. Another proposal is to require the divorcing spouses and their children to share the wealth that has been accumulated during the marriage in accordance with predetermined guidelines, primarily in order to give the children more financial security. Particularly useful are the provisions for pre- and postmarital counseling in the Louisiana and Arizona covenant marriage laws. Legislation can support marriage by encouraging counseling and providing resources for it, and by allowing sufficient time between the filing of a lawsuit and the entry of a divorce judgment for a spouse who opposes the divorce to have a fair chance through counseling to preserve the marriage.

What part can lawyers play? They can obviously work to help formulate more balanced legislation. Family lawyers who believe in marriage should seek to convince other family lawyers of the value of marriage. Lawyers should encourage and participate in professional seminars that teach support of marriages as well as those that teach the mechanics of taking them apart.

Family lawyers should explore with every client the potential for 25 reconciliation and the comparative costs and benefits of staying married or obtaining a divorce. Many clients come to their lawyers' offices in such a pell-mell rush toward divorce that they have hardly considered other possibilities or the downside of dissolving their marriage and family. Before the divorce dynamic takes over and establishes a life of its own, a lawyer can create a needed pause just by playing devil's advocate—a role to which lawyers should be accustomed. Marital therapy ought to be urged by lawyers in every case where there is a possibility of counseling. Meanwhile, a lawyer must be protective of a family's children.

The most obvious situation in which family lawyers interact with other professionals is that involving counselors or clergy. Communication among all the participants is critical. The wall of therapist or clergy confidentiality cannot be allowed to prevent vital communication concerning the marriage. Preservation of the marriage and the family is at least as important as most individual confidences. A balance can and should be struck.

A reformation of the money incentives to lawyers is also desirable. A reward for reconciling couples and a system other than the hourly rate (which encourages prolonged litigation) are not impossible and would be an improvement. But such changes are unlikely to come soon, and they are not absolutely necessary.

Lawyers are licensed by the state, as are marriages. The state has an interest in marriage. In acquiring his license to practice his trade, a family lawyer should be obliged to assist the state in preserving the marriages that the state sanctions. Lawyers need to be made aware of this obligation and taught how to discharge it. Lawyer support of marriages could produce large benefits to spouses, children and society at large, but benefits would also accrue to the lawyers themselves. The perception of family lawyers could undergo a dramatic change if they lent their good offices to the constructive preservation of marriages as well as to the activity of dissolving them.

Is the genie out of the bottle? America is inundated with divorce and its consequences. Divorce is part of the fabric of society. Ironically, however, even the pursuit of individual happiness is not always fulfilled: second and subsequent marriages have higher divorce rates than do first marriages. Yes, the genie is out of the bottle. But there are many reasons why we should try to push it back in.

What Did You Read?

1. According to Davis, what exactly is a "fault ground" action?
2. According to the author, many divorces are obtained by reaching an agreement that invariably involves *what*?
3. After a divorce, who usually ends up better off?

What Do You Think?

1. How do you feel about the statement "Divorce is selfish"?
2. Do you feel that there is much support for "hanging on" in marriage today?
3. In your opinion and observations, do children, after the initial divorce, seem to cope fairly well or not?
4. How do you think the proliferation of divorce can be stopped?
5. When divorce does occur, what kinds of mechanisms of protection need to be in place?

How Was It Done?

1. How does definition play into the development of this article?
2. In many ways, the basis for the article is the support of certain values. What are those values?
3. The conclusion of the article develops around certain proposals that might help to support and sustain marriage. What are some of these?

Warning: Living Together May Ruin Your Relationship

Stephanie Staal

Staal argues that recent research shows that couples who live together before marriage are more likely to divorce than couples who do not. This has become so established among researchers it is called "the cohabitation effect." Staal examines the possible reasons for this effect, including the idea that couples who live together first are not as committed to making a marriage work, or that living together makes couples less likely to want a family life with children. The notion that living together is a "trial run" for a later marriage is also debunked, as cohabitation creates the potential for social, financial, and legal snares that marriage does not.

Key Words

impasses	deadlocks; predicaments with no obvious escape
compatibility	having the ability to exist together harmoniously
cohabitate	living together as if being married
myriad	a great number; having a large number of aspects or elements
stigma	a mark of shame or discredit
accumulating	increasing gradually in number or amount
incubator	something that causes something to grow or develop
serial	belonging to a series of similar acts

When Kristina Mahaffey moved in with her boyfriend of a couple months, she didn't think twice about it. After all, she was only 22, she was having fun, and it seemed like the thing to do. But her carefree attitude began to change as the reality of living together sunk in. Besides sharing a home, she and her boyfriend opened a joint bank account to pay the bills. After a few years, her family started asking her about their plans for the future. "I remember going to bed with this cloud over my head," she says. "I would think, What are we doing?" When her boyfriend proposed a few years later, Kristina was excited and said yes. "We both felt like marriage was the next step, and because we had lived together for so long, we thought we were prepared to take that step," she says. "In retrospect, if it weren't for the fact that we were living together, I probably would have said no."

The transition from live-in girlfriend to wife was not easy. Kristina had dismissed many of the problems in the relationship while they were living together—they had very different upbringings and would often reach communication impasses. Once married, those problems became harder to ignore. At the same time, her new husband started to demand that she change. "When we met, I was wild and crazy and into the dance-club scene, but all those things that were attractive to him then were suddenly a no-no once we were married," she says. "I was expected to be a different person." A year and a half into their marriage, both Kristina and her husband were so miserable that they agreed to divorce. Today, at age 34, Kristina believes that her failed marriage was due to the unanticipated pressure to marry and the false sense of compatibility resulting from their decision to cohabitate.

The Cohabitation Effect

Living together has never been as popular as it is today. The number of unmarried couples who share the same roof jumped by 72 percent in the past decade, according to the 2000 census figures. Some women, like Kristina, move in with their boyfriends for the fun and convenience of it without even considering whether they'll one day want to tie the knot. Others see shacking up as a good trial run for matrimony. According to a recent Gallup poll, 62 percent of respondents aged 20 to 29 say that living together before marriage is a good way to avoid divorce.

But the generally accepted wisdom—that living together helps determine whether the relationship is meant to be—may be erroneous. In fact, numerous studies have shown the opposite to be true. "The rate of divorce is higher—about 50 percent higher—among those who live together before marriage," says Larry Bumpass, Ph.D., professor of sociology at the University of Wisconsin. Other studies show that, for myriad reasons, living with someone at any point in your life may make you more prone to divorce, regardless of whether that person becomes your spouse or not.

Dubbed the cohabitation effect, this link between living together   5 and relationship instability has garnered increased attention in academic circles in recent years. While the stigma attached to living together has all but faded, some experts warn that sharing a bed and a lease with a boyfriend creates far more risks than benefits to a relationship. "Based on the scientific evidence, I'd recommend people not live together," says Catherine Cohan, assistant professor of human development and family studies at Penn State University. "There is nothing to indicate that it'll help your marriage, and there is actually accumulating evidence that it could have negative consequences."

What's Causing It?

There are many different theories behind the cohabitation effect, but one possible explanation is that people who choose to live together have certain characteristics that make them more prone to divorce in the first place. They tend to have more liberal attitudes, are more nervous about tying the knot, and are less religious than those who don't cohabitate. "They don't see marriage as something that necessarily lasts forever, and they bring these attitudes with them into their marriages," says Paul Amato, Ph.D., a professor of sociology at Penn State University. "When things start going wrong, they might get divorced—not because their marriages are any worse but because they have fewer mental barriers to divorce."

Research also indicates that living together may actually change people's attitudes toward marriage over time. A study that tracked people from age 18 to 23 found that the longer couples lived together, the less enthusiastic they were about family life and the fewer children they wanted to have. And the couples who lived together and then broke up were more likely to believe that it's better to get out of an unhappy marriage than to try to stick together. "Cohabitations that dissolve have a big impact on making people more positive toward divorce, because the breakups are like minidivorces," says William G. Axinn, Ph.D., a University of Michigan sociologist and lead author of the study.

Abigail, 30, agrees that having lived with a boyfriend for two years in her mid-20s has left a lasting negative outlook. "We had been going out for a year and a half when we decided to get our own place to see how well we worked together," she says. "Well, it became clear that we brought out the worst in each other, but I stayed in it much longer than I should have because of our living situation. And when we finally broke up, I felt so burned that I avoided any serious relationships for two years afterward. I still feel somewhat doubtful that I'll ever find The One."

The Pitfalls of a Pretend Marriage

The most compelling explanation for the cohabitation effect is that the experience of living together seems to be an incubator for potential relationship killers. Since cohabitation is not a social institution like marriage, live-in couples often do not receive the same kind of support for their relationship from their families and friends. They also usually don't get the same kind of support from each other. "An uncertain outcome of the future of the relationship might make people feel less committed," says Cohan. And as a result of that lack of commitment, couples may develop bad relationship habits during the time they live together that then persist into their marriages.

Two years ago, Cohan interviewed 92 recently married couples 10 about their personal and marital problems and found that those who had lived together before they were married were not as good at listening to each other and solving problems together as those who hadn't. They were also more verbally aggressive toward each other. "If you're less committed to a relationship, you might be less motivated to work on your communication skills, and that decreased motivation might carry into your marriage," Cohan explains. "It might be a by-product of living together, since people in this kind of relationship often wonder Are we going to break up or are we going to get maried?"

The Runaway Relationship

Indeed, yet another factor may be that living together rushes people into marriages that either happen too soon or shouldn't be happening at all. "Cohabitation is seen as more casual—people are moving in with someone with much less consideration than they would if they were marrying that person," says Linda Waite, University of Chicago sociologist and coauthor of *The Case for Marriage*. "They don't realize that these situations are hard to get out of emotionally and financially, and so these poorly considered choices often become marriages. If people went more slowly, it would be easier to back up and break things off."

Sarah, 26, found that her relationship with her boyfriend Rick took on a momentum of its own as soon as they moved in together. "We felt a lot of pressure to figure out where things were going," she says. A few months later, they became engaged. With the stress of planning a wedding, Sarah had little time to focus on her uneasiness about getting married to Rick. "I even had misgivings when I was walking down the aisle," she says. Her doubts turned out to be well-founded. Two years later, she and Rick separated. Looking back, Sarah can see how living together pushed her into marrying someone who was not a good match. "If we had just been dating, I would've been able to see him more clearly and not as someone I need something from or have to negotiate with because we're living together," says Sarah.

When Living Together Last

While social scientists continue to research the cohabitation effect, many are quick to point out that not all unmarried couples are alike. Certain factors, such as the level of commitment and religious beliefs, can help predict the long-range success of the relationship. "It's the way couples go into their relationships that affects the level of stability you see in their marriages," says health scientist and demographer Lynne Casper. "I think treating cohabitants as one single entity can be problematic."

One group that seems to be exempt from the cohabitation effect are couples who are engaged or have definite plans to marry before they move in together. A 1996 study found that relationship quality did not differ between these couples and successfully married couples. "The people whom we have to be concerned about are the serial cohabitants," says Susan Brown, Ph.D., a sociologist at Bowling Green State University and lead author of the study. "Those are the kind of people who are going to have poorer relationship skills and an inability to sustain intimate relationships."

So should you or shouldn't you? If you're considering it, know 15 that one major success factor is to discuss openly and agree upon what your hopes for living together are to prevent any misunderstandings or resentment down the road. "It is really important for both parties to be clear about what they expect," says Dorian Solot, executive director of the Alternatives to Marriage Project, an advocacy group for unmarried couples. "A surprising number of people move in together where one partner expects to get married soon and the other one doesn't. That sets the stage for all sorts of trouble."

When Sophie, 28, first suggested to her boyfriend Scott that they live together, she was stunned when he said no. "We had been dating

---

Moving-In Mistakes

Steer clear of these three shacking-up pitfalls.

If you plan to set up house with your boyfriend, you have to be smart about it since cohabitation doesn't provide the same kind of insurances that marriage does. "If the relationship falls apart, there are no rules on how to divide the stuff you've collected," says Rosanne Rosen, author of *The Complete Idiot's Guide to Living Together.* To protect yourself . . .

> Don't make any major purchases together—like a car or a house—
> unless you are willing to have a written agreement drawn up de-
> tailing ownership. "It may seem like an unromantic thing to do,"
> says Ralph Warner, coauthor of *Living Together: A Legal Guide for
> Unmarried Couples,* "but if you don't, you may find yourself in
> court later on."
> Don't merge your money. Keep separate bank accounts, and don't
> pay each other's bills. "Many women offer to pay off their guys'
> credit-card debt because they think they will marry them eventu-
> ally," says Rosen. Likewise, don't get into a situation where you
> become dependent on your boyfriend's financial footing.
> Don't get sloppy with birth control. The unplanned pregnancy rate
> is high among couples who live together, and unlike belongings,
> children cannot be divided if you split up. "If you get pregnant,
> you may feel you should get married even if you're not happy
> with the relationship—and that's not the best way to start a fam-
> ily," says Rosen.

---

seriously for two years, and I was really upset, but then we talked about what living together meant. He explained that he saw it as a step toward marriage and he wasn't sure he was ready," she says. "It was interesting, because I didn't see it that way." So for the next six months, they continued to talk it over until they finally decided to live together with the intention of getting married when the time was right. "I wanted to move in together because I wanted more of a com-mitment. But I now see that if we had jumped in it too soon, it could have driven us apart."

What Did You Read?

1. What does Staal say ultimately about couples who cohabitate be-fore marriage?

2. According to the author, is cohabitation more popular today or not?

3. Identify some of the pitfalls of cohabitation that the author mentions.

What Do You Think?

1. Do you think that men and women look for different qualities in a girlfriend or boyfriend than they do in a marriage partner? Explain.
2. Do you think that before marriage, individuals overaccommodate their partners, and when the tendency to stop doing this occurs in marriage, trouble arises?
3. Do you believe that people who choose to live together have certain characteristics that make them more prone to divorce?

How Was It Done?

1. How do subtitles in the article help clarify its argument that cohabitation before marriage is much more likely to end in divorce?
2. What expert evidence does this article rely on?
3. Does the conclusion provide a good, effective summation of the main points?

Time, Sex, and Money

Michael G. Lawler and Gail S. Risch

Lawler and Risch report on a study done of newly married couples (together for five years or less). The study attempts to identify potential problem areas early in marriage, including worries about financial debt, sexual compatibility, and the demands of balancing job and family. Lawler and Risch examine how core problems tend to change over time, and that problems in marriages tend to get worse, not better, over time. The researchers point to the need for pre-marriage counseling for couples, especially in order to air problems early so they can be responded to effectively.

Key Words

conjunction	joined together
laity	people of a religious faith not in the clergy
friction	clashing between two parties; disagreement
interfaith	of two or more different religious faiths
practitioners	one who practices a profession
egalitarian	marked by the belief in human equality
per se	by, of, or in itself; as such
alluded	referred

Two of the most troubling aspects of American society today are the high rate of divorce and the fact that divorce in one generation increases the likelihood of divorce in the next. Current divorce statistics indicate that most divorces occur for couples married less than five years and that the proportion of divorces is highest for couples married three years. This is not surprising, since a recent study finds that couples face serious conflicts over the use of time, sex and money in their first years of marriage.

The national study of the first five years of marriage was conducted by the Center for Marriage and Family at Creighton University, in conjunction with the Secretariat for Family, Laity, Women and Youth of the United States Catholic Conference, the National Association of Family Life Ministers and Catholic Engaged Encounter. A sample was drawn from a national population of couples who between 1995 and 1999 had completed the premarital inventory known as FOCCUS (Facilitating Open Couple Communication Understanding and Study). The majority of respondents were Caucasian, Catholic and in first marriages; 54 percent were female and 46 percent were male.

Problem Areas

One part of the study asked respondents to rate 42 issues that might be problematic during the early years of marriage. The number one problem reported by newly married couples was balancing job and family. Since dual-career marriages now represent about 60 percent of all marriages in America, this is not surprising. The difficulty of juggling jobs, couple-time together and parenting (if there are children) requires serious attention.

The second area of concern to couples was frequency of sexual relations. Problems with sexual relations in the first years of marriage are often related to the spouses' struggles to understand each other's sexual needs and languages. That frequency of sexual relations is a major problem may also be related to the overall challenge of balancing the demands on time. The third, fourth and fifth most serious problems were economic: debt brought into marriage, the husband's employment and financial situation.

The sixth area of friction was expectations about household tasks. 5 Household tasks are major marital issues for today's dual-career newly marrieds.

Although the amount of household work done by modern husbands is almost double that of their grandfathers, it is still only about half the number of hours per week done by wives. Three decades of social change have produced dramatic increases in career opportunities for women but have left the traditional division of labor within the home relatively untouched.

Respondents were subdivided into seven groups according to gender, parental divorce, parental status, cohabitation, age, same-faith or interfaith marriage and number of years married. The top two issues in most groups were the same: balancing job and family and frequency of sexual relations. Here we will list only those issues on which there were interesting differences within the groupings.

Gender. Different recreational interests were listed as a highly problematic issue by male but not by female respondents, which suggests that recreation may be more important to men than to women. Females listed two issues that males did not list: parents/in-laws and time spent together with spouse. This suggests that relational issues were of more concern for female respondents.

Children. Many issues were problematic for both parents and nonparents, but the intensity of the problem was always greater for parents than nonparents. These results suggest the need for programs specifically for parents, a majority of whom expressed interest in pregnancy classes, parenting workshops, new-parent get-togethers and refresher marriage courses—but only if child care is also provided. The provision of child care is a must if practitioners wish to attract parents to marital and parental programs.

Cohabitation. Although there were similar responses from those who did and did not cohabit with their spouses prior to marriage, the intensity level was generally greater for those who cohabited than for those who did not. Balancing job and family did not appear as a problem for respondents who had never cohabited with anyone. The husband's employment was ranked as a top issue for them but not for those who had cohabited with their spouse or someone else. This finding may be related to traditional-versus-egalitarian attitudes toward gender roles. Non-cohabitors gave evidence of more traditional gender attitudes, which may explain their lack of concern for balancing job and family and their greater concern with the husband's employment.

Age. Analysis by age revealed major differences in marital problems. For those 29 and under, debt brought into marriage and finances were the top issues; for those 30 and over, balancing job and family and frequency of sexual relations were the top issues. Though financial matters were not the biggest problems for those 30 and over, they were still a concern. In general, issues that were problematic for both age groups were more problematic for those 30 and over than for those 29 and under.

Religious affiliation. For respondents in marriages in which only one spouse was Catholic, religious difference was a priority issue.

An earlier study by the Creighton Center for Marriage and Family showed that religious differences per se were not a major problem, but how couples dealt with their differences was an issue. Developing strategies to deal with religious differences in interchurch marriages is an important task for couples during the marriage preparation process and throughout their marriage.

Number of years married. For those married less than one year, the top two issues were related to money: debt brought into marriage and financial situation. The third and fourth most problematic issues were frequency of sexual relations and balancing job and family. For those married four to five years, balancing parent and couple time ranked as the number one issue, followed by balancing job and family. The issues included on these lists are similar from one year-group to the next, but the rank order varies from group to group. And as the number of years married increases, the intensity level of problematic issues also increases, reinforcing the increased marital distress alluded to earlier.

Marital Adjustment

When asked how they were doing in their marriages, respondents reported they were generally doing well. When their marital adjustment was assessed on a standardized scale, however, the picture was not so rosy: approximately 20 percent of both males and females were no better than slightly adjusted. This is a disturbingly high percentage in the early years of marriage. No significant differences in marital satisfaction were found between spouses who were male or female, spouses who cohabited or did not cohabit prior to marriage and spouses who were in same-faith or interfaith marriages. But a larger percentage who were 30 and over, who were in their fourth or fifth year of marriage and who were parents scored in the distressed range. Over time, marriage does not get easier; it gets more difficult, at least in the first five years of marriage covered by the study. Couples, and those who work with them, could profitably focus on strategies for balancing time between job and family and between spouse and children, sexual questions, financial questions, communication and conflict resolution problems, and the special problems faced by parents.

Conclusion

Amid the variety of marital issues uncovered in this study, balancing job and family and frequency of sexual relations were clearly the top issues for the majority of respondents. Couples need strategies to achieve a balance between job and family. Possibilities include placing limits on both job and family, trade-offs between wife and husband in family and career responsibilities over the life span, choosing a one-career marriage and limiting the combined work of both spouses to no more than 60 hours per week. Another possibility is expanding the marital frame of reference to embrace three careers, the separate careers of each spouse and their joint career as parents. This could be a useful strategy for contemporary newly marrieds.

Couples also need strategies to deal with sexual issues. It is not 10 surprising that there would be problems with sexuality in the early years of marriage, as couples learn each other's sexual languages and needs and as they learn the different approaches of men and women to sexuality. The likelihood of such problems is a clear signal of the need for effective premarital and postmarital resources to help couples recognize possible sexual problems, deal with them and move beyond them in their married lives.

The importance of dealing with these issues in marriage preparation and enrichment programs cannot be overemphasized. This study highlights problems that newly married spouses reported; the same issues were voiced in the focus groups that preceded the study. The best way to be truly helpful to couples in the early years of marriage is to listen and respond to their stated needs, rather than to fit all couples into a prepackaged program.

What Did You Read?

1. What do Lawler and Risch find troubling about the relationship between divorce and subsequent generations?
2. According to the authors, what is the number one problem reported by newly married couples?
3. According to the authors, over the first five years, does marriage get easier or more difficult?

What Do You Think?

1. Do you think it is important for at least one spouse to limit career options in order to leave time for parenting?
2. If both parties in a marriage have careers, is it realistic to expect the husband to do 50% of the household chores? Why or why not?
3. Do you think there is enough legitimate support for couples who need strategies to deal with sexual issues?

How Was It Done?

1. How do subtitles help to clarify and organize the material Lawler and Risch present, that in the first five years of marriage, common problems occur?

2. The evidence in this article is structured around what kind of survey or study?

3. In the conclusion, general prescriptions are given to help couples achieve a balanced, fulfilling marriage. Is this an effective method of providing closure to the article?

The Marriage Rehearsal

Peter Carter

In this article that appeared in the magazine Chatelaine, *the author details the weddings of Kiran Pal and Geoff Pross. Pal and Pross were married multiple times, traveling the globe to experience different traditional wedding ceremonies. By comparing experiences in places as varied as Borneo, Japan, and South Africa, Pal and Pross find interesting differences and some important commonalities.*

Key Words

eccentric	unusual; strange
obligations	things one is bound or obliged to do
consummate	to make marriage complete by sexual union
boors	rude or insensitive people
lexicon	the vocabulary of a language
salacious	lustful; arousing sexual desire or imagination
forbearance	patience; leniency
loincloth	an article of cloth worn about the lower abdominal areas and hips, often as a sole article of clothing
tiara	a decorative jeweled or flowered headband or semicircle for formal wear by women

The taxi ride between my house and Lester B. Pearson International Airport is about 15 minutes on a good day and on this particular Friday morning, traffic was light and the sky clear. So, for a quarter of an hour—and because I asked—I was treated to the story of a marriage as lived by one chatty Ethiopian cabbie. He had arrived in Canada a dozen years ago. Here, he met and fell in love with a woman, but his parents wanted him to follow his two older brothers and have a traditional arranged marriage. He ignored them, listened to his heart and married for love. Now, he and his wife have one little boy who needs extra help at school and Dad drives a cab about 60 hours a week to make ends meet. Life, he said as I was exiting his taxi, is hard. "You know," he said, "after all these years, I realize something. My father was right. I should have gone for the arranged marriage."

It seems that no matter where you go, marriage is complicated.

If I'd told the driver why I was catching a plane, he probably would have wanted to join me. I was flying to Whistler, B.C., to meet Kiran Pal and Geoff Pross, two self-styled marriage experts. Their claim to fame: Kiran, 30, and Geoff, 31, had been married eight times in traditional ceremonies around the world. Eight times. To each other. By the time you read this, they will have had a ninth wedding, scheduled for mid-July, in British Columbia.

Kiran and Geoff had been a couple for eight years since graduating from university. Then, in the fall of 2000, they decided to get married—but not until they thoroughly researched the roots of the institution. In the hope of learning as much about weddings—and each other—as they could, they took all their savings, left their Vancouver home and pursued this eccentric year-long project.

The pair moved to eight different countries sometimes for a few days, sometimes for a few months—made friends and shared their plans with the locals. They would ask about traditional wedding ceremonies, find someone to perform the rituals and then hire people to throw the parties. The price tag on this elaborate 12-month wedding? "The price of a new SUV," Geoff told me. "A really fancy SUV," Kiran added.

Their first ceremony was an Aboriginal affair in South Australia. There, they became honorary members of a tribe, adopted honorary godparents and sat around a fire while an elder wielded a flaming stick and told the newlyweds about their obligations. The sixth wedding was a Celtic celebration in County Leitrim, Ireland. For that one, Kiran and Geoff got bound to each other at the wrist. It's called a handfasting, and the couple is supposed to consummate the marriage tied up. (Each ceremony holds its unique appeal.)

At the Thai marriage, a pair of elders—spry ones, I might suppose—did the traditional job of warming up the marriage bed before the newlyweds hopped into it. (If experience is any teacher—I've got 16 years of matrimony under my belt—I bet the older married folks just read a bit, gave each other a peck on the cheek and nodded off.) Kiran and Geoff exchanged vows in a Shinto ceremony in Japan, watched a pig get slaughtered in Borneo and drank litre after litre of some horrid drink called Kill Me Quick in Africa.

I went to meet them not so much to hear details of their trips (I can wait until the book that they're writing comes out) but because I hoped they might answer a couple of simple questions.

First, what is up with marriage? Statistics show that most North American couples live together before they tie the knot, and even though some figures indicate a 42 percent divorce rate in this country, we never seem to give up. The wedding business is hotter than ever (see A Snapshot of Canada's Bridal Biz). Is it like this in the rest of the world, too? I once heard that the phrase "Till death do us part" was invented when a person's lifespan averaged 34 years. My question: are all cultures into this long-term business or are people who shill for the death-do-us-part thing out of their minds? Some days, you have to wonder.

The second question I had was about wedding ceremonies them- 10 selves. Are they worth it? Anybody who's been involved in planning a wedding knows how stressful it can be, that you sometimes have to tread the steps from engagement announcement to marriage vows as gingerly as if they were littered with landmines.

One group of relatives wants a big to-do, the other kind of hopes the couple elopes. The groom would like to invite his university pals, but the bride knows they're nothing but a bunch of hard-drinking all-night-partying boors.

I remember more about planning my wedding than I do about planning my career. I recall debating what kind of cutlery we would use at our reception but I don't ever remember talking about whether we'd raise the kids Catholic.

It strikes me as pretty weird. When you think about it, weddings are but one small part of marriage. Just like giving birth is one of the tiniest parts of raising a child. So, there's really no point knotting ourselves up over the details, right?

Wrong.

There must be something to this long-term marriage thing be- 15 cause everybody's into it. Kiran and Geoff discovered people everywhere have similar attitudes toward getting hitched. For example, here's what they were told when they got married in Australia: "With the Adnyamathanha people, if you break up you have to come back to where the marriage took place, find the burning sticks and throw them in opposite directions. And then you're not to see each other ever again and you cannot enter the community as a couple." Only the Celtic handfasting ceremony offered any chance of dissolution. The others were for life. And that answered my first question.

As for No. 2, I realized, after meeting Kiran and Geoff, that the wedding and everything that leads up to it is a preview—or a trailer as it's known in the movie biz—for the epic thriller called Married Life.

"The funny thing is," Kiran says, "we went on this journey because we wanted to get away from people fussing over little things, like brides freaking out when their bouquets don't arrive on time. But what we found were people interfering and fussing wherever we went."

And let's face it: the way you handle the interfering and fussing prepares you for life together. "They say travelling is living life in a hurry," says Geoff. "And we had all these experiences in a short period of time—and we had our differences. Kiran would want to do it one way, I'd want to do it another. We had to solve our differences, so we learned how to get past hurdles together."

Case in point: what's the most important word in the married person's lexicon? Compromise. A couple who gives in to each other once in a while stays together. And what teaches this better than hosting a wedding where you have to entertain 150 guests who include, for example, the bride's estranged stepfather, the groom's salacious brother-in-law and a few people both families deny even knowing?

If a couple doesn't compromise when it comes time to getting 20 married, they're doomed. Did Kiran and Geoff compromise? You're darn right they did. At their very first wedding, among the Australian Adnyamathanha, they had to eat kangaroo meat. Kiran and Geoff are both vegetarians. "Yeah, we agreed," says Kiran. "But at least it hadn't been domesticated." A pretty tiny compromise, you might think. But eating things you hadn't planned on—especially your words—is a huge part of staying married.

What about the generations-old marriage-saver called living in denial? Of course, marriage is based on love, acceptance, trust and forbearance, but sometimes indifference and ignoring things that just don't make sense go a long way to getting you through the day. Weddings are perfect practice for this. Everywhere.

When Kiran and Geoff were getting married in the Iban tradition in Borneo, they had to pick little candies off a banana tree. Only after they did this were they informed that the bananas symbolize shrunken enemy heads. "An Iban warrior," Geoff says, "had to take at least one head before being allowed to marry." We all adhere to traditions we ignore the meaning of. According to statistics, 96 percent of Canadian brides get married in a virginal white or ivory gown. As if.

Weddings also groom you for the little surprises that life never stops springing on you. Back in Borneo, Kiran and Geoff were dressed up—he in a loincloth and she in a beaded shimmering dress—and they put on a feast for more than 100 people. And just like at my wedding, one trusted guest was responsible for videotaping the affair.

At my wedding, my brother Alex was in charge of the camera and it became clear that he enjoyed our Polish dance band because during our ensemble's version of "I Just Called to Say I Love You," the camera starts polka-ing. That scene adds a grace note to the cherished video record of our special day.

"In Borneo," Geoff says, "the camera guy should have been zoom- 25 ing in on Kiran's sparkling new headdress—a silver tinkling thing with beads on it—and then you hear the squealing of the pig being slaughtered. So, guess what got videotaped? You guessed it—the pig intestines."

In life, as in wedding ceremonies, sometimes you get the tiara and sometimes you get the intestines.

Weddings also make a couple say "I do" several times. That can't be a bad thing. Kiran maintains that their year-long journey from wedding to wedding forced them to reiterate and demonstrate their love for each other on innumerable occasions. At least eight times they professed their undying devotion. "There's never too much reassuring the other person how much you love them," she says.

Their various weddings shared other characteristics. In Australia, the couple not only marries each other; in the Aboriginal tradition, once they marry into another family, they are responsible for the members of that other family. I, as well as anyone who's had a brother-in-law move in with them "until he gets a place," will agree that there isn't one society on the planet where you don't marry all the members of a family.

It goes on.

During the Iban ceremony in Borneo, Geoff had to do a warrior 30 dance. He recalls it this way: "I did my best, and the shrieks of laughter started up immediately." Like I said, I've been married 16 years. I have three children. I know from getting laughed at.

Finally, every ceremony that Kiran and Geoff found themselves involved in invoked unseen forces. Wherever they went, weddings were spiritual events.

Kiran again: "We had to believe we were spiritually connected to the land in the Aboriginal ceremony. In the Shinto ceremony, God was called to witness the event. It was like that wherever we went."

I recently read that almost 75 percent of Canadians who have traditional weddings include religion as part of the ceremony. And if nothing else preps you for life, that does. Because God knows, sometimes it's pure faith that gets married people through their daily lives.

Still, with all of Kiran and Geoff's experiences and rituals, I thought there was something missing. So, I'd like to add one detail—maybe a moment of silence or a boring rest period during which nothing happens—to every wedding reception, wherever it takes place. Because you might as well rehearse for marriage's best part, too.

En route to Whistler, I spent a night in an inexpensive hotel near 35 the airport. This place had walls so thin I could hear exactly what was going on in the next room. I'm not exaggerating. My neighbours were named John and, from what I could gather through the wall, Emmy.

I didn't mean to eavesdrop, but no sooner had I flopped down on my bed than I heard laughter coming through the flowery wallpaper.

And I'm not talking faint giggles, either. I could make out each tee and every hee as well as everything in-between.

Their mattress squeaked. While I don't know for certain that John and Emmy were a married couple, it sure sounded like it.

Because from what I could tell, Emmy was in bed reading the paper and eating chips and John was in bed beside her watching the game. He was also having a few beers. Which, apparently, he didn't do very often, because Emmy sweetly chided him. It was OK, though, because "This," she reassured him, "is a special occasion."

Then after a half-hour or so, I heard the newspaper rustle. She said, "I'm going to sleep. G'nite, dear. Don't forget to turn out the light."

"G'nite," said John.

Then there was silence, except for the sounds of two people getting comfy enough to nod off in peace. Ask any longtime married person, including my Ethiopian taxi driver—the one who works 60 hours a week and really needs a break. I'm sure he'd agree with me. It just doesn't get any better than that.

40

A Snapshot of Canada's Bridal Biz

Sept. 11 has sent people scurrying up the aisle. Wedding-industry types report a marked increase in reception-hall bookings and a return to traditional ceremonies. All those things that Kiran and Geoff were celebrating around the world have moved up the priority ladder—love, commitment, marriage, family, community.

Average age of first-time bride: 27
Average age of first-time groom: 29
Average number of guests per wedding: 170
Average size of wedding party: 12
Average number of functions—showers, stags, pre-nup suppers, etc., per wedding: 9
Estimated average wedding cost: $22,460
Average honeymoon cost: $4,650
Length of average engagement: 14 months
Average combined income of the engaged couple: $77,364
Percentage of brides who choose a long white or ivory gown: 96
Percentage of engaged couples who've known each other longer than three years: 69
Percentage of couples who've known each other less than a year: 3
Percentage of brides who say they'll change their surnames: 60
Percentage of couples cohabiting before they marry: 64

What Did You Read?

1. What is the average estimated cost of a wedding today?
2. What similar characteristics did Kiran and Geoff learn that other cultures share in their wedding ceremonies?
3. Did Kiran and Geoff find any positive benefits from so much "fussing" over the details of their wedding day? If so, what were they?

What Do You Think?

1. Do you feel compromise is the most important aspect of marriage or a good relationship? Why or why not?
2. Do you personally believe there is importance attached to the ritual of a wedding day?
3. Do you think it is important for a wedding to be a communal affair? Why or why not?

How Was It Done?

1. How important are factual statistics to the development of this article?
2. Does the large number of statistics trivialize the argument or give it credence? Discuss.
3. Does the story of Kiran and Geoff get lost in the statistical evidence or does it serve as an interesting story that "glues" the plethora of information together?

5

American Cities and Towns

Since the end of World War II, America has experienced a fundamental shift of the population from cities and rural areas into suburbs. One effect was that inner cities across the nation fell into decay. The initial response by cities was to expand their own borders, to incorporate the outlying bedroom communities. In recent years, however, cities have been fighting to get citizens and businesses to move back into their inner core. This new dynamic has the potential to create new, vibrant urban centers, but that result is far from certain. Cities across the nation also face their own special circumstances. For example, New York works to recover from the attacks of September 11, 2001; Los Angeles fights against nature to provide for its citizens; and Detroit struggles with high crime and high rates of illiteracy.

Of course, not everyone lives in a large city. Many live in suburbs or bedroom communities, often many miles from a city's center, creating issues of traffic congestion and pollution—the results of what has come to be referred to as "suburban sprawl." The suburbs themselves are also an issue in terms of the lifestyle they promote. This lifestyle, some have argued, has made America too soft and vulnerable to its enemies. Others see in suburbia crass commercialism and conformity. Still others see the American dream realized.

Small towns still dot the nation, but the image many Americans have of small town life, gleaned from decades' old television sitcoms, is often at odds with the new realities. In Hershey, Pennsylvania, a small company town was shaken to its core when a board of trustees, dominated by out-of-towners, sought to sell off Hershey Foods. Small towns also find themselves facing issues typically associated with large cities: immigration and an increase in single-parent homes. Yet most small towns do not have the resources or the experience to cope with these new problems.

Whether it is a big city, a suburb, or a small town, the issues matter—this is, after all, where we live. We need to know and confront the problems.

In this chapter, the Writing Lesson covers audience, tone, and purpose. Your use of language can improve with awareness of these aspects of writing. Audience focuses on the issue of who is going to read a work, so the use of appropriate diction and understanding any biases inherent in an audience need to be understood. Tone is an important part of conveying meaning as well, and you can shape your use of language to create the particular tone desired for a particular work. An author's purpose of writing is described in the following ways: to educate or inform, to express or entertain, and to persuade or argue. Developing a sense of purpose gives you, the writer, the best sense of what should be included in a work, why it should be included, and how it should be stated. The Chapter Writing Assignment emphasizes public discourse—a work of writing intended to be read by many in a public forum—since the theme of the chapter, America's cities and towns, gives rise to topics that are of concern to many.

THE MAIN EVENT READING

On the Playing Fields of Suburbia

David Brooks

Since the end of World War II, Americans have left their cities and moved into suburbs, housing tracts that exist outside of urban centers, connected often by freeways. These planned communities, peopled largely by the middle and upper-middle class of America, are remarkable in many ways for their uniformity: not only the tract houses but also the predictable strip malls, pocket parks, and SUVs. David Brooks reports on the virtues of such a life, and whether Americans raised and living in suburbia are made of the same mettle as farmers and others who work with their hands. He reviews the work of historian David Victor Hanson, who is critical of today's suburban man. Setting this discussion in light of the terrorist attacks of September 11, 2001, Hanson is pessimistic about America's ability to respond to terrorism, but Brooks sees reason for optimism.

Key Words

McMansions	large, expensive homes, yet all of a similar design so that they lack originality and distinction; very expensive tract homes
pachyderms	elephants

cosseted	pampered; treated as a pet
Jeffersonian	relating to Thomas Jefferson; a philosophy emphasizing individual self-reliance, as opposed to relying on institutions such as government or business to provide for one's needs
obsequiousness	subservient; extremely attentive in hope of gaining favor
surfeit	excess; an overabundant supply
agrarian	of or relating to farms and farmers
inculcates	teaches by frequent repetitions or admonitions; implants
yeoman	a person who owns and cultivates a small farm
meritocracy	a system in which the talented are chosen and moved ahead on the basis of achievement
abstemious	marked by restraint, especially from consuming alcohol

If you fly over Scottsdale, Arizona, and look down at the vast brown desert, here and there you see little ribbons of green fairways, with country-club communities clustered around them like reeds around ponds—tile-roofed McMansions with mouse-pad lawns and little blue dots where the backyard spas are. Along the nearby roadways you can see massive two-tier malls. In the front tier are strings of chain restaurants that, if they merged, could form Chili's Olive Garden Outback Cantina, serving enough chicken wings to fill a canyon. In the back tier a line of megastores stretches out like a parade of pachyderms: Target, Petsmart, OfficeMax, Lowe's, and Barnes & Noble. Gutting diagonally across the empty parking spaces in between are ninety-eight-pound women in aerobics outfits steering 4,000-pound SUVs (these days, the smaller the woman, the bigger the car). If a modern Pied Piper came down to round up all the kids, it would be called The Gathering of Ashleys, and hundreds of cheerful ten-year-old girls would pour out of the Gaps and Abercrombies and Wal-Marts, drawn by the piping of Britney Spears. They'd have their peach tank tops, their 2 Grrrls brand strawberry-scented spritz, and their pink backpacks, and they'd be led, mesmerized, to soccer practice.

    As I looked down on this scene from the air, one question popped into my head: Is this nation really ready to fight a war? From this vantage point America's culture seems better suited to produce Temptation Island 2 contestants than soldiers who can withstand the rigors of combat. From up here we seem too affluent and comfortable to be tough-minded, too cosseted by our own peace and prosperity to endure conflict. If one wonders about this sort of thing, it's helpful to consult the writing of the historian Victor Davis Hanson. In different guises Hanson comes down on both sides of the issue, and so is doubly illuminating.

[margin notes:]
McMansions— reveals sarcasm

mixing product names

the uniformity of the suburbs

commercialism

comparing the serious and the absurd

Hanson is a Jeffersonian, contemptuous of much of the commercial American culture he sees around him. The suburban information-age man, he writes in his book *The Land Was Everything* (2000), lives in a world of dross-"video games, romance novels, plastic Santa Clauses, and three-pound bags of Snickers." He is a pampered and conforming creature who "depends on someone else for everything from his food to his safety."

Brooks
directly
quotes
Hanson—
Why?
value of
the original
words

> Obsequiousness, rather than independence, is more likely to feed his family . . . his entire ideology [is] no ideology at all other than the expectation of material surfeit and liberty to enjoy his gains as he sees fit.

Hanson believes that farmers and people who work with their hands are the ones who embody the virtues that make countries strong. They are independent and resilient, stewards of the land in times of peace and courageous when called to war. And Hanson matches word with deed. He lives in the same farmhouse that his family has lived in for five generations. He leads a life half cerebral (he founded the classics program at California State University at Fresno) and half muscular (he still works his farm, growing grapes, apricots, plums, and peaches, which drains his academic income and then some). Farming for him, as for most family farmers, is no easy task. He writes in *The Land Was Everything*,

quotes
again

> Agriculture, I think, will always be war. At the conflict's most dramatic, during an unseasonable storm or foreclosure warning, the agrarian fight becomes real bloodletting, a brutal, horrific, yet sometimes heroic experience.

lessons
from
farming

Even in normal times there are struggles with weeds and pests, family squabbles, ruinous prices, developers, and sprawl. Hanson believes that the fundamental lessons in life are learned painfully, and that farming teaches that the land is permanent and individuals are temporary. Farming, he feels, inculcates a tragic view of life: bad things happen, and character is determined by how one accepts the hand of fate.   5

Reading Hanson the Jeffersonian, and observing how far the nation has traveled from the heroic, struggling life he celebrates, one may despair. But Hanson is also a military historian. He has noticed that Western constitutional democracies produce incredibly lethal armies. Though individualistic and loose, these democracies are able to defeat disciplined, fanatical and even barbarous dictatorships. They can do this, Hanson argues, because they have inherited Greek ideas: Science should not be subservient to religion, so democracies are usually technologically superior to their enemies. Citizens are entitled to private property, so democracies tend to be capitalist, and thus richer. Dissent is encouraged, so war aims and strategies are honed through argument, and junior officers can improvise. People are equal, so countrymen feel

connection
to military
history—
democra-
cies as
good fight-
ers

that they are all in the fight together—hence they battle with greater loyalty to one another. Hanson has explored these themes in a series of books, *The Western Way of War* (1989), *The Soul of Battle* (1999), and *Carnage and Culture* (2001). He is proud of how America has responded to the war against terrorism, and confident that it will triumph.

I phoned Hanson and asked him to reconcile his optimism about the current war effort with his pessimism about the state of American culture. He explained that America's institutions remain strong even if its culture is growing weak. Much as I admire Hanson, I'm not sure I was persuaded, because, as he himself emphasizes in his books, war is really a test of a nation's civilization. And yet I sense that many people share both Hanson's anxiety and his confidence. America does seem at once crass and materialistic and strong and indomitable. The problem is that we have lost the ability to explain our strength to ourselves. In the eighteenth century it was easy to see how a nation of yeoman farmers could put aside their ploughs and fight for independence. Their rugged lives prepared them for the struggle. In the nineteenth century it was easy to see how a nation of hardy pioneers could slog through a brutal civil war and then propel the nation to global pre-eminence. Even in the twentieth century it was easy to see how a population of tough factory hands and Depression-hardened workers could translate their survival skills to the battlefields of Europe. But what about now, in an age of mass affluence and office parks, an age in which so many people lead their lives in front of keyboards and video screens?

(margin note: Hanson's distinction between culture and institutions)

(margin note: rough life of past generations)

The comforting fact is that Americans have experienced that sort of cultural anxiety frequently in their history. When the agricultural economy gave way to the industrial economy, agrarians and pastoralists warned that the country was losing its soul. When Fredrick Jackson Turner pointed out that the frontier was closed, cultural pessimists argued that the country was losing its pioneer vigor. And now, when brain power is replacing muscle power, we are anxious once again.

And yet America is still somehow strong enough to be the world's dominant power. Our supposedly complacent suburban nation was able to endure, and win, a forty-year struggle with communism. Though we are fat and happy, our workers are still the most productive in the world. On average, we work 350 hours a year more than the Europeans, and longer hours than even the Japanese. Though we seem credit-card crazy, somehow there is little evidence that we are actually decadent. Crime rates have dropped dramatically over the past decade. Teenage pregnancy rates are down. Alcohol consumption is down.

The only plausible explanation, I think, is that suburban life is more 10 arduous than it appears, and provides more character-building experiences than we imagine. Sure, there's less drudgery and backbreaking labor than there was in the past, but there's also far more uncertainty, and life is far more competitive. Almost nobody grows up today

Brooks thinks suburban life is tough. Why? Does that really compare to past hardships?

assuming that he will work in the same profession, or at the same plant, as his parents. Almost nobody grows up thinking that she will work for one paternalistic organization all her life. Eighty years ago a person who grew up in a wealthy WASP family had a reasonably secure status. A person who grew up black or in an ethnic neighborhood encountered certain limits to opportunity. Those limits have been reduced, and although the field is more open, the burden on the individual is much greater. The essence of an information economy is that knowledge is not inheritable; each generation has to earn success over again.

why is meritocracy an ordeal?

Today's Americans face the ordeals of the meritocracy. Last year I wrote a piece for this magazine titled "The Organization Kid," about elite college students. During the reporting of that piece I developed some doubt about the quality of moral instruction on campus, but nobody would doubt that today's young people lead arduous lives. Since grade school many of them have been hitting the books, mastering skills, chasing down growth experiences. They grapple with the effects of divorce and the temptations of a media world that offers them access to excess. Yet when they get to college, their work ethic blows away that of any previous generation.

Talking with people in suburbs across America, one finds that as a nation we feel that the most pressing scarcity in life is not of money but of time. Hanson's farmers have callused hands; today's suburbanites have color-coded charts on the refrigerator indicating where each kid has to be at each moment of the week. They live in an over-communicated world; they have to be ruthless editors in the war for their attention. They are self-disciplined, too—this is surely the most abstemious moment in American history. (The yeoman farmers hit the moonshine, whereas caffeine, a stimulant, is the drug for our age.) Moreover, these suburbanites still find time to coach Little League teams, teach Sunday school, and take their kids hunting and fishing.

True, none of this meritocratic striving is proof of moral toughness. But as the Greeks taught us, good habits produce good virtues. I've been back on college campuses since September 11, and those striving kids are now having serious debates about the war effort. They were always morally earnest; now they're directing the determination they brought to their SAT prep courses to an examination of their life courses and the possibility of public service. Kids I met six months ago who had their eyes on investment-banking jobs are now suddenly thinking about careers in the CIA or the State Department.

affluence as a corrupting influence

America is perpetually on the brink of being corrupted by its own affluence—but only on the brink. We are less shallow than we appear. If you fly over Scottsdale, Arizona, you fly over homes owned by people who slogged their way through medical school and ER duty, or negotiated the booms and crashes of the high-tech industry, or handled a management team or a lifetime of divorce cases. They look stupid puttering around the fairways in their golf shorts, but they usually have something interesting to tell about their pasts. If we could understand how the lives they have lived have inculcated the virtues we admire, I think we would begin to appreciate that this nation has achieved a paradoxical and inexplicable condition: suburban greatness.

an oxy-moron?

What Did You Read?

1. Brooks describes suburbia as seen from an airplane at the start of this essay. What does his tone reveal about his feelings toward suburbia?

2. Why is Victor Davis Hanson contemptuous of the modern suburb and the people who live in it?

3. What does Hanson say about western democracies and war?

4. What is the basis of Brooks's assertion that life in the suburbs may be more arduous than Hanson believes?

What Do You Think?

1. Do you believe that suburbs produce and encourage conformity and uniformity? Why or why not?

2. Is Hanson's critique of a modern suburban man fair or unfair? Explain.

3. Brooks states that Americans are "fat and happy," and that previous generations who faced great turmoil—such as the Revolutionary War, the Civil War, and World War II—were raised in times of great hardship. Why then is Brooks optimistic about the character of today's Americans to fight war? Do you share that optimism? Why or why not?

4. What Brooks calls "suburban greatness" is a paradox. Explain this paradox.

How Was It Done?

1. Explain how descriptive language contributes to the development of this work. Does the descriptive language enhance the work or detract from it? Explain.

2. The article is structured around what piece of research? How does the author's point of view gravitate around it?

3. What virtues and values does the author appeal to?

4. How is the past compared to the present in the work? What purpose does such comparison with the past have in supporting the author's thesis?

THE MAIN EVENT WRITING ASSIGNMENT

Write an essay in which you respond to one of the following assignments. Write the essay so that it could be published in a public forum,
such as a newspaper's opinion section.

1. Argue whether suburbs have been ultimately beneficial or harmful to life in America. Be specific.

2. Should cities create policies to encourage urban development,
   such as spending millions of tax dollars to revitalize their inner
   cities, or should free market forces alone decide where people want
   to do business or live? Use specific examples to defend your position.

3. How can cities best fight the problems of urban decay, crime, and
   illiteracy?

4. Should city developers make more of an attempt to work with the
   limits of their natural environment, or should developers simply
   do whatever is necessary to meet the needs of people? Explain,
   using specific examples.

5. What should America's policy on immigration be? Take into account that there are both positive and negative effects from immigration. Use specific examples to defend your position.

6. Examine issues of importance in your own local community. Pick
   one, take a stance on the issue, and defend your position.

PREPARATION PUNCH LIST

Before you begin writing the essay, you need to prepare yourself to
write. One way to prepare is to work through the following strategies.
The following could be used to respond to Question #1.

Consider reasons why people move into the suburbs
in the first place.

- People are used to living in the suburbs; many of them grew up
  in suburbs themselves, and do not strongly consider any other
  alternative

- The perception is that suburbs are better places for raising children
  and are generally family friendly; they have better schools than in
  the city

- Cities are seen as crime-infested

- Convenience oriented

- Affordable for the middle class

- Land is cheaper in the suburbs than in urban environments; people can have yards that can be havens from the stresses of everyday life
- People like the organization and planning of a suburban community

Consider specific problems with the suburbs.
- Environmental stress, including habitat destruction, soil erosion, and increased pollution
- Traffic congestion and long commutes
- Loss of open space
- Isolated lives
- Ugliness—no concern for beauty or quality in the building of the homes
- Racial segregation

Policy Reform Suggestions
- New Urbanism—creating self-contained villages to encourage people to walk to stores, parks, and theaters. Making the home part of a real community.
- Design the communities and streets in ways that will encourage residents not to drive their cars when getting places.
- Make the suburbs serviceable to mass transit, such as light rail and buses.
- Green Belts—blocking off areas outside of the city from future construction so that a part of nature remains untouched and developers work within a confined area. One way to stop urban sprawl.
- Encourage independent stores instead of franchise establishments in the commercial areas that service the suburbs.
- Stop school policies of pressuring mothers to volunteer time in the school when many mothers are working in paid employment outside of the home.
- Encourage the building of daycare centers so that working parents have an affordable place for their young children.

THE MAIN EVENT WRITING LESSON: AUDIENCE, TONE, AND PURPOSE

In writing an essay meant to express an opinion on a public issue, such as those published in newspaper opinion pages, you should keep in mind issues of audience, tone, and purpose.

Audience

In all writing situations, you should have a sense of your audience, or to whom you are writing. In some writing situations, this is quite simple. If you're writing a diary or journal entry, your audience is yourself, and thus you can express yourself however you wish. A personal letter to a friend is written to someone whom you know well. You can choose language and allusions that are mutually understood between the two of you. In some business situations, you will write to others whom you do not know well personally, but the shared business environment shapes the way you express yourself.

In writing for the general public, however, you are writing in a situation in which you will not know your reader. You want to write so you can reach the broadest possible audience and be taken seriously by that audience. In order to do that, here are a few tips:

- Use Standard American English. Avoid the use of slang. The reader may be turned off by the use of overly familiar language. Also, avoid excessively formal English. That may be too difficult or off-putting for many readers. Use language that can be plainly understood.

- Avoid excessive use of contractions, as that will make your language appear too casual as well.

- Avoid excessive use of the first-person pronoun (i.e., I, me, my, mine) as that shifts the emphasis to the author rather than to the issues at hand. Your audience will be convinced of your points by the arguments you present, not by that fact that *you* hold that position.

- Avoid excessive use of "you" because you cannot be certain who your reader is, and thus how your reader will respond to any direct reference to him- or herself.

- Appeal to values and principles that you can expect the broadest possible audience to accept. Of course, you cannot expect everyone to agree with you, but try to find areas of common ground.

Tone

Think of tone in terms of vocal communication. When you talk, a lot of your meaning is expressed through your tone. You may be joyful, sarcastic, serious, mournful, light-hearted, ironic, fearful, cautious, or confident. In fact, as many different tones that we can think of in terms of talking can also be communicated in writing.

When writing to be read by a large audience, keep your tone generally serious, but occasional humor can be an effective tool as well. Audiences want to enjoy reading a piece even as they are being educated or persuaded on some important point. In other writing situations, other tones may be appropriate.

Purpose

Another factor to keep in mind in your writing is your overall purpose. Traditionally speaking, there are three purposes in writing: to entertain (or express), to educate (or inform), and to persuade (or argue). Most pieces of writing have elements of all three: a piece written as entertainment may often have a strong persuasive element, and those written to persuade often have quite a bit of education involved as well. Think, for instance, of a voter's information pamphlet, which features persuasive essays by proponents of a proposition, party, or candidate. The essays ultimately wish to persuade citizens to vote in their favor, but they must present credible information as part of that effort.

In writing an opinion essay for the general public, your primary purpose is to persuade. As such, you will want your reader to walk away from your essay in agreement with your stance. However, in order to get the reader into "head-nodding" agreement, you will need to present facts. In other words, you will need to inform or educate the reader about the issues in order for the reader ultimately to see the situation your way.

Thus, as a general strategy of writing an opinion essay, you will need to do the following:

- first establish that there is a problem,
- discuss the nature of the problem,
- and then present ideas for change.

If your facts are credible and your manner is convincing, the reader will more likely reach the conclusion in agreement with your position.

THE MAIN EVENT WRITING SAMPLE

The following is an essay written for this text in response to the Main Event Writing Assignment, Question #1.

The Myth of Suburbia

On the Statue of Liberty, there is a plaque that states "Give Me *Lead-in*

Your Hungry, Your Tired, Your Poor." I wonder how many of the

good people who landed at Ellis Island, New York, might have run

for their lives if they had known they were going to end up in

"Genericville." This place has been documented in Ira Levin's

Stepford Wives, in Gary Ross's film *Pleasantville,* and in the Rolling
Stones' song "Mother's Little Helper." In the suburbs, people live
in pumpkin-shell tract homes, with postage-stamp-sized yards,
drive their SUVs to the generic strip malls, and watch their children play in organized sports leagues from the age of five. I call this

Thesis
sentence

"dotted-line living." The suburbs are ugly, repressive, and antithetical to individuality; the problem is that once suburbs are established and people have lived in them, the drug of conformity takes
effect, and the residents become drones.

First
problem

The suburbs are a phenomenon of mass production, in which
quality of life and aesthetics are not considered. Tract homes look
and feel identical to one another. The advantage of tract homes is
that they are easier and cheaper to make. They feature plastic and

Examples
of ugliness

inorganic materials from faux marble and Pergo flooring to popcorn ceilings. The sameness of the homes is dulling. Often, due to
cost considerations, the houses built on the land make no sense for
the land—homes are stuck on spots without consideration for the
surrounding terrain—and if the terrain is too much trouble, the
land is simply bulldozed into submission. The tracts spread for

Problems
of cars

miles and miles, strategically placed along major freeway systems.
Because of the need for cars to reach those freeways, the streets are

McMan-
sions

not so friendly to children. For those with more money, McMansions are the newest development—an oversized tract home, built
to appear like a country mansion, yet placed on a spot of land far
too small for the building—and part of a development of other,
identical McMansions, like so many hamburgers coming down an
assembly line.

Second
problem

The suburbs have created environmental disasters. Suburbs are
almost always built on virgin land, not previously developed land.
Wetlands, farms, fields, and forests are all devoured by the sprawl of

the suburbs, to the tune of about 1.3 million acres a year (Chiras). *Environmental impact*
The suburbs also stretch the distances between two points. Suburbs
are connected by asphalt highways that create and foster a dependency on cars and discourage strolling, bicycle riding, and min-
gling with neighbors (Chiras). In fact, suburbanites spend much of *suburban sprawl and cars*
their lives in their cars: "The average American commuter now
spends 443 hours a year behind the wheel—the equivalent of 11
work weeks—often bumper to bumper on crowded highways,
breathing exhaust fumes and polluting the air with noxious chemicals while waistlines expand and blood pressures rise" (Chiras).
The sprawl of the suburbs has done great physical damage.

The suburbs are isolating places, with ramifications that are so- *Third problem*
cial, racial, and economic. By definition, suburbs are distant from a
city core. The city contains the center of business, industry, government, banking, and culture. Therefore, the suburbs are discon- *Isolation*
nected from these. The effect is to create a false split between those
aspects of civilization and the suburbs. However, not only is one
isolated from normal activity by living in the suburbs, but there
seem to be racial boundaries as well. Ironically, the prices for these *Segregation*
homogenous homes are expensive, catering to a small sector of the
population. Those who then move into the suburbs tend to live
with a psychology based on specific rules of conformity. In most
of America, the suburbs are overwhelmingly white; thus, minorities who move into the suburbs feel pressure to conform to a
white suburban culture. That culture is specifically middle class or
upper-middle class as well. Working-class families of any race will *Economic class*
have to find somewhere else to live.

The suburbs create a lifestyle imperative, meaning there is *Fourth problem*
pressure to conform one's lifestyle to the majority's. One effect is
that working women feel enormous pressure or isolation, since the

Suburbs are for stay-at-home mothers suburban dynamic is based on having a stay-at-home mother who can chauffer children after school to soccer practice or ballet lessons. The suburban schools reinforce this imperative by overloading children with homework and pressuring parents to volunteer in the classroom. Other imperatives foster in children a

Conformity in children conformist attitude, with pressure to buy what is marketed and owned by others. The notion of "keeping up with the Joneses" begins with children in elementary school making sure they have the same products—such as backpacks, dolls, and playing cards featuring the latest TV-inspired characters—that the others do. The reason is that in the suburbs, children seldom see anything that

Lack of diversity resembles diversity of lifestyle, life choices, or attitudes. It is a fast food, strip mall–oriented life, in which convenience is of prime importance, and sophistication and originality are not to be found.

First solution: Fostering diversity Cities and counties need to take an aggressive attitude to transform the suburbs into communities that foster diversity, creativity, and progressive roles for women and minorities. One solution is the development of sustainable, good quality daycare to support working women. Correspondingly, schools need to stop depending on mothers to supply their free time in the classroom, and recognize that many women today work. In the malls, fewer franchises and more unique boutique shops that reveal daring and bold creativity in the areas of food, clothing, and household decorations would be helpful. Until suburbs embrace diversity, the lifestyle and the attitudes they foster will be stifling.

Second solution: New urbanism Suburbs need to fit on the land, not the other way around. Suburban homes are often squeezed together on plots that have been created by large land-moving equipment. Instead, the developers should be required to work with existing terrain. Additionally, the plans for the homes should be arranged so as to emphasize communities or villages, not straight, open shots to the freeway. Reward homeowners with a community they can enjoy. This is called New Urbanism, creating old-fashioned neighborhoods, only in new areas. This is accomplished, as the *Indianapolis Monthly* states, "by putting work, shops, restaurants and recreation within walking distance of home" ("Here Comes"). This new emphasis in suburban design could create an entirely new feel for the currently homogenous suburban lifestyle.

A more fundamental change is to stop building suburbs alto- *Third solution: Green belts* gether and instead rebuild and renovate in areas that are already developed. Stopping the sprawl could have obvious environmental advantages, including reducing the need for additional freeways, lowering automobile emissions, and shortening commutes. Cities and counties may need to establish "green belts" around their city—essentially zones of undeveloped land where no development is allowed. This forces developers to work inside the belt, either in a city's center or its closer-in communities, rather than simply bulldozing more land.

We cannot continue to allow suburban sprawl. Americans *Conclusion* need to get out of their comfort zone with the suburbs and look at their true impact. We need environments that sustain the new American family—culturally and ethnically diverse, with a working mother, and children who need to be stimulated, not dulled, by their surroundings. People need places to live a good life, one that promotes creativity, growth, and community. The suburbs are out of date, and they need to be changed.

Works Cited

Chiras, Dan. "From Suburbia to Superbia!" *Mother Earth News* Jun/Jul 2002: 54+ *Masterfile Premiere.* EBSCOHost. San Diego Mesa College. 2 Oct. 2002.

"Here Comes the Neighborhood." *The Indianapolis Monthly* July 2001: 32+
    Masterfile Premiere. EBSCOHost. San Diego Mesa College. 2 Oct. 2002.
Levin, Ira. *The Stepford Wives.* New York: Random, 1972.
"Mother's Little Helper." *Flowers.* Perf. Rolling Stones. Writ. Mick Jagger
    and Keith Richard. ABCKO, 1966.
Pleasantville. Dir. Gary Ross. Perf. Tobey Maguire, Reese Witherspoon, and
    Don Knotts. New Line Cinema, 1998.

ADDITIONAL READINGS

Critical Mass or Incredible Mess?

Bill Manson

*Bill Manson, writing in San Diego, discusses problems faced by many American cities
that are attempting to revitalize their long-neglected downtowns. The phenomenon
carries with it great possibilities. Crime is down, new construction is booming, and an
influx of well-heeled residents holds the promise of a new era of downtown living.
However, downtowns are still seen as a difficult place to raise children, with few parks
and inadequate public schools, and prices for new homes are too high for working-class
or middle-class families. The result is that, for now, the boom is largely led by childless
adults in their 30s and older people whose children have already grown. Thus, downtowns have not yet created true communities.*

Key Words

esplanade	a open stretch of level paved or grassy ground
enclave	a distinct territorial, cultural, or social unit
vanguard	the forefront of an action or movement
whetted	stimulated
moored	anchored; secured
acclimated	accustomed to something
antithetical	being in direct opposition
impetus	incentive; stimulus
coagulated	gathered together to form a mass or group
elitist	a person who by position or education exercises much power or influence
glut	an excess or overabundance of something

BOOMTOWN, U.S.A.: Longtime San Diegans have never seen anything like the construction explosion that has rocked downtown. In a
few years the city's core is expected to have 2 million more square feet

of retail/office space, a 46,000-seat ballpark, 3,500 more hotel rooms, a new Main Library, a waterfront esplanade and more than 8,000 new condominiums, lofts and apartments.

But how does downtown stack up as a residential neighborhood?

Proponents say downtown is an exciting, safe place to live, with all the necessities of life a short walk away. They say it is becoming a real community, with diverse and numerous shopping, recreation, entertainment and dining options.

Critics say spiraling prices are turning downtown into an enclave for the wealthy—one that's unfriendly to kids and too expensive for young families and working stiffs, blue collar and professional. They say it's become a district torn between the haves and the have-nots.

This is the first of two stories that explore the issues that have   5
beset downtown.

Downtown Pioneers

Jacqueline Seavy King, a real estate broker and developer, has been at the vanguard of downtown experimental living since 1990. That's when she got a divorce and moved with her kids—her son, Sky, now 17, and daughter, Terra, 15—to live aboard an old power yacht in the San Diego Marriott's marina. They lived in the Marriott for four years.

That whetted her appetite for downtown.

Now she and her kids live in a three-bedroom, three-bath condominium on the fifth floor at CityFront Terrace. They look down Harbor Drive, over Seaport Village and can see the Navy's aircraft carriers, which are moored right across the bay.

What's it like bringing up a family, downtown in the midst of Empty Nesters Land? Not a problem, King says.

"When they were younger, my daughter wanted to move to the   10
suburbs. But my son's always been maybe more acclimated to the downtown. It's probably easier for a boy. A little more, oh, chin up when you're out there. Now they really love the downtown."

"The main problems with living downtown," says daughter Terra, "are not having a lot of other kids around, and the schools not being so great. The downtown schools are bad. Plus you grow up faster. You're more like an adult, living downtown."

She says the reason most of her friends come to her place, rather than vice versa, is because they think living downtown is "crazy," but oh so cool.

"They always want to come here."

Terra says she loves riding her bike all the way to Point Loma around the waterfront.

She admits it's harder to do homework, with the distractions, es-   15
pecially with the cool places to hang out, like Cafe Bassam, and the mushrooming number of downtown Starbucks.

Coffeehouses aren't the only places to get a little nibble. There are plenty of places to eat downtown.

"So far this week I had lunch at Faz," says King. "Then I had Sunday brunch with my daughter at Panevino (Osteria). On Friday we went to Indigo Grill. Then Old Town is just two or so trolley stops away."

The trolley and walking are the family's two main forms of transportation since King got rid of her car a year and a half ago.

"Downtown is a wonderful place to walk," says King. "I can get from the University Club to CityFront Terrace in 10 minutes. People think the distance is greater than it is. But we have very small blocks downtown."

And, says King, downtown is slowly but surely turning into a 20 community.

"We recently started a Presbyterian church service on Sundays in the Pacific Theater downtown," she says.

And yet architect/developer Kevin de Freitas says all is not as rosy as it may seem. Especially if you're an average wage earner who would like to live with his family downtown.

As one of the few architects who has actually lived for several years in East Village with a young family, de Freitas perhaps is uniquely qualified to cast a critical eye on what's happening.

"It's very expensive to live downtown," says de Freitas, who now lives in Point Loma. "It's the most expensive in the county besides very exclusive pockets like Rancho Santa Fe. You pay a premium to live there. Oftentimes the condo (owners) are paying $400 to $500 a month in homeowners' fees on top of (their mortgage). And then to spend an additional $6,000 a year per child to send them to Harborside, which is a private elementary school downtown—if you have multiple children, that's kind of a deal-breaker.

"Like what would be the benefit to do it? We don't have pocket 25 parks in many of the neighborhoods downtown either. We only have one supermarket. And it's not centrally located to the majority of downtown. Harborview was the closest hospital, but that went out of business. So we don't have a lot. And what we do have isn't kid-oriented. Even the children's park downtown: It's a series of mounds about 6 feet tall. If you have two children, they're both lost within about one minute. They have a wading pool approximately 2 feet deep that has a zillion signs saying 'no wading, or putting your feet in'—which is completely antithetical to the way children use the water element. There's no play structure. There's no flat area. You can't play Frisbee. It's all these grass mounds and gravel.

"The problem is, it's now financially impractical to spend $5 million for a block downtown to make it into a park. Some of those opportunities may have been missed, [and] are no longer financially feasible."

Bachelors and BMWS

Gary London, by contrast, lives right on the Edge of the Known World. He recently moved into de Freitas' Row Homes on F, between Seventh and Eighth streets.

"The East Village is unique in that we're kind of pioneers down here. I think this is the last downtown neighborhood where there are what we call real estate problems upside. In other words, I believe that all of downtown values will continue to appreciate. However, you always want to locate if you can—if your decision is mostly or strictly investment-oriented—in a neighborhood that you feel has an extra impetus to create value. And East Village is that neighborhood, principally because it's just beginning its redevelopment. It's the last neighborhood to be developed in all of downtown San Diego. And with the ballpark anchoring the south part of East Village, and this address being four blocks east of the Gaslamp [Quarter], I figure that ultimately this is a can't-lose neighborhood."

London is another realty expert who has voted with his feet.

"I'm a real estate economist. I do strategic studies and feasibility 30 studies for developers and investors. I'm my own guinea pig down there."

He admits he's out there on the edge of this brave new sophisticated downtown.

"You get an element here that you don't get in the suburbs. You see homeless. And you see a level of poverty that you don't see in the normal north city suburbs. But what you get also is a very colorful neighborhood, very interesting eating establishments, you're near everything that matters downtown with respect to eating, nightclubs, businesses, transportation and so forth. And it's not unsafe. It's just as safe as any other neighborhood. I find myself walking around downtown any time of the day or night and feeling extremely comfortable."

And, he says, the denizens of his new complex are very social.

"The units have sold principally to single males. And they're young. I'm 49. I'm the old guy. The average age is in the 30s. It really is amazing. At least three of the other owners are in the technology sector. One owner is 24 years old. It takes something to be 24 years old and be able to buy a townhouse. Prices for these were about $475,000, $500,000. When we moved in, we instantaneously changed the demographics of the neighborhood. Three of us have black BMWs. So we've created a real sense of neighborhood within the row home [complex]. We socialize and hold parties together. Kevin [de Freitas] calls the project 'Row Homes on F.' We nicknamed the project 'Bachelors with Black BMWs on F.'"

Rosy Retirement

Retiree William Keith until recently lived in modest circumstances in the Salvation Army's Silvercrest residence opposite the post office.

"I enjoy the Gaslamp Quarter tremendously, and I'm 82 years old. It's all the activity. I live almost in the Gaslamp area. I love it, because here, we're in the middle of *people.* You don't get lonely. There are things to do. I can pop across to the library. Go eat. Have a coffee. Talk with people.

"People think that seniors want to look at flowers and grass and trees. They don't! They want company. They want to be out with people. What we need are places here with more modest rent for seniors. Where I am is a good start. This could be the beginning of a real community."

Successes and Failures

"I think we've had some wonderful success downtown and some significant failures," de Freitas says. "The jury's still out. It's too early to tell."

Successes?

"Horton Plaza. There's no question that was the seed that got the 40 whole thing rolling. They did a really smart thing: they [poured] an enormous amount of money in a very, very concentrated spot, and it brought people downtown who hadn't been downtown in years, if ever. It started to create a sense of safety and energy that made it enjoyable for people."

The failures, de Freitas believes, are threefold. First, the west side—the Marina District, where Jacqueline King lives—got all the money, and the east side—East Village—became the dumping ground for homeless and other shelters. Second, most people have been left out of the equation—the middle-income people who can neither afford the luxury condos nor qualify for low-income assistance. And third, the infrastructure of a normal community—schools, libraries, parks, recreational centers, which don't directly make money—are not a priority.

"Traditionally cities like San Francisco or Chicago are a collection of neighborhoods that have coagulated and formed a city. And so they're somewhat complete with their own identity. They have their own shopping, their own churches, schools, everything that a community would need. We didn't have that [here]."

The San Diego Association of Governments (SANDAG) has estimated that there will be a million new residents coming into the county by 2025.

"Sixty percent of that million will be people who already live here," says de Freitas, "primarily our children and their children, people we will want to have living here: our families."

City Council members have suggested packing them in down- 45
town, bumping up their projections to 100,000, 150,000, even 200,000
inhabitants, a number de Freitas says would be impossible to absorb.

Whatever the figure, he says, downtown can't go on merely being
a crash pad for wealthy empty nesters and retreats for CEOs from
Phoenix and Vancouver. Sooner or later, it will have to accommodate
middle-income, family-creating folks who neither have it made, nor
are down and out.

Downtown architect Michael Witkin agrees. "Any balanced community needs schools, supermarkets, libraries and educational and institutional and cultural and medical facilities, in order to support the
housing.

"The housing is only one component of a healthy balance. You
need all those other things. And those are not happening. When they
built the first supermarket downtown, the Ralphs, which was extremely successful, everybody pooh-poohed it. 'Are you crazy? A
supermarket downtown?' They actually need a couple more, right
now, to feed those thousands and thousands of houses that are
under construction. And the housing that is being proposed is for
single, upwardly mobile professionals. There is nothing planned for
families.

"The lack of affordable housing is a big, big problem here. CCDC
is trying, but how does one change the mindset of the very elitist community that we are? It's a NIMBY (not-in-my-backyard) thing."

But Witkin believes downtown is in a bubble that can't last. "No- 50
body can afford to buy these huge 100-unit condo projects. Three, four
hundred thousand dollars for the tiniest, tiniest units, and that's what
they start at! What I personally think is going to happen, with a massive amount of units in the pipeline right now, is that there's going to
be a glut of product on the market, as there was before. One Harbor
Drive [now the Harbor Club] was empty for years and years. The market couldn't sustain it. Everybody's gung ho now, but there are thousands and thousands of units in construction."

A Public Market for Downtown?

When Dale Steele and her architect husband, Mark, saw North Market
when they were in Columbus, Ohio, around Christmas 2000, they said
to each other, "Why in the world do we not have one of these in San
Diego?"

"It was the coolest place," says Dale. "They had prepared foods
there, freshly farmed eggs, fresh chickens, a wine shop, a cheese shop,
bakeries, organic foods, on and on."

(continued)

Steele, a local entrepreneur and businesswoman, lost no time when she got back. She called in the nation's acknowledged expert on public markets, Theodore Spitzer, and with him started casting about for a downtown location.

The old Police Station at Dead Man's Point next to Seaport Village won hands down.

"It's perfect. The old garage with its trussed ceilings, the central courtyard—a great place for outside dining—the parkland surrounding it, its centrality to downtown."

Steele would have only local growers and food purveyors and craftspeople in it.

"No national brands—that's not its nature," she says.

It's on Port land so it would be administered by the Port as a public facility, and it would provide seafood and fresh, organic produce grown and sold direct by San Diego growers seven days a week.

Her only problem: convincing the Port District not to demolish the old Police Station and use the land for Seaport Village expansion. To get the ball rolling, she suggests an interim agreement to set the market up for a trial five years, "because whatever happens with Seaport Village expansion is going to take five years for entitlements anyway. Then the Port can make a permanent decision."

Steele's proposal is one of many that the Port has under consideration.

Milford Wayne Donaldson, the renowned preservation architect, says Steele's idea has been tossed around for years. In a report he prepared for the Port District earlier this year, he affirmed that the 1939 WPA-financed police building is salvageable, and outlined four possible plans.

"There were various alternatives," he says, "from demolishing most of the police station and creating a central park, to keeping all the buildings with no park."

There are other proposals including one for a boutique hotel.

"But I hope [the market] will happen," he says. The Port has been holding public meetings to help it make up its mind. One thing Donaldson—and the Police Historical Association—definitely want to see: the one intact jail cell in the building turned into a San Diego police museum.

What Did You Read?

1. What are the advantages to living downtown, according to Jacqueline King?

2. According to Kevin de Freitas, what are the problems with downtown living?

3. What got the whole "ball rolling" on urban development in downtown San Diego?

What Do You Think?

1. Would you want to live in a downtown environment? Why or why not?

2. Besides the "housing component," what other things are needed to make living in a downtown area possible?

3. In your opinion, what advantages are there in trying to rejuvenate cities? What are the drawbacks?

4. What are some of the problems with the urban–suburban dynamic that has existed since the end of World War II, in which middle-class and upper-middle class families live in the suburbs, and inner cities are business centers whose residents are largely poor or working-class families?

How Was It Done?

1. How is the article divided between proponents of downtown as a safe, stimulating, and diverse environment, and the critics who say that it has become an enclave for the wealthy?

2. What kinds of examples does the author use to substantiate his point? Are they credible? Why?

3. How do the subtitles help to organize this article? What organizational purpose do they serve?

Making Cities Civil

Joseph Dolman

In Atlanta, Joseph Dolman compares how his city deals with the problems of traffic congestion with what was done in Toronto, Canada. He sees Atlanta as still living with the frontier mentality that "resources are infinite." As such, Atlanta grows outward, resisting attempts at land-use planning. The result is congestion, very long commutes, and "edge cities." These are the strip malls and office complexes that exist at the outer edges of the city. He then looks back to 19th-century Paris, which underwent an extraordinary renovation, resulting in the large boulevards that have helped make Paris one of the most beautiful cities in the world. He suggests that Atlanta, too, is due for a major overhaul.

Key Words

aggregations	groups composed of many distinct parts
bounty	something that is given generously
seamlessly	perfectly smoothly

fiefdoms	feudal estates; something over which someone has rights to control
ceded	transferred or yielded
abyss	a bottomless pit or deep gulf; moral or intellectual depths
dysfunction	impaired or abnormal functioning
livery	a servant's uniform
zeitgeist	the general intellectual, moral, and cultural climate of an era
accretion	the process or growth or enlargement by a gradual buildup
decrepitude	the state of being run-down; diminished in quality
tenements	apartments or residences, often substandard and crowded
aerated	supplied with air
efflorescence	blossoming

Can America's sprawling, car-choked, urban wastelands be saved? Can the nation's great metropolitan areas ever become more than a joyless succession of edge cities—those bleak aggregations of office boxes that rise from asphalt parking lots in the middle of nowhere and help choke off the oxygen supply of older town centers?

It won't happen immediately. But sooner or later, when we run out of room for new expressways, when we run through the last oil deposits left on Earth, when we run out of land for shopping malls the size of Connecticut, we Americans will have to make some extreme changes in the way we live. We will have to lose our illusions of endless bounty, finally acknowledge that the last frontier is gone, and scrupulously abide by a few modest rules of urban civilization. The only real question is the magnitude of mayhem we create before that day arrives.

This first dawned on me about 15 years ago, when I accompanied a group of civic-minded Atlantans on a mission to inspect Toronto's mass transportation system. Those were happier days. Progressives—at least in the South—still thought they could save their boomtowns from the consequences of mindless and explosive growth, yet preserve their cherished go-to-hell attitudes about living and doing business. My little bubble of optimism burst on the spot.

As an editorial writer for the *Atlanta Constitution* at the time, I was actually with a committee from the Metropolitan Atlanta Rapid Transit Authority (MARTA), which runs a subway system through two of the region's 10 counties. We had trekked to Toronto to study how that city had managed to seamlessly integrate its new suburban light-rail network into its older, more traditional central-city subway system. As we zoomed out toward suburban Scarborough Centre, the head of the Toronto Transit Commission casually mentioned that a single fare could whisk a passenger across 13 different political jurisdictions.

Huh? I interrupted. How in the world did Toronto convince so 5 many governmental fiefdoms to cooperate on a single mass transit project? It was the only reasonable thing to do, he anserwed. He went on to explain—in the way that a parent might lecture a particularly slow 5-year-old—that without broad public commitments across bureaucratic and political borders, almost no important projects would ever materialize. Toronto, he said, had long ago ceded its most complex intergovernmental responsibilities—such as public transportation—to a consolidated form of regional administration.

My first reaction was a fleeting irritation at these smug Canadians. I also knew the truth: The Atlanta delegation might as well go home immediately. They could never duplicate Toronto's impressive achievement. Their let-'er-rip attitude toward politics and business would not allow it. For all its pretensions of sophistication, metropolitan Atlanta lacked the civic culture that could save it from the ravages of unrestrained exploitation. They say Southerners have a keen sense of place and a fierce love of the land, but this is a lie. Look no farther than Dallas or Houston or Orlando or Atlanta. In all of these places, the rules of the jungle seem to apply. Landowners will sell out in a heartbeat if the price is right, and no one will get too bossy about what you plan to build on your new expanse.

In places like New York City, centuries of cramped housing, jammed streets and chaotic growth finally drove home a vital lesson: An urban civilization requires vigorous rules, personal restraint, and a large measure of cooperation among people with varied interests. Until recently, though, much of America remained blissfully innocent of this realization. So at the end of the 20th century there was metro Atlanta, hypnotized by its sudden wealth, roaring straight into the abyss of urban dysfunction. Not once did it consider hitting the brakes. That would have been impossible in any event, Atlanta was too culture-bound.

In his new book, *The City in Mind: Notes on the Urban Condition* (Free Press, 272 pp., $25.00), James Howard Kunstler deftly describes the deadly coagulation of traffic that plagues Atlanta today. He probes the malignancy with a pathologist's precision and a comedian's irony. And in scathing prose he makes a strong case that the "drive-in utopias" Americans built over the last 80 years can't work.

By the late 1990s, he writes, Atlanta's traffic had become intolerable: "You dared not venture out anymore to a restaurant on a Friday evening in Buckhead, the Beverly Hills of Atlanta, unless you wanted to spend half the night listening to books on tape in your SUV. Routine midday trips to the supermarket now required the kind of strategic planning used in military resupply campaigns. Mothers with children were spending so many hours on chauffeuring duty that they

qualified for livery licenses. Motorists were going mad, literally, behind the wheel—one berserker tired of waiting at an intersection shot
out the signal light with a handgun. The people of Atlanta were clearly
driving themselves crazy with driving."

His bottom line: "With Atlanta, you can forgo agonizing over the   10
future, because the present doesn't even work there." Kunstler says
the city pushed the example of "car-crazy Los Angeles to its most ludicrous and terminal stage." A few of us scolds on editorial boards and
in university urban studies programs had been warning about this sort
of thing for years. It didn't matter. The local zeitgeist never had much
interest in cities. Eugene Talmadge—a racist demagogue of the 1930s
and '40s—used to declare that he would prefer not to campaign in any
town large enough to have streetcar tracks or sidewalks. Nor did the
local zeitgeist have much truck with outsiders. The problem was, an
outsider in Georgia could be an official from the neighboring county
two miles down the road. No county wanted to work with any other
county to set up consistent land-use policies. Anyhow, politicians figured, let the government that serves developers the best reap the most
in campaign contributions.

Meanwhile, no outer-ring suburban county wanted to let MARTA
roll inside its borders. The reason was starkly racial. Public transportation was viewed as an amenity for poor blacks and little more. Few
suburbanites wanted it anywhere near their plush subdivisions and
chichi malls. One retort often heard when MARTA tried to expand past
Fulton and DeKalb counties was, "If blacks want to come out here, let
them walk!"

Fear and loathing? Even the pitiable Atlanta Regional Commission—a toothless advisory agency—was widely suspected of plotting
to rise up one day, play martial music on the radio, and impose a
Soviet-style land-use plan on helpless suburbanites from the foothills
of the Appalachians in the north to the noise-racked counties around
Hartsfield International Airport in the south. No politician of the era
dared suggest that Atlantans drive less.

But what do we do now? Do we just administer last rites to some
of our most car-dependent cities and walk away? That is apparently
what Kunstler would do. "In my view," he insists, "Atlanta has become such a mess that really nothing can be done to redeem it as a
human habitat." Its only plausible destiny, Kunstler thinks, is to become "significantly depopulated." His verdict, I believe, is way over
the top—although it can't be proven wrong empirically.

"Edge City's problem is history. It has none," writes Joel Garreau
in his 1991 book, *Edge City: Life on the New Frontier*, the work that
coined the name for those awful traffic-intensive eruptions of office
towers and malls that ring the rims of American population centers.
"If Edge City were a forest, then at maturity it might turn out to be

quite splendid," Garreau says. "But who is to know if we are seeing only the first scraggly growth?" All new urban forms seem chaotic, he points out, but overtime many organize themselves into a high degree of order and success. He cites London.

For the record, Kunstler does not have a terrifically high opinion 15 of London. As the world's first great industrial city, it was a noxious pit of factory poisons for many years—a place where the rich tried to dilute the effects of foul urbanism with faux nature in locations like Hyde Park and Kensington Gardens. The legacy of this trend has not been good for America, Kunstler argues. We aren't content to let cities be cities. We try to graft nature into them. Simultaneously we want to urbanize our countryside.

Nevertheless, most of Kunstler's book tacitly seems to validate Garreau's point. Mid-19th century Paris, he writes, "was a rat-maze of poorly connected, narrow, disorienting streets, medieval in character, with a long accretion of tightly packed buildings falling into decrepitude." On the city's east end were working-class tenements so miserably overpopulated that they surpassed the later slums of lower Manhattan. "Disease flourished to the extent that births outnumbered baptisms," Kunstler says. In short, the city was one huge blob of an urban crisis—an unfit place for business and, as Kunstler puts it, "an increasingly dubious seat of a modern civilization."

Then, in 1853, Emperor Louis-Napoleon appointed one Georges Eugene Haussmann as prefect of Paris, and he set about transforming the cityscape. He remade Paris as one would create art, not from statistics or social service casebooks, but from an urge to capture the vibrancy of humanity itself. "It can justifiably be said that Haussmann's operations gave the old quarters new life" Kunstler observes. "The Paris that is beloved today is exactly that tapestry of narrow medieval streets aerated by the broad new boulevards supporting one another at appropriate hierarchies of scale."

Beyond Paris, other chapters in *The City in Mind* describe how Berlin is making itself into an appealing place once more and how—yes—London managed (imperfectly) to come back from the dead. If urban redemption is possible in Europe, why isn't it possible in America? Maybe it is, in a city like Boston, Kunstler allows.

Atlantans, however, he fumes, could not so much as grasp their plight: "It went against their current politics, their whole belief system, really, which boiled down to the notion that Atlanta was the ideal expression of democracy, free enterprise and Christian destiny. There couldn't be anything wrong with the form of the city, the way it had crept over the landscape in a dynamic efflorescence of money, power and personal freedom, like a pulsating slime mold. Atlanta was doing what every place in the country wished it could do, producing unprecedented new wealth." Its citizens have tended to see it as what the future will be all about.

They are wrong, of course. Even if you could cram all of metropol- 20 itan Atlanta's cars and trucks and SUVs onto its expressways every day, and even if you could learn to love the slick, soulless architecture of those barren glass rectangles that line the service roads, communities that are completely car-dependent have a primary problem: They have to rely totally on petroleum—and petroleum is a notoriously troublesome resource, volatile in price and irreplaceable when it's gone. When it does go, Atlanta's way of life will change, and so will the way of life in most American metropolitan areas.

Ninety-one years ago Frederick Jackson Turner, addressing a group of fellow historians in Indianapolis, told them two fundamental American ideals developed during the pioneer era: "One was that of individual freedom to compete unrestrictedly for the resources of a continent", the other was democracy. Unfortunately, Turner noted, these twin tenets were packed with mutual hostility. The pioneers who pushed America's frontiers ever westward hated government, but the establishment of democracy required government. Once the frontier closed, he continued, the tensions grew worse. The folks who hated government had nowhere left to go, and the people who sought to establish democratic civilizations needed government more than ever. What the nation faced, Turner said that night in December 1910, was a very delicate period of readjustment from a frontier society to a civilization.

We are still adjusting. When I visited Toronto with the MARTA group, 75 per cent of that city's work force used the public transportation system to get to their jobs. In Atlanta today—after major expansions of MARTA and a traffic problem that has exploded beyond belief—fewer than 7 per cent of the suburbanites in Fulton and DeKalb counties use the system's buses or trains. Throughout metropolitan Atlanta, the U.S. Census Bureau estimates, just 4 per cent of commuters use public transit.

The average commute in Atlanta is now 35 miles per day, a figure that far outdoes Los Angeles. Compared with 10 years ago, Atlantans have about doubled the amount of time they spend in their cars. No matter. Every week 500 acres of raw land in the region is bulldozed to make way for suburban development. Georgia has the lowest gasoline tax in the nation, Kunstler tells us, and the revenue can only be used to build more roads. Our fundamental American ideal of freedom based on infinite resources remains astonishingly resilient.

A recent *Atlanta Journal* editorial grousing about Governor Roy Barnes' transportation plan is an illustration. "Estimates are that 97 per cent of us will continue using personal vehicles throughout the first quarter of this century," it said. Yet more than 60 per cent of the state's investments will be "dedicated to transit, bicycle paths and sidewalks." In 25 years, the editorial explained, traffic volume will jump 60 per cent, while road capacity will grow by less than 10 per cent. Won't people finally abandon their cars for more efficient modes of transportation when gridlock becomes a constant difficulty? Georgians have no more willingness to give up their cars than they have to relinquish their phones or televisions, the *Journal* explained.

Under pressure from Washington, though, Georgia has already 25 swallowed its natural distaste for government and done something extraordinary. It has set up the Georgia Regional Transportation Authority, which has the power to build any kind of public transit system anywhere it wants, the power to kill local development projects, and the power to say no to more local roads.

This is big. The authority won't make Atlanta more person friendly, and it won't make its expressways pleasurable. But setting up the authority does signal a realization that land and its bounty are finite, and that with a tightly packed civilization comes rules. Maybe, as Kunstler maintains, this wisdom has arrived too late. Maybe it is not widely enough shared. Maybe metropolitan Atlanta is indeed doomed. But I don't think it is.

At some point it will hit bottom. Then, as in Paris and London and Boston, civic leaders will begin to rebuild in a way that works. Atlanta being Atlanta, I would not expect the esthetic triumph Haussmann brought to Paris. But I would expect its civic nervous breakdown to end.

And I would expect today's edge cities to take their rightful place among other urban fads that failed, such as urban renewal, high-rise housing for the poor and central business districts that suddenly "mailed" themselves. We have learned this much over the centuries: If the human capacity for folly is endless, so is the human capacity for resurgence and survival.

What Did You Read?

1. What vital rule about urban civilization does Dolman feel New York City finally learned?
2. According to James Kunstler (quoted by Dolman) what is one of Atlanta's biggest problems?
3. Why is it Atlanta has been so opposed to "across the counties consistent land use policies"?

What Do You Think?

1. What is your opinion about "faux nature" in cities? Cite examples.
2. Do you think that the U.S. is still philosophically a "frontier" society?

3. In your opinion, what urban fads that you have observed will fail? What developments do you see as successful?

How Was It Done?

1. What theme centers this article?

2. What two cities are compared in this article? In your opinion, were those two good cities to choose for the author's purpose?

3. What types of expertise does the author defer to in order to support and develop the thesis?

4. How does the author structure Atlanta's transportation problem around one's love for individual freedom and democracy?

The Ecology of Hollywood

Rory Spowers

Built on a desert, in an area capable of maintaining only 200,000 inhabitants, the city of Los Angeles has grown to be home to 15 million residents by fighting against nature. Rory Spowers points out that Los Angeles has long had a reputation of being antinatural, both in its image as a Hollywood dream machine and in its urban planning. In the 1930s, they cemented the Los Angeles River, and Los Angeles today depends on aqueducts to bring the city water. Now, however, there is a movement to bring more nature back to the city, including an attempt to reestablish the L.A. River to its natural state.

Key Words

seismic	relating to the earth or earthquakes
authenticity	the quality of being genuine; not fake or artificial
chaparral	a dense thicket of shrubs and dwarf trees, commonly found in southern California
ubiquitous	widespread; constantly encountered
apotheosis	elevation to divine status; being made into a god or god-like status
usurped	to take possession by force and without right; wrongful assertion of authority
thwarted	frustrated; defeated the hopes of
aquifers	a water-bearing level of permeable rock, sand, or gravel
tectonic	relating to the crusts of the earth, especially the formation of fault lines
hybrid	composed of two different species, races, varieties, or breeds
quintessential	the most typical example or representative
cartography	the science or art of making maps

Los Angeles is an unlikely city. Built over a major seismic fault, on the edge of one of the world's most inhospitable deserts, the city has developed like the extension of a Hollywood movie set, a sprawling urban fantasy which many people feel should not really exist. Scientists have estimated that the land and water in the area could naturally support 200,000 people, not the 15 million that live there. DJ Waldie, a city official and environmental spokesman, refers to the "persistent mythology of Los Angeles that doubts its reality, its legitimacy and authenticity as a place."

Since the 1880s, the Los Angeles basin has been transformed from desert chaparral, surrounding a sleepy cattle town with a population of 4,000, to a seething metropolis that now accounts for nearly one per cent of global greenhouse emissions. It is the car culture par excellence, with over 30 per cent of the landmass devoted to streets, freeways and parking, while nine million cars contribute to the ubiquitous smog and air pollution. It is somewhat ironic that, in a city where smoking cigarettes is almost illegal, 40 per cent of the population suffer from respiratory problems due to vehicle emissions. Surprisingly, LA is now becoming the forum for some of the most progressive environmental thought in the USA.

The city is full of contradictions. Often regarded as the pinnacle of the American dream, the apotheosis of consumerism and material extravagance, it is seen as the essence of anti-nature. Paradoxically, people often move to Los Angeles because of nature; attracted by the climate, the snowcapped mountains, the ocean and beaches. The movie industry came here because of the clarity of the light, the 270 days of sunshine per year and the diversity of locations close by. The fantasy which took shape in the early years, with the introduction of palm trees and orange groves, continues today in Hollywood gardens and the city's few green spaces; native trees are usurped in favour of exotic imports as nature is moulded to conform to an ideal.

The irony continues in the fact that no city in the world is more prone to natural disasters; the earthquakes, floods and mudslides are often interpreted as nature's vengeance against "the plastic society." In *Ecology of Fear,* prominent LA writer Mike Davis portrays a sort of modern-day Sodom and Gomorrah, drawing attention to the 49 nuclear strikes, 28 earthquakes, ten plagues, six floods and 35 other forms of destruction that the city has been subjected to by Hollywood's writers and film-makers.

The fantasy has always depended on one fundamental resource— 5 water. No metropolis on the planet has looked farther afield for its supply and the fact that there are "no more rivers to bring to the desert" is a cause of much concern. The natural water table was exhausted after four decades and, when the wells ran dry in the 1890s, watermelons were smashed at the base of trees in desperate attempts at emergency irrigation. In 1913, when the controversial Los Angeles Aqueduct was first opened, diverting water over 350 kilometres from Owens Valley, chief engineer William Mulholland proclaimed that it would supply Hollywood's lawns and swimming pools forever.

Within ten years the city needed more. In 1940 the aqueduct was extended 168 kilometres north to Mono Lake, while the completion of the Hoover Dam the following year allowed southern California to tap into Arizona, reducing the Colorado river to a sad, salty trickle. This was thwarted in the 50s, when the U.S. Supreme Court settled in favour of Arizona's claim to supply. Now the city is dependent on the above, together with the State Water Project, which brings more than a trillion gallons of water per year along the 720-kilometre Californian aqueduct. This effectively removes half the water that would otherwise flow into the San Francisco Bay area, altering the flow of fresh and saltwater in the Sacramento Delta but supplying irrigation systems for the vast agricultural base of the San Joaquim valley, a desert with less than 13 centimetres of rain per year.

Almost a third of the water feeding Los Angeles is now pumped from underground aquifers. However, a combination of illegal dumping, run-off from commercial fertilisers and leakage from garbage landfills, has left some 40 per cent of the wells in southern California contaminated above federal limits. To compound the problem, half of the considerable winter rainfall, which would permeate the soil and recharge the aquifers, is swallowed by concrete drainage systems and diverted into the Pacific. Since intensive farming methods require around 20,000 litres of water to produce what an average Californian eats in a day, the issue of water supply is never far away. Desperation has led to some ambitious proposals, ranging from a plastic pipeline from Alaska to towing icebergs up from Antarctica.

What few Los Angelinos are aware of today, is that the city is actually built on a river. The basin that surrounds, the city itself was originally created by four tectonic river plates and the so-called LA river, which stretches for kilometres from The Valley down to Long Beach, passing through the Hollywood studios and Chinatown, is the central natural feature of the city. At one time, it was shaded by sycamores, oaks and willows. However, as the city was paved over, the winter floods created a threat to economic expansion and, in the 1930s, work began to erase the river altogether. "The Army Corps of Engineers built a concrete trough, put the river inside it and fenced it off with barbed wire," explains Jennifer Price, an environmental writer working on a book about humans and nature in Los Angeles. "The river became the ultimate symbol of LA's destruction of nature."

Inevitably, the concrete flood control system had disastrous ecological consequences, destroying wetland areas, which provided an important staging area for migratory birds on the Great Pacific Flyway. The empty concrete channel is now used as an area for training municipal bus drivers to turn around and it has been suggested that it be used as a freeway during the dry season. Fittingly, it is best known today as the location for Hollywood car chases.

However, plans are now underway to restore the river, recreate 10 wetland areas to attract birds, and establish nature walks, cycle paths and equestrian trails. In true Hollywood style there has even been talk about whitewater rafting through the Sepulveda Basin. Led by the Friends of LA River, a pressure group formed by poet and filmmaker Lewis McAdams, the project has pulled people together from government agencies, environmental groups and neighbourhood associations, all working together in what is being seen as a symbolic attempt to heal the split between the population and the landscape of the city. "We're beginning to wake up to the fact that nature is not something 'out there' but 'in here'," says Price. "The population of LA had forgotten that it lives on a river. The resulting hybrid river, part concrete and part natural, again seems indicative of the 'fantasy' city and its intrinsic irony. "The LA River is a social construct in the purest terms," says DJ Waldie, a prominent campaigner for the project. "It was designed as a real estate protection device and flood control system. It is a quintessential LA product, a synthesis of reality and artifice. Consequently, its rehabilitation will be an interplay between these two factors, partly real and largely artificial."

California Dreaming

Waldie maintains that Los Angeles was always conceived in these terms, as a "unique interpenetration of nature and urban development." The early planners assumed that this would be "the perfect Arcadian place to build the ideal house and the ideal garden." Of course, this dream of a Californian utopia has constantly clashed with the realities of the landscape over the last hundred years, creating what has been cited as the epitome of a dystopia.

Perhaps the most prominent feature of this modern urban landscape is "the grid," first introduced during Spanish colonisation. Colonel Philippe de Neve, the governor of Upper California in 1781, laid out plans for the town in strict accordance with regulations derived from Roman models, believed to be part of a divine plan for imposing moral order on the natural world. With the advent of cartography, which coincided with the exploration of the continent, US President Thomas Jefferson divided the country up into a giant grid. However, when the early Anglo-American settlers arrived in California, they found that the Spanish grid was at 45 degrees to the compass points which determined the direction of the Jefferson grid.

Consequently, one can still find pockets of LA where the Spanish grid remains, slicing across the modern streets at an angle.

Waldie views Los Angeles as "a place where people have always come to fundamentally reinvent their lives." It therefore seems appropriate that the city has become the forum for redefining American environmental thought. The mainstream U.S. environmental movement has been predominantly concerned with wilderness preservation or "the green divinity of John Muir and Henry Thoreau," as Waldie puts it. Interestingly, now that we have become a predominantly urban species for the first time in our history, there seems to be a shift towards issues of urban sustainability. "The idea that nature can save your soul has always been the underpinning of American environmentalism," says Jennifer Price. "However, people increasingly realise that it's not possible to preserve wilderness without thinking about the areas where we use nature the most."

Being a prime example of nature's confluence with human culture, Los Angeles dearly provides the perfect platform to examine this interaction and make progress towards a sustainable urban environment. "If we actually rethought how to retain the water that falls from the sky, we wouldn't be so dependent on water sources hundreds of miles away," says Price. Various initiatives have now been implemented in this vein: a huge waste water recycling plant has been built in Santa Monica while environmental groups like The Tree People are redesigning drainage systems to collect run-off from buildings and re-direct it into underground aquifers.

There is a feeling of optimism about the future of nature in a city 15 which has always been regarded as being in fundamental opposition to it, leading to a more integrated vision of environmentalism in the 21st century. "The idea that LA shouldn't be here is rather like the belief that you either have nature or you don't," says Price. "We stand to gain a lot more by thinking of ourselves as part of nature." Therefore, those involved with the restoration of the LA river see it as not only important for ecological sustainability and a way of linking disparate communities, but also as being of tremendous significance symbolically. "There is a feeling that if you can fix the LA River, you can fix the city," believes Price. "And if you can fix this city, it seems possible that you can fix any city."

What Did You Read?

1. Why does the author refer to Los Angeles as an "unlikely city"?
2. From where does most of the water for Los Angeles come?
3. What has become the symbol of Los Angeles's destruction of nature?

What Do You Think?

1. Of all the cities you have visited, which one came closest to being a "utopia"? Why?

2. What kinds of the things can urban areas do to help sustain the water supply?

3. How is Los Angeles the city that in some way appeals to everyone?

How Was It Done?

1. How does the article structure itself around the paradox of L.A.: "the pinnacle of the American Dream [and] the apotheosis of consumerism and material extravagance"?

2. Explain how the concrete flood control system caused disastrous ecological effects.

3. What values does the author appeal to in order to substantiate what he claims to be true and desirable about L.A.?

The Future of New York

Jonathan Alter and Geoffrey Gagnon

The largest and arguably the most important city in the United States, New York City was a focal point for foreign terrorists on September 11, 2001. Since the attacks, New York has had a long struggle to return to normalcy. New York faced problems no other city in the United States has had to face since the Civil War, including not only the physical rebuilding of the destroyed areas, but the psychological recovery as well. Alter and Gagnon report on New York's recovery, and the efforts of its new mayor on the one-year anniversary of the attacks.

Key Words

deference	respect and esteem due to a superior or elder
insouciant	light-hearted unconcern
fatalism	a doctrine that events are fixed in advance so that human beings are powerless to change them
cross hairs	a fine wire or thread in an eyepiece used as a reference line in aiming at a target
infirm	weak of will, character, or body
toxin	a poison
simulations	imitating the functioning of a system; a test or trial run
blasé	unconcerned

It's not like Jerusalem or Tel Aviv. On most days, in most ways, New York City feels almost normal, as if it had all been a dream. Almost no one seems to fear sitting in an outdoor cafe or riding a bus. After treating each other with uncharacteristic deference for a few weeks last fall, New Yorkers have reclaimed almost all of that old insouciant swagger.

Almost. The shadow of September 11 hasn't fully lifted, and won't for some time. That's because the people who live here know in their bones that there's more trouble ahead. With the president, vice president and other authorities saying, "Not if but when," New Yorkers know the "where." They sense, as most terrorism experts predict, that the "evil ones" will at least try to strike their city again.

Mayor Michael Bloomberg, the no-fuss billionaire who succeeded Rudolph Giuliani on Jan. 1, calls that thinking "needless fatalism." But he, too, knows that New York remains in the cross hairs: "We're the target because we stand for everything they hate." Bloomberg's police commissioner, Raymond Kelly, recalls sitting in the lobby of the World Trade Center after the 1993 bombing, scoffing at the terrorists' claim that they could actually take the towers down. Now he and the world know better. "They go after symbols," Kelly says, reminding a visitor that plots against New York bridges, tunnels and landmarks were foiled in the 1990s.

The human and emotional toll of September 11 will take years to sort through, but the financial consequences are already clear. Everything is more expensive in New York, and September 11 was no different. All told, six buildings and 13.4 million square feet of space were destroyed, and a further 21 million square feet damaged. About 100,000 jobs were lost, and $1.6 billion in much-needed city taxes. The total economic losses by the end of the year have been calculated at more than $50 billion. That's not chump change, even in Manhattan.

But if anxiety still gnaws at New York, it hasn't changed behavior   5 here. "I know of no major company moving their headquarters out of the city, and several are thinking of moving in," Bloomberg says. Foreign tourism is down, but visits from other parts of the United States are up. Real estate is strong, and restaurants and theaters are hanging on, more worried about the impact of the bear market than of September 11. Mental-health officials estimated that 1.5 million New Yorkers would need psychological counseling, but only a tenth as many showed up for it between September and December. Experts caution that psychological aftereffects will extend far beyond the families of victims and will linger for years. But the posttraumatic stress disorder predicted by veterans of the Oklahoma City bombing hasn't been as acute or widespread as expected.

And yet the future feels infirm. While Ground Zero was cleared far ahead of schedule—an astonishing feat of civic teamwork—the plans for what to build there seem destined to be delayed for years. Bloomberg disliked the initial Port Authority plans because they focused on office buildings when that market is already glutted downtown; he prefers that housing be built there. As for the memorial, the mayor says, "It's too early to do it. A memorial built right away is a memorial nobody is going to remember. Every single one that was any good took many years." A popular temporary memorial, two towers of light, was too disruptive to area residents. Other ideas will be tried, including an eternal flame that Bloomberg will light next week on the first anniversary.

So far the mayor is getting surprisingly good marks, especially considering the act he had to follow. Within 48 hours of the attacks, Giuliani redefined crisis leadership, not only for New York but for the world. Bloomberg, by contrast, spent an unheard-of $70 million of his own money to impose his unimposing personality on the city last fall. With no political experience, he was perhaps best known for his stated intention (since fulfilled) to fly to his home in Bermuda without telling the press.

But by quietly reaching constituencies ignored by his predecessor and by avoiding much of the usual political gamesmanship, Bloomberg is showing that the same sharp business mind that built a financial-data empire can work in city government. Cops and firefighters are complaining again about pay (a sign of normalcy), but the overall volume of municipal noise has been turned down.

"He's a grown-up and a manager, who defuses time bombs as they come up," says Mark Green, his opponent last fall. Green adds that the mayor "has not yet used the public pulpit to show where the city should go." But it's still early for that. Bloomberg is a consensus man. He took e-mail suggestions from as far away as Australia on how to handle the anniversary. The result is a ceremony that promises to be moving and dignified, with rose petals strewn on the streets, an absence of speeches and the readings of inspiring historical words from Thomas Jefferson, Abraham Lincoln and Franklin Roosevelt, plus the names of all 2,819 who died.

When he's not commemorating the event or going to funerals 10 (even now, remains are still being identified), Bloomberg likes to put 9-11 in some larger perspective. "The big threats to Americans are not dirty bombs and bioterrorism," he says. "They're auto accidents and smoking." To that end, Bloomberg has hiked the local cigarette tax and is pushing to ban all smoking from local bars and restaurants. His biggest goal for the future is education. Bloomberg succeeded where Giuliani failed in getting mayoral control of the school system. Now he and his new schools chancellor, Joel Klein, have to deliver on what he calls the "centerpiece" of his administration.

First the mayor has to ease out of a budget jam caused more by the recession than by September 11. With creative borrowing and layoffs, Bloomberg is on his way to closing a $5 billion deficit. But the $20 billion promised from Washington to help the city recover from the terrorist attacks is not flowing as quickly as New York lawmakers would like.

Money for prevention of the next terrorist attack is even tighter. Sen. Hillary Clinton says that when she asks soldiers returning from Afghanistan if they have the training and equipment they need to fight terrorism, they answer yes. When she asks frontline responders at home the same question, they answer no. New York, by most accounts, has the best emergency-response teams in the country, in part because they are the most experienced at it. But along with Washington, D.C., the city is also the most vulnerable. "We have to get to the head of the line [for federal funding], not as a matter of New York arrogance but because of the risk," says Commissioner Kelly.

Kelly says he is focused on prevention and counterterrorism, but not at the expense of fighting crime, which has continued to drop (though budget cuts in community policing have some prosecutors worried). He's beefing up the NYPD's intelligence division (now headed by a former CIA director of operations), sending detectives as far as Yemen and Thailand to question suspects, posting officers with the FBI and Interpol, and using his own experience in Washington to break down the turf fights that have long hampered law enforcement.

A new hot line—staffed by 40 detectives—responds to tips from New Yorkers that the commissioner describes as usually "thoughtful." Police dogs and showy surveillance equipment are routinely sent to landmarks, synagogues and other possible targets to deter terrorists who might be casing them. Police are recruiting from the Muslim community, but also more closely monitoring mosques and Arabic papers, as well as immigration and census records. "We're doing a lot more identification of who is in New York," Kelly says. "For a long time we didn't have a handle on it."

But Kelly admits that fully securing the city is simply impossible: 15 "You could protect the place perfectly—and have no business here." He acknowledges that the sprawling subways—targeted in foiled plans in New York and actually attacked by terrorists in Japan—are "a real concern." While metal detectors in the subways wouldn't be practical, it's hard to discern what else is being done. The Washington, D.C., subway system is speeding up installation of a $22.5 million "toxin detection" apparatus that shows no signs of being installed in New York.

One example of insufficient preparation: dosimeters, pager-size devices that can detect radiation. The NYPD currently owns 100 of them, which rotate through police precincts and are used at big events. Bolstered by new technology that limits false positives, these devices should be standard for all police officers, some terrorism consultants believe. At a cost of $300 to $400 each for the 40,000 on the force, this would total up to $16 million, seemingly a small price to pay for enhanced security against a "dirty bomb" attack. Yet Kelly says the "money's not there" for more dosimeters, even as the department moves ahead with plans for a $270 million underground command bunker. Bloomberg thinks the meters will just burden police: "Everybody can't carry everything."

Overall, the city seems more focused on prevention than on response. The mayor and his high command have under-taken elaborate disaster simulations—so-called tabletop exercises—for containing a bioterrorism attack, and the huge hospital system seems well prepared. But massive evacuation of a city like New York is simply not practical. "You have 8 million people," Bloomberg says. "You could not get them all out of town."

While a few New Yorkers are making their own preparations, most are surprisingly blasé. There has been no run on gas masks or plastic sheeting and duct tape (to secure "safe rooms" in a bioterrorism attack). Bloomberg says "enormous efforts" are underway to respond in case of terrorism, though a random survey by *Newsweek* showed that large corporations are making antiterrorism preparations on their own, without coordinating with the city.

Even frontline forces are underprotected. Robin Herbert, codirector of the Occupational Medicine Clinic at Mount Sinai Hospital, says the "respiratory safety" of Ground Zero workers clearing the site was hampered by bulky equipment that was often in short supply.

The Fire Department of New York lost 343 souls—including a large chunk of top management. But now it is losing even more to retirement, particularly in the senior ranks. That's partly a result of the enormous trauma in the department, but partly a quirk: pensions are pegged to pay levels in the final year of service, which were as much as a third higher during the past year, thanks to overtime. So the exit began. Meanwhile, the faulty fire radios that cost lives are being replaced. And both the fire and police departments are overhauling their dispatch plans. The practice of rushing to the scene on their own (as so many did on September 11, with fatal consequences) will be barred. From now on, all New York City firefighters and police will be required to go only where they are told.

Help for the families of victims has been generous. Contributions for relief poured in from around the world, and a college-scholarship fund for the children of the dead is meeting its target of raising $100 million. For those families agreeing not to sue, a federal compensation fund is offering larger settlements than in any previous disaster. Others have filed suit against Saudi Arabia, arguing that while the Saudi kingdom opposes Osama bin Laden, it has underwritten charities that funded terrorism.

Down at city hall, Mayor Bloomberg still spends much of his day dealing with September 11 fallout. The billionaire's real office (not just for show) is a Dilbert-like cubicle in an open bullpen area, a symbol of his determination to stay connected. "There's almost a pride that we went through it," he says of the city's response to the attacks. "And we're tougher for it." Imagine that: the terrorists actually toughened up New Yorkers. That's what happens when they hit us where we're strong.

What Did You Read?

1. How much is the economic loss that New York suffered because of the attacks of September 11?

2. What kinds of things have been suggested to be built on Ground Zero?

3. According to the authors, what is the new mayor of New York, Michael Bloomberg, doing for his city?

What Do You Think?

1. What do you think is most important for cities like New York and Washington to focus on: the prevention of terrorism or the response to it? Why?

2. If you had to summarize what we have learned from the terror attacks, what would it be?

3. What would you suggest is the best way to commemorate or honor those who died in the attacks? What should be done with Ground Zero?

4. How has the "commercialization" of September 11 helped New York?

How Was It Done?

1. The article focuses its support primarily around what individuals?

2. If post-September 11 is the call to action in New York City, what are those resulting actions?

3. The September 11 trauma is compared briefly to what similar type of trauma experienced in the United States?

In Detroit, A Crusade to Stop Child Killings

Alexandra Marks

Decades ago, the city of Detroit was known as the murder capital of the United States. Since the 1970s, crime started to level, and then decrease. Lately, however, crime has been on the increase again. When the victims of those crimes are children, the public's concern skyrockets. Alexandra Marks reports on how Detroit is trying to cope with an increasing number of child deaths, looking at issues of law enforcement and the justice system. In a city in which almost 50 percent of the adults are functionally illiterate and a quarter of its available office space stands empty, it has precious few resources with which to fight back. Instead, some argue that true change needs to come in the shape of moral and spiritual change.

Key Words

pulpits	raised podiums from which ministers deliver sermons
indiscriminate	without concern or distinction
criminologists	people who study crime
demographic	statistical characteristics of the human population
felons	criminals; people who have been convicted of a serious crime
normalized	made normal; conformed or reduced to a standard
turf	a territory considered by a group to be under its control
spate	a large number; a flood or outburst

Sitting in the summer sun watching boat races from the beach at Detroit's Belle Isle, Sandy Gary keeps her daughter Shaliesha close by.

It's become something she does all the time. It's the way Ms. Gary helps ensure that the smiling 9-year-old with bows in her braids is safe. Keeping kids out of danger has become an overriding concern for many parents in Detroit. Since the beginning of the year, 15 children have been murdered in the Motor City—almost as many as were killed in all of 2000.

From neighborhoods to pulpits to city hall, the trend is fueling a determination that Detroit, for decades virtually synonymous with violent crime, not become the murder capital of the U.S. again.

The spate of child deaths—some innocents caught in gun crossfire, others unintentional victims of revenge—is part of an overall hike in the homicide rate that has ticked up in dozens of U.S. cities in the past year. In a handful of them—Detroit, Boston, and Memphis, Tenn.—the number of child victims has struck a deep chord, renewing fears of the rampant, indiscriminate killings that beset many American cities during the late 1980s and early '90s.

The reason criminologists cite for the hike in the overall murder   5
rate is a combination of the economic slump, a demographic bulge of
teens in their peak crime-committing years, and a large number of
felons now back on the streets after serving their time for crimes going
back to the '80s.

But in Detroit's distressed neighborhoods, parents, grass-roots activists, and civic leaders are looking for deeper answers. What they're
finding is a community in crisis due to several leading causes. The first
is a broken criminal justice system that cycles felons in and out of jail,
angry and unrepentant. Then there are sex- and violence-obsessed
music videos, blockbuster movies, and the like, with their hard-edge
rap lyrics and glorification of guns. Finally, they've found a dangerous
ignorance when children have children and are left to raise them on
their own in isolated poverty.

Combine them all in neighborhoods where drugs and guns are
easily available, and you get what criminologist Carl Taylor of Michigan State University calls the rule of the hood.

"We have a culture that has normalized violence and ignorance,"
he says. "Many kids here see having sex and being violent as a way of
getting notches on their belts."

Looking for Solutions

But Detroit is also a community full of people determined to heal. And
they're now looking inward for both the causes of the killings, as well
as the solutions.

"We're dealing with a cultural problem here . . . and the only way   10
we're going to solve it is to get the community to step up in a mighty
way and wrap our arms around our children," says Detroit Mayor
Kwame Kilpatrick. "What we need to have here is a spiritual movement in the city of Detroit."

This is the once-powerful Motown, the country's automotive engine that's now sputtering. In 30 years, half its population has fled—
most of the middle class, white and black. Well-maintained brick
homes now sit beside boarded-up, abandoned houses and vacant lots,
knee high with grass and weeds. Teenagers openly roll blunts—the
thick, potent marijuana cigarettes—while filling up their SUVs at the
corner gas station. Top-of-the-line assault weapons are as easy to buy
as Saturday night specials at a body shop just a five-minute drive from
downtown.

But in the past decade and a half, city leaders and community
groups have fought to turn around the city and its image. Under
Mayor Dennis Archer, economic development plans spurred more
than $13 million of investment in downtown. The Detroit Tigers—with
financing help from the city—built a 40,000-seat stadium. Three glittering new casinos are drawing people downtown and generating more

tax revenues. A few blocks closer to city hall, workers are soldering glass panels into Compuware's new international headquarters.

But a dozen art-deco skyscrapers still stand abandoned, and more than a quarter of the city's usable office space is vacant. They're physical reminders of the challenges that remain—from overhauling its inefficient police department to educating the almost 50 percent of adults who are functionally illiterate.

Turmoil in the '70s and '80s

Still, Detroit is far safer than it was 25 years ago. A common joke then summed up the city's prospects: The last person out should simply turn out the lights. The homicide rate, which had leveled off after spiraling up in the '70s, was ticking upward again. In 1986, 365 children under age 16 were shot. Forty-three of them died.

One of them was Clementine Barfield's 16-year-old son. Like several of the children killed this year, he was simply caught in crossfire, as one kid shot at another.

Ms. Barfield's response was to found a group known around the city as SOSAD. It stands for Save Our Sons and Daughters and is dedicated to helping victims of gun violence and promoting "peaceful communities."

"We have to think of Detroit as a city that's not well," she says. "[What we're seeing now] is the long-term impact that violence and homicide has had on our people. Detroit has had one of the highest homicide rates in the nation for 35 years. It started to increase right after the riots in 1967, when we had a huge influx of guns and drugs dumped into the city."

In a conference room next to her office, a three-sided bulletin board is papered with programs from the funerals of kids killed since the organization was founded in 1986. From the cover of one of the most recent ones, a smiling 10-year-old, DeAntoine Trammell, looks out. He wanted to be a basketball star and loved to sing blues and gospel songs on the way to school with his mother. He was at home sleeping on June 3 when his aunt and her boyfriend got into a drunken fight in the kitchen. The boyfriend allegedly threatened to kill himself, but instead fired into the wall. The bullet pierced it and killed DeAntoine in the next room.

That kind of senselessness marks many of the children's deaths here. In March, 3-year-old Destinee Thomas was killed while sitting at home watching TV. According to police, two petty drug dealers opened fire on the house with an AK-47 in a dispute over turf. In April, 8-year-old Brianna Caddell was also killed by an AK-47 sprayed indiscriminately into her house.

That was in revenge for an earlier shooting. She was asleep in bed at the time.

Then there's 16-year-old Alesia Robinson. She was sitting on her front porch with her boyfriend, a 19-year-old convicted drug dealer. He was playing with his gun. She'd asked him to stop. Instead, according to police, he pointed it at her and fired, killing her almost instantly.

In a less violent, but perhaps more chilling case, Tarajee Shaheer Maynor left her two children in a hot car for 3½ hours while she got a massage and her hair done. They suffocated to death. She told police she was "too stupid" to know that would cause them any harm.

Each Individual's Worth

"The real issue is that these young people have no value for others' lives, because there's no value on their own," says one of the city's leading black activists, the Rev. Horace Sheffield III, head of the National Action Network's Michigan chapter. "That's what we've got to work at, to find a way to let these people know they have some value, and they can contribute no matter what the circumstances are of their birth and upbringing."

Mr. Sheffield believes that can be accomplished without new money or programs, if all the city's churches work together and coordinate their efforts.

"The church really needs to find a way to take responsibility for 25 this," he says, "even if it means walking the streets at night and doing whatever is necessary to talk some sense into our young people."

But others say the city has a major role to play, too. Its police department is being overhauled and is working cooperatively with county and state law enforcement to stem the gun violence.

In addition, Mayor Kilpatrick is pledging to tear down as many as 4,000 abandoned houses near schools where he says drug dealers stash weapons and prey on nearby neighbors.

Yet his real focus, he says, is on the city's children. This fall, Detroit will start what's called "mayor's time" from 3 P.M. to 8 P.M. Adults will provide supervised programs for the estimated 50 percent of kids who say they take care of themselves either before or after school.

Although to pay for it in this cash-strapped city, in essence the mayor has had to go begging. He's trying to raise $30 million in private money to fund that and other priorities.

Needed: Positive Entertainment

Criminologist Taylor says such programs will help, but the media 30 have a key role to play in changing the hard-edge nature of youth culture as well. He wants rappers, in particular, to stop glorifying guns, violence, and rape, and begin sending positive messages to kids.

"When I play aggressive hip hop, it makes me very agitated," he says. "If the music is healing, then it sets the tone."

That was clear recently at Belle Isle, during the annual Metro Youth Day. Fifteen thousand elementary and junior-high kids from around the city descended on the Detroit River island park for a day of games, music, pie-eating contests, and wrestling matches.

Hundreds of them danced around a makeshift stage in a field while a local rap group got them to sing along. "When I say drugs, you say, 'No!' " the rappers shouted to the crowd of smiling, rocking kids, who sang back, "No, no!"

For 14-year-old Shardae Jones, who was helping with younger kids at the event, this is exactly the kind of thing adults should be doing more of. She's already seen some of the kids she's grown up with get heavily involved with drugs and drop by the wayside.

"I try to talk to them, but talking to them don't change anything. 35 They still feel the same way," she says.

That bothers her, just as it scares her when she walks to school, because of the recent spate of killings. Her friend Laquail Ramos doesn't like it either.

"Adults could do a lot more, but they don't, because they're lazy," Laquail says. "All of the parents should come together and work things out. They shouldn't just worry about just their own kids. They should worry about all of our kids."

What Did You Read?

1. According to the author, to what do criminologists and civic leaders attribute the hike in the overall murder rate in some of our cities, particularly Detroit?

2. What percentage of adults are functionally illiterate in Detroit?

3. What is SOSAD? What is it dedicated to?

What Do You Think?

1. When you think of Detroit, what do you think of? Why?

2. Do arguments suggesting that the way to fight crime is through moral and spiritual renewal have validity as public policy, or are these arguments merely wishful thinking?

3. In your opinion, what are the real issues as to why the city of Detroit seems so dysfunctional? What can be done to help reverse its problems?

How Was It Done?

1. The article centers on causes and effects of rampant killings and violent crime in Detroit. List some of both.
2. How is Detroit today compared to Detroit of thirty years ago?
3. What experts are referred to in the article? Are they credible? Why?
4. Do statistics play an important part of the development of this article? Why?

Bitterness Taints a Sweet Victory

David Lamb

The small town of Hershey, Pennsylvania, is famous for its connection to Hershey's chocolates. As perhaps the last, true "company town" in America, its residents either directly or indirectly owe their livelihood to Hershey Foods Company. When Hershey's board of trustees—many of whom do not live in Hershey—voted to explore the sale of the company, the residents of Hershey, a town created and run by Milton Hershey in the first half of the 20th century, beat back the challenge and saved itself and its very special way of life.

Key Words

collective	involving all members of a group as distinct from its individuals
capitulated	surrendered after negotiation of terms
benevolent	marked by goodwill
confectionery	a shop where sweets are sold
Utopia	an ideal society or city that exists only in fiction
fiduciary	held in trust or confidence
capriciousness	unpredictability
endowment	part of an institution's income derived from donations

When word leaked out two months ago that the Hershey Foods Corp. was for sale, residents here had a collective panic attack. Everyone prepared for the worst—new owners who would cut jobs, dismantle bits of the business and kill the soul of a company town that owes its very presence and prosperity to chocolate.

The town fought back. Lawsuits were filed and protests were held. Citizen groups were formed and Web sites were started. Placards declaring: "Derail the Sale" sprung up on the lawns of hundreds of homes. Edginess turned to anger. And Cathleen Lewis, president of the local historical society, said of the community-minded man who had founded the town: "Mr. Hershey must be turning over in his grave."

On Wednesday, Hershey's despair turned to jubilation as this town of 12,000 residents—half of whom work for the chocolate company or one of its entities—awoke to unexpected news: By a 10-7 vote late Tuesday night, the trust company that controls Hershey Foods had capitulated to public opinion and two unfavorable court rulings. Hershey Foods would not be sold.

"This is a day of celebration," said J. Bruce McKinney, an ex-member of the trust's board and an anti-sale activist. "It shows what a totally unified community can accomplish. But it's going to take time and effort on the part of a lot of people, particularly the board members, to reconstruct what has been fractured."

Robert Vowler, Hershey Trust Co. chairman and chief executive, 5 said Wednesday that the trustees had not bowed to community pressure, but decided not to sell because they didn't like the offers they got. One bid from chewing gum maker the Wm. Wrigley Jr. Co. was for $12.5 billion and the other—a joint offer from chocolate giants Nestle and Cadbury—was for $10.5 billion. Hershey Foods had been expected to receive bids as high as $15 billion.

Even with the sale scuttled and the jobs at Hershey's now secure, wounded feelings remain—as does a public sense of betrayal concerning the board's decision to look for buyers. Citizens have collected 6,000 signatures on a petition calling for the board's removal. It is an expression of distrust unimaginable in Milton Hershey's time.

Even 57 years after his death, Hershey often is referred to here in the present tense. It is as though his ghost walks the last of America's company towns, keeping watch over the well-being of his neighbors and the fortunes of his chocolate factory.

Hershey—who never got beyond the fourth grade and had failed as a candy maker in Philadelphia, Chicago and New York—ruled as a benevolent dictator here for 40 years after returning to his native township and, in 1905, opening a confectionery plant in a cornfield to produce Hershey's milk chocolate bars.

With the wealth from what would become the world's largest chocolate factory, he paid off churches' mortgages, built—and sold at cost—attractive, landscaped homes for his workers, set up a trolley system and a junior college and founded a school for orphaned boys. He operated the newspaper, the bank, the department store, the telephone and electric companies, the hotel and the drugstore, as well as the park and the ballroom where Glenn Miller and Harry James played in the summers. If it moved or breathed, people used to say, it belonged to Mr. Hershey.

He commanded such allegiance—he subsidized the town services   10
he owned and provided steady jobs, even through the Depression—
that when workers of a new union staged a sit-down in 1937 over issues of seniority, townspeople marched up Chocolate Avenue to
Hershey's mansion to demonstrate against their striking neighbors.
"Be loyal to Mr. Hershey," one sign said. "He was loyal to you."

"Let's face it, this was Utopia. Mr. Hershey took care of this town,"
said Robert Feaser, the current business manager of Chocolate Workers Local 464. Even now, he added, turnover at the plant is only 3% a
year. "Everyone was scared to death of what might happen [if the
company were sold]. And no one could understand why they'd sell. It
made no sense.

"You could understand if there had been a couple of bad years or the
stock wasn't growing or the dividends weren't holding up. But in good
times and bad, Hershey's been profitable. We're recession-proof. When
the economy goes down, our business goes up. When the economy recovers, we grow even more. It's like the goose that lays the golden egg."

Before he died in 1945, Hershey bequeathed his $60-million for-
tune to the Milton Hershey School for orphans. A 17-member board of
local citizens was set up to oversee the trust, which now is $5.8 billion.
The trust owns 31% of the chocolate company's shares and 77% of its
voting shares; 56% of the trust's assets are invested in Hershey Foods.

The board—most of whose members no longer live in Hershey, and
only five of whom own Hershey stock personally—said it had ordered
Hershey Food executives to explore a sale in March in order to diversify
the trust's holdings. To do otherwise, members said, could make them
susceptible to charges of failing to fulfill their fiduciary duties. (Hershey
Foods controls 32% of the chocolate market in the United States.)

"There's only one reason for exploring a sale: to diversify and sta-   15
bilize existing assets," Rick Kelly, a spokesman for the board, said last
week. "No one and certainly no foundation keeps 56% of assets in a
single company. The fact is, Hershey has to compete in a global economy. Everyone else is growing bigger. A strategic acquisition could
strengthen Hershey Foods, strengthen the brand and . . . benefit the
community."

Even Pennsylvania Atty. Gen. Mike Fisher joined the fight against
the board, saying any sale would cause "irreparable harm" to the company's hometown. In response to his filing, Judge Warren Morgan of
the Dauphin County Orphans Court, which oversees charitable trust
activities, issued a temporary injunction Sept. 4 to block the trust from
selling. Morgan said the trust's board showed "a capriciousness that is
an abuse of their discretion." The trust appealed his restraining order,
but a five-judge Commonwealth Court upheld the injunction.

In a town where the street lamps resemble Hershey's Kisses and
the spa at the Hershey Hotel offers milk chocolate baths, the imprint of

company largess is everywhere: on the five public golf courses, the minor-league hockey team, the new library, the country-club-caliber recreation center, the excellent public schools. The private Milton Hershey School—whose 1,150 students are financially needy but no longer have to be orphans to attend—has an endowment larger than that of Duke University and Dartmouth College combined.

"My concern was that a sale would have changed the character of Hershey and torn the heart out of our town," said Mike Pronio, who runs the grocery store that his grandfather, an immigrant from Italy, opened in 1918. "This is a company town, the last of its kind in America. People feel fiercely loyal to it. We all work to enhance Hershey. Visitors come and they say, 'What a beautiful little town you have.'"

On Wednesday, things in Hershey seemed to be getting back to normal. Restaurants gave diners Hershey's Kisses instead of after-dinner mints, and from the limestone Hershey plant, the fragrance of chocolate poured into the crisp autumn. Once again, the sweet smell of success hung over this company town.

What Did You Read?

1. How many residents live in Hershey and how many of them work for the chocolate company?

2. Who was Milton S. Hershey? What did he do for Hershey, PA?

3. What was the board's rationale for wanting to sell the Hershey Foods Company?

What Do You Think?

1. In a global economy, is it a luxury, and not very practical, for a company like Hershey not to diversify itself?

2. Do you think selling Hershey Foods Company would have destroyed the town of Hershey? Why or why not?

3. Do you think the residents of Hershey were upset about the sale of Hershey Foods because they feared for the loss of their jobs or they simply feared change?

How Was It Done?

1. The article revolves around what kind of conflict? Who are the two parties?

2. What values does the author use to support his claim?

3. What individual seems to embody the primary values set forth in this article? How is that developed in the article?

The Changing Heartland

Dean Foust, Brian Grow, and Aixa M. Pascual

Small town, U.S.A., idealized on television as a place of quiet, friendliness, family, and security, finds itself changed. Immigration is creating challenges once reserved for large cities. Economic prosperity in the 1990s attracted immigrants to small towns like Morganton, North Carolina. Now, with a high-skill economy, low-skilled immigrants have fewer job opportunities, creating an increased need for social services. Additionally, small towns are also experiencing other social problems: rising rates of divorce and single motherhood in areas traditionally known as the Bible Belt. Small-town America no longer looks like it did in the days of Mayberry.

Key Words

influx	a coming in
doles	gives as charity
askance	with disapproval or distrust
warp speed	extremely high speed
pragmatic	practical as opposed to idealistic
assimilating	absorbing into the culture
bonanza	an extremely large amount
stagnation	stale; not advancing or developing

It's a typical week in Morganton, N.C. At St. Charles Borromeo Catholic Church, the Reverend Kenneth Whittington delivers mass in English, Spanish, and Hmong, spoken by the growing Laotian community. At the nearby grocer, stock boys refill the shelves with the tortillas and guava nectar sold alongside the fresh wontons and egg-roll wrappers. Two school buses rumble through poor neighborhoods, loaded with computers and games to teach English to immigrant children.

But like so many melting-pot communities, Morganton is also grappling with a new set of social ills. At the Burke Mission Station, the soup kitchen doles out nearly 90 meals a day, 50% more than two years ago, while the nearby First Baptist Church employs a full-time parish nurse to call on the growing number of elderly in its congregation. And while St. Charles Borromeo has expanded its outreach services to include in-home family counseling, Whittington frets that the community doesn't have a handle on the rise in domestic violence, alcohol abuse, and prostitution he hears about in confession. "A lot of it we're just not dealing with," he sighs.

This isn't a hardscrabble corner of New York or Los Angeles. This is Morganton, population 17,310, a factory town in the same foothills region on which the 1960s TV utopia of Mayberry was based. While the scale of Morganton's problems still pale in comparison with, say, Philadelphia or Chicago's South Side, this rural community finds itself wrestling with the demographic and social forces once more common in America's urban corridors. "What we've viewed as big-city problems are here amongst us," says barber Tommy Sain.

Morganton's struggles are playing out not just across many other parts of North Carolina but also through swaths of the American heartland. One of the most fascinating social trends of recent years is the demographic revolution taking place in such traditionally rural states as Arkansas, Kentucky, North Carolina, and Nebraska. The booming economy of the 1990s did wonders for these states but also brought in its wake an unforeseen influx of immigrants eager to stake their claim, as well as upheaval in the manufacturing sectors that long buttressed Middle America.

As a result, rural towns such as Morganton that once looked askance 5 at the ills of the big city are confronting a rise in everything from out-of-wedlock births to divorces. "The heartland states are facing the same kind of social changes that urban areas encountered 20 years ago," says Barbara J. Risman, a sociologist at North Carolina State University and co-chair of the Council on Contemporary Families.

Combined, these changes are transforming this once-insular state at warp speed. On the political front, the influx of immigrant's and northern transplants, coupled with a growing professional class, are helping to usher in a new era of government. With the retirement of polarizing politicians such as Jesse A. Helms, more moderate candidates are running, including Democrat Erskine Bowles and Republican Elizabeth Dole, who are squaring off for Helms's Senate seat. At the same time, the flood of social transformations is taxing North Carolina's ability to provide Medicare and other services for the surging ranks of immigrants, elderly, and single mothers as the economy slows.

In many respects, the newfound problems can be linked to the growth pains that came with rising prosperity in the state, which now boasts the nation's second-largest banking hub, in Charlotte, and a thriving technology center, in Raleigh-Durham. Just as immigrants flocked to Detroit and New York during the first Industrial Revolution, the current wave of immigrants sees greater opportunity in the Sunbelt and the heartland. Thus, the share of immigration flowing into states such as North Carolina has nearly doubled over the past decade, according to the Census Bureau. Nor is the immigration clampdown from last September's terrorist attacks likely to reverse the trend. "Once a shift like this occurs, there's a certain momentum built in," says Urban Institute demographer Jeffrey S. Passel.

For the most part, the transformation has gone smoothly, particularly given North Carolina's relative inexperience in assimilating new groups. In the early 1900s, the state had the nation's lowest percentage of foreign-born residents. The economic boom of the 1990s changed all that. Because the job bonanza nearly dried up the state's pool of workers by the mid-1990s, immigrants provided the reinforcements that kept the good times rolling. State leaders put the welcome mat out by, for example, giving one of the nation's most liberal driver's-license tests, which can be taken in Chinese, Japanese, Korean, and Spanish.

To be sure, North Carolina's resolve has been tested in the year since last September's attacks. With the feds cracking down on fake IDs, two regional grocery chains, Food Lion and Harris Teeter Inc., let go dozens of Hispanic employees who couldn't produce valid Social Security numbers. Some recent immigrants also complain about growing discrimination. Reyna Chacon, a Guatemalan native living in Morganton, says "Hispanics are being told there are no jobs" even as whites are hired.

Still, recent arrivals say they aren't going home. "Work is slow, but it's still better here than in Mexico," says Victor Castellanos, a Mexican native who quit his $12.50-an-hour job as a house painter last year to open his own five-man painting business in Durham.

State officials also remain mindful of the economic importance of Hispanic workers whether they're here legally or not. While North Carolina tightened its driver's-license policy after September 11, it has since backed off by allowing undocumented workers to apply for an easily obtainable federal tax ID that can be used to get a license. Why? Despite the recession, the state still relies heavily on newcomers. Without immigration, "our economy would shut down," says Chatham County Commissioner Rick Givens. The Realistic Furniture Industries plant in rural Candor says it couldn't run a third shift without newly arrived Hispanics. Despite a local jobless rate near 7%, "we don't et any referrals from the unemployment office," notes human-resources manager Juan Guasque.

Law-enforcement officials are taking a pragmatic view, too. In Chapel Hill, Police Chief Gregg Jarvies says his officers turn illegal residents over to the Immigration & Naturalization Service for serious crimes but not for misdemeanors or traffic stops "We do not consider ourselves an arm of the INS," he says.

Longer term, the state must figure out how to assimilate largely low-skilled newcomers into an increasingly high-skill economy. Planners estimate that by 2020, the state's elderly will grow from 12% to 17% of the population, mostly due too the aging of baby boomers. These mostly skilled workers will exit the labor force at the same time that the ranks of immigrants and their children grow sharply, combining with other minorities to reach nearly 30% of the population by 2020. "A growing proportion of young workers will be immigrants," says Sarah Rubin, a senior associate at MDC Inc., a regional think tank. "It's important for North Carolina's economy that they [improve their] skills and meet the demands of higher-paying occupations."

As if that weren't enough, North Carolina already finds itself in the midst of other social challenges. Despite its Bible Belt image, the state saw the number of single mothers soar by 35% over the past decade, while nonfamily households rose 38%, and the number of households with unmarried partners ore than doubled—all changes that outpaced the national averages. Some attribute the breakdown of traditional family structures in rural sates to economic forces, such as the drop in many workers' real income that came with the stagnation of manufacturing jobs. Risman, the sociologist, also cites the spread of media such as cable and he Internet. "There's a decreasing difference between urban and rural cultures," she says.

Church leaders—agonizing over a divorce rate that, like those of other Bible Belt states such as Oklahoma and Arkansas, is higher than the national average—are promoting "Marriage Saver" programs that impose strict counseling requirements on newlyweds.

At the same time, local governments are struggling to fund services for single mothers in a region that despises handouts. With roughly 1 million North Carolinians living in poverty—25% more than in 1990—health officials are scrambling to provide medical care and other social services to the swelling numbers of people who lack the insurance or other means to pay for health care. It's not just undocumented workers, either, since roughly 40% of black families are headed by single mothers, who often rely on social services.

These traditionally rural states will continue to struggle, particularly in today's sputtering economy. In the process, they're likely to learn what much of the U.S. discovered decades ago—that diversity is inevitably a mixed blessing but that it can be an asset on which to build a thriving economy.

Which Has Lured a Flood of New Immigrants

States with the fastest percentage growth in Hispanic population, 1990 to 2000

North Carolina	394%
Arkansas	337
Georgia	300
Tennessee	278
Nevada	217
South Carolina	211
Alabama	208
Kentucky	173
Minnesota	166
Nebraska	155

Data: U.S. Census Bureau

And Creating a More Diverse Society

Change in North Carolina population, 1990 to 2000	
Hispanic	+392%
Asian	+117
Black	+19
White	+16

Data: U.S. Census Bureau

What Did You Read?

1. Describe the problems faced by Morganton, North Carolina.

2. How do small towns benefit from immigration? What problems does immigration bring?

3. What are some of the social challenges facing North Carolina today?

What Do You Think?

1. In your opinion, are small towns better to live in than big cities? Why?

2. Brooks describes a backlash against immigrants in Morganton. Is the backlash justified? Why or why not?

3. In your opinion, why are Bible Belt areas experiencing divorce, single motherhood, and unmarried households at rates higher than the rest of the country?

4. Why do you suppose the authors refer to diversity as a "mixed blessing"?

How Was It Done?

1. While the growing influx of immigration into small towns in America is the "big" topic, the issue centers on what city and state in the article? Do you feel it is a typical example? Why or why not?

2. The article develops what kinds of societal effects that the transformation of the population has caused?

3. The article is structured around the perspectives of several different groups of people. List some.

6

Technology and Society

One of the characteristics of our recent times has been the incredible speed at which technology is invented and apparently assimilated into our lives. History is full of inventions that have had a profound impact on human society: the wheel, the printing press, the steam engine, and the automobile come quickly to mind. But the speed and range at which changes are taking place, and the areas that are being affected—computers, health, education, entertainment, business, even crime detection—often push the limit of our society's ability to embrace change. Some people respond by rejecting these changes, arguing for a return to old-fashioned values and old-fashioned ways of doing things. Others embrace every new advance as a sign of improvement. A few things, however, seem clear: change happens, and when it does, its effects can range far beyond the immediate and the obvious.

The Writing Lesson in this chapter guides you through writing a critique of another text. This critique involves answering a series of specific questions that are designed to open up the text in ways that traditional methods of analysis often ignore. The questions are grouped by categories, with a sense of increasing complexity, taking you deeper into the analysis of the text. The Writing Assignment has you apply this critique format to a specific text based on the theme of this chapter, technology and society. The result is an analysis that achieves much greater understanding of the original text than would otherwise be possible—and gives you a tool for analyzing other texts in the future.

THE MAIN EVENT READING

DNA Detectives

Gunjan Sinha

Gunjan Sinha presents the newest development in criminal investigation techniques: DNA testing using a microchip device at the crime scene. On the one hand, such a development could lead to increased apprehensions and convictions of criminals. On the other hand, problems exist with DNA collecting and the potential abuse of an individual's right to privacy. After all, with DNA samples, police and other authorities could have access to the most personal information of all—your DNA code. Given more time and research, scientists may be able to discover more about genetic conditions, disease, and behavioral tendencies, and that could be turned over to the police. Our decisions about the future use of such technology may be based on our fears: our fear of a police state versus our fear of crime.

Key Words

unassailable	unable to be attacked
perpetrator	one who carries out an activity, especially a crime
inception	the act of beginning
exonerate	to relieve of responsibility or hardship; to declare innocent
prototype	an original model of something
infrastructure	the underlying framework or foundation of a system or organization
bipartisan	involving members of two political parties (in the United States, this usually refers to the Republican and Democratic parties)
expunged	deleted or destroyed
forensic	related to the application of scientific knowledge to legal problems, especially criminal investigations
mandate	an authoritative command

begins
with an
anecdote

In the early morning hours of April 4, 1993, a 30-year-old woman was awakened in her Roswell, Georgia, apartment by an intruder. Holding a hunting knife to her throat, the man blindfolded her and then, for two hours, terrorized and raped her. Over the next six years, the assailant would go on to rape five more women before unassailable DNA evidence would finally peg him as the perpetrator.

generalize
from the
example

The reality of brutal and violent crimes such as rape and murder is that more than 50 percent are carried out by repeat offenders. It's a reality that the U.S. National Institute of Justice (NIJ)—the research arm of the Department of Justice—wants to circumvent with high-tech advances in DNA analysis. In labs across the country, federal grant money offered by NIJ is helping scientists develop credit-card-size chips that will analyze the DNA from blood, semen, or flecks of skin right at a crime scene.

Such technology is part of a growing nationwide effort to store genetic information from convicted criminals. After a push by Congress begun in 1994, almost every state is now collecting DNA from violent offenders.

The data will be linked to a national database, unveiled last October by the Federal Bureau of Investigation, called the National DNA Index System, or NDIS. The database will allow authorities throughout the country to match traces of crime scene evidence to suspects.

The United States isn't the only country fighting crime with DNA. Great Britain, for one, has had a similar database in place since 1995 and has matched an estimated 16,000 suspects to crime scenes since its inception. Other efforts are developing internationally as well. [5 / compare to Great Britain]

The value of DNA in linking criminals to crime scenes is unquestionable. It was through DNA evidence, for instance, that last year a 12-year-old Phoenix girl convinced police that she had been molested by her grandfather. After watching an "NYPD Blue" segment, in which a rape victim collected semen left by her attacker, the girl used a cotton swab on herself. The evidence resulted in her 59-year-old grandfather's arrest.

And earlier this year in St. Petersburg, Florida, a police officer tailed a suspect named Charles C. Peterson, who resembled the description of the "Duck Robber" (who was named for his distinctive toe-out waddle)—a man who was suspected of 15 robberies and a double rape. Peterson was cruising on his motorcycle when he paused at a traffic light and spat on the road. The police officer who was following him grabbed a paper towel and then literally mopped up the evidence. A few days later, a laboratory reported a match with semen from the rape and Peterson was arrested. [example]

But despite hundreds of suspects DNA has helped put in jail—and the dozens more that DNA has helped to exonerate—a backlog of untested samples and outdated state laboratory techniques are keeping even more crimes from being solved. Today, detectives send crime scene samples such as hair, saliva, blood, or semen to a state lab for analysis—a process that can take several weeks, depending on the lab's caseload. A microchip, however, will enable detectives to analyze a piece of evidence right on the spot and immediately compare the DNA "fingerprint" with those stored in NDIS, bypassing the bureaucratic logjam that now enables hundreds of criminals to commit new crimes before they are caught. [problem with DNA testing]

While still in the developmental stages, a mobile chip system could be available within five years, says Bud Bromley, senior vice president of marketing and business development at San Diego-based Nanogen, a company that is developing such a chip ["Gene Readers," Nov. '98]. Nanogen is working specifically on a small, portable version. The Massachusetts Institute of Technology's Whitehead Institute in Cambridge is also developing a chip-based system to help solve crimes. Although it could be adopted for mobile analysis in the future, it's presently being used in labs to study the chemical components of DNA.

Nanogen's prototype microchip is packaged into a plastic cartridge. In a mobile unit, the cartridge would fit into a briefcase-size portable "reader" that would function as a reaction chamber and as a networked computer. The device would have the reagents needed to extract DNA and amplify, or make copies, for accurate study, as well as the software to analyze the results. 10

"Imagine the scenario," says Lisa Forman, deputy director of the National Commission on DNA evidence, part of NIJ. "In my most futuristic vision, the cops go to the crime scene. They pick up the evidence, drop it into the cartridge, and then stick it into their portable reader. The DNA extraction and amplification occur, and a timing device opens channels that mix up the chemicals. Electricity manipulates the DNA down the tubes until it moves onto the microchip, where it's analyzed. It's so futuristic that the cops no longer eat doughnuts; they have bagels and Starbucks coffee while they wait. And by the time they drink the froth off their lattes, out pops a DNA profile."

The exact pieces of DNA the system analyzes are recurring sections called short tandem repeats (STRs) strung along the DNA molecule. They reveal nothing about a person's hair or eye color, height, weight, or predisposition to disease because they are non-coding regions—genes that don't make proteins. But because they are unique, they will do a better job of catching a perp. The FBI has set a standard of using 13 different STRs that when used together can identify any person—a combination of genes that distinguishes an individual from all other people on the planet.

But while a portable system of some kind seems technically feasible within five years, a host of infrastructure issues must be addressed before the carry-anywhere mobile version envisioned by Forman can become a reality. For one thing, officers will have to learn how to collect evidence properly and then use the technology—and that requires a training program. "We used to talk over the heads of cops," recalls Forman. As a first step, the commission has put together information packets that will help teach police about the techniques of DNA collection and testing.

The biggest danger in proper DNA collection at the scene is cross- 15 contamination. A piece of skin or hair from the officer collecting evidence, for example, could greatly skew results. Material is collected with disposable tweezers, and cops must change gloves each time they pick up a sample; at a complex scene, an investigator might go through 100 pairs of gloves.

Also, DNA from a crime scene doesn't by itself identify an assailant; he or she must already be part of a database with which to compare samples. Right now, NDIS includes only about 140,000 DNA profiles from criminals that have been convicted in state courts; fewer than 15 states are currently linked to the system.

What's more, the FBI estimates that there is a backlog of about 400,000 DNA samples that must be analyzed, and another 200,000 that need to be reanalyzed with the new STR method for consistency's sake—the previous costlier and more time-consuming method characterized a completely different stretch of DNA.

Part of the problem has been an evolution in DNA identification technology, with which state labs have not kept pace. The FBI only mandated that state labs switch to using STRs in forensic analysis in January of this year—a technique that requires smaller amounts of sample material and is faster and cheaper than the older approach. Laboratories across the country are in the process of changing their protocols and updating their equipment and expect the backlog to be cleared within the next two to three years.

A bipartisan bill, sponsored by Senators Herbert Kohl (D-Wis.) and Mike DeWine (R-Ohio) and introduced to the Senate Judiciary Committee in April, also provides $30 million to the states for analyzing backlogged DNA samples. If approved, the Violent Offender DNA Registration Act of 1999 would also require federal agencies to collect DNA samples from some 15,000 federal prisoners. Plus, it would mandate DNA samples from offenders who are on parole, probation, or under supervision for violent crimes. A Congressional decision on the act is expected sometime this summer. *does "bipartisan" mean this is more reasonable?*

The NDIS effort is not without its critics. The American Civil Liberties Union, for example, has been particularly vocal about its opposition to a DNA database, arguing that very few states require that genetic material be destroyed after the DNA fingerprint is logged. Without such a step, the government would be able to reanalyze that DNA for more personal information about an individual at any point in the future, potentially threatening an innocent person's right to privacy. *20 opposition arguments*

"The DNA samples that are being held by state and local governments can provide insights into the most personal family relationships and the most intimate workings of the human body," says Barry Steinhardt, associate director of the ACLU. "This includes the likelihood of the occurrence of more than 4,000 types of genetic conditions and diseases, legitimacy at birth, and perhaps even tendencies for substance addiction, crime, and sexual orientation."

But perhaps most troubling to civil rights groups such as the ACLU is the notion of collecting DNA samples from mere suspects, who have not been tried before a jury of their peers and convicted. Many states have passed laws requiring individuals convicted of various types of crimes to give a blood sample, from which DNA is extracted. Arizona, for example, collects blood only from sex offenders, while Virginia, Alabama, and Wyoming collect blood from all convicted felons. But beginning this September, Louisiana will permit DNA testing of anyone arrested, even before conviction. "Louisiana also does not require that a person arrested for a crime of which he is not convicted automatically have his DNA records expunged," says Steinhardt.

referring to ConstitutionThe Fourth Amendment states the government must have "probable cause" to search someone's person, argues Steinhardt, and most crime suspects are never convicted and likely have never done anything wrong. "Arrest does not equal guilt," he adds, "and you shouldn't suffer the consequences of guilt until after you have been convicted."

prominent politiciansThe notion of testing unconvicted suspects has been considered in other states as well. New York City Police Commissioner Howard Safir, for example, has expressed his desire to see a similar law, and New York Mayor Rudolph Giuliani has even said he would back a citywide mandate to store DNA from all newborns.

While conceding that privacy issues need to be addressed, most states and the federal government do not share the ACLU's position, as their steadfast efforts to develop forensic DNA technology suggest. Beginning this year, NIJ has been making $5 million per year more in grant money available to scientists nationwide for the next five years toward developing forensic DNA technology.

Federal grant money has already helped Nanogen build a benchtop version of its cartridge system, which is presently being tested at the University of Texas Southwestern Medical Center in Dallas. Nanogen is also preparing to set up two additional test sites soon. The laboratory version requires a biological sample to be doused with chemicals in a test tube to extract DNA; that sample DNA then undergoes another reaction, called amplification, which generates thousands of DNA copies before it is placed on the cartridge. Nanogen is confident that it will be able to incorporate the DNA-extraction process into the cartridge within five years.

returns to anecdote at the startFor many crime victims, however, five years isn't soon enough. In the Roswell, Georgia, rape case, the assailant has now been identified as 47-year-old John Scieszka. He was convicted and given a life sentence for raping five University of Georgia women in 1995 and 1996. Upon that conviction, his DNA was compared with that collected at almost 1,000 unsolved crime scenes in Georgia—and only then was he linked to the 1993 rape in Roswell. Had a mobile chip system and the NDIS database been available, Scieszka would have been caught before he had a chance to rape again.

What Did You Read?

1. What is so remarkable about the crime "chip" in its analysis of evidence?
2. What are some of the things that must be done before a mobile crime reading system can become a reality?
3. What is the biggest danger in proper DNA collection at a crime scene?

What Do You Think?

1. Have you heard about any high-profile crimes in which DNA evidence would not help?
2. Is a DNA database of all violent offenders threatening to people's right to privacy? Why or why not?
3. Would you be willing to donate your DNA to create a DNA database that could be used to identify potential criminal suspects?

How Was It Done?

1. How effective is the short introductory paragraph as a lead-in to the author's claim? Explain.
2. The article is structured around what?
3. Does the author appeal chiefly to the audience using facts and logic or sentiment and values? Explain.

THE MAIN EVENT WRITING ASSIGNMENT

Find a recent article, preferably from an academic journal, on the general subject of Technology, and write a critique based on the following five categories.

Summary

Give the name of the author, the name of the article (in quotation marks), the name of the periodical (underlined), and the date of publication. Also, include any pertinent information about the author, if available. In about five to seven sentences, summarize the article, blending two quotations. Enclose the two quotations in quotation marks.

Questions of Author

1. What is the main idea of the article?
2. What seem to be the author's perceived "situation" and "strategic response" (that is, what is his or her purpose for writing)?
3. How does the author conceive his or her role? What persona, or mask, does the author put on: scholar, scientist, prophet, reformer, poet, judge, chronicler, wit, or what?
4. What mood or tone does the author write in? Does this change?

Questions of Craft

5. How is the article structured? Is it structured around a central theme? Individuals? Religions? Movements? Situations?
6. What single word (or two-word phrase) used by the author best crystallizes the article? Why?
7. How does the author give substance to explanations (by appealing chiefly to facts, logic, sentiment, ideology, tradition, values)?

Questions of Explanation

8. What kinds of connections does the author make among the disparate levels of experience? And how (e.g., literature with history, politics with art, novels with popular culture, the individual with the larger social environment, event with motives and consequences)?
9. What is the author's basic locus of cultural reality? What is the locus of control? (How does the author locate "where the action is"—in ideas? in politics? in lifestyles?)
10. How does the author explain what moves people? What are the shaping forces?

Conclusion

11. Is the article positive or negative? Why?
12. What two things did you learn from the article?
13. How would you have improved the article? For example, would a diagram, a better definition, or more examples have improved the article?

PREPARATION PUNCH LIST

Before you begin writing the essay, you need to prepare yourself to write. Begin by asking yourself a series of questions.

1. What is the author's main event? (Find the thesis.)

- In determining the author's thesis, make sure you don't simply jump on the topic the author is discussing. Try to narrow down to the specific argument the author is proposing concerning his or her subject.

2. How is the author able to support what he or she is saying?

- In other words, what experts, what professionals, what academic institutions, foundations, or scientists are mentioned? Those are the sources of credible support that make the argument of the author sound.

3. What is the basis for the article?

- To promote better environmental practices? Is the push to help experts do a better job in their particular field? Is the push to promote understanding in education? In other words, what is the driving or propelling force behind the article?

THE MAIN EVENT WRITING LESSON: CRITIQUE

The lead paragraph of your critique is a summary, which is described in Chapter 3. Be sure to include two quotations in which the words chosen are important and meaningful in relation to the essay as a whole. In the remainder of your critique, group different categories of questions together into different paragraphs.

Questions of Author

1. What is the main idea of the article?

This question requires that you determine the thesis of the article. In other words, what is the point of the article? The main idea may be stated explicitly, but other times it may only be implied.

2. What seem to be the author's perceived "situation" and "strategic response" (that is, what is his or her purpose for writing)?

This question requires that you go beyond the thesis itself and examine the broader importance or consequences of the thesis. The "situation" and "strategic response" involve questioning why the author has written that particular article. There may be some advancement or change in condition that creates the motivation for the article.

3. How does the author conceive his or her role? What persona, or mask, does the author put on: scholar, scientist, prophet, reformer, poet, judge, chronicler, wit, or what?

Often we refer to ourselves as playing a role at different points in our lives. Even within a single role, such as being an author, we can take many different approaches to the writing. Thus, an author may be a scholar, one who advances knowledge; a scientist, who investigates the physical universe; a prophet, predicting the future; a reformer, calling for change; a poet, bringing lyricism to a subject; a judge, assessing matters; a chronicler, recording events; or a wit, bringing humor. The roles an author can play are not limited to these categories. You may find others that fit your article better.

4. What mood or tone does the author write in? Does this change?

Just as we can speak of tone in terms of how we speak, we can also speak of tone in writing. The words writers choose can indicate moods such as solemn, serious, humorous, ironic, sarcastic, mournful, joyous, or fearful. During the course of the essay, this mood can change, particularly as the subject matter changes. If the mood does change, take careful note of when and why.

Questions of Craft

5. How is the article structured? Is it structured around a central theme? Individuals? Religions? Movements? Situations?

Examine the article to get a sense of what is at its core. The ideas or theme may be key, but other possibilities exist. The article may center on important people or ideologies. An event or condition could also be at the center of the article. In this question, you have to think not only of what the writer is bringing into the essay, but how the essay is organized in terms of its ideas.

6. What single word (or two-word phrase) best crystallizes the article? Why?

The crystalline word (or two-word phrase) is the word that most clearly encapsulates the overall sense of the essay. The word will reflect the most important aspects of the essay. As a comparison, think of the role of instant coffee to a cup of coffee: instant coffee is a crystallized form of coffee—all the water has been removed. So too with the crystalline word: it is the article reduced down to it bare essence.

7. How does the author give substance to the explanations (by appealing chiefly to facts, logic, sentiment, ideology, tradition, values)?

A critical reader does not accept an author's claims without sufficient support. Therefore, an author must make some sort of appeal to the reader. An appeal to fact involves the presentation of evidence, such as examples and statistics. Logic appeals to sound reasoning as a basis of proof. Sentiment appeals to a reader's emotions, and ideology appeals to a shared sense of beliefs. Appealing to tradition invokes a sense of heritage and custom. Appealing to values requires that the reader share the same fundamental sense of morals and ethics as the author.

Questions of Explanation

8. What kinds of connections does the author make among the disparate levels of experience? And how (e.g., literature with history, politics with art, novels with popular culture, the individual with the larger social environment, event with motives and consequences)?

The word "disparate" refers to something made from fundamentally different elements. For that reason, this question requires you to think of parts of the article that are not obviously connected, but that have been brought together in the article. Once you find those disparate elements, try to examine why they have been brought together.

9. What is the author's basic locus of cultural reality? What is the locus of control? (How does the author locate "where the action is"—in ideas? In politics? In lifestyles?)

The locus is the center point of activity. It is the point around which everything else revolves. The second part of the first question asks about "cultural reality"; that is, how someone looks at an event or condition is determined largely through issues of upbringing, education, religion, life experiences, and so forth. We might ask the question with the slang phrase, "Where is he or she coming from?"—meaning that social conditioning has influenced our sense of reality. The second question, about the locus of control, involves the issue of where power lies.

10. How does the author explain what moves people? What are the shaping forces?

People may be moved to action by a wide range of possible causes, including money, health, pursuit of knowledge, concern for others, a desire to be safe, selfishness, quest for power, and a variety of fears. These are usually applied to the specific situation in the article as a way to encourage people to embrace the author's perspective.

Conclusion

11. *Is the article positive or negative? Why?*

Was the article uplifting overall? Hopeful? Or was there a sense of trouble? Of problems that seem unsolvable? Examine the impression you had at the end of the article.

12. *What two things did you learn from the article?*

Reading is one way of learning, and if you have chosen a good, current article, you should be able to identify at least two things that you did not know before. Remember, if you didn't know those things, it is quite likely other readers did not know them as well.

13. *How would you have improved the article? For example, would a diagram, a better definition, or more examples have improved the article?*

If you had been able to lean over the author's shoulder as the article was being written, what would you have said that could have made the article better? Be specific—overly general advice is not helpful—and do not be afraid to criticize. There is no such thing as a perfect piece of writing.

THE MAIN EVENT WRITING SAMPLE

The following is an essay written for this text in response to the Main Event Writing Assignment.

Critique of "DNA Detectives"

Summary

The article "DNA Detectives" by Gunjan Sinha from *Popular Science,* August 1999, reports that "credit-card-size devices will soon analyze DNA right at a crime scene—identifying the perpetrators before they can strike again." More than 50% of violent crimes are carried out by repeat offenders, so the U.S. National Institute of Justice (NIJ) is helping scientists develop small chips that will analyze blood, semen, and skin at the crime scene. The idea is to store the data in a national database, called the National DNA Index System (NDIS), which would then allow the police to match traces of "crime scene evidence" to suspects. There are problems:

"The biggest danger in proper DNA collection at the scene is cross-contamination." Also, privacy issues are at stake. However, beginning this year NIJ has been spending $5 million per year to perfect forensic DNA technology so bureaucratic logjams can be avoided and criminals caught before they commit new crimes.

The main idea is that with dollars and political support, "credit-card-size devices" will soon analyze DNA right at a crime scene—matching up with samples from a national database and identifying perpetrators of crimes before they strike again. The thesis argues that DNA technology will revolutionize police work by identifying the DNA at the scene of the crime, by matching samples with a national database compiled of DNA from violent offenders, and by doing all of this quickly so offenders cannot repeat their crimes. The situation is the development of new technology that has the potential to change how police do their work. Sinha's strategic response is to investigate this development from the perspective of law enforcement, the companies that are creating these devices, and the civil rights groups and political leaders who must respond to the benefits and problems the new technology creates. Sinha is reporting the information in an objective and nonbiased way. Through background information, interviews, and research, he chronicles what the technology is, its problems as of now, and its future based on current political support. The tone is optimistic. Although Sinha points out how there has not always been money to keep the technology up to date, and how there has been criticism by the American Civil Liberties Union on Fourth Amendment rights (against illegal search and seizure), he points out the logical advantages of being able to pick up evidence at a crime scene and pop out a DNA profile. He points out how efficient and helpful this would be in finding criminals.

Questions of the Author #1

#2

#3

#4

Questions of Craft #5

The article is structured around a device—the crime chip and how it would work to identify a unique DNA fingerprint and the ability to match that fingerprint with its "match" from a central network containing stored DNA samples from thousands of criminals.

#6

"Fingerprint" is the crystalline word. The "fingerprint" is what is created by the device after the DNA is dropped into its cartridge.

#7

After the sample is analyzed, a DNA profile can be accessed. The author appeals chiefly to facts and dates as to when the U.S. and Great Britain began using forensic technology. Examples of how criminals have been caught with DNA samples were illustrated. Information was gleaned from experts including Bud Bromley, senior vice president of San Diego–based Nanogen, who says a mobile chip system could be available in the next five years. The author of the article also refers to MIT, which is developing a chip-based system as well. Lisa Forman, deputy director of the National Commission on DNA evidence, also shares her optimism about the viability of such technology. Logic was also implied; the technology is fast, effective, and efficient. Sinha alludes to sentiment when he describes how a rapist is caught and allowed to go free because of lack of evidence to convict. Lastly, Sinha links New York City Police Commissioner Howard Safir to supporting testing on convicted suspects.

Questions of Explanation #8
#9

The article connects technology and forensics. Police will be able to detect at the crime scene the suspect in question via the crime-chip device. The locus of control, or the power base, is in the technology itself, and the powers that be, the FBI as well as Congress, to support the forensic technology. The prime motive and shaping force is to be able to make quick and positive identification of violent criminals. The justice system has made too many mistakes in convicting those who are not guilty, and there are too many unsolved crimes.

#10

This is a positive article. We can look forward to technology *Conclu-*
that will assist police to make accurate and quick identifications of *sion #11*
criminals. I learned that fifty percent of all crimes are committed *#12*
by those who have committed crimes before. Also, the technology,
the mobile chip system, and NDIS database are in part already *#13*
being used. The article was logically presented with good diagrams
and explanations of the technology. It had some human interest as
well as covering certain obstacles that hinder the technology's use.
One area that could have been improved is the discussion of the
potential for abuse of this new technology either through incompetence or dishonesty on the part of the authorities.

ADDITIONAL READINGS

Welcome to the Snooper Bowl

Lev Grossman

*Lev Grossman discusses another innovation in crime fighting: video cameras out-
doors, taping everyone who comes before the lens. These inexpensive cameras have the
potential to put large areas under surveillance. Connected to computers that look to
match faces with those of wanted criminals, they have the potential to track down
criminals who dare to come out in public. However, the appearance of these cameras on
a large scale seems to foreshadow potential abuses—perhaps taking us another step
closer to George Orwell's nightmare vision of total state control.*

Key Words

decried	expressed strong disapproval of something
surveillance	close watch kept over someone or something
Orwellian	referring to George Orwell, 20th-century British author of *1984*, a novel in which an authoritarian government exerts total control over people's actions and thoughts
ubiquitous	widespread; existing everywhere
feasible	possible; able to be done

Happy, yelling faces. Red, drunken faces. Faces painted blue. Faces
painted purple. Tens of thousands of faces—accompanied by plastic

horns and giant foam hands—pouring into Raymond James Stadium in Tampa Bay last Sunday, ready to watch the biggest football game of the year. Meanwhile, someone—or rather, something—was watching them.

In a move that has been both hailed and decried, the Tampa Bay police department used the occasion of Super Bowl XXXV to conduct a high-tech surveillance experiment on its unsuspecting guests. In total secrecy (but with the full cooperation of the National Football League), the faces of each of the games' 72,000 attendees were scanned and checked against a database of potential troublemakers. The news, first reported in the St. Petersburg *Times,* raises some urgent questions: is this the end of crime—or the end of privacy?

The surveillance system, FaceTrac, is based on technology originally developed at the Massachusetts Institute of Technology to teach computers to recognize their users, and was installed by a Pennsylvania firm called Graphco Technologies. "It takes everything from forehead to chin," explains Tom Colatosti, CEO of Viisage, whose software drives FaceTrac. "It gets the distance between the eyes, then it calculates the other features: thickness of the lips, angle of the cheekbones, and so on." The beauty of the system is that it is disguise-proof. You can grow a beard and put on sunglasses, and FaceTrac will still pick you out of a crowd.

Tampa police insist that the experiment was harmless. The mugshots against which the fans were checked were drawn from state and federal computer files. According to police spokesperson Joe Durkin, they contained only "known criminals that are attracted to these large events," ranging from "pickpockets, scam artists, con-game players, all the way to terrorists." And the computers were carefully monitored by humans. When the software made a match, it alerted an officer who compared the two faces on screen. Although FaceTrac made 19 positive IDs, no one was arrested.

Everybody involved stresses that this was a test, not a serious at- 5
tempt to catch bad guys. For the police, it was a chance to gauge FaceTrac's effectiveness as a crime-fighting tool. For Graphco and its partners, it was a chance to see whether the system could capture tens of thousands of faces in difficult lighting and random angles and process them in real time—while grabbing a little free publicity. "It was a phenomenal success," says Colatosti. "If you had told me the day before that we'd get one, that would be great. The fact that we caught 19, that's astounding!"

Not everybody is so enthusiastic. Representative Edward Markey (D., Mass.) promptly declared himself "appalled" and issued a statement peppered with words like "Orwellian" and "nightmare." The American Civil Liberties Union is calling for public hearings and has requested all documents relating to the surveillance. "It's chilling, the notion that 100,000 people were subject to video surveillance and had their identities checked by the government," says Barry Steinhardt, associate director of the A.C.L.U. "We think the rights of the fans in Tampa were violated."

That may be a tough case to make. Under U.S. law, citizens have no reasonable expectation of privacy in public spaces like the Raymond James Stadium. Furthermore, as Colatosti points out, the Super Bowl surveillance isn't the first of its kind, only the most dramatic. The Viisage system is already deployed in some 70 casinos across the country, from Atlantic City to Las Vegas, to identify cheats and card counters. A similar system has been used for the past two years in a tough section of East London called Newham, where British police attribute a drop in crime to the 300 cameras.

Colatosti insists that the issue is not privacy. "It's simply the fear of change and technology," he says. "Once you've adapted, you look back and say, 'I was afraid of *what?*'" Perhaps. No one disputes that the deployment of cheap, ubiquitous video cameras has made an environment of near total surveillance technologically feasible. Whether that's a good thing or a bad thing, however, depends on how much you trust the cameraman.

What Did You Read?

1. How does a face scanner work?
2. What is the purpose of FaceTrac, the surveillance system?
3. Under U.S. law, in what type of places can citizens not expect to have the right to privacy?

What Do You Think?

1. What public places are you aware of where people are being videotaped? Do you think it is an invasion of privacy? Where can it be protective?
2. What does it mean to say something is "Orwellian"? Is it a knee-jerk reaction to suggest digital security is "nightmarish"?
3. What potential for abuse can you imagine with an abundance of security cameras in our society?
4. What are the obvious benefits of surveillance systems in our workplaces and public environments? What are the problems?

How Was It Done?

1. What single word best crystallizes the article?

2. How important are the experts the author uses to the credibility of this article? Explain.

3. How big a part does the appeal to values have in this argument? Explain.

Narcissus Cloned

John J. Conley

Another important technological development in recent years is cloning. John J. Conley argues against human cloning. He claims it violates human dignity and the respect for human life, that it subverts human diversity, and threatens to destroy human love.

Key Words

lay person	a person who does not belong to a particular profession or who is not an expert in a particular field
incipient	beginning to come into being
impoverishment	made poor; deprived of strength, richness, or fertility
corporeal	relating to the physical body
eugenics	the science of improving of hereditary qualities of a race or breed
anomalies	irregularities; something different or abnormal
dexterity	mental skill or quickness; readiness and grace in physical activity
conjugal	of or relating to the state of being married
discernment	the quality of being able to grasp or understand a difficult concept
nuanced	having subtle distinction or variation
intrinsic	belonging to the essential nature of a thing

The recent experiment in human cloning in Washington, D.C. has provoked moral unease in the public. Both specialists and laypersons sense that this new technology is fraught with ethical and political peril. The discussion of the ethics of human cloning, however, rarely moves from intuitive praise and blame to careful analysis of the moral values—more frankly, the disvalues—presented by this practice. The discussion also reveals the moral impoverishment of our culture's categories for dealing with biotechnological challenges because the key ethical issues are often obscured by a bland subjectivism that reduces moral values to the simple desire of the parent or researcher.

Here I will sketch out the moral debits of the practice of cloning and criticize the narrow types of moral reasoning that have prevented our society from collectively facing the incipient ethical and political dangers in this practice.

First, human cloning violates respect for the life of each human being, which is due from the moment of conception. While empirical science as such cannot determine the nature and extension of the person, it is indisputable that conception marks the radical beginning of the personal history of each human being. Many of the physical characteristics that clearly influence our interpersonal relations, such as gender, height and somatic constitution, are clearly shaped in the moment of conception. Contemporary genetic research continues to reveal how profoundly other more "spiritual" traits of the person, such as intelligence and emotive temperament, are molded by one's conceptive history. The insistence that respect for human life begin at the time of conception is not a sectarian doctrine. Until quite recently, it formed the keystone of medical ethics, as witnessed by the influential doctor's oath designed by the World Medical Association in the aftermath of World War II: "I will maintain the utmost respect for human life from the moment of conception."

Current experimentation in human cloning deliberately conceives a human being for the sake of research and then designates this human embryo for destruction. It is true that this pre-embryo represents a human being in an extremely primitive state of development. Nonetheless, this minute being remains clearly human (it can belong to no other species), uniquely human (due to its singular corporeal occupation of space and time) and, if placed in the proper environment, a being with an internal capacity to develop the distinctly human faculties of intellect and will.

The fabrication and destruction of human embryos may appear a   5
minor assault on life in a U.S. society numbed by 1.5 million abortions a year and Dr. Jack Kevorkian's house calls. The acid test of whether we corporately esteem human life, however, is not found primarily in our treatment of powerful adults. Rather, it emerges in our treatment of the vulnerable, like these fragile human beings at the dawn of gestation.

Second, the practice of cloning undermines one of the key values of social interaction: human diversity. Emmanuel Levinas, a contemporary French philosopher, argues that the central challenge in interpersonal contact is accepting the other person precisely as other, as something more than the mirror image of oneself. One of the oddest of the recent arguments in favor of human cloning went something like this: Childbearing will be easier for the parents if they can raise siblings hatched from the same egg, since the parents will always be dealing with children having the identical genetic code. (We could even save on the clothing bills.) It is hard to see how the family will benefit from becoming a hall of mirrors. The moral apprenticeship of family life consists precisely in the recognition of differences among siblings and the parents' recognition that their children are not simply the projection of their plans and wishes.

The possible reduction of human difference in a regime of routine cloning raises troubling political issues. Just who or what will constitute the model for the clonable human? Which race? Which physical composition? Which emotional temperament? Which kind of intelligence and at what level? The development of earlier biotechnologies, such as amniocentesis and eugenic abortion, has already begun to homogenize the human population.

Several sources indicate that up to 90 percent of fetuses with Down Syndrome are currently aborted in the United States. The tendency to eliminate those ticketed as "disabled" contradicts the gains of the disability fights movement, which correctly urges us to respect and include those who are different because of physical or mental anomalies. Certain enthusiasts for cloning appear to dream Narcissus-like of a uniform humanity created in their own idealized image, an amalgam of Einstein and the Marlboro Man. Our aesthetic values, which focus so frequently on the unique timbre of a human voice or the difference between two human faces, would fade in such a monocolor regime. One can only marvel at the moral dexterity of our generation, which valiantly defends everything from the whale to the snail-darter lest biodiversity be lost, yet calmly greets our growing destruction of the human other through eugenic technology.

Third, the practice of cloning undermines the integrity of human love. Human beings, until quite recently, have usually been conceived in the conjugal embrace of their parents. In marital intercourse, the two values of union between the spouses and the procreation of the family's children remain indissoluble. It is the same act unifying the couple and bringing forth the nascent child. Cloning, however, stands to radicalize the divorce between conjugal union and procreation already introduced by in vitro fertilization. A third person, the scientist in the laboratory, invades the once-intimate drama of the generation of children.

I have long been haunted by the remark of Louise Brown, the first 10 child successfully conceived in vitro, when the doctor who had artificially conceived her died. Louise was plunged into grief. She told the press: "I feel that I have lost the person who made me"—as if the role once reserved to God and parent had now passed to the scientist in the white coat. The ancient setting of procreation, the sacramental embrace of spouses, is abandoned in favor of the fertile/sterile laboratory.

The initial experiment in human cloning indicates how radically procreation has been divorced from conjugal union. The sperm and egg, provided by anonymous donors, were deliberately fused to fabricate a human embryo that would deteriorate within several days. It is true that in the future married couples struggling with infertility might resort to cloning technology. Even in this case, however, the wedge between unitive and procreative values remains. The intimate union between the conjugal gift of love and life remains severed.

The language employed by journalists to describe these new means of generation also indicates the sea change wrought by cloning and related techniques. "Procreation" becomes "reproduction." "The glimmer in my parents' eyes" becomes "the product of conception." "The act of love" becomes "reproductive technology." The reduction of the child, once the immediate evidence of romance, to a product of the laboratory suggests the assault on the integrity of human love implicit in this practice.

Cloning's infringements on the basic goods of life, love and otherness ultimately challenge human dignity itself. Immanuel Kant argues that human dignity entails the recognition that other human beings are ends in themselves, worthy of respect, rather than means to the ends of individual persons or society as a whole. Widespread cloning, however, would radically reduce humans to a eugenic mean. The human embryo would lose all claim to moral respect and legal protection by serving as an object of scientific curiosity or as an aid, easily discarded, to human fertility. In such a eugenic regime, human beings would increasingly be valued only for possessing certain socially desirable traits rather than for the simple fact that they exist as humans. By reducing the human person to an object stripped of intrinsic worth, routine cloning could threaten the ensemble of human rights itself.

The task of developing a moral response to the advent of human cloning is rendered all the more problematic by the superficial debate our society is currently conducting on this issue. Whether on the editorial page of *The New York Times* or on Phil and Oprah's television screen, the discussion tends to obscure the key moral problems raised by this practice. Certain popular types of reasoning prevent, rather than assist, the careful debate we deserve on this issue.

One common approach is the Luddite condemnation of all genetic 15 engineering. Jeremy Rifkin, the most visible critic of the cloning experiment, exemplifies this approach. This position argues that the moral and political risks of genetic engineering are so grave that we should simply censure and, where possible, ban all such technology. References to Pandora's Box, Frankenstein and the Third Reich decorate this blanket condemnation of all scientific intervention into human gestation. Such a categorical critique of biotechnology refuses to discern the different moral values present in the quite varied operations of genetic technology. While human cloning quite clearly appears to distort basic human goods, other therapeutic interventions can legitimately heal infertility and help an individual struggling with a genetic malady. Moral panic cannot ground a nuanced discernment of these disparate technological interventions.

Another approach, frequently offered by the proponents of cloning, contends that the current experiments are simply "scientific research." Since they are just research, they should not be the object of moral critique. In other words, the Pope & Co. should chill out. This aura of value-free science seriously constricts the scope of the moral enterprise. The object of moral judgment is any human action, i.e., any act of human beings rooted in intellect and will. Moral scrutiny of scientific action is eminently justified inasmuch as such action is patently the result of rational deliberation and choice. The effort to sequester human cloning from ethical judgment, like the earlier attempt to "take morality and politics out of fetal tissue research," simply blinds us to the moral values at stake.

Perhaps the most common reasoning used to justify human cloning is the subjectivist approach. As the editors of *The New York Times* argued, the producers of the material for cloning—I presume they mean the parents—should be the only ones to decide how the product is to be used. A thousand callers on radio talk shows claimed that "Father (or mother) knows best" and that no one could judge the clients and doctors who resort to this practice. Several proponents piously argued that these researchers sincerely wanted to help infertile couples. Such noble motives exempted them from moral censure.

In such a subjectivist perspective, the only relevant moral value is the motive of the parties concerned, and the only virtue is unqualified tolerance for the desire of the scientist or the parent. Such subjectivism systematically averts its gaze from the action of cloning itself, and the question of whether or how this practice destroys human goods can never be raised. Moral scrutiny of this action is suffocated under a sentimental veil of compassion or, worse, under the steely curtain of private property rights.

The subjectivists legitimately highlight the psychological plight of infertile couples who desire to bear children. They suppress, however, the salient ethical issue of which means, under what conditions, can properly be used to remedy this problem of infertility. An ancient moral and legal tradition tightly censures the buying and selling of infants as a just solution. There is a growing moral consensus that the violent battles over legal custody, not to mention the destruction of surplus embryos, have revealed the moral disvalues of surrogate mothering. Sentimental appeals to the pain of infertile couples "open to life" easily mask the ethical dangers of technologies that attempt to remedy infertility by the calculated manipulation and destruction of human lives.

The accompanying political debate must squarely question 20 whether this practice promotes or vitiates the common good. Conducting such a trenchant debate, however, is problematic in a society that increasingly perceives moral judgments as the arbitrary product of emotion or preference.

What Did You Read?

1. What does "subjectivism" mean? Is it possible not to be subjective?
2. What are some of the reasons for why the author believes human cloning is unethical?
3. Why does the author refer to Narcissus, a figure from Greek mythology?

What Do You Think?

1. Why do you suppose those skeptical of the benefits of cloning and those who label pro-cloners as "wishing to play God" do not attack other life-preserving technologies? Cannot many medical procedures, such as heart transplants and giving injections to mothers to prevent Rh babies, also be considered "playing God"?
2. Is it possible to stop advances in technology, such as cloning?
3. Is cloning a life-affirming advance or is it a dehumanizing technology?
4. If human beings are ultimately responsible for the creation of life, including by means of cloning, do we need to limit the definition of life and the apparatus of creation?

How Was It Done?

1. How does the title seem to catch the essence of Conley's moral stance over the issue of cloning in this article?
2. Does classification help to organize the political and ethical dangers of cloning?
3. How important is Conley's knowledge of those arguments about cloning that conflict with his own to the overall development of his point of view? Discuss.
4. Is the article primarily supported by facts or values? Explain.

Clear Thinking about Human Cloning

Terence Hines

Terence Hines offers an argument for human cloning that is based on rejecting what he feels are many misconceptions held both by the general public and by some in the scientific community. He approvingly comments on the work of Gregory Pence, a professor of philosophy, who argued that if human cloning ever becomes reality, it will be just simply another reproductive option. He argues that people's worst fears have no grounds in science or human behavior.

Key Words

fear-mongering	trying to stir up fear in a population
drivel	to talk stupidly or carelessly
cogently	convincingly; appealing to reason
nucleus	a central point; in a cell, the essential core governing its functions
intrauterine	from within the uterus
automaton	a mechanism that is self-operating; a robot
commemorate	to call to remembrance
bioethicist	someone who deals with the ethical implications of biological and medical research

Who's Afraid of Human Cloning? is the best thing I've seen written about cloning since the birth of Dolly the cloned sheep in 1997. The vast majority of post-Dolly writing on cloning, especially in the nonscientific press, has been near-hysterical fear-mongering drivel. Typically, commentators trot out the worst possible, and most unlikely, horrors that they think (hope?) might grow out of successful human cloning, such as being threatened with dozens of Hitlers (or Saddams, or whomever). Or the possibility that an army of mindless clones might be created by some ruthless warlord. Or the possibility that rich individuals might have themselves cloned, but leave out the genes for the brain, so that they would have a spare parts source.

Gregory Pence, a professor of philosophy at the University of Alabama in Birmingham, destroys such arguments against human cloning. He argues cogently that if and when human cloning becomes possible, it will represent little more than another step in reproductive technology and one that individuals should be free to choose if they desire.

Regarding the idea that a group of clones could be created from the cells of an evil ruler, Pence points out one of the most misunderstood aspects of cloning. This is the belief that a cloned individual would be genetically identical to the individual from whom the cell nucleus was obtained. To make this point clear, it is necessary to provide a bit of detail on how cloning is done. Basically, a cell (it need not be an egg) is obtained from a female and the nucleus of that cell is removed. Then a nucleus from a cell from the individual to be cloned is obtained and inserted into the enucleated cell from the female. This now nucleated cell is placed in a uterus and allowed to implant and come to term. The individual generated in this fashion will almost never be genetically identical to the individual who was cloned. This is because the female that donated the cell into which the nucleus is inserted will almost never be the mother of the individual who donated the cell nucleus. It is common knowledge in the biological sciences, but apparently almost totally unknown outside, that there is DNA not only in the cell nucleus, but in the cell's cytoplasm. This is known as mitochondrial DNA. Thus, a cloned individual will have the nuclear DNA of one individual, but the mitochondrial DNA of another. Mitochondrial DNA plays important roles in biological processes in the cytoplasm and in a number of serious diseases.

Only if the enucleated cell came from the nucleus donor's biological mother would the cloned individual be identical to the nucleus donor genetically. But this would certainly not mean that the cloned individual would be identical to the nucleus donor in every respect. Unless, that is, environment, both in utero and after birth, has absolutely no influence on any aspect of the individual's physical and behavioral development. In the case of humans, environmental influences have major effects on the more psychological aspects of an individual. Even if, as now seems likely, genetic factors can account for around half of the variance in different aspects of personality, intelligence, and the like, this means that environmental factors are responsible for the other half.

So, for Saddam, or whomever, to try to create himself over again, 5 he'd have to get cells from his mother, try to duplicate her intrauterine environment as it was 50 or so years ago, and recreate his own childhood experiences during at least the first 15 or so years of the clones' lives, just to have a reasonable shot at turning out someone like himself. Does this sound very likely? Not at all. Like conspiracy theories that fall apart when one considers how much effort would have had to be put into the conspiracy if it were true, so worries about cloning disappear when one considers the practical side of actually doing the cloning.

Another excellent example is the often-expressed fear that someone like Saddam could create an army of mindless automatons. First, no one would really want an army of automatons. They'd make lousy soldiers, being unable to make any decisions on their own. That aside, cloned humans would still be human in every respect. Each would have their own mind, personality, fears, dreams, and so on. Even if these objections aren't enough, cloning an army would be an astonishingly costly and inefficient way of getting an army. First you'd have to get lots of nuclei, and then lots of uteri. Then you'd have to let the embryos come to term. Then you'd have to wait another 18 years or so before the clone army would be old enough and trained enough to go into combat. Wouldn't it be a whole lot easier to raise an army the old fashioned way—draft young men when they are of age? Thus, the "army of automatons" objection turns out, with a little thought, to be just plain silly.

What if the cloning process turns out humans who are in some way abnormal? Perhaps there will be physical harm. But certainly, before it becomes generally available, human cloning would have been tested on primates to establish its safety, just like any other medical procedure. Or perhaps there will be psychological harm, with cloned children seen by their peers as "freaks." But how would anyone know if a given child (or adult) is a clone? They won't have a bar code birthmark on their forehead, or the word "clone" in big red letters on the backs of their hands!

Other, more scientific-sounding objections fare no better when subjected to Pence's penetrating analysis. For examples, maybe human clones would reduce human genetic diversity. But, if and when it becomes available, human cloning will be an expensive procedure to be used only in extreme situations. There will be few human clones out there. Most people will continue to produce their offspring via the considerably more enjoyable procedure of having sex.

Pence points out that the arguments against human cloning are very similar to those put forward against "test tube babies" (now known as in vitro fertilization—IVF) in the late 1970s. In fact, the clamor over IVF was nearly as great then as the clamor over cloning is now. But, twenty-one years after the birth of Louise Brown, the first IVF baby in 1978, IVF is so widely accepted that it has just been commemorated by the British Post Office. The 63 pence denomination in the BPO's "millennium" series of stamps noting great events of the century illustrates a small bronze statue of a baby commemorating Ms. Brown's birth.

In addition to the specific objections to human cloning, there has also been a lot of hand wringing with a more philosophical tone. Pence (p. 46) quotes Nigel Cameron, a bioethicist and theologian at Trinity International University (Deerfield, Illinois) as saying that human cloning "would be perhaps the worst thing we have ever thought of in the maltreatment of our species. It [sic] would be a new kind of slave class. You would have human beings who were made by other human beings for their purposes." But, as I've noted, there is no reason whatsoever to think that cloned humans would be slaves. The parents who went to all the trouble to have a child via cloning would, if anything, be especially loving of that child. And what about these children being made for their parents' "purposes"? Well, yes—but how is this different than when two people have sex to have a child? That child, also, was made for the parents' "purpose"—the purpose of having a child.

Another example: Well-known bioethicist Leon Klass of the University of Chicago (quoted on p. 46) has said, "It is not at all clear to what extent a clone will truly be a moral agent." Of course it's clear.

Cloned humans are going to be just as human as you and me and will have all the legal rights of any other human being in whatever society they are born into.

Along these lines, Pence is critical of the failure of most "physicians, distinguished scientists, and some well-known bioethicists" (p. 36) to reduce the misinformation that flooded the press after Dolly. Some of this misinformation, as the quotes above demonstrate, was actually produced by these very people.

Pence is especially scathing in his discussion of the National Bioethics Advisory Commission (NBAC), the board that President Clinton ordered to come up with a recommendation on human cloning following Dolly. The Commission recommended a total ban on human cloning. Pence notes that this was done with no real debate on the issue. The Commission knew that Congress wanted a total ban, and it provided one. Proponents of human cloning were not welcome to testify before the Commission, although a large number of individuals who objected on religious grounds presented their views.

Pence argues convincingly that the horrors and dangers of human cloning have been vastly exaggerated and that the procedure should be seen as nothing more than another reproductive option. In a free society government has no business limiting safe reproductive options, certainly not on religious grounds. He makes the most valuable suggestion that the emotionally charged word "clone" be dropped and replaced by the more accurate and descriptive term "nuclear somatic transfer" or NST, just as "test tube baby" was replaced by IVF.

What Did You Read?

1. What is an "enucleated cell"? What does it have to do with cloning?

2. According to Hines, why is it that a nucleated cell, placed in a uterus and allowed to come to term, will almost never be genetically identical to the individual who was cloned?

3. Why are so many of the anti-cloning arguments silly, according to Hines? Offer specific examples.

What Do You Think?

1. For what reasons might people opt for cloning when producing their offspring rather than choosing more conventional means?

2. Do you believe there would be any psychological trauma involved in being a clone (e.g., not having two real parents, being identical to someone else)? Explain.

3. Do you foresee cloning as another option that will separate the rich from the poor?

How Was It Done?

1. How does the article "Who's Afraid of Human Cloning" serve as an introductory springboard for a discussion about cloning?
2. How effective is Hines's use of the definition of cloning in the third paragraph of his article toward the development of his thesis?
3. How well organized are the author's counterarguments to the specific objections to cloning he lays out in the article?

The Virtualizing of Education

Samuel L. Dunn

In "The Virtualizing of Education," Samuel L. Dunn explores how technology combines with education to form "distance education," a form of education in which the traditional classroom is gone and courses are taken over by computers or by television. He predicts that the traditional university is on its way to becoming a relic, and that receiving education either through television or online will be the norm, not the exception. "Live faculty instruction" will not totally disappear, but it will occupy only a small niche in the education arena. The effect this will have on what it means to get an education will be enormous.

Key Words

imperative	necessary; not to be avoided or evaded
accredited	officially authorized or approved
antiquate	to make old or obsolete
asynchronous	not synchronous; not happening at the same time
commodity	a good or product for sale
certifying	confirming or guaranteeing
assessment	appraisal; determining the importance or value of something
consortia	associations or societies; groups that agree to pursue a course of action
methodologies	bodies of rules or procedures employed by a discipline

Education is an absolute imperative in the emerging global knowledge society, so new ways of providing access to education for a much higher percentage of the population are now being devised.

The most dramatic examples of access to education are found in the 11 distance-education mega-universities found around the world. In "distance education," the student is separated in time or space from the teacher or professor. The largest of these high enrollment universities is in China, the China Central Radio and Television University, with more than 3 million students. The English-speaking world has the British Open University, with 215,000 students, and the University of South Africa, with 120,000 students. In addition to the mega-universities, dozens of other national and regional systems are providing education at all levels to students. The Open University of Hong Kong, Universidade Aberta (Portugal), the Universidad Nacional de Education a Distancia (Spain), and the recently formed Western Governors University (United States) are just a few of those providing lower and/or higher education to needy citizenry.

Learning from Afar

The base delivery system for the distance-education mega-universities is television, supplemented by other technologies or even some onsite instruction in more-developed countries. Some distance-education systems use two-way interactive video connections to particular locations where students gather, others supplement with the Internet, and still others deliver only by Internet. With video- and audio-streaming now available, the Internet appears to be the technology of choice for systems where students have access to computers. Of course, these technologies merely add to the radio-delivered courses that have been offered for years in many countries around the world.

The programs and courses offered vary from basic literacy courses to the highest graduate-level programming. Hundreds of university degrees are now available through distance education, where 90% or more of the required credits are given at a distance, as are dozens of master's degrees and a small number of accredited doctoral degrees. One estimate suggests that 50,000 university-level courses are now available through distance-education delivery systems.

How will distance education affect traditional schools and universities? Primary and secondary schools have been a standard in most of the English-speaking world for at least a century. A large installed base of higher-education institutions provides adult and postsecondary educational services to students. In the United States, there are more than 3,600 accredited institutions of higher education, about half public and half independent. In addition, there are about the same number of other kinds of schools, colleges, and institutes that have access to federal funding for their students. The United Kingdom has approximately 120 recognized universities and hundreds of other educational institutions. It would seem that such a large installed base of traditional universities and schools would not be threatened by the new distribution channels of the knowledge society, but threatened they are.

Management theorist Peter Drucker has predicted that traditional universities as we know them will become a big wasteland in the next 25 years. The Association of Governing Boards predicts that one-third of the existing independent colleges and universities in the United States will close in the next 10 years.

I predict that 10% of existing public colleges and 50% of independent colleges will close in the next 25 years. Almost all colleges will be radically reshaped by the digital revolution.

The Virtual Student Body

The shape of the future of higher education in North America and Europe is starting to be visible. One of the most important features is that boundaries of time and space are being eliminated. When students had to go to a particular location to access their educational programs, it made sense to talk about regional accreditation, tuition areas, service regions, and semesters. The new delivery systems antiquate these notions. With asynchronous delivery on the Internet, for example, the same course can be taken by a student in Hong Kong or Helsinki, Pretoria or Peoria. These changes in delivery will make it necessary to develop new ways of accrediting or approving courses and programs that students may receive from many parts of the world.

There will be two main types of educational institutions: those that add value in coursework and those that are certifying agencies. The certifying colleges and universities are those that act as educational bankers for students. Students will earn credits from many places and have the credits or certifications of completion sent to the certifying university, then that certifying university will award the degree when enough credits of the right type have been accumulated. Regent's College of the University of the State of New York and Thomas Edison College of New Jersey are public certifying institutions that give accredited degrees.

One vision for some of the remaining residential colleges in the 10 United States, now serving mainly the 18-to 23-year-old population, is that many will become certifying colleges. Students will come to the colleges for their social, artistic, athletic, and spiritual programs. The basic commodity these colleges will sell is membership in the college community. Students will access their courses from colleges and universities around the world, transfer the credits to the college, then gain a degree. Faculty members will serve as tutors and advisers and may provide some courses live.

Most traditional colleges and universities already could be classified as certifying institutions. With more than 50% of all college graduates studying in more than one institution before graduating, most colleges readily accept the courses that are transferred in from other accredited institutions. In a majority of institutions, even now, a student has to take only one year of credits from that institution to get a degree.

The distinction between distance education and local education will become blurred. Almost all courses in the residential college of the future will be digitally enhanced. Because distance-education methodologies provide some advantages to student learning, those techniques will be incorporated into local teaching. By the year 2025, at least 95% of instruction in the United States will be digitally enhanced.

Digital courseware for most college-level courses will be available much sooner than 2025. Studies have shown that there are 25 college-level courses that get about 50% of the total credit enrollment across U.S. higher education. Among these are Introduction to Psychology, U.S. History, Introduction to English Composition, Statistics, Introductory Spanish, and Calculus. There will be "killer applications" for these 25 courses available by 2010. These killer apps—so-called because of their quality, their comprehensive character, and their widespread usage—will be available for both distance and local usage. Courseware publishers will realize huge profits from these applications.

As we make the transition to the new world of education, thousands of organizations will develop their own digitized courseware, thus reinventing the wheel over and over again. However, a general shakeout of courseware developers will leave a small number of courseware consortia and companies that will provide the bulk of courseware. These groups will sell courses directly to students and license courseware to colleges and universities.

While the number of traditional educational institutions will go 15 down, the number of providers of higher education will increase. The 7,000 current providers recognized by the U.S. Department of Education will grow to 10,000 by the year 2025. Publishers, corporations, for-profit and nonprofit entities will get into the education business, because there is big money to be made. Publishers will sell courses directly to students and thus eliminate the university middleman. The present 1,000 corporate universities will double by 2025.

Money is big in education. The United States alone spends $600 billion on education of all types each year, making it the second largest industry after health care. With estimates that the typical citizen will need the equivalent of 30 semester credits of coursework each 10 years to keep up with the changes that are coming, entrepreneurs see opportunities for large profits.

The need for continuing education is growing—a trend that will be compounded as the population base increases. The number of students needing traditional higher education in the United States is predicted to climb from the present 15 million to an estimated 20 million by the year 2010. Of the 6 billion people now on the globe, more than 1 billion are teenagers. It will be a gargantuan task to provide the education these people need to reap the benefits of the new world economy.

While entrepreneurs and for-profit organizations go after the profits available, governments will try to make education more efficient and save taxpayer dollars. Seamless education policies will make the transition from primary to secondary to higher education easier. Students will be encouraged to finish high school and college in six or seven years. States and provinces will provide financial incentives to institutions and directly to students to move through the system faster than normal.

The home-school movement will lead to the home-college movement. With the increased emphasis on educational outcomes, new systems of examinations and other assessment techniques will be made available to students who wish to study on their own. Certifying universities will provide the needed degrees and credentials.

Many independent colleges and universities will close, but there will still be a niche market for residential universities. Universities that provide a religious community or other special programming for older adolescents will still be viable and desirable. To survive, and to attract students who are willing to pay the differential price, these institutions must provide high-quality special-interest programming for the niche. Much more than coursework must be available and delivered.

Networked Education

We are moving away from the factory university, a place-bound, product-oriented institution that provides educational services—teaching, research, and service—to its clients at the time, place, and pace desired by the institution.

The virtual university is next—not a single institution, but a web of educational providers that collectively distribute services to the client at the time, place, pace, and style desired by the client, with quality determined by the client and a variety of approving and accrediting bodies. The virtual university has been born and is growing rapidly; it will be the predominant mode of higher education by the year 2025.

While higher education will enjoy the most dramatic changes, primary and secondary education will change as well. These levels of instruction will be heavily digitized in the years ahead, although more emphasis will be given to moving students out of the home in order to benefit from socialization and enculturation with live teachers and classmates.

Alternatives to the public schools will continue to grow and be more popular. Television- and Internet-delivered courseware to support home schoolers is already being written and disseminated. Increasing demands for quality will be heard and responded to by public schools, church schools, and both nonprofit and for-profit entrepreneurs.

These are exciting days in education. Education is an absolute ne- 25 cessity for the knowledge society. Change is rapidly altering the face of educational delivery, but one thing is sure: The English-speaking world will continue to invest large portions of its resources to assuring an educated citizenry for the future.

---

16 Predictions for Higher Education

1. The number of degree-granting institutions will continue to grow, while the number of traditional campuses will decline. By 2025, half of today's existing independent colleges will be closed, merged, or significantly altered in mission.
2. University degrees and programs at all levels will be available by information technologies from all quality levels of educational institutions.
3. Courseware producers will sell courses and award credits directly to the end user and thus, through intermediation, bypass the institutional middleman.
4. There will be two principal types of degree and certificate-granting institutions: value-added and certification institutions.
5. The distinction between distance and local education will be blurred. Almost all courses will be digitally enhanced. There will be a small group of colleges that will carve out a market niche by maintaining "live faculty instruction" in their course delivery.
6. Seamless education between high school, undergraduate college, and graduate programs will be the norm. Incentives will be given to students and institutions to move students through their programs at a fast rate.
7. The home-school movement will lead to a home-college movement.
8. The remaining campus-based colleges and universities will increasingly move to responsibility-center management and will outsource many functions now done by the institution.
9. Cities will expect colleges and universities to pay taxes or a "voluntary" equivalent for services rendered by the city.
10. The U.S. government will continue to certify institutions for access to student financial aid. By 2010, the number of eligible institutions will jump from about 7,000 at present to more than 10,000.

(continued)

11. Faculty in traditional colleges and universities will revolt against technological delivery of courses and programs and against the emerging expectations for faculty. Unionization and strikes will increase as faculty fight a rear-guard action to try to slow down or stop the inevitable.

12. Accreditation and program approval will be based more on educational outcomes. Testing programs will be put in place by discipline organizations, federal and state governments, corporations, and testing companies. Large corporations will develop their own approval systems. By 2025, there will not be one national accreditation system, although the U.S. Department of Education will provide a basic safety net for quality.

13. The big growth in adult and postsecondary education will be in degree and certificate programs for older adults. To be viable in the information society, the typical adult will need to take at least 30 semester credits every 10 years.

14. By 2005, there will be "killer" courseware applications covering the 25 college courses that enroll 50% of all credits.

15. Consortia of colleges, universities, and other kinds of institutions will increasingly band together to produce and deliver courses for students in their member institutions. Many of these consortia will seek their own accreditation and approval.

16. The distinctions between and among public and private, for-profit and nonprofit institutions of higher education will largely disappear.

What Did You Read?

1. What is "distance education"?

2. As described by the author, what will be the two main types of educational institutions?

3. Explain the sentence, "Money is big in education."

4. What are a few of the author's predictions for higher education?

What Do You Think?

1. How will distance learning affect the home-school movement?

2. In your opinion, how will distance learning enhance education? What will be the primary disadvantages of distance learning?

3. Do you think distance learning will dehumanize education?

How Was it Done?

1. How important are statistics to the overall support of this article?
2. Do the subtitles help to organize the support of this article?
3. Is the author's list of sixteen predictions for higher education at the end of the work instructional and convincing concerning his forecast that technology-based education is inevitable?

Look Out for the Luddite Label
Langdon Winner

Langdon Winner argues that those who question the value of many of today's techno-logical advances are scoffed at and pushed to the side. They are labeled "Luddites" in memory of the 19th-century workers who smashed textile machinery in a vain attempt to hold back progress (and keep their jobs). Winner says it is possible to be critical of technological change without being unreasonable and that the full-scale embrace of change and technology is not always for the best.

Key Words

skeptics	people with an attitude of doubt
juggernaut	a massive force that crushes whatever is in its path
tepid	lukewarm; lacking in passion or zeal
beneficence	the performing of acts of kindness
displaced	banished; driven out
ecological	referring to the branch of science concerned with the relationship between life forms and their environment
untrammeled	not beaten down; not restrained; having freedom
starkly	harshly; bluntly
opprobrium	contempt; public disgrace or fame
saturation	completely infiltrated; permeated

Society suffers when skeptics about the juggernaut of technological change are pushed to the policy-making sidelines.

"I'm no Luddite, but. . . ." we often hear people give this apology as they begin even the most tepid criticism about some technology or another. Evidently, it's important to let everybody know that you still affirm the overall beneficence of technological progress. How astonishing, then, to read in the *Wall Street Journal* and other recent press reports that a movement of "Neo-Luddites" is taking shape in the United States.

The original Luddites were displaced workers in early nineteenth-century England who resisted the destruction of their traditional, crafts economy by mechanized industrial production. In an era when labor organizing was illegal, the followers of the mythical "Ned Ludd" smashed textile machines as a protest against a system whose rise spelled their eventual doom. In the end, the British army brutally crushed the rioters.

Those who adopt the term Luddite today (or have it thrust upon them by others) turn out to be a diverse group of writers and social activists—Stephanie Mills, Jerry Mander, Wendell Berry, Chellis Glendinning, Kirkpatrick Sale, and Andrew Kimbrell, among others—whose views include a marked skepticism about what mainstream thinking considers economic and technical "advance." They argue that our technology-driven world is moving too fast in the wrong direction.

Among the beliefs they share are the following: 5

- Simple, conventional tools are often superior to the complex, high-tech instruments that replace them.
- Technical change ought to be guided by principles of social justice, ecological harmony, and personal dignity rather than the untrammeled pursuit of efficiency and profit.
- It is better to derive energy from renewable resources than from burning oil and coal.
- Methods of organic farming are superior to those of chemical-intensive agriculture.
- Local and regional economies are more sustainable than ones geared to global production and trade.
- The pursuit of a well-balanced life is not compatible with the speed and intensity of activity that today's digital electronics demand.

Neo-Luddite philosophers do not oppose technology per se; rather, they present a collection of arguments about what good technologies would look like and how to cultivate the wisdom needed to choose them. In fact, many enthusiastic techno-skeptics in this camp are deeply involved with highly sophisticated—though not necessarily modern—technical devices. Thus the writings of philosopher/novelist Wendell Berry describe in loving detail what the implements and methods of traditional agriculture mean for the soil, plants, and communities that use them. Eco-anarchist film-maker Godfrey Reggio employs state-of-the-art tools of cinematography in movies that starkly depict the dangers of today's global production system. Do these choices make Berry or Reggio "anti-technology"? Only zealots for technologies of a different brand would make that claim.

The ultimate purpose of labeling some approaches to technical practice as anti-technology or Luddism is not difficult to discern. Applying the decals of opprobrium—romantic, unrealistic, negative—to dissenters effectively excludes them from policy debates. When those who have serious reservations about the latest high-tech development are marginalized and stigmatized, the juggernaut of ill-considered change can proceed unimpeded.

President Clinton's National Information Infrastructure Advisory Council, for example, recently assembled a panel of luminaries from electronics and communications firms, the entertainment industry, and education to examine prospects for computerizing the nation's schools. But virtually all of the panelists convened were known in advance to be gung-ho for wired education. Not surprisingly, reports on the deliberations of the council stressed the unanimity of panelists' views; apparently few members expressed any fundamental doubts about the wisdom of the project they were considering.

This way of stacking the policy deck is lamentable. Many technologically savvy experts in education now fear that saturation of schools with electronic gadgets is doing more harm than good. But none of the prominent skeptics on this matter, such as New York University's Neil Postman and Stanford's Larry Cuban, were invited to join Clinton's advisory group. Thus, the planning of a grand strategy for American education proceeded smoothly, without any sour notes—and without meaningful debate.

In a climate like this, is it any wonder that people feel compelled 10 to beg forgiveness for occasional lapses into technology criticism? When mere boosterism is mistaken for serious advice, people of a different mind are dismissed as Neo-Luddites. Labels of this sort speed the onslaught of thoughtless innovation, crippling serious debate about the technological alternatives that confront us.

What Did You Read?

1. What does it mean to be a "Luddite"?
2. What are the principles of the neo-Luddites?
3. Why do policymakers exclude critics of technology from the decision-making process?

What Do You Think?

1. Why is it important to have people who doubt the wisdom of some technology seriously included in meaningful debate on our country's policy decisions?

2. What would be some examples of "good" technology? What would be some examples of "bad" technology? Explain your responses.

3. Do you believe that technology has overcomplicated, overchemicalized, and overstressed our daily lives? Explain.

How Was It Done?

1. Is the author's argument based solely on facts or on a philosophical perspective? Explain.

2. Does the bulleted list of beliefs of the "Neo-Luddites" make the information more readable?

3. Does much of this article seem to revolve around terms and labels? If so, how?

Technology as Magnifier of Good and Evil

Robert D. Kaplan

Robert D. Kaplan argues that technological changes are essentially not good or evil, but morally neutral. Instead, technology enhances the ability of people to do either good or evil. The true difference is that those with technology will grow more empowered, and those without technology will be weaker.

Key Words

innovation	introduction of something new
ambivalent	simultaneous and contradictory attitudes toward an object, a person, or an action
unleashing	letting loose
gadgetry	small mechanisms or electronic devices with practical uses but often thought of as novelties
warlordism	acting like a supreme military leader; engaging in the use of force, often excessively or unnecessarily
deteriorate	to impair; to make of inferior quality
ideologies	systematic bodies of ideas about human life and culture
proliferate	to grow rapidly; to increase in numbers quickly

The record of history is clear: Though technological innovations have changed the way we live, they have not changed man's essential nature. Strife is the origin of everything, the ancient Greek philosopher and scientist Heraclitus reminds us. Indeed, technology has always been a tool in man's struggle with other men, magnifying his capacity for both good and evil. The Industrial Revolution liberated man from the fields, but it also created the material framework for trench warfare in World War I and the mass murders perpetrated by Hitler and Stalin. The information revolution will, likewise, have an ambivalent impact, perhaps on an even greater scale: Few inventions have demonstrated the capacity for social and economic transformation like the computer. Yet history shows that rapid social development is often accompanied by violence and inequality.

A person writing at the end of the nineteenth century—when words like fascism and totalitarianism were still unknown—might have intuited the evils of the coming fifty years had he or she concentrated on how technology was increasing the power of the state in Europe and Japan. Bearing this legacy in mind, I worry about two consequences of the new information technologies: their tendency to widen the gap between those cultures that are already good at producing exportable material wealth and those that aren't; and the ability of these new technologies to enrich and complicate personal life at the expense of the community and the state. Whereas the Industrial Revolution constructed the massified state, the information revolution could deconstruct it, unleashing forms of benign and unbenign chaos at the same time that the computer revolution increasingly reveals how some cultures and subgroups are more technologically proficient than others. Therefore, group tensions will intensify, even as the state's ability to contain these tensions diminishes. Ultimately, the state may be replaced by something better. But this transformation, taking up most of the next century, will be cruel.

People are not passive actors who can be lifted up by their bootstraps with gadgetry. Technological innovations are useless if there is no civil order. What good are new vaccines in areas of Africa where health clinics are vandalized and there is no electric current for refrigeration because there is no tradition of maintenance? You can provide computers, but you cannot provide habits like maintenance, record-keeping, and returning messages on time—habits upon which a postmodern society depends. In a world where wealth will be less and less determined by muscle labor, technology's advance will further expose some racial and ethnic fault lines.

For example, Africa's per capita income growth rates are usually driven by price hikes in agricultural commodities, not by the attainment of the industrial and postindustrial skills that drive growth in Asia. In fact, large parts of Africa show few signs of undergoing even an industrial revolution, let alone a postindustrial one.

In the Indian subcontinent and China, meanwhile, the central state 5
apparatus is decomposing, leading to the rise of regional, economic warlordism. The acceleration of information technologies in these

areas is helping to create Westernized, middle-class bubbles, whereby businesses and home offices are maintained by private electricity generators, private water wells, and private security guards, even as state electricity, water, and police systems deteriorate. These middle-class bubbles are large, but the numbers of the poor and the subproletariat in the subcontinent and China are much larger. Information technology will certainly bring the middle classes of Asia and the rest of the world closer together, but they will become like the aristocrats of medieval Europe, who had more in common with each other than with their own peasant populations. Traditional state forms will not forever survive such crosscutting loyalties.

In postindustrial societies, information technologies will undermine the bureaucratic state in other ways. The federal government, as we know it, is not synonymous with the United States of America, but with the Gilded Age, when great increases in national wealth and population led to a complex society that required a huge bureaucracy to manage it. The building-down of the federal government will continue, whatever the fate of the 1994 Republican revolution, since the accelerating computer revolution will make many bureaucrats redundant while allowing millions of individuals to make end runs around the state. But this hopeful trend comes with a price.

As the late-eighteenth-century Scottish philosopher Adam Ferguson reminds us, human beings are most attached to each other where material conveniences are the least. The decline in civic spirit from the era of classical Greece (when Athenians regularly risked their lives in war and the average citizen took an intense, daily interest in city-state politics) to our own day, when many citizens do not serve in the military and invent excuses to avoid jury duty, is, as Ferguson would suggest, related to the growth in technological conveniences, which have enlarged the parameters of our personal lives, bringing an array of new choices and stresses that leave little time for communal concerns.

We are back to pure history then: the Darwinian struggle of individuals, each made more powerful than ever because of the computer. As the state withers, corporations grow in relative power because corporations—which are run by clusters of individuals committed to financial gain, and thus to efficiency and talent rather than to "politics" and "hiring quotas"—make better use of information technologies than do governments or universities.

But corporations have yet to establish a moral framework to the degree that Western governments have. And as the state proves increasingly unable to control our appetites, the search for new disciplinary values, religious and otherwise, will grow in importance. Remember that as new information proliferates, the past recedes ever faster and historical sensibility (and wisdom) consequently diminishes. Because of the speed at which this information travels, much of it will be unchecked and prove false. Given the greater cultural and material divides, the spread of both conspiracy theories and fierce ideologies has never before known such fertile conditions. We should be trembling.

The twenty-first century will certainly be more tumultuous than the twentieth. In *The Education of Henry Adams*, Adams writes that two thousand years after Alexander the Great and Julius Caesar, the fact that a simple and blunt man of action like Ulysses S. Grant—a type who "should have been extinct for ages"—had attained the presidency, is proof that human nature does not evolve. What future Alexanders, Caesars, Grants, and Hitlers will the computer age give us, I wonder?

What Did You Read?

1. What does Kaplan mean when he says, "Technology has always been a tool in man's struggle with other men, magnifying his capacity for both good and evil"?

2. How do Darwinian struggle and the computer relate?

3. What does Kaplan predict for the 21st century?

What Do You Think?

1. Is it your experience that in our advanced technological society today people are not community-oriented? Are people less involved in our schools, in our libraries, and in our neighborhoods than they used to be?

2. Should we halt our progress and growth because other countries have difficulty catching up to our level of technological development?

3. Is it possible that with the advance of technology and the growth of the Information Age human beings will become stunted in their emotional and spiritual growth? Why or why not?

How Was It Done?

1. How does the title, as well as the introductory paragraph, establish the focus of the article?

2. In your mind, is the comparison between recent technological advances and the Industrial Revolution logical? How so?

3. Do you see a connection, as the author has developed it, between growth in information technologies and a decline in civic spirit? Explain.

The Mike Mulligan Moment: Computers May Be Dumb, But They're Not Too Dumb to Take Your Job

Robert Wright

Robert Wright looks at job loss due to computers. Wright points out that while the computer may recreate new jobs, those new jobs are not easily held by those who lost their jobs in the first place.

Key Words

cognitive	the ability to be aware and show judgment
obsolete	no longer useful; outdated; old-fashioned
incessant	never ending; not stopping
pondering	questioning or wondering
endeavor	a serious and determined effort
dubious	doubtful; of questionable authenticity
impregnable	unconquerable; impenetrable
outmoded	not in style; no longer acceptable or current
tedious	tiresome because of length or dullness; boring

In the week since computers became the best chess-playing species on earth, we homo sapiens have proved that we remain world champs in at least one cognitive domain: rationalizing defeat. While Garry Kasparov was spending his post-match press conference accusing IBM of cheating, commentators around the world were finding other ways to minimize Deep Blue's triumph. CHESS, SHMESS! COMPUTERS STILL CAN'T HANDLE THE TOUGH STUFF, said the headline on a *Boston Globe* article that noted how much trouble machines have understanding a sentence or telling a dog from a cat. Britain's *Daily Telegraph* observed that computers "cannot be properly original" and that there is still no "decent tennis-playing robot." Thus were the *Telegraph*'s readers assured that they and their kind remain "nature's last word."

Maybe the idea here was to dampen the economic insecurity induced by Deep Blue. During the Kasparov match, there were many references to John Henry, who in legend died trying to defend his job against the incessant march of technology—in his case, the steampowered drill. After pondering that outcome, and Deep Blue's triumph, people naturally find it reassuring to be reminded that chess is an artificial endeavor, hardly central to our lives or our livelihoods, and that computers still can't make meaningful small talk.

But the reassurance is false, because computers don't take people's jobs by acting like people. There's no mistaking an automated-teller machine for a bank teller. Bank tellers can tell cats from dogs and play tennis—which they have plenty of time to do after they lose their jobs to ATMs. And the Website where I just bought some running shoes looks nothing at all like a salesperson at the Athlete's Foot. Similarly, if given the choice between lunch with an accountant and lunch with Turbotax, who among us would opt for Turbotax? (O.K., maybe a few people would.) But lunchtime conversation isn't what we want from an accountant anyway.

Often computers, rather than out-and-out stealing their victim's job, just nibble around the edges. The Bell Atlantic directory-assistance operator hasn't been entirely replaced. But with a machine asking you what listing you're after and then giving you the number, and the operator uttering about 4.6 words in between, fewer operators are needed. Even tax-preparation software works that way when accountants themselves use it instead of their old adding machine—the software raises their productivity, thus dampening demand for new accountants. (The use of professionals for tax preparation has so grown in recent decades, though, that you won't see many accountants in breadlines.)

In this sense, the real-world competition is rarely human vs. machine, as it was with Kasparov. It's one kind of tool vs. another kind of tool. Thus the steam drill wasn't really challenging John Henry; it was challenging his sledgehammer. It's the guy using the steam drill who was challenging John Henry. Similarly, the bank teller's competitor is not so much the ATM as the people who design the machine or those who build it or service it. Functionally speaking, they're just bank tellers using new tools. And that's all the old bank teller really needs: new tools—skill as an ATM programmer or servicer.

Of course, this is the refrain of technology's cheerleaders. Jobs don't disappear. They just change. Nimble people with can-do spirit can always find a new one. And on average, the jobs pay better and better. Life gets easier and easier. Actually, I'm one of technology's cheerleaders. Forced to choose between hunting buffalo with a bow and arrow and microwaving a cheese-steak hoagie, I'll take the sandwich. On balance, progress does make things better, at least materially, for most people. But the costs are real. Converting someone from a teller to an ATM servicer is not easy or cheap. And if we as a society are going to meet the challenge, we should avoid dubious reassurance about the impregnable uniqueness of our species.

After Kasparov's loss, a *Wall Street Journal* editorial issued a stern warning against viewing technology as a threat ("Sierra Club thinking"). After all, the *Journal* reminded us, Deep Blue is a product of human genius. So buck up! When you turnpike-toll takers lose your jobs to E-ZPass and other electronic systems, just remember: E-ZPass is a product of human genius. There. Feel better?

The *Journal* also noted that computers like Deep Blue can invent new drugs by "sorting quickly through hundreds of chemical

5

combinations that once required months of human tedium." Well, as some toll takers might observe, one human's tedium is another human's job. And although automating the tedious does raise average wages over time, it can lower wages for people with obsolete skills.

In the end, John Henry is too dramatic a metaphor. People rarely die trying to outrun technology. They usually adapt, moving either up the skills-and-income scale or down it. Perhaps a better metaphor is Virginia Lee Burton's classic children's story of Mike Mulligan and his steam shovel, Mary Anne. Outmoded by diesel models, Mary Anne retires in the cellar she has just dug for the new town hall. She becomes the building's heater. And Mike Mulligan finds gainful employment, though not by mastering diesel technology. He works contentedly alongside Mary Anne, as a janitor.

What Did You Read?

1. What was Deep Blue?
2. What is important about the chess match between Kasparov and Deep Blue?
3. In what ways does Wright feel technology enhances our lives?
4. How does computer technology make certain people's jobs obsolete?

What Do You Think?

1. Are you a "cheerleader for technology"? Why or why not?
2. In what ways do we suffer from technology? Explain.
3. Who are the people who suffer most from the technological advancement of society?
4. Is faster and cheaper always better? Can you think of examples of when that is not so? Explain.

How Was It Done?

1. What point is illustrated by the author's use of examples such as Deep Blue's chess triumph, John Henry's sledgehammer, and directory assistance operators only uttering four to six words?
2. How does the author give substance to his explanations in this article? Does he appeal chiefly to logic or sentiment? Explain.
3. How does the children's story of Mike Mulligan provide a metaphor for the author's thesis?

7

Your Body

Health is one thing everyone has a stake in. However, being healthy and staying healthy are often goals that many people have difficulty achieving. Things like eating right, exercising regularly, and getting plenty of sleep seem basic enough, but obstacles—both real and imagined—seem to prevent people from living healthy lives. Complicating matters is how society idealizes beauty and how it treats those who in some way do not live up to that ideal. Eating disorders and the popularity of cosmetic surgery are seen by some as responses to pressures to meet an ideal image. Magazines examine photos of celebrities who have nipped and tucked themselves into a more youthful and marketable appearance, and subtly criticize those who dare to look their age. Reality television shows take people who have physical disfigurements and transform them through plastic surgery for the whole world to watch. Underneath all of this is the virtually unquestioned idea that physical beauty is desirable and attainable—through whatever means necessary.

Whenever you are discussing whether something led to something else, such as why someone elected to have plastic surgery, you are involved in causal analysis. The writing lesson for this chapter guides you in how to conduct effective and convincing causal analysis, placing emphasis on the need to examine the possibility of multiple cause/effect relationships. Also, the lesson points out the logical fallacy of basing a causal argument on two events occurring in close proximity in time. The Writing Assignment then provides an opportunity to write a causal analysis in the area of health. In this area, cause

and effect relationships are important to everyone, yet they often remain controversial because of the difficult nature of causal analysis.

THE MAIN EVENT READING

The Pursuit of Beauty: The Enforcement of Aesthetics or a Freely Adopted Lifestyle?

Henri Wijsbek

*Henri Wijsbek explores the issues related to cosmetic surgery, and questions the true
source of people's desire to surgically change their appearance. Wijsbek examines what
it means to talk about "choosing" to have cosmetic surgery, and whether what many
people think of as their free choice may simply be a response—knowingly or not—to
society's never-ending pressures to conform to a certain ideal of how people (especially
women) are supposed to look. He examines how the concept of free will and the process
of decision making enter into the discussions of whether women are doing what they
want when they get cosmetic surgery, or simply doing what society (particularly men)
want them to do (in order to enhance their attractiveness to men).*

Key Words

duped	tricked; fooled; conned
existential	grounded in existence; having being in time and space
paradigmatically	based on a pattern or example; based on a framework within a school of thought or discipline
paradox	a statement that is seemingly contradictory or opposed to common sense yet seems true
coerced	forced; compelled by force or threat of force
colonization	control by one group over another dependent area or group
orthodox	conventional; conforming to established doctrine
contracausal	the ability to act against or in opposition to a causal force
metaphysical	supernatural; beyond the reality that is perceptible to the senses
ambiguous	unclear; capable of being understood in two or more possible senses
diametric	completely opposed; at opposite extremes

Introduction

Considering the amount of time, money and effort some people spend
on clothes, cosmetics and their looks in general, the pursuit of beauty
is a lifestyle if anything is. One feminist aptly calls it "a deeply signifi-

cant existential project"[1]; not a bad definition of "lifestyle" actually. We current take an enormous interest in the way our body looks: we paint and situation pierce it, we keep it in shape through exercise and diet, and we take it to the cosmetic surgeon if we're really dissatisfied with some specific part of it. People do go to considerable lengths and are willing to incur serious risks, to change the appearance of their bodies for what they take to be the better.

Concern about their looks guides people's lives. So in one impor- question tant sense the pursuit of beauty is clearly a lifestyle. But paradigmati- of choice cally, in order to qualify as a lifestyle, a way of life should also be something you have chosen yourself. A lifestyle is a way of showing the world which things in life you deem important, what kind of life you want to live, what kind of person you want to be. This goes for men as well as for women. But the massive pressure on women to live up to some ideal standard of beauty, makes it particularly doubtful whether women's choices concerning appearance are anything but mere reflections of fashion, or worse still, of male-dominated power relations. Can women's pursuit of youth and beauty, then, ever really qualify as a freely adopted lifestyle?

Morgan and the Technological Beauty Imperative

At least one feminist answers the last question with a resounding "No"! In an article entitled "Women and the Knife; Cosmetic Surgery appearance and the Colonization of Women's Bodies," Kathryn Pauly Morgan sets versus out to investigate whether cosmetic surgery is liberating or coercive. reality? As the title suggests, she has no doubts about the outcome. What makes her article interesting therefore, is rather what makes her think that, despite appearances to the contrary, women are coerced into cosmetic surgery. The key to her answer lies in what she calls "paradoxes of choice" that is, situations that leave women no real options at all. She distinguishes three such paradoxes.

The first is the paradox of conformity: women do not use the medical technology to underscore their uniqueness or eccentricity, rather they all let the one and the same "Baywatch" standard determine their looks. "More often than not, what appear at first glance to be instances of choice turn out to be instances of conformity."[2]

Secondly, women who involve themselves in the pursuit of youth 5 and beauty do not take their body as something natural or given, but rather as raw material to be shaped and pruned to fit some external standard. Their bodies are transformed for others to exploit them. And it is men who are wielding the power, either actual men or merely

---

[1]Morgan KP. Women and the knife: cosmetic surgery and the colonization of women's bodies. *Hypatia* 1991; 6: 36.
[2]Ibid.

imagined men who occupy the consciousness of women and make them into self-surveying subjects. This is the paradox of colonisation. It looks as if women are cultivating their own bodies, whereas in fact their bodies are being colonised by men.

Finally, there is an overwhelming pressure to undergo cosmetic surgery. The technological beauty imperative enforces itself in numerous ways: through advertising, articles in the media, in so-called success stories, in Miss America pageants. At the same time, the beauty imperative sets a new norm: those who refuse to submit to it will become stigmatised. What used to be normal is rapidly becoming deviant, problematic, inadequate and deformed. Eventually, Morgan ventures, "the 'ordinary' will come to be perceived and evaluated as the 'ugly.'"[3] The fact that women are coerced to avail themselves of these techniques and the ensuing pathological inversion of the normal constitutes the third paradox, the paradox of coerced voluntariness and the technological imperative.

Whenever a woman conforms to some single, external standard imposed on her, the conditions of genuine choice have not been met. If any of these paradoxes prevail therefore, she is not making a choice of her own, but is being forced to adapt herself to men's norms. Actually not just men's norms, nor just "white, western and Anglo-Saxon" norms, but norms that are "male-supremacist, racist, ageist, heterosexist, anti-Semitic, ableist and class biased" and to be on the safe side, Morgan adds the ominous "eugenicist" as well.[4]

Davis and the Desire to Be Ordinary

In her very interesting book, *Reshaping the Female Body*, Kathy Davis offers a totally different picture of cosmetic surgery and the partial freedom women enjoy to avail themselves of its mixed blessings. Davis has investigated the actual decision process of women contemplating undergoing cosmetic surgery. Typically, they take the step of consulting a cosmetic surgeon only after having pondered the decision for years. Often they seek support from a woman who has had cosmetic surgery herself, rarely from a husband or lover. Usually they have to overcome opposition, from friends, family and colleagues. All the women Davis talked with insisted they wanted the surgery for themselves. Interestingly, even women with very bad side effects and permanent disfigurement were happy they had finally taken their lives into their own hands.

The women Davis spoke to, mostly women who had had their breasts augmented or reduced, invariably described years of suffering before even thinking about consulting a cosmetic surgeon. Their suf-

Marginal notes:
What is genuine choice?

Is the author defensive?

What is "partial freedom"?

examples

---

[3]See reference 1:41.
[4]See reference 1:36, 38, 42.

fering, so convincingly rendered by Davis, had pervaded the whole of their lives: when buying clothes, when going to the beach, when doing sport, when having sex. They had been constantly reminded that their breasts were too big or too small.

One of the women, Sandra, complained that her breasts made her seem like somebody else: "Big breasts are supposed to be sexy. So you got to be a sex-bomb, whether you want to or not." She spent years hiding her breasts under bulky sweaters and leather jackets, trying to avoid being reduced to "just a pair of tits."[5] Ellen suffered from the opposite "problem." One story she tells is particularly poignant. She had just given birth to her first child and was lying in a hospital bed, on top of the world, feeling one hundred percent woman. Then the nurse came in to sponge her off. She started washing Ellen's face, then her breasts, and she blurted out: "Gee, you're flat as a pancake, aren't you?" Even as she was telling this to Davis she began to cry. "It was like being stabbed with a knife; it was, it was so awful, just really awful."[6]

Sandra and Ellen didn't want to become beautiful, they wanted to become ordinary. They wanted to put an end to their suffering, and cosmetic surgery had come to be the only way to achieve their goal.

In the last chapter of her book, Davis takes issue with Morgan about the nature of cosmetic surgery and the freedom of choice. Davis does not deny that there is pressure on women to have their bodies altered, but throughout her book she stresses women's agency. Cosmetic surgery is not simply imposed, it is fervently desired by its recipients. Women having cosmetic surgery are knowledgeable and responsible agents, no "more duped by the feminine beauty-system than women who do not see cosmetic surgery as a remedy to their problems with their appearance."[7] At the same time, she regrets the fact that women are willing to undergo risky operations. She wishes that circumstances would be otherwise and that women would choose a different course of action.

The Problem

I find this controversy between Morgan and Davis fascinating. Who is right? And if either is, how can it be established which one? On the face of it, Davis's conclusions seem to be by far the more plausible. They are based on sound, empirical research, whereas Morgan has done little more by way of empirical investigation than skim a few glossy magazines featuring interviews with knife-happy surgical dopes. Moreover, Davis, somewhat to her own surprise and against

Margin notes: 10 / desire to conform / critique of the methods of Morgan and Davis / slanted language

---

[5]Davis K. *Reshaping the female body. The dilemma of cosmetic surgery.* New York: Routledge, 1995: 77.
[6]See reference 4: 82.
[7]See reference 4: 163.

her own will, comes up with a balanced, not to say ambiguous view of cosmetic surgery. She weighs the pros and cons carefully and draws a conclusion that is almost shocking to the feminist she considers herself to be, let alone to more orthodox feminists with whom she has indeed experienced some troubling and unpleasant confrontations because of her liberal outlook. In that sense, her book is open-minded and courageous. Morgan's article on the other hand, smacks of lopsided exaggeration. She knew all along what she thought about cosmetic surgery, and drives home the politically correct analysis with force once again.

I'm afraid, however, that the controversy cannot be so easily settled in favour of Davis. It is not at all an easy job to decide how the data should be interpreted. Morgan could acknowledge all of Davis's results and yet stick to her own theory. Women may well say or think they make their own choices, whereas in fact they are only doing what the sexist, anti-Semitic, ageist, etc., etc., system requires them to do. It is hard to see how this disagreement about the interpretation of the empirical data could be solved empirically.

can women avoid responsi-bility?
One of Davis's main objectives is to find a way of being critical of a 15 beauty-system that treats women as inferior, without blaming the women who partake in it. But how can she do so while at the same time stressing women's agency? Her formula—own choice, bounded circumstances—is not very satisfactory, because choices are always made with less than complete information, under conditions not wholly of the agent's own making, and with few if any ideal options available. It seems to follow from her assumptions that women are blameable after all. How could anyone choose to partake in a blameable practice, without her- or himself incurring any blame?

Actually, Morgan's views seem to be more condoning of women. If they do not choose to undergo cosmetic surgery, but are rather coerced into compliance by an oppressive beauty-system, they can hardly be blamed for being so coerced. It is the system that should be blamed, not its victims. But Morgan's views have some nasty implications as well. Not only are women victims, they are duped victims at that, surgical dopes, not real agents responsible for their own doings.

women as victims

Underlying the disagreement between Morgan and Davis is a conceptual problem about freedom and responsibility. Before we can answer the question whether women who participate in the beauty system are blameable agents or innocent zombies, or whether yet a third characterisation is more appropriate, we must become clear about the conditions of freedom, agency and blame.

Freedom, Agency and Blame

criticism of Morgan's suggestion
Neither Morgan nor Davis makes it very clear how the beauty-system actually sustains its coercive influence. Morgan has not empirically investigated the matter, but she makes two suggestions. In the first place, its evil influence is spread by men, "brothers, fathers, male

lovers, male engineering students who taunt and harass their female counterparts, and by male cosmetic surgeons." And if not by actual men, then by "hypothetical men" who live "ghostly but powerful lives in the reflective awareness of women."[8]

Davis, who has painstakingly investigated women's actual decision process, concludes that contrary to what is assumed by Morgan and many others, women are not pressed into the operation by actual men. As a matter of fact, husbands and boyfriends more often than not try to talk their partners out of it. For that reason, some women even concealed that they were planning to have an operation from their husbands or boyfriends. Actually, when Davis describes what makes women try cosmetic surgery as a last resort, other women figure prominently not only as support, but also as catalysts. Many of the painful remarks about their appearance were made by other women, either out of jealousy, or condescension or mere thoughtlessness. I have already mentioned the nurse's remark about Ellen, but Davis quotes some others as well, for instance: "Gosh, I thought you had more than that!" and "Big breasts are so-o-o uncomfortable dear. I wish I had yours."[9]

Davis's research

However, Davis does think a considerable pressure is being exerted by something much more abstract and far less tangible than real men or women, something she calls "the beauty-system" or "the gender society," and sometimes still less specific "the social order," without elaborating on the content or working of this "social order." I suppose this is the same as what Morgan refers to when she uses the more picturesque phrase "hypothetical men." But according to Davis this pressure is not so strong as actually to coerce women into cosmetic surgery. They are left with a choice. Her formula for this ambiguous situation was: choice, constrained by circumstances which are not of the agent's own making. The constraints she refers to are the relative lack of information about the operation and its possible consequences and secondly, the lack of viable alternatives for women in a society organised by gender and power hierarchies.

20

coercion versus choice

Lack of information is something that is inherent in all choice situations. People do not have perfect foresight: some options are apt to be overlooked, and the ones considered can always turn out to be different from what was being imagined. Notoriously this holds for medical interventions. But only if the surgeon withholds available and relevant information on purpose could the situation be called coercive. In that case, women would be forced to make a decision on a skewed set of data. If this actually happens, they cannot make a free decision and therefore they cannot be held responsible for it. But this is hardly a controversial case. I take it that literally everybody agrees that the

[8]See reference 1: 36, 37.
[9]See reference 4: 80, 82.

surgeon should give the woman all the relevant data. If he does not, he is to be blamed, not she.

The complaint about lack of viable options is much more difficult to deal with. What options are lacking, what circumstances should be different? I have no reliable figures, and they would be very hard to come by, but the number of women who do opt for cosmetic surgery is almost negligible compared to the number who do not. In order to make the claim that women have no viable options except cosmetic surgery at all plausible, the category of women to whom it applies has to be made much more precise. Suppose such a category could be defined: women with characteristics a, b and c all opt for cosmetic surgery under circumstances x, y and z. Even if this claim could be vindicated, nothing as yet would have been established as to what actually causes them to do so. Physical and psychological characteristics such as size of breasts and lack of self-assurance would presumably figure on the one side, and stereotypes and role models are among the things that would figure on the other side of some such explanation.

why no figures?

Causal Explanation

speculation

Suppose then that the statistically significant correlation could be dressed up to a causal explanation for this well-defined category of women, would that make them into the unfree and irresponsible zombies Morgan takes them to be? Not necessarily. Being caused to do something is not in itself a threat to either freedom or responsibility. It would only be so if you hold that free and responsible agency implies the ability to act in defiance of the causal network that makes up the rest of the world. It is a wildly implausible claim that people have such a contracausal metaphysical power and I have nothing to say to its credit. If you were to trace the antecedents of any act far enough, you would always find that its causes lie outside the agent. Usually acts are considered to flow from some combination of beliefs and desires. But of course one can always push the inquiry one step further back and ask where these beliefs and desires come from. Ultimately, they will be caused by something the person is not in control of. If being the ultimate cause of one's actions were a necessary condition for agency, nobody would ever be an agent.

all choices involve some lack of control

According to a metaphysically less extraordinary view, agency is compatible with people being subject to all the laws that govern the rest of nature. A feeling of thirst normally causes me to try and quench it. I think I am very lucky to be caused to act in that way and I do not wish it were otherwise. The fact that I am caused to act in a certain way, does not imply that I must act in an insensible or mechanical way. I do not drink just anything; depending on further circumstances I take something hot or cold, sweet or bitter, alcoholic or nonalcoholic. And if I am attending a lecture, I wait until it is over before having my drink, because I think it would be ill-mannered to walk away in the middle of the lecture for such a reason. Normally, what I will actually do and when I will do it, is the outcome of my deliberation. As long as my acts are sensible responses to the requirements of the situation, as long as I am able to respond adequately to all its relevant features, I have all the freedom I can possibly wish. If these relevant features leave me no option but the right (or a right) one, that is no more a serious constraint on my freedom than the analogous constraint on belief formation would be. Our freedom would not be diminished if we were always caused to have only true beliefs.

importance of decision-making

Best Chances

The way Davis describes the women who take recourse to cosmetic surgery, fits this picture very well. These women have a problem—an indisputable kind of suffering—they survey their options, and they pick that option that promises them the best chances to overcome their problem. They respond sensibly to the situation, make an intelligible decision and act accordingly. In particular, they don't expect the operation to work miracles, for instance that it will save a broken marriage. Admittedly, it is a somewhat risky option, but not an outrageously risky one. It seems therefore, that their decisions are based on a prudent cost–benefit analysis. What reasons could there be to call even this particular category of women innocent zombies and their decisions unfree or coerced? They do indeed seem to have all the characteristics of knowledgeable and responsible agents.

25

It might be countered that even if the "gender society" leaves women's capacity to reason instrumentally unimpaired, it distorts their capacity to form values to act on. Although I find this very hard to believe, it is conceivable that women or a category of women are manipulated in such a way that they are no longer able to discern which features of their lives really matter. In that case, they would be duped by magazines, advertisements and all the rest into putting beauty and appearance at the top of their preference-ordering. They would value beauty more than they should, spend more time and money on cosmetics than is proper and accord too little weight to other important things in life. To put it briefly, they would have become obsessed by their appearance, and obsession does not sit well with free agency.

But who can tell what the proper amount of attention is to pay to your appearance? Is lipstick OK? Going to the hairdresser? Being choosy about the clothes you wear? Dieting? Fitness? Twice a week? Two hours a day? Everybody can come up with extreme examples of paying either too much or too little attention to appearance, but in between all causes are hard cases. And I think that is how it should be. All lifestyles can give rise to misgivings. Who can ever be sure she is not according too much importance in life to something not really worth it? How can you know that you would not be happier or lead a

differences in lifestyle choices

more satisfying life if you had chosen something completely different? To take up a lifestyle is to forsake other lifestyles that are equally worthy of being chosen. That is one of the reasons Morgan's description of the pursuit of beauty is such an appropriate definition of a lifestyle in general: it is "a deeply significant existential project," with all the meaningfulness and uncertainty that usually go with such projects.

refutes
Morgan's
paradoxes

After this, what is left of Morgan's three paradoxes? As to the first, women, except perhaps for a very small category of women, do not conform to a single standard. But even for this category, that fact in itself is no more significant than that a large number of Victorian men had whiskers or that nowadays some men practise body-building. Secondly, that this standard can be traced back to external influences is a property it shares with many, if not all, of our beliefs and desires. Finally, if you actually look at the decision process of these women, you will find that it forms a reasonable and adequate response to their problems and so is an expression of their freedom rather than an obstacle to it.

Alternative Explanation

This is the
author's al-
ternative

But even if women who have cosmetic surgery have all the characteristics of full-blown agents, the possibility is still left open that they are blameable agents, a possibility I took to be a consequence of Davis's position. That would be so if they knowingly and willingly were involving themselves in a morally reprehensible practice. Is cosmetic surgery reprehensible? According to Davis, the women who have cosmetic surgery do so in order not to be constantly looked at or made the object of offensive remarks, whether well meant or not; and they want to feel at ease in their own bodies. An alternative explanation would be that they want to look more beautiful. Both the ordinary and the beautiful are respectable and it is hardly blameworthy to strive for either.

If you want to become a proficient piano player, you must practise 30 daily; if you write a scientific article, you don't expect the first draft to qualify as the final version; only with effort do we learn to become a good friend, parent, partner. Usually, to actualise values—be it artistic, scientific or moral values—is hard work. Why then should we have to accept our appearances as given?

Lingering Doubts

Still, I can imagine that not everybody will be persuaded that women have a free choice in these matters. Given that circumstances are as they are, women are free to choose whether they want to have recourse to cosmetic surgery. To be free in a practical sense does not mean to be the uninfluenced originator of all your thoughts and actions; whoever fits that description is doomed to act in a haphazard and unintelligible way. Rather, it means to be able to respond adequately to the circumstances in which you find yourself. We want "a freedom within the world, not a freedom from it," in Susan Wolf's apt phrase.[10]

But sometimes we want the world to be different, rather than just to be able to respond adequately to the way it happens to be. Ideals of beauty and stereotypes differ from biological needs such as thirst, since they are not given in the same inescapable way. Different cultural ideals for women (and men) come and go, for example take fashion: slim in the twenties, buxom in the fifties. In a sense you could say these cultural ideals are made by human beings, albeit not in any direct or simple way. They would be very hard to influence for individuals, but perhaps governments or non-governmental organisations should do their utmost to change them. Or rather, to get rid of them altogether. After all, changing them would only change the category of women that could not live up to them and hence the category of women that would suffer from falling short of these ideals.

I suppose that this is what Davis meant when she said she wished circumstances could be different. Plastic surgery should not be an eligible way for women to overcome their problems with their appearance, because in Davis's ideal world, women would not have any problems with their appearance to begin with.

What would the world look like if Davis's wish were realised? It is *specula-tion* very hard to imagine a world without such ever-changing beauty norms, but nevertheless, let me end with some speculations. It would be a world in which no woman ever suffered from the way she looked, because no woman, nor anybody else, would care about how she looked. Everybody would have become insensitive to aesthetic properties; nobody would be moved by Vermeer's Girl with the pearl or Schubert's Schone Mullerin. There would be no poetry, only social realistic prose. It would be a paradise for pigs, and a boring place for people. In my view, that is too high a price to pay to get rid of cosmetic surgery.

What Did You Read?

1. What is the "paradox of conformity"?
2. Explain the "colonialism of men" as defined by Wijsbek.
3. What is meant by a beauty-system that sustains a coercive influence?

---

[10]Wolf S. Freedom within reason. New York: Oxford University Press, 1990: 93. I have benefited from this book in writing this paper.

What Do You Think?

1. If you are a woman, when you think about your choices of clothes, makeup, and even cosmetic surgery, do those choices reflect what pleases you and only you, or what pleases you and others, including men? Has that changed over time?

2. Do you agree that we are "invaded" with men's attitudes about women, thereby causing women to want to conform to those attitudes?

3. Morgan states, "The 'ordinary' will come to be perceived and evaluated as the 'ugly.'" Could that also be said for achieving the peak of excellence in anything? Does it sometimes mean those who cannot achieve the same excellence appear inferior in the minds of some?

4. Do women make lifestyle choices to "please" men other than getting cosmetic surgery? What are they? Do men make lifestyle choices to please women? What are they?

How Was It Done?

1. Around what is the article structured?

2. How important are terms such as "paradox of conformity" and "beauty imperative" to the development of the support? Does much of the argument revolve around the definition of these terms?

3. Is the debate and analysis of the article organized well with the use of subtitles and enumeration? Explain.

4. Are enough facts and research incorporated into the development of the article? Explain.

THE MAIN EVENT WRITING ASSIGNMENT

Write an essay in which you respond to one of the following assignments:

1. Write a causal analysis of a topic within the general subject area of Health.

2. Why are we at the same time an incredibly knowledgeable society in terms of medicine and yet an unhealthy society as judged by levels of obesity?

3. How does the rest of the world view the United States as contributing to solving the world's problems? For example, other countries are further along in stem cell research. Also, many coun-

tries feel the United States' contributions to solving the problems of AIDS have been insufficient.

4. Are more people interested in their health or in their appearance? Is there a difference? Do these interests sometimes come into conflict with each other?

PREPARATION PUNCH LIST

Before you begin writing the essay, you need to prepare yourself to write.

1. The first thing you need to determine is finding health issues that you would be interested in writing about.

- Anorexia, bulimia, obesity, plastic surgery, steroid usages, health supplements, diets

2. Are you interesting in examining effects or causes in terms of your particular health interest?

- For example, if one were interested in eating disorders, you might first narrow it down to anorexia, and then decide to investigate the causes of this disorder. Most people are aware already of the effects (the symptoms), but there is controversy about the cause of anorexia.

3. Virtually everyone has a story related to dieting, and many people have personal theories of how to diet best. However, we need experts to support diets with factual evidence.

- For example, have you known someone with an eating disorder? A personal connection can lead you to more precise academic discussions.
- When examining an event in terms of causal analysis, it is very important to get as much evidence as possible.
- Studies, as opposed to personal experiences, make for more credible support for a position.

THE MAIN EVENT WRITING LESSON: CAUSAL ANALYSIS

Have you ever wondered why something happens the way that it does, or how something can be affected by something else? If you have, you already are showing the beginnings of causal analysis.

Causal analysis examines the cause and effect relationship between two or more things, and it is a critical aspect of how we think.

Fairly simple types of cause and effect relationships are easy to understand. If you stub your toe and feel pain, you know that the action of stubbing your toe caused the pain. One action occurred, and then another followed.

Stubbed your toe ⟶ felt pain

However, most events or conditions that you may be asked to analyze are not nearly so simple. An event or condition can have more than one cause, or more than one effect can result from that condition. In complicated political or social situations, there are multiple causes and effects. In the human body, too, causal analysis can be quite complex, often because there are so many uncontrollable variables (or different situations) that make understanding what is going on troublesome. For example, if you have a headache, and you take an aspirin pill for the headache, you cannot be positive that the pill *caused* the headache to go away. After all, the source of the headache, such as tension or an annoying sound, may have also gone away. You may also have relaxed on a couch upon taking the pill. You may also have experienced a "placebo" effect, in which the headache went away because you expected it to go away. This is one reason why the government agency in charge of testing new drugs must run so many tests and trials with them: determining causal relationships can be very difficult.

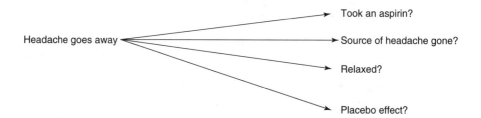

When you are examining an event or condition in terms of causal analysis, you need to have as much connection between events as possible to make the connections convincing. Remember that merely having two events occur in close proximity in time does not by itself mean that one event caused the other to occur. Look to see how frequently the two events happen in relation to each other. If the two events frequently occur one after the other, a causal connection is more likely.

Much superstition is a result of faulty causal analysis. Everyone has heard of the famous Friday the 13th superstition, but how often do bad things happen on other days? Breaking a mirror does not cause seven years' bad luck, deaths do not always come in threes, and black cats do not bring bad luck. Adherence to these types of superstitious beliefs has its basis not in logic but in fear and ignorance.

Such matters can become particularly important when one examines the human body. In recent years, a growing trend toward "alternative medicine" has led people to reject traditional Western medicine and instead use such practices as acupuncture and aromatherapy. Critics, especially within the Western medical establishment, have long maintained that there is no clear causal link between these practices and healing. The debate is essentially over whether the cause-and-effect claims of alternative medicine can be verified.

Within the medical field, debates over causal analysis are constant. One debate is over the causes of eating disorders, such as anorexia and bulimia. Some point to unrealistic media images, especially of women, as pressuring young women to be too thin. On the other hand, data clearly show that a large portion of Americans, including young women, is overweight, and that rates of obesity are increasing, not decreasing. Thus, critics point out, the media cannot be blamed for causing people to be too thin when more people actually have a problem with being too big.

When you organize your causal analysis, you will want your thesis statement in the introduction to make the general statement of the causal relationship. Then, each paragraph of the main body must develop a separate and distinct aspect of that relationship. For instance, if you wanted to write an essay about fad diets, you might develop your essay in the following manner:

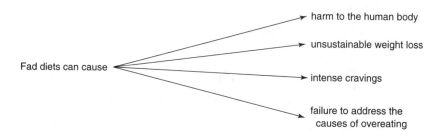

To put these relationships in a thesis sentence, you might write the following: "Fad diets are an ineffective and potentially harmful approach to losing weight because they have the potential to produce long-term harm to the body, they cause weight loss that cannot be sustained, they produce intense cravings on the part of the dieter, and they fail to understand the causes behind a person's overeating."

THE MAIN EVENT WRITING SAMPLE

The following is an essay of causal analysis written for this text in response to the Main Event Writing Assignment, Question #1.

Fad Diets: A Craze You Should Avoid

One can hardly walk past a supermarket checkout counter without seeing the ads: "I lost 55 pounds in five weeks!" or "I eat everything I want and still lose weight!" Many people have a strong desire to lose weight, but they usually want to do so without effort or change in their lifestyle. In a society that loves quick-fixes for serious problems, nothing has greater popularity than the quick-fix "fad diet." Fad diets—ones that propose to cause dramatic weight loss quickly—often fail to deliver on their promises. The history of weight loss is filled with examples of diets that ultimately caused more harm than good, including diets that restricted people to eating just one type of food, or encouraged eating extremely high amounts of carbohydrates, or very low amounts of carbohydrates, or drinking lots of water or little water, of having "shake" substitutes for meals or drinking "formulas" at night before bed and having the weight simply disappear. The truth, however, is that attaining one's ideal weight is best done through a healthy, balanced approach to diet that can be sustained.

Thesis Fad diets are an ineffective and potentially harmful approach to losing weight because they have the potential to produce long-term harm to the body, they cause weight loss that cannot be sustained, they produce intense cravings on the part of the dieter, and they fail to understand the causes behind a person's overeating.

Cause 1 Fad diets often confuse the human body's chemistry, and over the long term, can produce harmful effects on the human body. Sometimes the damage done is irreversible. For example, in *Make the Connection,* by Bob Greene and Oprah Winfrey, Greene states that he believes Oprah Winfrey's crash diet using a liquid supplement caused permanent changes in her body's chemistry. These changes caused her metabolism to slow down, meaning that she has to exercise harder than the normal person in order to produce the same effects of weight loss (37–38). Barry Sears, PhD, and Bill Lawren, in *The Zone,* argue that a high-carbohydrate diet can, in fact, be dangerous to a person's health. One of the newer fad diets, the high-protein, low-carbohydrate diet, is so new that, Marion J. Franz reports, no long-term studies have been done yet, but he reminds us that "popularity is not credibility." *Time* magazine reports that losing weight too rapidly produces gallstones. The reality is the best way to lose weight is still to reduce caloric intake and exercise more ("It's Never Too Late"). Fad diets are more likely to do the body more harm than good, even if weight is lost.

Losing weight is one thing, but sustaining weight loss is some- *Cause 2* thing else. Many fad diets do work, in the short term. However, keeping that weight off over a long period of time is something that fad diets usually fail to do. The public has seen how famous people, such as Oprah Winfrey, former baseball manager Tommy Lasorda, and singer Luther Vandross, have "yo-yoed" their weight up and down over the years because of an inability to keep lost weight off. As Franz points out, even in the best weight loss programs only 60% retain their weight loss for one year. Presumably, the lesser quality programs have even lower percentages of keeping weight loss. The trouble comes because the dieter cannot live with the strict or odd regimen imposed by fad diets. Of those who are successful, Franz reports, ". . . their lives are devoted to weight loss!" He says they eat less and exercise more on a daily basis. Fad diets do not teach people how to eat right for the rest of their lives; they just teach people how to eat to lose weight in a short period of time.

Cause 3   Fad diets break down a dieter's discipline because they can cause intense cravings. This is a result of throwing the dieter's eating habits out of balance, and the dieter's body naturally wants what it is being denied. As Sears and Lawren report, "People on restrictive diets get tired of feeling hungry and deprived" (11). Additionally, there seems very little consistency on the part of the fad diets as to what should be denied. Franz reports that the U.S. Department of Agriculture did a study of diet books and found that diet books recommended either a low-carb diet, a moderate-fat, moderate-carb diet, or a low-fat, high carb diet. These completely contradictory diets accounted for 90% of the diet books! The apparently arbitrary control of one aspect of the human diet makes it easy for the dieter to reject the diet. Kathiann M. Kowalski, writing for *Current Health 2,* points out that better than focusing on diets that eliminate one food type, people should instead focus on eating well-balanced meals. They can refer to the U.S. Department of Agriculture's Food Guide Pyramid, use the food labels found on most food products, pay attention to serving size. In other words, people should develop a daily diet they can live with that is healthy.

Cause 4   Finally, fad diets fail to work because they often fail to address the causes of overeating. True, some people gain weight simply through bad lifestyle choices: they eat too many processed foods, and they fail to get enough physical exercise. But often, especially with those who suffer from obesity, there is more to the problem than simply becoming knowledgeable about food. Like alcohol or illegal drugs, food has the potential to be abused. Sears and Lawren write that food *"has a more powerful impact on your* body—*and your health*—*than any drug your doctor could ever prescribe* [italics are the authors']" (77). As a result, some people may, as the saying goes, "confuse love and lasagna." Many emotional problems may manifest themselves in eating disorders. Lori Gottlieb, writing for *Cosmo Girl,* describes how, in her obsession with food, she forgot about the importance of her more human qualities. Kowalski emphasizes that overeaters need to think more positive thoughts about themselves. Franz stresses that people who struggle with their weight need to learn to "like themselves." Clearly, the psychology behind eating problems must be addressed.

Fad diets cause more problems than they solve. The best *Conclusion* method for people to lose weight and sustain that weight loss is not easy—they have to change their lives. Eating right and exercising on a regular basis are the only real ways to get and stay healthy. In a society that wants a pill for every problem, that hardly seems like an exciting solution. The truth is, however, that nothing else will work in the long run. So, stay away from those supermarket tabloids and their false promises of easy weight loss. Get to work on changing your life!

Works Cited

Franz, Marion J. *Clinical Diabetes* 19.3 (2001): 105+. *MasterFILE Premier.* Ebscohost. San Diego Mesa College Lib. Aug. 28, 2001.

Gottlieb, Lori. "Eating Disorders." *Cosmo Girl* Apr. 2001: 148+. *MasterFILE Premier.* Ebscohost. San Diego Mesa College Lib. August 28, 2001.

Greene, Bob, and Oprah Winfrey. *Make the Connection.* New York: Harpo, 1996.

"It's Never Too Late To . . ." *Time* 5 Feb. 2001. 54+. *MasterFILE Premier.* Ebscohost. San Diego Mesa College Lib. Aug. 28, 2001.

Kowalski, Kathiann M. "Fuel or Fixation: What Role Does Food Play in Your Life?" *Current Health 2* Dec. 2000: 6+. *MasterFILE Premier.* Ebscohost. San Diego Mesa College Lib. Aug. 28, 2001.

Sears, Barry, with Bill Lawren. *The Zone.* New York: Regan-Harper, 1995.

ADDITIONAL READINGS

Body Envy

Nora Underwood

Nora Underwood examines the link between popular culture and body image. Underwood examines how images from the media influence what sorts of cosmetic surgeries will be popular. More people than ever before are dropping their inhibitions about cosmetic surgery, equating it with hair coloring. The idea of growing old gracefully has simply been dumped. Women are not the only ones affected either—men want their bodies to look bulkier and more muscle-bound than ever before.

Key Words

augmentation	being made bigger; supplement
conformity	to act in agreement with some standard or authority
tubular	shaped like a tube
insidious	treacherous; harmful but enticing
archeological	related to the study of the material remains of human life

Dr. Stephen Mulholland is no psychic, but he can make astoundingly accurate predictions about what his clients are going to want. All he has to do is run through the movie listings and keep on top of popular television shows, and the Toronto plastic surgeon can anticipate at least some of the business that will be coming his way. Angelina Jolie is on the cover of several magazines and starring in a couple of movies? Requests for lip augmentations will soar. Jennifer Lopez displays her assets in a barely there dress at an awards ceremony and breast implants become even more of a must-have. Leonardo DiCaprio strips down in *Titanic* or *The Beach,* and requests for hair removal shoot up 20 per cent. "I have been amazed by the call of Hollywood," says Mulholland. "Younger people want to look done. They want to take on the physical attributes and characteristics of the stars of the day."

American writer Allen Ginsberg once said: "Whoever controls the media—the images—controls the culture." Truer words were never spoken. The media, and those they celebrate, have always influenced fashion and body shape. But what's remarkable now is how profoundly body image is affected by popular culture, and how willing— no, eager—people are to mess with Mother Nature.

Why the rush to retool? For one thing, baby boomers—the demographic group that can usually be counted on to rewrite the rules—are stampeding across the 50-year mark. They have long been obsessed with youth and vitality, and even before researchers mapped a rough draft of the human body's genes earlier this year, the prospects for a longer, healthier life were increasing all the time. So were the options for making changes, be they profound or merely skin-deep—from celebrity-endorsed diets and exercise crazes to fitness trainers, weight-loss or muscle-building drugs and sophisticated cosmetic surgery procedures.

There are best-seller lists packed with diet books (Dr. Atkins' *New Diet Revolution*, Barry Sears' *The Zone*), magazines filled with the beauty secrets of the stars ("Never eat bread!" "Do three hours of yoga every day!") and, everywhere, famous thin women and body-hair-free, heavily bicepped men. "We place such a big premium on what-ever the designers and image-makers have created as what's beautiful," says Mulholland. "That inspires conformity, it inspires the concept of self-worth through physical attractiveness. 'Beauty fades' just isn't true anymore."

During the 1920s, thin women were briefly in vogue, but their 　5 popularity was usurped by the likes of Mae West, Jean Harlow, Rita Hayworth and Marilyn Monroe. In the 1960s, model Twiggy helped usher in the next era of thin—one that has never completely abated. Some of that trend, notes Dr. Paul Garfinkel, head of the Toronto-based Centre for Addiction and Mental Health, "is an emulation of the higher social classes. Some relates to extreme health consciousness, some to a desire to control, some to a narcissistic preoccupation with youth and appearance." But much of it, he adds, "has to do with media and advertising—the notion that appearance is the self. The world has become much more superficial."

And because we have truly become a global village, particularly as a result of the Internet, there are few corners of the world left un-touched by western popular culture—or impervious to its influences. In fact, two researchers travelled to a corner of Peru that had little ex-perience with western culture and showed men there a variety of im-ages of women—fat and skinny, shapely and tubular (bodies with less differentiation between waist and hip). The results, which were pub-lished in the journal *Nature* in November, 1998: the men found the heavier, tubular women more attractive and healthy looking. Peruvian men from less remote villages who had had more exposure to western culture regarded thinner, smaller-waisted women as more desirable.

How thin is too thin? The average North American woman is five-foot-four and weighs 140 lb., the average model, on the other hand, is five-foot-11 and weighs 117 lb. In May, the British medical establish-ment issued a report that blamed the media's preoccupation with the ultra-thin on the growing numbers of eating disorders among young women. "Female models are becoming thinner at a time when women are becoming heavier, and the gap between the ideal body shape and the reality is wider than ever," the British Medical Association wrote. "There is a need for more realistic body shapes to be shown on television and in fashion magazines." At a summit in London a month later, British editors pledged to monitor images that appeared in their magazines and use "models who varied in shape and size."

That's exactly what editor Cyndi Tebbel had in mind when she published her April, 1997, "Big Issue" of the Australian edition of *New Woman* magazine, which featured size-16 model Emme Aronson on the cover and photographs of average-size women inside. Despite the positive response from many readers, big-money advertisers hated it, complaining so much, in fact, that Tebbel—who has since written a book called *The Body Snatchers: How the Media Shapes Women*—was forced to resign.

Others are also challenging the thin-is-in ethic. Three years ago, Allyson Mitchell and Mariko Tamaki founded Pretty, Porky and Pissed Off, a Toronto-based fat activist group. They initially handed out flyers and candy outside a fashionable clothing store that sold only small-sized items. They have since put on plays, organized regular clothing swaps with other large women and are now working on a documentary. They approach the subject of fat in a humorous way, but their message is serious. "It's important to reach out to other people because our stories are all very similar—like never having clothes that fit, crazy yo-yo diets," says Tamaki. "So we're trying to tell kids that beauty is more than fitting into a size-4 pant."

Sure, but try telling that to fashion writer Dick Snyder, who, in a   10 recent column in *The Globe and Mail*, extolled the virtues of thin women. "Magazines with sexy, skinny girls on the cover sell like crazy," he wrote. "Very few guys will admit it, but these magazines attract them like bees to honey. And women buy them as well. Slap a heavy model on the cover and that magazine will sit around collecting a month's worth of dust. You can't blame that on skinny girls."

According to Greek myth, when Eos, goddess of the dawn, fell for the mortal Tithonus, she begged Zeus to give her beloved immortality. But she neglected to ask for eternal youth as part of the deal. As Tithonus aged, Eos lost interest in him—eventually ending the union by turning him into a cicada.

In the non-mythological world, it seems, a long, healthy life alone is not enough. People want to look as good as they feel. In 1920, the average Canadian lifespan was 59 years; today it is 79. And once the genes responsible for aging can be manipulated, anything, conceivably, is possible. "No one wants to prolong life if it means sitting in some home and being cared for," explains Dr. Claudio De Lorenzi, president of the Canadian Society of Aesthetic Plastic Surgery. "People want to play golf and tennis and then die with their boots on."

In other words, growing old gracefully just isn't much of an option anymore, particularly for the boomers and succeeding generations. "This is the fastest-growing group of men and women seeking cosmetic surgery," says Mulholland. "They created jogging, the tennis club, the cult of youth and vitality. And now they're finding that genetics is not allowing them to maintain that edge."

Louisa, a 64-year-old German-born woman who asked not to be identified, was always slim and looked and felt young for her age. Since her retirement six years ago, she put on a little weight and developed a few more wrinkles than she would have liked. Her body no longer reflected how she felt inside. With $25,000 she inherited, Louisa made some changes, starting with a tummy tuck, then laser surgery on her face to remove wrinkles, rhinoplasty (nose job), an eyelid tuck and finally a face-lift. "When I was growing up, 64 was ancient," she says. "But I'm the type who wears miniskirts and lots of makeup. I jog, I'm a very active person." She knows her decision would have shocked her parents. "There's so much that we take for granted these days that was absolutely taboo in the olden days," adds Louisa. "We know so much more about nutrition and exercise. Why shouldn't we do something about our bodies? We look at ourselves and we see our mothers. Now, when I wake up, I look at myself and I think, 'Hey woman, you look great.'"

For the generation now entering the labour force, cosmetic surgery 15 is simply another lifestyle choice, and having it done involves little more introspection—and certainly no more guilt—than changing hair colour. Younger people, says Mulholland, have "embraced the concept of physical manipulation as an improvement of what has been given to you. There are almost no ground rules as to who you can be and what you can be." In 1998, 22,000 American teenagers had cosmetic surgery—a 95-per-cent increase from 1992. Among the most popular procedures were liposuction, rhinoplasty and breast implants; the latter have been controversial, although a *New England Journal of Medicine* article in March concluded that gel-filled implants were unrelated to connective tissue disease or other autoimmune or rheumatic conditions.

What they're seeking has changed too, says Dr. Robert Thompson, a plastic surgeon in Vancouver. "With the young group, there's less fear of cosmetic surgery than ever before," he says, "with women who want to not only have a breast augmentation, but a very large augmentation." If Thompson points out to a patient that what she wants isn't in proportion with the rest of her body, he adds, "many say they don't care—they don't mind if people know they have implants. 'Natural' often doesn't enter into the equation."

Sophia is five-foot-six and 115 lb., but already the 23-year-old woman has had cosmetic surgery to enhance a body she felt was imperfect. At 20, she had breast augmentation to increase her less-than-A cup to a B. Last fall, she had liposuction to smooth out her thighs—and to head off coming trouble. "There were certain areas I didn't like that I thought were going to get progressively worse as I got older," she says. "I look at the older generation and I wonder how did they get that way. They lost the bodies they had."

Sophia researched the procedures, saved the money to pay for them—$11,000 to date—working three part-time jobs, and then took the plunge. And she makes no apologies for her decision. Half a dozen of her friends have also had breast implants. "They're common," says Sophia matter-of-factly. And if she feels she needs more work in the future, she'll do it. "It's not that I'm a high-school dropout doing pornos," she adds. "I went to university, I have a great job, I own my car, I plan to get married one day and have children. I am a normal 23-year-old who's just had work done to better myself—for nobody else."

Anyone who thinks men are somehow spared body-image angst hasn't looked closely at the covers of men's magazines lately, with their photo spreads and advertisements featuring brawny, chiselled studs. Not that such pressures are new—Montreal's Weider brothers began pumping up their body-building empire in the 1940s. But Dr. Harrison Pope Jr., a professor of psychiatry at Harvard Medical School and one of the authors of *The Adonis Complex*, published earlier this year, believes that men's insecurities are becoming as insidious as women's. "Men are now beginning to get a taste of the same medicine that women have had to put up with for decades," explains Pope, "namely seeing pictures of unattainably perfect bodies in the media."

Pope and his colleagues devised a test for college men in the 20 United States and Europe. Each man was shown a computerized image of a male body and was asked to change it to create the look he wanted and the one he thought women would like the best. On both sides of the Atlantic, the college students wanted an average of 30 lb. more muscle than they had, which they also felt would make them more attractive to women. When the researchers asked women to choose the male bodies they found attractive, they generally picked men with only slightly more muscle than average.

Part of what is fuelling male insecurity, says Pope, is the advent of anabolic steroids. "It's now possible to create male bodies that are more muscular and leaner than any natural male," he says. Pope also argues that many men have focused on their bodies as one of the few remaining ways to express their masculinity. "Women now can fly combat aircraft, they can go to military academies, they can be CEOs of multinational corporations," he adds, "so that men's traditional roles as soldiers and defenders and breadwinners have gradually been eroded." But no matter how much women can do, says Pope, they can't benchpress 300 lb.

Mark knows all about body-image pressures. He exercises like mad, is careful about what he eats and still wasn't happy with how he looked. "I wanted to look thinner and I didn't want to look quite so old," says the 45-year-old man, who does not wish to be identified. "I didn't want to look like I was 27. I wanted to look like a good 45." Mark had liposuction from his chest and abdomen, and had fat removed from under his chin and injected under his eyes to take away his tired look. Men, in fact, now comprise nine per cent of cosmetic surgeons' clients; men's liposuction procedures alone have increased 200 per cent since 1992.

But as John Xiros Cooper points out, obsessions with the body long predate Hollywood. "You just need one visit to the archeological museum in Athens to be impressed by how good-looking the Greeks were," laughs Cooper, an associate English professor at the University of British Columbia in Vancouver, who is interested in the cultural impact of mass media. "But the body has become a commodity and like all commodities it's in constant need of updates. Now we have the technological means of changing its shape and the genome project has opened the door to unimaginable things. So the question is, how far are we going to go?" Bodies that are more perfect? Now there's something to feel insecure about.

What Did You Read?

1. What is meant by the statement: "Whoever controls the media—the image—controls the culture"?

2. What is the fastest growing group of people seeking cosmetic surgery?

3. What are some of the more popular procedures people are having done?

What Do You Think?

1. Do you agree that physical manipulation in order to feel good about who you are and what you can be is a good thing? Why or why not?

2. Have thin women always been the preferred aesthetic in this country? Explain.

3. How many women do you know who have had cosmetic surgery? How many men do you know who have had it?

How Was It Done?

1. How much research went into the crafting of this article? Identify at least three different sources and explain how they contribute to the argument.

2. How effective is the contrasting of past generations' body images with those of the present?

3. Does the article include enough examples that are typical and representative in order for the argument to be effective?

Does He or Doesn't He?

Pat Haire

Pat Haire points out that more men than ever before are pursing cosmetic surgery, and the most popular surgery is liposuction. Generally, the two main groups of men getting cosmetic surgery are aging baby-boomers and much younger men who want "body contouring." Importantly, men face different risks than women because of physiological differences in their bodies, including greater risks of bleeding and developing bruises.

Key Words

contouring	shaping
hematomas	blood clots
incisions	cuts
post-operative	after an operation
penile	related to the penis
elasticity	springiness; resilience; the ability to be adaptable

Plastic surgery isn't just for women anymore. More men are visiting plastic surgeons for a variety of treatments and procedures.

When Ponce de Leon discovered Florida in 1513, it was reportedly during an expedition to locate an elusive fountain of youth. The intrepid Spaniard never found that fountain, but today's cosmetic surgeons have more than compensated.

Over the years, doctors have created a variety of skin-tightening, nose-chiseling, tummy-tucking, ear-pulling and fat-suctioning techniques that peel decades off individuals—mostly women—who seek to defy the ravages of time and gravity.

Times are changing, though. Now thousands of men are drinking from this modern medical fountain of youth, making up more than nine percent of the million or so cosmetic surgeries performed annually in the United States. In 1999, more than 100,000 men had some type of cosmetic surgery, and a lot of them did it right here in Florida, which ranks third behind New York and California in its ratio of plastic surgeons to population.

Obviously, those men aren't requesting breast augmentations, but 5 they are undergoing many of the same procedures women discovered years ago—and these days they aren't as shy about showing up at a plastic surgeon's office.

Dr. Mark P. Solomon, a board-certified cosmetic surgeon outside of Philadelphia and the former chief of plastic surgery at Hahnemann University Hospital in Pennsylvania, claims the stigma attached to males having plastic surgery died long ago. He says most of his male patients fall into two groups. First there are the affluent baby boomers, 50 years and older, who are trying to keep up with the young guns in the office by having facelifts and eyelid surgery. Then there are the younger, more body-conscious men who actively work out but want body contouring surgeries such as liposuction of "love handles" that do not respond to regular diet or exercise.

According to the American Society of Plastic and Reconstructive Surgeons (ASPRS), liposuction is the most popular procedure among men, followed closely by eyelid surgery, nose reshaping, breast reduction and facelifts. (For women, liposuction and breast augmentation followed by eyelid surgery, facelifts and chemical peels are the five favorites.) The ASPRS says that in most cases, surgery for men is a modification of the standard cosmetic surgeries, and most procedures cost the same regardless of gender. But there are physical differences. For example, because men retain their skin elasticity longer than women do, certain procedures, like liposuction in the neck, are usually very effective for them. Perhaps a more critical difference between the sexes is the significant post-operative considerations for men.

This is especially true when it comes to facelifts. Men's skin is thicker, and because the facial area contains hair, the blood supply is greater. This can pose a higher risk of bleeding; men are more prone than women to forming hematomas that may require additional surgery to remove. Also, depending on where the excess skin is moved, hair-bearing skin may be relocated behind the ears or to the back of the neck. "Men may have to deal with removing hair in places they've never had it before," says Dr. Solomon. And unlike women, few men are comfortable wearing makeup to cover post-operative redness, although some get relief with tinted sunscreens.

"There are definitely nuances" to performing this operation, says Dr. David L. Mobley of Sarasota Plastic Surgery. "The good part about men is that they are looking for a more moderate, natural appearance. They generally seek less dramatic changes than women."

Scarring can be another problem for men. Incisions in facelifts are 10 usually placed in front of the ear or along the hairline. Some doctors recommend you let your hair grow a bit before surgery to hide this scarring. Some men choose to grow sideburns. The ASPRS says men who are balding or have thinning hair may have a harder time hiding these incisions.

Finally, men who have been socialized to get back to work quickly are often surprised to find they face extended recovery periods. Men who choose to have a full abdominoplasty, or "tummy tuck," can be out of commission for as long as four weeks. Studies show men frequently deny having pain and feel foolish about asking for help, but those who attempt too much too soon or who reject post-operative instructions will find themselves facing a difficult recovery.

Never before has the fountain of youth been so available to so many people of both sexes. As one 45-year-old patient told Solomon, "It's because of you that I can go to dinner with a 21-year-old woman." Solomon predicts that in the years to come, cosmetic surgery for men will become even more prevalent, in the form of hair transplants, eyelid surgery, facelifts and penile enhancements.

"The market is growing all the time," agrees Dr. Mobley. "People consider this just an extension of everything else they do to look good. It's no longer a dramatic leap of faith."

But with availability comes the need for caution. Dr. Solomon urges patients to look for board-certified surgeons who have undergone extensive training and peer review. Be sure to ask if the surgeon has privileges at a local hospital and if he or she has medical malpractice insurance. "People tend to think of cosmetic surgery as cosmetic," says Dr. Solomon, "while I tend to think of it as surgery." After all, he says, "We're not just hairdressers with a scalpel."

What Did You Read?

1. What are the two types of men who want cosmetic surgery today?
2. What kinds of procedures are most popular for men? What is the most popular procedure for men?
3. What are some of the problems particular to men who choose cosmetic surgery?
4. What should people watch out for if they are interested in or thinking about having cosmetic surgery done?

What Do You Think?

1. In your opinion, is there still a social stigma against men seeking cosmetic surgery?

2. Why do you think there is more pressure on women to maintain a youthful appearance while men are allowed (even expected) to grow old "gracefully"?

3. Is our culture's emphasis on youthful appearances ultimately helpful or destructive? Explain.

How Was It Done?

1. What phrase best crystallizes this article? Why?

2. Do you feel the article is fully developed? Is length necessarily a testament to how credible and thorough the research is? Explain.

3. Is there enough scientific and medical expertise supporting the claim of the author, or are there numerous generalizations that have been arrived at without the benefit of actual facts?

Exercise That Fits Your Body

Kimberly Wong

Kimberly Wong presents the idea of three main body types, first described by William H. Sheldon in 1940, and how people should exercise according to their body type. The three types—ectomorph (thin), endomorph (round), and mesomorph (muscular)— have different qualities, so that some forms of exercise work better than others for each. Underpinning Wong's article is the importance of accepting your body for how it is, and working with what you already have.

Key Words

duped	tricked; fooled; conned
jarring	unsettling; shaking
physiologists	people who study the organic processes of an organism, especially of a human
aesthetic	related to the concepts of beauty
aerobic	activity that causes a marked increase in respiration and heart rate
willowy	graceful, tall, and slender
voluptuous	suggesting sensual pleasure by fullness and beauty of form
proclivity	an inclination or predisposition to something

Jennifer Carton Wade had loathed her pear shape ever since high school. "I hated my butt," she says. She ran for years, but the miles she put in did little for her shape, and the extra weight she carried on her hips ended up causing pain in her knees. Looking for a less jarring way to work out, she happily accepted a friend's invitation to a spin-bicycling class. She assumed the class was for novices, but it wasn't. "I was tricked," says the 31-year-old occupational therapist from San Francisco. "When I got there, I realized the only 'beginner' thing about the class was me."

To Carton Wade's surprise, she managed to keep pace with the group. Biking, it turns out, tapped her body's natural strength—her legs and rear. "Something clicked inside of me when I started cycling," says Carton Wade. "It was much easier than going for a long run. By accident, I found something that I'm actually pretty good at."

All that pedaling held another reward: Her rear slimmed down, and she gained definition and tone in her thighs. "Everything just feels firmer," says Carton Wade. "I love that my legs look muscular and strong." These days, there's no getting her off a bike. In the two years since she was duped by her friend, she's barely missed a cycling class.

Sounds like the impossible dream: a workout that comes naturally and gives you the aesthetic results you're after? Well, pinch yourself—it's not just wishful thinking, according to the experts, even though few of us ever figure this out. "People beat themselves up over the fact that they're not good at something," says Leigh Crews, a personal trainer and spokesperson for the American Council on Exercise, "or that they work really hard but don't seem to get anywhere. They could be fighting their body type." Some people are just made to be runners, say, while others have a build that favors swimming or weight training. If you haven't found the right workout for your body, you probably know firsthand the frustration exercise can cause. But once you identify your body type, you can tailor your workout to your abilities, Crews says. What's more, you can start working on ways to balance your figure; you may even find, as Carton Wade did, that doing what comes naturally will give you the shape you've always wanted.

Body typing was developed in 1940 by psychologist William H.   5 Sheldon. He had a theory that body shape determines personality. After scouring thousands of photographs, he came up with three basic shapes. The personality link didn't pan out, but the differences he charted turned out to be useful to nutritionists and exercise physiologists.

Sheldon's three body types have unwieldy scientific names, but their characteristics are easy to grasp: ectomorph (thin), endomorph (round), and mesomorph (muscular). Often, a person falls mainly into one of the three categories, but some people are an even mixture of two types.

You can either thank or curse your parents for your shape; for the most part, genetics determine body type. But knowing Mother Nature's no-exchange policy up front has an advantage: "Accepting that you're stuck with your body type helps you set realistic goals," says Alan Mikesky, an exercise physiologist at Indiana University–Purdue University at Indianapolis. "You may not be able to change your genetics, but you can certainly do the best with what your genes have dealt you."

How to know which category you fall into? Figuring it out isn't too tough, though you will have to stand naked in front of a mirror. If your parents passed down ectomorphic traits, chances are you're not harboring too many bitter feelings toward them at this moment. Ectomorphs have lean bodies; they're built like sticks. Picture Gwyneth Paltrow, with her willowy arms and narrow frame. They can even have a hard time gaining weight. (Crocodile tears, everyone.) Look in the mirror and flex your biceps and calves: An ectomorph's muscles, if visible at all, are long and thin.

For these string beans, it's building muscle that's challenging. The thousands of long microscopic fibers that constitute a muscle fall into one of two categories: fast-twitch or slow-twitch. Ectomorphs' muscles tend to have a high ratio of slow-twitch fibers, and these fibers simply don't thicken in the same way fast-twitch ones do, no matter how much work they get. However, the slow variety use energy and oxygen conservatively, and that translates into plenty of stamina. (Marathoners tend to be ectomorphic.)

At the other end of the scale are voluptuous endomorphs. Their 10 bodies hoard fat, favoring the hips and thighs as storage sites. They often look like a pear, though they can have an hourglass shape—think Marilyn Monroe. In the mirror test, endomorphs may not be able to make out their muscles, since body fat can conceal definition. But if your build is pear shaped, or you store weight in your hips, you're endomorphic.

Although endomorphs constantly battle the bulge, their muscles tend to be a more even mix of slow- and fast-twitch muscle than ectomorphs'. That means exercise can give endomorphs the best of both worlds: nice results from strength training and satisfaction from aerobic work, says Dixie Stanforth, an exercise physiologist at the University of Texas. Endomorphs can also use their powerful lower bodies to advantage in skating and cycling.

Lucky mesomorphs are born with the ability to build muscle quickly and burn fat easily. A mesomorph's muscular build makes her a natural athlete. Think of Olympian Marion Jones with her muscular arms, broad shoulders, and narrow waist and hips. Anything that calls for strength and short bursts of energy is going to favor the mesomorph, since her muscles have lots of fast-twitch fibers to provide the quick spark needed for explosive sports like racquetball and tennis.

Because these muscle fibers get thicker in response to any work— be it swinging a racquet or pumping iron—a sharply defined bicep or calf is a giveaway that you're mesomorphic. So is a V-shaped build and a proclivity for tossing around bales of hay.

As you read more about your type, you'll learn which activities suit you and which you might not find as satisfying. The prescribed workout falls within the recommended range of 20 to 60 minutes of aerobic exercise, three to five days a week. But each combines activities that come naturally with moves that will help balance your shape. If you happen to love something that isn't recommended for your body type, don't panic. It may be that you're a combination of two types or that you've simply overcome some inherent limitations. Combos such as ecto-endo or meso-endo are common. If, from the mirror test, you think you're a mixture of two types, read both sections and follow the advice that addresses your needs.

For more help planning a personalized workout schedule, go to 15 www.health.com, click on "Fitness" and check out our Fitness Planner.

Endomorphs

What Comes Naturally

Pear-shaped women don't carry just fat on their lower body; some of that extra heft is pure muscle, which can power you through activities such as in-line skating, swimming, dancing, and snow skiing. Also, short- to middle-distance fitness walking is good, but go longer and you're risking injury. Endomorphs tend to be more buoyant because of their padding, an advantage while swimming.

What You May Find Frustrating

Sports that involve running or jumping.

How to Improve Your Shape

Your goal is to do long-distance, low-impact exercise to burn off extra fat and slim your hips. Adding a little upper-body strength training can help balance out a bottom-heavy endomorph.

Your Ideal Regimen

Skate, swim, walk, or cycle, 30 to 45 minutes, 3 to 5 times a week.
Lift weights, 8 to 12 repetitions, 1 to 2 sets, 2 to 3 times a week.

Ectomorphs

What Comes Naturally

Your slight build lends itself to distance running, fitness walking, cross-country skiing, snowshoeing, and hiking. Most ectomorphs are extremely flexible, so you'll find stretching activities such as yoga and pilates rewarding.

(continued)

Ectomorphs (continued)

What You May Find Frustrating

Most ball sports, anything requiring sudden bursts of speed or strength.

How to Improve Your Shape

If ectomorphs complain, it's about their lack of curves. Full-body activities such as swimming or rowing can round you out with muscle. Weight training can also provide the definition you may crave, but don't overdo it, use weights you can lift 12 to 15 times. By the way, weight-bearing exercise is a must, because most ectomorphs are small boned, which can put you at a higher risk of osteoporosis.

Your Ideal Regimen

Walk or jog, 30 to 60 minutes, 2 to 3 times a week.
Cross-train on a rowing machine or swim, 30 to 60 minutes, 2 to 3 times a week.
Lift weights, 10 to 12 reps, 2 sets, 2 to 3 times a week.

Mesomorphs

What Comes Naturally

Muscular mesomorphs are good at just about everything they try. You'll enjoy tennis, basketball, and soccer; your build is also great for kickboxing or martial arts.

What You May Find Frustrating

Because of mesomorphs' preponderance of fast-twitch muscle fibers, endurance activities may prove to be a challenge.

How to Improve Your Shape

Be careful when weight training; you could easily overdevelop specific muscle groups, making you look out of proportion. And even though you burn fat easily, if you don't watch your diet and exercise, you could pile on the pounds.

Mesomorphs should stretch out regularly, since all that muscle can make you stiff. "Mesomorphs need to balance high-energy activities with something more mellow like yoga, pilates, or tai chi to help with the flexibility," says Crews.

Your Ideal Regimen

Choice of aerobic exercise, 30- to 45-minute sessions, 3 to 5 times a week.
Regular stretching, such as yoga.
Lifting weights isn't as crucial for mesomorphs; strength-train as needed to reach your goals.

What Did You Read?

1. What does it mean to fight your body type?
2. What are Sheldon's three body types? Which are you?
3. What mostly determines body type?

What Do You Think?

1. Depending on your body type, what kind of exercise program best suits you?
2. Do you think it is beneficial to have a professional help you arrange a workout plan just for your body?
3. Do you feel like you are maintaining a healthy lifestyle for your body type?

How Was It Done?

1. Around what is this article structured?
2. Most of the experts referred to in this article have training in what areas?
3. How helpful is the chart of the three body types at the end of the article? How does it improve the overall presentation of the material?

The Answer to Weight Loss Is Easy— Doing It Is Hard!

Marion J. Franz

Marion J. Franz discusses the seemingly never-ending problem of how to lose weight. He notes that current dieting practices are not successful since as more people diet, more people also become overweight. One aspect of the problem is that many diets supply temporary weight loss, but few people are able to sustain that weight loss over a long period of time. Thus, the truly important issue is not how to lose weight, but how to maintain weight loss. Simply put, Franz argues that quick fixes do not work, and that weight loss maintained over a long period of time results from eating right and regular exercise—in other words, a sustained commitment to weight loss.

Key Words

prevalence	the degree to which something is dominant or widespread
self-monitoring	watching over oneself to see that one conforms to certain rules, procedures, or expectations

obese	excessively overweight
registry	an official record book, or an organization keeping such books
cardiovascular	relating to the heart and blood vessels
innovative	being new; having a new idea, method, or device
insulin	a hormone required to metabolize carbohydrates
secretion	a fluid such as saliva that is released from the body
metabolism	the process by which products (such as food) are changed within the body into other forms that the body can use directly
oxidation	the state of changing into oxygen, such as rusting
chronic	marked by long duration or frequent occurrence

The rate of obesity and the number of "dieters" are increasing in parallel! Surveys consistently show that most adults are trying to lose or maintain weight.[1] More than 54 million Americans are currently on a diet,[2] yet the prevalence of overweight and obesity continues to increase. If dieting worked, obesity should be decreasing or at least not increasing. It is true that many dieters succeed in taking weight off, but very few—maybe just 5%, but at most 10%—manage to keep the weight off over the long term.[3–5]

Statistics suggest that about half of the adult population in the United States is overweight (body mass index [BMI = weight/height^2] 25–30), and 16% are obese (BMI > 30).[6] It is not surprising that so many consumers are searching for the "magic bullet" that will allow them to lose weight quickly and effortlessly. Unfortunately, health professionals also contribute to this phenomenon by constantly warning the public and their patients about the perils of being overweight. And herein lies the quandary—how to solve the problem of increasing obesity and its related health risks without making the problem worse.

Many Professionals Claim to Have the Solution to Weight Loss

There seem to be many "authorities" out there who have the answer—buy their book, buy their product, come to their program, and you will lose weight. A search of Amazon.com using the words "weight loss" revealed 1,214 matches with 58% published after 1999 and 85% since 1997.[5] Many of the 20 best sellers at Amazon.com promote some form of carbohydrate restriction—*Dr. Atkins' New Diet Revolution, The Carbohydrate Addict's Diet, Protein Power, Lauri's Low-Carb Cookbook*. So people do buy their books and products and attend their programs and do lose weight.

But although there appear to be easy solutions to the weight-loss problem, these solutions tend to be, at best, temporary. Even the "gold standard" behavioral weight-loss programs—those involving 16–24 treatment sessions over 6 months including self-monitoring, low-fat diet, and exercise—consider an average weight loss of 18–20 lb a success, but also report that participants retain only 60% of their initial weight loss 1 year after treatment.[3] Another study[4] reported the average duration of weight-loss programs to be 18 weeks, with moderately obese individuals losing 10% of their body weight. However, at 1 year, 34% had regained the lost weight, and at 3- to 5-year follow-up, there was a gradual return to baseline weight.

To determine what is required to maintain weight loss, a national registry searched nationwide and found a small number (in comparison to the number of people who diet) of successful weight losers. In a descriptive study of 784 participants,[7] the investigators reported that participants who lost an average of 66 lb (30 kg) and kept off at least 30 lb (13.6 kg) for an average of 5.5 years expend an average of 2,800 kcal per week through physical activity or an average of 1.5 h of exercise daily and eat less than 1,400–1,500 kcal with −20 of their calories from fat. In other words, their life is devoted to weight loss! But we all want an easier answer, so the parade of quick fixes continues.

Given the beneficial effects of weight-loss treatments on medical conditions such as type 2 diabetes and cardiovascular disease, reputable researchers continue to search for innovative ways to improve treatment outcomes.[8] As researchers continue to search for solutions to the problem of weight regain after weight loss, other medical professionals "buy into" the claims made for the high-protein, low-carbohydrate diets, and without any research documenting the long-term effectiveness of this solution, they recommend the latest book to their patients.

The Latest Solution: High-Protein, Low-Carbohydrate Diets

The current diet fad promises results with a high-protein, low-carbohydrate diet (which in actuality is a high-fat, low-carbohydrate diet). With only three macronutrients—carbohydrate, protein, and fat—to manipulate for changes in energy intake, there are not many options left to sell a new diet book. We have gone through the high-carbohydrate phase—bagels, pretzels, and low-fat cookies. It is unlikely that the current fad diet will be blatantly promoted as a high-fat diet—everyone has heard about the perils of eating fat. So, we are left with recycling the concept of a high-protein diet.

High-protein, low-carbohydrate diets claim to promote weight loss and improve blood glucose control. And while such diets are followed, they usually do both. Weight loss and improved glucose control are both important goals for people with type 2 diabetes, so why not recommend such diets to all persons with type 2 diabetes?

Advantage Claims for High-Protein, Low-Carbohydrate Diets

The advantages of the high-protein, low-carbohydrate approach are that diets that eliminate a whole category of nutrients—in this case, carbohydrate—are lower in calories and thus result in weight loss. With a high-protein intake and strict limitation of carbohydrate, water stored with glycogen (carbohydrate) is released. This rapid loss of fluid is an initial boon to dieters looking for fast results.

Fasting ketosis, which results in loss of appetite, may also develop. 10 Furthermore, few people can eat endless amounts of animal protein and fat for weeks on end, and so they eat less and less. The good news is that with a high-protein diet, weight is lost, insulin needs drop, and blood glucose and sometimes even lipid levels improve. It works, at least temporarily.

Although the authors of the popular books all take a slightly different approach, the basic premises are fairly similar. Eating a high-carbohydrate diet, they claim, makes people "fat" because carbohydrate increases blood glucose levels, causing a greater release of insulin, and higher insulin levels cause carbohydrate to be stored easily as fat (in adipose cells). Eating a high-protein diet, the argument goes, leads to weight loss, decreased insulin levels, and improved glycemia. However, neither this nor the claim to "cure" insulin resistance—the oversecretion of insulin that proponents of these diets say causes the lipogenesis—with a low-carbohydrate, high-protein diet is supported by scientific evidence.

Nor is there good evidence that insulin resistance from eating a diet rich in starchy foods and sugar is the cause of obesity. It is more likely the other way around—it is obesity that is associated with insulin resistance. Increased physical activity, energy restriction, and/or moderate weight loss have been shown to improve insulin sensitivity—not changes in the protein-to-carbohydrate ratio.[9–11] A high fat intake, regardless of the type of fat (saturated, polyunsaturated, or monounsaturated) has also been linked to insulin resistance,[10,12–15] so reducing fat intake may also help.

High-protein diets claim to offer other benefits. For example, protein stimulates the release of glucagon, a hormone that raises the level of blood glucose and counteracts the action of insulin; so eating right means balancing insulin and glucagon levels. Therefore, the argument goes, if you don't eat enough protein, your body releases too much insulin and not enough glucagon. It is true that the balance of insulin and glucagon release is important in the metabolism and storage of nutrients. But it is doubtful that you can change the balance by eating more protein.

Another claim is that, if the right kinds of fat are eaten, individuals will not become fat. However, there appears to be a hierarchy for the autoregulation of substrate utilization and storage that is determined by storage capacity and specific fuel needs of certain tissues.[16] Alcohol has the highest priority for oxidation because there is no body storage pool for it, and conversion of alcohol to fat is energetically expensive. Amino acids and carbohydrates are next in the oxidative hierarchy. Body proteins are functional, and there are no storage depots for amino acids. There is also a limited capacity to store carbohydrate as glycogen, and conversion of carbohydrate to fat is energetically expensive, as well. In contrast, there is virtually unlimited storage capacity for fat, largely in adipose tissue, and the storage efficiency of fat is high.

Because of the oxidative priority of alcohol and protein, the body has an exceptional ability to maintain their balance across a wide range of intakes of each. Carbohydrate oxidation closely matches carbohydrate intake.[17,18] Therefore, the amount of fat oxidized or stored is the difference between total energy needs and the oxidation of the other priority fuels—alcohol, protein, and carbohydrate.

Proponents of these diets also claim that more protein in the diet increases the satiety value of the meal, leading people to eat less. Although the effects of dietary fat and carbohydrate on regulation of energy intake, weight loss, and satiety have been studied, only limited research has been conducted related to protein. Short-term studies have suggested that protein per calorie exerts a more positive effect on satiety than both carbohydrate and fat.[19-21] However, this may not translate into eating fewer calories. Stubbs et al.,[21] in a 1-day study, reported that although subjective hunger was less after a high-protein breakfast compared to a high-fat or high-carbohydrate breakfast, lunchtime intake 5 h later and energy intake for the rest of the day were similar after all three breakfasts.

Skov et al.[22] studied the effect on weight loss in obese subjects by replacement of carbohydrate with protein in ad libitum fat-reduced diets. All foods were supplied to the 50 subjects for 6 months and could be consumed ad libitum. Subjects were randomly assigned to either a high-protein (25% protein, 45% carbohydrate) or high-carbohydrate (12% protein, 58% carbohydrate) diet. Both diets were low in fat (30% of energy). At 6 months, the high-protein group had lost an average 8.9 kg (20 lb) with a fat loss of 7.6 kg (17 lb), compared with the high-carbohydrate group average loss of 5.1 kg (11 lb) with a fat loss of 4.3 kg (9 lb).

Over the course of the study, energy intake was lower in the high-protein group by 8,000 calories (similar to 42 kcal/day), which probably accounted for the difference in weight loss. The researchers attributed the decrease in calories to the higher satiating effect of protein compared with carbohydrate. The real test of effectiveness would be to follow these subjects for the next 2 years to identify food choices after the completion of the study and to determine whether weight lost during the study was maintained.

Disadvantages of High-Protein, Low-Carbohydrate Diets

Aside from the problem that no long-term research is available to document that high-protein, low-carbohydrate diets maintain weight loss any better than traditional weight loss diets,[3–5] what are other concerns posed by these diets?

A major concern is that foods with proven health benefits are elim- 20 inated. There are health needs for the nutrients found in grains, fruits, vegetables, milk, and other carbohydrate-containing foods.[23–27] When analyzed,[5] these diets are low in calories—e.g., 1,152–1,627 kcal/day. However, they are also high in fat (55–60%), especially saturated fat; cholesterol; and protein (25–30%), mainly animal. The excess protein also has the potential to cause the body to lose what little calcium is ingested. They provide lower than recommended intakes of vitamin E, vitamin A, thiamin, vitamin B6, folate, calcium, magnesium, iron, potassium, and dietary fiber, which can contribute to constipation. Taking a supplement to replace missing nutrients is not the complete solution either, because all of the essential nutrients found in foods have not yet been identified and so cannot be replaced.

The long-term effect on lipids from these diets is unknown. A study of subjects following a high-protein, low-carbohydrate diet for 12 weeks reported substantial increases in plasma levels of both uric acid and LDL cholesterol, decreases in triglycerides, but no increase in HDL cholesterol levels, despite effective weight loss.[28]

We are reminded that popularity is not credibility. There is little research published in peer-reviewed journals to support low-carbohydrate, high-protein diets. High-protein diet books are based on personal experiences and testimonials and contain theories that usually would not survive peer review. Authors quote their own studies as proof of their diet's effectiveness. However, even their own studies have not shown this to be an approach that individuals can follow over the long term. Long-term studies are necessary to determine how long individuals can comfortably consume a high-protein diet in the real world.

The bottom line: people are obese not because they eat too much carbohydrate, but because they eat too many calories. Eating carbohydrate does not make people fat unless they overeat on carbohydrate (just as it would to overeat on protein or fat). There is evidence that high levels of dietary fat are associated with high levels of obesity,[29] but there is no evidence that high intake of "simple" sugars or carbohydrate causes obesity, hyperglycemia, or insulin resistance without dietary fat.[30]

Furthermore, should medical professionals be recommending a diet known to be nutritionally inadequate to people with diabetes in an effort to improve blood glucose control? This is an ethical question that deserves an answer.

Does Habitually Following a Low-Carbohydrate Diet Correlate with Lower Weight?

The U.S. Department of Agriculture initiated a research program to as-   25
sess the relationship between prototype popular diets and diet quality, food consumption patterns, and BMI.[31] To do this, researchers analyzed the food intake of 9,372 adults from the 1994–1996 Continuing Survey of Food Intake by Individuals. These data were used because they illustrate what people in the United States are actually eating. Popular diets were divided into three categories that represent more than 90% of the popular diet books now on the market: 1) low-carbohydrate diets (defined as <30% of energy from carbohydrate); 2) moderate-fat, moderate-carbohydrate diets (30–55% of energy from carbohydrate); and 3) very-low-fat, high-carbohydrate diets (>55% of energy from carbohydrate).

The largest portion—64%—fell into the middle group. Energy intake, total fat, saturated fat, protein, and mean BMI for subjects consuming these diets are listed in Table 1. Diet quality was highest for the high-carbohydrate group; diets high in carbohydrate and low to moderate in fat also tended to be lower in energy. BMIs were significantly lower for the high-carbohydrate diets, and the highest BMIs were noted for those on a low-carbohydrate diet. Their conclusion: weight loss is independent of diet composition. Energy restriction, not manipulation of macronutrients, is associated with weight reduction in the short term.

Focus on Blood Glucose Control, Not Weight Loss

There may be better advice, but it isn't very new or exciting. Moderation is generally the best approach—eating a healthful diet, being more physically active, and, if an individual has diabetes, keeping food records along with blood glucose records so that blood glucose levels can be kept under optimal control.

Perhaps we need to even ask why we have focused lifestyle changes for type 2 diabetes on weight loss instead of on improving blood glucose control. All of us would like to be able to help individuals lose and maintain weight loss, but research reveals little long-term

Table 1 Daily Intake and BMI for Adults Who Consume Diets with Differing Percentages of Carbohydrates

A	B	C	D
Energy (kcal)	2,026	2,166	1,895
Total fat (% kcal)	46	37	25
Saturated fatty acids (% kcal)	16	12	8
Carbohydrate (% kcal)	25	45	62
Protein (% kcal)	22	17	14
Mean BMI, men	26.9	26.6	26.1
Mean BMI, women	26.8	25.9	25.4

Legend for Chart:
A—Variables
B—Less than or equal to 30% of energy from carbohydrate
C—30–50% of energy from carbohydrate
D—>55% of energy from carbohydrate
Source: U.S. Department of Agriculture Continuing Survey of Food Intakes by Individuals, 1994–1996. Adapted from ref. 32.

success. Research is clarifying why weight loss is difficult[32-34] and documenting the psychological problems associated with the dieting process.[35] Obesity is associated with the development of chronic diseases, such as type 2 diabetes, and prevention of chronic diseases may require a better understanding of what controls appetite and better tools, including medications, to prevent weight gain or assist in weight loss. However, treatment for individuals who already have type 2 diabetes needs to focus on lifestyle strategies for the improvement of the associated metabolic abnormalities.

Early in the course of the disease when insulin resistance is present, energy restriction not related to weight loss and moderate weight loss (5–10% of body weight or 10–20 lb) have been shown to improve glycemia.[36] But as the disease progresses and insulin deficiency becomes the central issue, it may be too late for weight loss to be helpful.[37]

Fitness, Not Thinness, Reduces the Risk of Mortality

Blair and associates[38-40] evaluated the relationship between changes in physical fitness, obesity, and risk of mortality in 25,000 men. Baseline physical fitness and mortality during 8 years of follow-up within various BMI strata were reported.[39] In all BMI categories, men who were fit had lower death rates compared with men with low fitness levels. Differences in mortality were not caused by differences in body weight but rather by differences in fitness.

In a follow-up study,[40] the health consequences of body fatness and cardio respiratory fitness in relation to all-cause and cardiovascular mortality were reported. The investigators found that obesity did not appear to increase mortality risk in fit men regardless of their BMI. Fit men had greater longevity than unfit men regardless of their body composition or risk factor status. In fact, obese fit men had a lower risk of all-cause and cardiovascular mortality than lean unfit men. Their conclusion: for long-term health benefits, we should focus on improving fitness by increasing physical activity rather than relying only on diet for weight control.

What Advice Should We Give to Individuals Who Struggle with Weight Issues?

The first message to give individuals with weight problems should be to eat healthfully. Today, we may not know how to help individuals maintain weight loss, but we do know what constitutes a healthy diet. Studies have documented the importance of foods containing carbohydrate—fruits, vegetables, whole grains, low-fat milk products—in a healthy lifestyle. However, it is true that carbohydrate foods containing a large amount of sugars are not essential to good health—even if they are enjoyable. They should be eaten with caution. Low-fat diets have also been shown to contribute to weight maintenance.[41–43]

Encourage physical activity. Studies have also shown that individuals can become fit by accumulating only 30 min of physical activity throughout the day.[44] Having a dog that requires walking several times a day can contribute not only to psychological well-being through the enjoyment of having a pet, but also to improved physical health.

If you think individuals with type 2 diabetes must lose weight, remember that all that is required is a 10-lb loss. The challenge for health professionals is to convince individuals that this should be their goal. Foster et al.[45] reported that women participating in a weight-loss program expected to lose 34% of their body weight. However, after 48 weeks of treatment, they had lost only 16% of their initial weight, and they reported being unsatisfied with their weight loss.

Perhaps the most helpful thing we can do is to help individuals who struggle with their weight to "like themselves." They are important people both for themselves and for those who they care about. Even if we can't help them maintain weight loss, we can help them make changes for a healthier lifestyle, and we can help them manage their diabetes better.

Acknowledgment

Portions of this article originally appeared in: Franz MJ: Protein controversies in diabetes. *Diabetes Spectrum* 13:132–141, 2000.

References

1. Serdula MK, Mokdad AH, Williamson DF, Galuska DA, Mendlein JM, Health GW: Prevalence of attempting weight loss and strategies for controlling weight. *JAMA* 282:1353–1358, 1999.
2. Fad diets: look before you leap. *Food Insight* March/April, 2000, pp. 1,4,5.
3. Wing RR: Behavioral approaches to the treatment of obesity. In *Handbook of Obesity*. Bray G, Bouchard C, James PT, Eds. New York, Marcel Dekker, 1998, pp. 855–873.
4. Foreyt JP, Goodrick GK: Evidence for success of behavior modification in weight loss and control. *Ann Intern Med* 119:698–701, 1993.
5. Freedman MR, King J, Kennedy E: Popular diets: a scientific review. *Obes Res* 9 (Suppl. 1):1S–40S, 2001.
6. National Task Force on the Prevention and Treatment of Obesity: Overweight, obesity, and health risk. *Arch Intern Med* 160:898–904, 2000.
7. Klem ML, Wing RR, McGuire MT, Seagle HM, Hill JO: A descriptive study of individuals successful at long-term maintenance of substantial weight loss. *Am J Clin Nutr* 66:239–246, 1997.
8. Smith CF, Wing RR: New directions in behavioral weight-loss programs. *Diabetes Spectrum* 13:142–148, 2000.
9. Mayer-Davis EJ, D'Agostino R, Karter AJ, Haffner SM, Rewers MJ, Saad M, Bergman RN, for the IRAS Investigators: Intensity and amount of physical activity in relation to insulin sensitivity. *JAMA* 279:669–674, 1998.
10. Mayer-Davis EJ, Monaco JH, Hoen HM, Carmichael S, Vitolins M, Rewers MJ, Haffner SM, Ayad MF, Bergman RN, Karter AJ: Dietary fat and insulin sensitivity in a triethnic population: the role of obesity. The Insulin Resistance Atherosclerosis Study (IRAS). *Am J Clin Nutr* 65:79–87, 1997.
11. Markovic TP, Jenkins AB, Campbell LV, Furler SM, Kraegen EW, Chisholm DJ: The determinants of glycemic responses to diet restriction and weight loss in obesity and NIDDM *Diabetes Care* 21:687–694, 1998.
12. Lovejoy JC, DiGirolamo M: Habitual dietary intake and insulin sensitivity in lean and obese adults. *Am J Clin Nutr* 55:1174–1179, 1992.
13. Lovejoy JC, Windhauser MM, Rood JC, de la Bretonne JA: Effect of a controlled high-fat versus low-tat diet on insulin sensitivity and leptin levels in African-American and Caucasian women. *Metabolism* 47:1520–1524, 1998.
14. Mayer EJ, Newman B, Quesenberry CP Jr, Selby JV: Usual dietary fat intake and insulin concentrations in healthy women twins. *Diabetes Care* 16:1459–1469, 1993.
15. Maron DJ, Fair JM, Haskell WL: Saturated fat intake and insulin resistance in men with coronary artery disease. *Circulation* 84:2070–2074, 1991.
16. Stubbs RJ: Macronutrients effects on appetite. *Int J Obes* 19 (Suppl. 5):SI 1–S-19, 1995.
17. Hudgins LC, Hellerstein M, Seidman C: Human fatty acid synthesis is stimulated by a eucaloric low fat, high carbohydrate diet. *J Clin Invest* 97:2081–2091, 1996.
18. Schwarz JM, Neese RA, Turner S: Shortterm alterations in carbohydrate energy intake in human: striking effects on hepatic glucose production, de novo lipogenesis, lipolysis, and whole-body fat selection. *J Clin Invest* 96:2735–2743, 1995.

19. Hill AJ, Blundell JE: Macronutrients and satiety: the effects of a high-protein or high carbohydrate meal on subjective motivation to eat and food preferences. *Nutr Behav* 3:133–144, 1986.

20. Barkeling B, Rossner S, Bjorvell H: Effects of a high-protein meal (meat) and a high-carbohydrate meal (vegetarian) on satiety measured by automated computerized monitoring of subsequent food intake, motivation to eat and food preferences. *Int J Obes* 14:743–751, 1990.

21. Stubbs RJ, van Wyk MCW, Johnstone AM, Harbron CG: Breakfasts high in protein, fat or carbohydrate: effect on within-day appetite and energy balance. *Eur J Clin Nutr* 50:409–417, 1996.

22. Skov AR, Toubro S, Ronn B, Holm L, Astrup A: Randomized trial on protein vs carbohydrate in ad libitum fat reduced diet for the treatment of obesity. *Int J Obes* 23:528–536, 1999.

23. Liu S, Manson JE, Lee I-M, Cole SR, Hennekens CH, Willett WC, Buring JE: Fruit and vegetable intake and risk of cardiovascular disease: the Women's Health Study. *Am J Clin Nutr* 72:922–928, 2000.

24. Anderson JW, Hanna TJ, Peng X, Kryscio RJ: Whole grain foods and heart disease risk. *J Am Coll Nutr* 19:291 S–2995, 2000.

25. Liu S, Manson JE, Stampfer MJ, Hu FB, Giovannucci E, Colditz GA, Hennekens CH, Willett WC: A prospective study of whole-grain intake and risk of type 2 diabetes mellitus in U.S. women. *Am J Public Health* 90:1409–1415, 2000.

26. Hu FB, Rimm EB, Stampfer MJ, Ascherio A, Spiegelman D, Willett WC: Prospective study of major dietary patterns and risk of coronary heart disease in men. *Am J Clin Nutr* 72:912–921, 2000.

27. Appel LJ, Moore TJ, Obarzanek E, Vollmer VW, Svetkey LP, Sacks FM, Bray GA, Vogt TM, Cutler JA, Windhauser MM, Lin PH, Karanja N: A clinical trial of the effects of dietary patterns on blood pressure. *N Engl J Med* 336:1117–1124, 1997.

28. Larosa JC, Gordon A, Muesing R, Rosing DR: Effects of high-protein, low-carbohydrate dieting on plasma lipoproteins and body weight. *J Am Diet Assoc* 77:264–270, 1980.

29. Lissner J, Levitsky DA, Strupp BJ, Kalkwarf HJ, Roe DA: Dietary fat and the regulation of energy intake in human subjects. *Am J Clin Nutr* 46:886–892, 1987.

30. Surwit RS, Feinglos MN, McCaskill CC: Metabolic and behavioral effects of a high-sucrose diet during weight loss. *Am J Clin Nutr* 65:908–915, 1997.

31. Kennedy ET, Bowman SA, Spence JT, Freedman M, King J: Popular diets: correlation to health, nutrition, and obesity. *J Am Diet Assoc* 101:411–420, 2001.

32. Brownell KD, Rodin J: The dieting maelstrom: is it possible and advisable to lose weight? *Am Psychol* 49:781–791, 1994.

33. Brownell KD, Wadden TA: Etiology and treatment of obesity: understanding a serious, prevalent, and refractory disorder. *J Consul Clin Psychol* 60:505–517, 1992.

34. Liebel RL, Rosenbaum M, Hirsch J: Changes in energy expenditure resulting from altered body weight. *N Engl J Med* 332:621–628, 1995.

35. Polivy J: Psychological consequences of food restriction. *J Am Diet Assoc* 96:589–592, 1996.

36. UKPDS Study Group: UK Prospective Diabetes Study 7: Response of fasting plasma glucose to diet therapy in newly presenting type II diabetic patients. *Metabolism* 39:905–912, 1990.

37. Watts NB, Spanheimer RG, DiGirolamo M, Gebhart SS, Musey VC, Siddiq K, Phillips LS: Prediction of glucose response to weight loss in patients with non-insulin-dependent diabetes mellitus. *Arch Intern Med* 150: 803–806, 1990.

38. Blair SN, Kohl HW, Barlow CE, Paffenbarger RS, Gibbons LW, Macera CA: Changes in physical fitness and all-cause mortalilty. *JAMA* 273:1093–1098, 1995.

39. Barlow CE, Kohl HW, Gibbons LW, Blair SN: Physical fitness, mortality and obesity. *Int J Obes* 19 (Suppl. 4):S41–S44, 1995.

40. Lee DC, Blair SN, Jackson AS: Cardiorespiratory fitness, body composition, and all-cause and cardiovascular disease mortality in men. *Am J Clin Nutr* 69:373–380, 1999.

41. Carmichael HE, Swinburn BA, Wilson MR: Lower fat intake as a predictor of initial and sustained weight loss in obese subjects consuming an otherwise ad libitum diet. *J Am Diet Assoc* 98:35–39, 1998.

42. Larson DE, Ferraro RT, Robertson DS, Ravussin E: Energy metabolism in weight-stable postobese individuals. *Am J Clin Nutr* 62:735–739, 1995.

43. Kendall A, Levitsky DA, Strupp BJ, Lissner L: Weight loss on a low-fat diet: consequence of the imprecision of the control of food intake in humans. *Am J Clin Nutr* 53:1124–1129, 1991.

44. Pate RR, Pratt M, Blair SN, Haskell WL, Macera CA, Bouchard C, Buchner D, Ettinger W, Heath GW, King AC, Kriska A, Leon AS, Marcus BH, Morris J, Paffenbarger RS, Patrick K, Pollock ML, Rippe JM, Sallis J, Wilmore JH: Physical activity and public health: a recommendation from the Centers for Disease Control and Prevention and the American College of Sports Medicine. *JAMA* 273:402–407, 1995.

45. Foster GD, Wadden TA, Vogt RA, Brewer G: What is reasonable weight loss? Patients' expectations and evaluations of obesity treatment outcomes. *J Consul Clin Psychol* 65:79–85, 1997. Acknowledgment Portions of this article originally appeared in: Franz MJ: Protein controversies in diabetes. *Diabetes Spectrum* 13:132–141, 2000.

What Did You Read?

1. Why does the author seem unimpressed with most diet fads and diet books?

2. Why do many people initially think high-protein, low-carbohydrate diets are effective?

3. What are problems with high-protein, low-carbohydrate diets?

What Do You Think?

1. What should people focus on to lose weight and be healthy?

2. What kinds of diets have you tried? Were they successful or not? Explain.

3. In your opinion, do people overcomplicate eating and dieting? Explain.

How Was It Done?

1. Is the article supported well with facts and data? How so?

2. Is the chart easy to read and helpful in supporting the claim?

3. Is the article too technical in its discussion of how some low-carb/high-protein diets are dangerous? Are the facts overwhelming and confusing when more emphasis or analysis would be easier to digest? Explain.

I Had an Eating Disorder . . . and Didn't Even Know It!

Lori Gottlieb

Lisa Gottlieb presents the story of a woman who was too thin. In a confessional tone, Julie Weaver recalls her increasingly strict diet regimen and excessive workouts. She began to eat less and less while maintaining a rigorous workout schedule. She eventually recognized that she had developed a problem—her life had begun to revolve around food and her body. She dealt with her problem by becoming more involved in other parts of her life, eating smarter and exercising regularly but not excessively.

Key Words

pared-down	trimmed or diminished
obsess	to be preoccupied
anorexia	a disorder marked by excessive dieting, leading to unhealthy and potentially fatal weight loss
bulimia	a disorder marked by binge eating followed by purging of the food from the body
regimen	a systematic plan designed especially to improve and maintain health

Julie Weaver, 21, watched what she ate, got tons of exercise, and had a body other girls envied. But something was wrong. Seriously wrong.

You don't nibble on celery sticks all day, or starve yourself until you're stick-thin. You don't binge on ice cream and boxes of

Oreos, then make a beeline to the nearest bathroom stall to toss your, well, cookies. Okay, so maybe you do count calories and are super-careful about what you eat. But it's not like there's anything wrong with you.

Or is there? For the past several years, doctors have been research-ing that very question. What they've discovered is that sometimes a pared-down diet and a simple desire to be thin can cross the line into something dangerous: an eating phenomenon called disordered eat-ing. It hasn't been officially classified as an eating disorder by the American Psychological Association (yet), but don't be fooled. Disor-dered eating is something to be concerned about.

So what is it? Basically, it's when food starts to play a really impor-tant part in your life—almost like you're obsessed with it. Some exam-ples: You're so afraid of gaining weight that you constantly think about what you can or cannot eat. You skip early meals (breakfast and lunch), then feel so famished later on that you pig out during dinner. You talk about food a lot with your friends. You're always trying some weird diet, where you only eat one or two kinds of food. Or you feel so guilty after eating that you just have to work out (now!).

Hannah, 14, from Evansville, Indiana, has been there. "I hardly   5 ever eat breakfast," she says. "For lunch, I'll munch on fast-food french fries or a Twix bar. As soon as I get home, I'll have a small bowl of ce-real. By the time dinner rolls around, I'll be so hungry, I'll load up my plate, then have a bowl of ice cream afterward. I know I'm not eating right. For one thing, I'm always tired. It's hard for me to get up in the morning, and I have trouble concentrating in class. And when it comes time for soccer practice after school, I start out strong and then gradu-ally fizzle out."

Worth the Weight?

Just like with other eating problems, this illness can do really bad things to your health . . . and body. (Dry hair, broken-out skin, chapped lips, constant fatigue. Attractive, huh?) But what's even scarier is this: Left untreated, disordered eating can lead to more seri-ous eating disorders, like anorexia (starving yourself to stay thin) and bulimia (bingeing and purging to keep off the pounds).

According to Eating Disorders Awareness and Prevention, Inc., at least 40 percent of all women suffer from some form of disordered eat-ing. But since the symptoms aren't as severe as those associated with anorexia or bulimia, most girls are unaware they even have a problem. Until three years ago, 21-year-old Julie Weaver was one of them. The Barnard College student wasn't concerned with her strict eating habits and fitness regimen. She just wanted to stay thin and look good. But then, things got out of control.

Julie's Story . . .

Growing up, I was always a little overweight. What made it worse was that it seemed like everyone else around me was skinny. I'd see how great my friends looked in their Florida "uniforms" (tank tops and jeans). I'd thumb through fashion magazines and come across Kate Moss modeling skimpy summer dresses, or see tiny little Michelle Pfeiffer looking amazing in those elaborate period costumes in *Dangerous Liaisons.* It didn't take a genius to realize that skinny was the thing to be.

I guess it was in the eighth grade when I began losing weight. I started playing soccer, and the baby fat just came off. The first thing I noticed was how good I looked. The next thing I noticed was the positive feedback people were sending my way. Friends, teachers, family—they couldn't stop commenting on my new, "improved" body. All of a sudden, people noticed me. The attention made me feel more confident, more important.

My body became a big deal to me. If it came down to a choice between being told I was smart or being told I had a great body, I'd take the "great body" compliment any day. Does that sound vain? Maybe. But the sad thing is, people really do treat you differently when you have a certain type of body. Here's an example: In high school, I worked as a waitress to earn extra money for college. And it was obvious that some customers were nicer to me than they were to the other girls. It was always "Hi, sweetheart! How are you?" (And yes—they tipped better too.)

Getting in Deeper

The summer after my junior year of high school, I went backpacking in Colorado for four weeks. I was doing volunteer work for Rocky Mountain National Park, and six days a week, we would hike uphill, then work all day hauling logs to clear pathways. This big care package of food—vegetables mainly—was brought to us once a week.

In the month I was away, I lost ten pounds. That may not sound like much. But believe me, when you're 5'4", ten pounds in one month is a lot. I remember standing in a stall in the airport bathroom after leaving Colorado and looking down at my thighs. They were so skinny! I decided to do whatever it took to keep them that way.

I started an exercise routine to keep the weight off. I'd wake up at 4:30 every morning and work out for about an hour and a half before school. I'd start by doing a couple of miles on a stationary bike, then a half hour on the Stairmaster at the gym. I'd also use weights to tone up. After every workout, I weighed myself to see if I had lost weight. Those little numbers on the scale were so important to me. Depending on what I saw, it could affect my mood for the rest of the day. My friends were always telling me they wished they had my discipline. I also got compliments on how great my body looked. When you're getting all of this positive feedback, it only makes you want to work harder. It got to the point where I wouldn't miss a day of exercise. If I couldn't work out in the morning, you'd better believe I'd be out there running or pedaling after school.

Food for Thought

I also become hyperconscious of what I ate. Because I started getting involved in animal rights, I decided to become a vegan. (That's a really strict vegetarian who doesn't eat meat, fish, milk, cheese, eggs, honey, or anything that comes from an animal.) I had the whole routine down and it hardly ever changed. I was careful to control the amount of food I ate. Just one medium-sized serving. Period. And I was dedicated. I had this whole list of foods that I'd never dare eat, like french fries. My "reward" for all the hard work: By my senior year, I'd lost another ten pounds. It was such an amazing feeling of power—knowing that I had the ability to control my body. To me, it was a huge accomplishment—every bit as impressive as the A's I was getting in school. Maybe more so.

Pretty soon, I was staring into every mirror I passed. I'd spin 15 around and look at myself from all angles. Do my thighs look thin? Are my arms toned? If I went to the bathroom, I wouldn't just look at my face, I'd step back so I could check out my entire body. It never occurred to me that I was obsessed. I mean, what's so strange about wanting to look good? Besides, I wasn't doing anything my friends weren't doing. We'd work out together—like a buddy system, to spur each other on. If you weren't in the mood to exercise one day, there'd be someone there to say, "Come on—you should do it!" You knew if you wanted to keep up and look as good as everybody else, you couldn't goof off.

The hard work seemed to pay off—and I was so psyched. I really wanted to be skinny. I figured people wouldn't notice me if I didn't look this way. Not once did it occur to me that they could be attracted to me for other things.

Facing the Truth

After high school, I moved to New York City to attend Barnard. I continued to work out and added something new to my routine: Capoeira, an intense form of Brazilian martial arts. I did that two hours a day, three days a week. Since I was busy with classes, my eating routine became more basic. I'd skip breakfast; then whenever I felt hungry, I'd munch on plain bagels in the dining hall.

My first semester, I took a women's studies course, and one day, my classmates and I started talking about body image. As we went around the room, every woman in my class confessed that she had an issue with food and body image. Some hated the way their bodies looked. Others went from diet to diet to drop pounds. One woman was even hospitalized for anorexia. I was stunned. I mean, here were these strong, smart women who seemed so together—and yet every one of them felt insecure about her body. How sad was that? Then it hit me: I was one of them.

Seeing myself reflected in their eyes and listening to them speak so honestly about their insecurities helped me reexamine my own relationship with food. Being able to talk about my weight was the first step in admitting that something was wrong. And I needed to deal with it.

Little by little, I made an effort to take my attention away from food—and my body—and redirect it to other parts of my life. I got a part-time job tutoring kids who were in danger of dropping out of school. I also got a place off-campus, and made an effort to explore the city. The busier I got, the less I seemed to obsess about food. 20

The Body Fantastic

Yes, I'm still a vegan. But I've learned to relax my eating habits. I'm not about to dig into a container of Haagen-Dazs anytime soon. But since I've moved into an off-campus apartment, I've made a promise to actually start cooking for myself and eating smarter. I've branched out a bit. Now I eat three full meals a day. For breakfast, it might be a bagel topped with tofu cream cheese, a bowl of cereal, and a piece of fruit. Lunch usually means a dish of pasta topped with veggies. I eat out four times a week—maybe at a cool Japanese place around the corner. If I want a late-night snack, I'll open up some salsa and dip. Food is a treat for me now—not something to worry about or stress over, but something to enjoy.

I'm also more relaxed about exercising. If I'm busy with classes and I can't work out for a few days, I'm cool with that. Do I have a perfect body? No, probably not. But I feel good, I'm healthy, and I'm comfortable with the way I look. That's all that I'm striving for now.

Sometimes I look at old photos of myself. In one junior high picture, I'm wearing a blue tank top. You don't have to look close to see my collarbone jutting out from underneath my skin. Back then, I thought I looked great. Now I go, "Too skinny!" I wish that girl in the picture could've known what I know now. There's nothing wrong with looking good, or wanting to be thin. But if you spend all your time obsessing about your body, you're neglecting some important things that exist on the inside:

Your humor. Your intelligence. Your kindness. Your soul. And when you think about it, that's so sad.

No, my friends and I didn't have life-threatening eating disorders. 25 Not anorexia. Not bulimia. But I don't think the way we acted was normal, either. Or maybe it was . . . and that's what's so scary.

Girls in Trouble

If these girls sound like you, check out the box.

"I don't eat breakfast. For lunch, I'll munch on potato chips or Little Debbie's snack cakes. By dinner I'm hungry, so I'll drive to Arby's for a beef and cheddar melt. My mom gives me a hard time about not eating better. I guess she's right. I'm always tired, and sleep all the time."

—Sara, 17, Munfordville, KY

"The day before yesterday, I ate an entire loaf of bread, with nothing on it. Yesterday, all I ate was a can of chickpeas. (I figured the fiber would clean out my colon.) I know I should go on a healthy diet, instead of eating just one thing all day. But that's all I have the discipline to do."

—Marae, 17, Yorktown, VA

"I figured the way to drop pounds was to eat four bowls of soup a day, and nothing else. Then a friend who was dieting got so sick. It scared me, and I started eating three meals a day. I thought guys would like me if I was thin. But I was so miserable, they didn't want to be around me."

—Michelle, 15, Woodbridge, VA

"It started out with me skipping lunch. It got to the point where I'd only eat pretzels till dinner. Then I'd be so hungry I'd pig out till my stomach hurt. But my grandma's moved in with us and she's started making delicious food. Now I spread my meals throughout the day."

—Lynda, 15, Wilmington, DE

Busting the Boy Myth

Think girls are the only ones obsessing about their bodies? Turns out guys struggle with the same eating problems we do, and for similar reasons (like pressure to live up to the buff bodies they see in action movies and sporting events). Check it out: In one study, 95 percent of all college-age guys say they're dissatisfied with their bodies. About two million are battling bulimia. And more than one million suffer from anorexia.

Ryan, 18, of Lexington, KY, was one of them. "My dad used to say, 'Don't eat so much, you're going to be fat,'" says Ryan. "It started getting to me. I tried to lose weight by going three days without eating anything but fruit. Every couple of days, I'd end up bingeing—and getting sick."

Know any guys like Ryan? To help, or to get more information on guys and eating disorders, check out www.something-fishy.org.

—*Kristen Oldham*

What Did You Read?

1. How many women suffer from some kind of eating disorder?
2. What made Weaver realize she had an eating disorder?
3. What were some of the symptoms of Weaver's eating disorder?

What Do You Think?

1. Is it important to have "disordered eating" officially classified by the American Psychological Association? Why or why not?
2. Gottlieb says at least 40 percent of women suffer from an eating disorder. Why do you suppose this number is so high?
3. In your experience, are attractive people treated better, as Weaver claims? What specific examples of preferential treatment have you witnessed?
4. Weaver says that her eating habits were not normal even though they were not life threatening. What would constitute "normal eating"?

How Was It Done?

1. Is the checklist of symptoms at the end of the article helpful in clarifying what eating disorders are?
2. Does the article present a balanced cause/effect logic of eating disorders, or is the emphasis simply on the effects of eating disorders so you can determine if you have one?
3. Did the article appear to be constructed primarily with scientific evidence or anecdotal support?

The Fattening of America

Barry Sears with Bill Lawren

In this excerpt from The Zone, *Sears and Lawren argue that diets based on eating less fat and eating more carbohydrates are not working. Evidence shows that Americans are fatter than ever, despite well-publicized advice to cut down on fatty foods. The authors argue that high-protein, low-carbohydrate diets create changes in the body chemistry that make it virtually impossible for people to lose weight and keep that weight off.*

Key Words

noble	aristocratic; famous or notable
prestigious	honored
macronutrients	chemical elements of which relatively large quantities are needed for good health
carbohydrate	a compound of carbon, hydrogen, and oxygen, such as sugars and starches
radicals	people who adhere to an extreme position or view
plateau	a level of attainment or achievement with relative stability
visceral	felt deeply; not intellectually but emotionally
mystical	having spiritual meaning not obvious to the senses or reason
metabolic	referring to the process by which products (such as food) are changed within the body into other forms the body can use directly
heresy	dissent or deviation from a dominant theory

You fatten cattle by feeding them lots and lots of low-fat grain. How do you fatten humans? Same way: you feed them lots and lots of low-fat grain. So if you've been eating more pasta and bread (both made from grain) than ever before, and you're still gaining weight, think about those grain-fed cattle the next time you sit down to a big plate of pasta.

The Great Carbohydrate Experiment

For the past fifteen years, the people of this country have been unwitting participants in a massive scientific experiment. The goal of that experiment was exceptionally noble—the reduction of excess body fat in the American population. If such a goal was attainable, our healthier population would dramatically decrease the burdens on the existing health-care system, especially for an aging population. (By conservative estimates, the cost of treating conditions related to obesity in 1986 was $39 billion.)

But how to achieve that goal? The message, from top scientists, nutritionists, and the government, was simple: Americans were told to eat less fat and more carbohydrates. That, said the experts, is how you get skinnier.

We're now fifteen years into the experiment, and one doesn't have to be a rocket scientist to see that it isn't working. In fact, all data analysis during the last fifteen years of this experiment shows that in spite of the fact that the American public has dramatically cut back on the amount of fat consumed, the country has experienced an epidemic rise in obesity.

The sad truth is that Americans are getting fatter. A recent study by scientists at the National Center for Health Statistics in the Centers for Disease Control and Prevention showed that the number of overweight adults in America—one-quarter of the population from 1960 to 1980—suddenly jumped between 1980 and 1991 to one-*third* of the population. That's a 32 percent increase in obesity in just ten years. If there were a 32 percent increase in heart disease or a 32 percent increase in breast cancer in a similar time period, it would be a national emergency. (Actually, as I'll show later, within another ten to twenty years this increase in obesity is likely to manifest itself in similar increases in those disease states as well.)

Researchers at the National Institutes of Health recently revealed that during the last seven years, while the dietary intake of saturated fats and cholesterol was decreasing, the average weight of young adult Americans has actually *increased* by ten pounds!

"Shocking," said the experts who conducted the study. "Totally unexpected." And indeed it's obvious that something is very wrong. If we're eating supposedly "healthy" diets that supply less fat and less cholesterol, why in the world are we gaining weight?

That straightforward question has a straight answer: we're getting fatter because many of our dietary "laws" are wrong.

In addition, many of today's fashionable recommendations are confusing. If you read enough of these low-fat, high-carbohydrate dietary formulas, you'll find little agreement—even among the scientific experts—as to precise definitions for "low" and "high."

The National Research Council's prestigious Committee on Diet and Health, for example, recommends that most Americans get 30 percent of their total daily calories from fats, and 55 percent or more from carbohydrates—especially so-called "complex" carbohydrates like pasta and bread. That's one set of recommendations.

But when *Consumer Reports* magazine—a highly respected, even authoritative publication—asked a panel of sixty-eight scientific experts on nutrition (some of whom sit on the NRC Committee on Diet and Health), they got a different answer. The panel assembled by *Consumer Reports* recommended limiting fat intake to as little as twenty percent of daily calories, and a vague "more than half" of daily calories from carbohydrates.

And protein? The National Research Council Committee tells you to "maintain protein intake at moderate levels." What's a moderate level? Who knows? Meanwhile, the *Consumer Reports* panel says, "Don't worry about protein one way or the other. Most Americans eat at least as much protein as they need."

These differences are confounding people who want a simple, standard set of figures. But the confusion's just starting. The National Research Council's committee and the *Consumer Reports* panel represent the conservative end of what is actually a wide spectrum of low-fat, high-carb recommendations. At the other end of the spectrum are the people I think of as the low-fat radicals. Led by the late Nathan Pritikin, author of *The Pritikin Program for Diet and Exercise,* these dietary extremists advocate that only 5 to 10 percent of total calories should come from fats, 10 to 15 percent from protein, and a whopping 75 to 85 percent from carbohydrates.

No wonder the average American is confused.

But the confusion caused by these conflicting recommendations is 15 only one problem. The greater problem is the terrible paradox: people are eating less fat and getting fatter! No medical authority will tell you that excess body fat makes you healthier. There is but one alarming conclusion to reach: a high-carbohydrate, low-fat diet may be dangerous to your health.

To understand why that is, we need a new perspective on food. We need to understand the relationship between the food we eat and our potential to live in the Zone. If you're not in the Zone, one major consequence may be the relentless accumulation of excess body fat—even with an almost fat-free diet.

To get a new perspective on food, here's some information you need to know. Some of it may surprise you.

- *Eating fat does not make you fat.* It's your body's response to excess carbohydrates in your diet that makes you fat. Your body has a limited capacity to store excess carbohydrates, but it can easily convert those excess carbohydrates into excess body fat.

- *It's hard to lose weight by simply restricting calories.* Eating less and losing excess body fat do not automatically go hand in hand. Low-calorie, high-carbohydrate diets generate a series of biochemical signals in your body that will take you out of the Zone, making it more difficult to access stored body fat for energy. Result: you'll reach a weight-loss plateau, beyond which you simply can't lose any more weight.

- *Diets based on choice restriction and calorie limits usually fail.* People on restrictive diets get tired of feeling hungry and deprived. They go off their diets, put the weight back on (primarily as increased body fat), and then feel bad about themselves for not having enough will power, discipline, or motivation.

- *Weight loss has little to do with will power.* You need information, not will power. If you change *what* you eat, you don't have to be overly concerned about *how much* you eat. Adhering to a diet of Zone-favorable meals, you can eat enough to feel satisfied and still wind up losing fat—without obsessively counting calories or fat grams.

- *Food can be good or bad.* The ratio of macronutrients—protein, carbohydrate, and fat—in the meals you eat is the key to permanent weight loss and optimal health. Unless you understand the rules that control the powerful biochemical responses generated by food, you will never reach the Zone.

- *The biochemical effects of food have been constant for the last forty million years.* All mammals, including man, have essentially the same responses to food. These responses have been genetically conserved throughout evolution, and are unlikely to change in the near future.

Bottom line: the key to losing fat is not a matter of cutting calories, it's a matter of reaching the Zone. In the Zone losing body fat is virtually automatic. But to reach the Zone and stay there on a permanent basis, you'll first need to understand the difference between weight loss and fat loss.

Fat Loss versus Weight Loss

Nutrition, like religion, is extremely visceral. For many people, it's a matter of faith that a pound lost is a pound lost, and it doesn't really matter where that lost weight came from. So let me make something clear: there's a big difference between weight loss and fat loss.

Obesity is not simply weight gain. It's the accumulation of *excess* body fat. Thus, reaching an ideal body weight is not just a matter of losing weight. It involves the reduction of *excess* body fat.

Your body weight is composed of many factors—water content, fat content, muscle content, and structural component (bones, tendons, etc.). For simplicity, though, you can treat the body as a two-part system: pure fat on the one hand, and lean body mass (everything else) on the other. Your percentage of body fat is simply your total fat content divided by your total weight (Total Fat ÷ Total Body Weight = Body Fat).

When you want to calculate your *ideal* body weight, you're not looking for some mystical number. Your ideal body weight is simply the appropriate percent of body fat for a healthy male or female. That figure is usually accepted to be 15 percent body fat for males and 22 percent body fat for females. (The higher amount of body fat for females is a reflection of the genetic differences between men and women.)

(The old Metropolitan Life Tables for ideal body weight—which have consistently revised upwards over the years and which almost no one in America comes close to matching—are included in Appendix G.)

How do current Americans stack up in terms of body fat? Today's average American man has 23 percent body fat, while the average American woman has 32 percent body fat. This means the average male in this country is 53 percent fatter than his ideal, and the average female 50 percent fatter than hers. Americans are without question the fattest people on the face of the planet.

Why are our body-fat percentages so high? Because the experts who are telling us what to eat don't really understand the relationship between diet and fat loss. Specifically, the experts don't quite understand how body fat is influenced by the *macronutrient* content of the food we eat.

What are macronutrients? Very simple: protein, carbohydrates, 25 and fat.

This concept may seem mundane. Of course food consists of protein, carbohydrates, and fat—you've been told that since the fourth grade. But the truth goes much deeper. The fact is that every time you eat these macronutrients generate complex hormonal responses in your body. These responses ultimately determine how much body fat you will store. In terms of weight loss, knowing how to control these responses is the real power of nutrition, and hence the gateway to the Zone.

So let's take a look at the macronutrients, one by one:

Carbohydrates—The Reason You're Fat

Over the past fifteen years, our dietary establishment has made a virtual industry of extolling the virtues of carbohydrates. We're constantly told that carbohydrates are the good guys of nutrition, and that, if we eat large amounts of them, the world should be a better place. In such a world, the experts tell us, there will be no heart disease and no obesity. Under such guidance, Americans are gobbling breads, cereals, and pastas as if there were no tomorrow, trying desperately to reach that 80 to 85 percent of total calories advocated by the high-carb extremists.

Unfortunately, many people don't really know what a carbohydrate is. Most people will say carbohydrates are sweets and pasta. Ask them what a vegetable or fruit is, and they'll probably reply that it's a vegetable or fruit—as if that were a food type all its own, a food type that they can eat in unlimited amounts without gaining weight.

Well, this may come as a surprise, but all of the above—sweets and 30 pasta, vegetables and fruits—are carbohydrates. Carbohydrates are merely different forms of simple sugars linked together in polymers— something like edible plastic.

Of course, we all need a certain amount of carbohydrates in our diet. The body requires a continual intake of carbohydrates to feed the brain, which uses glucose (a form of sugar) as its primary energy source. In fact, the brain is a virtual glucose hog, gobbling more than two thirds of the circulating carbohydrates in the bloodstream while you are at rest. To feed this glucose hog, the body continually takes carbohydrates and converts them to glucose.

It's actually a bit more complicated than that. Any carbohydrates not immediately used by the body will be stored in the form of glycogen (a long string of glucose molecules linked together). The body has two storage sites for glycogen: the liver and the muscles. The glycogen stored in the muscles is inaccessible to the brain. Only the glycogen stored in the liver can be broken down and sent back to the bloodstream so as to maintain adequate blood sugar levels for proper brain function.

The liver's capacity to store carbohydrates in the form of glycogen is very limited and can be easily depleted within ten to twelve hours. So the liver's glycogen reserves must be maintained on a continual basis. That's why we eat carbohydrates.

The question no one has bothered to ask until now is this: what happens when you eat *too much* carbohydrate? Here's the answer: whether it's being stored in the liver or the muscles, the total storage capacity of the body for carbohydrate is really quite limited. If you're an average person, you can store about three hundred to four hundred grams of carbohydrate in your muscles, but you can't get at that carbohydrate. In the liver, where carbohydrates are accessible for glucose conversion, you can store only about sixty to ninety grams. This is equivalent to about two cups of cooked pasta or three typical candy bars, and it represents your total reserve capacity to keep the brain working properly.

Once the glycogen levels are filled in both the liver and the muscles, excess carbohydrates have just one fate: to be converted into fat and stored in the adipose, that is, fatty, tissue. In a nutshell, even though carbohydrates themselves are fat-free, *excess carbohydrates end up as excess fat.* 35

That's not the worst of it. Any meal or snack *high* in carbohydrates will generate a rapid rise in blood glucose. To adjust for this rapid rise, the pancreas secretes the hormone insulin into the bloodstream. Insulin then lowers the levels of blood glucose.

All well and good. The problem is that insulin is essentially a storage hormone, evolved to put aside excess carbohydrate calories in the form of fat in case of future famine. So the insulin that's stimulated by excess carbohydrates aggressively promotes the accumulation of body fat.

In other words, when we eat too much carbohydrate, we're essentially sending a hormonal message, via insulin, to the body (actually, to the adipose cells). The message: "Store fat."

Hold on; it gets even worse. Not only do increased insulin levels tell the body to store carbohydrates as fat, they also tell it not to release any stored fat. This makes it impossible for you to use your own stored body fat for energy. So the excess carbohydrates in your diet not only make you fat, they make sure you *stay* fat. It's a double whammy, and it can be lethal.

To put it another way, too much carbohydrate means too much insulin, and too much insulin takes you out of the Zone. Out of the Zone, you put on excess body fat, and you can't get rid of it. 40

That's the carbohydrate picture in outline. Let's sharpen the focus. The real key to all this is the speed at which carbohydrates enter the bloodstream, because that's what controls the rate of insulin secretion. You see, the stomach is basically an indiscriminate vat of acid that takes all carbohydrates—whether they're puffed-rice cakes, refined table sugar, carrots, or pasta—and breaks them down into simple sugars for absorption. What distinguishes one kind of carbohydrate from another is the rate at which the carbohydrate enters the bloodstream.

Before 1980 no one bothered to ask about the entry rates into the bloodstream of various types of carbohydrates. When this question was finally studied, the implications should have turned the nutritional community on its head. Somehow supposedly "simple" sugars like fructose were entering the bloodstream at far slower rates than supposedly "complex" carbohydrates like pasta. This fact has major consequences if you ever hope to reach the Zone.

The entry rate of a carbohydrate into the bloodstream is known as its *glycemic index*. The lower the glycemic index, the slower the rate of absorption. Believe it or not, refined table sugar has a lower glycemic index than typical breakfast cereals. Actually, the carbohydrate that turned out to have one of the highest glycemic indices—that is, the fastest recorded entry rates into the bloodstream—was the basic centerpiece of many weight-reduction programs: puffed-rice cakes. In fact, puffed-rice cakes have a much higher glycemic index than ice cream, which is supposed to be the weight watcher's worst enemy.

Say it ain't so.

What determines the glycemic index? The primary factors are (1) the structure of the simple sugars in the food, (2) the soluble fiber content, and (3) the fat content. I'll come back to the fat content in a moment; for now let's talk about the other two. 45

How does the structure of the simple sugar that makes up the carbohydrate affect the sugar's rate of entry into the bloodstream? Remember that all "complex" carbohydrates must be broken down into simple sugars for absorption. There are only three common sugars that comprise all edible carbohydrates, and each one has a different molecular structure, which ultimately determines its rate of entry into the bloodstream. Glucose is the most common of these sugars, followed by fructose and galactose.

Glucose is found in grains, pasta, bread, cereals, starches, and vegetables. Fructose is primarily found in fruits. Galactose is found in dairy products. However, while all of these simple sugars are rapidly absorbed by the liver, only glucose can be released directly into the bloodstream. This is why glucose-rich carbohydrates like breads and pasta virtually sprint from the liver back into the bloodstream, while galactose and fructose, which must first be converted to glucose in the liver, enter the bloodstream at a slower rate.

For fructose especially, this a very slow process. That's why even though they're primarily made up of simple sugars, fructose-containing carbohydrates (primarily fruits), have a very low glycemic index compared to glucose and galactose-containing carbohydrates.

What about the fiber content? Fiber (which is nondigestible carbohydrate) is not absorbed, and therefore it has no effect on insulin directly. However, it does act as a brake on the rate of entry on the absorption of other carbohydrates into the bloodstream. The higher the fiber content of a carbohydrate, the slower the rate of entry into the bloodstream. Remove the fiber of the carbohydrate and the rate of entry accelerates. So fiber is a significant factor in controlling the speed at which the body absorbs carbohydrate. In effect, fiber acts as a control rod to prevent a runaway rate of carbohydrate absorption. (This, by the way, is the same reason that there are control rods in nuclear reactors—to prevent potentially dangerous runaway reactions.)

That's why the recent popularity of juicing (the removal of fiber 50 from fruits to make easy-to-drink juices) has been a disaster. Juicing simply removes a primary control rod (i.e., fiber) from the carbohydrate, meaning that the carbohydrate enters the bloodstream too fast.

When a carbohydrate enters the bloodstream too fast, the pancreas responds by secreting high levels of insulin. While that brings the blood-sugar level down, it also tells the body to store fat and keep it stored.

So too many high-glycemic carbohydrates can not only make you fat, they will also keep you that way. A complete listing of the glycemic index of carbohydrates is given in Appendix H; you can use these simple rules to determine whether a carbohydrate's glycemic index is high or low. Virtually all fruits (except bananas and dried fruits) and virtually all fiber-rich vegetables (except carrots and corn) are low-glycemic carbohydrates. Virtually all grains, starches, and pasta are high-glycemic carbohydrates.

Ironically, high-glycemic carbohydrates like grains, breads, and pasta are the base of the new and supposedly healthy "food pyramid" established by the U.S. government. Yet these are precisely the types of carbohydrates that promote increased insulin secretion, and, as you've found out, higher insulin levels make you fat.

So if you're trying to lose weight, eating too many carbohydrates, especially high-glycemic carbohydrates—and the resulting increase in insulin levels—can have exactly the wrong effect. Instead of burning off your stockpiles of stored fat, you're actually increasing them. Instead of getting leaner, you're getting fatter.

The next time you reach for a fat-free puffed-rice cake, you may 55 want to keep that in mind.

Protein—The Neglected Macronutrient

If carbohydrates are the good-guy macronutrients in contemporary nutritional mythology, the two bad guys are fats and proteins. Let's take proteins first. The justification for protein's bad rap is that two of our most popular protein sources, red meat and whole dairy products, also contain large amounts of saturated fats. These fats can be unhealthy.

But instead of simply restricting the amounts of these two *types* of protein, some of today's trendy diets tend to lump *all* types of protein together and restrict them all. This is a case of throwing out the baby with the bath water. Protein's recent bad reputation—and the restrictive dietary recommendations that accompany it—is a misleading overreaction.

Proteins are the basis of all life. In our bodies, protein is more plentiful than any other substance but water. As much as one-half of your dry body weight—including most of your muscle mass, skin, hair, eyes, and nails—is made up of protein.

Protein is the main structural ingredient of our cells, and the enzymes that keep them running. Even our immune systems are essentially composed of protein. Amino acids, the building blocks of protein, are the foundation of all life.

There are twenty of these vital amino acids. Nine of them, known 60 as the essential amino acids, cannot be synthesized by the human body, and must be supplied by the diet. Without these essential amino acids constantly entering the body, the rates of new protein formation will slow down, and in the extreme case stop altogether. You can see why having adequate levels of protein on a daily basis is critical. You must constantly provide the building blocks for new protein formation. Without bricks, you can't have walls.

All right, if protein is a necessary fact of life—and if excess carbohydrate makes you fat—why not eat lots of protein and very little carbohydrate? Wouldn't that help you lose that excess body fat?

In fact, high-protein, low-carbohydrate diets are the basis of many quick weight-loss programs, whether they're sold over the counter or medically supervised. The typical slogan of these programs: "Eat all the protein you want and all the fat you want, just cut back on the carbohydrates."

At first glance, these quick-loss programs look good. Almost everyone who tries them does lose weight at first. Unfortunately, those people are losing the wrong kind of weight, and for the wrong biological reasons.

The truth is that these high-protein, quick-loss diets induce an abnormal metabolic state known as *ketosis*. This occurs when you have insufficient carbohydrate stored in the liver to meet the requirements of the body and the brain. (Remember that even when "full" the liver stores only small amounts of carbohydrate.) Once that stored carbohydrate is used up, which takes less than twenty-four hours on a low-carbohydrate diet, the body turns to fat to supply energy. Great, you say—isn't that what we want?

Unfortunately, with a high-protein, low-carbohydrate diet, that's 65 often not what you get. The process of converting fat into energy gets short-circuited on a low-carbohydrate, ketogenic diet. As a result, your cells manufacture abnormal biochemicals called *ketone bodies*.

The body has no use for these ketone bodies. It tries like mad to get rid of them through increased urination. That spells weight loss—at first—but the vast bulk of that weight loss is merely water. That high-protein diet hasn't really touched most of your excess body fat.

These high-protein, quick-weight-loss programs have you losing the wrong kind of weight. And that's not even the worst of it. If you eat too much protein at a meal, your insulin levels will also start to increase because your body doesn't want a lot of excess amino acids floating around in the bloodstream. What will the increased insulin levels do? They now help convert the excess protein into fat.

It's also been discovered recently that high-protein, ketogenic diets may cause changes in the fat cells, making them ten times more active in sequestering fat than they were before you went on the diet. So when you go off the diet, you continue to accumulate fat at a frightening rate. (This is commonly known as the "yo-yo syndrome.")

Add insult to injury. The body isn't stupid. When it has to deal with a high-protein, low-carbohydrate diet, it says, "Hey, I didn't fall off the turnip truck. The brain needs carbohydrate to function, so I'll start ripping down muscle mass, and I'll turn much of the protein in that muscle mass into carbohydrate." You might say, "That's fine; I can live with losing some muscle until I lose my body fat." But remember: because of those increased insulin levels, you're not losing fat at anywhere near the rate you expect, and you eventually reach a weight plateau.

Put all this together, and you'll see why more than 95 percent of the people who have ever lost weight using high-protein, ketogenic diets have gained that weight back and more. Why? Is everyone who ever tried a quick-weight-loss program a weak-willed ninny? I don't think so. It's just that their high-protein, low-carbohydrate diets have caused permanent changes in their fat cells, changes that virtually guarantee increased body-fat accumulation in the future.

What Did You Read?

1. According to the authors, what is the one thing causing Americans to gain weight?
2. What is a "complex" carbohydrate?
3. Why is protein important to the human diet?
4. What is the problem with a high-protein, low-carbohydrate diet, according to Sears and Lawren?

What Do You Think?

1. What is your response to the information that Americans are getting heavier and heavier? Were you surprised or not? Why?
2. Sears and Lawren state that what you eat is more important than how much you eat. Do you agree or disagree? Why?
3. If there is so much social pressure to be thin, as argued by other authors, and health professionals have made clear the dangers of obesity, why are Americans getting fatter and fatter?

How Was It Done?

1. Is the integration of rhetorical questions helpful in the presentation of the material and its logical flow?
2. Does the "bottom line" tone balance well with the steady flow of facts, percentages, and expert opinions in this article?
3. Do the subtitles and bullets help to organize the material so a reader can understand it better?
4. Are definitions used effectively?

Sports Supplement Dangers

From *Consumer Reports*

"Sports Supplement Dangers" looks at the increasingly popular use of sports supplements and studies whether they are effective or dangerous. The article suggests that scientific studies have shown little evidence that they provide more than slight improvements in performance, yet they have the potential to cause dangerous side effects. The article examines the three most popular sports supplements—androstenedione, creatine, and ephedra (also known as "ma huang")—and the dangers they pose.

Key Words

supplements	something that completes or makes an addition
metabolizes	changing products such as food within the body into other forms that the body can use directly
puberty	the condition of first being able to reproduce sexually
potent	powerful
efficacy	the ability to produce an effect
cessation	a stopping of an action
exacerbation	to make more violent, bitter, or severe
stringent	tight, constricted; rigid

Americans spent an estimated $1.4 billion on sports supplements in 1999, hoping that the pills, drinks, and powders would help them bulk up, slim down, or compete more effectively. But people who take these products are actually conducting what amounts to a vast, uncontrolled clinical experiment on themselves with untested, largely unregulated medications.

The few good scientific studies available on these "dietary" supplements suggest that they either are ineffective or, at best, produce only slight changes in performance. More disturbing, they can contain powerful and potentially harmful substances, such as:

- Androstenedione, which can upset the body's hormonal balance when it metabolizes into testosterone and estrogen, and may cause premature puberty and stunted growth in adolescents.
- Creatine, a substance produced by the body that can help generate brief surges of muscle energy during certain types of athletic performance. It may also cause kidney problems in susceptible individuals.
- Ephedra, an herbal stimulant that acts like an amphetamine ("speed") and that some investigators hold responsible for dozens of deaths and permanent injuries.

"All you have to do to get these products is walk into a food-supplement store," says Gary Wadler, M.D., a New York sports-medicine specialist and adviser to the White House Office of National Drug Control Policy. That's because a federal law, the 1994 Dietary Supplement Health and Education Act, allows supplements to be sold to consumers of any age without rigorous safety testing and without meaningful oversight of product quality.

Little is known about the long-term safety of these products in adults, and even less about their effect on youngsters. But if the supplement industry has its way, at least some of these products will be consumed by ever-increasing numbers of weekend athletes and even nonathletes.

"Sports nutrition isn't just for hard-core athletes any more," 5 Anthony Almada, president of a California supplement company, told an industry journal recently. It's for anyone seeking energy improvement, he said, or "a woman who wants to tone her body and lose a few pounds, or a person who rides a bike and wants to perform like an athlete."

Into the Mouths of Babes

Nutrition Business Journal, a trade publication that tracks the industry, estimates that 4 percent of American adults have taken a sports supplement at least once, including 1.2 million who use the products regularly.

Adolescents are using sports supplements at least as enthusiastically as adults, according to a national survey conducted in 1999 for the Blue Cross and Blue Shield Association. The survey found that 6 percent of youths ages 15 to 16 and 8 percent of 17- and 18-year-olds, had taken a sports supplement; the vast majority of users were male. About one in four respondents said they knew someone who took the products.

Teenagers and adults seem to be taking the supplements for the same reasons. The first is to develop bigger muscles. Bodybuilding magazines such as *Muscle & Fitness* bulge with ads from supplement makers pushing these products.

To Benjy, 15, creatine "seems like a magical way to gain muscle effortlessly, to look good, impress girls and guys, etc." (Kids quoted here responded to a *Consumer Reports* questionnaire and are identified by first name and age only, to protect their privacy.) Benjy said he was tempted to try creatine because a friend, who "seemed unnaturally muscular for his age," said it was from taking the supplement.

But sometimes it's adults who push youngsters to take the pills. 10 "My football coaches suggested I take creatine to bulk up for this year's season," said Cyrus, 17.

The second motivation for using such supplements is to have energy to burn, either to improve athletic performance or as an aid to losing weight.

Heather, 16, said friends who use an ephedra supplement "are always telling everyone how much weight they have lost, and bragging and bragging."

Easy Access

You don't need to live near a nutrition specialty store to purchase these products. According to industry estimates, 28 percent of sports supplements are sold in mass-merchandise stores and another 17 percent by trainers and through direct marketing and the Internet.

Of the teenage Blue Cross and Blue Shield survey respondents who knew someone using such supplements, half said they were "very easy" or "pretty easy" to get.

Here's a sample of the products we easily found online and in retail stores: 15

- 3-Andro Xtreme, whose recommended dose contains large amounts of androstenedione and ephedra plus the caffeine equivalent of two cups of coffee.

- Teen Advantage Creatine Serum. The manufacturer of this product claims that it's "specially formulated for teens from ages 11–19" and delivers "the benefits of creatine supplementation safely." When we asked for research to back those claims, the manufacturer sent us sales brochures with no references to any study.

- LifeSmart's Creatine Chews, advertised as tasting "like candy." "We feel it's totally safe for kids in high school, but we're not actively marketing it to them," says Darren Lopez, vice president of LifeSmart Nutrition, the product's manufacturer.

- Yellow Jacket, a blister pack of three capsules we picked up at a gas station. The label failed to specify the quantities of ephedra and caffeine contained in its "proprietary blend," but it did promise that users would "feel the sting of extreme energy!"

Untested, Unrestricted

Any dietary supplement can be marketed without advance testing under current federal law. The only restriction: The label can't claim the product will treat, prevent, or cure a disease. But the label can traffic in vague claims like "enhances energy" or "supports testosterone production." If serious problems are reported, it's up to the Food and Drug Administration (FDA) to prove they're real before it can order a supplement off the market or impose other restrictions. So far, that has not happened. (However, a few manufacturers have voluntarily re-called their supplements after the FDA warned them of possible dangers.)

Sports-medicine researchers have tested androstenedione, crea-tine, and ephedra in adults. There has been no systematic testing in minors and, for ethical reasons, there probably won't be.

Here, then, is what's known about these supplements and their effects:

Androstenedione

Androstenedione—"andro" to its enthusiasts—is a pro-hormone, one of several compounds formed in the body during production of testos-terone, the male hormone, a potent muscle-building steroid. To sports aficionados, it's the Mark McGwire drug, the supplement that the brawny Cardinals slugger took on the way to hitting 70 home runs in 1998.

"The first time I ever heard of these supplements was on TV, when 20 Mark McGwire broke the home-run record," wrote Kevin, 14, respond-ing to our questionnaire. "Soon after, I heard kids in school talking about it, wondering whether they should take them."

But andro flunked the two most rigorous studies of its efficacy. In both studies, volunteers took daily doses of andro while on a strength-training program; control groups followed the same training, but without taking andro.

One of the studies, published in 1999 in the *Journal of the American Medical Association,* involved young men ages 19 to 29; the other, pub-lished last November in the *Archives of Internal Medicine,* involved men 35 to 65. In both studies, those who didn't take andro gained just as much muscle and strength as those who took the supplement.

For the younger group, taking andro didn't even increase the aver-age testosterone level. The older men experienced a temporary rise in testosterone, which subsided to normal levels by the end of the 12-week study. That's because taking the supplement for more than a few weeks disrupts the normal feedback that signals the body to produce its own sex hormones, says Craig Broeder, Ph.D., director of the human performance laboratory at East Tennessee State University and leader of the study involving the older men. "The body says 'I've got too much testosterone' and starts shutting off its own production of the hormone."

In both age groups, the androstenedione also produced unwel-come changes in blood-cholesterol levels, with an increase in the harmful kind and a decrease in the protective kind.

But perhaps the most disconcerting result of both studies was a 25 marked increase in levels of the female hormone estrogen. In theory, that could lead to feminization, including the development of breast tissue, in long-term male users—a common side effect of prolonged steroid use.

Andro use in boys before or during puberty hasn't been studied formally. "We're just hypothesizing," Broeder says, "but based on everything we know, the minute a child took andro, his normal hormonal development would go awry." Among the possible results, depending on whether the andro ends up mainly as estrogen or testosterone: feminization, premature puberty, male-pattern baldness, and premature growth cessation.

Creatine

Of the sports supplements, creatine is the only one that careful, published research has shown to improve performance of certain athletic tasks.

Creatine is an amino acid made by the liver, kidneys, and pancreas; it also occurs naturally in meat and fish. It's stored in muscle and elsewhere in the body and plays a key role in producing immediate bursts of energy.

Taking supplemental creatine causes a rapid weight gain of perhaps one to four pounds. Scientists believe the extra weight is mainly water retained in muscles.

A few well-designed studies have found that creatine enhances 30 performance requiring brief, intense bursts of strength, as in high jumping and weight lifting. But it doesn't improve the endurance needed for sports like distance running or soccer.

There has been no systematic study of creatine's side effects, but there have been case reports in the medical literature of muscle cramping and the exacerbation of existing kidney problems. Most studies of creatine involved short-term use, so "long-term effects are completely unknown," says Bernard Griesemer, M.D., director of a pediatric sports-medicine practice in Springfield, Mo.

Ephedra

The herbal supplement ephedra (also known as ma huang) may be the most hazardous of the major sports supplements.

It contains several stimulants, including ephedrine and pseudoephedrine, active ingredients in over-the-counter cold and sinus drugs. But while the drugs contain just one active ingredient, almost all the supplements combine multi-ingredient ephedra with at least one other stimulant, usually caffeine or guarana (an herb containing caffeine).

"Ephedrine and caffeine work synergistically," says Bill Gurley, Ph.D., associate professor of pharmaceutical sciences at the University of Arkansas. "The effect is similar to taking amphetamines." The FDA found the combination so dangerous that it banned it from over-the-counter drugs in 1983.

In March, the *International Journal of Obesity* published the first 35 well-controlled clinical trial of the herbal combination ephedra and guarana. By the eighth week, the supplements had produced moderate weight loss. (Two very small studies have found that ephedra plus caffeine slightly increases endurance as well.) But side effects, notably heart palpitations, forced 8 of the 35 users to drop out of the study. And in the real world, where no one is overseeing the dosages, the risks may be more serious.

Last December, scientists from the University of California, San Francisco, published a study, partly funded by the FDA, of 140 "adverse event" reports the agency had received on ephedra products. The agency concluded that 87 of the events were "definitely," "probably," or "possibly" caused by the ephedra.

Nearly half of those cases involved cardiovascular symptoms such as sudden high blood pressure or a racing heartbeat. There were 17 strokes and seizures, 13 cases of permanent impairment, and 10 deaths, including a 15-year-old girl.

Another group of physicians recently wrote *The New England Journal of Medicine* about a 19-year-old male bodybuilder with no apparent cardiovascular risk factors who suffered a heart attack 15 minutes after taking an ephedra-caffeine energy supplement.

For the past four years, the FDA has been trying to exert its limited authority under the 1994 law to limit the maximum doses in ephedra supplements to 24 milligrams a day.

The industry has vigorously disputed the idea that ephedra is un- 40 safe and has proposed an alternative maximum of 100 milligrams a day, with a label saying "not for use by anyone under the age of 18."

Recommendations

Weekend warriors, young athletes, and people who want to lose weight or gain energy should not take sports supplements. Evidence for the products' effectiveness is sketchy at best, and concerns about their safety are too numerous.

Adults and youngsters alike should focus instead on the basics of fitness and nutrition. "You can accomplish your goals with a well-balanced diet, a disciplined workout program, and sports-specific training," says Wadler, the sports-medicine specialist.

Parents who are concerned that their children may be taking any of these supplements should familiarize themselves with some of the most common brand names and ingredients (see box).

Consumers Union urges the FDA to continue pursuing stringent nationwide restrictions on the use of ephedra. At least ten states and several local governments have imposed various limitations, such as requiring a prescription, outlawing sales to minors, or limiting the maximum dose. We've testified in favor of several state and local laws restricting ephedra sales. States and municipalities that have not moved to control ephedra should consider doing so.

How to Spot the Ingredients

As this table shows many products sold in stores or on the Internet contain androstenedione, creatine, or ephedra—and the names often provide no tip-off about those ingredients.

Androstenedione*

3-Andro Xtreme
Andro-Gen
Andro-Stack
Androstat
Animal Stak
Nor Andro Ripped Fuel Stack
Nor-Stak
Nor-Tek

Creatine

Animal Max
ATP Advantage
Cell-Tech
Creaject
Crea-Tek
Creatigen
Creatine Booster
Creatine Fizz Fuel
CreaVate
Effervescent Creatine Elite
LifeSmart's Creatine Chews
Mass Action
Micronozed Creatine
Perfect Creatine
Phosphagen
Power Creatine
Synthvol
Teen Advantage Creatine Serum
Xtra Advantage Creatine Serum

Ephedra (Ma Huang)

3-Andro Xtreme
Adipokinetix

(continued)

How to Spot the Ingredients *(continued)*

Amphetra-Lean
Animal Cuts
BetaLean
Clenbutrx
Diet Boost
Diet Fuel
Dyma-Burn Xtreme
Dymetadrine Xtreme
Energel
Herbalife
Herbal Phen-Fen
Hydroxycut
Metabolife 356
Metab-O-Lite
Metacuts
Ripped Force
Fipped Fuel
Thermadrene
ThermaPro
Thermo Speed
Trim Fast
Ultimate Energizer
Ultimate Orange
Ultra Chromaslim
Xenadrine RFA-1
Yellow Jacket

*Related compounds include 19-norandrostenedione, androstenediol and dehydroepiandros-
terone (DHEA)

What Did You Read?

1. Why do adolescents take sports supplements?
2. How easy are sports supplements to get? Explain.
3. How are sports supplements advertised? What is alarming about it?
4. Based on research, what are the dangers of:
   Androstenedione?
   Creatine?
   Ephedra?

5. What does the article recommend about sports supplements?

What Do You Think?

1. Do people assume that because supplements can be gotten easily that they must be safe? Explain.

2. Have you or someone you know ever taken any product containing androstenedione, creatine, or ephedra? Describe your or others' experiences with the product.

3. In your opinion, why do you think people use supplements even when dangerous side effects are well known?

How Was It Done?

1. If you have had no prior exposure to the subject of sports supplements, do you find the information in this article credible and thorough?

2. Is it helpful to have each supplement individually analyzed, or do you find that too repetitious?

3. Is the substance of the article based primarily on facts and data, or on the author's agenda to outlaw sales of certain supplements and the products that contain them?

8

Youth Culture

Since the birth of the Baby Boom generation in the wake of World War II, the media, educators, sociologists, and parents have tried to label and understand young people as a distinct group. Today's young people, born since 1977, have been called Generation Y, the Net Generation, the Echo-Boom Generation or the E-generation, but whatever their label, they are different from the Baby Boomers (who are often their parents) and their immediate predecessors, Generation X. Today's young people are growing up in a nation in which only about 15 percent of the households are made up of a married couple, in which the father works and the mother stays home. Among married couples with children, two-income households are far more prevalent now than one-income households. Additionally, many more children are raised in single-parent households than in the past. Thus, today's young people are more independent, which may also make them less loyal. They go it alone rather than working with others. They embrace diversity, not uniformity. They are more comfortable with the technological advances that are changing how we work, play, and go to school. They are more apt to skateboard or snowboard than play baseball or ski, listen to rap than rock, and expect to work for many employers rather than stay a lifetime with one firm—if they aren't starting their own companies. Like other young people before them, they rebel against their parents and the status quo, searching to make the world their own. One can only guess what that world will look like.

425

In this chapter, the emphasis in the Writing Lesson is on critical analysis. As such, the lesson examines the various rules of logic, including discussions of induction and deduction. The lesson also presents a series of logical fallacies. The point is to see how strong, logical arguments are formed, and to recognize when arguments are weak and fallacious. Another part of the lesson is learning to distinguish between facts and inferences. Often inferences masquerade as facts, and a good critical thinker must recognize when this occurs. The Writing Assignment then gives you the opportunity to use the logic lessons in the creation of an essay that examines a particular aspect of youth culture.

THE MAIN EVENT READING

Born in Fire: A Hip-Hop Odyssey
Jeff Chang

Jeff Chang examines the historical background to hip-hop. He starts with its roots in the Bronx of the 1970s, a place where economic collapse created an environment in which a new music needed to be created. From there, hip-hop spread west, notably bursting out with N.W.A.'s 1989 hit album, Gangsta Gangsta. *Hip-hop moved from the ghetto to the suburbs, replacing rock as the music of the young. It remains a music of potential, although savvy marketers and companies have been quick to use hip-hop as a way to make their pitch to a new generation of young people.*

Key Words

odyssey	an intellectual or spiritual wandering or quest
borough	a political division of areas within New York City
slumlords	landlords who make high profits on substandard properties
entrepreneurs	people who start up their own businesses
aesthetic	relating to beauty
satiated	overly filled; glutted
braggadocio	boasting; cockiness
transcendent	extending beyond the limits of ordinary experience
nexuses	connections or links; points of focus
conflating	combining together to make a new whole
homophobic	someone who is fearful of homosexuals; expresses hatred toward homosexuals
misogynistic	someone who hates or degrades women

During the summer of 1975, the South Bronx was burning. New York City officials admitted that they couldn't battle all the fires, let alone investigate their origins. Chaos reigned. One long hot day in June, 40 fires were set in a three-hour period.

These were not the fires of purifying rage that ignited Watts in 1965, Newark in 1967, or St. Louis and a half dozen other U.S. cities after the assassination of Martin Luther King, Jr. These were the fires of abandonment.

As hip-hop journalist S.H. Fernando notes, the Bronx had been a borough of promise for African American, Puerto Rican, Irish, Italian and Jewish families after World War II. But as industry moved north to the suburbs during the sixties, housing values collapsed and whites fled, leaving a population overwhelmingly poor and of colour.

So slumlords were employing young thugs to systematically burn the devalued buildings to chase out the poor tenants and collect millions in insurance. Hip-hop, it could be said, was born in fire.

As rapper Grandmaster Flash and the Furious Five's "The Message" would describe it, the New York ghettoes that fuelled hip-hop's re-creative project were spaces of state neglect and fading liberal dreams. "Got a bum education," the narrator rhymed, "double-digit inflation, can't take a train to work there's a strike at the station." But these would also be spaces of spiritual and creative renewal.

In an earlier era, say the 1920s and 30s when jazz legends like Charles Mingus grew up, a youth might find an extended web of peers, mentors, patrons, bands and venues through which he or she might master an instrument and find a vocation. But by the late 1970s, such music education was a luxury for most families.

Jamaican Connection

The result? Play, as African American author Robin D.G. Kelley has put it, became an alternate form of work for a new generation. Adapting the Jamaican tradition of outdoor dance parties to the grid and grit of New York, young black and Puerto Rican entrepreneurs illegally plugged their stereo systems into street light power supplies, and started the party.

With vinyl grooves as sheet music, and a rig of two turntables, a mixer and an amplifier as instruments, Black Art began reinventing itself in 1974 and 1975. That's when a Jamaican immigrant disc jockey named Kool Herc started gaining a reputation in the Bronx for filling the smoky air with "the breaks"—that portion of the song, often as short as two seconds, where the singer dropped out and let the band immerse itself in the groove.

Punching back and forth between two copies of the same record's breaks, then ratcheting up the excitement by shifting to ever more intense breaks, DJs like Herc and Afrika Bambaataa were creating a new aesthetic, which simultaneously satiated and teased the audience.

Escaping the Chaos on the Streets

On the one hand, a loop (of beats) became a metaphor for freedom: 10
through movement, dancers stretched within the space sculpted by
the break. A new canon of songs—drawn from funk, disco, rock, jazz,
Afrobeat and reggae—launched new, athletic forms of dancing, which
would become known as breakdancing or b-boying. Rather than being
passive spectators, the audience engaged in a real dialogue with the
disc jockey.

The New York DJs began employing MCs—masters of ceremony—to affirm the crowd's response to proven breaks, win them
over to new breaks, divert them during bad records and generally
keep spirits high. In time, the MCs became attractions in their own
right. Rocking memorized poems ("writtens") or improvising them on
the spot ("freestyles"), the MC became Everyman, the representative
of the audience onstage. They reacted to the MC's flow, laughed at his
cleverness, cheered his braggadocio, thrilled at his tall-tale spinning,
felt his bluesy pain, riding the riddims with words (or "rapping").

The Black Arts poets, the Black Panther messiahs and other revolutionary firebrands sharpened their words into spears to attack. This
new generation of rappers let the words flow generously, in search of a
moment that might serve as a shield of protection, or a transcendent
escape from the chaos on the streets.

Popular culture in America is one space where the trope (expression) of working-class creativity is still firmly lodged. American markets are good at providing poor audiences of colour easy access to
goods such as music, video and clothing. In the last three decades, a
whole class of middlemen entrepreneurs have made fortunes by charting the rapidly shifting terrain of black and brown ghetto chic.

By the late 70s, black and Jewish record label owners in Harlem
noted the popularity of hip-hop and rushed to record leading crews.
Basically, these owners were geographically and personally close to
the music. When a novelty record by the Sugar Hill Gang, "Rapper's
Delight" became a surprise international smash, major labels began
sniffing around uptown for the next hit. In 1980, Kurtis Blow released
rap's first full-length album on a major label. The stage was set for the
ascendance of hip-hop culture into the most powerful international
youth culture of the late twentieth century.

Until the late 80s, the undisputed centre of this culture was New 15
York. The visual signifiers were provided by the vibrant graffiti movement, whose young renegade artists braved electrified razor-wire
fences and armed Metropolitan Transit Authority guards to apply
bright spraypaint hieroglyphics onto the city's subways. Every time a
train pulled into a station, hip-hop was in respectable society's face,
like a middle-finger.

Margin notes:

audience has active participation

role of MC

working class has expression in pop culture

Remember the backdrop to the 1980s: the Reagan administration was launching an attack on the "welfare state", wiping out subsidies for the poor, allowing housing agencies to become dens of corruption while closing down entire categories of government programmes. Hip-hoppers were on the counter-offensive. As the Furious Five warned: "Don't push me 'cause I'm close to the edge. I'm trying not to lose my head. It's like a jungle sometimes, it makes me wonder how I keep from going under." political context— connecting to national trends

On the technological front, hip-hoppers racked up one breakthrough after another. While most rock musicians of the mid-80s were perplexed by new sampling technology, rap producers were turning their new toys into unrelentingly dense, reflexive grooves. Then, as the anti-apartheid movement crested in the U.S., groups like Boogie Down Productions and Public Enemy extended rap's social realism into broader discussions of political action.

But the lofty views of revolutionary nationalism and hardrock spiritualism veered back to the streets in 1989. A group of barely twenty-somethings, who not so ironically called themselves Niggas With Attitude, released what would become an anthem for a generation, *Gangsta Gangsta*. Within six weeks of its release, the album went "gold", selling over 500,000 copies. Hip-hop shot itself into the heart of world culture.

The album, *Straight Outta Compton*, decentered hip-hop from New York to Los Angeles. By the middle of the Reagan administration, Compton was one of a growing number of inner-city nexuses where deindustrialization, devolution, the cocaine trade, gang structures and rivalries, arms profiteering and police brutality combined to destabilize poor communities. Chaos was settling in for a long stay and gangsta rap would be the soundtrack. By conflating myth and place, the narratives could take root in every 'hood (neighbourhood). From Portland to Paris, every 'hood could be Compton; everyone had a story to tell, a cop to fight, a rebellion to launch. shift to Los Angeles

Ironically, gangsta tales populated with drunken, high, rowdy, irresponsible, criminal, murderous "niggas"—its practitioners likened it to journalism and called it "reality rap"—seemed to be just what suburbia wanted. As student populations diversified, youth were increasingly uninterested in whitewashed cultural hand-me-downs. The 1988 advent of the MTV show, "Yo MTV Raps", made African American, Chicano, and Latino urban style instantly accessible across the world. With its claims to street authenticity, its teen rebellion, its extension of urban stereotype and its individualist "get mine" credo, gangsta rap fit hand-in-glove with a generation weaned on racism and Reaganism. These were not the old Negro spirituals of the civil rights era. They were raw, violent, undisciplined, offensive, "niggafied" rhymes, often homophobic, misogynistic. 20
appeal to white suburbia

Gangsta rap drew new lines in the culture wars. As the music crossed over to whiter, more affluent communities, gangsta rap inflamed cultural conservatives like Bob Dole and neoliberals like C. Delores Tucker into demanding new corporate and state repression. Gangsta rap was even showing up in presidential debates.

Progressives often speculate that gangsta rap was foisted on a young public by reactionary record labels. But to a great extent, the rise of these popcultural trends was completely unplanned. Well into the 1990s, major recording labels had no idea what kind of hip-hop would sell. Unlike rock music, which had long before matured into a stable and culturally stale economy, hip-hop was like a wild child whose every gesture and motion was a complete surprise.

reaction to Rodney King beating

In the wake of the Los Angeles riots after the brutal police beating of motorist Rodney King in 1991, gangsta rap and hip-hop marched toward their greatest commercial success. Dr. Dre's album *The Chronic* topically moved gangsta rap away from ghetto commentary to druggy hedonism, and, with its polished chrome sound, onto mainstream radio playlists. As cast by MTV and the expanding hip-hop press, artists such as the late Tupac Shakur, the son of a Black Panther revolutionary, made rebellion less a battle in the culture wars, and ever more a mere marker of youth style.

increasing appeal to youth makes hip-hop less threatening

The shrinking music industry also transformed the hip-hop scene. Between the early to mid-90s, several of the independent record label owners who had been instrumental in launching the music sold their companies to major labels, which also began consolidating and reducing the size of their rosters. As a result, grassroots acts no longer went from the streets to the top of the charts. Management firms guaranteed polished stars and funded the farm teams that would take those stars' places in turn. The new hip-hop sound, crisply digitized and radio-ready, became mainstream pop.

hip-hop goes main-stream. What will the effect be?

With the massive major label distribution juggernauts behind 25 them, it became routine for the biggest hip-hop acts to debut with gold (half-million) or more sales. A half-dozen magazines were launched to take advantage of the new wealth of advertising dollars. Hollywood's big money came calling, making multimedia stars of rappers LL Cool J and Ice Cube. Commercial tie-ins with products such as Sprite or the Gap clothing proliferated for second-level artists. Producer Russell Simmons began calling the hip-hop generation "the biggest brand-building generation the world has ever seen". The audience had matured into a marketable demographic.

Rebellion or Capitulation?

As U.S. author Don DeLillo has written, "Capital burns off the nuance in a culture." To be sure, hip-hop has transformed popular culture across the world. In Kenya, youngsters wear Adidas baseball caps, Nike shoes and stage rowdy rap concerts that look like versions of

Bambaataa's romps in the Bronx of yore. It's unclear whether such performances reflect a hybrid youth rebellion or capitulation to global capitalism.

Yet somewhere within the culture lies the key to understanding an entire generation. This culture forged in fire still keeps its hand near the match. Rap rewards those who "represent" its audiences' realities. If this often appears as caving in to baser impulses, hip-hop's defense is that it speaks to young people as they are and where they are.

Is this conclusion justified, or is Chang overstating the effects of hip-hop?

And yet a growing movement believes that the culture is liberating. In cities across the world, youths use hip-hop to organise the struggles against racism, police brutality, and the prison-industrial complex. For them, the culture and the politics are inseparable—they are all part of a cohesive world-view. Therein finally lies the story: hip-hip, born of the destructive fires of the 1960s and 70s, has rekindled creative flames of hope in a new generation. The cleansing fires are still to come.

What Did You Read?

1. What caused the economic decline of the Bronx in the 1970s?
2. What in essence fueled hip-hop?
3. What did the lyrics in early rap music have to do with?
4. How are "gangsta" tales like journalism?
5. How is gangsta rap a musical form launched within a particular socioeconomic class?
6. Name some of the early hip-hop artists and their albums.

What Do You Think?

1. If hip-hop was born out of chaos and destruction in the 1960s and 1970s, has hip-hop contributed to any healing since that time?
2. Has hip-hop transformed youth culture in positive or negative ways? Explain.
3. How has hip-hop transformed the music industry? How has the music industry affected hip-hop artists themselves?

How Was It Done?

1. What strategy does Chang use to introduce the reader to the subject of hip-hop?
2. How do the subtitles help organize Chang's material?
3. Does the author's use of time frames (for example, referring to the '70s and the '80s) help to clarify the political context of hip-hop and connect it to national trends?

4. Does Chang cite enough hip-hop artists and their lyrics to develop his argument? What artists does he mention?

THE MAIN EVENT WRITING ASSIGNMENT

Write an essay in response to one of the following assignments:

1. Explain how a particular aspect of culture serves as an adequate symbol for describing today's young generation.
2. Are today's youth, sometimes called Generation Y, substantially different from the youth of Generation X or the Baby Boom generation? Explain, being as specific as possible.
3. Is there validity in media-generated labels, such as "Generation Y" or the "Net Generation"? If so, what is the benefit of such labels? If not, are labels misleading and inadequate? Be specific in your response.
4. Is American society's fascination with youth and youth culture a positive quality, or are there serious dangers in being youth-oriented? Explain, being as specific as possible.

PREPARATION PUNCH LIST

Before you begin writing the essay, you need to prepare yourself to write. Jot down some notes on what you know in general.

1. What are the characteristics of today's youth, as you see them?

- Today's young people seem more individualistic, less interested in groups, and more interested in the pursuit of personal goals.
- Today's youth seem less concerned with advancing in materialistic ways. They're more willing to delay completion of college, delay advancing in jobs; they're more knowledge-oriented than promotion-oriented in the workplace.
- Young people today are more interested in individual expression, such as in wearing tattoos with messages, wearing unconventional clothes and hairstyles. They're also more accepting of individual expression in others as well.

2. How are young people similar to young people of prior generations?

- Like young people before, they seek to establish themselves as different from their parents in terms of fashion, music, and other forms of entertainment. While the styles are different today than in the past, the fact that they search out new styles is similar to what young people have done before.

- Young people are concerned about their future, and what the world is going to look like.

- Like young people before, many young people are socially conscious about issues like the environment and the distribution of wealth around the world.

3. How are today's young people different from prior generations?

- Today's young people more frequently grow up in nontraditional homes, especially in single-parent households. They're less likely to go to church. They're far more likely to be accepting of alternative lifestyles than their predecessors.

- Young people are more likely to start working in jobs themselves at an earlier age in order to earn their own money than did Generation Xers or Baby Boomers.

- Today's youth are exposed to a far greater amount of electronic media—dozens of cable television stations, video games, VCRs and DVDs—than the youth of the past. This exposes them to a much greater quantity and variety of media images and messages.

- The preponderance of electronic entertainment makes many young people less active. Fewer play sports; more young people are overweight.

- Today's young people are more technologically savvy than any prior generation; they don't just learn the technology, they help invent it. They may be the first generation in which the younger teach the older.

THE MAIN EVENT WRITING LESSON: CRITICAL ANALYSIS

Often in our daily lives, the word "critical" can take on negative connotations: it suggests disapproval or dislike of something. However, in the academic arena, the word "critical" means to assess or evaluate. To analyze a work critically, or to create a critical analysis of your own, does not mean to dislike or disagree with the subject of the work. It does mean that you read the material closely, paying attention to main ideas and supporting ideas, assessing the details used as evidence, examining the word choice of the author, and evaluating any underlying meanings or implications.

In order to write a critical analysis, you should be aware of the different ways in which people think. In other words, you must examine how we know what we know. Two processes of reasoning are induction and deduction. Understanding how each of these processes works can be helpful in analyzing a work critically.

Induction

Inductive logic means that you form a general conclusion after the observation of a series of specifics. That is, a person has specific experiences of a certain type, and from that experience, forms a generalization. For example, if you know several people who have recently visited Hawaii, and all of them say that their visit was wonderful, you might conclude that Hawaii is a wonderful place to take a vacation. Many of our most basic thought patterns are based on induction. Indeed, the more experiences one has, the better or more accurate the general conclusions will be. Whenever you drive a car, for instance, you use your past driving experiences to inform your decisions on the road. Thus, you know how to handle speed, how to brake in bad weather, how to deal with erratic behavior by other drivers, because you have experience. This is one reason why younger drivers have more accidents than older ones: their lack of experience leads them to form bad or faulty generalizations about driving, which can lead to accidents on the road.

However, induction can only give you probability, not certainty. No matter how much experience you have driving, you can never know exactly what might happen on the road. If you notice a car weaving on the freeway, you might conclude, because you know that erratic driving is a sign of a drunk driver, that the driver is impaired, and thus should be avoided. However, you may be mistaken, and the driver may be driving erratically for other reasons. Clearly, the more examples or experiences one has, the better, more reliable the conclusions are, but induction can never provide 100% certainty. Problems arise when conclusions are made without observing enough examples, or the examples are not typical. When this occurs, you have formed a "hasty generalization," which is a logical fallacy.

Deduction

The other form of reasoning is called deduction. In deductive logic, you work through a three-sentence formula called a "syllogism." The syllogism begins with a major premise, which is an assumption or general statement about something. The major premise may be based on a definition, but often the major premise is based on induction. Then, the premise can only state probability. The second statement is called a minor premise, and it is a specific instance of the major. The third statement is the conclusion, reached by applying the minor to the major. A syllogism looks like this:

Major premise:	All students enrolled at this college can use the computing center.
Minor premise:	Ramon is a student enrolled at this college.
Conclusion:	Ramon can use the computing center.

If the major premise is true, and the minor premise is true, the conclusion must be true.

However, things can go wrong with syllogisms. For example, a common problem is when the major premise is an absolute statement. If the statement is based on induction, the premise cannot be an absolute.

Major premise:	All young people enjoy listening to hip-hop music.
Minor premise:	Michelle is young.
Conclusion:	Michelle enjoys listening to hip-hop music.

The conclusion reached is not valid because the major premise is wrong. Even if many young people enjoy listening to hip-hop music, not *all* young people do. The absolute statement needs to be qualified to make it more accurate.

Major premise:	Many young people enjoy hip-hop music.
Minor premise:	Michelle is young.
Conclusion:	Michelle is likely to enjoy hip-hop music.

Another possible problem with a syllogism occurs when both the major premise is true and the minor premise is true, but the way they are brought together is illogical. This is called "guilt by association," another logical fallacy.

Major premise:	The September 11 terrorists were Arabs.
Minor premise:	Amir is an Arab.
Conclusion:	Amir is a terrorist.

This type of logical fallacy rests on the mistake of putting the two premises together by their common factor, in this case, being an Arab. The conclusion is illogical because not all Arabs are terrorists. "Guilt by association" does not recognize that the two premises can both be individually true without the conclusion being justified. This form of logical fallacy is at the root of many prejudices that rely on stereotypes.

Distinguishing between Facts and Inferences

For the purpose of writing essays, you must be able to distinguish between facts and inferences in the reading that you do and in your own writing. Knowing when a statement is one of fact and one of inference goes to the heart of understanding the logical development of an argument. Confusion on this issue might lead one to accept statements as fact that are actually only expressing someone's opinion.

A *fact* is a statement that can be verified. Facts include statistics and examples. An *inference* is an opinion reached after the observation or consideration of facts. Inferences include any statements of opinion, value, cause/effect relationship, or probability. An inference is essentially an educated guess. As long as the authorities are credible, facts are generally not arguable; however, inferences always are.

Consider the following example of how facts and inferences work. You have probably heard people claim that excessive television viewing has caused obesity in many children. While this statement may be intended to be taken as a fact, in reality it is only an inference. The facts that can be verified are the number of hours per day children on average watch television, and the average weight of children. The cause/effect relationship between those two facts, however, is an inference. Someone has looked at the time children spend in front of a television and their obesity and inferred that one is the cause of the other. On the other hand, other researchers note that the causes for the rise in obesity may be complex and involve factors beyond television viewing habits, such as eating habits and other lifestyle choices.

To see how this confusion between facts and inferences can occur, examine the following statements:

Fact: McDonald's moved from serving their hamburgers in Styrofoam shells to using paper wrappers.

Inference: McDonald's is interested in saving the environment.

Fact: The voters approved a recent proposition to legalize marijuana for medicinal use.

Inference: Most voters don't think there is anything dangerous about marijuana.

Remember, inferences are made *after* the observation of facts, but they are not facts themselves. The more credible facts a person has at hand, the more reliable the inferences are likely to be. A good critical writer (and reader) needs to be aware of when inferences are being made, and on the basis of what facts the inference was made.

Logical Fallacies

There are numerous logical fallacies to avoid in your writing, and to be aware of when you are analyzing materials. You may come across these fallacies by different names, but they all represent an important breakdown in logical reasoning.

- **Hasty Generalization.** This problem occurs in inductive logic when the observer uses too few examples, or the examples are not typical of the group. The conclusion reached may focus on the exceptions rather than the rule. Many stereotypes are based on hasty generalizations.

Example:

I know someone from my hometown who never finished school and went on to run a successful business. Therefore, most successful businesspeople did not finish school.

Explanation:

One person is not a large enough sample from which to form the conclusion.

- **"Post hoc" or Doubtful Cause.** The question of what caused one thing to happen can often be a difficult one, especially if complicated issues are involved. The post hoc error typically occurs when someone tries to link together events that occurred close to each other, either in time or space. Keep in mind, however, that determining the cause of something can be quite complicated, often involving more than one cause. Superstitious beliefs are often based on doubtful cause reasoning.

Example:

When I accidentally slammed the door, the power in the entire building went out.

Explanation:

Slamming a door is unlikely to have caused the power in an entire building to go out. Another cause is more likely.

- **"Ad hominem" or Attacking the Messenger.** This error ignores the content of a statement and instead directs attention to the qualities or character of the person giving the message.

Example:

My doctor says I should quit smoking, but I noticed she's overweight. She must not know much about how to be healthy, so I'm going to keep smoking.

Explanation:

Even if the doctor is not herself living a healthy lifestyle, that does not mean that she does not know what people should do to be healthy.

- **Guilt by Association.** Seen in faulty deductive logic, this error draws together two statements by something in common. The error is in not seeing that there are additional possibilities.

Example:

Skateboarders damaged a nearby park with their irresponsible behavior. Tony is a skateboarder. Thus, Tony skateboards irresponsibly.

Explanation:

Just because other skateboarders have acted irresponsibly does not mean Tony is irresponsible when he skateboards.

- **Faulty Use of Authority.** When a person makes a statement without sufficient authority. Sometimes a person has authority in one area but uses that as a springboard to make a statement in another, unrelated area.

Example:

A famous actor said he had some new ideas about global warming and its impact on the environment.

Explanation:

An actor is not a scientist and thus is not qualified to speak on scientific matters.

- **Faulty Comparison.** Comparing one thing with something else of its same type can be limited in its effectiveness if the two things do not have enough in common. Sometimes the differences between two things of the same type can be enough to make comparisons difficult or meaningless.

Example:

If Sweden can have universal health coverage, the United States should just copy their system here.

Explanation:

The differences between the two countries, the United States and Sweden, may be substantial enough to make such a comparison unreliable.

- **Begging the Question.** When a person assumes something in making an argument that is actually still unproven, that person is said to be "begging the question." This means that the statement remains unproven.

Example:

Students should not be required to take worthless general education courses.

Explanation:

The fact that general education courses are "worthless" is not proven. Indeed, the argument cannot proceed without a discussion of the value of general education courses.

- **False Analogy.** An analogy is a comparison between two unlike things, usually for descriptive purposes. An analogy can be said to be false when the differences in the two things are substantial enough that the comparison becomes misleading.

Example:

Schools should start treating students like customers, and design courses and give degrees according to what students want.

Explanation:

The relationship of a business to a customer is not the same as a school to a student; for example, a customer pays money and receives a particular product or service, but students do not pay money to receive a particular grade. Also, students are not educational experts, and may not know best what should be in courses or what courses should qualify one for a degree.

- **Glittering Generality.** This logical fallacy is a "positive prejudice" in the sense that one takes a small, single positive point and uses that to form a "glittering" or positive conclusion.

Example:

The famous athlete donated his jersey for the charity auction; thus, we can say that he is a great humanitarian.

Explanation:

A single act of charity does not qualify one as a "great humanitarian."

- **Exigency.** This argues that something must be done immediately. It ignores the possibility of waiting or delay.

Example:

We must buy this stereo equipment today because the prices may never be this low again.

Explanation:

The statement ignores the likelihood of future sales. Indeed, advertisers often try to create a sense of exigency in customers to encourage impulse purchases.

- **False Dilemma.** This fallacy tells a person that only two options exist in a certain circumstance. Usually one option is undesirable, essentially forcing the person to accept the other option. However, the statement is fallacious if it does not admit for additional options.

Example:

You can do what I told you to do and become a great success, or you can ignore my advice and become an utter failure.

Explanation:

The statement does not allow for a third alternative: to ignore the speaker and still become a success.

- **"Ad populum" or Appealing to the People.** This is a form of misdirection, used to flatter an audience and avoid criticism of a point. There are different forms of ad populum arguments, including appealing to people's sense of patriotism or flattering the audience directly by suggesting their virtues are superior.

Example:

I know I speak today to those good, loyal Americans who are unwilling to be swayed by negativity and doubt, but who embrace my proposal because it stands for what is right in this country.

Explanation:

Rather than defend the proposal on its merits, the speaker attempts to flatter the audience by linking positive words such as "good," "loyal," and "right" with both the proposal and the audience.

- **Red Herring.** This form of argument diverts attention from a substantial issue to a false issue. For example, in detective fiction, the detective (and the reader) must sort through many clues, some of which are diversionary, in order to figure out who committed the crime. The red herring avoids the real issues.

Example:

Critics claim that cartoons on television are too violent for today's children. However, cartoons seldom feature blood and other types of real injuries. Thus, their violence is largely unreal and cannot be a problem.

Explanation:

The issue is not whether the violence is depicted in a realistic manner, but whether watching the depiction of violence is healthy for young viewers.

- **Straw Man.** Another diversionary tactic, drawing attention away from the real issue at hand. The speaker attacks and "wins" an easy point while avoiding the true issues.

Example:

My opponent has accused me of taking money under the table to do the bidding of special interests. If by this they mean the gift of a young puppy that I received and gave to my daughters, I can tell you this: I will not rip that puppy out of the arms of my children.

Explanation:

By drawing attention away from the issue of money, and directing the attention to the relatively safe issue of the gift of a pet, the speaker "wins" the point by standing up for his children and avoiding having to answer about the money.

- **Non sequitur.** From Latin, this means "does not follow." A non sequitur happens when a disruption in logic occurs. This can usually be traced to a faulty assumption the speaker is making.

Example:

I'm sure to make it as a Hollywood star. After all, I'm a huge movie fan already.

Explanation:

Being a fan of the movies does not qualify one as a "sure bet" to be a Hollywood star.

THE MAIN EVENT WRITING SAMPLE

The following is a sample essay written for this text in response to the Main Event Writing Assignment, Question #1.

Fashion as the Symbol of a New Generation

Youth culture is shaped by many things. When we think of young people, we think of cell phones, e-mail, digital cameras; we think of technology. We also think of raves and concerts and music stores—anywhere that plays the music they listen to, which is largely hip-hop. We also think of celebrity—youth idealized and turned into an art form. Hollywood is a Mecca for the young, beautiful, and talented; the silver screen is the altar they go to to pay their dues. Teenagers want to look like Reese Witherspoon or Brittany Murphy. Fashion has become the great arena where all these shaping forces come together to adorn our youth. Adornment, in this case, is the primary vehicle that allows our youth to celebrate who they are and who they want to be. Like the young, the fashion industry is an ever-changing, egocentric, heavily hyped, scandalously trendy playground. Fashion serves as a symbol for today's young generation as seen in gangsta styles, retro chic, and celebrity worship.   *Thesis based on Induction*

One of the most distinguishing styles of today's young people is the embracing of gangsta-style clothing. These clothes are a symbol for the hip-hop generation. The clothes go along with the rap. The men wear clothes that are baggy: exaggerated, hanging down

Inference below the waist revealing boxer shorts. They are reminiscent of jailhouse pants (in which belts are not allowed). As such, the clothing is a form of protest, a way of identifying with those who live outside the mainstream. Nevertheless, as Jeff Change notes in his article, "Born in Fire: A Hip-Hop Odyssey," gangsta has become a

Specific detail "marker of youth style" (25). National clothing brands such as Gap embraced hip-hop (Chang 25). Other brands, such as the popular

Specific detail FUBU clothing line, owe their inspiration to gangsta rap. On the FUBU website, amongst the awards they have received is the "On-line Hip-Hop Award," and they use hip-hop stars like LL Cool J to promote their products. They began by selling t-shirts, hats, hockey jerseys, and rugby shirts; now they are a nationally prominent brand that is incredibly popular with young people today. Wear-

Inference ing gangsta-style clothing is clearly a statement of the younger generation.

Retro chic calls upon the fashions of the past, but in a new way for a new generation. In this respect, fashion calls to mind

Inference today's music. "Like the hip-hop stars, designers love to sample the works of those who have gone before them" (Singer 198). To para-phrase an old saying, fashion today is déjà vu all over again. Youth have a nostalgic interest in what has gone before them. Just as the

Specific detail music world has seen a resurgence of interest in Santana and Tony Bennett, fashion has also mined its own history. Zac Posen, a hot 21-year-old designer is doing dresses with a 1940s style: shaped, heavily darted, flared hems, enhanced bust, and tight waist (Lus-

Specific detail combe 78). Sally Singer reports in *Vogue* that Marc Jacobs is doing long skirts, bohemian layers, and boots reminiscent of the early 1990s grunge era. At a recent show, he played Nirvana music, re-

Specific detail minding everyone of how he initially started his career (198). Tie-dye, bell-bottoms, hip huggers, and the little Diane Fustenberg

dress are all making a comeback with young women who were not even alive when these styles came around the first time.

Celebrities are to fashion for the young what icing is to cake. Not only do celebrities such as Penelope Cruz and Julianne Moore model for Ralph Lauren and Revlon, but also they have the best seats in the house at the fashion shows themselves. Celebrity models such as Naomi Campbell model for the young and hip fashion designers, sometimes simply for clothes rather than pay (Luscombe 78). Fashion aficionados who double as movie stars, like Gwynth Paltrow, Jennifer Lopez, and Julia Stiles, are heartily documented as to what specific designers they wear. Entire magazines, such as *In Style* and *W,* not only feature such stars, but also help bridge the gap between what stardom can afford and what the normal everyday person can. These magazines tell the audience what terrifically priced items the stars wear, and where readers can buy knock-offs to help them look like the celebrities. Reese Weatherspoon plays a Manhattan fashion designer in the film *Sweet Home Alabama,* a romantic comedy. The fashion-conscious movie star has become the perfect symbol of the female American dream—rich, talented, beautiful, and young. The movies and the media sell it, and our youth buy it.

From haute couture to the local strip mall, fashion designers have done all they can to gain entrance into the temple of youth, and it is smart that they do. Young people, and there are about 31 million teenagers in this country today, spend on the average $116 per week on themselves (Ebenkamp and Greenberg). Any business in America needs not only to cultivate but also consistently appeal to this group. Clothing often has symbolized attitudes; this generation is no different in that respect. The fashions of the young today symbolize the youth of today: individualistic, alternative, celebrity,

specific detail

specific detail

specific detail

Statement based on Induction

and market-oriented. Today's fashion junkies have not only shaped and symbolized youth culture, but in many ways have shaped and controlled the big piece of corporate America that goes with it.

Works Cited

Chang, Jeff. "Born in Fire: A Hip-Hop Odyssey." *UNESCO Courier.* July/Aug. 2000: 23–25.

Ebenkamp, Becky, and Karl Greenberg. "Youth Shall Be Served." *Brandweek* 24 June 2002: 20+. *MasterFile Premiere.* EBSCOHost. San Diego Mesa Coll. Lib. 1 Sept. 2002.

FUBU. FUBU Inc. 22 Nov. 2002 <www1.fubu.com>

Luscombe, Belinda. "Boy In Vogue." *Time* 30 Sept. 2002: 78–80.

Singer, Sally. "Revamp, Rethink, Recycle." *Vogue* Oct. 2002: 198–204.

Sweet Home Alabama. Dir. Andy Tennant. Perf. Reese Witherspoon, Josh Lucas, and Patrick Dempsey. Touchstone, 2002.

ADDITIONAL READINGS

Rave Fever
Susan Oh and Ruth Atherley

Oh and Atherley examine raves, the all-night dance parties favored by many young people. They look at the positive atmosphere of love and acceptance, and the underlying drug use that also permeates the environment. They compare raves with the rock festivals of the 1960s and 1970s, and note their common desire for peace, love, and unity. The effect of Ecstasy is also an issue. Still, raves appear to experience fewer problems in the forms of violent acts or drug overdoses than other types of large parties or festivals.

Key Words

motley	composed of diverse elements
amphetamine	a drug frequently abused as a stimulant
eschew	to avoid something regularly, especially on moral grounds
yore	time past
protocols	rules governing proper behavior
illicit	illegal
regimented	organized rigidly
luminescent	light producing

It's 2:30 A.M. on a Saturday night, and Amanda Mondoux is just hitting her party stride. All smiles and a swirl of flapping clothes and damp ponytail, the 17-year-old is swaying like someone in a voodoo trance, brandishing glow sticks to carve arcs of light through the shooting lasers. Amanda, a Grade 12 student, is among some 7,500 young people—a motley crowd dressed in brightly coloured "fun" fur, pants that hang like sacks and baseball caps—gathered to dance till morning in a cavernous Toronto exhibition hall. The sea of grinning faces and flailing arms bobs in sync with the jackhammer beats. Door-sized speakers pump out music so loud that it registers more through the soles of the feet than the numbed eardrums.

Hours later, awash in glitter makeup and sweat, Amanda visits the "chill" section, a rest area just quiet enough for conversation. She and the other young people greet old friends and make new ones. Modern-day flower children, the kids exchange not just nods and handshakes but also hugs, kisses, massages, glow-in-the-dark toys, bracelets and candy. Then, in a corner of the women's washroom, Amanda introduces herself to a chubby 15-year-old girl named Max.

"Hey, what's up?" says Amanda. "How long you been partying?"

"It's my second party," Max replies, adding, "I had to sneak out of a window. My mom thinks I'm still home."

"No way! For real?" Amanda groans and gives her another hug. 5 They exchange e-mail addresses.

It all seems sweetly mischievous. But then Amanda asks, "Are you dosing?"—rave-speak for "Have you taken drugs?"—which draws a nod from Max.

That many kids like Amanda and Max dose is the foremost concern of parents, police and legislators now that raves are an entrenched—and growing—part of youth culture. With the increased popularity of the all-night parties has come increased consumption of rave drugs, most notably the amphetamine-like substance MDMA, known as ecstasy or "E." Their use is by no means confined to raves—those stimulants can be found at concerts, nightclubs and many private parties. But wherever they are taken, they can be deadly. Ecstasy has been implicated in at least 14 Canadian deaths in the past two years—10 in Ontario, three in British Columbia and one in Halifax. The victims ranged in age from 19 to 43, but most were in their 20s. One of the latest was 21-year-old Allan Ho, a business student at Toronto's Ryerson Polytechnic University, who collapsed at a rave in a former shoe factory last Oct. 10. Traces of MDMA were found in his body. A coroner's inquest into his death beginning on May 3 will look at overall safety issues surrounding raves.

Many more kids have become sick from rave drugs. Earlier this month in Edmonton, at a rave at Northlands Sportex attended by more than 5,000 people, eight partyers suffered seizures and had to be taken to hospital.

Because of the drugs, because of the inherently worrisome aspect of kids staying up all night, far from parental scrutiny, "rave" has become one of those red-flag words. "Oh, my God, I worry to death what goes on at those things," says 44-year-old Janet Cacchioni, a marketing co-ordinator in Vancouver whose 18-year-old daughter, Holly, goes to raves. "I know all the trouble I got into at her age, but I also know that nothing could have stopped me—and I expect nothing will stop her."

Like the rock festivals of the Sixties and Seventies, raves are one- 10 off celebrations of youthful exuberance, gatherings of the idealistic tribe. They draw anywhere from hundreds to thousands, most between the ages of 15 and 29, to party to electronic music played and sometimes created by DJs using synthesizers and turntables. Much like their hippie predecessors, ravers preach peace, love and unity, and eschew violence. Unlike the counterculturists of yore, they frown on alcohol. "You can develop a sense of community," observes 26-year-old Will Chang, a corporate lawyer in a downtown Toronto law firm who's been going at least once a month for the past four years. Chang, also a founding member of the Toronto Dance Safety Committee, which helped set up protocols for the safe operation of raves, says they "have made me more open-minded and accepting of others—no one cares about colour, sex or age."

Some ravers, however, believe the scene is losing its joy and innocence. They cite commercialization, profiteering venue owners creating unsafe conditions, and the gangs that have taken control of rave drugs, adding more lethal substances to the psychedelic menu. "There's no vibe anymore," complains Matt Whalley, a 20-year-old Toronto DJ, referring to a sense of positive energy and goodwill. "I remember a time when I'd go there and just feel happy—no drugs, just the music, and everybody was happy."

In trouble or not, raves are common in major cities across the nation. There are parties almost every Saturday in Toronto, considered by many devotees to be the rave capital of North America. Last Halloween, in the largest rave ever in Canada, about 16,000 gathered at a Toronto entertainment complex. Those events attract people from as far away as Wisconsin and New York City. Meanwhile, ravers can dance till dawn most weekends in the Vancouver area, Calgary, Edmonton, Montreal and Halifax, and less often in smaller locales. Yet the events still draw only a tiny fraction of young Canadians. A recent Angus Reid survey into youth trends and values found that five per cent of 3,500 subjects aged 16 to 29 had attended one or more raves in the past year, and only one per cent went to them on a regular basis.

Applied to the overall population, those findings mean roughly 50,000 Canadians are committed ravers.

The numbers are substantial enough, however, for raves to be the focus of big business, both legitimate, and illicit. With tickets running from $25 to $50, rave organizers stand to net—or lose—as much as $40,000 from one event alone. Raves have also spawned numerous spin-off enterprises, including shops specializing in rave music and garb.

Trafficking in ecstasy and other rave drugs, meanwhile, has become a virtual epidemic. By no means are all those pills, vials and capsules being consumed at raves, but their association with the all-night parties—and the deaths—have made raves a hot-button issue in municipal politics across the country. Vancouver and Toronto have both struck committees to help regulate raves, and Calgary is considering doing the same. Toronto raves must now adhere to safety protocols and guidelines pertaining to water, security and numbers, though they are difficult to enforce.

"In many ways, the concerns raised over the rave scene are not 15 that much different than for rock concerts in the 1970s," says Edward Adlaf, a research scientist at the Centre for Addiction & Mental Health in Toronto. Adlaf maintains it's a myth that everyone who attends raves is heavily into hard drugs, citing his organization's ongoing study of drug use in middle- and high-school students, which found that 57 per cent of students who had attended a rave in the past year had used cannabis but no other illegal substance. But two-thirds of those who had been to a rave are heavier drug users than non-ravers. And 4.4 per cent of all the students surveyed had taken ecstasy in the past year. He does concede, however, that the study, based on voluntary disclosure, comes with a degree of underreporting.

Meanwhile, 30 per cent of the students in Adlaf's study had had one heavy-drinking episode in the past four weeks alone. And he notes that young people are far more likely to cause themselves short- or long-term harm with the much more pervasive drugs tobacco and alcohol. Despite the far greater risks involved with alcohol abuse, Adlaf is nonetheless very concerned about ravers buying drugs increasingly cut with poisonous chemicals, or mixing substances to create a lethal dose. He also notes that illegal crowding and a lack of running water at many raves puts kids at risk. Water, experts say, is crucial. Without it, a person cannot control the body heat generated by rave drugs and dancing, and the liver and kidneys can shut down. Until recently in Toronto, some landlords who had maintained the right to sell water would cut off the water supply and air-conditioning in order to maximize sales.

Informed kids like Amanda make sure to drink constantly, convinced that it will protect them. "And I only do E," she says, taking a break from playing with her tongue stud. "I don't touch any of the dirty stuff." She's referring to drugs like gamma hydroxy-butyric acid (also known as GHB), one of the so-called date-rape drugs, and Ketamine, an animal tranquillizer known as "Special K." Highly addictive crystal methamphetamine, a type of speed also called "ice," has also become popular. With such drugs, the trip from euphoria to overdose can be swift—especially when kids combine substances, as they often do. "I don't like the e-tards," says 18-year-old Chris Pettitt as he drags on a marijuana joint and points to some kids lying on the floor. "They're the people who take too much drugs and act stupid." Says an indignant Amanda: "People have offered me Special K, and I'm like, 'Cat tranquillizers? Do I look like a cat to you? No way.' "

Those dangers aside, ravers protest that their culture is about the music and the love-fest factor, not drugs. "I found a family at raves," says Becky, a 19-year-old Toronto student who attended her first one, in 1994. Taken into foster care at age 12, she says she kept going because of the accepting environment. But for a few years, Becky took ecstasy every other week, and she still indulges every couple of months. "I respect myself and my body," she says, "but everybody does something that's bad for them."

Given the rave-drug equation, many parents simply forbid their children from going. Others—baby boomers who remember the excesses of the Sixties and Seventies—believe it's pointless to try to deny young people their own tribal celebrations, or even their own drugs. Rebecca Ientile started to accompany her three children (Chris, 20, Kathleen, 17, and Ashley, 15) to raves five months ago. "At least I know where my kids are," says the 43-year-old Toronto single mother, who owns a landscaping company. "I know what they do and what they're on. We've sat down as a family and discussed it. As long as everything is in moderation and we're open about it, I'm not worried." Ientile is quick to point out raves' positive aspects. "The kids are wonderful. There's never any fights or bullying. Everyone's friendly and respectful of one another."

Rose Ker, a federal civil servant, sometimes accompanies daughter   20 Danielle, 17, to raves, where the teen and her best friend, Meghan Shepherd, have for the past two years operated a booth selling jewelry, toys and clothing they make themselves. "I was amazed," the 40-year-old mother says of her first rave experience. "Usually kids can be so judgmental and cruel to each other, but there was none of that. There seemed no barriers. It reminded me of the hippie age."

Many ravers savour the self-expression that is central to the culture. So-called candy ravers cultivate a childlike look, dressing in bright colours and big hats and decking themselves with toys and candy. "Liquid kids" wear white gloves and move in a fluid, mime-like fashion. Dancing at raves is less regimented than at clubs: people tend not to pair off as they move in quirky, even comical, ways. The clothes tend to be fun and comfortable rather than sexually provocative.

Sociologist Tim Weber, who authored a 1999 study on raves for Toronto's Centre for Addiction & Mental Health, notes that today's teens are looking for positive experiences to offset the comparatively stressful climate they've grown up in. "I was surprised at the number of kids in high school who saw raves as mini-vacations away from daily stressors," says Weber, who is now working for the pollster Angus Reid. "Some enjoyed being allowed to act like small children, doing things like wearing costumes, eating candy and playing with toys." Raised by done-it-all, seen-it-all boomers, they are also the generation that grew up with latchkey-ism, AIDS, the dominance of clothing brands and the pressure to start planning a career during adolescence. Jessica Hafekost, a 19-year-old Toronto salesclerk, says of the first rave party she and a friend attended four years ago: "We walked in and saw people dressed and just moving in ways we'd never seen before. There was a bubble machine, toys and tubing on the ceiling filled with luminescent green goo—a fantasy quality to the whole thing. Where else are you going to see that?"

Shawn Parsons, now 33, has worked in security since he was 15, first in clubland, and since 1993, at raves with his own security company. "At a bar on any given night, you can guarantee a member of my staff will be physically attacked," says the burly Toronto father of three preteen children. "With ravers, that just doesn't happen. The parties attract the same group of people as they always have: intelligent, respectful kids who feel like outsiders in the real world."

Often, raves get an undeservedly bad rap because of confusion over what they are. A Vancouver shooting in early February, reported to be at a rave, in fact occurred outside a Chinese new year party at a banquet hall, and was gang-related. "What you're seeing is a knee-jerk reaction where they're calling everything a rave," says Sgt. Steve Clark, in charge of downtown special events for Toronto police. Meanwhile, conventional nightclubs don't necessarily fare any better in terms of safety. Last year, the 1,800-capacity Toronto club The Guvernment was the source of 37 emergency calls on Friday and Saturday nights—24 medical problems, seven acts of violence and six accidental overdoses. At the Toronto rave attended by 16,000 last Halloween, there was just one emergency call when a table fell on a person's leg.

At 7:30 A.M., Amanda is waiting for friends at the coat check as 25 orange sunlight filters into the hall. The music is still loud, but most of the few hundred kids remaining have put on their coats and are dancing their way across the trash-strewn floor towards the exit.

Amanda and her pals are about to go to one of their houses to talk or listen to music as they come down off the drugs. Soon, there will be another rave, another all-nighter. "I won't become a bum and do this when I get old, like 26," she shrugs. "But for now this is what it's about."

An Inquiry into the Agony of Ecstasy

Kieran Kelly's death got the most headlines, but Allan Ho's is considered the most typical. Both of the 21-year-old Ontarians had been to raves, and both had taken the drug ecstasy. The bookish Kelly, a native of Brampton, disappeared last summer from an outdoor rave held near Sauble Beach, a popular Lake Huron holiday spot 250 km northwest of Toronto. For a month, his anguished father carried on a highly publicized search—until Kelly's body was finally found in dense bush almost two kilometres from the rave site. Ho, a business student at Ryerson Polytechnic University, collapsed at a Toronto rave in a former shoe factory last October. Rushed to hospital, he lay unconscious for 14 hours, and then died.

The two deaths added to the provincial coroner's growing file on ecstasy-related deaths. By the end of 1999, the toll in Ontario, home to more raves than any other province, had reached nine for the year (with just one other in the rest of Canada). That number marked the sudden emergence of a new way of dying—in 1998 Ontario had recorded only one ecstasy-related death, its first ever—and prompted the coroner's office to call an inquest, scheduled to begin in Toronto on May 3. The inquest will focus on Ho, because the coroner considers him the most representative of the nine Ontario cases: all were healthy males between 19 and 28, and most died at raves in the Toronto area. But the inquest will also look at the entire urban rave scene and its dangers.

Adding to deputy chief coroner Jim Cairns's sense of urgency is the fact that two more such deaths have already been confirmed in 2000 and others suspected, putting the province on track to match or exceed last year's total. "Look, I know this is not the most dangerous thing going on," Cairns allows. "Many more young people die from alcohol every year. But it is new, it's continuing, and we need to collect what we know and make it public."

That means Ho's inquest will have "a broad mandate," Cairns says. "It will examine not just his death, but the larger questions about ecstasy, by hearing testimony from police about the problems they deal with, and from medical professionals about what they see in emergency wards on weekends." It's an exercise in public health and safety that Cairns hopes will help keep others from the fate of Kieran Kelly and Allan Ho.

Wild Ones through the Ages

Some of the youth movements that have captivated kids—and, in most cases, scandalized parents—over the past 80 years:

Flappers 1920s

> **Music:** Dixieland
> **Look:** short, bobbed hair and slim-cut dresses for women, fedoras for men
> **Drug of choice:** alcohol and roll-your-own cigarettes
> **Ritual:** dance-hall parties and the Charleston

Swing Kids 1940s

> **Music:** big-band jazz
> **Look:** sleekly coiffed hairdos, fitted blouses and skirts for women, pleated trousers and sports jackets, or the clean-cut GI Joe look for men
> **Drug of choice:** alcohol and cigarettes
> **Ritual:** music-hall parties and cutting a rug with the jive and the jitterbug

Rock 'N' Rollers 1950s

> **Music:** Elvis Presley and other early rockers, Paul Anka
> **Look:** bouffant hairdos and bobby socks for women, greasy duck-tails and white T-shirts for men
> **Drug of choice:** alcohol and cigarettes
> **Ritual:** parties in darkened rec rooms, group excursions to drive-ins and pool halls, high-school dances

Hippies 1960s

> **Music:** folk and acid rock, the Beatles
> **Look:** tie-dyed garments, ethnic wear, jeans, bell-bottoms, miniskirts
> **Drug of choice:** just about every legal and illegal mind-altering drug going, especially cannabis, LSD and alcohol
> **Ritual:** love-ins, happenings, rock concerts and festivals

Disco Diehards 1970s

> **Music:** mindless dance music
> **Look:** platform shoes, loud shirts, big collars, halter tops and hot pants
> **Drug of choice:** cannabis, cocaine, heroin, alcohol
> **Ritual:** dancing till you dropped at discotheques

(continued)

Wild Ones through the Ages (continued)

Punkers Late-1970s to Mid-1980s

Music: The Sex Pistols and other punk rock
Look: safety pins, mohawks, studded leather
Drug of choice: cannabis, heroin, speed, alcohol
Ritual: concerts and mosh pits

Hip-Hop Kids 1980s to the Present

Music: rap music
Look: extremely baggy sportswear, sometimes worn backwards
Drug of choice: cannabis, crack
Ritual: parties, concerts

What Did You Read?

1. What are some of the youth movements that the authors identify?
2. According to sociologist Tim Weber, why are young people attracted to raves?
3. What are some of the things that cause people to feel that raves are *not* the idealistic rock festivals of the new millennia?

What Do You Think?

1. Is it realistic to think that any mass grouping of young people is going to be alcohol, drug, or gang free?
2. What happened to private parties? What needs do raves meet that private parties do not?
3. Why do young people attending raves have a social life that is programmed like their school and work life: as public institutions? What is the appeal of this?

How Was It Done?

1. What introductory technique do the authors use to introduce the subjects of raves, drugs, and youth culture?
2. How important are statistics to the development of the article?
3. What kind of expertise and support is used to support the authors' argument?

4. How important to the authors is the contrast between the raves of today and the rock festivals of the 1960s and 1970s?

5. Does the chart at the end of the article chronicle well youth movements over the past eighty years? Does it add or detract from the article?

Get Ready for the Net Generation
Mark L. Alch

Mark Alch creates the term "Net Generation" and argues that this generation of young people, born from 1977 to 1997, is distinctly different from both their baby boomer parents and their Generation X predecessors. They are comfortable with change and chaos, being largely the products of nontraditional family structures. They have grown up with the PC as an ordinary, everyday tool; they are savvy with technology; they are unlikely to see a stable work environment as necessarily desirable. Businesses in the future will have to change their workplace habits and cultures if they wish to hold on to this new generation of workers.

Key Words

savvy	practical knowledge
conversant	having knowledge or experience
synthesizers	people who can bring together different ideas or skills to create a new whole
configurations	shapes; arrangements of elements
contingency	something that is liable but not certain to happen
distance learning	education that takes place over the computer, often a class conducted using the Internet as the prime means of contact
intrapreneurs	employees who develop new enterprises within a company
pervasive	becoming diffused or spread out among all parts of something

The group following on the heels of Generation X is being called the Net or Echo-Boom Generation—people born between 1977 and 1997. Employers will have to face the new realities of the Net Generation's culture and values, and what it wants from work if they expect to attract and retain those talents and align them with corporate goals. As this 80 million-strong generation enters the workforce in stages, it will easily displace the baby boomers, who number 77 million, and the 44 million baby busters, Gen X. Netters—like their parents, the baby boomers—will redefine business as they stream into the corporate world.

The oldest members of the Net Generation—those just turning 22 and graduating from college with a baccalaureate degree—are starting to slip quietly past Gen Xers to occupy center stage. Not only is the Net Gen more populous than Gen X, it's also the first generation to grow up in the digital age. Due to their number and influence soon to be felt in the business arena, they're destined to shake up current management practices and have a great effect on how work is done.

In the 1960s, the generation gap was over differences in values, lifestyles, and ideology between parents and their children. A yawning generation gap between boomers and their children is that the offspring have a huge edge on information technology. Bombarded with information and media-savvy, the newest generation displays a strong work ethic and has grown up understanding the electronic economy. They're comfortable with changes brought about by new technologies and e-commerce. More than any previous generation, they're conversant with a communications revolution transforming business, education, health care, entertainment, government, and every other institution.

But rather than reject wholly the lifestyle choices, values, and outlooks of previous generations, they accept some of the old with the new. In that respect, they're synthesizers.

Netters exhibit several major differences from boomers and   5 busters.

> **Sharing the load.** Netters have held part-time jobs in high school and college and haven't been as overindulged as busters. As the cost of a college education has risen, they have had to help defray the expense.
>
> **Global orientation.** Netters have grown up understanding the need for interconnectivity to the worldwide community. They're aware of global warming and the eroding of the ozone layer. They've observed how the Asian financial market crisis is affecting the American economy. And they've been connected globally via the Internet.
>
> **Not the Cleavers.** The concept of how a family is defined has changed. Fifty years ago, the typical unit was a working father and a mother who stayed at home to rear the two children. Now, only about 15 percent of U.S. households fit that description. Many baby busters are children of divorce, but Netters tend to view various family configurations as normal.
>
> **Reality bound.** Members of the Net Generation have seen their parents cut from organizations one or more times due to downsizing, mergers and acquisitions, takeovers, and closings. They've witnessed little company loyalty or job security. They

understand that their training, skills, and abilities are the currency for a getting a job and establishing a career path.

Cool with chaos. The Net Generation has come to regard constant and turbulent change as normal. As a result, they're more attuned to the need to make adjustments in midstream and have contingency plans.

A Domino Effect

The generational changing of the guard in the workforce will have wide-ranging HR and OD implications.

As a group, the Net Generation mixes creativity with an investigative bent regarding electronic media. The resulting culture is one of free expression and strong views. That free form allows a great deal of independence without restraint or hindrances. Because of that, Netters tend to use a blend of collaboration, interdependence, and networking to achieve their ends. The American educational system has had a lot to do with that. Students learned to work together to prepare and deliver group or team projects. That will serve them well in companies with team-based environments. As much as Netters are helping redefine and restructure the new workplace, they'll be looking to use their talents in companies that pose no barriers to freedom.

It's not surprising that a new kind of worker would emerge—one who would rather work for him- or herself or for companies that provide development opportunities project by project. After a project ends, they're ready to move on to new challenges and opportunities. That can create a problem for companies trying to direct employees in traditional ways. Many managers face the difficulty of guiding cross-functional team members who don't care about hierarchy and career ladders. These new employees view themselves as contract workers lending their services and expertise for a time. Middle and senior managers need to understand that such employees are at their best in terms of productivity, creativity, and work satisfaction when they work on projects that enhance their skills and competencies.

As these workers move from one company to another, it will be up to them to ensure that their assemblage of training and areas of expertise is up-to-date and portable. Likewise, companies have the responsibility to keep employees current with new technologies and bleeding-edge training.

Ease with computers as a business and personal tool places the Net Generation on a plane no previous generation has been. It lets companies orient, train, retrain, and develop new programs without having to teach these workers how to use a PC. Online delivery of learning over an intranet is and will continue to be highly acceptable to these new workers. 10

Netters are strong advocates of lifelong learning. They understand that they need to update and maintain their training at cutting edge to ensure their employability. More than previous generations, they accept and recognize that they'll go through numerous job changes and perhaps five to eight different careers in their lifetimes—aided by distance learning.

Netters will use the Internet to obtain a formal degree or certification, or just take courses on topics of interest. These working adults want to be able to join a class online when it suits their schedule.

Companies with self-managed, self-directed teams will find the new labor force well equipped to work individually as well as in groups. Merit increases in salaries and bonuses, usually a sore point in the context of group efforts, will have a better chance in the short-term teams of the future, in which office politics won't have a chance—or time—to intrude.

Recognizing that company loyalty is a relic of the past, employers mustn't judge or feel betrayed when employees ready for their next work role leave for other offers. Empowered employees, accountable to their companies for results, can operate best.

This new breed of change-hardy and change-ready intrapreneurs   15 will be a welcome addition to companies going through transformation. With more emphasis on teamwork and group performance, companies that gear their systems to the new economic realities will come out ahead. Those that don't understand the makeup of the new workforce entrants will have trouble assimilating and keeping employees. Bosses who think they can act as an authority on everything will turn off the new employees. Netters respect people who demonstrate expertise and knowledge; they don't care about organizational rank, age, or tenure. One can't expect this generation to be interested in ladder climbing. They're interested in using their knowledge and skills, participating in decision making, collaborating, and establishing interconnectivity with others. Companies using such traditional motivators as promotions, bonuses, and merit-pay increases will find they need other rewards to retain high performers.

Evidence suggests the Net Generation will thrive in environments where they have a direct say in how work is done and where they can add, innovate, or create in order to turn out the best product or service possible. The new workers readily accept the accountability all of that requires. As for managers, they must help keep the objectives of self-managed teams aligned with corporate goals, through effective strategic planning and constant internal communications. The new way of working will require flexibility, multitasking, the running of numerous projects or programs concurrently, and working with different people as they enter and leave the company.

Companies can prepare for the newest workforce entrants, not forgetting to upgrade the skills of baby boomers still working. Many U.S. schools have had computers for a long time and are hooked up to the Internet, but there's still an information lag. Business communities need to support local school board initiatives to get technology into the classrooms. It's also imperative for schools to offer additional time on computers for children who don't have them at home. Companies can help by setting up and staffing computer training centers to instruct teachers on new technology. Employers can underwrite the purchase of home computers for employees. In a bottom-line sense, when employees take home a computer, their children will learn how to use it and teach the parents, thus closing the digital gap. And the computer literacy of the company's workforce will rise dramatically.

The new wave of 80 million young people entering the workforce during the next 20 years are technologically equipped and, therefore, armed with the most powerful tools for business. That makes their place in history unique: No previous generation has grown up understanding, using, and expanding on such a pervasive instrument as the PC. It will be up to HR and OD professionals to lead their companies in understanding the needs, motivations, and behaviors of the Net Generation.

What Did You Read?

1. How does the author identify the newest generation, the "Net Generation"? Describe them.
2. How will the Net generation affect companies in the future?
3. What does it mean that Netters are not the Cleavers?
4. What can companies and schools do to help prepare the Net generation for their future?

What Do You Think?

1. What will motivate the Net generation at work if it is not the things that motivated past generations (such as promotions or bonuses)? How can companies keep their top performing employees?
2. Do you think schools are encouraging the kind of innovation, cooperative learning, and self-management that will be so important to the future labor force?
3. What pitfalls do you see in the business arena that is so dependent on cutting-edge technology?

How Was It Done?

1. What purpose does the use of bold lettering serve?
2. Alch begins his article with a definition of the "Net Generation." How does he define this term?
3. How does the classification of differences between "boomers" and "busters" help to develop his investigation of the Net generation?
4. Does Alch use any outside sources to develop his ideas of how the current generation of youth will affect the business sector in the future?

Understanding Youth, Popular Culture, and the Hip-Hop Influence

Patricia Thandi Hicks Harper

Patricia Thandi Hicks Harper examines hip-hop as a clue to understanding today's young people. Her interest is based on bridging the gap of understanding between older adults and America's youth, so that educators, medical professionals, and others can reach the young with their messages. She argues that the values of hip-hop are the values of this new generation: emphasis on diversity, technology, urban, color, and spirituality. She argues that without understanding the culture of hip-hop, older adults with a message, no matter how well-intentioned, will not get that message across.

Key Words

permeates	spreads through
contextualizes	places in a context; relates something to its external conditions
pertinent	relevant
conglomerates	widely diversified corporations
contemporary anthropologist	someone who studies the culture and workings of today's peoples
predilection	a preference for something
cognitive	related to the process of knowing
schemata	outline; a structured framework
risqué	verging on indecency

America's youth represent a distinct group with their own unique popular culture—a culture within which Hip-Hop recurrently permeates.

Despite adult attitudes (both positive and negative) about youth culture, we know we must have a working knowledge of this culture that engulfs and contextualizes our young people's lives if we are to effectively communicate with them. It is important to understand the information that they process. The rules of social marketing are pertinent and suggest that effective communication begins with knowing your target audience.

Collectively, youth in America represent a powerful movement that transcends race, ethnicity, gender, and social or economic status. America's youth are a walking depiction of their worldview that is externally manifested through clothing, art, attitude, style, movement, music, video, television, film, language, and the World Wide Web.

Youth are big business, and everyone is struggling for their attention: advertisers; large and small businesses; media conglomerates; the sports, fashion, and entertainment industries; faith communities; health arenas; schools; community-based organizations; families; and even local, state, and federal governments.

Many of America's youth need adult assistance, nurturing, supervision, and resources because they are at-risk for making negative and harmful behavioral choices. Those entities that will succeed in reaching these young people with their messages or products are those who are the most culturally competent in youth popular culture and who use this knowledge and experience as a foundation for their education and information dissemination outreach strategies.

The need for cultural competence in understanding and appreciating racial and ethnic diversity is well recognized in corporate, community, and governmental arenas. The influx of international racial and ethnic groups over the past 20 years has made it necessary for America to develop communication efforts that are targeted, authentic, culturally sensitive, and designed to speak appropriately to cultural nuances.

Yet, America has not voiced the same urgency in understanding the culture of youth. It is time that we understood that culture is not limited to race, ethnicity, gender, or sexuality. Programs targeting youth must demonstrate a sensitivity to and an understanding of young people and their design for living and interpreting their environment.

By examining youth culture, we can form a guide for predicting behavioral choices and for determining the strategies necessary to change and influence those choices.

Youth Popular Culture Competence

Youth popular culture is simply defined as that which is "in," contemporary, and has the stamp of approval of young people. It is that which has mass appeal; it is nonlinear and eclectic. The culture dictates what become the shared norms that provide young people "with a deep sense of belonging and often with a strong preference for behaving in certain ways." It is "psycho-socio-cultural" in that its primary elements involve the reciprocal interaction of individual, social, and cultural forces.

Youth popular culture has aspects that cross racial, ethnic, and ge- 10 ographical boundaries, and while all youth do not behave or think in the exact same ways, many similarities suggest that the vast majority of adolescents fit somewhere within the mainstream of an American youth popular culture. How youth spend their time; what they value; their attitudes, styles, and behaviors; their concerns; and how they interact with mass mediated messages, their peers, and society-at-large constitute youth popular culture.

Because our mass popular culture is the most influential in the world, youth, as the drivers of the culture, are very powerful. While some scholars maintain that today's youth are extremely diverse in terms of their culture (whether they be heroes, nerds, urban martyrs, or valley girls), we contend that the strength of youth popular culture today is in what young people have in common with each other. The challenge for health professionals, educators, and others who intend to effectively communicate with youth is to get a good read on what is happening within this culture and to recognize the commonalities. The key, again, is to become and/or remain youth popular culture competent.

The U.S. Department of Health and Human Services' Center for Substance Abuse Prevention (CSAP) defines cultural competence as:

> A set of academic and interpersonal skills that allow individuals to increase their understanding and appreciation of cultural differences and similarities within, among, and between groups. This requires a willingness and ability to draw on community-based values, traditions, and customs and to work with knowledgeable persons of and from the community in developing focused interventions, communications, and other supports.

CSAP stresses the importance of cultural competence for effectively maximizing substance abuse prevention and intervention efforts. The point is that health professionals, educators, and anyone else targeting youth must honestly address the following questions:

- "How well do I really know the target audience?"
- "How much do I really know about their racial, ethnic, and adolescent culture?"
- "How much do I really understand about their worldview and how they interact within society?"
- "How much do I really know about how young people use media?"

- "How important is it for me to be culturally competent about youth popular culture?"
- "Do I base my responses on newly obtained information about today's youth culture, or do I make judgments based on speculation or the opinions of others and/or media?"

Once these questions are addressed, the knowledge, understanding, and appreciation gaps must be filled. The related issues must be explored by taking the most appropriate actions (based on the definition), which will lead to increased cultural competence. The result would be more effective communication with youth populations because health professionals and educators would be more cognizant of their psycho-socio-cultural realities. Communication would be more directly targeted.

A 17-year-old female living in an urban area of Washington, DC, 15 describes effective communication from her perspective. She states:

> Sometimes when young people are being criticized, they get so angry [that] they're not actually listening to what these people have to say. The older generation is not communicating because they're being so critical without really looking and listening. If they would just listen to what matters to us, they might be able to communicate better. We're not that bad. But the younger people have to check themselves too and listen to what the older generation is saying. They do know a lot. Everybody has to listen to each other. Maybe then we'll get on the same page.

We at the Institute maintain that it is imperative for those who work with youth to seriously explore and consider the potential effectiveness of using what we call youth popular culture's inherent and associated "formal features," contexts, and appropriate content for effective communication. We contend that it is important to move beyond society's and professionals' negative associations with the culture and to explicate how its characteristics and attributes can best be utilized in the interest of those who are captivated by it on a daily basis. At the same time, we know we must clarify that we are not implying that anyone should give his or her blessing to all aspects of youth popular culture or that anyone should encourage an unexamined conformism by young people.

The Formal Features

Formal features are those elements that give communicative strength to messages and are usually discussed within the context of visual media. The formal features of youth popular culture, for purposes of this article, include elements and characteristics that can be manifested through all media and personal communication.

The role that youth popular culture's formal features play in the everyday lives of youth suggests them as integral factors of youth popular culture. Leading contemporary anthropologist C. P. Kottack discusses the "features" of popular culture, indicating that these "features are sometimes regarded as trivial and unworthy of serious study." We beg to differ, as does Kottack, and contend that ideology, predilection, belief, language, and formal features (which to some degree encompass the other cultural aspects) constitute youth culture— which influences the choices youth make.

The features allow for the shaping and customizing of messages and materials that target youth and that illustrate the creative relationship between distinct styles of form and content. The formal features of youth popular culture provide resourceful pathways for effective and affective communication with target audiences. Examples of these formal features include:

- bold
- "rhythm" driven
- eclectic
- colors
- urban
- non-governmental
- "popular music" driven
- "attitude" driven
- humorous
- power-to-the-youth centered
- family connected
- spiritual
- celebrity-icon driven
- non-linear
- jargon specific
- dance
- "sports" focused
- to the point
- technological
- "keeping it real" driven
- full of verve
- "posse" driven

The formal features of youth popular culture are multidirectional, 20 eclectic, familiar, and nontraditional (compared to European standards of traditional culture, which may be described as linear, hierarchical, standardized, individualistic, and rule-oriented).

The use of these features in designing pro-health and education messages would make a youth's cognitive processing and sanctioning of these messages more likely because of the features' cultural appropriateness and relation to a youth's already existing mental frameworks of prototypical experiences (schemata).

Youth will respond positively to information couched within a cultural context that genuinely acknowledges their worldviews. Knowledge of youth popular culture's formal features will assist educators and health professionals:

- in more creatively facilitating their students' learning process
- in their efforts to develop and design messages targeting youth
- in their efforts to get youth interested about sexuality education and living healthy lifestyles
- in their efforts to effectively communicate using a variety of formats
- in enhancing their cultural competence as it relates to youth as a cultural group

Hip-Hop Culture

Hip-Hop culture is America's dominant youth popular culture today. This is the reason why adults who target youth must be clear about it. Hip-Hop is a cultural phenomenon in the American mainstream. Noted writer of popular music culture, Nelson George, suggests that we all exist in what can legitimately be called a "Hip-Hop America." While some may argue that other youth cultures (e.g., Rock and Punk youth culture) are just as pervasive in the lives of youth, we at the Institute profess that the masses of young people are engulfed in selected aspects of Hip-Hop and that other popular youth cultures have embraced its vastness, thereby creating an interchange of styles for popularity.

Hip-Hop's legacy lies in the old and ancient traditions of African people, however, its contemporary status has evolved from a subterranean Bronx (NY) expression in the early 1970s to a profitable commodity worldwide. The origin of what is now contemporary Hip-Hop lies in the backyards, basements, and communities of inner-city Black and Hispanic/Latino youth.

The name Hip-Hop also has a distinct origin. According to R T. 25 Perkins and the nationally and internationally acclaimed founder of the "Universal Zulu Nation Movement" and "Godfather of Hip-Hop and Rap" Afrika Bambaataa:

The term Hip-Hop was taken out of verses that Love Bug Starski used to say "to the Hip-Hop you don't stop" and it was the Zulu Nation that took it and named the whole culture Hip-Hop. Hip-Hop is something that's the whole culture, the whole picture of the movement which is the break dancing, the graffiti art, the rapping, the scratching, the deejaying, the style of dress, the lyrics, the way you look, the walk, it's all this combined . . . the attitude.

Hip-Hop is an "all encompassing" culture for many of America's youth. It includes forces that affect and influence the choices these youth make in their everyday lives. Hip-Hop represents a strong and unified youth consciousness; it is a powerful and pervasive movement among youth worldwide. Youth, regardless of who they are or where they come from, very likely will identify with at least some aspect of Hip-Hop culture.

Today, the formal features of Hip-Hop are successfully used to communicate a myriad of messages and to sell products which profitably, ethically, and unethically target the masses of young people. The understanding of Hip-Hop and its influence within popular culture has proven to be very effective for influencing behavioral choices and drawing the attention of young people to various subject areas. An exploration of Hip-Hop music (particularly Rap music) will show that youth of various races and ethnic groups are purchasing the music to significant degrees. Research indicates that white American teens purchase Rap in larger numbers than do their African-American counterparts. "More than 70 percent of Hip-Hop albums are purchased by Whites," all of whom contribute to the fact that the music is now a billion dollar industry.

Rap music continues to lead the way in album sales growth when compared to other music genres (e.g., R & B, Country, Alternative). According to Byran Turner, president and CEO of SoundScan:

> Rap album sales shot up 32 percent in just 12 months, first time. That jump makes for the largest single-year gain by any genre since SoundScan began collecting sales data eight years ago.

Hirschorn, past editor of *Spin* music magazine, compares Hip-Hop and rock music sales data. He supports the argument that "the energy now days is in Hip-Hop" and contends that:

> When Hip-Hop albums as strong as Lauryn Hill's or Outcast's sell as well as they did, it's hard to argue about the quality. The question is whether rock is going to lose a whole generation of young listeners, who are naturally gravitating to Hip-Hop now.

Hip-Hop's pervasive influence within the fashion, film, television, 30 and dot.com industries clearly show the culture as one of choice for many of America's youth. It is a culture that must not be ignored because of its mainstay status within the American mainstream. It is a culture whose elements must be explored as a useful contextual backdrop for effective communication. (See "Reaching the Hip-Hop Generation with 'Pro-Social' Behavior Messages" in the June-July 1999 issue of the SIECUS Report.)

Cultural Competency in the Classroom

Many of America's educators, regardless of their subject area, still fail to consider culture when determining their teaching methodologies and exploring the best ways to communicate with and to their students.

Consequently, there is an evident lack of cultural responsiveness, relevance, and significance in classroom environment, and too many students remain uninterested and lack the motivation required to process important information.

Those educators who continue to conduct classroom "business as usual"—failing to realize that "traditional approaches to pedagogy have tended to be rigid and uncreative [and that] they are far from exhausting the wonderful possibilities for teaching and learning"—must work hard to take the classroom experience to higher heights by increasing their youth popular culture competence and, therefore, creativity. As a result, their relationships with students will be enhanced; and students will more readily enjoy their learning experience.

Summary and Conclusion

Today's youth popular culture has evolved into a phenomenon much different from what it was 40 years ago.

Unlike the days of *Ozzie & Harriet*, when youth listened to one popular radio station and looked forward to the annual school dance, many of today's youth are taking risque spring breaks at summer resorts; going to clubs that cater to adult audiences; participating in gang-related activities; surfing the Net; experiencing peer pressure to use drugs and to have sexual relationships; choosing from over 100 television channels and at least four popular radio stations; having direct access to images of pornography, violence, and drug-use live and via broadcast media; and much more. 35

Given these realities, and in order to stimulate critical thinking, influence attitudes and behaviors, and maintain the attention, curiosity, and interest of today's young generation, we need a revolution in the way that health and education-related information and messages are designed and delivered. We must supplement our traditional communication strategies with ones that are more sensitive to the worldviews of our youth.

Hip-Hop culture can be convincingly argued to be the leading force within youth popular culture nationwide. It is the pipeline for effectively communicating to and with young people. The pipeline connects to the mental, social, and cultural tenets of the vast majority of America's youth. As legendary rapper, activist, and author Chuck D puts it: for many young people Hip-Hop is their CNN.

It is my hope that this article will stimulate professional dialogue around the related issues and that all of us will focus even more thoroughly on increasing our youth popular culture competence in an effort to enhance and improve our relationships and communication targeting this very vulnerable population.

What Did You Read?

1. Name some "formal features" of our youth's popular culture?
2. How will knowledge of some of these formal features assist educators and health professionals?
3. How has hip-hop been mass marketed?

What Do You Think?

1. How are today's youth different from how they were twenty or even forty years ago?
2. How has hip-hop influenced fashion?
3. How can receptiveness to hip-hop culture increase or enhance education in the classroom?

How Was It Done?

1. In trying to itemize formal features of youth culture, is the authors' use of bulleting effective?
2. Of all the experts integrated into the support of the authors' argument, which ones in your mind were best qualified and most convincing?
3. In the conclusion, is the particular call to action relevant? Do the authors overstate the need to understand youth culture? If so, why?

The Kids Are All Right

From *The Economist*

This article from the British magazine Economist *discusses how the work environment in the United States is becoming more youth oriented. In the past, young people at work attempted to make themselves appear older in order to be taken seriously; now, being young is a distinct advantage. Companies are creating work cultures that appeal to the young, as the younger employees are considered more valuable because of their technical skills and their ability to adapt to change. Thus, younger is perceived as better to the point that older employees try to make themselves appear younger and participate in youth culture.*

Key Words

lift	elevator (British)
gravitas	high seriousness
spliff	marijuana cigarette
hierarchies	classifications of groups of people according to rank or standards
meritocracies	systems in which advancement is made by value or accomplishment
implicit	capable of being understood even though not expressed
dystopian	a world in which everything is wrong or bad; in which people live in fear or war

Youth is a time for fun and frolic, and nowhere more than in one American playground in Florida. Outside, there are basketball courts and volleyball nets. Inside, there are bright colours, Nerf guns and a talking life-size Austin Powers cut-out in the lift; in the games room, pingpong and pinball. Children of all ages run amok, from the pre-schoolers in the day-care centre to the 40-year-old vice-president with the robot collection.

This particular romper room happens to be not a school, but the offices of CapitalOne, one of America's largest credit-card firms. A decade or two ago, a big financial institution such as CapitalOne would have had all the gravitas of, well, a bank. Now the firm allocates each department a monthly "fun budget," and managers are graded on their "coaching" skills. The same sort of thing can be found across corporate America these days. The kids—in spirit, if not always in age—have taken over. It is technology that drives business today, and dot.com culture has infected everyone. The carriers of this virus are the young, who are emerging as the rising power in the workplace.

Take Microsoft, a 25-year-old business with 40,000 mostly youngish employees, where the dress code, in its entirely, is "bathe" (i.e., anything goes as long as you're clean). Extreme body piercing, shorts and blue hair abound, sometimes even in management. The only firm rules on campus are no guns and no smoking (this is America, after all). And the typical workplace scene at most dot.coms would not be tolerated at any high school or politically correct university: no-holds-barred Nerf warfare, mid-afternoon hall hockey, videogames, pumping techno on headphones, and the occasional spliff.

As the frenetic pace of today's working life blurs the distinction between personal time and work time, so it increasingly mixes up personal lifestyle and work style. And as companies concentrate on attracting and keeping a younger workforce for its technical skills and enthusiasm for change, office culture is becoming an extension of youth culture. This may be no bad thing. Along with the football table and company toy budget come things that matter more deeply to young people: opportunity, responsibility, respect. Their parents could never have hoped to enjoy those at such a tender age.

For most of human history the middle-aged have ruled. From 5 Confucian ideals to the old boys' club, maturity has almost always trumped youth. With years came wisdom, experience, connections and influence. At work, like everywhere else, grey hair, years of loyal service and seniority counted most. Now the tables are turning, maybe for good. Older workers will not disappear, or even necessarily shrink in numbers, but they will now have to share power with fresh-faced youths.

There has been nothing like this since the advent of the railroads and the "Go west, young man" spirit they created, from which rose

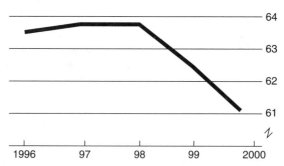

Golden not-so-oldies: Average age of the richest 400 Americans

Source: Forbes

the Rockefellers, Morgans and Carnegies. But what is happening now is, if anything, bigger: after all, the railroads were not primarily the domain of the young, as the Internet is. Don Tapscott, author of "Growing Up Digital," calls this a "generation lap": the effect, in technology at least, is not so much to level the playing field as to reverse the slope.

The Original Whizz-Kids

Generations come in waves, some of which are more favoured than others because of the vagaries of demographics, economics, business cycles, even wars. But the current rise of youth is not so much the result of a birth boom, a thriving economy or a tight labour market, although those certainly help; its main cause is a remarkable constellation of factors in the business world. It's cool.

The most dramatic of these is technology. The Internet has triggered the first industrial revolution in history to be led by the young. As it has swept through corporate America, the Internet has brought along its infantry of young things, from hard-core programmers (any computer language learnt more than a decade ago is obsolete, as are many of those who learnt it) to the young generalists to whom thinking in web terms is second nature. Virtually all American university students today have Internet access, as do more than 60% of pre-college kids in their own home. "We had the blind luck to grow up on a precipice," says Rebecca Smith, who at 23 is the number two at a fast-growing New York dot.com public-relations agency.

This is the age group that created Netscape, the first commercial web browser; Napster, the music-sharing technology that has rocked the music industry; Yahoo! and many of the other web giants. "Never trust anyone over 30," the rallying cry of the hippies, has become sage advice for any chief executive staffing his dot.com spin-out.

There have been youth revolutions before, from 20s flappers to 50s rock'n'roll to 60s radicalism, but none of them made the leap from teen bedroom to boardroom the way the Internet has. Throughout the 20th century, to enter corporate America was to leave your youth behind. You got a haircut, and probably a suit or at least a tie. Now the office cubicle is the new dorm: same hair, same clothes, even nearly the same hours. Technology has bridged the generation gap.

But not by itself. If those twentysomethings are now enjoying a warm welcome in the workplace, T-shirts and all, they have to thank the corporate restructurings of the 1980s and 90s for breaking down the traditional hierarchies. In the old days companies grew slowly and stayed on top when they got there; with success came conservative corporate values. Now corporate order can be overturned in a

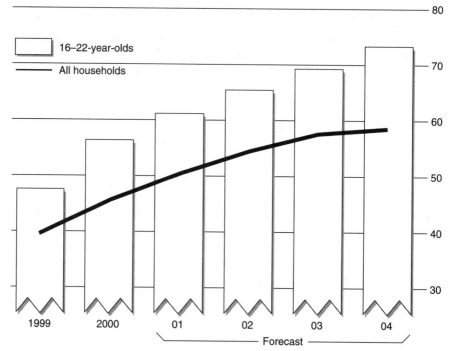

Young netheads: Online in America, %
Source: Forrester Research

financial quarter, and the world's largest firms turn on a dime. The pace of change is relentless, with no end in sight. And change favours the young: they learn and relearn faster and, unencumbered by families and mortgages, can afford to risk more to try new things.

In many companies, rigid seniority-based hierarchies have given way to meritocracies. No longer is the ability to navigate internal bureaucracies and pay dues the most valued skill. The restructuring of the past two decades has overturned the implicit corporate compact of mutual loyalty that existed as long as men wore suits. Today's fast risers do not have to spend years sucking up to their superiors, as long as they are able to understand e-business or have the naive courage to ask "why?". Corporate devotion counts for less than talent. Employees are free agents who stay only as long as they are challenged and rewarded; flitting from job to job, once a trait of fickle youth, is now an admired sign of ambition and initiative.

Not convinced? Ask yourself these questions: Will technology play more or less of a role in the future? Will business slow down, or continue to speed up? And, now that the old corporate hierarchies have been torn down, what are the chances that they will grow up again? The answers to all of these are bound to be encouraging for the young.

But the new ascendancy of the young should not conjure up some Lord-of-the-Flies vision of a dystopian future where immaturity rules. This revolution is not just about the chronologically young. Youth itself is being redefined.

We're All Young Now

Once, when you grew up you put away childish things. Today, the 35-year-old Wall Street analyst who zips to work on his push-scooter, listening to Moby on his headphones and carrying annual reports in his backpack, has far more in common with a 20-year-old than he would have done a generation ago. Then, he would probably have been married for a decade already, with children at school; his many suited years of service at the firm would have placed him mid-way up the corporate ladder. Today, it is becoming harder to find suits in Manhattan, much less corporate ladders, and both marriage and kids now come far later in life.

The old premium on maturity, from the age-based seniority of the office to the uniforms of adulthood, is disappearing. Increasingly, 35-year-olds listen to the same music as 20-year olds, dress like them, snowboard and mountain-bike like them and, thanks to hard work at the gym, even look almost like them. What with plastic surgery and anti-ageing therapies, they may be able to keep this up for many years. Ponce de Leon came to the New World looking for the fountain of perpetual youth; in exercise, antioxidants and Viagra, his spiritual descendants may have found the next best thing. Imagine a society converging on a virtual age somewhere between 20 and 30, and you have a fair picture of New York or San Francisco now, with other American cities not far behind.

But what of the rest of the world? Most of it is still nothing like this. In Japan, still held back by a decade-long economic slump, things have improved, but remain deeply frustrating for most young adults. Much of Europe, hamstrung by restrictive labour policies that have hampered corporate change, is slow to abandon its age-bound traditions of apprenticeships and corporate paternalism. And remember that most of the world's young people live in the developing world, and may never get to touch a computer in their lives.

But the time will come. If this generation of young people in Asia and Europe did not grow up with a computer in every bedroom, the next generation will. Or perhaps they will skip the computer entirely, and will instead have endless video chats with friends on pocket wireless devices. Whatever technology dominates, it is sure to change so quickly that those who have never known anything else will have the advantage, just as growing up speaking a language is much easier than learning it as an adult.

Thanks to the pressures of globalisation, the business trends that have made the workplace so receptive to the young in America are spreading to other parts of the world. That applies not just to technology, but to all the other characteristics of the new, informal office culture as well, from meritocracy to free-agentry. As a later chapter will show, different countries are progressing at different paces, but there is nowhere in the developed world—or indeed in much of the developing world—that is not already moving that way.

This survey will argue that the rise of the young is a good thing, 20 not least because it gives people at their most creative stage in life more opportunity to put their ideas and energy into practice. But there are also serious risks involved in handing the inmates the keys to the asylum.

What Did You Read?

1. How is office culture becoming an extension of youth culture?
2. Explain this statement: "The Internet has triggered the first industrial revolution in history to be led by the young."
3. What has "bridged" the generation gap?

What Do You Think?

1. If society is becoming more youth oriented or youth controlled, how will this affect older generations, including Generation X?
2. Does the Net generation encourage more meritocracy than past generations? Explain.
3. Can you identify some areas of "business" in which the youth revolution will not be embraced?

How Was It Done?

1. How well do the graphs bring home the point that younger people are claiming power?
2. In the last third of the article, is the refining of youth in America described well for the reader?
3. How well does the article contrast the youth in the country to that of other areas of the world, such as Europe or Japan?

Going to Extremes
Joan Raymond

Joan Raymond examines the phenomenon of extreme sports and their appeal to today's young people. She shows how traditional team sports, such as baseball, basketball, volleyball, and softball, are losing participants, while skateboarding, snowboarding, motorcycle jumping, and other individual sports are becoming increasingly popular. The argument is presented that the rejection of team sports is a symptom of the young's rejection of the traditional values of working together, sportsmanship, and group competition. Marketers for national brands have been quick to notice this trend, and their sponsorship of extreme sports (and their sales) has increased dramatically.

Key Words

authentic	real; actual
elusive	hard to understand; difficult to catch
aficionados	fans who are highly knowledgeable about a sport and are fervent in following it
anemic	weak; lacking interest or spirit
hardy	bold or brave; strong in spirit
kindred	a group of related individuals
diametrically	being at opposite extremes

Andrew Royal isn't your typical couch potato. The 26-year-old from Cleveland, who works two jobs to finance his new mortgage payments, rarely sits glued to the tube—even when his hometown team, the Cleveland Browns, is playing on *Monday Night Football*. But when the *X Games* or the *Gravity Games* are on, Royal not only makes time to watch, he actually schedules his day around what's on TV. "These athletes are so on the edge that it actually makes watching TV enjoyable," says Royal, who hung up his skis more than 10 years ago in favor of a snowboard. "Extreme sports are my *Monday Night Football.*"

For those who still think a half pipe is something you light up, wake up and smell the Mountain Dew. Extreme sports, once considered the sole province of the multi-pierced, tattooed slacker, have entered the mainstream. These high-intensity, individualistic sports, which involve everything from the ultrahip snowboarding to Moto-X (a strange, scary contest that has motorcyclists attempt ski jumps) have encroached upon traditional sports—especially group sports-in popularity. While *Monday Night Football*, for example, has recently struggled for an audience, viewership has steadily increased each year for such sports events as the *X Games* on ESPN and the *Gravity Games* on NBC. "These new sports are an authentic slice of the wider youth culture and not just a fad," says Harvey Lauer, president of American Sports Data, Inc. (ASD), a sports marketing research company in Hartsdale, N.Y.

This youth culture consists of some 58 million Americans between the ages of 10 and 24. Horizon Media Research in New York City estimates this group's annual buying power at more than $250 billion. That's one reason why giants such as PepsiCo, AT&T Broadband, Motorola, Ford and Morningstar Foods—and even the U.S. Marines—have focused a chunk of their marketing budgets on capturing the elusive Gen X and Gen Y male consumers, who make up the bulk of extreme sports aficionados. PepsiCo's Mountain Dew, for example, has been a sponsor of the X Games, widely considered the Olympics of the extreme sports world, and the Gravity Games. (American Demographics' corporate parent, PRIMEDIA, is part owner of the Gravity Games.)

Introduced in the 1960s, Mountain Dew was perceived as a hillbilly drink, says Dave DeCecco, spokesman for PepsiCo. That changed in 1992, when "Do the Dew" was born. The edgy ads, showing people engaged in various extreme activities, made Mountain Dew the fastest-growing soft drink of the 1990s. "The involvement was a natural extension of our advertising," DeCecco says. PepsiCo reports that the number of teens who said "Mountain Dew is a brand for someone like me" increased 10 percentage points between 1998 and 2001.

In an otherwise anemic sports-viewing market, extreme sports   5 have a hardy following. Although they can't match the numbers of *Monday Night Football,* ratings for the *X Games* and *Gravity Games* are rising—albeit from a much smaller base. *Monday Night Football* is one of the strongest sports broadcasting franchises, often ranking among the top 10 prime-time programs. But the show's standing has been declining for several years: Ratings for the ABC staple fell to an average of 12.7 percent of the nation's 100-million plus homes with televisions in 2000, and then fell to 11.5 percent in 2001, according to Nielsen Media Research. By contrast, the 2001 Gravity Games, held in Providence, R.I., averaged a 1.7 household rating—which corresponds to about 2 million households—up from 1.6 in 2000. The Winter X Games VI held in Aspen, Colo., earlier this year, resulted in record viewership for ESPN and ESPN2: The telecast on February 3, 2 P.M. Eastern time, on ESPN, scored a 1.04 rating (894,640 households), making it the highest-rated and most-watched Winter X Games telecast ever on the network. (The sports network has been televising the X Games for seven years.) Last year, the Summer X Games VII, in Philadelphia, also posted increases. In an X Games record, the 2001 event attracted an average audience of 465,905, an increase of 48 percent over the prior year.

Moreover, the demos are young and male—an elusive target group for most marketers. The 2001 Gravity Games, for instance, attracted more male viewers, 18 to 34, than any other action sports program.

Among males ages 12 to 17, the Gravity Games drew a 1.7 household rating, corresponding to more than 200,000 male teens, up from 1.2 in 2000. Among males ages 12 to 24, the games drew a 1.3 rating, nearly 320,000 males, up from 1.1 in 2000. Last year's Summer X Games had some big air too: Within the 12- to 17-year-old demographic, ratings were up 86 percent (to 0.93 from 0.50), about 219,000 boys and girls, while numbers for males ages 12 to 17 were up 72 percent (to 1.48 from 0.86), about 178,000 boys. Within the coveted 18- to 34-year-old male demographic, ratings were up 40 percent, nearly 330,000 young men (to 1.05 from 0.75). Compare those demos with baseball's median age of 46.4 or even ESPN's total-day median age of 40.7.

"This is a demographic sweet spot," says Brad Adgate, senior vice president and corporate research director at Horizon Media. "The games are an incredible success story in combining sports with entertainment while targeting a specific market. If you look at the continually increasing participation numbers in these sports, viewership is going to continue to grow. I'm an entrenched Baby Boomer, and even I know who Tony Hawk is."

For those who don't, Tony Hawk is the undisputed god of skateboarding, the most famous alternative athlete of all time. He's the guy who took the skateboard out of the closet, placing it into the hands of an estimated 8 million boys and girls, ages 7 to 17. Indeed, skateboarding, snowboarding and wakeboarding are among the fastest-growing alternative sports in the U.S., according to the 14th annual Superstudy of Sports Participation, conducted by ASD, which surveyed 14,772 Americans nationwide.

Snowboarding—once the stepchild of the ski slopes—now claims 7.2 million participants, up 51 percent from 1999. The kindred activities of skateboarding and wakeboarding surged 49 percent and 32 percent, respectively (to 11.6 million and 3.5 million participants). The subgenre of "board" sports thus gets a clean sweep of the top three growth positions among all alternative sports. This has occurred as membership in team sports is declining. Participation in baseball is down 28 percent since 1987, to 10.9 million players. Basketball declined by 5 percent in 2000 and 17 percent from its 1997 peak. Since 1987, involvement in softball and volleyball has plunged by 37 percent and 36 percent, respectively.

ASD's Lauer says that part of the growth spurt in extreme sports 10 stems from a rejection of the traditional values reflected in team sports, like working together, character-building and group competition. Alternative sports, he points out, are "rooted in a diametrically opposite set of values," including fierce individualism, alienation and defiance. But as Maria Elles, ESPN X Games marketing manager says: "You don't have to have a tattoo to like an action sport. The athletes are really setting the trends."

On the Edge . . . of Their Seats

Three out of five U.S. kids and teens (61 percent) watch extreme sports on TV, more than the number who watch most other sports. Those living in the West are the most likely of all to tune in to extreme TV.

Sports Watched	Total	Northeast	Midwest	South	West
Olympics	84%	90%	89%	80%	81%
NFL football	80%	78%	83%	81%	75%
NBA basketball	71%	62%	76%	72%	72%
Baseball—major/ minor	63%	68%	64%	64%	57%
Extreme sports/ X Games	61%	64%	61%	58%	66%
College football	60%	54%	61%	67%	51%
Basketball—men's college	57%	48%	57%	64%	48%
Professional wrestling	50%	47%	47%	60%	38%
Gymnastics	48%	45%	48%	50%	47%
Soccer	47%	40%	50%	46%	52%
Auto/motorcycle racing	46%	40%	49%	47%	45%
Ice skating	46%	53%	48%	42%	41%
Boxing	44%	28%	39%	55%	43%
Swimming/ diving	43%	47%	42%	44%	39%
NHL hockey	41%	51%	41%	37%	38%
Tennis	34%	32%	31%	40%	26%
Skiing	31%	29%	33%	30%	31%
Basketball—women's college	30%	31%	27%	35%	22%
Basketball—WNBA	29%	28%	25%	33%	29%
Golf	27%	31%	27%	24%	28%

Source: The Amateur Athletic Foundation of Los Angeles, ESPN Inc., and Statistical Research, Inc.

Wherever bleeding-edge athletes go, marketers are sure to follow. As a firsttime X Games sponsor last year, Hershey's was looking for a spot to sample its new single-serve Hershey's Milk. According to Patty Herbeck, marketing director for Dallas-based Morningstar Foods, which markets' the Hershey's product, the X Games sponsorship fit into the company's overall sports marketing initiative targeting 16- to 19-year-olds. Hershey's ran spots, on ESPN during the X Games—the first national advertising campaign for the product. It then followed up with print ads in *ESPN The Magazine* and an on-site sampling campaign that "was bang for the buck," says Herbeck, citing that demand for samples was so high that Hershey's couldn't keep enough milk on site during the games.

With all the emphasis on all things extreme, isn't there a chance that the buck-convention status the sports enjoy will soon be as appealing to the young male demographic as cricket? In any sport, there are the mainstream and then the core enthusiasts, who set the standard and push the envelope. If extreme sports start to lose the "how did they do that?" factor, the hard-core fan will simply "set another standard, which will then trickle down to the mainstream," says Bill Carter, the 33-year-old president of Fuse Integrated Marketing, a Burlington, Vt.-based company which designs sponsorship programs for marketers.

But Carter is confident that it will be a while before the mainstream demands more than big backside air, with frontside air, along with a McTwist and an Indy grab. "A lot of viewers of snowboarding don't have a clue about the names of the tricks," says Carter. "What they see on television are elite athletes who are doing something that nobody's ever done before. And when it comes to these kinds of athletes, that's not going to change."

What Did You Read?

1. How many Americans are there between the ages of 10 and 24?
2. What are extreme sports? How popular are they with youth culture? Name some extreme sports.
3. According to Raymond, why are people attracted to these alternative sports?

What Do You Think?

1. Do you believe that most hard-core fads of something (hiphop, body piercing, etc.) will eventually "trickle down to the mainstream"?
2. What happens often to the purity of something when it goes mainstream? Provide examples.
3. Why is interest in traditional sports fading?

How Was It Done?

1. Does most of the evidence in this piece come from marketing spokespeople from large companies? Why?

2. Does the chart at the end provide powerful support that Extreme Sports/X Games are growing in popularity?
3. Are there sufficient statistics to substantiate that X Games are re-defining entertainment and marketing?

Habla English?

Rebecca Gardyn

Rebecca Gardyn discusses Hispanic youth and how they differ from other young people today and from the Hispanic youth of the past. She says that today's Hispanic youth are more comfortably bilingual than any previous generation of Hispanics; they resist assimilation into the mainstream culture, yet they move comfortably through it as well. Not only are today's young Hispanics bilingual and bicultural, but also they have held on to their cultural values, including maintaining a strong family orientation. Advertisers wishing to reach young Hispanics must recognize that these young people want to have the best of both worlds—and they see little contradiction in that.

Key Words

renowned	famed; highly honored
discontent	unhappiness
niche	a specialized market
mainstream	the prevailing current of activity or influence
assimilated	absorbed into a culture
differentiation	expressing specific distinguishing characteristics
optimize	to make as effective as possible
nuances	subtle distinctions

When Spanish-language cable station Galavision launched two week-day prime-time blocks of bilingual programs last spring, the move provoked some controversy. Galavision's parent company, Univision, the Spanish-language broadcast network targeted at Hispanic adults, is renowned for its strict ban on English-language programming and advertising messages. When the new shows initially aired, several long-time viewers called in to express their discontent. But as a cable station, Galavision had the freedom to reach out to what it perceived to be a growing yet ignored niche: bilingual and bicultural Hispanic youth.

Hispanics under the age of 18 constitute one of the largest and most complex demographics in the nation. Unlike their parents and grandparents, who felt compelled to, at least publicly, melt into the

American pot, this generation of consumers—representing 35 percent of all Hispanics—wants the best of both worlds. As a result, the Spanish-only media channels that keep their parents entertained and informed are not always enough, and marketing to them in their own language no longer means simply translating general market strategies into Español. More culturally relevant media vehicles and advertising messages, better media planning, and bigger budgets are a must for any marketer trying to build brand loyalty with tomorrow's "mainstream" consumers, as those consumers are and will increasingly be of Hispanic origin.

By 2005, Hispanic youth will overtake blacks to become the largest ethnic youth population accounting for 17 percent of all those under age 18, and 45 percent of all minority minors in the U.S. This segment is helping to fuel the growth of the entire youth market: By the end of the decade, 1 kid in 5 will be Hispanic, amounting to a 22 percent increase in nine years, while during the same period, the proportion of white youth will experience a decrease of 5 percent. In fact, in several top urban markets—breeding grounds for consumer trends—Hispanic kids and teens already constitute the majority: 58 percent of the under-20 crowd in Los Angeles are Hispanic, and their share is expected to reach 80 percent by 2003.

While all kids and teens today are hard to reach, with the ever-growing assortment of media channels at their disposal, Hispanic youth are even more difficult to target. Unlike their non-Hispanic counterparts, more than three-quarters of them are bilingual, and thus they have another set of media to consume—the Spanish-language media. "When you talk about targeting today's youth, there's all this talk about marketing to their individuality," says Daisy Exposito, president of the Association of Hispanic Advertising Agencies (AHAA) and of The Bravo Group, Young & Rubicam's Hispanic shop. "For young Latinos, their bilingualism is a huge part of their individuality."

One of the biggest misperceptions about U.S. Hispanic teens, says 5 Olivia Llamas, project director of the Yankelovich Hispanic MONITOR, is that they will eventually be completely assimilated into American culture, in language, social habits, and media consumption, and become indistinguishable from their general market counterparts. In fact, a look at the top five English-language TV programs and magazines for Hispanic teens (aged 12 to 17) and kids (aged 6 to 11) matched against their white counterparts reveals little differentiation. In any given week, for instance, the No. 1 show for both Hispanic and white teens is *The Simpsons*, capturing 41 percent and 31 percent respectively, according to Simmons Market Research. Similarly, the No. 1 magazine perused by Hispanic and white kids is *Nickelodeon* magazine, capturing 23 percent and 20 percent of each group. These comparisons can be misleading, however. "Marketers think that eventually

they will only need to advertise in English in order to reach U.S. Hispanic youth," says Llamas. "But what we are finding is the opposite,
they're not losing that language or culture."

On the contrary, they are increasingly embracing it. Fifty-four percent of U.S. Hispanic teens identify themselves as "Hispanic Only" or
"More Hispanic than American." Another 36 percent perceive themselves as being equally grounded in both cultures, according to TNS
Market Development. Only 6 percent consider themselves "more
American than Hispanic," and just 4 percent say they are "American
only."

While their elders are still much more likely to prefer Spanish to
English in all aspects of their lives, including media consumption,
there has been a significant jump in Spanish-language preference
among Hispanic youth in recent years. Twenty-nine percent of 16-to
24-year-olds say they prefer Spanish, up from 23 percent in 1997, according to the MONITOR. And even though 45 percent of this group
prefers English, 65 percent still watch Spanish-language TV—for an
average of 1.7 hours per day—and 59 percent listen to Spanish-
language radio.

So while reaching the adult Hispanic population is a no-brainer—
an ad on Univision or Telemundo usually does the trick—reaching
today's Hispanic youth can cause some serious headaches. "For the
18- to 49-year-old Hispanic group, we go directly to Spanish-language
media," says Graziella Flathers, media planning supervisor at Hispanic ad agency Bromley Communications, in San Antonio. "But
when targeting Hispanic youth, you can't make any assumptions."

Flathers had her work cut out for her last spring when she began
to develop the Hispanic youth media plan for her client, The American
Legacy Foundation, a Washington, D.C.-based organization established to reduce smoking as part of the 1998 settlement against major
tobacco companies. By conducting extensive research and analysis of
ratings data for individual programs, she found that WWF Smack-
down, in English, on UPN, delivered a huge chunk of their target audience. The show reaches about 35 percent of all Hispanic teens in any
given week, according to Simmons. Flathers also found that in many
of the top 10 markets, the three most popular radio stations for Hispanic teen delivery were in English. And yet, according to a recent
analysis by Starcom Worldwide, 9 of the top 15 rated shows among
Hispanic teens are on Univision, and thus Spanish TV also needed to
be included. "For an advertiser to be effective with today's Hispanic
youth market, he needs to be everywhere they are, and with a message
that is relevant to them, both in Spanish and in English," says Monica
Gadsby, senior vice president and director of Hispanic media for Starcom. Advertisers targeting the general youth market should also take
note: The inclusion of Spanish-language TV in teen-targeted schedules
will not only optimize delivery of Hispanic teens, but will increase a

plan's total teen-market reach by as much as 4 to 5 percentage points, according to Starcom's analysis.

Media planning and buying may start to get a little easier, thanks 10 to a slew of new media vehicles aimed at reaching this group. In addition to Galavision's bilingual programming efforts, the past year was filled with English-language cable stations launching new youth-oriented shows with Hispanic themes and characters. In February, the FOX Kids Network premiered Los Luchadores, a kids' adventure series that has characters such as Lobo Fuerte and an eyepatch-wearing villain Chihuahua. Nickelodeon also launched three new programs this season: The Brothers Garcia, Dora the Explorer, and Taina, all of which feature Hispanic kids as main characters. And SITV, an English-language, 24-hour cable network devoted to Latino-themed programming, is expected to launch this fall. While Bromley's Flathers is still taking a wait-and-see attitude toward SITV, she has high hopes. "It's not something I would jump into headfirst, but I'm anxious to see what happens," she says. "Whenever there are new opportunities to reach this youth market, we're all on the edge of our seats. The options today are very limited."

In addition to new program content, major TV networks are giving marketers options in the form of more flexible advertising policies. Last September, for what is thought to be the first time ever, CBS accepted Spanish and bilingual ads during their prime-time broadcast of the Latin Grammy Awards. Adding fuel to the trend, in January, Nickelodeon became the first major English-language cable network to accept bilingual advertising during regular programming. Chuck E. Cheese's, the child-oriented pizza and entertainment chain, owned by CEC Entertainment, was the first advertiser to bite. But considering that the network attracts 66 percent of all Hispanic children aged 2 to 11 each month, or about 4 million, others are expected to follow.

That is, of course, if they can afford it. The out-of-pocket costs for English-language media tend to be about 10 times more than for Spanish-language media, so buying it on a traditional Hispanic marketing budget (which is often pennies compared with general market dollars) may be a problem for some companies. "Just to buy English local radio in the top 10 markets could eat up Hispanic dollars for a year," says Flathers. And since reaching the segment and getting through to them are two different things, more production money will be needed to develop relevant creative that speaks to them, regardless of language.

Unlike prior generations, messages targeted to today's Hispanic teens do not have to be in Spanish to be understood. But marketers who use the language in their ad messages may reach them on a more emotional level. The California Wellness Foundation's "Get Real About Teen Pregnancy" print campaign series, called "The Word," did just that. Each execution featured one Spanish word, in bold, at the top

We Are the World

Ethnic kids and teens are fueling growth in the youth market.

(Under Age 18)	2001	2010	2020	2030	% Change (2001–2030)
Total Youth	71.0 mil	72.5 mil	77.6 mil	83.4 mil	+18%
Hispanic*	11.3 (16%)	13.7 (19%)	17.2 (22%)	21.0 (25%)	+85%
Non-Hispanic White	45.2 (64%)	42.7 (59%)	42.4 (55%)	42.3 (51%)	−6%
Non-Hispanic Black	10.7 (15%)	11.3 (16%)	12.2 (16%)	13.2 (16%)	+24%
Asian/Pacific Islander	3.2 (5%)	4.0 (6%)	5.0 (7%)	6.1 (7%)	+94%
Other Non-Hispanic	0.7 (1%)	0.7 (1%)	0.8 (1%)	0.9 (1%)	+27%

(in millions, % of total youth)
Percentages may not equal 100 due to rounding.
*Hispanics can be of any race
Source: *U.S. Census Bureau; calculations by American Demographics.*

Read All About It

Hispanic teens are 120 percent more likely than the average U.S. teen to peruse *Shape* magazine.

Top Five English–Language Magazine Titles, by Index*

Hispanic Teens (12 to 17)	Index	Hispanic Kids (6 to 11)	Index
Shape	220	Thrasher	145
InStyle	161	Totally Fox Kids	134
Beckett Sports Collectibles	153	Child Life	132
Jump	149	Children's Playmate	118
GamePro	134	Disney Adventures	114

*An index of 100 is the national average.
Source: *Simmons Market Research, Spring 2000.*

of each ad, for instance: "Educacion," "Salud," "Futuro," while the rest of the text, explaining the problem of teen pregnancy, was in English. "We know that most of these teens, and the policymakers we're trying to target, speak English, but we wanted to do something to connect to their roots and grab their attention," says Dawn Wilcox, public educa-

Latin America

From 1998 to 2003, the fastest-growing Hispanic youth population will be in the Dallas-Fort Worth area, where the share of Hispanic kids and teens will increase 21 percent.

Total Hispanic Youth, 1998–2003 (Aged 0 to 19, by Metro Area), in Millions.

	1998	2003	% Change
Los Angeles	2.48	2.78	12%
New York	1.18	1.33	12%
Chicago	0.48	0.55	13%
San Francisco/Oakland/San Jose	0.47	0.52	12%
Houston	0.44	0.52	18%
Miami	0.36	0.43	19%
San Antonio	0.31	0.36	15%
Dallas-Fort Worth	0.31	0.37	21%
San Diego	0.28	0.32	13%
El Paso	0.21	0.25	16%

Source: TGE Demographics, 1998; Marketing to American Latinos *by M. Isabel Valdes.*

A Family Affair

Hispanic teens tend to watch Spanish television with their parents and English television with their siblings or friends.

Percentage of Hispanic Teens Who Say They Usually Spend Time Watching TV with . . .

	Spanish TV	English TV
Mom or dad	62%	21%
Brothers or sisters	23%	64%
Other adults in the home	11%	2%
Friends	9%	17%

Source: Starcom Worldwide's Kidscope Study.

tion director for the campaign and vice president of Ogilvy Public Relations Worldwide.

But speaking their language isn't necessarily about language at all, it's about being "in-culture," a term coined by Hispanic marketing strategist Isabel Valdes, co-chair and partner of Santiago & Valdes

Solutions, in Newport Beach, California. Valdes identifies core values among Hispanic youth that set them apart from their general market counterparts, such as Familismo, or a strong family orientation, which influences how they use and respond to media. For instance, Hispanic teens are more likely to watch television with their parents than non-Hispanic teens "at least some of the time" (46 percent vs. 35 percent) and "most of the time" (18 percent vs. 12 percent), according to Starcom Worldwide's Kidscope study. And 50 percent of Hispanic teen girls and 27 percent of teen boys say they admire their mother more than anyone else in their lives, according to TNS Market Development.

Being "in-culture" with today's youth is something with which 15 most marketers and traditional Hispanic ad agencies have little experience. That's why Roberto Ramos launched Ruido Group, a Hispanic-youth-focused communications agency in New York City, last fall. Ramos' first project, a bilingual TV, print, and radio effort for the Office of National Drug Control Policy, will launch in September. It will attempt to tap into kids' sense of Familismo, not to mention good old-fashioned guilt. The theme: If you do drugs, you're letting down your immediate family and friends.

In addition to promoting core Hispanic values in their marketing, Ramos also stresses that businesses need to pay more attention to the nuances that separate youth from different countries, and capture those cultural, religious, and idiomatic differences in their messages when targeting specific geographic locales. Fifty-four percent of Hispanics in the MONITOR, for example, say they feel there are, some important differences between themselves and other Hispanic groups. "For many clients, knowing about these differences is not necessarily to guide them in targeting, but in trying to avoid mistakes," says the MONITOR's Llamas. Marketers who want to use soccer in all their Hispanic-targeted advertising, for example, need to wake up. "Soccer may work for some, but on the East Coast, most Hispanics are from the Dominican Republic and Cuba, where baseball is king."

As Hispanic youth become a bigger portion of the American pie, the group will need to be sliced in ways that better resemble the segmentation of the general market, in which ads are targeted more to interests, lifestyles, and attitudes. Indeed, experts expect that the overall diversity of America's youth—already 36 percent of all children are of a race or ethnicity other than white—will force market segments not only within the Hispanic, black, Asian, and other ethnic communities, but across them. The use of "attitude" or "psychographic" research to define those new boundaries will take on a larger role in market research, creative execution, and media buys in the future, experts say.

"Hispanics, and other ethnic kids, have multiple categories for themselves," says Ben Gervey, a psychologist and a director at Applied

Research & Consulting in New York City, which conducts attitudinal research. "They may consider their Hispanic heritage as being more or less central to their identity, but it is not their only identity, and they shouldn't be marketed to as if it is."

What Did You Read?

1. What percentage of today's youth is Hispanic? Is this percentage increasing or decreasing? Is the percentage of white youth increasing or decreasing?
2. What is one of the biggest misconceptions about U.S. Hispanic teens?
3. For an advertisement to be effective with today's Hispanic youth market, what must advertisers do?

What Do You Think?

1. How do you think knowledge about one's culture helps advertisers and promoters of certain kinds of social policy (e.g., anti-drug messages)?
2. How will the growing percentage of younger minorities force advertisers and businesspeople to be much more conscious of everyone's individuality?
3. Do you think it is a good idea for TV networks to accept more Spanish and bilingual ads? Why?

How Was It Done?

1. How is the appeal to statistics in the beginning of the article particularly powerful? What does it articulate about Hispanic youth?
2. If you had to crystallize the concept of this article in one word, what would it be? Why?
3. What values does this article center itself on? Do these values of the target group, Hispanic youth, surprise you at all?

9

Biographies

Can we get to know history by knowing people? Some individuals seem to embody their time periods: what they experienced and what they produced in their work have come to be seen as symbols of their own eras. Other people changed the times, with the force of an idea, an invention, or even a personality. Looking at the lives of important individuals is one way a reader can learn about the past, and in so doing, also learn about the present. After all, while from the present-day perspective everything about the past seems orderly and neat— we know what happened next—in our present time we lack such foreknowledge. However, by seeing how others lived their lives, we can at times see models of how to live our own.

In this chapter on biographies of famous people, the Writing Lesson addresses historical analysis. As distinct from other types of analysis, historical analysis requires careful attention to research, to avoid the myths, prejudices, and biases that may have been picked up over time. Writing about history and historical persons requires a certain discipline, to avoid the tendency to give information without understanding, and to avoid one-source research that does little more than repeat what has already been written. The Writing Assignment then gives you the chance to write about a historical figure or the study of history itself.

THE MAIN EVENT READING

Out West

Andrew Jay Hoffman

The famous American novelist and humorist known as Mark Twain was born and raised as Samuel Clemens. Born in 1835 and raised in Hannibal, Missouri, Clemens started working as a printer's apprentice when he was still a boy. Later, he worked as a riverboat pilot on the Mississippi, and in 1862, he moved to Virginia City, Nevada, then a thriving boomtown, thanks to the discovery nearby of gold and silver. Clemens worked as a reporter in this Wild West town, and from this experience he learned not only about the people of the west, but also of his own skill at writing imaginative works. This talent would later pay off in the classic works of Mark Twain, such as The Adventures of Tom Sawyer, The Adventures of Huckleberry Finn, Roughing It, The Prince and the Pauper, *and* A Connecticut Yankee in King Arthur's Court. *This excerpt is from the biography* Inventing Mark Twain.

Key Words

terraced	rows of houses put onto a hillside
hierarchy	classification of groups of people according to ability, wealth, or social standing
burgeoning	flourishing; expanding rapidly
tribute	payment given as an acknowledgment of submission
entrepreneurs	people who organize and assume the risk of a business
brigands	people who live by stealing; thieves
gentry	upper or ruling class
Bohemians	people who live an unconventional life, usually in a colony with others
hoax	trick intended to accept as real something that is fake or fictional
petrified	converted into stone
squib	a short, humorous, or satiric writing or speech

Virginia City was the West's most prominent boomtown. It was a strange and violent place. Not quite five years old in 1862, Virginia boasted more than forty thousand residents. Set into the side of Mount Davidson, the streets of the city terraced the hillside and gave a physical manifestation to its social hierarchy. C Street, the main commercial road, led south to neighboring Gold Hill and north to the Henness Pass route to San Francisco. Farther up the hill on A and B streets lived

the wealthy and respectable. D Street offered bars, whorehouses, and
plan of city other amusements for the hardworking miners. Below that were
slums, then Chinatown, and at the bottom of the hill the Indians who,
it was said, lived off the white man's trash. No one planned cross
streets for this burgeoning metropolis; people literally and figuratively
clawed their way up chance alleys from the depths toward A Street.
Virginia City was San Francisco's far-flung counterpart. San Francisco
money built Virginia City, and Virginia City sent back as much as $20
million a year in tribute. The goal of every miner was to have a house
on Nob Hill; the A Street mansions merely provided luxurious way
stations until their residents could live well in San Francisco.

Local lore held that the first twenty-six graves in the Virginia City
dangerous cemetery were occupied by murdered men. The search for sudden
town wealth had turned these entrepreneurs from the settled states to the
east into desperate and marginal creatures. The major mines—the
Ophir, the Gould and Curry, the Spanish or Mexican, and a few others—operated around the clock, as did the enormous and noisy ore
mills just outside of town. After twelve hours of scraping rock out of a
hole in the ground, the miners needed raucous fun, so the saloons and
brothels never closed. A panorama of prostitutes plied the streets, from
the raging siren "Buffalo Jo" Dodge, who physically attacked rivals in
public, to the refined madam Julie Bulette, who brought Paris fashions
to the Nevada desert. Among the men, disagreements often ended in
blood, unless they involved mining money, in which case they went
into the courts. (There were over three hundred lawsuits during Sam's
first year in Virginia.) The murders received little notice from newspapers or from the law. Sam interrupted a letter to his mother with "I
have just heard five pistol shots down the street—as such things are in
my line, I will go and see about it." He concluded the tale in a second
postscript: "5 A.M.—The pistol did its work well—one man . . . shot
two of my friends, (police officers), through the heart—both died
within three minutes." The murderer, Missourian John Campbell, es-
connection caped. Virginia City's untamed quality came straight from San Fran-
to San cisco, which had established a vigilance committee in 1856 to force its
Francisco brigands out of town. By 1860, San Francisco had shipped its dark and
violent recklessness inland and rebuilt itself as a cosmopolitan city of
100,000 people; when San Francisco could no longer afford despera-
does, it provided the money to build Virginia City for them.

The town's unique birth resulted in an odd mix of democracy and
aristocracy. Everyone smoked and drank, but what you smoked or
drank defined your social position—cigarettes for the Mexicans, fine
pipes for the gentry. Entertainment included several theaters and several more hurdy-gurdy houses, with rowdy music and dancing girls.
The rich settled their differences with pistols as commonly as did ruffi-
ans, but the elite observed the rules of dueling—involving challenges,
seconds, and rhetorical indignity—while the lower classes simply shot

one another. Duels exacted more legal retribution in Virginia City than did outright murders. People from all strata mixed freely, and the myth that a sudden find could elevate a filthy prospector to social eminence kept snobbery to a minimum.

The *Territorial Enterprise* gave Sam a partial immunity from the violence of Virginia City; he was a witness to the scene, a commentator on it, not an actor in it. He found the culture at the *Enterprise* uplifting and gratifying. His fear that returning to newspaper work would mean another period of servitude proved false. Writers at the *Enterprise* saw themselves as a desert outpost of cosmopolitan Bohemians, whose challenge to traditional values created a stir in New York and San Francisco. Joe Goodman, Rollin Daggett, Dan De Quille, and Steve Gillis showed him how to wash the miner's dirt from his hands and replace it with printer's ink. Writing all together at one long and broad wooden table, the reporters at the *Enterprise* did not even have to leave to eat, since the paper's Chinese cook tossed bowls of oriental cuisine in front of them. Dan showed Sam, who had never reported regularly, what constituted news for the paper, while Joe set the journalistic standards. After they put the paper to bed for the night, the staff headed to their favorite establishment, a D Street brewery that sold beer at a dollar a gallon and served it with platters of Limburger cheese, radishes, and mustard. [Clemens's status]

The facts and figures of the mining beat bored Sam—he'd had enough of holes in the ground during his four months in Esmeralda— but Dan De Quille's fanciful sketches, which he called "quaints," intrigued him. Dan, at thirty-three the old man on the paper, had a kindly, gentle manner both personally and in print, and people appreciated and admired even his most outrageous hoaxes. One article, titled "The Travelling Stones of Pahrangat Valley," minutely detailed the mysterious and random movements of some boulders in the Nevada desert. When newspapers around the country and around the world reprinted the article without qualification, it created a scientific stir. Sam loved hoaxes, and hardly three weeks into his tenure he wrote "The Petrified Man," reporting that a corpse had been found "in the mountains south of Gravelly Ford," as petrified as the rock around it. Judge Sewall, who had annoyed Sam during his brief stay in Humboldt, rushed to the spot to hold an inquest. Sam's description of the deceased hid the clues to the hoax: "The body was in a sitting posture . . . the attitude was pensive, the right thumb resting against the side of the nose; . . . the right eye was closed and the fingers of the right hand were spread apart." The petrified man was thumbing his nose at his readers, but few editors noticed and the squib found gullible audiences in newspapers hundreds of miles away. Sam confessed to his brother that the story was "an unmitigated lie, made from whole cloth. I got it up to worry Sewall. Every day, I send him some California paper containing it." Sam discovered from the episode his awesome journalist's power. For the first time in his life, [humorous pose] he had colleagues who could help him develop his imagination and literary skills.

What Did You Read?

1. Describe Virginia City in 1862. Why would this be an exciting place for a young reporter to live?
2. How did being a reporter help shield Clemens from some of the violence of Virginia City?
3. What is the point of Clemens's story of the Petrified Man?

What Do You Think?

1. Explain what the author means when he says that Virginia City provided an "odd mix of democracy and aristocracy"?
2. What is the idea of Bohemianism, and how does that connect to the life that Clemens led at this time?
3. As Mark Twain, Clemens would later be the author of many popular books, including *Tom Sawyer* and *Huckleberry Finn*. How did life in Virginia City help prepare Clemens to be a novelist?

How Was It Done?

1. Why is it that Mark Twain (Clemens) isn't mentioned in this five-paragraph excerpt until the fourth paragraph?
2. If you divided the article into two parts, how would you identify each part?
3. Identify the piece of evidence or example that demonstrates Mark Twain's ability to satirize, be imaginative, and be humorous.

THE MAIN EVENT WRITING ASSIGNMENT

Using multiple sources, write an essay in response to one of the following assignments:

1. Analyze one particular time or episode in a historical person's life and determine how it relates to the larger historical context. Then show how that time period is reflected in the person's work. This may include political, social, legal, economic, religious, or other contexts.
2. How does reading a biography humanize history? Be specific.
3. Do you think most people's great success has hinged on one event, situation, or even choice? Cite specific examples.

4. Choose a historical figure and argue whether that person embodied his or her time, or changed it. Be specific.

5. Do most great people somehow transmute great pain or anxiety into great art or great accomplishments? Be specific.

PREPARATION PUNCH LIST

Before you begin writing the essay, you need to prepare yourself to write. Jot down some notes on what you know in general. You may want to consider some of the following suggestions.

1. Pick a historical person. Read about that person. Look up biographies and criticisms of that person's work.

For example: Bill Blass, Frida Kahlo, or Samuel Clemens

2. Pick a particular time period of interest in that person's life.

For example, Bill Blass in his war years; Frida Kahlo during her tempestuous marriage with Diego Rivera. Samuel Clemens during his years as a reporter in Virginia City, Nevada.

3. Examine what was going on in the world at that same time that had a profound effect on that person.

World War II for Bill Blass

The uncertain aftermath of the Mexican Revolution and the sweep of left-wing ideologies for Frida Kahlo.

For Samuel Clemens, the settlement of the west by Americans searching for wealth; also, the Civil War.

4. Connect those years to the person.

For Bill Blass, serving in World War II gave him a sense of freedom and camaraderie. It gave him a feeling that he could negotiate and navigate the world.

For Frida Kahlo, the radical left-wing politics of her age influenced her relationship with Rivera and the larger art world.

Samuel Clemens found his writing voice in the exaggerated stories of the Wild West.

5. How did this profound change or effect translate itself into the accomplishments or art of the individual?

Bill Blass found himself able to negotiate among the men of the world as a confident person who could accommodate and absorb the average yet style-conscious American.

Frida Kahlo produced powerful art that translated her emotional states—painting herself bleeding, weeping, and cracked open. Her art provides a statement of the sexual power of her relationship.

Sam Clemens created vignettes that were excellent preparation for the immortal characters he created in his books, *Tom Sawyer* and *Huckleberry Finn*.

6. Can we determine something about a historical time frame by looking at a person and what he or she did?

In the case of Bill Blass, it reveals both the inherent optimism of the post-war time period and the celebration of classical forms.

For Frida Kahlo, her feminism and socialism inform her art by empowering her to express her pain in dramatic and forceful ways.

For Samuel Clemens, the time period became his subject matter for decades, contributing to the mythology of the American West, a mythology still at work to this day.

THE MAIN EVENT WRITING LESSON: HISTORICAL ANALYSIS

Analyzing history requires you to use many of the same critical thinking skills that are used in writing about other subjects. However, sometimes writers fall into certain bad habits when writing about history, so keep the following ideas in mind:

- **Have a point.** A common mistake is to write about history as a plot summary. (Someone did this, then he did this, then he did this, and so on.) Instead, make sure that your writing leads to a point or thesis. The whole idea of historical analysis is to have an insight into your subject, not merely repeat a list of well-known or documented events.

- **Understand the bigger picture.** People do not exist in isolation, but rather within a large number of contexts, including political, social, economic, legal, and religious contexts. These contexts are not merely external factors: they are part of the fabric of life in which historical persons existed. No one avoids them or lives outside of them anymore than someone can live without oxygen. Even Ishi, the last known "wild" Native American, had context— including the fact that he was the very last of his kind.

- **Use multiple references or sources for your research.** Understanding the bigger picture may mean consulting a number of different sources so that you can better understand all of these contexts. Some texts may address only certain contexts, such as a war, while ignoring other happenings of a less dramatic yet important nature.

  Also, historians, biographers, and other writers have different assumptions and preconceptions that they bring to their work, and these influence their writings. Indeed, one instructive exercise can be to examine biographies of the same person written in different eras, and see how attitudes about that person have changed over time.

- **Document your materials carefully.** Any time you do research, you must document your findings. In historical analysis, this is especially important so that a reader can determine what facts and inferences are your own, and which ones are from other sources. The reader will also want to know about the sources you used to double-check the quality of the research.

    Most historians use the documentation system based on the *American Psychological Association Handbook* (or APA) in their professional papers. This documentation system is unfamiliar to many students of English, who learn the *Modern Language Association Handbook* (or MLA) system. While this text uses the MLA system for documenting research in all its sample essays, both systems are described in two appendixes to this text. Use the system your instructor prefers.

THE MAIN EVENT WRITING SAMPLE

The following is an essay written for this text in response to the Main Event Writing Assignment, Question #1.

Mark Twain: Samuel Clemens in the Wild West

In 1862, in Virginia City, Nevada, a young man by the name of Samuel Clemens went to work for the *Territorial Enterprise*. This young man, who eventually became famous as Mark Twain, had already worked as a printer's apprentice and a riverboat pilot on the Mississippi. During this time, the Civil War was raging. In August 1862, while Clemens was in Nevada, Confederate troops defeated Union troops at the second Battle of Bull Run. Clemens was certainly not the only young man not to be serving either side in the war, but as one of the most well known American writers ever, Clemens's stance on the war and the conditions of the west as he found them are of special interest. This is especially important since his most famous works, *The Adventures of Tom Sawyer* and *The*

Adventures of Huckleberry Finn, memorialized and, at times, idealized the image of life in the United States before the war. Samuel

Thesis   Clemens's experiences in Virginia City helped him become one of America's greatest writers and humorists because there he learned how to write with imagination and humor, observed the darker aspects of human nature, and learned to integrate humor and cynicism.

Clemens in the Civil War
Having left for Nevada the year before, Clemens was no longer part of the war. He had served a mere two weeks as a volunteer in the Confederate army (Neider 11). Despite Clemens's failure to help, 1862 was for the most part a good year in the war

The state of the war in 1862
for the Confederacy. In June, Robert E. Lee took command of the Army of North Virginia. Besides the victory at the second Battle of Bull Run, Confederate forces also defeated the Union at Cedar Mountain, Virginia; Harper's Ferry, Virginia; and Fredericksburg, Virginia. Lee also crossed the Potomac and began an invasion of Union territory. President Abraham Lincoln issued the Emancipation Proclamation in September 1862. However, while these important events were occurring, little is known about what Clemens actually said or did. He was from Missouri, which was a slave state and had seceded from the Union; the Nevada Territory and the nearby state of California were aligned with the Union. Interestingly, in 1864 (by which time Clemens had moved to San Francisco), San Francisco was "teeming with men in their twenties

Clemens was not very political
who had declined to die for the Union cause" (Hoffman 92). At best, it can be said that Clemens had no strong political feelings one way or the other, and thus removed himself from the war.

What Virginia City was like
Later, though, his stance on slavery would be clearer.

In 1862, Virginia City was booming, and the source of the boom was silver. Slightly more than a decade earlier, the California

Gold Rush had induced thousands to come west in search of their fortunes. Once California's rush settled down, Nevada became the place for miners. According to Phyllis Zauner, author of *Virginia City: Its History . . . Its Ghosts,* in 1859 two prospectors found gold and "heavy black stuff," which turned out to be silver (8). Once the word was out, miners were flocking to stake claims. Warren Hinckle and Frederick Hobbs state that the mines outside Virginia City

Origins of the Silver Rush

> changed the face of the west, enriched the North in the Civil War, built San Francisco into a Pacific Paris, laid the Atlantic cable, founded the Hearst newspaper empire . . . and fattened the lean meat of the American dream with the carbohydrate of success stories about lumpen mining stock speculators who struck it rich. . . . (vii–viii)

The men who came to Virginia City were of the roughest sort; indeed, it was said that San Francisco had virtually pushed their criminal element out of the city and out to Virginia City, and in return, Virginia City gave San Francisco its wealth (Hoffman 72). Virginia City was the embodiment of today's image of an old west town: murders, duels, and bar fights were everyday occurrences. Legend had it, repeated by Twain himself, that the first twenty-six graves in the Virginia City cemetery were for murdered men. (Twain 76). If one were looking for a true center of life in North America away from the Civil War in 1862, one would surely have looked at Virginia City.

Rough and tumble Western town

Virginia City provided an excellent opportunity for Samuel Clemens to become Mark Twain. What the west provided Clemens with were two things: subject matter and audience. According to his biographer, Andrew Jay Hoffman, Clemens had come to Nevada with his brother, Orion, in 1861 after the Union troops had essentially shut down the Mississippi (63). His brother had received a political position with the new governor in charge

Clemens goes west

of the Nevada territory, so Sam went with him to Carson City, the capital. Sam tried prospecting, struck it rich, and then lost all of his money (Geismar 2, 26). Sam sent in a few pieces to the *Territorial Enterprise* under the pseudonym "Josh." These were largely "fron-

Clemens as a reporter tier sketches" (Hinckle and Hobbs 75). He was offered a job. Clemens stayed for about two years, and during his time working as a reporter, he was exposed to a rough and violent life. He wrote that a man wasn't considered to be much until he had "killed his man" (Twain 76). The town provided a reporter with the opportunity for plenty of stories. It was during this time that Clemens

Becomes Mark Twain took on the pen name "Mark Twain," which according to Hoffman was given to Clemens because he frequently ordered that two drinks be put on his tab in the local saloon, as in "mark two drinks." In addition to the real life happenings, Clemens and his cohorts printed hoaxes. Some of these hoaxes were humorous, but some did not consider others funny, such as a short piece that insulted the honor of the women in Carson City (Hinckle and

Flees from a duel Hobbs 76–77). Eventually, Clemens had to flee Virginia City for California because so many Carson City husbands had threatened to challenge Clemens to a duel (Hoffman 89). However, by that time, Clemens had already established himself as Mark Twain, the great western humorist.

Importance of experience to Twain's writing Virginia City had a profound impact on the work of Samuel Clemens as Mark Twain. Twain's book *The Jumping Frog of Calaveras County and Other Sketches* came out just two short years after the end of the Civil War (Hoffman 121). These stories sprang from the exaggerated humor of the west that he had learned in Nevada;

Importance of Roughing It its success was said to have "put all of New York in a roar. It was voted the best thing of its day" (qtd. in Hoffman 101). The travel book *Roughing It* showed the eastern audience what life in the west was like, a life that was dirty, violent, passionate, dangerous, and most of all, different from civilization on the east coast. Twain was on his way. His fame and success would last for the rest of his life, during which time he would write the works today's audiences read more frequently, including *Tom Sawyer* and *Huckleberry Finn*. While in these books children are the central characters, the world around them is cruel and violent. In fact, violence and cruelty are consistent undercurrents in much of Twain's writings. Especially in *Huckleberry Finn,* with its murderers, con-men, drunkards, and cowards, human beings are exposed as deeply flawed, incompetent, and at times evil creatures. In an important moment in the novel, Huck decides that he'll help Jim escape slavery. Of this decision, he says, in a twist of the expectation of good and evil: "All right, then, I'll go to hell" (169). In Huck's mind, *Huck* freeing a slave was wrong, although he was determined to do it. In *rejects slavery* the Civil War, Clemens had volunteered to serve the Confederacy, yet had held no strong convictions on slavery. By the time of his writing *Huckleberry Finn,* his writing clearly shows a condemnation of the institution of slavery. As Huck says in a later passage, "Human beings *can* be awful cruel to one another" (182). Twain's sensitivity to human cruelty can be traced back at least in part to *sensitivity to human* his exposure to the great violence of the west. *cruelty*

Samuel Clemens found his literary name and voice in the cold mountain town of Virginia City during the height of the Civil *Conclusion* War. To say that without this experience Mark Twain would never have existed is to state the obvious; the nature of that voice, one that was concerned about the human condition, but deeply pessimistic about human nature, reflects the experiences of Clemens at a time in the west when the rule of law was only a second or even third thought. The Mark Twain created in the 1860s, and the works Twain later created, have deeply enriched American literature.

Works Cited

Geismar, Maxwell. *Mark Twain: An American Prophet.* Boston: Houghton, 1970.

Hinckle, Warren, and Frederic Hobbs. *The Richest Place on Earth: The Story of Virginia City and the Heyday of the Comstock Lode.* Boston: Houghton, 1978.

Hoffman, Andrew Jay. *Inventing Mark Twain: The Lives of Samuel Langhorne Clemens.* 1997. London: Phoenix, 1998.

Neider, Charles, ed. *The Travels of Mark Twain.* New York: Coward-McCann, 1961.

Twain, Mark. *Adventures of Huckleberry Finn.* Ed. Sculley Bradley, et al. 2nd ed. New York: Norton, 1977.

Twain, Mark. "At Home: Virginia City." Neider 74–86.

Zauner, Phyllis. *Virginia City: Its History Its Ghosts.* Sonoma: Zanel, 1998.

ADDITIONAL READINGS

It's Going to Happen

James Wallace and Jim Erickson

Possibly the richest man in the world today, Bill Gates is both much admired and much hated. As the successful leader of Microsoft, he has played a huge role in the personal computer revolution. Starting his company at a time when, for most people, computers meant large, unyielding, and comparatively slow machines, his software company created products that, used with a personal computer, helped bring computers into everyday people's workplaces, schools, and homes. More importantly, Gates saw the importance of software as the driving force of the computer revolution. His phenomenal success has made him much admired, but also hated and despised by those who oppose him and his aggressive business practices. In this passage from Hard Drive, *the authors take a look at what kind of young man Gates was when he was first beginning his college years at Harvard.*

Key Words

mystique	an air or attitude of mystery
conjured	summoned as if invoked by magic
rarefied	related to a select group
algorithms	step-by-step procedures for solving a problem, especially by computer

Bill Gates would later tell a friend he went to Harvard University to learn from people smarter than he was . . . and left disappointed.

He had arrived in Cambridge in the fall of 1973 with no real sense of what he wanted to do with his life. Although he listed his academic major as prelaw, he had little interest in becoming a lawyer like his father. Nor did his parents have any expectations that he would. There was no pressure on him to be this or that. They only insisted he go to college and mix with other students. And what better environment for their son than Harvard, America's oldest institution of higher learning? There was a mystique about the place. It conjured up images of success, power, influence . . . greatness. Supreme Court justices went to Harvard. So did presidents. Now their son had ascended into this rarefied intellectual atmosphere. Any plans he had to form a software company with Paul Allen would have to wait, his parents insisted.

"I was always vague about what I was going to do, but my parents wanted me to go to undergraduate school," Gates said. "They didn't want me to go start a company or just go do graduate work. They didn't have a specific plan in mind, but they thought I should live with other undergraduates, take normal undergraduate courses . . . which is exactly what I did."

At Harvard, most first-year students live in dormitories in and near what is known as the Yard, next to Harvard Square in Cambridge. The Yard is the center of what was the original college, founded in 1636, just 16 years after the Pilgrims landed at Plymouth. At the end of their first year, students can apply to live in twelve residential houses.

Gates was assigned to one of the dorms his freshman year and 5
roomed with two other students, Sam Znaimer and Jim Jenkins. They had been assigned the same room by chance. They didn't know each other. The three came from vastly different backgrounds and cultures—just the kind of environment Gates' parents were hoping for. Gates was a rich white kid from Seattle. Znaimer was a poor Jewish kid from Canada whose parents had immigrated to Montreal after the Holocaust. He was attending Harvard on a scholarship, majoring in chemistry. Jenkins was a middle-class black kid from Chattanooga, Tennessee, whose father was in the service.

"I found Bill fascinating," recalled Znaimer, who today is a venture capitalist in Vancouver, British Columbia. "I had not run into too many people from fairly affluent, WASP backgrounds. I didn't know those kinds of people in Montreal. Bill was someone who came from a comfortable family and had gone to a private school. He would talk about how some governor of the state of Washington used to hang out with his grandfather . . . which was not the world I was used to. On the other hand, Bill was very down-to-earth. There was not a lot of bullshit or pompousness about him. We all lived more or less the same lifestyle. We all ate together, worked together, and as a group we were all interested in science, engineering and that kind of stuff. We also all loved science fiction."

When he enrolled at Harvard, Gates received permission to take both graduate and undergraduate courses. That was not unusual for gifted students. What was unusual was that he was allowed to set aside those graduate-level courses in math, physics, and computer science and apply the credits toward a graduate degree later. "About two-thirds of my courses were toward my undergraduate degree and about a third were set aside for my graduate degree, although it all doesn't matter now since I didn't complete either one," said Gates.

That first year he took one of Harvard's most difficult math courses, called "Math 55." Almost everyone in the class had scored a perfect 800 on the math portion of the Scholastic Aptitude Test. Gates did well in the course, but he was not the best. Two other students finished ahead of him, including Andy Braiterman, who lived in the same dorm as Gates. Braiterman had entered Harvard as a sophomore. He and Gates became good friends and later roomed together.

Gates took the typical undergraduate courses in economics, history, literature, and psychology. His attitude toward class work was much the same as it had been at Lakeside. He worked hard and did well in those courses he cared about. He didn't work hard in courses that didn't interest him. However, he still did well because he was so smart. In Greek literature his freshman year, Gates fell asleep during the final exam but still managed to receive a "B" in the class. "He was really very proud of that," recalled Braiterman. "It was a story he liked to tell on himself."

That Gates would fall asleep in class was not surprising. He was 10 living on the edge. It was not unusual for him to go as long as three days without sleep. "How he coped with lack of sleep I never figured out," said Znaimer. "I would kind of wimp out after 18 to 24 hours, but his habit was to do 36 hours or more at a stretch, collapse for ten hours, then go out, get a pizza, and go back at it. And if that meant he was starting again at three o'clock in the morning, so be it."

His sleeping habits were just as bizarre. Gates never slept on sheets. He would collapse on his unmade bed, pull an electric blanket over his head and fall asleep instantly and soundly, regardless of the hour or activity in his room. (Gates still falls asleep instantaneously. When he flies, he often puts a blanket over his head and sleeps for the entire flight.)

"He didn't seem to pay much attention to things he didn't care about, whether it was clothes or sleep," said Znaimer.

To his roommates and the small group of students he hung out with, Gates was a very intense character. He would often work himself into a frenzy of energy and start rocking back and forth, head in his hands, during a conversation or while reading or concentrating on a mental problem. Sometimes, he would wave his arms madly about to make a point in conversations.

Much of this energy was directed toward computers, just as it had been at Lakeside. Although Gates may not have decided what he was going to do with his life when he entered Harvard, to those who knew him there was little doubt about his real passion. He worked for weeks during his first year there on a BASIC program for a computer baseball game, which required that he figure out highly complex algorithms that would represent figures on the computer screen hitting, throwing, and catching a baseball. Even when he was sound asleep under his electric blanket, Gates was dreaming about computers. Once, about three o'clock in the morning, Gates began talking in his sleep, repeating over and over again, "One comma, one comma, one comma, one comma . . ."

He spent many nights that year in the Aiken Computer Center at 15 Harvard, which also had a PDP-10. Znaimer would sometimes drop by the computer building and find Gates hacking away at one of the machines. There were several games on the computers, including Steve Russell's "Space Wars," and Gates and Znaimer would play computer games into the early morning hours.

To unwind and relax, Gates, Znaimer, and Braiterman would go to movies in Cambridge or play pinball in an upstairs lounge in their dorm. The lounge also had an early version of the video game "Pong." (This game had been designed by Nolan Bushnell, and it made him rich and famous. He sold the game through his startup company, Atari.)

As usual, when it came to games the competitive Gates almost always won. He became an exceptional player at both pinball and "Pong."

"Other than playing pinball and going to a lot of movies," said Znaimer, "we were all doing our share of sex, drugs and rock 'n' roll . . . with the exception that the rest of us were more overwhelmed by our hormones than Bill. I don't remember him chasing any women, and there were lots of opportunities."

No one who knew Gates at Harvard can recall him ever dating anyone while he was there. He did see one young woman occasionally when he returned home on holiday breaks to Seattle, but they were not romantically involved. The woman was Karen Gloyd, a freshman at Whitman College in Washington State. Gloyd was a couple years younger than Gates, having entered college early, at age 16. They met through their parents. Her stepfather was on the state bar association's board of governors, as was Gates' father. Gates did not make a very good impression on Gloyd. He lacked the social graces a young lady would have expected of a Harvard man. It was clear to Gloyd that Gates had had little experience with women. The first thing he wanted to know when they met was the score she made on her college SAT.

"It didn't strike me as being a great pickup line at the time," re- 20 called Gloyd, now married. "It's kind of amusing looking back on it, but at the time I really wasn't that amused. I thought maybe I hadn't heard him right. I thought it rather odd to say the least." Gates then proceeded to explain to Gloyd that he had taken his Scholastic Aptitude Test twice so he could make a perfect score of 1600. (Math and verbal scores each count a maximum of 800 points.) Gates told her that when he first took the test, he breezed through the math portion but made a silly mistake and ended up with 790 points. The second time he took the test he got a perfect math score of 800. "At that point in the conversation," said Gloyd, "I assumed we had very little in common."

They did see each other a few more times. Once, when both were home from college, they accompanied their fathers on a bar association trip to Friday Harbor in the scenic San Juan Islands. Gloyd and several other young people on the trip took off in their parents' cars and went into town at night to dance and party. Gates, however, stayed behind and played poker with the adults.

"Bill and I played tennis together a few times, but we really didn't have much in common socially," said Gloyd. "I always thought he was really nice, but I just thought he was sort of a brain, and I was more into partying, sororities, and that kind of thing. Bill was real shy. I didn't get the impression at the time that he had a lot of experience dating girls and going out and doing social things. I may have thought of him then as being nerdy, but I think he just didn't want to spend a lot of time doing things he wasn't interested in."

Although Gates may not have had much experience with girls, he did have experiences of another kind that set him apart from many of his peers at Harvard. He had already been out there in the "real world." He even had his own company, Traf-O-Data.

"That was one of the more interesting things about Bill," said Znaimer. "Compared to the rest of us at Harvard, he was much more broadly grounded. You could find other people who were really good mathematicians or really good physicists. But Bill had a lot more hands-on experience. He had gone and worked in various environments, like TRW."

Znaimer remembered Gates spending several nights in his dorm 25 room in early 1974 working on an IRS tax return for his Traf-O-Data business. "I could not have told you which way was up on a tax form. It was something my parents did," Znaimer said. "But Bill sure knew."

What Did You Read?

1. What kind of socioeconomic background did Gates come from?
2. Why did Gates's parents choose to send him to Harvard?
3. What is Gates's favorite story from his college days?
4. In what ways was Gates a typical college student? In what ways was he not?

What Do You Think?

1. Do you agree that broadly grounded people (i.e., people who have worked in a variety of environments) tend to be more successful than those who are very good at just one thing? Explain.
2. Do you think Gates fits the profile of the typical genius or not?
3. What were some of Gates's personality traits that were evident in college that would later help him to be successful leading Microsoft? Be specific.

How Was It Done?

1. Besides Bill Gates, the article centers on what individuals?
2. What examples or anecdotes are offered to support the idea that computers were always Gates's passion?
3. How many connections are made in the development of this piece between Gates's Harvard years and who he is now. Identify them.

Prologue

Edmund Morris

Taking office in 1901, Theodore Roosevelt was the youngest man ever to become president. Roosevelt had been a political maverick: a young Republican from a wealthy New York family who opposed the political machines that dominated both parties at that time. His foes had essentially tried to "hide" him by making him vice president (and ending his service as governor of New York), but after the assassination of William McKinley, this robust president became a political force like no other president had been for decades. Roosevelt had a charismatic personality, which he was able to use to galvanize public support for his positions. He made brilliant use of the press, so his political enemies could not work against him without exposing themselves to criticism. His presidency saw a great expansion of the power of the United States on the international scene. He was a popular and respected president, to such a degree that his face is one of only four carved onto Mount Rushmore. This excerpt is taken from the biography, The Rise of Theodore Roosevelt.

Key Words

sincerity	honesty
linguists	scholars who study the nature of language
novel	new; different
virtuoso	expert
mirth	laughter; fun; humor
raconteur	an excellent storyteller
inimitable	not able to be imitated
roan	hair having a base color, such as red, brown, or black, which is lightened by white hairs
seismic	related to an earthquake

No Chief Executive has ever had so much fun. One of Roosevelt's favorite expressions is "dee-lighted"—he uses it so often, and with such grinning emphasis, that nobody doubts his sincerity. He indeed delights in every aspect of his job: in plowing through mountains of state documents, memorizing whole chunks and leaving his desk bare of even a card by lunchtime; in matching wits with the historians, zoologists, inventors, linguists, explorers, sociologists, actors, and statesmen who daily crowd his table; in bombarding Congress with book-length messages (his latest, a report on his trip to Panama, uses the novel technique of illustrated presentation); in setting aside millions of acres of unspoiled land at the stroke of a pen; in appointing struggling poets to jobs in the U.S. Treasury, on the tacit understanding they are to stay away from the office; in being, as one of his children humorously put it, "the bride at every wedding, and the corpse at every funeral."

He takes an almost mechanistic delight in the smooth workings of political power. "It is fine to feel one's hand guiding great machinery." Ex-President Grover Cleveland, himself a man of legendary ability, calls Theodore Roosevelt "the most perfectly equipped and most effective politician thus far seen in the Presidency." Coming from a Democrat and longtime Roosevelt-watcher, this praise shows admiration of one virtuoso for another.

With his clicking efficiency and inhuman energy, the President seems not unlike a piece of engineering himself. Many observers are reminded of a high-speed locomotive. "I never knew a man with such a head of steam on," says William Sturgis Bigelow. "He never stops running, even while he stokes and fires," another acquaintance marvels, adding that Roosevelt presents "a dazzling, even appalling, spectacle of a human engine driven at full speed—the signals all properly set beforehand (and if they aren't, never mind!)." Henry James describes the engine as "destined to be overstrained perhaps, but not as yet, truly, betraying the least creak . . . it functions astonishingly, and is quite exciting to see."

At the moment, Roosevelt can only be heard, since the first wave of handshakers, filing through the Red Room into the Blue, obscures him from view. He is in particularly good humor today, laughing heartily and often, in a high, hoarse voice that floats over the sound of the band. It is an irresistible laugh: an eruption of mirth, rising gradually to falsetto chuckles, that convulses everybody around him. "You don't smile with Mr. Roosevelt," writes one reporter, "you shout with laughter with him, and then you shout again while he tries to cork up more laugh, and sputters, 'Come, gentlemen, let us be serious. This is most unbecoming.'"

Besides being receptive to humor, the President produces plenty of 5 it himself. As a raconteur, especially when telling stories of his days among the cowboys, he is inimitable, making his audiences laugh until they cry and ache. "You couldn't pick a hallful," declares the cartoonist Homer Davenport, "that could sit with faces straight through his story of the blue roan cow." Physically, too, he is funny—never more so than when indulging his passion for eccentric exercise. Senator Henry Cabot Lodge has been heard yelling irritably at a portly object swaying in the sky, "Theodore! if you knew how ridiculous you look on top of that tree, you would come down at once." On winter evenings in Rock Creek Park, strollers may observe the President of the United States wading pale and naked into the Potomac, followed by shivering members of his Cabinet. Thumping noises in the White House library indicate that Roosevelt is being thrown around the room by a Japanese wrestler; a particularly seismic crash, which makes the entire mansion tremble, signifies that Secretary Taft has been forced to join in the fun.

Mark Twain is not alone in thinking the President insane. Tales of Roosevelt's unpredictable behavior are legion, although there is usually an explanation. Once, for instance, he hailed a hansom cab on Pennsylvania Avenue, seized the horse, and mimed a knife attack upon it. On another occasion he startled the occupants of a trolleycar by making hideous faces at them from the Presidential carriage. It transpires that in the former case he was demonstrating to a companion the correct way to stab a wolf; in the latter he was merely returning the grimaces of some small boys, one of whom was the ubiquitous Quentin.

Roosevelt can never resist children. Even now, he is holding up the line as he rumples the hair of a small boy with skates and a red sweater. "You must always remember," says his English friend Cecil Spring Rice, "that the President is about six." Mrs. Roosevelt has let it be known that she considers him one of her own brood, to be disciplined accordingly. Between meetings he loves to sneak upstairs to the attic, headquarters of Quentin's "White House Gang," and thunder up and down in pursuit of squealing boys. These romps leave him so disheveled he has to change his shirt before returning to his duties.

A very elegant old lady moves through the door of the Blue Room and curtsies before the President. He responds with a deep bow whose grace impresses observers. Americans tend to forget that Roosevelt comes from the first circle of the New York aristocracy; the manners of Gramercy Park, Harvard, and the great houses of Europe flow naturally out of him. During the Portsmouth Peace Conference in 1905, he handled Russian counts and Japanese barons with such delicacy that neither side was able to claim preference. "The man who had been represented to us as impetuous to the point of rudeness," wrote one participant, "displayed a gentleness, a kindness, and a tactfulness that only a truly great man can command."

Roosevelt's courtesy is not extended only to the well-born. The President of the United States leaps automatically from his chair when any woman enters the room, even if she is the governess of his children. Introduced to a party of people who ignore their own chauffeur, he protests: "I have not met this gentleman." He has never been able to get used to the fact that White House stewards serve him ahead of the ladies at his table, but accepts it as necessary protocol.

For all his off-duty clowning, Roosevelt believes in the dignity of 10 the Presidency. As head of state, he considers himself the equal, and on occasion the superior, of the scepter-bearers of Europe. "No person living," he curtly informed the German Ambassador, "precedes the President of the United States in the White House." He is quick to freeze anybody who presumes to be too familiar. Although he is resigned to being popularly known as "Teddy," it is a mistake to call him that to his face. He regards it as an "outrageous impertinance."

What Did You Read?

1. Roosevelt is compared to a "high-speed locomotive." What are some of the characteristics shared by the two?
2. Why does one of his friends say, ". . . the President is about six"?
3. What was the advantage of being from "the first circle of New York society"?

What Do You Think?

1. Is it important for presidents to have a charismatic personality in order to serve effectively? Explain.
2. The author emphasizes Roosevelt's great energy. In what ways can such energy not be a benefit but a problem?

3. Is the emphasis on the personalities of politicians good or bad for this country? Explain.

How Was It Done?

1. The article centers on what basic description of Theodore Roosevelt?
2. The evidence provided by the authors to support his character descriptions comes in the form of what?
3. How are quotations used effectively in substantiating explanations? Who speaks them?

Outside the Slaughterhouse

Theodora Kroeber

By the start of the 20th century, the westward expansion of the European Americans was over. The frontier was closed in 1893, and the Native American tribes had been decimated by decades of warfare with the United States Army, as well as hunger, disease, and despair. Survivors had been removed to reservations. However, in 1911, a "wild man" showed up at a slaughterhouse in Oroville, California. Ishi, as this man became known, was the last surviving member of a small tribe, called the Yahi. His story is a link to a past on this continent that is gone forever. This excerpt is taken from Ishi in Two Worlds.

Key Words

roused	awakened
emaciated	made thin and weak from hunger
poncho	a blanket with a slit in it so that it can be slipped over the head and worn as a sleeveless garment
unwonted	out of the ordinary
diffidence	distrust; reserved and unassertive
lurid	sensationalistic
indifferent	without care or concern
subjected	brought under control; being forced to endure something

The story of Ishi begins for us early in the morning of the twenty-ninth day of August in the year 1911 and in the corral of a slaughter house. It begins with the sharp barking of dogs which roused the sleeping butchers. In the dawn light they saw a man at bay, crouching against the corral fence—Ishi.

They called off the dogs. Then, in some considerable excitement, they telephoned the sheriff in Oroville two or three miles away to say that they were holding a wild man and would he please come and take him off their hands. Sheriff and deputies arrived shortly, approaching the corral with guns at the ready. The wild man made no move to resist capture, quietly allowing himself to be handcuffed.

The sheriff, J. B. Webber, saw that the man was an Indian, and that he was at the limit of exhaustion and fear. He could learn nothing further, since his prisoner understood no English. Not knowing what to do with him, he motioned the Indian into the wagon with himself and his deputies, drove him to the county jail in Oroville, and locked him up in the cell for the insane. There, Sheriff Webber reasoned, while he tried to discover something more about his captive he could at least protect him from the excited curiosity of the townspeople and the outsiders who were already pouring in from miles around to see the wild man.

The wild man was emaciated to starvation, his hair was burned off close to his head, he was naked except for a ragged scrap of ancient covered-wagon canvas which he wore around his shoulders like a poncho. He was a man of middle height, the long bones, painfully apparent, were straight, strong, and not heavy, the skin color somewhat paler in tone than the full copper characteristic of most Indians. The black eyes were wary and guarded now, but were set wide in a broad face, the mouth was generous and agreeably molded. For the rest, the Indian's extreme fatigue and fright heightened a sensitiveness which was always there, while it masked the usual mobility and expressiveness of the features.

It should be said that the sheriff's action in locking Ishi up was   5
neither stupid nor brutal given the circumstances. Until sheriff Webber took the unwonted measure of keeping them out by force people filled the jail to gaze through the bars of his cell at the captive. Later, Ishi spoke with some diffidence of this, his first contact with white men. He said that he was put up in a fine house where he was kindly treated and well fed by a big chief. That he would eat nothing and drink nothing during his first days of captivity Ishi did not say. Such was the case; nor did he allow himself to sleep at first. Quite possibly it was a time of such strain and terror that he suppressed all memory of it. Or he may have felt that it was unkind to recall his suspicions which proved in the event groundless, for Ishi expected in those first days to be put to death. He knew of white men only that they were the murderers of his own people. It was natural that he should expect, once in their power, to be shot or hanged or killed by poisoning.

Meanwhile, local Indians and half-breeds as well as Mexicans and Spaniards tried to talk to the prisoner in Maidu, Wintu, and Spanish. Ishi listened patiently but uncomprehendingly, and when he spoke it was in a tongue which meant no more to the Indians there than to the whites.

The story of the capture of a wild Indian became headline news in the local valley papers, and reached the San Francisco dailies in forms more or less lurid and elaborated. The story in the *San Francisco Call* was accompanied by a picture, the first of many to come later. In another newspaper story, a Maidu Indian, Conway by name, "issued a statement" that he had conversed with the wild man. Conway's moment of publicity was brief since the wild man understood nothing of what he said.

These accounts were read by Professors Kroeber and Waterman, anthropologists at the University of California, who were at once alerted to the human drama behind the event and to its possible importance, the more particularly because it recalled to them an earlier episode on San Nicolas Island, one of the Channel Islands of the Pacific Ocean some seventy miles offshore from Santa Barbara.

In 1835, the padres of Mission Santa Barbara transferred the San Nicolas Indians to the mainland. A few minutes after the boat, which was carrying the Indians, had put off from the island, it was found that one baby had been left behind. It is not easy to land a boat on San Nicolas; the captain decided against returning for the baby; the baby's mother jumped overboard, and was last seen swimming toward the island. Half-hearted efforts made to find her in subsequent weeks were unsuccessful: it was believed that she had drowned in the rough surf. In 1853, eighteen years later, seal hunters in the Channel waters reported seeing a woman on San Nicolas, and a boatload of men from Santa Barbara went in search of her. They found her, a last survivor of her tribe. Her baby, as well as all her people who had been removed to the Mission, had died. She lived only a few months after her "rescue" and died without anyone having been able to communicate with her, leaving to posterity this skeletal outline of her grim story, and four words which someone remembered from her lost language and recorded as she said them. It so happens that these four words identify her language as having been Shoshonean, related to Indian languages of the Los Angeles area, not to those of Santa Barbara.

Another reason for the anthropologists' particular interest in the 10 wild man was that three years earlier, in 1908, some surveyors working a few miles north of Oroville had surprised and routed a little band of Indians. After hearing of this incident, Waterman with two guides had spent several weeks in an unsuccessful search for the Indians: the wild man of Oroville might well be one of them.

On August 31, 1911, Kroeber sent the following telegram: "Sheriff Butte County. Newspapers report capture wild Indian speaking language other tribes totally unable understand. Please confirm or deny by collect telegram and if story correct hold Indian till arrival Professor State University who will take charge and be responsible for him. Matter important account aboriginal history."

The sheriff's office must have confirmed the report promptly: Waterman took the train to Oroville the same day. That he and Kroeber correctly "guessed" Ishi's tribe and language was no *tour de force* of intuition. The guess was based on field work with Indians all up and down California; they knew that Oroville was adjacent to country which formerly belonged to the Yana Indians; presumably the strange Indian would be a Yana. He might even be from the southernmost tribe of Yana, believed to be extinct. If this were true, neither they nor anyone so far as they knew could speak his language. But if he were a Northern or Central Yana, there were files of expertly recorded vocabularies for those dialects from two old Yanas, Batwi, called Sam, and Chidaimiya, called Betty Brown.

With a copy of Batwi's and Chidaimiya's vocabularies in his pocket, Waterman arrived in Oroville where he identified himself to Sheriff Webber and was taken to visit the wild man. Waterman found a weary, badgered Indian sitting in his cell, wearing the butcher's apron he had been given at the slaughter house, courteously making what answer he could in his own language to a barrage of questions thrown at him in English, Spanish, and assorted Indian from a miscellaneous set of visitors.

Waterman sat down beside Ishi, and with his phonetically transcribed list of Northern and Central Yana words before him, began to read from it, repeating each word, pronouncing it as well as he knew how. Ishi was attentive but unresponding until, discouragingly far down the list, Waterman said *siwini* which means yellow pine, at the same time tapping the pine framework of the cot on which they sat. Recognition lighted up the Indian's face. Waterman said the magic word again; Ishi repeated it after him, correcting his pronunciation, and for the next moments the two of them banged at the wood of the cot, telling each other over and over, *siwini, siwini!* . . .

Ishi was the last wild Indian in North America, a man of Stone 15 Age culture subjected for the first time when he was past middle age to twentieth-century culture. He was content that it should be so, participating as fully as he could in the new life. Before examining more closely those astounding few years and what one Stone Age man contributed in so short a time to our understanding of man as such, let us go back to the years of childhood, young manhood, and middle age— almost a whole lifetime. These were years spent by him without experience or understanding of a way of life other than that of a tiny fugitive band of fewer than a dozen souls at most, opposing their ancient Yahi skills and beliefs to an unknown but hostile outside world.

There came the time—months, perhaps two or three years before August, 1911—when Ishi was the only one remaining of the little band, violence from without, old age and illness from within, having brought death to the others.

Ishi's arrival at the slaughter house was the culmination of unprecedented behavior on his part. A few days earlier, without hope, indifferent whether he lived or died, he had started on an aimless trek in a more or less southerly direction which took him into country he did not know. Exhaustion was added to grief and loneliness. He lay down in the corral because he could go no farther. He was then about forty miles from home, a man without living kin or friends, a man who had probably never been beyond the borders of his own tribal territory.

What Did You Read?

1. Why did Ishi come in from the wild into the "white man's world"?
2. Why were anthropologists particularly interested in Ishi?
3. How did the media contribute to the treatment of Ishi?
4. What was the mutually understood word that enabled Waterman to begin communicating with Ishi?

What Do You Think?

1. Does reading the biography of Ishi make you more sympathetic to the plight of Native Americans today? Why or why not?
2. Does the author's use of the word "wild" unfairly characterize Ishi?
3. How does understanding the Indians of North America help to the understanding of our own history?
4. What is the significance of being the last person of one's own race or tribe?

How Was It Done?

1. Most of the article is structured around what event?
2. The concluding three paragraphs identify Ishi as what?
3. The evidence provided in this article, including the information about Professors Kroeber and Waterman as well as information about Indians in California, is all based on what? Explain.

Portraits of a Marriage

Hayden Herrera

Frida Kahlo is one of the most famous artists of the 20th century, yet her personal life history is perhaps as interesting as the art she created. Kahlo had an explosive, intense, and passionate marriage to muralist Diego Rivera. Not only their art, but also their high-profile left-wing politics caused them to gain international notoriety. These two Mexican artists fought with each other, took other lovers, separated, and reunited while at the same time producing art that is vibrant, evocative, and enjoyed to this day. This excerpt is taken from Frida.

Key Words

escapades	adventures, frequently running counter to conventional morality
eccentricities	odd behaviors
condoned	pardoned or overlooked; excused behavior
imperiousness	domineering; commanding
deities	gods
vicissitudes	changes or fluctuations in life; difficulties and hardships in life
limner	someone who creates outlines of figures; paints on a surface
symbiotic	intimate living together of two different beings; a cooperative relationship
clods	lumps of mud or dirt
panorama	a comprehensive presentation of a subject
contagious	able to spread a disease

Years after Frida and Diego died, friends remembered them as "sacred monsters." Their escapades and eccentricities were beyond the petty censurings of ordinary morality; not simply condoned, they were treasured and mythologized. As for being "monsters," the Riveras could harbor Trotsky, paint paeans to Stalin, build pagan temples, wave pistols, boast of eating human flesh, and carry on in their marriage with the vast imperiousness of Olympian deities. By the 1940s, Diego, of course, was an ancient myth. Frida, on the other hand, was new to mythic stature, and during this decade their myths meshed.

After the remarriage, while the bond between Frida and Diego deepened, so did their mutual autonomy. Even when they lived together, Diego's absences were frequent and long. Both had love affairs: his were open, hers (with men) she continued to keep secret because of his wild jealousy. Not surprisingly, their life was full of violent battles followed by bitter separations and tender reconciliations.

Starting with the "wedding portrait" of 1931, Frida recorded the vicissitudes of her marriage. The various paintings that show her and Diego together, or that include Diego only by implication—for example, in tears on Frida's cheeks—reveal the extent to which the Riveras' relationship changed with the years even while certain underlying realities remained constant. *Frida and Diego Rivera*, 1931; *Self-Portrait as a Tehuana*, 1943; *Diego and Frida 1929–1944*, 1944; *Diego and I* and *The Love Embrace of the Universe, the Earth (Mexico), Diego, Me and Señor Xolotl*, both 1949, all express Frida's great love and need for Rivera. Tellingly, he connects with her in a different way in each painting. In the earliest, the wedding portrait, their relationship is a little stiff. Like figures in a double portrait by a folk limner, they face forward, rather than toward each other. This, together with the large sliver of space between them and the light clasp of their hands, makes the couple appear like new partners who have not yet learned the elaborate, interlocking steps of the marriage dance. By contrast, in the 1943 *Self-Portrait as a Tehuana*, Frida's obsessive love for her unpossessable husband has made her trap his image in her forehead in the form of a "thought." One year later, in *Diego and Frida 1929–1944*, she has intertwined herself so closely with Diego that their faces form a single head—a symbiotic state that is clearly not a comfortable, harmonious union. In *Diego and I*, Frida's despair over Rivera's philandering is almost hysterical; his portrait is lodged in her forehead, but he himself is elsewhere, and Frida seems to be strangling in the swirl of her own hair—a woman drowning in solitude. When she painted *The Love Embrace*, she still wept, but the relationship appears to have found some resolution; Frida holds Diego in an embrace rather than a stranglehold. Whereas in the 1931 marriage portrait Frida played a daughterly role, and in 1944 the couple seem to have achieved, if not mutuality, at least a more or less matched battle, in *The Love Embrace* Frida finally possesses Diego in the way that presumably worked out best for them both—he is a big baby lying contentedly in her maternal lap.

The Riveras had much in common: humor, intelligence, Mexicanism, social conscience, a bohemian approach to life. But the greatest bond may have been their enormous respect for each other's art. Rivera took pride in his wife's professional successes and he admired her growing artistic mastery. He would tell people that before he or any of his colleagues had had a painting hung in the Louvre, Frida had had that honor, and he loved to show her off to friends. One visitor recalls that the first thing Rivera did when she met him was to say that she must meet Frida. "There is no artist in Mexico that can compare with her!" Rivera said, beaming. "He immediately told me that when he was in Paris, Picasso had taken a drawing by Frida, looked at it for a long time, and then said: 'Look at those eyes; neither you nor I are capable of anything like it.' I noticed that in telling me this his own bulging eyes were shining with tears."

Expounding on Frida's genius, Rivera would say, "We are all clods 5 next to Frida. Frida is the best painter of her epoch." In his 1943 article "Frida Kahlo and Mexican Art," he wrote: "In the panorama of Mexican painting of the last twenty years, the work of Frida Kahlo shines like a diamond in the midst of many inferior jewels; clear and hard, with precisely defined facets." Frida was, he said, "the greatest proof of the renaissance of the art of Mexico."

Frida reflected the compliment back to Diego. To her, Diego was the "architect of life." She listened to his stories and theories with amused skepticism, sometimes interjecting, "Diego—it's a lie," or bursting out with her contagious belly laugh. When he talked she often made odd little movements with her hands. These were signals to let his listeners know what was true and what was false in his conversation. In her "Portrait of Diego," she wrote:

> His supposed mythomania is in direct relation to his tremendous imagination. That is to say, he is as much of a liar as the poets or as the children who have not yet been turned into idiots by school or mothers. I have heard him tell all kinds of lies: from the most innocent, to the most complicated stories about people whom his imagination combined in fantastic situations and actions, always with a great sense of humor and a marvelous critical sense; but I have never heard him say a single stupid or banal lie. Lying, or playing at lying, he unmasks many people, he learns the interior mechanism of others, who are much more ingenuously liars than he, and the most curious thing of the supposed lies of Diego, is that in the long and short of it, those who are involved in the imaginary combination become angry, not because of the lie, but rather because of the truth contained in the lie, that always comes to the surface.
>
> . . . Being the eternally curious one, he is at the same time the eternal conversationalist. He can paint hours and days without resting, chatting while he works. He talks and argues about everything, absolutely everything, like Walt Whitman, enjoying talking with everyone who wants to listen to him. His conversation is always interesting. It has sentences that astonish, that sometimes wound; others are moving, but never do they leave the listener with an impression of uselessness or emptiness. His words disturb terribly because they are alive and true.

Frida tolerated and even indulged Rivera's egocentric idiosyncrasies, and was extremely protective of him, coming to his defense, for example, when he was under attack for making art for millionaires, or when people accused him of being a millionaire himself. In "Portrait of Diego," she challenged his critics with rhetoric that seems to flare at the nostrils.

> Against the cowardly attacks that are made on him, Diego always reacts with firmness and with a great sense of humor. He never compromises or

yields: he faces his enemies openly, the majority of them are sneaky, and a few are brave. He counts always on reality, never on elements of "illusion" or of "the ideal." This intransigence and rebelliousness are fundamental in Diego, they complement his portrait.

Among the many things that are said of Diego, these are the most common: they call him mythmaker, publicity-seeker, and the most ridiculous, millionaire. . . . It is unbelievable, surely, that the lowest, most cowardly and stupidest insults to Diego have been vomited in his own house: Mexico. By means of the press, by means of barbaric and vandalous acts in which they have tried to destroy his work, using everything from the innocent umbrellas of "decent" señoras who scratch his paintings hypocritically, and as if they were doing it in passing, to acids and table knives, not forgetting common ordinary spit, worthy of the possessors of so much saliva and so little brains; by means of groups of "well-brought-up" youths who stone his house and his studio, destroying irreplaceable works of pre-Cortesian Mexican art—which form part of Diego's collection—those who run away after having their laugh by means of anonymous letters (it is useless to speak of the valor of their senders) or by means of the neutral and Pilate-like silence of people in power, charged with guarding or importing culture for the good name of the country, not giving any importance to these attacks on the work of a man who, with all his genius, his unique creative effort, only tries to defend liberty of expression not only for himself, but also for all. . . .

But the insults and the attacks do not change Diego. They form part of the social phenomena of a world in decadence, and nothing more. The whole of life continues to interest, to amaze him, with its changeability, and everything surprises him with its beauty, but nothing disappoints or intimidates him because he knows the dialectical mechanism of phenomena and of events.

Frida was prepared to defend her husband physically as well as with words. Once, in a restaurant, a drunk at the next table picked a fight with him, calling him a damned Trotskyite. Diego knocked the man down, but one of his companions pulled a gun. Furious, Frida jumped in front of him, yelling insults. She was felled by a blow to her stomach. Fortunately, waiters intervened, but in any case, Frida had drawn so much attention that the assailants fled.

What Did You Read?

1. How does Frida Kahlo's great love and need for Diego Rivera connect to her painting? Explain.
2. What personality traits did Kahlo and Rivera have in common?
3. How is, according to Kahlo, Rivera's "mythomania" related to his tremendous imagination?

What Do You Think?

1. Do you think rebelliousness is fundamental to great artists?
2. The author relates the story of how Rivera loved to tell people that Frida had had a painting in the Louvre before he did. What does this anecdote show about people's biases about women as artists?
3. Does sexual pathology create tension for creativity? Cite examples.

How Was It Done?

1. In the structuring of the essay, what two voices do we hear? How is the second voice indicated?
2. What evidence is used in the article to support the author's claim that the marriage and relationship evolved with time?
3. How important are the articles written by Kahlo and Rivera to the development of this work? Explain and identify by name the articles each wrote.

Excerpt from *Shakey: The Neil Young Story*

Jimmy McDonough

Rock musicians sometimes have a way of becoming heroes in the minds of many. Certainly one of those heroes from the 1960s and beyond has been Neil Young, first a member of Buffalo Springfield, and then a major star on his own. Young's music has gone through many reincarnations over the decades, but his public persona has often been of the artist committed to his craft, without much concern for commercial success. Such individuals can, however, be quite difficult and demanding on those around them. The following passage from Young's biography details the rather unusual and at times insensitive approach Young took toward those who worked for him.

Key Words

racehorse	slang for commercially successful artist
cohort	band or group
gig	a job, usually a show for an entertainer
vibe	vibration or feeling
petrified	converted into stone

With Joni Mitchell and various members of Crosby, Stills and Nash constantly flitting about, the scene in Laurel Canyon was a rich one. But Neil Young wasn't really part of the gang. "Neil never dealt with *anyone*," said Elliot Roberts. "Neil very rarely called anyone and never socialized—Neil just doesn't go to parties. He will go a year without talking to you, 'cause he doesn't initiate phone calls."

Roberts would first encounter Young during the tail end of the Springfield. "Even then, you knew he was his own person. Neil didn't hang with the band, wasn't friendly with the band, wasn't nice to the band—'cause they weren't cooperating with him. They were always afraid of Neil. He had this vibe like Clint Eastwood—he was like death. You saw him ride into town. You didn't know a thing about him, but you knew not to fuck with this guy. Everyone was petrified of Neil."*

But Roberts detected a frailty that others missed. "Instantly—from the first day—I knew that Neil was physically very, very weak. Neil was sickly. He was so vulnerable—you could blow him away with a word, you could hurt his feelings with the drop of a hat. It was so easy to get Neil—so fuckin' easy—it was really sorta weird."

Although Joni Mitchell was Elliot Roberts's "first racehorse," it was Neil Young who would go the distance. Ironically, Mitchell put the pair together. She was in the studio working on her first album when she discovered her cohort from the Canadian folk scene, still in the Springfield at the time, was recording in the next studio over. Mitchell called Roberts, telling him, "You've got to meet Neil Young. He's the only guy who is funnier than you are."

The pair so hit it off that Roberts—still sleeping on B. Mitchell   5 Reid's floor at this point—got an invitation from Young to stay in his Laurel Canyon guest house. By this time the Springfield were without a manager and floundering. Roberts badly wanted to manage the band and accompany them on a southern California bus tour as sort of a test run. It was just before his first gig with the Springfield that Roberts discovered how difficult a client Young could be.

"Neil fired me 'cause I took off a half hour to play golf. We went to the hotel and right next to the hotel was a driving range. Everyone goes to their rooms and I go to the golf range. I don't know it, but Neil's not feeling well, he's calling around for me to get him a doctor, and when I get back, Dickie Davis said to me, 'Well, you can split. Neil fired you. He doesn't want a manager who's playin' golf—he wants a manager who's lookin' after the band.'

"And Neil won't see me. I'll tell ya what a lunatic this guy was— Neil won't see me, but I'm *there,* I'm on the bus! So I hang out, try and avoid him like the plague. Neil won't look at me. And that's how he treats me all night long—like I'm dead. The other guys are talking to me, but to Neil I'm not even in the *room.* I'm tryin' to get in his good graces—'Can I get you somethin', some aspirin? Do you want some

---

*When I asked Roberts where he thought Young got this vibe of doom, he had a one-word answer: "Rassy."

water?' Neil doesn't turn around. I don't exist. When he needed me, I was playing golf."

Somehow Roberts slipped back in Young's good graces, or so he thought, and put together a management contract for the Springfield through Chartoff-Winkler. But when the time came to sign, the deal fell through—because of Young. "Neil refused to sign, even though the band voted four to one," recalls Roberts, thoroughly confused and hurt by the artist's behavior. He was still living with Young, who hadn't offered a word of complaint on the deal. "He *drove* me to the meeting," said Roberts.

Undaunted, a day or two later, Roberts tracked the Springfield down to a rehearsal at the Variety Arts Center in Santa Monica. "I go to the rehearsal and it's just the band and Dickie. And Neil stops playing and said to me, 'Get the fuck outta here.' I walk all the way up to the stage and I go, 'Neil, please don't do this'—I'm yelling now, 'Don't do this, I *know* I can make this band happen.' And Stephen is like 'Let Elliot talk.' Neil said, '*FUCK* Elliot! Fuck him!'

"Now I start to cry. I really loved the Springfield, and I had gotten   10 to really like Neil—and I can't believe he's doing this to me. He was so bad to me I was *crying in front of the band.* I couldn't believe it, it was so off the wall. Neil's screaming at me—he said to the band, 'Either he leaves now or I leave now. You wanna play, or you wanna listen to this fuckin' shit?' Now everyone's stopped, they're all staring, and Neil's cursing me and telling me to just get the fuck out. And the band goes, 'No, we wanna play.' I'm in tears and I leave.

"A week later Neil shows up. At one o'clock in the morning, there's a knock at the door—and it's Fuckface. I go, 'What do *you* want?' I didn't know if he wanted to hit me or if he heard I bad-mouthed him—which I had. And he goes, 'I wanna talk to you for a few minutes.' I go, 'FINE.' He comes in and goes, 'I want you to manage me. I left the Springfield. I told them today. I didn't want you to manage the Springfield because I knew I was leaving and I'd rather you manage *me* than manage the Springfield.' I go, 'This guy's like *Geffen.*'"

First of all, I fired Elliot from Buffalo Springfield because he was out playing golf. I was in a bad mood or somethin'. It was just before the Springfield was gonna break up, so everything pissed me off. So you could even say I was like a spoiled little brat or whatever and it would probably be true. No problem with that. Because I know how long it took me to learn some things—to grow up.

But still—my feelings were "This guy's a fucking jerk." *I liked him, but he was a jerk. No way I wanted him to manage Buffalo Springfield. Then later, when I quit the Springfield, I was looking for a manager, and I remembered, "This guy's pretty good." But when I said, "I don't want him to man-*

age the band," I wasn't thinking to myself, "I'm gonna get this guy. He's gonna manage me."

Now, to tell ya the truth, I don't exactly *remember* every *detail about this. It's twenty-six years ago—what the fuck do you want?*

How did I know Elliot was the one? It was obvious. He was a lotta fun. 15
Just like that.

As long as I give Elliot good direction, he does what he has to do to protect me. Elliot, he's a character, boy. Hard to find. One in a million. He's a soulful guy. That's all. Elliot's got soul.

The night Young came knocking on the door, "he ended up staying, just smoking pot and talking about his hopes and his fears, what he really wanted to do," said Roberts, who described the Young of those days as a primitive, instinctual artist without the savvy of a Joni Mitchell. "Joni really had a much clearer vision. Neil was into his thing and thought that being too much into the business end of it perverted you. He only knew that he had more to give than he was able to give."

Folksinger Dave Van Ronk—playing a gig at the Ice House in nearby Pasadena—was staying at Roberts's house, and the next night Elliot convinced Young to open for him. "Neil was scared to death—he wanted to do it, but he didn't have the balls to do it," said Roberts, who maintains that this impromptu gig was a turning point.

Young "played all these new songs and kicked ass. Everyone loved him. Had they booed him, life would've been a hundred percent different. It was after that night that Neil's vision became clearer, because he was resolved that he could do his own material better than anyone else—and that there was an audience for it."

Roberts took Young to Reprise (Jack Nitzsche also deserves credit, 20 having talked up Young to label head Mo Ostin every chance he got). Under the guidance of Ostin and Lenny Waronker, Warner/Reprise was thriving on the singer/songwriter boom of the early seventies. "You could be sort of ugly and not have a traditional voice and it was okay," said Reprise veteran Randy Newman. With its counterculture advertising and hip roster, Reprise was the record company of the era. "Of course, Reprise was never as different as it purported to be—they always cared about sellin' records—but they left us alone," said Newman. "Lenny was passionate about music."

Roberts would make an unusual deal for Young at Reprise. "We took very little money, and I took a lot of points. Everyone else was front-loading their deals, taking short points and taking the bread up front. I really thought Neil was gonna sell big records. I believed in Neil."

Young's first record would flop, but within a year he would link up with Crosby, Stills and Nash and, with Elliot Robert's careful orchestration, emerge a superstar. In the meantime, Neil Young would meet his greatest producer, David Briggs, and his greatest rock and roll band, Crazy Horse.

What Did You Read?

1. What was the importance of Neil Young's mother, Rassy, to his personality?
2. According to Roberts, what was the turning point in Neil Young's career?
3. How is Neil Young's personality a paradox?

What Do You Think?

1. Who is a contemporary successor to Neil Young? Explain.
2. Does one have to change (e.g., images, bands, producers, managers) to stay artistic and creative?
3. Why do we consider some musicians more as artists and others more as "stars"?

How Was It Done?

1. What event does this article center on? What does it accomplish in telling us who Neil Young is?
2. What voice besides the author's is integrated into this work? How is it typographically signaled in the text?
3. How does the concluding paragraph give purpose and drama to the whole selection?

Politics

Sidney Poitier

Sidney Poitier is one of the most accomplished actors of his generation. He was arguably the first black actor to become a major star, reaching the height of his career during the turbulent 1960s. He won an Oscar in 1963 for his role in Lillies of the Field. *About ten years before that, however, Poitier got caught up in one of the darkest episodes in the history of the United States: the communist witchhunts of Senator Joe McCarthy and the House Committee on Un-American Activities. These witchhunts accused and slandered Americans, often on little or no evidence, ruining people's lives. In Hollywood, an actor or actress could wind up on an infamous "blacklist"—meaning that they were considered "unhirable." Poitier talks about that time period and*

how he managed to land the role that jump-started his career. This excerpt is from
This Life.

Key Words

fringes	marginal or extremist views, away from mainstream views
permeates	penetrates something
cronies	close friends
cells	small groups as basic units of a larger group
demagoguery	using prejudice to make false claims and gain power
blacklisted	placed on a list of persons who are to be boycotted
hierarchy	classification of a group of people according to ability, wealth, or social standing
persona non grata	an unwanted or unwelcome person

The years 1952, 1953, and all but four weeks of 1954 were a dry spell
for me in terms of the movies and the theater. Nothing, absolutely
nothing. I didn't know exactly why it was nothing, but I had my suspicions; with the racial situation being what it was I didn't need three
guesses. During that period I was being introduced to many people
who were very politically aware. Among them were a lot of white people who seemed to be strikingly different from the majority of whites I
had encountered before. They were friendly and sympathetic on the
racial question, when most other people were decidedly not. They
seemed more willing to grant me an equal opportunity for economic,
cultural, and political expression, with no strings attached. Of course
most of those new white people were actors, actresses, writers, producers, directors, and people generally on the fringes of a world
bound on one side by the theater, on the other by motion pictures, and
somewhere, in the back of the bus, television, in its infancy.

I took care to nurture these relationships because through them I
was exposed to new ideas, new concepts, and new points of view on
old troubling issues. And in the process of airing these ideas and questions I eventually began—slowly, on a gut level—to develop my own
political ideas. I began to realize that politics is an integral part of how
we lead our daily lives. It has an influence on everything: education,
health, art, economics, the attitudes of one group to the other—it just
permeates everything. I began to realize more and more, and in time,
shooting the breeze with old cronies about girls and getting laid was
replaced by political discussions. My interest in the political views
swirling about me in this new circle of acquaintances attracted invitations to numerous homes for dinners or parties or cocktails, all of
which had an underlying political motive reaching far beyond eats

and drinks. At these friendly gatherings of Democrats, Republicans, Progressives, Liberals, Socialists, Communists, and FBI informers I would always sit and listen. I would join in the discussions occasionally, depending on the extent of my information, but mostly I would listen—I would learn. I would learn about politics—I would learn about America—I would learn about urban life—about all kinds of things that otherwise I wouldn't have been exposed to. On many occasions I would be invited to cells of left-wing political activists who said, "Come and hear what we have to say." I would go to somebody's house and there would be half a dozen or a dozen other people, some of whom I might have seen somewhere before, others total strangers. The talk would be Progressive, Socialist, Communist, or a mixture of all three, aimed at developing new converts.

My initial introduction to politics came at a furious time when a political upheaval of hurricane force was battering the country at large, while slamming itself with particular force at the high-visibility areas of art and intellect, with theater, film, and television absorbing the lowest blows. While that period, known as the McCarthy era, was scaring people in mighty places, I didn't even know who the hell McCarthy was—so removed was I from the mainstream of American politics—he was just a Senator who was white and mean to other white people, especially those who had black friends. But I was to learn in detail about the period in American history that he symbolized. I was to see his hurricane touch down around me, striking friends who were not Progressives, Liberals, or Communists as well as friends who were. Blacks who had white friends were in as vulnerable a position as whites who had black friends. So before I had learned enough about politics to get a fix on McCarthy, I found myself victimized by the indiscriminate gusts from his demagoguery. With a long arm that was never ready to help but always ready to hurt, the Senator smeared and paralyzed much of the area I had by now chosen to spend my life in. Before I could understand any of it, I was blacklisted. I wasn't able to work.

Mind you, I don't think if affected me as much as it did others, because I wasn't working anyway. And I couldn't really say for sure whether it was a blacklist or my black face that was keeping me out of work. I do know that I was considered an upstart, left-wing troublemaker by the hierarchy of the Negro Actors Guild of America. The president of the Guild on several occasions had threatened me about my politics, and later declared me persona non grata at the Guild, informing me that on at least one network I was on a list of unhirables.

During that dry spell of nearly two and a half years I just worked 5 in our tiny little restaurant, plunged into the role of new father, while I took three classes a week at the Paul Mann/Lloyd Richards Actors Workshop and made the rounds religiously and unsuccessfully.

In 1953 I got a call from the casting director at MGM in New York. Since I had visited him many times in search of jobs, he was familiar with my credentials. "You're too old for what I'm looking for, but I wonder if you'll help me out. I'm looking for a sixteen- or seventeen-year-old kid who can play a juvenile delinquent in a picture we're doing called *Blackboard Jungle*." "I'll certainly give it some thought and call you back," I said. A few days later I phoned him back with a list of eight or ten names of teenage black actors. He thanked me and that was that. About a month later he called me up again, saying, "We haven't been able to find that boy yet. We just wondered if you could come down and we could talk about it—maybe you know someone else who might fit the bill. So drop by my office and let's have a talk."

I "dropped" by his office that very same afternoon. Seated behind his desk in a big leather chair, he stared silently at me, nodding his head as if in agreement with some conclusion reached in the not too distant past. He smiled apologetically and said, "I'm sure by now you've guessed that I really wanted you to come by so I could take a look at you—well, now having seen you let me tell you, you don't look too bad. Would you make a screen test for me?" "Yes, sir, I sure will." "Okay, in a couple of days we'll run a test and I'll send it on to California." Two days later he directed me in a short test that was sent to Pandro Berman, the producer, and Richard Brooks, his director, for a final decision. They approved, and I was hired. I flew to California, and went straight to the MGM Studios to meet the fiery Richard Brooks. He was a strong, tough, agile man of about forty-two years who looked and dressed like a bum most of the time because he hated the codes of the front-office contingent. But were those flashes of street survival instinct that dominated his personality in unexpected moments the real Richard Brooks, or were they a meticulously nurtured camouflage that a forceful personality had chosen in order to ward off, and forever frustrate, simple definitions of itself? Puzzlement. Yet could he not be both? Surely no one of us is one of anything. Well, time itself will ultimately render a judgment as to the many sides of Richard Brooks's personality—provided Richard doesn't find a way to frustrate even time's efforts.

"I'm very glad to have you aboard," he said to me with those fierce, penetrating eyes boring into me. "Thank you very much," I said. "While you're here today, drop into Wardrobe for a fitting and I understand the producer wants you to come up to his office. Tell his secretary to give you a revised script. Read it and if you have any questions, let me know." Off I went for a fitting and then to the office of Pandro Berman, the producer. The secretary said Mr. Berman was away from his desk for a moment, but that my appointment was really at the legal department. She gave me directions and I made my way through the maze of corridors to the legal department, where I was taken into the office of a young lawyer fellow who closed the door behind me and got right down to business. "You know we have your name on a list of people whose loyalty is questionable." "Who, me?" "Yes sir, you. And in order to do this picture you will have to sign a loyalty oath." "Me? A loyalty oath? To who? For what?" "It's just a piece of paper that says you have no intention of overthrowing the Government." "I see. Well, let me think about it." "You'll have to sign it before you can start work." "Yeah? Well, okay, I'll have to let you know." I was perplexed. He stood up, extended his hand, I shook it, and I left.

I never went back to that office. I just put it off, because I didn't want to face that. I didn't want to have to deal with whether or not I was going to sign—because deep down I didn't want to sign. I don't want to feel that my livelihood depends on that kind of a compromise. I mean if I'm loyal—and I'm loyal—I don't have to put it on paper. Who the hell am I to overthrow the Government by force or violence? Is the Government going to sign a loyalty oath in terms of *my* rights? I didn't go back and I didn't call. The day came for the start of the picture and I reported for work. All day I looked for that guy to come down or for someone to send me up to his office, but I didn't hear from him all that day. The next day for sure, I thought. But no—no word. In fact I never heard from him again. I thought it very strange, but then I got to thinking: Did they trick me? I know I signed my contract. Could they have slipped that in the contract? But I say no—because by now I can read pretty fucking good. I can tell a loyalty oath from anything else, and I don't remember signing a loyalty oath in my contract. So how come they're not after me?

One day Richard Brooks said to me out of the blue, "You're a good 10 actor and you've had an interesting life." I said, "Oh?" He said, "Yeah. I've read your whole dossier." I said to myself: Oh, shit—what the hell is this? I know what "dossier" means—like I'm some kind of international spy or something. I said, "I see." He said, "Yeah, I guess they asked you all those things up in the office." He didn't give me a chance to answer—he continued with, "Fuck 'em." Such was his attitude about front offices, that guy from the trenches. I believe he knew I was on the blacklist when he hired me. I believe to this day, though I never discussed it with him, that he said, "I want that kid and don't give me all that bullshit that he knew Paul Robeson or he knew Canada Lee." Those were the charges against me. That I knew Paul Robeson intimately—that I knew Canada Lee—and that I used to get up in union meetings in New York and ask for equal rights for black actors. I'm sure he said, "I don't want to hear all that crap, I just want that actor. Get him for me."

What Did You Read?

1. Explain what Poitier means in the following: ". . . I eventually began—slowly, on a gut level—to develop my own political ideas. I began to realize that politics is an integral part of how we lead our daily lives."
2. How did McCarthyism affect Poitier's career?
3. How did Poitier finally find work as an actor?

What Do You Think?

1. Can politics and art be separated? Explain.
2. Are entertainers still persecuted for expressing their beliefs? Cite specific examples.
3. Would you be willing to sign a loyalty oath as a condition for employment? Why or why not?

How Was It Done?

1. What central "nonact" does the article revolve around? What is revealed about which two people?
2. What do the beginning paragraphs accomplish as far as introducing the theme of Sidney Poitier and his "dry spell"?
3. How is the excerpt developed? Is the narrative chronological or not? Explain.

Then and Now

Bill Blass

Bill Blass, who died in 2002, was a giant of the fashion world. His styles were elegant, classic, and expensive. He established Bill Blass Limited, and expanded his fashion line to include such non-high fashion items such as airline uniforms and chocolates. Essentially, the Blass look was classic and conservative. Blass was raised in the Midwest and served in World War II. In this passage from his autobiography, he talks about how his roots influenced him in some surprising ways to become a world-famous designer. This excerpt is from Bare Blass.

Key Words

bedazzled	enchanted
unambiguously	clearly; without question
wholesomeness	soundness of body, mind, and morals
penthouse	an apartment or condominium on the top floor of a building; often the most expensive unit in the building

the Depression	weak economic times of the 1930s, noted for high unemployment and lack of business growth
gaudy	tastelessly ornamental; showy or extravagant
innocuous	innocent; not threatening
memoir	autobiography; a narrative of personal experiences
insolently	insulting; showing contempt
enigmatic	puzzling; unclear and uncertain

Childhood bores the hell out of me.

I think it bored me even as a child, although I am certainly aware that had it not been for the joylessness, colorlessness, and fatherlessness of my small-town Indiana childhood, I might not have gone anywhere. People today speak about the character-building qualities of the miserable childhood, but I can tell you from experience: There is nothing like the dull, unattractive childhood to give a bedazzled boy the *right* push.

Of course, the beauty of my upbringing was in its plainness. And there was this consoling feature: Everyone we knew in Fort Wayne, and everyone they knew, were in the same plain boat. As a consequence of having little money ourselves and no social standing above my mother's widowed respectability—and even here we might have stood to gain some ground if my father had died instantly and unambiguously in a highway crash rather than by a self-inflicted gunshot in our front parlor—I learned, perhaps in that single isolating moment (I was five), how to occupy myself. In this stiff-upper-lip wholesomeness there was surely somewhere a budding genius for avoiding anything unpleasant or ugly (what else am I to make of a drawing I did at the age of six showing a butler serving drinks in a Manhattan penthouse, other than, perhaps, an advanced knowledge of where the better customers lodged?). But at that time, in a life-in-general way, I was happy. And don't forget the world was a different place then. It didn't take much to amuse a kid, and everybody had troubles, on account of the Depression, so there was no point complaining about that. I used to spend hours up in my room, flopped on my bed, reading the latest *Vogue* or *Delineator* and marveling at the unapproachable glamour of "Lady in Emerald Hat, coiffure of ostrich." Fashion held such mystery then. On Saturdays, I and my friends would go down to the local movie house, with its aromas of sweat and cigarettes and drugstore perfume, and watch in gundy silence as Marlene Dietrich breezed through sixteen costume changes in *The Garden of Allah*. Even food had wondrous possibilities. I remember once being at the cottage we had on a lake, about sixty miles from Fort Wayne, and after a quick evaluation of our supplies, settling on sandwiches made of cold leftover mashed potatoes, with lavish swirls of Miracle Whip (this was before we knew about Hellmann's) and lots of black pepper on the soft white bread. You can't imagine how delicious those sandwiches tasted. There would be other meals as wonderful and bad, like the spur-of-the-moment dishes we made in the army during the Second World War when a fresh egg was available. But I think that day at the lake was the first time I realized that the taste of food depends not just on the ingredients, but also on where you are at the time and how hungry you are.

I was lucky in one respect. My type of looks, which were the opposite of the type that appealed to me, were wholesomely innocuous to fit into several local categories, sissy to jock, while belonging to none. This may strike you as a bit of very un-American foot-dragging toward the inevitable main event—sex, and sex with *whom?*—and given the expectation today that every memoir writer will conduct himself with the thoroughness of a House Committee on Un-American Activities investigation, telling all, I suppose I am ducking (for the moment) the question of sexual category, though, even then, I didn't believe in them. Sexual encounters between men were far more prevalent among my classmates at Southside High School than encounters with women, in part because so few of the girls were willing to do it with their boyfriends, and because homosexuality, being so forbidden, was so tempting to accomplish. I recall a Sunday-school teacher gathering a group of us boys around for what we assumed would be another grim lesson about the Apostles and him saying rather jovially, "Let's do something different for a change. You guys know what a circle jerk is?" Some of us did and some of us didn't. Needless to say, none of us saw a religious tie-in. But I doubt that the teacher, or the kindly men posing as father figures or even the more sweetly observant boys that I knew, most of them destined for marriage, considered themselves homosexuals.

As for myself, I was much more interested in joining worlds that 5 before the war would have been denied to a middle-class boy with only a high school education, and this meant, at the very least, getting out of Fort Wayne. Luckily, as I say, my looks, along with a sense of humor, helped me to straddle the different divides, and by the time I was nineteen, I had added, for good measure, the polish of a slight British accent—no doubt lifted from Frederick Austerlitz, a.k.a. Fred Astaire, another Midwesterner. Yet, curiously, it wasn't until I was in the army, living for the first time among men, that I experienced real happiness. And freedom.

Also, I could draw. The beauty of being able to draw, or paint, from an early age is that you never feel trapped, least of all by your immediate circumstances. When I was fifteen, I began selling sketches of evening dresses, at $25 a pop, to a manufacturer in New York called

Kalmour (long gone) that did a brisk business selling to women who plainly saw themselves, as I saw Dietrich and Swanson, entering a room and insolently flinging their wraps down on the couch. I didn't make much off the Kalmour people, but it was enough to help pay for fashion school in New York. A few years later, in Europe during the war, I managed to fill several of the small notebooks that we all carried—all of us being creative types assigned to a rather enigmatic outfit called the 603rd Camouflage Battalion—with miniature drawings of ladies hats, shoes, gloves, and dresses. I still have those notebooks. The man closest to me in the army, Bob Tompkins, who today lives in Gardnerville, Nevada, recently told me that I drew my first sketch of my company logo, a pair of mirrored B's, while lying on a bunk in a convent in Luxembourg as we were waiting to go up to the Battle of the Bulge. I have no memory of this. He also reminds me that from the day we first met in boot camp, at Fort Meade, Maryland, until the night we came home from the war, on July 5, 1945, and took the elevator up to the apartment in Greenwich Village where my mother and sister had moved from Indiana (and where Bob's wife, Bunny, now waited, too), I seemed to be smiling for dear life, and, according to the photographs I have, he is right.

In retrospect, I can see how certain influences of my childhood and youth entered my unconsciousness and remained there, like a fine fog, while I steered unaware, and apparently grinning, toward the only city I have ever wanted to live in (New York) to do the only thing I have ever wanted to do (fashion). For all my ardent interest in movies, I must have recognized that Hollywood was no place for a relatively insecure lad still lean and scared from the Depression; it all looked *too* easy and glamorous, and that made me nervous. I needed the beat and grind of New York, the feeling of being hemmed in, the discomforts, and the macaroni and cheese you could only get at the Automat. Inevitably, my clothes displayed a similar taste for realism—admittedly, a jazzy, expensive realism—that occasionally put me on the outs with fashion editors, especially Diana Vreeland, who in the sixties kept *Vogue* filled with the Turkish delight numbers that appealed to her love of fantasy, but which generally were unavailable in stores. I minded the rejection—up to a point. Some years ago, at a meeting with other Seventh Avenue designers to discuss a show, it became clear to me that they were only interested in showing novel or outrageous clothes, and not the kind their customers actually bought. Finally, someone said, "We don't want those kind of people." To which I replied from my place at the back of the room, "I'll take 'em."

What Did You Read?

1. How does Blass describe himself as a child?
2. Why did Blass like being in the Army so much?
3. What is the only city he ever wanted to live in? Why?
4. What kind of customer appealed to Blass?

What Do You Think?

1. Do you think an attractive or an unattractive childhood does more to help one be successful in the future? Explain.
2. How does his passage on eating the mashed-potato sandwich serve as a metaphor for what he learned about life?
3. What kinds of things did you do as a child to transcend your own immediate circumstances?

How Was It Done?

1. How does the first sentence, "Childhood bores the hell out of me," center the entire excerpt? Explain.
2. What word best crystallizes this excerpt? Explain.
3. The first half of the excerpt reveals how certain influences led him to New York and to fashion. The second half of the article establishes what?

10

Fairy Tales

Many people associate fairy tales with their childhood: watching Disney movie versions of famous tales, listening to fairy tales read to them at bedtime, and hearing innumerable references to fairy tale characters in popular culture. Fairy tales seem uniquely associated with childhood in part because the fairy tale world itself seems almost childlike in its simplicity. In the tales, characters are good or evil, with no gray area between. Magic is used—a way of making what one wishes to happen actually happen. Most fairy tales resolve themselves in satisfactory ways: the good are rewarded and the bad are punished. We can also look at the messages that fairy tales send children, and us, about how the world is supposed to be. Young girls listening to "Cinderella" are given an idea that the goal for young women is to be beautiful so they can marry a prince. Boys hear tales of bravery, such as the young prince fighting through thorns and thickets to rescue Sleeping Beauty. Underneath these messages are perhaps deeper psychological messages. Some critics, such as Bruno Bettelheim, have argued that fairy tales are a way for children to resolve disturbing and often unacceptable messages about sex, sibling rivalry, and conflict with parents. Because of their prevalence throughout the world, fairy tales and the messages they send us are an interesting and rewarding field of investigation.

In this chapter, the Writing Lesson is centered on literary analysis. As an introduction, the lesson first presents common literary terms and their meanings. The terms cover aspects of character, plot, setting, theme, and symbolism. Then, the lesson provides help in how you can do research specifically geared to the discussion of literature. The practical advice in the lesson prepares you for the Writing Assignment, which incorporates the material from literary texts and from texts that criticize or comment on the literature. In this way, you can form your own fresh and original perspective about a literary work.

THE MAIN EVENT READING

Cinderella, Or the Little Glass Slipper
Charles Perrault

One of the oldest and most popular fairy tales, the story of Cinderella has been told in many different ways in many different times and countries. This version, by the 17th-century Frenchman Charles Perrault, served as the basis for the famous Disney movie of the same name. Cinderella is a rags-to-riches story: the young girl is forced by a wicked stepmother to live like a slave and sleep in the cinders. She, with the help of a fairy godmother, is able to attend the prince's ball and win his love. This version also features the pumpkin carriage, animal helpers, and most important of all, the glass slippers.

Key Words

haughty	excessively proud
odious	hateful
meanest	lowest
looking glass	mirror
liveries	servants' uniforms
collation	a light meal
adieus	good-byes
citrons	a citrus fruit similar to a lemon

Once upon a time there was a gentleman who married, for his second wife, the proudest and most haughty woman that ever was seen. She had two daughters of her own, who were, indeed, exactly like her in all things. The gentleman had also a young daughter, of rare goodness and sweetness of temper, which she took from her mother, who was the best creature in the world. `traditional opening`

The wedding was scarcely over, when the stepmother's bad temper began to show itself. She could not bear the goodness of this young girl, because it made her own daughters appear the more odious. The stepmother gave her the meanest work in the house to do;

she had to scour the dishes, tables, etc., and to scrub the floors and clean out the bedrooms. The poor girl had to sleep in the garret, upon a wretched straw bed, while her sisters lay in fine rooms with inlaid floors, upon beds of the very newest fashion, and where they had looking-glasses so large that they might see themselves at their full length. The poor girl bore all patiently, and dared not complain to her father, who would have scolded her if she had done so, for his wife governed him entirely.

can't trust father

When she had done her work, she used to go into the chimney corner, and sit down among the cinders, hence she was called Cinderwench. The younger sister of the two, who was not so rude and uncivil as the elder, called her Cinderella. However, Cinderella, in spite of her mean apparel, was a hundred times more handsome than her sisters, though they were always richly dressed.

her real name is not revealed

It happened that the King's son gave a ball, and invited to it all persons of fashion. Our young misses were also invited, for they cut a very grand figure among the people of the country-side. They were highly delighted with the invitation, and wonderfully busy in choosing the gowns, petticoats, and head-dresses which might best become them. This made Cinderella's lot still harder, for it was she who ironed her sisters' linen and plaited their ruffles. They talked all day of nothing but how they should be dressed.

"For my part," said the elder, "I will wear my red velvet suit with French trimmings."   5

"And I," said the younger, "shall wear my usual skirt; but then, to make amends for that I will put on my gold-flowered mantle, and my diamond stomacher, which is far from being the most ordinary one in the world." They sent for the best hairdressers they could get to make up their hair in fashionable styles, and bought patches for their cheeks. Cinderella was consulted in all these matters, for she had good taste. She advised them always for the best, and even offered her services to dress their hair, which they were very willing she should do.

As she was doing this, they said to her:—

"Cinderella, would you not be glad to go to the ball?"

"Young ladies," she said, "you only jeer at me; it is not for such as I am to go there."

"You are right," they replied; "people would laugh to see a   10 Cinderwench at a ball."

Any one but Cinderella would have dressed their hair awry, but she was good-natured, and arranged it perfectly well. They were almost two days without eating, so much were they transported with joy. They broke above a dozen laces in trying to lace themselves tight, that they might have a fine, slender shape, and they were continually at their looking glass.

importance of beauty

At last the happy day came; they went to Court, and Cinderella followed them with her eyes as long as she could, and when she had lost sight of them, she fell a-crying.

Her godmother, who saw her all in tears, asked her what was the matter. <small>enter fairy godmother</small>

"I wish I could—I wish I could—" but she could not finish her sobbing.

Her godmother, who was a fairy, said to her, "You wish you could 15 go to the ball; is it not so?"

"Alas, yes," said Cinderella, sighing.

"Well," said her godmother, "be but a good girl, and I will see that you go." Then she took her into her chamber, and said to her, "Run into the garden, and bring me a pumpkin."

Cinderella went at once to gather the finest she could get, and brought it to her godmother, not being able to imagine how this pumpkin could help her to go to the ball. Her godmother scooped out all the inside of it, leaving nothing but the rind. Then she struck it with her <small>magic</small> wand, and the pumpkin was instantly turned into a fine gilded coach.

She then went to look into the mouse-trap, where she found six mice, all alive. She ordered Cinderella to lift the trap-door, when, giving each mouse, as it went out, a little tap with her wand, it was that moment turned into a fine horse, and the six mice made a fine set of six horses of a beautiful mouse-colored, dapple gray.

Being at a loss for a coachman, Cinderella said, "I will go and see if 20 there is not a rat in the rat-trap—we may make a coachman of him."

"You are right," replied her godmother; "go and look."

Cinderella brought the rat-trap to her, and in it there were three huge rats. The fairy chose the one which had the largest beard, and, having touched him with her wand, he was turned into a fat coachman with the finest mustache and whiskers ever seen.

After that, she said to her:—

"Go into the garden, and you will find six lizards behind the water-pot; bring them to me."

She had no sooner done so than her godmother turned them into 25 six footmen, who skipped up immediately behind the coach, with their liveries all trimmed with gold and silver, and they held on as if they had done nothing else their whole lives.

The fairy then said to Cinderella, "Well, you see here a carriage fit to go to the ball in; are you not pleased with it?"

"Oh, yes!" she cried; "but must I go as I am in these rags?"

Her godmother simply touched her with her wand, and, at the same moment, her clothes were turned into cloth of gold and silver, all decked with jewels. This done, she gave her a pair of the prettiest glass slippers in the whole world. Being thus attired, she got into the carriage, her godmother commanding her, above all things, not to stay till after midnight, and telling her, at the same time, that if she stayed one moment longer, the coach would be a pumpkin again, her horses mice, her coachman a rat, her footmen lizards, and her clothes would become just as they were before.

She promised her godmother she would not fail to leave the ball before midnight. She drove away, scarce able to contain herself for joy. The King's son, who was told that a great princess, whom nobody knew, was come, ran out to receive her. He gave her his hand as she alighted from the coach, and led her into the hall where the company were assembled. There was at once a profound silence; every one left off dancing, and the violins ceased to play, so attracted was every one by the singular beauties of the unknown newcomer. Nothing was then heard but a confused sound of voices saying:—

"Ha! how beautiful she is! Ha! how beautiful she is!"   30

The King himself, old as he was, could not keep his eyes off her, and he told the Queen under his breath that it was a long time since he had seen so beautiful and lovely a creature.

All the ladies were busy studying her clothes and head-dress, so that they might have theirs made next day after the same pattern, provided they could meet with such fine materials and able hands to make them.

The King's son conducted her to the seat of honor, and afterwards took her out to dance with him. She danced so very gracefully that they all admired her more and more. A fine collation was served, but the young Prince ate not a morsel, so intently was he occupied with her.

duplicity   She went and sat down beside her sisters, showing them a thousand civilities, and giving them among other things part of the oranges and citrons with which the Prince had regaled her. This very much surprised them, for they had not been presented to her.

Cinderella heard the clock strike a quarter to twelve. She at once   35 made her adieus to the company and hastened away as fast as she could.

As soon as she got home, she ran to find her godmother, and, after having thanked her, she said she much wished she might go to the ball the next day, because the King's son had asked her to do so. As she was eagerly telling her godmother all that happened at the ball, her two sisters knocked at the door; Cinderella opened it. "How long you have stayed!" said she, yawning, rubbing her eyes, and stretching herself as if she had been just awakened. She had not, however, had any desire to sleep since they went from home.

"If you had been at the ball," said one of her sisters, "you would not have been tired with it. There came thither the finest princess, the most beautiful ever was seen with mortal eyes. She showed us a thousand civilities, and gave us oranges and citrons."

Cinderella did not show any pleasure at this. Indeed, she asked them the name of the princess; but they told her they did not know it, and that the King's son was very much concerned, and would give all the world to know who she was. At this Cinderella, smiling, replied:—

"Was she then so very beautiful? How fortunate you have been! Could I not see her? Ah! dear Miss Charlotte, do lend me your yellow suit of clothes which you wear every day."

"Ay, to be sure!" cried Miss Charlotte; "lend my clothes to such a 40 dirty Cinderwench as thou art! I should be out of my mind to do so."

Cinderella, indeed, expected such an answer and was very glad of   duplicity the refusal; for she would have been sadly troubled if her sister had lent her what she jestingly asked for. The next day the two sisters went to the ball, and so did Cinderella, but dressed more magnificently than before. The King's son was always by her side, and his pretty speeches to her never ceased. These by no means annoyed the young lady. Indeed, she quite forgot her godmother's orders to her, so that she heard the clock begin to strike twelve when she thought it could not be more than eleven. She then rose up and fled, as nimble as a deer. The Prince followed, but could not overtake her. She left behind one of her glass slippers, which the Prince took up most carefully. She got home, but quite out of breath, without her carriage, and in her old clothes, having nothing left her of all her finery but one of the little slippers, fellow to the one she had dropped. The guards at the palace gate were asked if they had not seen a princess go out, and they replied they had seen nobody go out but a young girl, very meanly dressed, and who had more the air of a poor country girl than of a young lady.

When the two sisters returned from the ball, Cinderella asked them if they had had a pleasant time, and if the fine lady had been there. They told her, yes; but that she hurried away the moment it struck twelve, and with so much haste that she dropped one of her little glass slippers, the prettiest in the world, which the King's son had taken up. They said, further, that he had done nothing but look at her all the time, and that most certainly he was very much in love with the beautiful owner of the glass slipper.

What they said was true; for a few days after the King's son caused it to be proclaimed, by sound of trumpet, that he would marry her whose foot this slipper would fit exactly. They began to try it on the princesses, then on the duchesses, and then on all the ladies of the Court; but in vain. It was brought to the two sisters, who did all they possibly could to thrust a foot into the slipper, but they could not succeed. Cinderella, who saw this, and knew her slipper, said to them laughing:—

"Let me see if it will not fit me."

Her sisters burst out a-laughing, and began to banter her. The gen- 45 tleman who was sent to try the slipper looked earnestly at Cinderella, and, finding her very handsome, said it was but just that she should try, and that he had orders to let every lady try it on.

He obliged Cinderella to sit down, and, putting the slipper to her little foot, he found it went on very easily, and fitted her as if it had been made of wax. The astonishment of her two sisters was great, but it was still greater when Cinderella pulled out of her pocket the other slipper and put it on her foot. Thereupon, in came her godmother, who, having touched Cinderella's clothes with her wand, made them more magnificent than those she had worn before.

duplicity— she allowed her sisters to go first

And now her sisters found her to be that beautiful lady they had seen at the ball. They threw themselves at her feet to beg pardon for all their ill treatment of her. Cinderella took them up, and, as she embraced them, said that she forgave them with all her heart, and begged them to love her always.

She was conducted to the young Prince, dressed as she was. He thought her more charming than ever, and, a few days after, married her. Cinderella, who was as good as she was beautiful, gave her two sisters a home in the palace, and that very same day married them to two great lords of the Court.

What Did You Read?

1. Why is Cinderella hated so much by the stepmother and the stepsisters?
2. How is Cinderella's goodness portrayed?
3. What does the Prince admire about Cinderella?
4. Over how many nights does the ball occur?

What Do You Think?

1. What is significant about this statement regarding Cinderella's father: "his wife governed him entirely"?
2. How is women's power regarded in this story? Cite specific examples of the use of power by women.
3. Is Cinderella an active or passive agent in the story?
4. What is the symbolic importance of Cinderella's small foot size?

How Was It Done?

1. Does Cinderella start in a traditional manner? Explain.
2. How is the story structured around tasks? How many?
3. How does the use of adjectives help to shape the individual characterizations?
4. What single artifact does the story revolve around?

THE MAIN EVENT WRITING ASSIGNMENT

Write an essay in response to one of the following assignments:

1. How are women portrayed in fairy tales? Examine different female roles in a variety of fairy tales, and argue how they relate to each other, to men, and/or to the natural world.

2. How is sexuality signified in fairy tales? How is sexuality disguised? How is it used to propel the storyline?

3. How is childhood presented in fairy tales? Examine parent/child relationships. For instance, who protects children and who harms them?

4. How does social class function in fairy tales? What is class associated with? For instance, what is poverty associated with? What is wealth associated with? How can characters move from one social class to another?

PREPARATION PUNCH LIST

Before you begin writing the essay, you need to prepare yourself to write. Jot down some notes on what you know in general. You may want to ask yourself some of the following questions.

1. What do you know about fairy tales?
- Some were written down by the brothers Grimm, who transcribed them from storytellers who passed them down orally.
- Writers, such as Hans Christian Andersen and Marie Le Prince de Beaumont, created some fairy tales.
- Fairy tales occur in many times and cultures.

2. Read some fairy tales that have women as central characters:
- Thumbelina
- The Little Mermaid
- Snow White
- Rapunzel
- Cinderella
- Beauty and the Beast
- The Snow Queen

3. Determine how women are portrayed in fairy tales.
- beautiful
- virtuous

- productive
- as good fairy godmothers
- as evil mothers and stepmothers
- evil sisters
- jealous
- competitive
- cunning

4. Do additional library research on fairy tales and the literary criticism written about them.

THE MAIN EVENT WRITING LESSON: LITERARY ANALYSIS

Perhaps you have enjoyed reading since you were a little child, books of fairy tales, mysteries, adventure, or family. You likely read these stories simply for pleasure. However, you can look at stories more closely, going beyond the surface level meaning to discover other, richer interpretations. This requires a careful, close reading of the text; then you will want to analyze the text. The word "analyze" means to look at the parts of something and how they work together to create the whole.

The biggest mistake beginning writers make in analyzing literature is to fall into plot summary. Plot summary is simply retelling the story in your own words. That is not a substitute for analysis. When you write about a literary work, you may assume that your reader has already read the work as well. Your job is to explain it.

Here are five areas that you can examine: character, plot, setting, symbolism, and theme.

Character

Characters are the figures that inhabit the world of the story. Some important terms related to the discussion of character are protagonist, antagonist, round characters, and flat characters.

The *protagonist* in a story is the main character, the one whom the story is about: Cinderella, Aladdin, and the Ugly Duckling are examples of protagonists. Sometimes the protagonist is called a *hero* when that character embodies the virtues of a given culture.

Opposed to the protagonist is the *antagonist*. This is the character who works against the protagonist. The evil stepmother in Cinderella is her antagonist, and to a lesser extent, so are her stepsisters. Outside of the world of fairy tales, not all antagonists are evil in their motives. They may have legitimate, reasonable motives for opposing the protagonist, such as in a sports story in which one athlete is trying to defeat another.

Round characters are characters who undergo a fundamental change in their ways of thinking and acting during the course of the story. In other words, they change as a result of something in the story. *Flat characters* are characters who remain unchanged throughout a story. Many literary works are concerned with examining the change of one character, while the other characters remain flat. This allows the reader to focus on that change. The Ugly Duckling is a round character because the Duckling undergoes not only a physical change, but he gains self-esteem, too.

Plot

In stories, things happen. The series of events in a story form the *plot* of the story. Plots generally are described as having certain periods. There is the introduction, in which the central *conflict* begins. The conflict may be between two persons; a person against him or herself, as in struggling to overcome a fear or addiction; a person against a larger group, such as society; and a person against larger forces, such as nature. After the introduction, additional complications occur; this phase is called the *rising action.* The action then comes to a *climax,* the most dramatic point of the story. After the climax is the *falling action,* in which the events lead to the final position. The end is typically referred to as the *denouement.* In traditional storytelling, the denouement occurs because the conflict is fully resolved. You may recognize the phrase, "And they lived happily ever after" as a common ending in fairy tales.

In many stories, of course, plots may be more complicated. Some stories involve the use of *flashbacks,* in which a character recalls events of a time before the beginning of the story. In longer works, such as novels, plots may be complicated by *subplots,* in which the actions of other characters intersect with the main plot.

Setting

Setting is where a story occurs, both in time and place. Some stories occur entirely in one setting, but most have a variety of settings for the action. Setting can do a lot to create atmosphere: a forest in fairy tales, for example, can be spooky and dangerous. Bad things happen in the forest, such as getting captured by a witch or encountering a dangerous beast. On the other hand, a grand palace in the fairy tale can exude a sense of luxury, wealth, and power. Where things happen in stories can be crucial to understanding their larger meaning.

Setting refers not only to place but also time. In fairy tales, time is often unclear, hinting at an idealized version of the past. Things are just simply said to have happened—when they occurred is not important. In other works of fiction, time periods can be enormously important: a story that takes place during wartime is not the same one that takes place during a time of peace.

Settings can often be symbolic. While the forest may be literally a place of danger, it may also represent the unknown, or any dangerous person or situation. A city can represent new hope, new possibilities. Think of the Land of Oz and how it represents an imaginative place of escape for Dorothy, away from her gray, humdrum farm life in Kansas.

Symbolism

Many stories employ *symbols* as a way to create levels of meaning beyond the strictly literal. A symbol is something that stands for something else. Some symbols are easily recognized, such as the use of a flag to symbolize a nation or state. In literary works, the symbols writers use may be easy to see, such as the use of a rose in "Beauty and the Beast" to symbolize love, or the symbols can be more difficult to decipher. Nevertheless, most symbols must be reasonably clear, or the author takes the risk that the reader will not understand their meaning.

Determining symbolism within a story requires the reader to pay close attention to details. In "From an Ounce of Sorrow," the author uses a number of devices that can be seen as symbolic: the plant that grows from the seeds and then is destroyed by birds may represent the young princess's adult sexuality. She cries when the plants are ravished. Her happiness is only restored when she learns that the prince, who had, in the form of the bird, destroyed the plant, loves her and wishes to marry her.

An interpretation of the use of symbols is typically just that: an interpretation. Other readers may develop other interpretations. The key is to stay grounded in the text as much as possible. Look for things that are emphasized, such as the plant. Another way to determine symbols is to look for unusual things, such as a tree that grows where someone has cried. Carefully examine aspects of a story that are repeated, or things that are described that don't seem important at first glance. These may have symbolic importance.

Readers who look too deeply and too far for symbolism may be adding more into a story than is supportable. However, a reader who only reads for literal meaning is likely to miss important implications of additional meanings left by the author.

Theme

The theme of a story is what the story is about. Some have called the theme the central argument of the story. For example, in Aesop's Fables, each fable ends with a short moral, intended to teach a lesson to the reader. "The Boy Who Cried Wolf" teaches the reader the importance of telling the truth. Today, many readers reject such simple moral lessons as being too child-like, as unsatisfactory for adults. Often, we look to a work of literature to give us a new vision or understanding of the world. An author may convey a message that is complicated by the uncertainties of life, rather than reflecting the simple moral dynamics of older stories. Nevertheless, the concept of theme involves some idea or concept that can be explicit (but is usually implied) that is conveyed to the reader.

Using Research to Support Your Analysis

Readers of literature need to develop their own ability to read and interpret text. Nevertheless, making use of criticism written about a text can be helpful and enlightening. The following points may be helpful:

- **Read the literature first.** This may sound like a statement of the obvious, but too often students fall into the trap of reading professionally written study notes as a substitute for reading the primary text itself. This shortchanges your ability to learn and think about literature. There is no substitute for the actual work itself. Studying literature can be immensely rewarding, but only to those who are willing to put in the time and effort to read it first.

- **If you are producing an essay in which you use ideas received from reading criticism, always cite the material.** Remember, borrowing someone else's ideas without proper acknowledgment is plagiarism, just as much as directly copying someone else's words is.

- **Look for criticism in books.** Your local or college librarian can assist you in finding materials. You may wish to look up criticism written about a particular work, or you may wish to expand your search to examining criticism about the author. After that, you may want to find what is available that is written about the literature of the general time period.

  When you locate a book, look at the copyright year. Knowing how current the text is can be helpful. While older criticism may still be valid (since literature is not as time sensitive as other subjects, such as science), you will want to acquaint yourself with material that has been written more recently. After all, critics read and respond to the criticism that has already been written.

  Check to see if the book has an index. That can be of practical help, as you may not be in a position to read an entire book. You might want to focus just on particular works or subjects covered within a book. A book that does not contain an index may still have value, but it may also demand more of your time.

- **Look at criticism in periodicals.** There are a number of literary journals that publish literary criticism. Again, speak with a librarian on the best way for you to locate articles on your chosen subject. Articles in periodicals can be helpful because they may be more narrowly focused on a work or author than in a book, and the criticism found in periodicals also is likely to be more current. Keep in mind, too, that far more criticism is published in periodicals than in books.

- **Synthesize the material.** The general purpose of using research is to help you better understand the text in front of you. However, this does not mean that you should simply parrot what you have read. A good reader needs to learn how to interact with both the literary work and the criticism to formulate his or her own ideas about the work. In other words, your essay presents your informed analysis.

THE MAIN EVENT WRITING SAMPLE

The following is an essay written for this text in response to the Main Event Writing Assignment, Question #1.

Women in Fairy Tales

Fairy tales have universal appeal. Not only are children enchanted by the stories of "Jack and the Beanstalk," "The Story of Aladdin,"

Insight from a secondary source "Snow White," and "Sweet Rampion," but also fairy tales are the only art form readily accessible to children (Bettelheim 12). They promise meaning to a child. Even newer fairy tales have this quality of trying to create meaning. In the 19th century, Hans Christian Andersen himself lived something of a fairy tale—he was the son of a shoemaker, homely, and a little odd; his fears and passions seemed to be transcended by his ability to write stories

Insight from a secondary source (Whitcomb). Interestingly, in Andersen's desire to discover and transform himself, he is able to take archetypical truths, such as the abandoned orphan in "The Little Match Girl," and somehow move from worldly realities into innocence and wonder. One of these realities is the role of women. Within the tales, women are beautiful daughters, evil stepmothers and stepsisters, trusted servants, and even fairies themselves. Women are at the center of the action of most fairy tales, and their actions and relationships with each other and the world around them tell a lot about how women are expected to be. Women in fairy tales are portrayed as being in sympathy with the natural world, being in competition with other women, and being beautiful and good to men.

Roles of women

Thesis sentence

The natural world aids good women in fairy tales. Cinderella has her animal helpers: rats are turned into servants for Cinderella's night at the ball, mice become horses, lizards become footmen (Perrault 19). On the other hand, even though it appears in many ways that the evil woman is aided and supported by the natural world, such as when the witch gives Snow White the poisoned apple, it is nevertheless the sympathy the natural world has for the good woman that ultimately wins out. The evil stepmother in Snow White uses the apple to entice and poison Snow White; however, near the end of the story, when the good dwarves give Snow White in her coffin to the king's son and his servants, they stumble over a bush, and the poison apple flies out of Snow White's throat. Thus nature, seen in the bush, ultimately is on the side of the good woman. As easily as it is to see virtue wins out in Cinderella, evil is overtaken in "Sweet Rampion" (a version of the Rapunzel tale). After the prince leads his dear wife and children back to his own kingdom, the witch who had imprisoned Rampion was caught in a forest by a wolf who "ate every scrap of her except her yellow, claw-like hands and feet which it spat out. But the worms and beetles finished those off" (32). Nature sides with the good woman.

First example

Second example

Third example

Women are each other's enemies in fairy tales. This is largely because they are in competition with each other for men, and

*First
example* their entire base of competition is beauty. At the very beginning of
Snow White, the queen asks the famous question, "Mirror, Mirror,
on the wall, who's the fairest of them all?" When the answer is
Snow White, the queen decides that Snow White must die, so that
she can remain the most beautiful. The entire story, motivated by
this jealousy, begins. Cinderella is in competition with her stepsis-
*Second
example* ters for the hand of the prince. Because of her beauty, Cinderella is
a clear threat to the stepsisters; thus, the stepmother tries to insure
that Cinderella cannot attend the ball. Of course, Cinderella does,
and her beauty is enough to win the prince. In "Beauty and the
*Third
example* Beast," Beauty's two sisters, when grieving for the loss of their fortune, find their sister to be stupid and mean-spirited in her contentment with the "low way of life" (25). They also are very eager
to send her off with their father because "they were jealous of her
and because everybody loved her" (27). In the end, the fairy transforms the beast back into a handsome, graceful young prince, and
rewards Beauty. The fairy says, "You have chosen well, and you
have your reward, for a true heart is better than either good looks
or clever brains" (31). But when she turns to the two elder sisters,
she says,

> I know all your ill deeds, but I have no worse punishment for you
> than to see your sister happy. You shall stand as statues to the door of
> her palace, and when you repent of and have amended your faults,
> you shall become women again. But, to tell you the truth, I very
> much fear you will remain statues forever. (32)

Competition, between sisters, or between daughters and stepmothers, is a common theme in fairy tales.

Women in fairy tales are valued by men for their beauty and
their moral goodness. Indeed, a woman's physical beauty is a sign
*First
example* of her moral goodness. In "Beauty and the Beast," the youngest
daughter was so very beautiful that everyone called her the Little

Beauty, and Beauty, in her tender expression of love, transforms the Beast's palace into a place of light and rejoicing. This happens because Beauty, forgetting the Beast's physical ugliness because she is not only beautiful but also equally virtuous, expresses her love for the Beast. In that moment he changes back into a handsome, graceful young prince, reversing a curse. This curse had been placed on the Beast because he had been so mean-spirited and beastly. Thus, Beauty redeems the Beast. In "Cinderella," Perrault describes Cinderella as a "girl of rare goodness and sweetness of temper, who is the best creature" (18). This is foiled by the step- *Second example* mother's bad temper and her own foolish, ill-mannered, ugly step- sisters. Although Cinderella is treated like a lowly servant throughout the story, it is she that the king's son so desperately wants to marry after spending time with her at the ball. His attrac- tion to her is based on her great beauty, which is the admiration of everyone there; however, her goodness is also shown in her friendly treatment of her stepsisters at the ball. Finally, after the prince marries Cinderella, because she is as charming and good as she is beautiful, she arranges for her two stepsisters to be married to "two great lords of the court" (21). In "From an Ounce of Sor- row," a king has a beautiful daughter who grows lovelier by the day. When a prince from the secret garden sees her in all of her *Third example* sensitivity and compassion and beauty, he falls in love with her. Beauty is a sign of goodness, and thus the beautiful woman is de- serving of a prince's love.

Women are central figures in fairy tales, in large part because fairy tales were an oral art form passed down largely by women. *Fairy tales as a form of instruc- tion* Thus, the roles of women in fairy tales show young girls what women are to be like, and what they are not to be like. Girls are taught to be like Cinderella—to be virtuous, talented, beautiful, and sensitive. The ultimate goal for the women in many fairy tales is marriage, particularly to a prince—Cinderella, Snow White, Sleeping Beauty, Little Beauty, Anna, the princess in the Algerian tale—and girlhood ends with marriage. The messages are largely that women can seek security and advancement through men (and marriage). The prince is handsome and royal, and equally kind and loving; more importantly, the men search for the good women and save them from some undeserved fate. The prince in Sweet Rampion, blinded, wanders through the forest, crying for his Sweet Rampion until finally tears fall from the prince's eyes, washing away the witch's spell. This cleanses the spell from his eyes, allowing him to see again and find his family. And they lived happily ever after.

Works Cited

Andersen, Hans Christian. "The Little Match Girl." Griffith and Frey 132–34.

Beaumont, Marie Le Prince de. "Beauty and the Beast." Griffith and Frey 24–32.

Griffith, John W., and Charles H. Frey, eds. *Classics of Children's Literature.* 3rd ed. New York: MacMillan, 1992.

Grimm, Jacob, and Wilhelm Grimm. *Grimm's Fairy Tales.* Trans. Peter Carter. Oxford: Oxford UP, 1982.

"Hansel and Gretel." Grimm and Grimm 208–218.

Knappert, Jan. "From an Ounce of Sorrow." *The World & I.* Aug 2002: 188–195. ProQuest. San Diego Mesa Coll. Lib. 10 Nov. 2002. <http://www.umi.com/proquest>.

Perrault, Charles. "Cinderella, or the Little Glass Slipper." Griffith and Frey 17–21.

"Rumpelstiltzskin." Grimm and Grimm 13–20.

"The Story of Aladdin; Or, The Wonderful Lamp." *The Arabian Nights.* Illustrated Junior Library. 1946. New York: Grosset, 1974. 213–69.

"Sweet Rampion." Grimm and Grimm 27–32.

Whitcomb, Claire. "The Fairy Tale Lady." *Victoria.* Dec. 2001: 114+. *MasterFILE Premier.* EbscoHost. San Diego Mesa Coll. Lib. 10 Nov. 2002. <www.ebscohost.com>.

ADDITIONAL READINGS

Hansel and Gretel

Jacob and Wilheim Grimm

In the early 1800s, two German scholars, Jacob and Wilheim Grimm, set about copy-ing down oral folktales. They were interested in setting down in print these tales lest they be lost to history. They were interested in preserving German traditions and lan-guage. Thus, the brothers Grimm cannot be said to be truly the "authors" of the tales so much as transcribers of an oral tradition. The tale of "Hansel and Gretel" contains some common fairy tale character types: an evil mother figure, a weak or powerless fa-ther, and a cunning enemy—in this case, a witch who tricks the children into believing she is good and then tries to eat them.

Key Words

dearth	scarcity; famine; extreme lack of food
morsel	a tiny bit of food
bough	a large branch of a tree
cauldron	a large kettle or boiler
kneaded	pressed into a mass with one's hands

Hard by a great forest dwelt a poor wood-cutter with his wife and his two children. The boy was called Hansel and the girl Gretel. He had little to bite and to break, and once when great dearth fell on the land, he could no longer procure even daily bread. Now when he thought over this by night in his bed, and tossed about in his anxiety, he groaned and said to his wife: "What is to become of us? How are we to feed our poor children, when we no longer have anything even for ourselves?" "I'll tell you what, husband," answered the woman, "early tomorrow morning we will take the children out into the forest to where it is the thickest; there we will light a fire for them, and give each of them one more piece of bread, and then we will go to our work and leave them alone. They will not find the way home again, and we shall be rid of them." "No, wife," said the man, "I will not do that; how can I bear to leave my children alone in the forest?—the wild ani-mals would soon come and tear them to pieces." "O, you fool!" said she, "then we must all four die of hunger, you may as well plane the planks for our coffins," and she left him no peace until he consented. "But I feel very sorry for the poor children, all the same," said the man.

The two children had also not been able to sleep for hunger, and had heard what their stepmother had said to their father. Gretel wept bitter tears, and said to Hansel: "Now all is over with us." "Be quiet,

Gretel," said Hansel, "do not distress yourself, I will soon find a way to help us." And when the old folks had fallen asleep, he got up, put on his little coat, opened the door below, and crept outside. The moon shone brightly, and the white pebbles which lay in front of the house glittered like real silver pennies. Hansel stooped and stuffed the little pocket of his coat with as many as he could get in. Then he went back and said to Gretel: "Be comforted, dear little sister, and sleep in peace, God will not forsake us," and he lay down again in his bed. When day dawned, but before the sun had risen, the woman came and awoke the two children, saying: "Get up, you sluggards! We are going into the forest to fetch wood." She gave each a little piece of bread, and said: "There is something for your dinner, but do not eat it up before then, for you will get nothing else." Gretel took the bread under her apron, as Hansel had the pebbles in his pocket. Then they all set out together on the way to the forest. When they had walked a short time, Hansel stood still and peeped back at the house, and did so again and again. His father said: "Hansel, what are you looking at there and staying behind for? Pay attention, and do not forget how to use your legs." "Ah, father," said Hansel, "I am looking at my little white cat, which is sitting up on the roof, and wants to say goodbye to me." The wife said: "Fool, that is not your little cat, that is the morning sun which is shining on the chimneys." Hansel, however, had not been looking back at the cat, but had been constantly throwing one of the white pebble-stones out of his pocket on the road.

When they had reached the middle of the forest, the father said: "Now, children, pile up some wood, and I will light a fire that you may not be cold." Hansel and Gretel gathered brushwood together, as high as a little hill. The brushwood was lighted, and when the flames were burning very high, the woman said: "Now, children, lay yourselves down by the fire and rest; we will go into the forest and cut some wood. When we have done, we will come back and fetch you away."

Hansel and Gretel sat by the fire, and when noon came, each ate a little piece of bread, and as they heard the strokes of the wood-axe they believed that their father was near. It was not the axe, however, but a branch which he had fastened to a withered tree which the wind was blowing backwards and forwards. And as they had been sitting such a long time, their eyes closed with fatigue, and they fell fast asleep. When at last they awoke, it was already dark night. Gretel began to cry and said: "How are we to get out of the forest now?" But Hansel comforted her and said: "Just wait a little, until the moon has risen, and then we will soon find the way." And when the full moon had risen, Hansel took his little sister by the hand, and followed the pebbles which shone like newly-coined silver pieces, and showed them the way.

They walked the whole night long, and by break of day came once more to their father's house. They knocked at the door, and when the woman opened it and saw that it was Hansel and Gretel, she said: 5

"You naughty children, why have you slept so long in the forest?—we thought you were never coming back at all!" The father, however, rejoiced, for it had cut him to the heart to leave them behind alone.

Not long afterwards, there was once more great dearth throughout the land, and the children heard their mother saying at night to their father: "Everything is eaten again, we have one half loaf left, and that is the end. The children must go, we will take them farther into the wood, so that they will not find their way out again; there is no other means of saving ourselves!" The man's heart was heavy, and he thought: "It would be better for you to share the last mouthful with your children." The woman, however, would listen to nothing that he had to say, but scolded and reproached him. He who says A must say B, likewise, and as he had yielded the first time, he had to do so a second time also.

The children, however, were still awake and had heard the conversation. When the old folks were asleep, Hansel again got up, and wanted to go out and pick up pebbles as he had done before, but the woman had locked the door, and Hansel could not get out. Nevertheless he comforted his little sister, and said: "Do not cry, Gretel, go to sleep quietly, the good God will help us."

Early in the morning came the woman, and took the children out of their beds. Their piece of bread was given to them, but it was still smaller than the time before. On the way into the forest Hansel crumbled his in his pocket, and often stood still and threw a morsel on the ground. "Hansel, why do you stop and look round?" said the father, "go on." "I am looking back at my little pigeon which is sitting on the roof, and wants to say goodbye to me," answered Hansel. "Fool!" said the woman, "that is not your little pigeon, that is the morning sun that is shining on the chimney." Hansel, however, little by little, threw all the crumbs on the path.

The woman led the children still deeper into the forest, where they had never in their lives been before. Then a great fire was again made, and the mother said: "Just sit there, you children, and when you are tired you may sleep a little; we are going into the forest to cut wood, and in the evening when we are done, we will come and fetch you away." When it was noon, Gretel shared her piece of bread with Hansel, who had scattered his by the way. Then they fell asleep and evening passed, but no one came to the poor children. They did not awake until it was dark night, and Hansel comforted his little sister and said: "Just wait, Gretel, until the moon rises, and then we shall see the crumbs of bread which I have strewn about, they will show us our way home again." When the moon came they set out, but they found no crumbs, for the many thousands of birds which fly about in the woods and fields had picked them all up. Hansel said to Gretel: "We shall soon find the way," but they did not find it. They walked the whole night and all the next day too from morning till evening, but they did not get out of the forest, and were very hungry, for they had nothing to eat but two or three berries, which grew on the ground. And as they were so weary that their legs would carry them no longer, they lay down beneath a tree and fell asleep.

It was now three mornings since they had left their father's house. 10 They began to walk again, but they always came deeper into the forest, and if help did not come soon, they must die of hunger and weariness. When it was mid-day, they saw a beautiful snow-white bird sitting on a bough, which sang so delightfully that they stood still and listened to it. And when its song was over, it spread its wings and flew away before them, and they followed it until they reached a little house, on the roof of which it alighted; and when they approached the little house they saw that it was built of bread and covered with cakes, but that the windows were of clear sugar. "We will set to work on that," said Hansel, "and have a good meal. I will eat a bit of the roof, and you Gretel, can eat some of the window, it will taste sweet." Hansel reached up above, and broke off a little of the roof to try how it tasted, and Gretel leant against the window and nibbled at the panes. Then a soft voice cried from the parlour:

"Nibble, nibble, gnaw,
Who is nibbling at my little house?"

The children answered:

"The wind, the wind,
The heaven-born wind,"

and went on eating without disturbing themselves. Hansel, who liked the taste of the roof, tore down a great piece of it, and Gretel pushed out the whole of one round window-pane, sat down, and enjoyed herself with it. Suddenly the door opened, and a woman as old as the hills, who supported herself on crutches, came creeping out. Hansel and Gretel were so terribly frightened that they let fall what they had in their hands. The old woman, however, nodded her head, and said: "Oh, you dear children, who has brought you here? Do come in, and stay with me. No harm shall happen to you." She took them both by the hand, and led them into her little house. Then good food was set before them, milk and pancakes, with sugar, apples, and nuts. Afterwards two pretty little beds were covered with clean white linen, and Hansel and Gretel lay down in them, and thought they were in heaven.

The old woman had only pretended to be so kind; she was in reality a wicked witch, who lay in wait for children, and had only built the little house of bread in order to entice them there. When a child fell into her power, she killed it, cooked and ate it, and that was a feast day with her. Witches have red eyes, and cannot see far, but they have a keen scent like the beasts, and are aware when human beings draw near. When Hansel and Gretel came into her neighbourhood, she laughed with malice, and said mockingly: "I have them, they shall not escape me again!" Early in the morning before the children were awake, she was already up, and when she saw both of them sleeping and looking so pretty, with their plump and rosy cheeks she muttered to herself: "That will be a dainty mouthful!" Then she seized Hansel with her shrivelled hand, carried him into a little stable, and locked him in behind a grated door. Scream as he might, it would not help him. Then she went to Gretel, shook her till she awoke, and cried: "Get up, lazy thing, fetch some water, and cook something good for your brother, he is in the stable outside, and is to be made fat. When he is fat, I will eat him." Gretel began to weep bitterly, but it was all in vain, for she was forced to do what the wicked witch commanded.

And now the best food was cooked for poor Hansel, but Gretel got nothing but crab-shells. Every morning the woman crept to the little stable, and cried: "Hansel, stretch out your finger that I may feel if you will soon be fat." Hansel, however, stretched out a little bone to her, and the old woman, who had dim eyes, could not see it, and thought it was Hansel's finger, and was astonished that there was no way of fattening him. When four weeks had gone by, and Hansel still remained thin, she was seized with impatience and would not wait any longer. "Now, then, Gretel," she cried to the girl, "stir yourself, and bring some water. Let Hansel be fat or lean, tomorrow I will kill him, and cook him." Ah, how the poor little sister did lament when she had to fetch the water, and how her tears did flow down her cheeks! "Dear God, do help us," she cried. "If the wild beasts in the forest had but devoured us, we should at any rate have died together." "Just keep your noise to yourself," said the old woman, "it won't help you at all."

Early in the morning, Gretel had to go out and hang up the cauldron with the water, and light the fire. "We will bake first," said the old woman, "I have already heated the oven, and kneaded the dough." She pushed poor Gretel out to the oven, from which flames of fire were already darting. "Creep in," said the witch, "and see if it is properly heated, so that we can put the bread in." And once Gretel was inside, she intended to shut the oven and let her bake in it, and then she would eat her, too. But Gretel saw what she had in mind, and said: "I do not know how I am to do it; how do I get in?" "Silly goose," said the old woman. "The door is big enough; just look, I can get in myself!" and she crept up and thrust her head into the oven. Then Gretel gave her a push that drove her far into it, and shut the iron door, and fastened the bolt. Oh! then she began to howl quite horribly, but Gretel ran away and the godless witch was miserably burnt to death.

Gretel, however, ran like lightning to Hansel, opened his little stable, and cried: "Hansel, we are saved! The old witch is dead!" Then Hansel sprang like a bird from its cage when the door is opened. How they did rejoice and embrace each other, and dance about and kiss each other! And as they had no longer any need to fear her, they went into the witch's house, and in every corner there stood chests full of pearls and jewels. "These are far better than pebbles!" said Hansel, and thrust into his pockets whatever could be got in, and Gretel said: "I, too, will take something home with me," and filled her pinafore full. "But now we must be off," said Hansel, "that we may get out of the witch's forest."

When they had walked for two hours, they came to a great stretch of water. "We cannot cross," said Hansel, "I see no foot-plank, and no bridge." "And there is also no ferry," answered Gretel, "but a white duck is swimming there: if I ask her, she will help us over." Then she cried:

> "Little duck, little duck, dost thou see,
> Hansel and Gretel are waiting for thee?
> There's never a plank, or bridge in sight,
> Take us across on thy back so white."

The duck came to them, and Hansel seated himself on its back, and told his sister to sit by him. "No," replied Gretel, "that will be too heavy for the little duck; she shall take us across, one after the other." The good little duck did so, and when they were once safely across and had walked for a short time, the forest seemed to be more and more familiar to them, and at length they saw from afar their father's house. Then they began to run, rushed into the parlour, and threw themselves round their father's neck. The man had not known one happy hour since he had left the children in the forest; the woman, however, was dead. Gretel emptied her pinafore until pearls and precious stones ran about the room, and Hansel threw one handful after another out of his pocket to add to them. Then all anxiety was at an end, and they lived together in perfect happiness. My tale is done, there runs a mouse; whosoever catches it, may make himself a big fur cap out of it.

What Did You Read?

1. Why do the father and mother abandon Hansel and Gretel in the forest?
2. What did the children find in the witch's house in the chests in every corner?
3. How do Hansel and Gretel cross the river to get home?

What Do You Think?

1. How is the father portrayed in relationship to his wife and to his two children? What is significant about that?

2. What is significant about nature? Is it sympathetic or not to the plight of the children?

3. What is the role or importance of food in this story?

How Was It Done?

1. How does the integration of short verses help to add interest to the story?

2. How is the story structured around animals? Explain.

3. Is the storyline a traditional one—with beginning conflict, action rising to climax, and denouement?

4. How does the dynamic of evil and innocent participants operate in the story?

Rumpelstiltzskin

Jacob and Wilheim Grimm

In this classic tale, a young girl is put into a precarious position by the vanity of her father, who has bragged to the king that she can spin straw into gold. The king puts her to the test, and if she fails, she will be put to death. A strange little man saves her by spinning the gold himself, but he exacts a steep price: her first-born child.

Key Words

spin	to twist fiber into yarn or thread
manikin	a little man
jeered	mocked; taunted

By the side of a wood, in a country a long way off, ran a fine stream of water; and upon the stream there stood a mill. The miller's house was close by, and the miller, you must know, had a very beautiful daughter. She was, moreover, very shrewd and clever; and the miller was so proud of her, that he one day told the king of the land, who used to come and hunt in the wood, that his daughter could spin gold out of straw. Now this king was very fond of money; and when he heard the miller's boast his greediness was raised, and he sent for the girl to be brought before him. Then he led her to a chamber in his palace where there was a great heap of straw, and gave her a spinning-wheel, and said, "All this must be spun into gold before morning, as you love your life." It was in vain that the poor maiden said that it was only a silly boast of her father, for that she could do no such thing as spin straw into gold: the chamber door was locked, and she was left alone.

She sat down in one corner of the room, and began to bewail her hard fate; when on a sudden the door opened, and a droll-looking little man hobbled in, and said, "Good morrow to you, my good lass; what are you weeping for?" "Alas!" said she, "I must spin this straw into gold, and I know not how." "What will you give me," said the hobgoblin, "to do it for you?" "My necklace," replied the maiden. He took her at her word, and sat himself down to the wheel, and whistled and sang:

"Round about, round about,
 Lo and behold!
Reel away, reel away,
 Straw into gold!"

And round about the wheel went merrily; the work was quickly done, and the straw was all spun into gold.

When the king came and saw this, he was greatly astonished and pleased; but his heart grew still more greedy of gain, and he shut up the poor miller's daughter again with a fresh task. Then she knew not what to do, and sat down once more to weep; but the dwarf soon opened the door, and said, "What will you give me to do your task?" "The ring on my finger," said she. So her little friend took the ring, and began to work at the wheel again, and whistled and sang:

"Round about, round about,
 Lo and behold!
Reel away, reel away,
 Straw into gold!"

till, long before morning, all was done again.

The king was greatly delighted to see all this glittering treasure; but still he had not enough: so he took the miller's daughter to a yet larger heap, and said, "All this must be spun tonight; and if it is, you shall be my queen." As soon as she was alone that dwarf came in, and said, "What will you give me to spin gold for you this third time?" "I have nothing left," said she. "Then say you will give me," said the little man, "the first little child that you may have when you are queen." "That may never be," thought the miller's daughter: and as she knew no other way to get her task done, she said she would do what he asked. Round went the wheel again to the old song, and the manikin once more spun the heap into gold. The king came in the morning, and, finding all he wanted, was forced to keep his word; so he married the miller's daughter, and she really became queen.

At the birth of her first little child she was very glad, and forgot the dwarf, and what she had said. But one day he came into her room, where she was sitting playing with her baby, and put her in mind of it. Then she grieved sorely at her misfortune, and said she would give him all the wealth of the kingdom if he would let her off, but in vain; till at last her tears softened him, and he said, "I will give you three days' grace, and if during that time you tell me my name, you shall keep your child."

Now the queen lay awake all night, thinking of all the odd names that she had ever heard; and she sent messengers all over the land to find out new ones. The next day the little man came, and she began with TIMOTHY, ICHABOD, BENJAMIN, JEREMIAH, and all the names she could remember; but to all and each of them he said, "Madam, that is not my name."

The second day she began with all the comical names she could hear of, BANDY-LEGS, HUNCHBACK, CROOK-SHANKS, and so on; but the little gentleman still said to every one of them, "Madam, that is not my name."

The third day one of the messengers came back, and said, "I have travelled two days without hearing of any other names; but yesterday, as I was climbing a high hill, among the trees of the forest where the fox and the hare bid each other good night, I saw a little hut; and before the hut burnt a fire; and round about the fire a funny little dwarf was dancing upon one leg, and singing:

"Merrily the feast I'll make.
Today I'll brew, tomorrow bake;
Merrily I'll dance and sing,
For next day will a stranger bring.
Little does my lady dream
Rumpelstiltskin is my name!"

When the queen heard this she jumped for joy, and as soon as her little friend came she sat down upon her throne, and called all her court round to enjoy the fun; and the nurse stood by her side with the baby in her arms, as if it was quite ready to be given up. Then the little man began to chuckle at the thought of having the poor child, to take home with him to his hut in the woods; and he cried out, "Now, lady, what is my name?" "Is it JOHN?" asked she. "No, madam!" "Is it TOM?" "No, madam!" "Is it JEMMY?" "It is not." "Can your name be RUMPEL-STILTSKIN?" said the lady slyly. "Some witch told you that!—some witch told you that!" cried the little man, and dashed his right foot in a rage so deep into the floor, that he was forced to lay hold of it with both hands to pull it out.

Then he made the best of his way off, while the nurse laughed and 10 the baby crowed; and all the court jeered at him for having had so much trouble for nothing, and said, "We wish you a very good morning, and a merry feast, Mr. RUMPLESTILTSKIN!"

What Did You Read?

1. What seems to be the magic number in this story?
2. How does Anna find herself in the predicament of having to spin straw into gold?
3. Who are the innocent victims?
4. How does Anna learn the name of Rumpelstiltzskin?

What Do You Think?

1. How are men portrayed (i.e., the father, the king, the dwarf) in this story?
2. What does this story say about women?
3. How do you reconcile Anna being able to marry a man who was willing to put her to death if she did not produce gold?
4. Do you feel sorry for Rumpelstiltzskin? Why or why not?

How Was It Done?

1. How is rhyming central to the construction of the plot line?
2. What values provide the foundation of this story?
3. How is the number three central to the storyline?
4. What is the point of publicly humiliating Rumpelstiltzskin at the end of the story?

Beauty and the Beast

Marie Le Prince de Beaumont

Beaumont was an 18th-century Frenchwoman living in London when she wrote this tale. The lesson of looking beyond surface appearances to find the true value in a person reminds one of Cinderella's situation, and later, of Hans Christian Andersen's "Ugly Duckling." This tale also features ungrateful and jealous sisters, again reminiscent of "Cinderella." However, Cinderella is seeking the love of a handsome prince; in Beaumont's tale, the prince has been transformed into a hideous beast, and the love test is more Beauty's than the Beast's—his curse can only be lifted if she loves him. The symbolic depth of the fairy tale, centering on the love test, has provided rich ground for philosophical and moral inquiry.

Key Words

airs	an artificial or affected manner
affront	insult
arbors	trees; forests

atone	to make amends; reconcile
entreated	begged
obstinately	stubbornly
melancholy	sadness
vexed	troubled; puzzled
amended	changed; fixed

There was once a very rich merchant, who had six children, three boys and three girls. As he was himself a man of great sense, he spared no expense for their education. The three daughters were all handsome, but particularly the youngest; indeed, she was so very beautiful, that in her childhood everyone called her the Little Beauty; and being equally lovely when she was grown up, nobody called her by any other name, which made her sisters very jealous of her. This youngest daughter was not only more handsome than her sisters, but also was better tempered. The two eldest were vain of their wealth and position. They gave themselves a thousand airs, and refused to visit other merchants' daughters; nor would they condescend to be seen except with persons of quality.

They went every day to balls, plays, and public walks, and always made game of their youngest sister for spending her time in reading or other useful employments. As it was well known that these young ladies would have large fortunes, many great merchants wished to get them for wives; but the two eldest always answered, that, for their parts, they had no thoughts of marrying anyone below a duke or an earl at least. Beauty had quite as many offers as her sisters, but she always answered, with the greatest civility, that though she was obliged to her lovers, she would rather live some years longer with her father, as she thought herself too young to marry.

It happened that, by some unlucky accident, the merchant suddenly lost all his fortune, and had nothing left but a small cottage in the country. Upon this he said to his daughters, while the tears ran down his cheeks, "My children, we must now go and dwell in the cottage, and try to get a living by labor, for we have no other means of support." The two eldest replied that they did not know how to work, and would not leave town; for they had lovers enough who would be glad to marry them, though they had no longer any fortune. But in this they were mistaken; for when the lovers heard what had happened, they said: "The girls were so proud and ill-tempered, that all we wanted was their fortune; we are not sorry at all to see their pride brought down; let them show off their airs to their cows and sheep." But everybody pitied poor Beauty, because she was so sweet-tempered and kind to all, and several gentlemen offered to marry her, though she had not a penny; but Beauty still refused, and said she could not think of leaving her poor father in this trouble. At first Beauty could not help sometimes crying in secret for the hardships she was now obliged to suffer; but in a very short time she said to herself, "All the crying in the world will do me no good, so I will try to be happy without a fortune."

When they had removed to their cottage, the merchant and his three sons employed themselves in plowing and sowing the fields, and working in the garden. Beauty also did her part, for she rose by four o'clock every morning, lighted the fires, cleaned the house, and got ready the breakfast for the whole family. At first she found all this very hard; but she soon grew quite used to it, and thought it no hardship; indeed, the work greatly benefited her health. When she had done, she used to amuse herself with reading, playing her music, or singing while she spun. But her two sisters were at a loss what to do to pass the time away; they had their breakfast in bed, and did not rise till ten o'clock. Then they commonly walked out, but always found themselves very soon tired; when they would often sit down under a shady tree, and grieve for the loss of their carriage and fine clothes, and say to each other, "What a mean-spirited, poor stupid creature our young sister is, to be so content with this low way of life!" But their father thought differently; and loved and admired his youngest child more than ever.

After they had lived in this manner about a year the merchant received a letter, which informed him that one of his richest ships, which he thought was lost, had just come into port. This news made the two eldest sisters almost mad with joy; for they thought they should now leave the cottage, and have all their finery again. When they found that their father must take a journey to the ship, the two eldest begged he would not fail to bring them back some new gowns, caps, rings, and all sorts of trinkets. But Beauty asked for nothing; for she thought in herself that all the ship was worth would hardly buy everything her sisters wished for. "Beauty," said the merchant, "you ask for nothing: what can I bring you, my child?"

"Since you are so kind as to think of me, dear father," she answered, "I should be glad if you would bring me a rose, for we have none in our garden." Now Beauty did not indeed wish for a rose, nor anything else, but she only said this that she might not affront her sisters; otherwise they would have said she wanted her father to praise her for desiring nothing. The merchant took his leave of them, and set out on his journey; but when he got to the ship, some persons went to law with him about the cargo, and after a deal of trouble he came back to his cottage as poor as he had left it. When he was within thirty miles of his home, and thinking of the joy of again meeting his children, he lost his way in the midst of a dense forest. It rained and snowed very hard, and besides, the wind was so high as to throw him twice from his horse. Night came on, and he feared he should die of cold and hunger, or be torn to pieces by the wolves that he heard howling around him. All at once, he cast his eyes toward a long avenue, and saw at the end a light, but it seemed a great way off. He made the best of his way toward it, and found that it came from a splendid palace, the windows of which were all blazing with light. It had great bronze gates, standing wide open, and fine courtyards, through which the merchant passed; but not a living soul was to be seen. There were stables, too, which his poor, starved horse, less scrupulous than himself, entered at once, and took a good meal of oats and hay. His master then tied him up, and walked toward the entrance hall, but still without seeing a single creature. He went on to a large dining parlor, where he found a good fire, and a table covered with some very nice dishes, but only one plate with a knife and fork. As the snow and rain had wetted him to the skin, he went up to the fire to dry himself. "I hope," said he, "the master of the house or his servants will excuse me, for it surely will not be long now before I see them." He waited some time, but still nobody came: at last the clock struck eleven, and the merchant, being quite faint for the want of food, helped himself to a chicken, and to a few glasses of wine, yet all the time trembling with fear. He sat till the clock struck twelve, and then, taking courage, began to think he might as well look about him: so he opened a door at the end of the hall, and went through it into a very grand room, in which there was a fine bed; and as he was feeling very weary, he shut the door, took off his clothes, and got into it.

It was ten o'clock in the morning before he awoke, when he was amazed to see a handsome new suit of clothes laid ready for him, instead of his own, which were all torn and spoiled. "To be sure," said he to himself, "this place belongs to some good fairy, who has taken pity on my ill luck." He looked out of the window, and instead of the snow-covered wood, where he had lost himself the previous night, he saw the most charming arbors covered with all kinds of flowers. Returning to the hall where he had supper, he found a breakfast table, ready prepared. "Indeed, my good fairy," said the merchant aloud, "I am vastly obliged to you for your kind care of me." He then made a hearty breakfast, took his hat, and was going to the stable to pay his horse a visit; but as he passed under one of the arbors, which was loaded with roses, he thought of what Beauty had asked him to bring back to her, and so he took a bunch of roses to carry home. At the same moment he heard a loud noise, and saw coming toward him a beast, so frightful to look at that he was ready to faint with fear. "Ungrateful man!" said the beast in a terrible voice. "I have saved your life by admitting you into my palace, and in return you steal my roses, which I value more than anything I possess. But you shall atone for your fault—die in a quarter of an hour."

The merchant fell on his knees, and clasping his hands, said, "Sir, I humbly beg your pardon: I did not think it would offend you to gather a rose for one of my daughters, who had entreated me to bring her one home. Do not kill me, my lord!"

"I am not a lord, but a beast," replied the monster. "I hate false compliments: so do not fancy that you can coax me by any such ways. You tell me that you have daughters; now I will suffer you to escape, if one of them will come and die in your stead. If not, promise you will yourself return in three months, to be dealt with as I may choose."

The tender-hearted merchant had no thoughts of letting any one of his daughters die for his sake; but he knew that if he seemed to accept the beast's terms, he should at least have the pleasure of seeing them once again. So he gave his promise, and was told that he might then set off as soon as he liked. "But," said the beast, "I do not wish you to go back empty-handed. Go to the room you slept in, and you will find a chest there; fill it with whatsoever you like best, and I will have it taken to your own house for you." 10

When the beast said this, he went away. The good merchant, left to himself, began to consider that, as he must die—for he had no thought of breaking a promise, made even to a beast—he might as well have the comfort of leaving his children provided for. He returned to the room he had slept in, and found there heaps of gold pieces lying about. He filled the chest with them to the very brim, locked it, and, mounting his horse, left the palace as sorrowful as he had been glad when he first beheld it. The horse took a path across the forest of his own accord, and in a few hours they reached the merchant's house. His children came running round him, but, instead of kissing them with joy, he could not help weeping as he looked at them. He held in his hand the bunch of roses, which he gave to Beauty, saying, "Take these roses, Beauty; but little do you think how dear they have cost your poor father"; and then he gave them an account of all that he had seen or heard in the palace of the beast.

The two eldest sisters now began to shed tears, and to lay the blame upon Beauty, who, they said, would be cause of her father's death. "See," said they, "what happens from the pride of the little wretch; why did not she ask for such things as we did? But, to be sure, Miss must not be like other people; and though she will be the cause of her father's death, yet she does not shed a tear."

"It would be useless," replied Beauty, "for my father shall not die. As the beast will accept one of his daughters, I will give myself up, and be only too happy to prove my love for the best of fathers."

"No, sister," said the three brothers with one voice, "that cannot be; we will go in search of this monster, and either he or we will perish."

"Do not hope to kill him," said the merchant, "his power is far too great. But Beauty's young life shall not be sacrificed; I am old, and can- 15 not expect to live much longer; so I shall but give up a few years of my life, and shall only grieve for the sake of my children."

"Never, father," cried Beauty; "if you go back to the palace, you cannot hinder my going after you! Though young, I am not over-fond of life; and I would much rather be eaten up by the monster, than die of grief for your loss."

The merchant in vain tried to reason with Beauty who still obstinately kept to her purpose; which, in truth, made her two sisters glad, for they were jealous of her, because everybody loved her.

The merchant was so grieved at the thought of losing his child, that he never once thought of the chest filled with gold, but at night, to his great surprise, he found it standing by his bedside. He said nothing about his riches to his eldest daughters, for he knew very well it would at once make them want to return to town; but he told Beauty his secret, and she then said, that while he was away, two gentlemen had been on a visit at her cottage, who had fallen in love with her two sisters. She entreated her father to marry them without delay, for she was so sweet-natured she only wished them to be happy.

Three months went by, only too fast, and then the merchant and Beauty got ready to set out for the palace of the beast. Upon this, the two sisters rubbed their eyes with an onion, to make believe they were crying; both the merchant and his sons cried in earnest. Only Beauty shed no tears. They reached the palace in a very few hours, and the horse, without bidding, went into the stable as before. The merchant and Beauty walked toward the large hall, where they found a table covered with every dainty and two plates laid already. The merchant had very little appetite; but Beauty, that she might the better hide her grief, placed herself at the table, and helped her father; she then began to eat herself, and thought all the time that, to be sure, the beast had a mind to fatten her before he ate her up, since he had provided such good cheer for her. When they had done their supper, they heard a great noise, and the good old man began to bid his poor child farewell, for he knew that it was the beast coming to them. When Beauty first saw that frightful form, she was very much terrified, but tried to hide her fear. The creature walked up to her, and eyed her all over—then asked her in a dreadful voice if she had come quite of her own accord.

"Yes," said Beauty.   20

"Then you are a good girl, and I am very much obliged to you."

This was such an astonishingly civil answer that Beauty's courage rose: but it sank again when the beast, addressing the merchant, desired him to leave the palace next morning, and never return to it again. "And so good night, merchant. And good night, Beauty."

"Good night, beast," she answered, as the monster shuffled out.

"Ah! my dear child," said the merchant, kissing his daughter, "I am half dead already, at the thought of leaving you with this dreadful beast; you shall go back and let me stay in your place."

"No," said Beauty, boldly, "I will never agree to that; you must go 25 home tomorrow morning."

They then wished each other good night, and went to bed, both of them thinking they should not be able to close their eyes; but as soon as ever they had lain down, they fell in to a deep sleep, and did not awake till morning. Beauty dreamed that a lady came up to her, who said, "I am very much pleased, Beauty, with the goodness you have shown, in being willing to give your life to save that of your father. Do not be afraid of anything; you shall not go without a reward."

As soon as Beauty awoke she told her father this dream; but though it gave him some comfort, he was a long time before he could be persuaded to leave the palace. At last Beauty succeeded in getting him safely away.

When her father was out of sight, poor Beauty began to weep sorely; still, having naturally a courageous spirit, she soon resolved not to make her sad case still worse by sorrow, which she knew was vain, but to wait and be patient. She walked about to take a view of all the palace, and the elegance of every part of it much charmed her.

But what was her surprise, when she came to a door on which was written, BEAUTY's ROOM! She opened it in haste, and her eyes were dazzled by the splendor and taste of the apartment. What made her wonder more than all the rest, was a large library filled with books, a harpsichord, and many pieces of music. "The beast surely does not mean to eat me up immediately," said she, "since he takes care I shall not be at loss how to amuse myself." She opened the library and saw these verses written in letters of gold in the back of one of the books:

"Beauteous lady, dry your tears,
Here's no cause for sighs or fears.
Command as freely as you may,
For you command and I obey."

"Alas!" said she, sighing: "I wish I could only command a sight of 30 my poor father, and to know what he is doing at this moment." Just then, by chance, she cast her eyes upon a looking-glass that stood near her, and in it she saw a picture of her old home, and her father riding mournfully up to the door. Her sisters came out to meet him, and although they tried to look sorry, it was easy to see that in their hearts they were very glad. In a short time all this picture disappeared, but it caused Beauty to think that the beast, besides being very powerful, was also very kind. About the middle of the day she found a table laid ready for her, and a sweet concert of music played all the time she was dining, without her seeing anybody. But at supper, when she was going to seat herself at table, she heard the noise of the beast, and could not help trembling with fear.

"Beauty," said he, "will you give me leave to see you sup?"

"That is as you please," answered she, very much afraid.

"Not in the least," said the beast. "You alone command in this place. If you should not like my company, you need only say so, and I will leave you that moment. But tell me, Beauty, do you not think me very ugly?"

"Why, yes," said she, "for I cannot tell a falsehood; but then I think you are very good."

"Am I?" sadly replied the beast. "Yet, besides being ugly, I am also 35 very stupid; I know well enough that I am but a beast."

"Stupid people," said Beauty, "are never aware of it themselves."

At which kindly speech the beast looked pleased, and replied, not without an awkward sort of politeness. "Pray do not let me detain you from supper, and be sure that you are well served. All you see is your own, and I should be deeply grieved if you wanted for anything."

"You are very kind—so kind that I almost forgot you are so ugly," said Beauty, earnestly.

"Ah! yes," answered the beast, with a great sigh; "I hope I am good-tempered, but still I am only a monster."

"There is many a monster who wears the form of a man; it is better 40 of the two to have the heart of a man and the form of a monster."

"I would thank you, Beauty, for this speech, but I am too senseless to say anything that would please you," returned the beast in a melancholy voice; and altogether he seemed so gentle and so unhappy that Beauty, who had the tenderest heart in the world, felt her fear of him gradually vanish.

She ate her supper with a good appetite, and conversed in her own sensible and charming way, till at last, when the beast rose to depart, he terrified her more than ever by saying abruptly, in his gruff voice, "Beauty, will you marry me?"

Now Beauty, frightened as she was, would speak only the exact truth; besides her father had told her that the beast liked only to have the truth spoken to him. So she answered, in a very firm tone, "No, beast."

He did not get into a passion, but sighed deeply and departed.

When Beauty found herself alone, she began to feel pity for the 45 poor beast. "Oh," she said, "what a sad thing it is that he should be so very frightful, since he is so good-tempered!"

Beauty lived three months in this palace very well pleased. The beast came to see her every night, and talked with her while she supped; and though what he said was not very clever, yet, as she saw in him every day some new goodness, instead of dreading the time of his coming, she soon began continually looking at her watch, to see if it were nine o'clock; for that was the hour when he never failed to visit her. One thing only vexed her, which was that every night before he went away, he always made it a rule to ask her if she would be his wife, and seemed very much grieved at her steadfastly replying "No." At last, one night, she said to him, "You wound me greatly, beast, by forcing me to refuse you so often; I wish I could take such a liking to you as to agree to marry you; but I must tell you plainly that I do not think it will ever happen. I shall always be your friend; so try to let that content you."

"I must," sighed the beast, "for I know well enough how frightful I am; but I love you better than myself. Yet I think I am very lucky in your being pleased to stay with me; now promise, Beauty, that you will never leave me."

Beauty would almost have agreed to this, so sorry was she for him, but she had that day seen in her magic glass, which she looked at constantly, that her father was dying of grief for her sake.

"Alas!' she said. "I long so much to see my father, that if you do not give me leave to visit him, I shall break my heart."

"I would rather break mine, Beauty," answered the beast; "I will 50 send you to your father's cottage: you shall stay there, and your poor beast shall die of sorrow."

"No," said Beauty, crying, "I love you too well to be the cause of your death; I promise to return in a week. You have shown me that my sisters are married, and my brothers are gone for soldiers, so that my father is left all alone. Let me stay a week with him."

"You shall find yourself with him tomorrow morning," replied the beast; "but mind, do not forget your promise. When you wish to return, you have nothing to do but to put your ring on a table when you go to bed. Good-bye, Beauty!" The beast sighed as he said these words, and Beauty went to bed very sorry to see him so much grieved. When she awoke in the morning, she found herself in her father's cottage. She rang a bell that was at her bedside, and a servant entered; but as soon as she saw Beauty, the woman gave a loud shriek; upon which the merchant ran upstairs, and when he beheld his daughter he ran to her, and kissed her a hundred times. At last Beauty began to remember that she had brought no clothes with her to put on; but the servant told her she had just found in the next room a large chest full of dresses, trimmed all over with gold, and adorned with pearls and diamonds.

Beauty, in her own mind, thanked the beast for his kindness, and put on the plainest gown she could find among them all. She then desired the servant to lay the rest aside, for she intended to give them to her sisters; but, as soon as she had spoken these words, the chest was gone out of sight in a moment. Her father then suggested, perhaps the beast chose for her to keep them all for herself: and as soon as he had said this, they saw the chest standing again in the same place. While Beauty was dressing herself, a servant brought word to her that her sisters were come with their husbands to pay her a visit. They both lived unhappily with the gentlemen they had married. The husband of the eldest was very handsome, but was so proud of this that he thought of nothing else from morning till night, and did not care a pin for the beauty of his wife. The second had married a man of great learning; but he made no use of it, except to torment and affront all his friends, and his wife more than any of them. The two sisters were ready to burst with spite when they saw Beauty dressed like a princess, and looking so very charming. All the kindness that she showed them was of no use; for they were vexed more than ever when she told them how happy she lived at the palace of the beast. The spiteful creatures went by themselves into the garden, where they cried to think of her good fortune.

"Why should the little wretch be better off than we?" said they. "We are much handsomer than she is."

"Sister," said the eldest, "a thought has just come into my head; let 55 us try to keep her here longer than the week for which the beast gave her leave; and then he will be so angry that perhaps when she goes back to him he will eat her up in a moment."

"That is well thought of," answered the other, "but to do this, we must pretend to be very kind."

They then went to join her in the cottage, where they showed her so much false love that Beauty could not help crying for joy.

When the week was ended, the two sisters began to pretend such grief at the thought of her leaving them that she agreed to stay a week more; but all that time Beauty could not help fretting for the sorrow that she knew her absence would give her poor beast; for she tenderly loved him, and much wished for his company again. Among all the grand and clever people she saw, she found nobody who was half so sensible, so affectionate, so thoughtful, or so kind. The tenth night of her being at the cottage, she dreamed she was in the garden of the palace, that the beast lay dying on a grass plot, and with his last breath put her in mind of her promise, and laid his death to her forsaking him. Beauty awoke in a great fright, and she burst into tears. "Am not I wicked," said she, "to behave so ill to a beast who has shown me so much kindness? Why will I not marry him? I am sure I should be more happy with him than my sisters are with their husbands. He shall not be wretched any longer on my account; for I should do nothing but blame myself all the rest of my life."

She then rose, put her ring on the table, got into bed again, and soon fell asleep. In the morning she with joy found herself in the palace of the beast. She dressed herself very carefully, that she might please him the better, and thought she had never known a day pass away so slowly. At last the clock struck nine, but the beast did not come. Beauty, dreading lest she might truly have caused his death, ran from room to room, calling out: "Beast, dear beast"; but there was no answer. At last she remembered her dream, rushed to the grass plot, and there saw him lying apparently dead beside the fountain. Forgetting all his ugliness, she threw herself upon his body, and finding his heart still beating, she fetched some water and sprinkled it over him, weeping and sobbing the while.

The beast opened his eyes. "You forgot your promise, Beauty, and 60 so I determined to die; for I could not live without you. I have starved myself to death, but I shall die content since I have seen your face once more."

"No, dear beast," cried Beauty, passionately, "you shall not die; you shall live to be my husband. I thought it was only friendship I felt for you, but now I know it was love."

The moment Beauty had spoken these words, the palace was suddenly lighted up, and all kinds of rejoicings were heard around them, none of which she noticed, but hung over her dear beast with the utmost tenderness. At last, unable to restrain herself, she dropped her head over her hands, covered her eyes, and cried for joy; and, when she looked up again, the beast was gone. In his stead she saw at her feet a handsome, graceful young prince, who thanked her with the tenderest expressions for having freed him from enchantment.

"But where is my poor beast? I only want him and nobody else," sobbed Beauty.

"I am he," replied the prince. "A wicked fairy condemned me to this form, and forbade me to show that I had any wit or sense, till a beautiful lady should consent to marry me. You alone, dearest Beauty, judged me neither by my looks nor by my talents, but by my heart alone. Take it then, and all that I have besides, for all is yours."

Beauty, full of surprise, but very happy, suffered the prince to lead 65 her to his palace, where she found her father and sisters, who had been brought there by the fairy lady whom she had seen in a dream the first night she came.

"Beauty," said the fairy, "you have chosen well, and you have your reward, for a true heart is better than either good looks or clever brains. As for you, ladies," and she turned to the two elder sisters, "I know all your ill deeds, but I have no worse punishment for you than to see your sister happy. You shall stand as statues at the door of her palace, and when you repent of and have amended your faults, you shall become women again. But, to tell you the truth, I very much fear you will remain statues forever."

What Did You Read?

1. What does the merchant take from the Beast's house that jeopardizes his life?
2. Does the beast allow Beauty to leave?
3. What does the fairy tell the two sisters of Beauty at the end?

What Did You Think?

1. How is "work" portrayed in this story?
2. What is the significance of the statement, "But, to be sure, Miss [Beauty] must not be like other people, and though she will be the cause of her father's death, yet she does not shed a tear."
3. How does this story differ from the Disney version? What is important about the differences?
4. What other literary works does this tale remind you of?

How Was It Done?

1. What values seem central to the structure of the storyline?
2. What two environments is the story structured around?
3. What artifacts are central to the story? Explain.
4. How important is "magic" to the construction of the story?

The Ugly Duckling

Hans Christian Andersen

Andersen lived in 19th-century Denmark, and saw his own life as a type of Ugly Duckling story. He found fame and success from writing fairy tales, but never shook off his personal insecurities. In this simple tale, the ugly duckling seems poorly suited for the world around him: he does not look like the other ducklings, he cannot find friends or acceptance from the other birds around him, and even his own mother appears to reject him. Ultimately, however, the reasons for this awkwardness are revealed in a most dramatic transformation.

Key Words

moat	a deep trench filled with water surrounding a building as protection from invasion
broods	groups of young birds hatched at the same time
drake	a male duck
ganders	male geese

pert	lively; forward and flippant
askance	scornfully
tongs	a grasping device joined at one end by a pivot or hinged like scissors
tribulation	experience of distress or suffering

The country was very lovely just then—it was summer. The wheat was golden and the oats still green. The hay was stacked in the rich low meadows, where the stork marched about on his long red legs, chattering in Egyptian, the language his mother had taught him.

Round about field and meadow lay great woods, in the midst of which were deep lakes. Yes, the country certainly was lovely. In the sunniest spot stood an old mansion surrounded by a deep moat, and great dock leaves grew from the walls of the house right down to the water's edge. Some of them were so tall that a small child could stand upright under them. In among the leaves it was as secluded as in the depths of a forest, and there a duck was sitting on her nest. Her little ducklings were just about to be hatched, but she was quite tired of sitting, for it had lasted such a long time. Moreover, she had very few visitors, as the other ducks liked swimming about in the moat better than waddling up to sit under the dock leaves and gossip with her.

At last one egg after another began to crack. "Cheep, cheep!" they said. All the chicks had come to life and were poking their heads out.

"Quack, quack!" said the duck, and then they all quacked their hardest and looked about them on all sides among the green leaves. Their mother allowed them to look as much as they liked, for green is good for the eyes.

"How big the world is, to be sure!" said all the young ones. They 5 certainly now had ever so much more room to move about than when they were inside their eggshells.

"Do you imagine this is the whole world?" said the mother. "It stretches a long way on the other side of the garden, right into the parson's field, though I have never been as far as that. I suppose you are all here now?" She got up and looked about. "No, I declare I have not got you all yet! The biggest egg is still there. How long is this going to take?" she said, and settled herself on the nest again.

"Well, how are you getting on?" said an old duck who had come to pay her a visit.

"This one egg is taking such a long time!" answered the sitting duck. "The shell will not crack. But now you must look at the others. They are the finest ducklings I have ever seen. They are all exactly like their father, the rascal!—yet he never comes to see me."

"Let me look at the egg which won't crack," said the old duck. "You may be sure that it is a turkey's egg! I was cheated like that once and I had no end of trouble and worry with the creatures, for I may tell you that they are afraid of the water. I simply could not get them into it. I quacked and snapped at them, but it all did no good. Let me see the egg! Yes, it is a turkey's egg. You just leave it alone, and teach the other children to swim."

"I will sit on it a little longer. I have sat so long already that I may 10 as well go on till the Midsummer Fair comes round."

"Please yourself," said the old duck, and away she went.

At last the big egg cracked. "Cheep, cheep!" said the young one and tumbled out. How big and ugly he was! The duck looked at him.

"That is a monstrous big duckling," she said. "None of the others looked like that. Can he be a turkey chick? Well, we shall soon find that out. Into the water he shall go, if I have to kick him in myself."

Next day was gloriously fine, and the sun shone on all the green dock leaves. The mother duck with her whole family went down to the moat.

Splash! into the water she sprang. "Quack, quack," she said, and 15 one duckling plumped in after the other. The water dashed over their heads, but they came up again and floated beautifully. Their legs went of themselves, and they were all there. Even the big ugly gray one swam about with them.

"No, that is no turkey," she said. "See how beautifully he uses his legs and how erect he holds himself. He is my own chick, after all, and not bad looking when you come to look at him properly. Quack, quack! Now come with me and I will take you out into the world and introduce you to the duckyard. But keep close to me all the time so that no one will tread upon you. And beware of the cat!"

Then they went into the duckyard. There was a fearful uproar going on, for two broods were fighting for the head of an eel, and in the end the cat captured it.

"That's how things go in this world," said the mother duck, and she licked her bill, because she had wanted the eel's head herself.

"Now use your legs," said she. "Mind you quack properly, and bend your necks to the old duck over there. She is the grandest of us all. She has Spanish blood in her veins and that accounts for her size. And do you see? She has a red rag round her leg. That is a wonderfully fine thing, and the most extraordinary mark of distinction any duck can have. It shows clearly that she is not to be parted with, and that she is worthy of recognition both by beasts and men! Quack, now! Don't turn your toes in! A well brought up duckling keeps his legs wide apart just like father and mother. That's it. Now bend your necks and say quack!"

They did as they were bid, but the other ducks round about 20 looked at them and said, quite loud, "Just look there! Now we are to have that tribe, just as if they were not enough of us already. And, oh dear, how ugly that duckling is! We won't stand him." And a duck flew at him at once and bit him in the neck.

"Let him be," said the mother. "He is doing no harm."

"Very likely not," said the biter. "But he is so ungainly and queer that he must be whacked."

"Those are handsome children mother has," said the old duck with the rag round her leg. "They are all good looking except this one, but he is not a good specimen. It's a pity you can't make him over again."

"That can't be done, your grace," said the mother duck. "He is not handsome, but he is a thoroughly good creature, and he swims as beautifully as any of the others. I think I might venture even to add that I think he will improve as he goes on, or perhaps in time he may grow smaller. He was too long in the egg, and so he has not come out with a very good figure." And then she patted his neck and stroked him down. "Besides, he is a drake," said she. "So it does not matter so much. I believe he will be very strong, and I don't doubt but he will make his way in the world."

"The other ducklings are very pretty," said the old duck. "Now 25 make yourselves quite at home, and if you find the head of an eel you may bring it to me."

After that they felt quite at home. But the poor duckling who had been the last to come out of the shell, and who was so ugly, was bitten, pushed about, and made fun of both by the ducks and the hens. "He is too big," they all said. And the turkey cock, who was born with his spurs on and therefore thought himself quite an emperor, puffed himself up like a vessel in full sail, made for him, and gobbled and gobbled till he became quite red in the face. The poor duckling was at his wit's end, and did not know which way to turn. He was in despair because he was so ugly and the butt of the whole duckyard.

So the first day passed, and afterwards matters grew worse and worse. The poor duckling was chased and hustled by all of them. Even his brothers and sisters ill-used him. They were always saying, "If only the cat would get hold of you, you hideous object!" Even his mother said, "I wish to goodness you were miles away." The ducks bit him, the hens pecked him, and the girl who fed them kicked him aside.

Then he ran off and flew right over the hedge, where the little birds flew up into the air in a fright.

"That is because I am so ugly," thought the poor duckling, shutting his eyes, but he ran on all the same. Then he came to a great marsh where the wild ducks lived. He was so tired and miserable that he stayed there the whole night. In the morning the wild ducks flew up to inspect their new comrade.

"What sort of a creature are you?" they inquired, as the duckling 30 turned from side to side and greeted them as well as he could. "You are frightfully ugly," said the wild ducks, "but that does not matter to us, so long as you do not marry into our family." Poor fellow! He had not thought of marriage. All he wanted was permission to lie among the rushes and to drink a little of the marsh water.

He stayed there two whole days. Then two wild geese came, or rather two wild ganders. They were not long out of the shell and therefore rather pert.

"I say, comrade," they said, "you are so ugly that we have taken quite a fancy to you! Will you join us and be a bird of passage? There is another marsh close by, and there are some charming wild geese there. All are sweet young ladies who can say quack! You are ugly enough to make your fortune among them." Just at that moment, bang! bang! was heard up above, and both the wild geese fell dead among the reeds, and the water turned blood red. Bang! bang! went the guns, and flocks of wild geese flew from the rushes and the shot peppered among them again.

There was a grand shooting party, and the sportsmen lay hidden round the marsh. Some even sat on the branches of the trees which overhung the water. The blue smoke rose like clouds among the dark trees and swept over the pool.

The retrieving dogs wandered about in the swamp—splash! splash! The rushes and reeds bent beneath their tread on all sides. It was terribly alarming to the poor duckling. He twisted his head around to get it under his wing, and just at that moment a frightful big dog appeared close beside him. His tongue hung right out of his mouth and his eyes glared wickedly. He opened his great chasm of a mouth close to the duckling, showed his sharp teeth, and—splash!— went on without touching him.

"Oh, thank Heaven!" sighed the duckling. "I am so ugly that even 35 the dog won't bite me!"

Then he lay quite still while the shots whistled among the bushes, and bang after bang rent the air. It only became quiet late in the day, but even then the poor duckling did not dare to get up. He waited several hours more before he looked about, and then he hurried away from the marsh as fast as he could. He ran across fields and meadows, and there was such a wind that he had hard work to make his way.

Towards night he reached a poor little cottage. It was such a miserable hovel that it could not make up its mind which way even to fall, and so it remained standing. The wind whistled so fiercely around the duckling that he had to sit on his tail to resist it, and it blew harder and ever harder. Then he saw that the door had fallen off one hinge and hung so crookedly that he could creep into the house through the crack, and so he made his way into the room.

An old woman lived here with her cat and her hen. The cat, whom she called "Sonnie," would arch his back, purr, and give off electric sparks if you stroked his fur the wrong way. The hen had quite tiny short legs, and so she was called "Chickie-low-legs." She laid good eggs, and the old woman was as fond of her as if she had been her own child.

In the morning the strange duckling was discovered immediately, and the cat began to purr and the hen to cluck.

"What on earth is that?" said the old woman, looking round, but 40 her sight was not good and she thought the duckling was a fat duck which had escaped. "This is a wonderful find!" said she. "Now I shall have duck's eggs—if only it is not a drake. We must wait and see about that."

So she took the duckling on trial for three weeks, but no eggs made their appearance. The cat was master of this house and and the hen its mistress. They always said, "We and the world," for they thought that they represented the half of the world, and that quite the better half.

The duckling thought there might be two opinions on the subject, but the cat would not hear of it.

"Can you lay eggs?" she asked.

"No."

"Have the goodness to hold your tongue then!"   45

And the cat said, "Can you arch your back, purr, or give off sparks?"

"No."

"Then you had better keep your opinions to yourself when people of sense are speaking!"

The duckling sat in the corner nursing his ill humor. Then he began to think of the fresh air and the sunshine and an uncontrollable longing seized him to float on the water. At last he could not help telling the hen about it.

"What on earth possesses you?" she asked. "You have nothing to 50 do. That is why you get these freaks into your head. Lay some eggs or take to purring, and you will get over it."

"But it is so deliciouis to float on the water," said the duckling. "It is so delicious to feel it rushing over your head when you dive to the bottom."

"That would be a fine amusement!" said the hen. "I think you have gone mad. Ask the cat about it. He is the wisest creature I know. Ask him if he is fond of floating on the water or diving under it. I say nothing about myself. Ask our mistress herself, the old woman. There is no one in the world cleverer than she is. Do you suppose she has any desire to float on the water or to duck underneath it?"

"You do not understand me," said the duckling.

"Well, if we don't understand you, who should? I suppose you don't consider yourself cleverer than the cat or the old woman, not to mention me! Don't make a fool of yourself, child, and thank your stars for all the good we have done you. Have you not lived in this warm room, and in such society that you might have learned something? But you are an idiot, and there is no pleasure in associating with you. You may believe me: I mean you well. I tell you home truths, and there is no surer way than that of knowing who are one's friends. You just set about laying some eggs, or learn to purr, or to emit sparks."

"I think I will go out into the wide world," said the duckling.   55
"Oh, do so by all means," said the hen.

So away went the duckling. He floated on the water and ducked underneath it, but he was looked at askance and was slighted by every living creature for his ugliness. Now autumn came. The leaves in the woods turned yellow and brown. The wind took hold of them, and they danced about. The sky looked very cold and the clouds hung heavy with snow and hail. A raven stood on the fence and croaked "Caw, caw!" from sheer cold. It made one shiver only to think of it. The poor duckling certainly was in a bad case!

One evening, the sun was just setting in wintry splendor when a flock of beautiful large birds appeared out of the bushes. The duckling had never seen anything so beautiful. They were dazzlingly white with long waving necks. They were swans, and uttering a peculiar cry they spread out their magnificent broad wings and flew away from the cold regions to warmer lands and open seas. They mounted so high, so very high, and the ugly little duckling became strangely uneasy. He circled round and round in the water like a wheel, craning his neck up into the air after them. Then he uttered a shriek so piercing and so strange that he was quite frightened by it himself. Oh, he could not forget those beautiful birds, those happy birds. And as soon as they were out of sight, he ducked right down to the bottom, and when he came up again he was quite beside himself. He did not know what the birds were, or whither they flew, but all the same he was more drawn towards them than he had ever been by any creatures before. He did not envy them in the least. How could it occur to him even to wish to be such a marvel of beauty? He would have been thankful if only the ducks would have tolerated him among them—the poor ugly creature.

The winter was so bitterly cold that the duckling was obliged to swim about in the water to keep it from freezing over, but every night the hole in which he swam got smaller and smaller. Then it froze so hard that the surface ice cracked, and the duckling had to use his legs all the time so that the ice should not freeze around him. At last he was so weary that he could move no more, and he was frozen fast into the ice.

Early in the morning a peasant came along and saw him. He went   60
out onto the ice and hammered a hole in it with his heavy wooden shoe, and carried the duckling home to his wife. There he soon

revived. The children wanted to play with him, but the duckling thought they were going to ill-use him, and rushed in his fright into the milk pan, and the milk spurted out all over the room. The woman shrieked and threw up her hands. Then he flew into the butter cask, and down into the meal tub and out again. Just imagine what he looked like by this time! The woman screamed and tried to hit him with the tongs. The children tumbled over one another in trying to catch him, and they screamed with laughter. By good luck the door stood open, and the duckling flew out among the bushes and the newly fallen snow. And he lay there thoroughly exhausted.

But it would be too sad to mention all the privation and misery he had to go through during the hard winter. When the sun began to shine warmly again, the duckling was in the marsh, lying among the rushes. The larks were singing and the beautiful spring had come.

Then all at once he raised his wings and they flapped with much greater strength than before and bore him off vigorously. Before he knew where he was, he found himself in a large garden where the apple trees were in full blossom and the air was scented with lilacs, the long branches of which overhung the indented shores of the lake. Oh, the spring freshness was delicious!

Just in front of him he saw three beautiful white swans advancing towards him from a thicket. With rustling feathers they swam lightly over the water. The duckling recognized the majestic birds, and he was overcome by a strange melancholy.

"I will fly to them, the royal birds, and they will hack me to pieces because I, who am so ugly, venture to approach them. But it won't matter! Better be killed by them than be snapped at by the ducks, pecked at by the hens, spurned by the henwife, or suffer so much misery in the winter."

So he flew into the water and swam towards the stately swans. 65 They saw him and darted towards him with ruffled feathers.

"Kill me!" said the poor creature, and he bowed his head towards the water and awaited his death. But what did he see reflected in the transparent water?

He saw below him his own image, but he was no longer a clumsy dark gray bird, ugly and ungainly. He was himself a swan! It does not matter in the least having been born in a duckyard, if only you come out of a swan's egg!

He felt quite glad of all the misery and tribulation he had gone through, for he was the better able to appreciate his good fortune now and all the beauty which greeted him. The big swans swam round and round him and stroked him with their bills.

Some little children came into the garden with corn and pieces of bread which they threw into the water, and the smallest one cried out, "There is a new one!" The other children shouted with joy, "Yes, a new one has come." And they clapped their hands and danced about, running after their father and mother. They threw the bread into the water, and one and all said, "The new one is the prettiest of them all. He is so young and handsome." And the old swans bent their heads and did homage before him.

He felt quite shy, and hid his head under his wing. He did not 70 know what to think. He was very happy, but not at all proud, for a good heart never becomes proud. He thought of how he had been pursued and scorned, and now he heard them all say that he was the most beautiful of all beautiful birds. The lilacs bent their boughs right down into the water before him, and the bright sun was warm and cheering. He rustled his feathers and raised his slender neck aloft, saying with exultation in his heart, "I never dreamt of so much happiness when I was the Ugly Duckling!"

What Did You Read?

1. What is the first comment the little ducklings make after they are hatched?
2. What does the mother say about the ugly duckling? What is the relationship between the mother and the ugly duckling?
3. How do the siblings treat the ugly duckling?
4. Who tells the ugly duckling "home truths"? What are those truths?

What Do You Think?

1. How is the experience of privation, misery, and sadness that the ugly duckling goes through during the hard winter significant?
2. Describe the importance of this quotation: "He was himself a swan! It does not matter in the least having been born in a duck-yard, if only you come out of a swan's egg!"
3. How does this story reflect Judeo-Christian teachings?

How Was It Done?

1. Why are the seasons of particular importance to this story?
2. How does the story revolve around Judeo-Christian values?
3. Why is it interesting that the story is told from the first-person vantage point?
4. Why are the many different reactions to the Ugly Duckling central to the plot?

Excerpt from *The Uses of Enchantment*

Bruno Bettelheim

This groundbreaking book of literary criticism of fairy tales attempted to explore the psychological depths of many well-known fairy tales. Bettelheim's book argued that fairy tales promise meaning to the children who hear them. In this passage, Bettelheim examines the tale of "Cinderella" from the psychological viewpoint of a child, including the experiences of sibling rivalry and rejection by parents. The child can identify with Cinderella and her predicament. The child sees his or her own position, and can judge Cinderella's to be worse. In a sense, Cinderella serves as a model of how bad things can be yet still end happily.

Key Words

sibling	a brother or sister
degradation	decline to a low or demoralized state
animosity	hatred toward someone or something
tribulations	experiences of distress or suffering
condone	to pardon or overlook
overt	open; not hidden
welter	a state of wild disorder
infirmities	frailties; diseases
credence	believability; credibility

Cinderella

By all accounts, "Cinderella" is the best-known fairy tale, and probably also the best-liked. It is quite an old story; when first written down in China during the ninth century A.D., it already had a history. The unrivaled tiny foot size as a mark of extraordinary virtue, distinction, and beauty, and the slipper made of precious material are facets which point to an Eastern, if not necessarily Chinese, origin.* The modern hearer does not connect sexual attractiveness and beauty in general with extreme smallness of the foot, as the ancient Chinese did, in accordance with their practice of binding women's feet.

"Cinderella," as we know it, is experienced as a story about the agonies and hopes which form the essential content of sibling rivalry; and about the degraded heroine winning out over her siblings who abused her. Long before Perrault gave "Cinderella" the form in which it is now widely known, "having to live among the ashes" was a symbol of being

---

*Artistically made slippers of precious material were reported in Egypt from the third century on. The Roman emperor Diocletian in a decree of A.D. 301 set maximum prices for different kinds of footwear, including slippers made of fine Babylonian leather, dyed purple or scarlet, and gilded slippers for women.

debased in comparison to one's siblings, irrespective of sex. In Germany, for example, there were stories in which such an ash-boy later becomes king, which parallels Cinderella's fate. "Aschenputtel" is the title of the Brothers Grimm's version of the tale. The term originally designated a lowly, dirty kitchenmaid who must tend to the fireplace ashes.

There are many examples in the German language of how being forced to dwell among the ashes was a symbol not just of degradation, but also of sibling rivalry, and of the sibling who finally surpasses the brother or brothers who have debased him. Martin Luther in his *Table Talks* speaks about Cain as the God-forsaken evildoer who is powerful, while pious Abel is forced to be his ash-brother *(Aschebrüdel)*, a mere nothing, subject to Cain; in one of Luther's sermons he says that Esau was forced into the role of Jacob's ash-brother. Cain and Abel, Jacob and Esau are Biblical examples of one brother being suppressed or destroyed by the other.

The fairy tale replaces sibling relations with relations between step-siblings—perhaps a device to explain and make acceptable an animosity which one wishes would not exist among true siblings. Although sibling rivalry is universal and "natural" in the sense that it is the negative consequence of being a sibling, this same relation also generates equally as much positive feeling between siblings, highlighted in fairy tales such as "Brother and Sister."

No other fairy tale renders so well as the "Cinderella" stories the inner experiences of the young child in the throes of sibling rivalry, when he feels hopelessly outclassed by his brothers and sisters. Cinderella is pushed down and degraded by her stepsisters; her interests are sacrificed to theirs by her (step)mother; she is expected to do the dirtiest work and although she performs it well, she receives no credit for it; only more is demanded of her. This is how the child feels when devastated by the miseries of sibling rivalry. Exaggerated though Cinderella's tribulations and degradations may seem to the adult, the child carried away by sibling rivalry feels, "That's me; that's how they mistreat me, or would want to; that's how little they think of me." And there are moments—often long time periods—when for inner reasons a child feels this way even when his position among his siblings may seem to give him no cause for it.

When a story corresponds to how the child feels deep down—as no realistic narrative is likely to do—it attains an emotional quality of "truth" for the child. The events of "Cinderella" offer him vivid images that give body to his overwhelming but nevertheless often vague and nondescript emotions; so these episodes seem more convincing to him than his life experiences.

The term "sibling rivalry" refers to a most complex constellation of feelings and their causes. With extremely rare exceptions, the emotions aroused in the person subject to sibling rivalry are far out of proportion to what his real situation with his sisters and brothers would justify, seen objectively. While all children at times suffer greatly from sibling rivalry, parents seldom sacrifice one of their children to the others, nor do they condone the other children's persecuting one of them. Difficult as objective judgments are for the young child—nearly impossible when his emotions are aroused—even he in his more rational moments "knows" that he is not treated as badly as Cinderella. But the child often feels mistreated, despite all his "knowledge" to the contrary. That is why he believes in the inherent truth of "Cinderella," and then he also comes to believe in her eventual deliverance and victory. From her triumph he gains the exaggerated hopes for his future which he needs to counteract the extreme misery he experiences when ravaged by sibling rivalry.

Despite the name "sibling rivalry," this miserable passion has only incidentally to do with a child's actual brothers and sisters. The real source of it is the child's feelings about his parents. When a child's older brother or sister is more competent than he, this arouses only temporary feelings of jealousy. Another child being given special attention becomes an insult only if the child fears that, in contrast, he is thought little of by his parents, or feels rejected by them. It is because of such an anxiety that one or all of a child's sisters or brothers may become a thorn in his flesh. Fearing that in comparison to them he cannot win his parents' love and esteem is what inflames sibling rivalry. This is indicated in stories by the fact that it matters little whether the siblings actually possess greater competence. The Biblical story of Joseph tells that it is jealousy of parental affection lavished on him which accounts for the destructive behavior of his brothers. Unlike Cinderella's, Joseph's parent does not participate in degrading him, and, on the contrary, prefers him to his other children. But Joseph, like Cinderella, is turned into a slave, and, like her, he miraculously escapes and ends by surpassing his siblings.

Telling a child who is devastated by sibling rivalry that he will grow up to do as well as his brothers and sisters offers little relief from his present feelings of dejection. Much as he would like to trust our assurances, most of the time he cannot. A child can see things only with subjective eyes, and comparing himself on this basis to his siblings, he has no confidence that he, on his own, will someday be able to fare as well as they. If he could believe more in himself, he would not feel destroyed by his siblings no matter what they might do to him, since then he could trust that time would bring about a desired reversal of fortune. But since the child cannot, on his own, look forward with confidence to some future day when things will turn out all right for him, he can gain relief only through fantasies of glory—a domination over his siblings—which he hopes will become reality through some fortunate event.

Whatever our position within the family, at certain times in our lives we are beset by sibling rivalry in some form or other. Even an 10 only child feels that other children have some great advantages over him, and this makes him intensely jealous. Further, he may suffer from the anxious thought that if he did have a sibling, his parents would prefer this other child to him. "Cinderella" is a fairy tale which makes nearly as strong an appeal to boys as to girls, since children of both sexes suffer equally from sibling rivalry, and have the same desire to be rescued from their lowly position and surpass those who seem superior to them.

On the surface, "Cinderella" is as deceptively simple as the story of Little Red Riding Hood, with which it shares greatest popularity. "Cinderella" tells about the agonies of sibling rivalry, of wishes coming true, of the humble being elevated, of true merit being recognized even when hidden under rags, of virtue rewarded and evil punished— a straightforward story. But under this overt content is concealed a welter of complex and largely unconscious material, which details of the story allude to just enough to set our unconscious associations going. This makes a contrast between surface simplicity and underlying complexity which arouses deep interest in the story and explains its appeal to the millions over centuries. To begin gaining an understanding of these hidden meanings, we have to penetrate behind the obvious sources of sibling rivalry discussed so far.

As mentioned before, if the child could only believe that it is the infirmities of his age which account for his lowly position, he would not have to suffer so wretchedly from sibling rivalry, because he could trust the future to right matters. When he thinks that his degradation is deserved, he feels his plight is utterly hopeless. Djuna Barnes's perceptive statement about fairy tales—that the child knows something about them which he cannot tell (such as that he likes the idea of Little Red Riding Hood and the wolf being in bed together)—could be extended by dividing fairy tales into two groups: one group where the child responds only unconsciously to the inherent truth of the story and thus cannot tell about it; and another large number of tales where the child preconsciously or even consciously knows what the "truth" of the story consists of and thus could tell about it, but does not want to let on that he knows. Some aspects of "Cinderella" fall into the latter category. Many children believe that Cinderella probably deserves her fate at the beginning of the story, as they feel they would, too; but they don't want anyone to know it. Despite this, she is worthy at the end to be exalted, as the child hopes he will be too, irrespective of his earlier shortcomings.

Every child believes at some period of his life—and this is not only at rare moments—that because of his secret wishes, if not also his clandestine actions, he deserves to be degraded, banned from the presence of others, relegated to a netherworld of smut. He fears this may be so, irrespective of how fortunate his situation may be in reality. He hates and fears those others—such as his siblings—whom he believes to be entirely free of similar evilness, and he fears that they or his parents will discover what he is really like, and then demean him as Cinderella was by her family. Because he wants others—most of all, his parents—to believe in his innocence, he is delighted that "everybody" believes in Cinderella's. This is one of the great attractions of this fairy tale. Since people give credence to Cinderella's goodness, they will also believe in his, so the child hopes. And "Cinderella" nourishes this hope, which is one reason it is such a delightful story.

Another aspect which holds large appeal for the child is the vileness of the stepmother and stepsisters. Whatever the shortcomings of a child may be in his own eyes, these pale into insignificance when compared to the stepsisters' and stepmother's falsehood and nastiness. Further, what these stepsisters do to Cinderella justifies whatever nasty thoughts one may have about one's siblings: they are so vile that anything one may wish would happen to them is more than justified. Compared to their behavior, Cinderella is indeed innocent. So the child, on hearing her story, feels he need not feel guilty about his angry thoughts.

On a very different level—and reality considerations coexist easily 15 with fantastic exaggerations in the child's mind—as badly as one's parents or siblings seem to treat one, and much as one thinks one suffers because of it, all this is nothing compared to Cinderella's fate. Her story reminds the child at the same time how lucky he is, and how much worse things could be. (Any anxiety about the latter possibility is relieved, as always in fairy tales, by the happy ending.)

The behavior of a five-and-a-half-year-old girl, as reported by her father, may illustrate how easily a child may feel that she is a "Cinderella." This little girl had a younger sister of whom she was very jealous. The girl was very fond of "Cinderella," since the story offered her material with which to act out her feelings, and because without the story's imagery she would have been hard pressed to comprehend and express them. This little girl had used to dress very neatly and liked pretty clothes, but she became unkempt and dirty. One day when she was asked to fetch some salt, she said as she was doing so, "Why do you treat me like Cinderella?"

Almost speechless, her mother asked her, "Why do you think I treat you like Cinderella?"

"Because you make me do all the hardest work in the house!" was the little girl's answer. Having thus drawn her parents into her fantasies, she acted them out more openly, pretending to sweep up all the dirt, etc. She went even further, playing that she prepared her little sister for the ball. But she went the "Cinderella" story one better, based on her unconscious understanding of the contradictory emotions fused into the "Cinderella" role, because at another moment she told her mother and sister, "You shouldn't be jealous of me just because I am the most beautiful in the family."

This shows that behind the surface humility of Cinderella lies the conviction of her superiority to mother and sisters, as if she would think: "You can make me do all the dirty work, and I pretend that I am dirty, but within me I know that you treat me this way because you are jealous of me because I am so much better than you." This conviction is supported by the story's ending, which assures every "Cinderella" that eventually she will be discovered by her prince.

What Did You Read?

1. Why does Bettelheim think Cinderella is an excellent story for explaining the problems of sibling rivalry?

2. What are some other stories of sibling rivalry that Bettelheim cites, and why are they important?

3. According to Bettelheim, why do children sometimes believe they "deserve to be degraded"?

What Do You Think?

1. Why do you suppose Cinderella has been so popular for over one thousand years?

2. How do you respond to Bettelheim's contention that the real source of conflict for the child experiencing sibling rivalry is not with the brothers or sisters, but with the parents?

3. Bettelheim cites Djuna Barnes's observation that "the child knows something about them which he cannot tell" such as "Little Red Riding Hood and the wolf being in bed together." What examples can you think of from other fairy tales that might qualify as a similar example?

4. Does Bettelheim's analysis of the story of Cinderella go too far in its attempts to explore the psychology underneath the tale? Why or why not?

How Was It Done?

1. What theme does the author construct his criticism around?

2. What experts does the author use to help give substance to his explanations?

3. Explain how the author's appeal to the child's sensibility is very important to the development of this article.

4. Does the author examine the straightforward style of the Cinderella tale as well as the unconscious associations? Explain how this contributes to the development of the article.

The Fairy Tale Lady

Claire Whitcomb

Whitcomb examines the views of Jackie Wullschlager, an expert on fairy tales. Wullschlager talks about the importance of fairy tales for children in that fairy tales are entertaining, but they also reveal "enduring truths." Childhood as we know it, she claims, is an invention of the 19th-century Victorians. Wullschlager sees the works of Hans Christian Andersen as essentially creating children's literature, and how the magical world of fairy tales influenced our current celebrations of Christmas (Santa Claus) and other fantastical characters (such as the Easter Bunny and the Tooth Fairy). Fairy tales are renewed even today in new tales and new tellings of old tales.

Key Words

treatise	a systematic exposition in writing including a methodical discussion of facts and principles
archetypes	original patterns of which all other things of the same type are copies
sanitized	cleaned up; made less offensive or shocking
forlorn	nearly hopeless; miserable
transcriptions	the writing down of the words of someone else
venerated	honored; revered
peasant genre	an art form of the peasant class, which was a social class of people who worked the land as laborers; the art form of the pre-industrial age working class
warp and weft	the foundation or base

Once upon a time, recounts Jackie Wullschlager, a mother asked Albert Einstein what she should read to her scientifically minded son. "Fairy stories," he replied, nodding his cloud of white hair. "And then what?" the mother asked, awaiting the names of complicated treatises. "More fairy stories," Einstein answered.

Tales of Jack and his beanstalk, Aladdin and his lamp teach "enduring truths, all in a few pages," says Jackie, the European arts correspondent for the *Financial Times*. She's struck by the power of the archetypes—the orphan in the cupboard, unaware of his noble heritage; the young lion wandering in exile, learning what he needs to learn in order to be king. And she says, "I'm always interested in the questions fairy tales inspire." Recently, she read her three children *The Little Mermaid*, which is based on an ancient tale of mermaids turning into mortals. "At the end, my daughter asked, 'What does "an immortal soul" mean?'"

Jackie argues that we live in a sanitized culture that sometimes leaves "a void in the lives of children in terms of spiritual discussion."

Fairy tales, while surely not a substitute for religion, "do encourage," she says. "They promise meaning."

Stories of forlorn stepchildren and prince charmings have always been told, but it wasn't until the eighteenth century that they were written down. The initial transcriptions by the brothers Grimm were often terrifying—toes were chopped off to fit into glass slippers, a wicked queen danced in red-hot shoes at Snow White's wedding. But when the nineteenth century arrived, fairy tales, doused with the proverbial spoonful of sugar, entered the nursery.

"The Victorians invented childhood as we know it," Jackie says 5 quite emphatically. Their increased affluence and leisure made a cult of motherhood—witness all those Mary Cassatt paintings. Stunned by the industrial age, they venerated the innocence and unworldliness of children—and eagerly retreated into the enchanted Eden-like worlds of Never-Never-Land, Wonderland and the Hundred Acre Wood.

As Jackie set about analyzing Alice, Peter, Pooh and assorted other characters for her 1995 book *Inventing Wonderland* (Free Press), she realized children's literature stood in the shadow of one man: Hans Christian Andersen. The first writer to treat the fantastical world of folktales as literature, he not only transformed what Jackie calls a "peasant genre" but changed children's books forever.

"I . . . have written [my stories]," Andersen said, "exactly the way I would tell them to a child." His prose, always carefully worked, was chatty, funny and surprisingly devoid of preachiness. Animals talked, toys walked and great truths were expressed. It's astonishing to think how his best tales—*The Emperor's New Clothes, The Ugly Duckling, Thumbelina, The Princess and the Pea, The Red Shoes*—have become part of the warp and weft of our imaginations.

The son of a poor Danish shoemaker, Andersen lived something of a fairy tale himself. Homely, odd and desperate to be a poet, he was sent to school at seventeen by a group of kind businessmen. He grew up to write a novel, a play and plenty of poems, but didn't find his voice until he channeled all his fears and passions into the folktale. Fame quickly arrived on his doorstep. "I covet honor in the same way as a miser covets gold," he said at age thirty-two.

Andersen became the darling of European royalty, the confidant of singer Jenny Lind (*The Nightingale* tells of his love for her) and the inspiration for writers such as Thomas Mann and Charles Dickens. But he never shook the feeling of being an outsider, a forgotten match girl barred from the warmth of holiday celebrations.

Andersen wrote only two holiday stories—*The Little Match Girl* 10 and *The Fir Tree*, both of which end tragically—but he always issued his story collections in December. There is something about the fairy tale, with its ability to venture into the heart of darkness, that seems particularly poignant in a season of love and abundance. Dickens recognized this when he created the immortal Scrooge. "He set about attacking bourgeois complacency," Jackie says, "at the same time depending on it." He pricked the plum-pudding veneer of Victorian society, "all the time knowing he was going to sell cart-loads of books."

Jackie goes on to explain that the Victorians' intense interest in fairy tales changed Christmas. Santa became part of the popular imagination, along with the tinsel-trimmed fir tree. The return to "a shared inventory, a bedrock of fantasy," also led Victorians to embrace the Easter bunny, the tooth fairy—and novels with a decidedly archetypal turn. Where, asks Jackie, would Jane Eyre be without Cinderella? Or Dickens' Dombey? Eliot's *Middlemarch* without Bluebeard as a model for Casaubon?

Naturally the fairy tale casts its spell today. The Harry Potter books rest at the top of the best-seller list. *The Lion King* rules Broadway. "I think it's fascinating how Disney was launched on the fairy tale," says Jackie, who considers its *Snow White* "terribly good" and doesn't mind watching it a hundred times with her kids. Fairy tales, she says, "are always satisfying. You can tell them by heart. If you're stuck on a train, you don't even need a book."

They explain life, coming of age, even nations. She points out that the United States started out as the archetypal orphaned child and rose to greatness. In Hans Christian Andersen, she quotes Dickens, who said, "Everyone who has considered the subject knows full well that a nation without fancy, without some romance, never did, never can, never will hold a great place under the sun."

What Did You Read?

1. How do fairy tales reflect the historical century they come from?
2. What are some contemporary fairy tales?
3. How did Hans Christian Andersen live something of a fairy tale life himself?
4. What does Jackie Wullschlager feel that fairy tales do for children?

What Do You Think?

1. Explain Wullschlager's comparison between fairy tales and the role of religion. Do you agree or disagree with her? Why?
2. Do you think the archetypal orphaned child is still a significant image?
3. Do you think fairy tales give children a distorted view of the world? Explain.

How Was It Done?

1. What individual is this article structured around?
2. How is the emphasis of Victorian culture central to what Wullschlager is saying about fairy tales and children in general?
3. How does the comparison to Dickens contribute to the development of this essay?

From an Ounce of Sorrow
An Algerian Fairy Tale
Jan Knappert

Knappert translates an Algerian fairy tale that contains many of the same elements found in European fairy tales: magic, princes and princesses, and journeys. A sheltered princess does not even know enough of life to know what misery is, so she buys an ounce of sorrow, which comes in the form of seven seeds. These seeds grow into a beautiful flowered plant, but the plant is wrecked repeatedly by two birds, one white and one black. Her sorrow moves her to hear the sorrows of all the other women in her kingdom, but that leads her to a very unexpected revelation.

Key Words

marrow	the soft part inside the bone; the choicest or best food
hawkers	people who sell goods, often on the street or in bazaars
wares	goods for sale
ravished	destroyed; raped
diadem	a royal headband
perchance	by chance
vexed	troubled; puzzled
chamberlain	a chief officer in the household of a king or nobleman; a treasurer
equerry	an officer of a nobleman in charge of the care of horses
tiara	a jeweled, semicircular headband worn by women

Long ago there was a king who had a beautiful daughter. She grew lovelier by the day. The king decided she had to be protected from the covetous eyes of the people. He confined her to a wing of the palace where she could not be seen by anyone. She had only one trusted servant, a woman who brought her food. This was always carefully prepared: meat without bones and bread without crusts.

One day the servant forgot to close the door to her quarters properly. An urchin walked in from the street and saw her as she ate. "O princess!" he said. "They serve you bread without crusts and meat without bones? Yet everybody knows that the crust is the best part of the bread, and the bones make the meat tastier!"

The boy ran out to the street and disappeared. When her servant came back, the princess demanded: "From now on I want bread with the crust on it and meat with the bones in it!"

She got what she asked for. At her next meal, she discovered marrow in a piece of bone and knocked it against the table. This caused such a noise that the building shook and the window of her room shattered. Suddenly the princess was exposed to the noises that penetrated from the outside. She could hear the sounds of the marketplace, where hawkers were loudly praising their wares. Fascinated, the princess listened. She tried to look outside, but the high window permitted her to see little. Then she heard one merchant shout: "Buy from me an ounce of sorrow!"

Her curiosity aroused, the princess excitedly ordered her servant   5
to ask the merchant in. He soon appeared and showed the princess his wares. These appeared to be the seeds of some unknown plant. The princess decided to buy seven seeds. The merchant gratefully invoked God's blessings upon her.

The princess decided to plant them on the terrace in a large flowerpot, which had once held a plant from Egypt. She and her maid watered the seven seeds regularly, and soon the first green shoots appeared. The stalks rose up and formed buds. These opened one fine morning, becoming large and splendid flowers. The princess was overjoyed and could look at nothing else.

Alas! Their delicious fragrance attracted two large birds, one pitch black and one snow white. They suddenly alighted and trampled on the flowers until nothing remained except crumpled petals. The princess was furious. She chased the birds with shouts and cries; she even threw her golden ring after them, since she had no other way to punish them. The white bird skillfully caught the ring in flight, then disappeared from the terrace with its crumpled flowers.

The princess was desolate. Suddenly she understood that she had indeed bought sorrow, for she had acquired something she loved for its beauty, only to see it ravished. The princess mourned her flowers until darkness fell.

Two Magical Birds

Lo and behold! The next morning the broken stalks stood erect once again. New flowers were rapidly expanding and opening, until they were as large and numerous as before. Overjoyed, the princess contemplated them. But alas! The two birds descended again. They quickly picked some flowers and trampled the others. Once again, none were left standing. The princess chased the birds, even throwing her diadem after them, but the white bird caught it skillfully before flying away.

The princess shed tears for her lovely flowers but lo! The next 10 morning new flowers opened on new stalks, as fresh and fragrant as ever. No sooner had the princess begun to admire them, however, then the birds returned and quickly set about destroying the blooms. The princess threw the only thing she had nearby at that moment, her golden necklace, to chase them away. The white bird caught the necklace in the air, and both birds disappeared.

On the fourth morning, new flowers adorned the terrace. The princess rejoiced until the birds arrived and destroyed them all. She threw a jewel at them, but the white bird caught it and took it away. Indeed, each morning thereafter the same thing happened. Finally, the poor princess had not a single jewel or ornament left. The big birds had uprooted the plants so completely that they would never grow again.

The princess wept until she fell deathly ill, so her servant went to warn her parents. The king and queen came at once, and when they saw how serious her illness was, they asked their daughter if she had perchance one last wish. "Yes, I have a wish," she said. "Namely, that you ask all the women of the city to come here and tell me their life history, every single one of them. I want to know if even one of them is suffering a grief that is greater than mine."

She had bought an ounce of sorrow. Now she was going to hear the sorrow of the entire city.

Her parents consented. Soon a procession of all the women in the town, young women, married women, widows, divorced women, and old women, came to the palace. Every single one approached the princess' bedside and told a sad story. One woman complained about her husband, another about her mother-in-law, a third was vexed by her child, a fourth complained that she had neither a son nor a daughter. Many young ones wanted to marry, many older ones regretted having done so. Every woman was convinced that her suffering and sorrow were greater than those of the others. The princess, in turn, was convinced that her own sorrow was much greater than that of any of the women who had spoken to her.

One last visitor appeared. This woman, the slave of a rich family, 15 told a curious story. "I was at the riverside, doing the washing of the family," she explained, "when I saw a camel approaching. There was no camel driver in sight, and no one was riding it. The camel walked into the river. There it stopped. It just stood there in the water.

"The camel was loaded with pots and pans and other kitchen utensils. All of them were dirty and heavily used. One after another these utensils disengaged themselves, fell into the water, washed and rinsed themselves clean, then refastened themselves to the camel's back. All the time there was no one to be seen, no man and no woman.

"When all the utensils had washed themselves and were back in place, the animal began to return from whence it had come. Quickly I ran into the water and grabbed its tail. The camel dragged me out of the river and up the other bank. It did not seem hindered by me, so I let myself be towed along a path through the desert.

"After a long time we came to the foot of the mountains. There, in front of a sheer rock wall, the camel halted. I thought this must be the end of the journey. Suddenly a gate opened in the rock, and the camel entered a spacious garden. In the garden there was a pond with a fountain and behind it stood a lovely castle. At once the gates of the castle swung open, and all the utensils flew through the air and disappeared into the castle's kitchen. All the while the pots and pans were talking to each other: 'You go in first.' 'No, you go first. I'll follow you.'

"I let go of the camel's tail and walked into the kitchen. All the utensils there were made of silver and gold. Suddenly, I heard a rustling above me as two big birds alighted by the pond. One bird was a beautiful creamy white; the other was shining jet black, like ebony or india ink, beautiful! At once they plunged into the pond, splashed around, and emerged from the water, miraculously transformed into two tall young men. Both were very handsome. One was dressed richly, like a prince, all in white. The other was dressed in black velvet and seemed to be his companion's chamberlain or equerry.

"When the men entered the palace together, I followed them and 20 hid behind the curtains. They sat at a table. I saw no servants, but refreshments came in, suspended in the air, carried by invisible hands. Silver plates were loaded with the choicest delicacies and cups with the most delicious beverages, tea and coffee. When the young men had finished eating and drinking, the invisible servants carried the trays away again.

"The prince then asked his companion for his jewel box. When it was brought to him, he opened it and took out a very pretty ring. 'She threw this ring at me,' he said, 'but why? Does it signify that she rejected me? If only I could marry her!'

"As he was speaking, the ring shed tears and sobbed sadly. Then the prince took out a golden anklet. 'Why did she throw me this lovely anklet?' he wondered. 'Did she mean that she wanted me to come and put it on her ankle adoringly, to show her my love?'

"The anklet, too, shed tears and sobbed sadly. Then he took out a tiara, a lovely dainty diadem, and exclaimed: 'Why did she throw this priceless jewel at me? Did she mean to say that her title of princess was worth less to her than the love I feel? Or did she reject both me and her title?'

"The diadem sighed and sobbed audibly in his hand. The prince went on lamenting his forsaken love: 'Her cheeks, now pale with illness, were once like rose petals: delicately beautiful. Her mouth has a perfect shape and color, her nose is as straight as a sword, her eyebrows are like two bows, her hair is like shining silk, her hands are sculpted like ivory, her whole being is perfect. She has enchanted me forever!'

"While the white prince was thus expressing his love for the 25 princess, the jewels lay in their box, sobbing disconsolately."

To the Secret Garden

The princess, captivated by her visitor's tale, wept with longing for the man who loved her. The slave girl continued her enthralling story. "I spent the night in that room," she said. "The prince and his companion soon left, presumably to sleep in some other part of the castle. The next morning I went to the kitchen. I saw what I expected to see. The kitchen utensils, used and dirty again, were flying out—one after the other—in the direction of the camel, which was waiting outside.

"The moment it departed, with all the spoons, knives, and silver plates on its back, I got hold of its tail and let myself be towed as far as the river. There the camel stopped, as it had done before. I found my laundry untouched on the bank.

"It was on my way home that I learned that all the women of the town had been invited by you. They had gone to tell you of their lives and sorrows. So I decided that I, too, should go and tell you this story, the strangest of my life. So there you have it. I am not sure whether it presages good luck or misfortune, perhaps both."

The princess thanked the young lady for her story and dismissed her, saying, "Come back tomorrow morning before dawn. Please do not fail me."

That evening the princess asked her parents for permission to go 30 on a journey. Of course, the king and queen had many questions, but the princess would only answer some of them: "Yes, I'll have company. A nice young woman will come tomorrow to act as my guide to the mountains. She has been very good to me, so much so that I feel much better now."

Believing that their daughter had been on the brink of death only a little while before, and seeing that she now seemed almost recovered, the king and queen agreed that a trip to the mountains might do her health good. So they gave their consent.

At dawn the next morning, the guide arrived. Together the two women walked to the river. Soon they saw the camel approach. All the dirty cups, plates, and pans were on its back. When the magical washing up was done, and all the utensils had resumed their places on its back, the animal departed with measured stride. At once the two women grasped its tail and were dragged along behind. The camel did not seem to be bothered in the least by their weight.

After several hours they arrived at the sheer rock wall. This opened at once when the camel approached, so it could walk into the garden. There, the utensils left its back. The women hid behind some flowering shrubs in the garden. They were just in time. The two big birds arrived, with a loud flapping of wings. They alighted beside the pond, then plunged into the water. A few moments later they reemerged as two handsome men, one dressed in black and the other in white. The man in white was so attractive that the princess fell in love with him as soon as she saw his human shape.

The two women followed the men inside and hid behind the curtains. Soon, the prince opened his jewel box and began lamenting his love for the princess. But a strange thing happened: the gems and jewels neither sobbed nor shed tears. Startled, the prince asked them, "What has happened?"

"Our mistress is here, so we are happy and cheerful," the jewels 35 replied.

The prince did not believe his ears. He gave himself over to his laments once again: "Oh! How lovely she is, that princess! I love her!"

The princess did not wish to hear another word. She stepped out from her hiding place and declared: "And she loves you, my prince!"

She ran up to him and threw herself into his arms. They covered each other with tears of joy. The prince asked if she would marry him. "Of course," she said.

Meanwhile, the prince's companion was enamored of the woman who had guided the princess. He asked her to marry him and she, too, said yes. So, from an ounce of sorrow, the princess who had been denied all knowledge of the world and the woman who had lived a life of servitude both found happiness and bliss.

What Did You Read?

1. Why did the princess buy the seeds from the merchant?
2. How many times did the black and white birds destroy her flowers?
3. Why do the jewels sob disconsolately?

What Do You Think?

1. What is the significance of the "ravished flowers" and the discarded ring, diadem, and necklace?

2. What is the cultural message and moral we learn from reading this story? What does this say about women?

3. How does this story symbolize the interaction of the socioeconomic class system?

How Was It Done?

1. How many structural parts are there to this story? How are they divided?

2. What artifacts does the story center on?

3. Does the tale within the tale device work well in the crafting of the fairy tale?

4. How does the ending provide symmetry to this tale?

11

The Justice System

Headlines announce new, horrific crimes daily, and society responds with increasing harshness toward those accused of these crimes. Underpinning much of society's response is the assumption that justice is blind—meaning it is fair and free of bias or prejudice. With blind justice, we argue, we can measure out harsh penalties to those found guilty. However, what if the justice system is not blind, but troubled: that the justice system is different for the poor and the rich, that minorities are likely to be punished more harshly, and that children who cannot drive a car are treated like adults in the courtroom and prison? Fear and anger about crime have driven many to accept these practices, but the question of fairness must be addressed. So, too, must the question of whether our justice system actually provides justice, or just punishment.

Because this chapter's theme, the Justice System, involves an area of life that is frequently and heatedly debated, the Writing Assignment for this chapter discusses the creation of a proposal for change. There are distinct aspects to a policy paper—including the assessment of the need for change, the opposition to the argument, the characteristics of the actual changes needed, and the benefits of such a change. To meet the challenge of this assignment, the Writing Lesson focuses on presenting the opposition to an argument—the concession paragraph. By conceding that the opposition to your argument has valid points, you can often make your own position more convincing. That is, your reader becomes aware that you have considered the alternative position before advancing your own side.

THE MAIN EVENT READING

Reasonable Doubts

Stephen Pomper

Stephen Pomper, offering a number of specific ideas for reform, examines issues such as changing the exclusionary rule, creating DNA databases, protecting witnesses, monitoring prosecutors, and dumping the insanity defense. Pomper questions the wisdom of certain mandatory sentencing laws and the attempt to fight drugs with incarceration. His policy proposals provide an excellent ground for discussing many of the issues facing our justice system today.

Key Words

ransacked	searched thoroughly, as during a robbery
loci	centers of activity, attention, or concentration
sleuthing	acting like a detective; searching for information
intimidation	to frighten into compliance by threats; to make timid or fearful
prosecutor	the attorney who brings charges against a suspect in court
incentive	something that urges someone into action or to a determination
clunker	someone or something notably unsuccessful
adjourned	suspended indefinitely or until another time or place
kibbitzes	looks on and offers unsolicited advice
continuances	adjournments of court cases until later dates

Crime may be down but the criminal justice system remains something of a mess. If you've ever spent time on a jury, if you've worked in a criminal court, or if you caught even 10 minutes of the O.J. trial on TV, you've seen some of the problems. The system has an Alice-in-Wonderland quality: The guilty are over-protected, the innocent are under-served, and much of the time the public interest simply fails to enter the picture. Jurors spend days in court dozing through endless delays and witnesses who dare come forward find their lives imperiled. When all is said and done, too many violent and dangerous felons wind up with Get-Out-of-Jail-Free cards and too many non-violent and just-plain-innocent people wind up doing time. *(Is this true or just public perception?)*

How do we make it better? Read on for the *Monthly*'s guide to criminal justice reform.

Get the Truth Out

examples
of reform
Courts are supposed to be finders of fact. Yet there's an awful lot about the criminal justice system that keeps them from ever getting to those facts. Some of the obstacles are straight-forwardly bad laws. Others are more a question of resources and oversight. We could help our courts get past some of these obstacles and here's how:

reference
to pop
culture
1. End "Two Wrongs Make a Right" Criminal Procedure. The judicial system labors under rules crafted by the Warren Court, which protect defendants even if it's at the expense of the truth. In a 1997 law review article, University of Minnesota law professor Michael Stokes Paulsen casts this as the "Dirty Harry" problem. In the movie of the same name, Detective Harry Callaghan gets increasingly violent as he goes after a serial murderer named "Scorpio." He busts into his place without a warrant, nabs the murder rifle, and savages Scorpio until he spits out the location of a kidnap/rape/murder victim. But here's the kicker: Although Scorpio is a monster, and Harry does some monstrous things, neither of them is actually punished. Scorpio goes free because all the evidence against him is tainted by Harry's antics, and Harry slides by because cops get away with stuff.

origins of
current
laws
Decades later, this lose–lose approach is still at the heart of criminal procedure. To be sure, the failing has noble origins. Back in the Civil Rights era, the Supreme Court, concerned about segregationist states deploying policemen to harass and imprison minorities, developed a set of constitutional principles that stopped them from doing that: Ill-gotten evidence was treated like fruit from a poisoned tree and had to be discarded. If the police ransacked your car without a warrant, the resulting evidence could not be produced at trial. 5

objections
to current
laws
But the days of officially-sponsored police racism are over. And while there's still racism and police abuse on a different scale, it's hard to see why they are best dealt with by excluding otherwise helpful evidence. It's one thing to say that forced confessions should not be considered: That protects innocent people who might be beaten into confessing crimes they did not commit. But what kind of protection does an innocent person get from an "exclusionary rule" that prevents a court from considering ill-gotten evidence? If Harry busts into an innocent person's apartment and doesn't find anything to seize, then there won't be any evidence for a court to exclude, and there won't be any negative consequence for the police. Not that exclusion is such a negative consequence anyway: when police are evaluated in cities like New York, the emphasis is on the number of arrests to their credit—

is the
author
assuming
a suspect
is guilty?
not convictions. If Scorpio goes free because Harry trashes his place, Harry still may be eligible for a promotion.

Part of the problem with the exclusionary rule is that it assumes that the Bill of Rights is focused on protecting the guilty rather than the innocent. But some leading constitutional scholars have begun to suggest that this assumption is backwards—protecting the innocent is in fact the top priority. The correct way to control police abuse is not by tossing potentially useful evidence onto the compost pile. It is by punishing the policeman or the police department through a lawsuit or through criminal charges. But the court should, by all means, be allowed to consider Scorpio's rifle and any other relevant evidence that Harry has managed to dig up.

In 1995 Congress considered a bill that would have gone in this direction—by getting rid of the exclusionary rule and making it easier to sue delinquent cops—but it fizzled. Supporters of the status quo argue that it doesn't really matter: There are so many exceptions to the exclusionary rule that only a small percentage of arrests are lost as a result. They also argue that the rule is useful because it provides at least some check on police abuse—and that creating an alternate system of checks would be a real challenge. This, however, ignores the problems in the current system. Read the recent coverage about the Los Angeles and New York police departments and you will see that the exclusionary rule is not an especially effective mechanism for controlling police brutality. Meanwhile, courts and lawyers waste their time on motions to suppress evidence that can only undermine the truth-seeking process.

Getting to the truth should be the court's foremost objective. And this principle doesn't apply just to the exclusionary rule. For example, a majority of states have deadlines after which a convict cannot introduce new evidence to prove his innocence. In Virginia, the deadline is a scant 21 days after trial. The idea is to keep appeals from dragging out endlessly, but that's not a good rationale for keeping innocent people in jail. If a convict can present credible new evidence, then a court should review it. But if a case reopens for this reason and the state has come up with new evidence of guilt, the court should look at that too. another problem with excluding evidence

It's time to end the lose–lose cycle that we create by excluding evidence. A court must get the information it needs to send Scorpio to Alcatraz. If he can prove his innocence later, it must hear the evidence it needs to spring him. And the Harrys of this world must pay for their brutality through some mechanism that punishes them directly—rather than one that punishes the community by putting guilty people back on the street. 10

2. Create a Universal DNA Database. This is an idea that Rudy Giuliani has endorsed and the ACLU has said could usher in a "brave new world" of genetic discrimination—but looking past the rhetoric, it's a winner. 2nd reform

The idea is to take full advantage of the enormous power of DNA evidence. Because it's so much more reliable at identifying people than eye-witnessing, DNA evidence can keep innocent people from going to death row and guilty people from going free. And because it is such Is getting DNA like getting a fingerprint?

powerful proof, it can help shorten trials, relieve problems with witness intimidation, and generally lend itself to a more efficient and reliable criminal justice system. But in order to maximize its usefulness, you need to be able to check crime scene DNA samples against the biggest possible database. The government is already coordinating a database that will include mostly convicted felons' DNA samples. That's decent start: Convicted felons have a high probability of returning to their old ways when released from prison. Still, plenty of crime is committed by people who have never spent time behind bars. So why not do it right and create a database that includes everybody?

is this reasonable?   The idea is simple and non-discriminatory. Upon the birth of any child, a hospital would take a DNA sample using a simple procedure that involves swabbing cells off the inside of a cheek with a bit of cotton and then analyzing their genetic material for patterns at 13 separate points, called loci. The information recorded at these loci is referred to as "junk" by geneticists because it doesn't say anything interesting about whether a person is likely to be an insurance risk, is likely to win a Nobel Prize, is a cat or a dog person, or anything of the sort. Like a fingerprint, it would simply identify who a person is. This information would be sent to a federal database where it could be used only by law enforcement authorities when trying to establish the identity of a criminal.

Civil libertarians get hysterical over the privacy issues, but where's the beef? Given the restricted information that we're talking about, and the limited access that would be afforded, the main privacy right at stake is the right to commit crimes anonymously. It's also worth noting that millions of hospital patients leave blood and tissue samples when they come for treatment. Some hospitals keep these on file. So if your local homicide chief decides that he wants to get a DNA profile on you, he may very well be able to go down to City General, retrieve some old cells of yours, and do his own genetic analysis. This analysis could wind up furnishing information that is much more sensitive than the information that would be recorded in the national database. Wouldn't it be preferable to require the police to limit their DNA sleuthing to one tightly controlled source?

benefits to suspects of DNA evidence   One more point on DNA evidence: It can help us correct past mistakes, and we should use it to do so. States should be required to take DNA samples from all convicts in all cases where it could prove their innocence and the prisoner wants it. Given that no fewer than 67 prisoners have already been found innocent using DNA testing, states should be working overtime to find other innocents who have been wrongly imprisoned. The flip side of this position is that states and courts should do whatever it takes to make certain that statutes of limitations don't stop victims and prosecutors from going after violent offenders where DNA technology for the first time allows guilt to be established.   15

3. Save the Witnesses. If you watch too many movies of the week, 3rd reform
you can get a highly distorted view of what this country does to protect its witnesses. There is a romantic idea that once you agree to testify in a dangerous case, the FBI rushes in with a team of plastic
surgeons, draws up new papers, and moves you to the furthest corner
of the furthest possible state—where it continues to keep a watchful
eye on you for the rest of your natural born days. But there's a problem: The FBI program is for federal witnesses—it was designed to help
U.S. attorneys bust up organized crime. It doesn't do a thing to help
out at the state and local levels where most crime, and most witness
intimidation, occurs.

And a shocking amount of witness intimidation does occur at
those levels. According to a 1995 report published by the National Institute of Justice (their latest on this subject), some prosecutors were
able to identify gang-dominated neighborhoods where between 75
and 100 percent of violent crimes involved intimidation—from knee
capping potential witnesses to staring them down in court to actually
rubbing them out. That's an unsettling figure when you consider that
a court's fact-finding machinery can grind to a halt without witnesses.

Consider the following example: A Baltimore jury recently acquit- example
ted three men who had been accused of shooting one Shawn L. Suggs
in a street fight that spilled out into rush hour traffic. At first, the prosecution seemed to have a good case—but then the key witnesses
started dropping out of the picture: The first was killed in his home.
Another disappeared without a trace. And the third (Suggs' former
girlfriend) claimed at the last moment to have lost her memory to
heroin addiction. "I think she is afraid to tell the truth," Suggs' mother
told the *Baltimore Sun*. "I think I would be afraid too."

How do you fight that kind of fear? Many states and communities 20
have created their own witness protection programs that try to offer
some measure of security—from posting police cars outside witnesses'
homes to moving witnesses out of their old neighborhood until the
trial is over. But the programs often lack adequate funding. And on top
of that, it can be a lot tougher to protect state and local witnesses than
it is to deal with mob rats. Street and gang crime witnesses are frequently reluctant to abandon their homes and neighborhoods. They
get bored, lonely, and afraid when they're pulled away from their families. And even if they can be persuaded to move a short distance—say
a few towns away—the temptation to look in on friends and relatives
back in the old neighborhood can be both irresistible and dangerous.

More could be done. Improving funding and stiffening penalties potential
would be a good start. When prosecutors can persuade a witness to solutions
cooperate, they should have the money they need to pay for motel
bills, replace locks on doors, and pick up the tab for gas and groceries.
Because it can be tough to come up with the scratch to do this on short

notice, some states, like California, have set aside funds that communities can use to foot the bill. Other states should follow their lead, and the federal government should set up an emergency fund to help communities pick up the slack when there's a shortfall. And with regard to penalties, states should rank intimidation right up there with the gravest non-capital offenses. Under Washington, D.C. law, intimidators can get up to life imprisonment. That sounds about right.

4th reform   **4. Police the Prosecutors—As Well As the Police.** Police and prosecutors are the gatekeepers of the criminal justice system. But although police brutality gets a lot of attention—as it has recently in New York and Los Angeles—prosecutors tend to escape scrutiny.

lack of   We should pay closer attention to the prosecutors. They, after all,
account-   are the ones who decide which cases go to trial and how they're pre-
ability   sented. If they misrepresent the facts, they can wind up sending innocents to jail. And that's a problem for two reasons. First, there are a lot of powerful incentives that make prosecutors want to win—sometimes even at the expense of the truth. ("Winning has become more important than doing justice," complained Harvard Law School professor Alan Dershowitz in a 1999 *Chicago Tribune* interview. "Nobody runs for Senate saying 'I did justice.'") Second, when a prosecutor does step over the line, he rarely faces serious punishment.

research   How do we know? In 1999, *The Chicago Tribune* published a nationwide survey. They looked at all the murder cases in the past 40 years that had to be retried because a prosecutor hid evidence or permitted a witness to lie. They found 381 in all. What happened to the prosecutors in those cases? Almost nothing. About a dozen were investigated by state agencies, but only one was actually fired—and he was eventually reinstated. And not a single one of the offending prosecutors was ever convicted of either hiding or presenting false evidence. Indeed, not a single prosecutor in the history of the Republic has ever been convicted on those grounds—even though they're both felony offenses. As Pace University law professor Bennett Gershman told the *Tribune:* "There is no check on prosecutorial misconduct except for the prosecutor's own attitudes and beliefs and inner morality."

But isn't the defense bar a check on prosecutorial misconduct? 25 Don't count on it. In December 1999, *The New York Times* noted that the number of legal aid lawyers in New York City's Criminal Court had dropped from 1,000 a decade ago to 500 today. And it quoted Manhattan defense attorney Ronald Kuby as saying that "No competent criminal defense lawyer zealously representing his clients can make a living on [legal aid rates]." This problem is obviously not limited to New York.

All this suggests that if we want to make certain prosecutors are doing the right thing, we have to police them more aggressively. That means creating well-muscled independent agencies that have strong incentives to find out when prosecutors misbehave—and to fine, press charges, and/or fire them when they do. Judges should help them out by publishing the names of prosecutors who commit misconduct in their orders and opinions (not a common practice)—and circulating them to the independent watchdogs. And while we're on the subject, states should also set up similar watchdogs to police the police—both for abuse and sheer incompetence. There should be independent civilian commissions that not only have responsibility for overseeing police departments, but that also have the power to impose discipline on the departments when they stray.

5. Abolish the Insanity Defense. It is true that you have to be a bit crazy to shoot the President like John Hinckley, or to cut off your husband's penis like Lorena Bobbit—but should that affect the state's ability to keep you separated from the rest of society, where you might do further harm? If you are rich or high profile or just plain lucky enough to find a defense lawyer who can successfully argue the insanity defense on your behalf, it can.

5th reform

How often is the insanity defense used? Is it a major problem?

Consider the case of Tomar Cooper Locker, who opened fire on a crowded D.C. hospital ward, killing a boxer named Ruben Bell and wounding five bystanders. The apparent motive for the shooting was that Locker had a vendetta against Bell, whom he thought had killed his girlfriend. But Locker pled insanity based on the claim that he was suffering from a momentary attack of post-traumatic stress disorder— a claim endorsed by the same psychiatrist who testified in the Lorena Bobbit incident. The jury bought it. Locker was then committed to St. Elizabeth's hospital, where he was treated for two whole months until, earlier this spring, doctors declared him fit to reenter society.

Michael Lazas is another example of someone who slipped through the system as a result of the insanity defense. In 1993, Lazas was found not guilty by reason of insanity for strangling his infant son and sent to Maryland's Perkins Hospital Center. It was his second violent assault; two years earlier he had stabbed a picnic companion in the throat. In 1998, Perkins officials thought Lazas was ready for a group home, so they moved him to an essentially zero-security facility in Burtonsville, Maryland. In February of this year, Lazas simply walked away from the Burtonsville facility. He was reportedly gone for four days before anyone notified the authorities he was missing.

In both cases, the public would have been better served if there were no insanity defense. There is no dispute that Locker and Lazas did what they were accused of doing. As a society, we've made a judgment that people who do these things need to be separated from the rest of us for a certain amount of time. Locker and Lazas should each have been found guilty and served the requisite time for his offenses—

30

in an appropriate treatment facility to the extent necessary. The law should not force chronic schizophrenics to do hard time in maximum-security prisons. But it should be adamant about finding ways to keep those who commit violent crimes at a safe distance from the rest of society.

Lock Up the Right People

6th reform   Politicians who vote for mandatory minimum sentences stake a claim to being tough on crime. Politicians who vote against them run the risk of appearing weak. Of course in a perfect world, "toughness" would be assessed by whether you put the right (i.e., most dangerous) people in jail—rather than how many people you put in jail. But the world of sentencing statutes is far from perfect.

one cause   The political blindness that surrounds these laws can be partly
of the laws   traced to the death of Len Bias—a Maryland basketball star who had been the Celtics' first pick in the NBA draft. When Bias overdosed on cocaine in his college dorm room in 1986, he became an overnight poster child for the war on drugs. It was an election year and Beltway legislators, who were close enough to Maryland to be caught up in the public horror at Bias' death, wanted to make a statement. So they replaced a set of temporary federal sentencing guidelines that had been in place with permanent "mandatory minimum" sentencing requirements. States followed suit with their own iterations of these requirements. And in 1994, California and Washington added a new wrinkle when they passed so-called "three strikes laws" that require courts to give 25 year minimum sentences to any two-time felony offender who steps out of line a third time—even if to commit a misdemeanor offense.

what is just   These laws have generated some spectacularly unfair results. For
punish-   example, a California court recently sentenced Michael Wayne Riggs, a
ment?   homeless man, to 25 years in jail for stealing a bottle of vitamins. His most serious prior offense was snatching a purse.

But if Riggs' story is maddening at the individual level, the major concern at the policy level is what all this chest-thumping legislation is doing to our nation's prison system. There are roughly 2 million Americans behind bars, of whom more than half are there for nonviolent (in most cases drug-related) crimes. The country spends $31 billion per year on corrections—twice what it spent 10 years ago. There is still not enough room in America's prisons.

effects of   Even looking past the overcrowding issues, however, sentencing 35
sentencing   laws have proven to be losers. Sending minor drug offenders to jail
laws   exposes them to hardened criminals and increases the risk of them committing more serious felonies when they get out. The Rand Corporation has found that mandatory minimums are the least cost-

effective way to reduce drug use and crime—as compared to treatment programs and discretionary sentencing. Even White House Drug Czar Barry McCaffery has acknowledged that "we can't incarcerate our way out of the drug problem." It is therefore unsurprising that a dozen or so states have formed commissions to reconsider their rigid sentencing policies and several, like Michigan, have begun to repeal them. And on the progressive front, Arizona recently became the first state to offer the option of drug treatment, rather than prison, to its non-violent offenders convicted on drug charges.

Arizona's program is both cost efficient and makes sense. A Cali- example fornia study found that one dollar spent on drug treatment saves seven dollars in reduced hospital admissions and law enforcement costs. These savings can be put to better use elsewhere in the criminal justice system. For example, they can be used to help communities develop facilities to siphon off non-violent offenders from the heart of the system. Roughly two percent of the nation's drug offender traffic is processed in special "drug courts," which dole out a combination of light sentencing—such as short jail terms, community service, and probation—plus mandatory drug treatment. More drug courts would almost certainly be a good thing.

Communities also do themselves a service when they set up tough example probation programs that actually help minor offenders steer away from trouble. Orange County, California has had substantial success with a program that involves 6 A.M. inspection visits to all participants from program officers, surprise drug testing, counseling, and monthly evaluations by the supervising judge. Anecdotal evidence suggests that in order to work these programs have to be ready to dish out real discipline to participants who fail to live up to their end of the bargain. Orange County participant Dale Wilson, who had been addicted to cocaine for three decades before joining the program, told the *Los Angeles Times* that he was sent to jail for nine days when he had a relapse. "It's a strict program," he said. "But I never would've gotten to the point to keep me sober if I hadn't been faced with these punishments."

Put More Order in the Courts

Finally, we shouldn't forget that the best laws and policies in the 7th reform world aren't going to do a whole lot of good unless we have reliable, industrious, and smoothly administered courts. And while there are lots of hard-working judges with the same objective, there are also plenty of clunkers.

In a 1996 San Francisco case, for example, two municipal court example judges batted a domestic violence case back and forth on an October Friday. According to *The Recorder*, a legal newspaper, Judge Wallace Douglass was supposed to hear the case—but he double-booked another trial for the same day. So he sent it across the hall to Judge Ellen Chaitin, who held a mid-day conference—and then sent it back to Douglass when it failed to settle by the early afternoon. Douglass then said that he couldn't find a jury to hear the case (it was Friday afternoon, after all) and, because a delay would have violated the defendant's speedy trial rights, he dismissed it. This calls to mind the story of the Manhattan judge who in 1971 adjourned a robbery trial to catch a flight to Europe. Another trial would have violated the defendant's constitutional rights, so he walked away scot-free.

lazy judges The problem is two-fold. One is that judges don't always push 40 themselves that hard. In 1989, *Manhattan Lawyer* correspondents observed that, on average, the judges in Manhattan's criminal court were in session about four and a half hours a day. Sixty-two percent spent less than five hours in session, and 42 percent started after 10 A.M. In Baltimore, which has more than 300 homicides per year, you can
is this a
typical day
in court? sometimes walk through a criminal courthouse around 3:30 or 4:00 P.M. and find courtrooms that have adjourned for the day.

But the additional problem is that judges are too often inclined to schedule things first for their own convenience, second for the convenience of lawyers, and last of all for the convenience of the people the system should be bending over to accommodate—jurors and witnesses. One prosecutor said that there are days in D.C. Superior Court that unfold as follows: The jury is instructed to arrive at 10 A.M. and sits for hours while the judge kibbitzes with the lawyers over technical legal issues. Sometimes the kibbitzing runs right into lunch. Then everybody trundles off for a two hour break. The trial starts in earnest at 3 P.M. And court adjourns between 4:30 and 5 P.M.—sometimes earlier.

Lack of organization is another problem. Washington D.C.'s Superior Court has no central scheduling mechanism. Judges control their own dockets and are allowed to book two or three trials for the same day, anticipating that there will be pleas and continuances. Policemen who are supposed to testify wind up milling around the courthouse for days on end, waiting for their trials to be called, and—if they otherwise happen to be off-duty—collecting overtime.

It has to be possible to run a tighter ship because some judges already do. As noted in last month's "Tilting at Windmills," for example, a Tennessee judge named Duane Slone has adopted a policy that he won't hear plea bargains on the day a trial is scheduled to begin. This saves the jury from having to sit and wait while lawyers haggle over a plea and allows trials to start promptly at 9 A.M. Common sense courtesies like this could kill a lot of the inefficiencies that you see in courtrooms today. But more importantly, disciplinary panels need to keep better tabs on the courts and punish (by fines or demotions if necessary) those judges who fail to show up on time, stay all day, and run an orderly docket.

What Next?

Wholesale reform of the criminal justice system obviously isn't going to happen overnight. Some reforms can only be made by Supreme Court decision. Others will have to be effected through new laws and practices at the federal, state, and local levels. Still, it's a set of tasks well worth facing. It's great that crime is down but if we want it to stay there, and if we want to make sure that we're sending the right people to jail, then we need a system that we can really trust beyond a reasonable doubt.

What Did You Read?

1. What exactly does the "exclusionary rule" mean?
2. Why does the author think it useful to create a universal DNA database?
3. What does it mean to "police the prosecutors"?
4. What is Arizona doing to reform its prison system?

What Do You Think?

1. Why do you suppose it is difficult to "sue" delinquent police officers? Do you see police corruption as a severe problem? Why or why not?
2. Do you think the insanity defense should be abolished? Why or why not?
3. What other reforms can you think of to improve the justice system? Explain.

How Was It Done?

1. Structurally, what does Pomper's article revolve around?
2. In crafting this article, how big a part do the "opening remarks" and "conclusion" play? Why?
3. What kind of facts and data does the author use to back up his claim? Provide examples. How useful are they?
4. What single word best crystallized this essay?

THE MAIN EVENT WRITING ASSIGNMENT

Write an essay in which you respond to one of the following assignments:

1. Write a policy of your own explaining the need for change, the policy for reform, and the benefits. When you organize your essay, organize it in the following fashion:
   • Introduction, with thesis
   • Concession paragraph with citations to research
   • A Needs section
   • A Policy section
   • A Benefits section
   • Conclusion
   One way to help yourself is to use subtitles for the "Needs," "Policy," and "Benefits" sections. Each section should be roughly equal in length, with no section slighted. A common error is to devote too much space to the development of the Needs section and not enough in the Policy or Benefits sections.

2. Critique a recent proposal in your community for fighting crime or improving public safety. Write a critique that is either critical or supportive. Consider the proposal's constitutionality.

3. Write an argument on what you consider to be one of the largest miscarriages of justices going on in this country right now. It could be on such issues as treatment of the homeless, corporate fraud, or police brutality.

4. Are court television shows, with celebrity judges, beneficial to society, or do they mislead the general public about how the real justice system works?

5. Argue whether or not court proceedings should be on television. Does the fact of televising a trial affect the trial itself?

PREPARATION PUNCH LIST

Before you begin writing the essay, you need to prepare yourself to write.

1. Begin with a passion you have for making a change that would help society and help fill in some obvious holes that you have seen in the justice system based on breaking news, articles in magazines, or other media reports.

• For example, if recently there have been numerous examples of kidnappings of young children, what policy might you suggest to fix that problem? You might suggest a policy based on taking a DNA sample from every child, at birth, and placing that information into a DNA database. This would allow for nearly instant recognition of forensic evidence at a crime scene.

2. *Anticipate objections to your policy.*

- Although creating a universal DNA database might to you seem reasonable, comprehensive, and much needed, some people might object to the invasion of privacy, the cost of building and maintaining the database, and the cost of training detectives in how to collect evidence.

3. *You need to make sure that you go beyond simply eliminating certain proposals (that in itself is not a policy). Indeed, if you choose to reform a policy already in existence, you need to understand that original policy and the problems with it.*

4. *In many ways, this assignment is an exercise in cataloguing research. Once you determine your proposal, you need to compile your research in terms of three different areas. Why do we need the reform? (List all the problems that exist that make it necessary.) What are the ideas proposed by the experts? What are the anticipated beneficial results if said proposal were implemented?*

THE MAIN EVENT WRITING LESSON: THE CONCESSION PARAGRAPH

One of the issues you face in many writing situations is that reasonable people can disagree. If you fail to acknowledge the presence of opposing views, your reader is likely to have one of two reactions: the reader may assume you are ignorant of opposing arguments and therefore cannot be trusted; or the reader may assume you are being deceitful by hiding these arguments and therefore cannot be trusted. This problem is known as "card stacking" and should be avoided.

The concession is how you deal with the problem of card stacking. In brief, a concession acknowledges the other side of your argument's points. That is, if you are arguing for one side, you must recognize the other side has some legitimate points; otherwise, intelligent people would not need to debate the issue.

The concession normally follows the introduction of the essay. This allows the writer the full length of the main body of the essay to present his or her own arguments. The writer needs to begin with a transitional word or phrase that signals to the reader that what follows is not the writer's position, but that of the opposing side. If this transition is not provided, the writer seems confused—arguing for both sides of the same issue. Concession arguments must represent the real arguments, not misleading or unfair arguments that the opposition does not actually present. One way to ensure this is to include quotations or paraphrases from opposition sources. Be careful also to end the concession with a wrap-up that prepares the reader for your main arguments.

For instance, if you were to argue in favor of abolishing the use of the death penalty, your concession would have to acknowledge the fact that a large majority of people favor the use of the death penalty and believe that it is important to execute those convicted of the worst offenses. Still, you would turn those claims around and argue that the popularity of a punishment is not by itself a reason for having it, and that the problems associated with the death penalty outweigh any perceived benefit.

Consider the following pattern of argument:

Thesis:

We should put an immediate stop to the use of the death penalty in this state.

Concession Paragraph:

Granted, the death penalty has many supporters. It has been reported that 73% of the adults in this state favor the use of the death penalty for murder in which special circumstances are involved (Walker A-3). Additionally, many of those supporters believe that the death penalty deters those who would otherwise commit murder (Smith 12). Sheriff Gwen Perkins of Central County, in a personal interview, suggests that if the death penalty were abolished, career criminals from other states might relocate here to avoid a possible death penalty. However, the popularity of the death penalty is not reason enough to keep it, the deterrence effect of the death penalty is greatly overestimated, and the idea that career criminals relocate according to the perceived risk of punishment seems illogical at best.

Note the following features:

- The first sentence concedes that the death penalty enjoys a lot of public support. This allows the writer to present the evidence about that.
- The concession paragraph contains three pieces of evidence derived from research.
- The end of the paragraph helps the reader anticipate the direction the writer will be going in the main body of the essay.

THE MAIN EVENT WRITING SAMPLE

The following is a sample policy essay written for this text in response to the Main Event Writing Assignment, Question #1.

Desperately Needed Prison Reforms

When the judge's gavel falls and the jury pronounces the suspect *Intro-* "guilty," many people think the justice system has done its job. The *duction* suspect, now a convict, is led off to incarceration, and society can breathe a little easier. However, in most cases, that convict will eventually be freed—and the question is, will the convict, based on his or her experience, change? Or does the justice system create a revolving door of crime, punishment, and more crime. Because of society's fear of crime, laws have gotten tougher and tougher on suspects and convicts. Children are being tried as adults and incarcerated with adults. The poor receive inadequate defenses, and the public is unconcerned (Wypijewski). Minorities are incarcerated at rates vastly exceeding their numbers in the general population, and the death penalty is more popular now than it has been in decades. The "throw away the key" mentality of the public's approach to criminals will ultimately force the incarceration of unprecedented numbers (driving up state and federal costs) unless meaningful reforms in the justice system can be made to incarcerate only those who truly deserve it. The justice system should implement some *Claim* policies of reform that separate addicts from violent criminals, protect the civil rights of inmates, and make the death penalty less common.

However, there are those who praise the justice system for the *Concession* work it has already done. What most people want out of a justice system is safety, deterrence, and punishment for the guilty, and this is being provided. According to an article by John J. DiIulio, Jr., a senior fellow at the Manhattan Institute, between the years 1973 and 1986, the Rockefeller Drug Law and the Second Felony Offender Law earned New York its reputation as the state with the toughest drug laws in the country. DiIulio reports that those were mandatory anti-drug laws that required giving drug offenders a mandatory state prison term, with second offenders receiving even steeper terms. The RDL has for years been seen as a model of how to deal with the problem of drugs. People also point out that new technology makes it possible for the innocent to be distinguished from the guilty. For example, with new DNA technology, eighty-seven inmates on death row have been freed in the state of Texas alone (Bach). The poor are not forgotten either, they claim. For instance, the Georgia Supreme Court created a commission to study indigent defense and propose recommendations from its legislature (Bach). Simply put, the opposition argues that money and time have been spent to provide adequate defense to the needy in this country. Many people feel that in conjunction with community policing, better recruitment of police officers, and constant scrutiny by the media, the justice system is doing its job.

Needs

Although some people think that the current system is working, the justice system is actually an area that requires urgent evaluation and sweeping reforms. This statement is made in response to sexual assaults on inmates in incarcerated settings, the number of drug offenders incarcerated with violent criminals, the inequity of justice for minorities and the poor, and the self-destructive and self-defeating acts of incarcerating juveniles in adult institutions.

Need #1   First, a large problem with prisons is that the prison population has exploded with nonviolent drug offenders. For example, since the mid-1990s, a large fraction of New York's incoming prison population "has consisted of offenders whose only past felony crimes, recorded and undetected, were genuinely low-level, nonviolent drug crimes" (DiIulio). Many of these drug-only offenders are drug abusers or addicts who have never been in a well-structured community-anchored substance abuse program. Other states such as New Jersey, Wisconsin, New Mexico, and Arizona have found that these drug-only offenders are simply drug-dependent (DiIulio). As far as deterrence goes, as soon as one offender is incarcerated, another one will assume his sales and effectively take his place. The drug laws have not increased public safety, but have only overcrowded the prison system. There is also a socially divisive racial rub to the RDL and its mandatory minimum rules. In 1997, about ninety-five percent of all persons in New York prisons whose last and most serious conviction was for a drug offense were black or Hispanic (DiIulio). Ironically, most of the people in the communities where these prisoners came from strongly oppose drug legalization and want drug dealers out of their neighborhoods (DiIulio). This is not justice. Alternatives have to be found to deal with first-time drug offenders while still punishing those guilty of more serious crimes.

Another current problem is the unconscionable treatment of *Need #2* children in the justice system. Over a hundred years ago, the juvenile justice system was created because children who were incarcerated were subjected to unspeakable atrocities and returned to society as hardened criminals. Despite the lessons of history, Congress is getting ready to pass the Violent and Repeat Juvenile Offenders Acts (S-10), which calls for housing juveniles with adult inmates, and would "force states to transfer large numbers of young offenders to adult prisons in order to be eligible for federal funds" (Ziedenberg and Schiraldi). Common sense suggests that a 13-year-old locked up with murderers and rapists will tend to grow up with a similar profile. Even conservatives recognize that without adult guidance and proper role models, children do not have a chance to become productive citizens. Just as disturbing is the knowledge that young people slated for prison are more likely to be raped, assaulted, or commit suicide (Ziedenberg and Schiraldi). In Ohio, a 15-year-old girl was sexually assaulted by a deputy jailer after she was put into an adult jail for a minor infraction; in Kentucky, thirty minutes after a 15-year-old was put in a jail following an argument with his mother, the youth hung himself (Ziedenberg and Schiraldi). Some states lump suicide deaths under the category of "unspecified cause," making the problem invisible. Other states list rape among "inmate assaults," effectively masking the problem. Statistics on rape are conservative at best, and documentation of the behavior is obviously compromised by the culture of the prison itself and staff attitudes. There are obvious incentives for prison officials to underreport the incidents of rape and suicide because it embarrasses the system and could be used as evidence for lawsuits (Ziedenberg and Schiraldi). Thus, it is likely that no one knows the true extent to which children are victimized in prisons.

Need #3   Society's response to juvenile crime is based more on media hype than reality. According to Adam Rich, author of "Adult Consequences for Young Offenders," between the years of 1993 and 1998, juvenile homicide declined 56 percent; however, a Gallup poll found that Americans *think* juveniles commit 43 percent of violent crime when in fact the actual amount is 12 percent. There seems to be an emotional reaction to punish young offenders across the board because of a very few violent but well-publicized crimes by youths. It almost appears like as one criminologist from the University of California told the *Christian Science Monitor,* "there is a solution in search of a problem" (qtd. in Rich). Clearly, a new approach to youth crime is called for since the current response is unwarranted.

The poor and minorities face a continuous uphill battle to get *Need #4* a fair trial. Often unable to pay, the indigent are given public defenders who fall asleep, who often do not know the names of their clients, who are overworked and underpaid, who cannot hire private detectives to dig past what appears to be and the pressure to find the guilty (Bach). JoAnn Wypijewski tells the story of Ernestina Rodriguez, a poor woman living in Texas, who was accused of intentionally killing her baby by starvation. She was charged with capital murder. Although her family hired defense attorneys for $10,000, the attorneys appeared incompetent, opening doors to speculation they did not close, never hiring an investigator, and never calling witnesses to testify on behalf of Rodriguez. She was sentenced to 38 years in prison. The assumption of people in the town was that people like Rodriguez were "inbred sons-of-bitches" (qtd. in Wypijewski). Life for the poor, as far as justice goes, seems to be an endurance test.

Finally, there is the problem with capital punishment. There is *Need #5* the issue of the morality itself, but the most disturbing aspect of the death penalty is the risk and known incidents of executing the innocent. There have been so many problems with killing the innocent that the governor of Illinois, George Ryan, called a moratorium on capital punishment until the system could be cleaned up. Carl M. Cannon, writing for the *National Review,* recounts the story of four black men from Detroit (convicted of abducting a white couple, raping the woman, and killing both her and the man) who were exonerated by evidence unearthed by journalism students at Northwestern. This evidence got the men off of death row. Cannon reports that the students discovered the prosecutor's star witness had an IQ of less than 75, and that prosecutors had fed her details of the crime and coached her into testifying about them. These men were fortunate the students took an interest in their case; if not, they would have been executed. Most likely there are other innocent people on death row, too.

Policy

The presence of a large number of problems with the current justice system points out the need for change. The changes need to be specifically addressed to deal with the problems of placing non-violent drug offenders in with violent criminals, of placing young offenders in situations where they will be abused and not rehabilitated, and of the unequal application of justice that minorities and the poor experience, and of the problems associated with capital punishment. The following are recommendations for change:

Policy 1
- The first priority is to invest serious resources in the prevention of child abuse and neglect. If we prevent these tragedies, we can reduce violent crime later when these children, warped by abuse, grow old enough to commit their own crimes. Four priorities seem especially critical: preventing child abuse and neglect, enhancing children's intellectual and social development, providing support and guidance to vulnerable adolescents, and working intensely with juvenile offenders. Child abuse itself is the worst and most tragic of violent crimes. Elliott Currie reports that nationwide, child abuse results directly in up to 5,000 deaths per year, 18,000 permanent disabilities, and 150,000 serious injuries. It is the fourth leading cause of death for American children age 1–4 (82). Currie argues that programs like PEIP (Prenatal Early Infancy Program) need to be available to low-income parents to help prevent abuse in a deprived environment. Programs like Healthy Start enroll families considered at risk to help with housing, education, single parenthood, depression, and substance abuse. The Perry Project and other similar programs have helped to expand and enhance early intervention for children at risk of impaired cognitive development, behavior problems, and early failure in school (91). We also need programs for vulnerable adolescents, to build skills and keep them on track to higher education and training. The Quantum Opportunity Program and others have provided a mix of services to high school–age minority youth to help them overcome inadequacies of earlier training programs (Currie 91). Finally,

we need to prevent crime in youth by connecting family, peers, schools, and the broader community to treat youth, to empower them, and to help them take control of their own lives. Programs such as the Family and Neighborhood Services hire trained case workers to work with troubled youth where they get counseling, curfews, and required school attendance, to help get them back on track (Currie 91). Community-based programs work, and more of them are needed.

- Children under the age of 18 should not be incarcerated in *Policy #2* adult prisons. Recidivism has been too high, rape and assault too frequent, and suicide alarmingly common. Other alternatives that are punitive, yet also focused on rehabilitation, must be tried first. Often high-profile violent youth crimes, from Columbine to Santee, happened because individuals felt completely disenfranchised from their world. Support systems need to be put into place for these children so that at a later date they may return to society as productive citizens. Boot camp, community service, juvenile detention centers, and drug treatment programs, if well organized, can effectively treat the youth (Anderson 77). Society needs to use appropriate programs for children and stop throwing them into prison.

- Drug treatment for nonviolent offenders offers a better ap- *Policy #3* proach than incarceration. These programs can work to separate the nonviolent from those who represent a violent threat to the community, and provide treatment to remove them from drugs. David A. Anderson reports on a model program started in Brooklyn in 1989 called the Drug Treatment Alternative Program (DTAP). He records how this program, started by Charles Hynes, the Brooklyn District Attorney, has successfully dealt with obstacles, including initial hesitation from the court and the public. The program has "earned solid praise," and the only real complaint is that the program cannot handle all who might be eligible (77–85). Defense attorney Alan Abrahamson is quoted by Anderson: "Nobody ever benefitted from doing prison time for selling crack on the street" (85). If drug offenders do get prison time (due to connection with other crimes), they can benefit from drug treatment in prison. As Elliot Currie notes in *Crime and Punishment in America,* ". . . the most effective programs have shown substantial success in keeping offenders out of crime once they leave prison" (166). A new attitude toward drug offenders will pay off in the long run.

- Representation of the indigent has to improve in order for *Policy #4* our justice system to be fair. Clearly, revisions to budget priorities must be made. When politicians seek election on "tough on crime" planks, they have a hard time spending the tax dollars needed for public defenders. However, the system is based on the assumption that everyone is innocent until proven guilty, and that means public defenders are not automatically the defenders of criminals. States also need to monitor the effectiveness of "contract defenders." Public funds should not be wasted on defenders who do not defend their clients competently.

Policy #5 • A national DNA database with information from *all* persons convicted of a felony, on a state or federal level, should be established. This would include all currently incarcerated people, and as others are convicted, their DNA would be added. There should be no constitutional challenge to this move since the DNA collection would essentially be no different from fingerprinting. This would help in the investigations of crimes as a relatively small, criminal class of people commits the large percentage of crime. Common sense dictates that having more information available to investigators would help to solve more crimes accurately. It would also help cut down on false accusations, based on one's race, gender, or social class. DNA evidence would be an excellent way to help our justice system be color-blind.

Policy #6 • There needs to be greater equality in sentencing. Often there are race and class biases in sentencing. This means that more minorities and more poor go to prison, while those with greater resources receive alternative sentences, particularly in cases where judicial discretion is greatest (Mauer 49). Laws need to be rewritten so that sentencing guidelines are clearly based on the crime and the criminal's past, so large disparities in sentencing can be overcome.

Policy #7 • Capital punishment should once again become the exception, not the rule. In truth, no one can be assured that innocent people are not executed. That fact alone should be enough to stop using capital punishment, but other reasons exist as well. Capital punishment is a poor man's penalty because the poor cannot afford competent legal representation. Capital punishment has a visceral appeal—an eye for an eye—but, as the American Civil Liberties Union points out, there is no credible evidence that capital punishment deters crime (2). It is not needed to protect the public, since a life sentence without parole will effectively do that. Capital punishment is expensive too, including the cost of the appeals, which are inevitable and routine. As the great American lawyer Clarence Darrow said:

In the end, this question is a simple one of the humane feelings against the brutal feelings. One who likes to see suffering, out of what he thinks is a righteous indignation, or any other, will hold fast to capital punishment. One who has sympathy, imagination, kindness and understanding, will hate it and detest it as he hates and detests death. (qtd. in Spencer 162)

Benefits

Successful implementation of these policies would lead to a much improved justice system. The public's trust in the system is based on the idea that the system provides for public safety in a fair manner, but too frequently the desire to increase public safety is being done at the cost of that fairness; the irony is that elusive safety may not even be achieved.

By developing a new, more humane attitude toward our children, including those who break the law, we have a better chance of ensuring a safer future. Our children are at risk, either because of pressures due to racial or class discrimination, abusive home environments, or neglect. Intervening in these children's lives is an effort and expense that will pay dividends in the long run. If those children do commit crimes, we need to remember they are still children. A punitive and rehabilitative juvenile system is the best way to handle juvenile crime—punishing children as adults does nothing for them except ensure a future of abuse and deprivation. Society must remember to care for its children, or society itself will pay. *Benefit #1*

Separating nonviolent drug offenders from other convicts will be a more cost-effective way of dealing with a problem that is more behavioral than criminal. Indeed, these offenders show greater promise for rehabilitation than most other criminals (DiIulio). Putting drug offenders with hardened criminals can make the formerly nonviolent offender a career criminal. To stop *Benefit #2* this, society needs to take advantage of the opportunity to help the nonviolent drug offenders turn their lives around. Missing this opportunity means risking more crime in the future.

Benefit #3   Creating a DNA database will solve several problems, as long as it can be done in a constitutionally valid manner. By requiring samples only from those convicted of felonies, the system can be assured of meeting any constitutional challenge. The benefits of such a database are potentially enormous—even more than fingerprints, DNA samples will identify perpetrators of crimes, and as the database grows, law enforcement will be able to match DNA crime scene evidence with suspects. Additionally, the use of DNA is likely to reduce the incidence of false accusations brought by biased police and prosecutors.

Benefit #4   More financial support of competent legal services for the accused will help the public to know that only the truly guilty are convicted, not just the truly poor. When the innocent are convicted, society's moral stature is undermined, but it also means that a criminal is still on the loose. Therefore, there is a two-fold payoff for better legal representation for the accused: greater assurance that the process is fair and greater assurance that the need for public safety is being met.

Benefit #5   The elimination of capital punishment will also raise the moral standing of the judicial system. Simply put, no guarantees can be given that the innocent are not found guilty, and since the death penalty is irrevocable, undoubtedly innocent people have been executed—and not just in the distant past. With DNA evidence leading to the exoneration of a number of wrongly convicted people, one can only wonder how many people are facing the death penalty today who are innocent. The only moral stance is to follow in the footsteps of Illinois Governor George

Ryan and suspend all executions (Cannon). No other alternative is acceptable.

No justice system can ever be made that is perfect. Some crimes will go unpunished, some young criminals cannot be rehabilitated, some drug offenders will never break their addictions, and some innocent people will be wrongly convicted. However, this is not a justification for standing pat and accepting the flaws in the system. The justice system can work better than it now does, and attempts at its improvement must be continually made. To do otherwise would be criminal.

Works Cited

American Civil Liberties Union. "The Death Penalty." *ACLU Briefing Paper.* 14 (Spring 1999): 1–2.

Anderson, David C. *Sensible Justice: Alternatives to Prison.* New York: New Press, 1998.

Bach, Amy. "Justice on the Cheap." *Nation* 21 May 2001: 25+. *MasterFILE Premier.* Ebscohost. San Diego Mesa College Lib. 22 Aug. 2001.

Cannon, Carl M. "The Problem with the Chair." *National Review* June 19, 2000: 28+. *MasterFILE Premier.* Ebscohost. San Diego Mesa College Lib. 22 Aug. 2001.

Currie, Elliott. *Crime and Punishment in America.* New York: Owl-Holt, 1998.

DiIulio, John, J., Jr. "Against Mandatory Minimums." *National Review* May 17, 1999: 46+. *MasterFILE Premier.* Ebscohost. San Diego Mesa College Lib. 22 Aug. 2001.

Mauer, Marc. "The Racial Dynamics of Imprisonment." May 47–50.

May, John P., ed. *Building Violence.* Thousand Oaks, CA: Sage, 2000.

Pomper, Stephen. "Reasonable Doubts." *Washington Monthly* June 2000: 21+. *MasterFILE Premier.* Ebscohost. San Diego Mesa College Lib. 22 Aug. 2001.

Rich, Adam. "Adult Consequences for Young Offenders." *State Government News* April 2000: 10+. *MasterFILE Premier.* Ebscohost. San Diego Mesa College Lib. 22 Aug. 2001.

Spenser, Steven S. "Death Penalty: The Ultimate Violence." May 156–163.

Wypijewski, JoAnn. "Death and Texas." *Nation* July 16, 2001: 20+. *MasterFILE Premier.* Ebscohost. San Diego Mesa College Lib. 22 Aug. 2001.

Ziedenberg, Jason, and Vincent Schiraldi. "The Risks Juveniles Face." *Corrections Today* Aug. 1998: 22+. *MasterFILE Premier.* Ebscohost. San Diego Mesa College Lib. 22 Aug. 2001.

ADDITIONAL READINGS

Death and Texas

JoAnn Wypijewski

JoAnn Wypijewski details the story of a poor woman in Texas accused of murdering her infant child. She recounts the death of the baby, and how, through legal incompetence, Ernestine Rodriguez was found guilty under circumstances that should have aroused substantial doubt. The article details how the poor have a very difficult time getting a fair trial and adequate legal representation; as a consequence, they are more likely to wind up in prison.

Key Words

bawdy	obscene; lewd; humorously indecent
demarcating	setting apart; separating
dude ranches	vacation resorts offering activities typical of western ranches
maquiladora	a U.S.-owned factory in Mexico, employing low-cost labor to manufacture goods previously made in the U.S.
corrugated	made up of alternating ridges or grooves
autopsy	an examination of a dead body to determine the cause of death
appellate	having the power to review the judgment of another, lower court
notorious	generally known and talked about, especially unfavorably
provocative	tending to excite or stimulate
stoicism	a philosophy emphasizing indifference to pleasure or pain; impassive

Bandera, Texas

Men in spurs still ride on horseback to the Eleventh Street Cowboy Bar here, hitch Smokey or Pancho to the post and, after enough beers, sing songs of their own making that are wry or a bit bawdy but, above all, stake the singer's claim to the "real" in a region too open to infection from potpourriana and the bric-a-brac of kowboy kulture. Bandera, "Cowboy Capital of the World," has only 975 people, but it's getting dicey to take a horse through town now that some 13,000 cars travel up Main Street every day.

Thirty-seven miles northwest of San Antonio, Bandera is in the heart of the Hill Country, where dude ranches outnumber the working variety and No Trespassing-signs sprout like bluebonnets in the spring, demarcating the property of "Winter Texans" or city folk with money to invest in the rustic experience. It is the fourth-fastest-growing county in Texas, outpacing those that hold Dallas and Austin. Realtors' brochures tout premium property in an area that's "on the way to nowhere," and people mention that a nearby ranch of 300-some acres recently sold for $3.2 million, but the houses most easily in view in Bandera are modest affairs with scrappy yards that speak of too little money and too little time. Local men work for ranches or work construction or "work for each other," according to a real estate agent in town, "but how much are you going to make shoeing horses?" Women work mostly in the services. Father Stanislaw Oleksy of St. Stanislaus Church says the churches in the area have a well-coordinated relief system to pay a heating or electric bill or cover a prescription or distribute food if once in a while someone doesn't make payroll and families need something to help them hold on. "Of course you have a lot of roads where you never see these people. You never know they exist."

Off Highway 173 five miles to the north and not far from a ranch where the rich pay to shoot exotic creatures is one of those places you won't see unless you're looking. It's a colonia, unincorporated, unregulated territory not too different in appearance from the pictures of maquiladora communities that Ross Perot held up as an argument against NAFTA back in 1992. Three years ago a baby died to a Chicana/Mexican family living there in a one-room shack attached to animal pens of similar design, and before the grief-struck mother knew what was happening the state had transformed her personal tragedy into a case of capital murder.

Ernestina Rodriguez lived in that colonia off 173, in that shack measuring ten feet by fourteen feet, with her husband and four little children, without plumbing or running water, a place patched together out of wood and corrugated metal for which they paid $200 a month rent. On February 11, 1998, her two-and-a-half-month-old son, Ramiro, stopped breathing. Now at 28 she's serving a life sentence at the Hobby Unit in Marlin, Texas, for knowingly, intentionally killing him by starvation.

Last year's presidential campaign directed enough unwelcome 5 light on the more outrageous features of the Texas criminal justice system that the state legislature spent a fair portion of its session this spring trying to make some face-saving adjustments, but this is not one of those cases that would cause a politician embarrassment. Nor is it the kind of case, like the one involving the Texas woman recently charged with drowning her five children, that whips up national comment. Except for the relatively rare allegation of starvation, it is crushing in its ordinariness. Like most prisoners in Texas, which ranks tenth in the country for poverty and third in the world for having a population in chains (after the United States and Russia), Rodriguez is poor. And as in most cases in which someone dies mysteriously and the people involved are poor, the first assumption was murder. At the Eleventh Street Cowboy Bar a perfectly nice rodeo rider said he'd been called for jury duty in the case but was excused after he admitted he was sure of the mother's guilt before hearing any evidence. "I know these people," he said at the bar—not Rodriguez and her family per se but these people, "inbred sons-of-bitches."

In the autopsy, baby Ramiro was found to have milk in his stomach, which suggests he had been fed, and throughout his short life the family's neighbor heard him cry the way any baby does, which is inconsistent with death by starvation. Recall the stock image of a thousand famine stories in which the African village has "an eerie silence, the babies too weak even to cry." Rodriguez says she fed the baby alternately at the breast and by bottle, with formula or watered-down cow's milk, not the best approach but hardly murderous. She says he was a hungry baby, yet he didn't grow. When he stopped breathing and she ran to her landlord's trailer to use the phone, she was hysterical. But the coroner presumed the child had been starved from the get-go, and alternative explanations were never pursued. Rodriguez was charged with capital murder.

Overcharging, getting a grand jury to indict on the most severe rap in hopes that a defendant will take a plea and do some jail time, is a common prosecutorial tactic; in Texas it is practically the rule. Rodriguez has always insisted on her innocence. After she was sentenced to life, her husband, Noel Perez, pleaded guilty—he says his lawyer demanded it—and avoided the same outcome. He was sentenced to twenty-five years and could be out in 2012. Unless she wins on appeal, it will be thirty-eight years before Rodriguez is eligible for parole.

Although it has become a commonplace to associate Texas with miscarriages of justice with capital punishment, the three linked as if by some perverse force of nature, the state didn't ask for the death penalty in this case. In fact, it rarely does in small counties, where the mechanics involved could be financially ruinous and politically problematic, as resources would be strained and other cases would have to go waiting. So Rodriguez had a standard trial, before a white male judge and a jury of twelve men. The only women involved in the trial besides herself were a prosecutor, a Latina who displayed contempt for her and her entire family, and an alternate juror, who is so upset over the verdict that her husband has asked Rodriguez's appellate lawyer, Adrienne Urrutia, not to call anymore, since discussing it rips her up.

Rodriguez didn't have a court-appointed lawyer who fell asleep at trial or was senile or drunk or about to be indicted for a crime himself, all conditions that have attended some of the state's most notorious cases. Instead, her family members pooled all the money they had, $10,000, and hired attorneys (also men) who didn't know what they were doing or didn't feel it was worth it to care. Defense attorneys called the most damaging witness, Rodriguez's landlady, who, they learned too late, had a vendetta against her and handed the prosecution its theory of the case: that this mother just didn't want her baby. They repeatedly opened doors to speculation that they didn't close, or allowed the prosecution to make speculations that went unchallenged. They never hired an investigator, never called their own expert witnesses to rebut the starvation charge, never called witnesses who could testify that Tina Rodriguez welcomed the birth of Ramiro. Again and again they asked questions whose answers they didn't know, each time giving the prosecution's experts more credence than they deserved.

Urrutia has noted this and more in her appeal brief, and has pre- 10 sented testimony of a nutrition specialist and a pediatric expert in malnutrition who studied the autopsy report and concluded that Ramiro may have died from something more rare than starvation: a genetic defect that prevented him from metabolizing the milk he drank; that caused it, in effect, to ferment rather than build flesh and bone and keep him alive. She calls this the "most compelling case" she's had in twelve years of practice. To take it on, working day and night under deadline, hiring an investigator, finding experts and filing a motion for a new trial, she put her entire practice on hold for more than a month. "Clients came and went; it cost me everything." And she was appointed to this case, paid $3,280, including expenses.

Urrutia says there are plenty of people in Texas who defy the stereotype of court-appointed lawyers being lazy or worse, but it's not a surprise, given the rate of payment, that so many cut corners. The Court of Appeals has ordered the district court to hold a hearing on Rodriguez's motion for a new trial, and the state is resisting all the way. "I shouldn't have to fight this hard just for a hearing," Urrutia says. "People forget, but the state's job isn't to win; the state's job is to secure justice."

Back in Austin legislators were tinkering with the mechanisms of what passes for justice. Bills to place a moratorium on the death penalty didn't have a chance (though they got farther than anyone had expected), but legislators did manage to ban executions of mentally retarded persons, a ban Governor Rick Perry, like George W. Bush before him, recently vetoed. Outside the Capitol before that bill was finalized, Perry was on hand, with police, FBI, DEA, highway patrol, various county officers and a gaggle of prison wardens, all representatives of the institution that has guys with IQs of 57 and such sitting on death row, for the symbolic kickoff of the Texas Law Enforcement Torch Run for Special Olympics. Texas is first in the country in executions, first in executions of the retarded, first in fundraising for Special Olympics. Perry made some treacly remarks about "the special in Special Olympics" and then lit four torches with the Flame of Hope, sending runners out on the Austin streets. It was all phony (after a few blocks the runner-lawmen would quench their torches and go back to work), a photo-op for Perry to show off Texas as a bighearted place that rewards the "good retards" for hard work—run! jump!—while holding the needle in reserve for the bad ones. Now some in the State Senate vow they'll try to override Perry's veto.

The legislators did succeed in granting convicts access to state-paid DNA testing in cases where the results might determine innocence, a law that could benefit 13,000 incarcerated people. They set minimum standards for lawyers appointed to defend poor people in criminal cases and allocated $20 million to counties to help pay those lawyers. They banned racial profiling and barred judges and expert witnesses in the course of sentencing from using a defendant's race or ethnicity to determine his or her future dangerousness. They increased money damages for persons wrongfully convicted of a crime, to $25,000 for each year of imprisonment plus legal fees.

In Bandera, Richard Trevino, overhearing talk on the legislature's newfound interest in civil rights, said, "I'm a Yellow Dog Democrat and I voted for Gore. But I wish I'd voted for Bush so I could take credit for getting him out of Texas." As Susan Smith of the *Austin American-Statesman* points out, though, it lets Democrats off the hook to attribute all the ills of Texas to Bush's nearly six-year governorship. And significant as the new measures are, with the possible exception of the law regarding wrongful conviction, none of them will affect people like Tina Rodriguez. There are things more intractable than the law, more deeply rooted, things that politicians, Democrats and Republicans alike, have come to accept almost as part of the landscape. Trevino himself is a lawyer, representing working-class people in civil actions, work he says he's able to pursue only because his wife's salary as a nurse covers the family's bills. For Trevino, his clients, anyone on the short end, there's no mistaking that law is the handmaid to power, and power is something the vast majority of people here haven't got enough of.

Tina Rodriguez didn't have enough of it—a woman yoked with   15 poverty, isolation, a body weakened from successive birthings, a jealous and abusive husband who kept her on a psychic short leash and sent a large portion of the family's money to his other wife and children in Mexico. If there was a way out, she couldn't see it. Even if she could, as a woman ill disposed to discuss her problems, she was a good daughter of Texas, whose boosters strain to present stoicism in the face of the stuck life as a virtue.

In Austin I had visited the newly opened Bob Bullock Texas State History Museum, dedicated to the late Democratic lieutenant governor who was vital in establishing the Bush "legacy." For the most part the museum's permanent exhibit presents the state's history as a provocative saga of colonial, racial and class conflict, but ticket-sellers were eager to steer tourists to a special installation called "It Ain't Braggin' if It's True," designed to cement the state in the caricature of

Wild West individualism. "Texas is no place for the faint-hearted," reads one panel. In addition to drought, floods, hurricanes and boom and bust cycles, "it tests the individual with social structures that resist change." For this, "Texans have one tool that gets them out of most tight spots: perseverance."

Paul Robbins and Andrew Wheat of Texans for Public Justice have put together a list of things to which Texas can claim bragging rights. Among the fifty states, it ranks second in hunger; third in malnourishment; fifth in children living in poverty; forty-sixth in prenatal care; forty-seventh in child immunizations. It ranks first in almost every category of environmental hazard; first in people without health insurance; second in poor children without health insurance; forty-fourth in public health spending; and fiftieth in per capita state spending. If Texas were a person, someone would move to take away its kids.

As it is, the state's fitness is never on trial, and it decides who gets to be a parent. The day before Tina Rodriguez and Noel Perez buried Ramiro, Child Protective Services seized their three other children. In Kerrville, twenty-eight miles north of Bandera, Tina's mother, Lionora, remembers how the family was just returning home when a white van and a police car came into view. In a flash, a woman grabbed 4-year-old Paublo and 3-year-old Kassandra. Another woman was pulling at eighteen-month-old Noel Jr., trying to rip him from Tina's arms, while the older ones screamed, "Mommy, Mommy," and the little one clutched on in terror. That was February 13, 1998. No one in the family—not their parents or grandparents, not their five aunts and five uncles, not their twenty-six cousins—has seen them since.

The State of Texas terminated Tina and Noel's parental rights. Lionora Rodriguez says that when she asked Judy Brown of CPS if she and their grandfather could have the children, "she told me no because there were too many people living here, plus my house was too poor and we were too old." Lionora, 56, whose house is crowded and down at the heels but vibrant with well-loved, good-tempered grandchildren, says she was never allowed even to propose how she might make room for more. "They just went around us as if we were nothing." Now Paublo, Kassandra and Noel Jr. have been adopted out, severed permanently from their parents and familial roots, lost through a proceeding known as "the capital punishment" of civil law.

Amid the Hill Country's ranchettes and antique shops, people 20 don't know the half of it. The only serious press treatment of the Rodriguez case was an excellent story by Debbie Nathan in San Antonio's alternative paper, the *Current*. Otherwise, there's just rumor and shards of fact and fiction, half-remembered. Someone wandering in the Guadalupe Cemetery in Kerrville might pause at the coincidence of names and dates on two little graves there. Ramiro Perez 1997–1998. Roman y Fabian Perez, 1998–1998. Now, what was that about?

Tina Rodriguez was pregnant again when she was arrested, and at five-and-a-half months, while awaiting trial in the county jail—her family, tapped out from retaining lawyers, couldn't make bail—she gave birth to twins. They lived about an hour and a half. Their grandmother learned of this in a call from a funeral home; by then her daughter had been transported back to the cell. Lionora says Tina sleepwalked through the trial; "she wasn't with us." Grief is another country.

When she first got to the Marlin prison, about 175 miles from Kerrville, Rodriguez worked in the fields picking fruits and vegetables; sometimes she was part of a gang that would be driven out to clean local parks. Now she works in the print shop. She is allowed no personal phone calls, and can receive two visitors for two hours once a week. She has found Jesus. No longer the mother of six children, she is a Texas prisoner. Life as an endurance test.

What Did You Read?

1. What were some of the problems facing Ernestina Rodriguez?
2. Why was $10,000 not enough to pay for an adequate defense for Rodriguez?
3. How is Texas rated in its treatment of children?

What Do You Think?

1. What does the long anecdote about Rodriguez say about poverty and justice? Why?
2. In order to have a completely fair trial, what is necessary to ensure a competent and thorough defense?
3. What is the irony in the state of Texas taking civil rights away from Rodriguez? In other words, how does Texas measure up as a provider for its people?
4. What aspects of the Rodriguez trial seem racist and sexist?

How Was It Done?

1. Why are the introductory paragraphs critical to this essay? Why is the anecdote central to the theme of the article?
2. In crafting his article, besides facts, what kind of values and sentiment does Wypijewski appeal to in order to convince you of the inequality of justice in Texas?
3. How do the facts concerning Texas's poor track record concerning children contribute to the development of the thesis?

Justice on the Cheap

Amy Bach

Amy Bach examines the problem of finding adequate defense for the poor. Public defender offices are typically underfunded, with attorneys taking on too many cases. Public support for defenders is being directed to "contract lawyers" who are private attorneys who bid for the defense work. The results are fairly predictable: cut-rate lawyering for cut-rate prices. The system is accepted because to do anything more would cost the state more, and taxpayers have little sympathy for those accused of crime.

Key Words

indigent	impoverished
sanction	explicit or official approval
privatization	to turn over to private businesses functions previously done by the government or agencies of the government
vouched	given a guarantee or personal assurance
phlebotomist	someone who draws blood
grist	a matter of interest or value forming the basis of a story or analysis
fiefdom	an area of which one has rights or control
ensconced	sheltered; concealed

It's right after lunch in Greene County, Georgia, about an hour east of Atlanta, and the old courtroom, with its still ceiling fans and creaky floors, is full to bursting. More than 100 people, mostly African-Americans, have packed the dark wooden benches, and the corridor outside is overflowing with those who didn't land a seat. Judge Hulane George calls for a woman who has been knocking at her chambers to complain about her lawyer.

Tasha McDonald, 30, freely admits her crime—a credit-card fraud of $1,895.35—but refuses to plead, she says, until she gets a lawyer she can talk to for more than two minutes. But even two minutes is hard to get from Robert Surrency, the attorney who has been handed her case. Surrency meets his clients, almost always for the first time, on the courthouse stairs or in the hallway with a dozen others surrounding him like frustrated fans outside a stage door. "Everybody back up. Back up," he says. "I'll talk to you all individually before you go to the judge." Representation means checking a list of plea offers from the district attorney and appearing before the judge, who clinches the deal by ticking off some rights.

"You have a right to a lawyer of your choice," the judge says primly to Tasha McDonald, ordering the case revisited in another three months. Outside the courtroom, McDonald, in a neat white blouse and a black leather blazer, puts her face in her hands and begins to sob inconsolably. "They don't even know me," she says.

Tasha McDonald's problem is a common one. It's no secret that public defender services are desperately underfunded, especially in poor Southern states. But thanks to a growing breed of "contract attorneys" who win the right to represent all of a county's defendants by offering the least costly bid, the minimum standard for legal assistance has sunk to new lows. As if on a conveyor belt, defendants are uniformly processed to plead guilty. The lawyers representing them often don't know their names, let alone any facts that would affect the outcome of their cases. Frequently, Surrency is not even in court when his clients plead. Another lawyer who knows even less stands in. In a country where little is expected of attorneys for the poor—where it is a matter of debate as to whether a lawyer who falls asleep during his client's death-penalty trial provides effective assistance—contract lawyers are a cheap way for counties to acknowledge their obligation under the Constitution. In reality, their work renders the equal protection clause and the Sixth Amendment right to counsel virtually meaningless.

Contact defenders were born more than a decade after the $_5$ Supreme Court's landmark 1963 ruling in *Gideon v. Wainwright,* which declared that poor defendants are entitled to lawyers but left it up to the states to decide how they would be provided. At first, states used one of two systems. Some places, like Washington, DC, and Kentucky, established highly esteemed public defender systems staffed by investors, social workers, secretaries and veteran lawyers capable of training new ones. But many states, like Georgia, Alabama, Mississippi, Texas and New York, never developed statewide indigent defense systems with the structure, resources and independence to do the job. Most used court-appointed counsel, a system with its own set of problems. At best, judges are able to choose from a list of lawyers with expertise in criminal defense, but often, inexperienced lawyers sign up. Since rates are low, they tend to accept more cases than they can handle.

Beginning in the late 1970s, Congress and state legislatures criminalized more behavior and increased sanctions for crimes, creating mandatory minimum sentences and life imprisonment without parole. They also extended the death penalty to more crimes and provided for the prosecution of children as adults. As the number of indigent defendants soared, so did costs to the counties, since most used court-appointed lawyers systems with contract systems. They held auctions where lawyers or firms could offer to do all the work for a period of years—no matter how many cases or how difficult, including death penalty cases—for the lowest lump sum. "It's part of the privatization movement," says Scott Wallace, director of defender legal services at the National Legal Aid & Defender Association in Washington, DC. "Counties like the concept of flat fees. It's a way of controlling costs."

Nobody knows exactly how many counties employ contract defenders, but 21 percent of the nation's 100 largest counties use them, according to a 1999 report by the Bureau of Justice Statistics. Last December Texas Appleseed, a nonpartisan group that works on issues of legal representation for poor people and minorities, reported "a slow but sure movement" to replace assigned counsel systems with contract lawyers systems. The largest increases in the past ten years have occurred in rural states like South Dakota, North Dakota, Oklahoma, Nebraska, Idaho and Georgia, according to Robert Spangenberg, president of the Spangenberg Group, an indigent-defense consulting firm in West Newton, Massachusetts. A few major metropolitan areas have instituted contract systems, Spangenberg explains, but most look to factors other than cost, such as experience, in awarding contracts, and put a cap on the number of cases an agency can perform without obtaining additional funds—as in New York. "[New York's] is one of the best ones," Spangenberg says of the contract system Mayor Rudolph Giuliani created in 1995, which shoulders 18 percent of the city's caseload. (The Legal Aid Society of New York carries an additional 50 percent, while the rest must endure court-appointment lawyers paid at the second-lowest rate in the country.)

In Greene County, Surrency's winning bid was $40,000 to represent as many poor people as the sheriff can charge (others bid between $60,000 and $70,000), making the county pay out in 1999 an average of $75.38 per case in a state that spent $242.34 per case on average. From 1997 to 1999, Surrency served as a lawyer in 1,455 cases, nearly twice as many per year as the American Bar Association recommends. In the past four years, only thirteen of his clients refused to take the state's plea offer and go to trial.

Pleas are a moneymaking venture for Greene County. Most defendants avoid prison time in exchange for paying county fines and surcharges, which sometimes amount to $100 a month for years. As in other states, a judge can sentence a defendant who either ignores his pay schedule or fails to explain to the court that he can't afford to pay to a "diversion center," where he is required to work for money that is automatically turned over to the county.

Surrency, the judge and the prosecutor form a triangular tag team 10 that pushes people to accept pleas so a full-blown trial can be averted. But even plea agreements require spending time with a client. Missing in Greene County is the ration of justice that is supposed to be meted out between the time of being charged and sentenced, when it becomes clear whether the defendant was the ringleader or acted with intent—the distinctions that make the difference between a severe sentence and a lenient one, or none at all. It can happen in court or out, under the watchful eye of a judge who can make inquiries and pressure lawyers, or in a phone call between the defense lawyer and the prosecutor. If the other blinks, or they duke it out in trial, where relevant facts are the grist for a good defense. "The criminal justice system does a huge amount of sorting out once guilty," says Steve Bright, director of the Southern Center for Human Rights in Atlanta, who worked as a public defender in Washington, DC, for three years. "Whether it's probation, death penalty, boot camp, the punishment depends on the nature of the act." But not in a low-budget contract system.

With his scruffy, uncombed red hair and rumpled clothes, Robert Surrency appears either distracted and professorial, or jaded and tired. "We have successfully done a ten-page calendar in one day," he boasts. In two days, Surrency pleaded forty-eight people, which he refers to as "a uniquely productive way to do business." "No defendant wants to go to trial, because of the possibility that you look more guilty than you really are," Surrency said, explaining that most cases are really "open and shut." However, Marie Boswell, former clerk of the court where he operates, knows otherwise. "We are going to get hit with a lawsuit one day that is going to rock the world."

Watching the proceedings intently in the last row is "H.," 29, a heavily built black man with a shaved head, charged with aggravated assault and battery. H., a restaurant manager about to start nursing school, has never before been in trouble with the law, but his crime is grim. In October he ran his car over his then-boyfriend, ripping off one of his ears. Ben Mitcham Jr., the laid-back assistant DA, initially offered five years in prison and thirty years' probation.

What Mitcham didn't know, because Surrency never raised it, was that H., who is HIV-positive, claims that the victim knowingly exposed him to the virus without telling him. In addition, H. says his crime was without intent: The two were sitting in a parked car arguing and in the process of breaking up when H.'s boyfriend walked off down the highway. "I guess I panicked," he says. "A lot of emotions were going through me. And I don't know how to drive." (H.'s former boyfriend declined to comment for this story.) Mitcham, informed of these facts, said that had he known there was a possibility that H.'s crime was done "in the heat of passion," he would have thought about the case differently. "I didn't make my offer with that knowledge. I wish I had known," he said.

Because an assistant district attorney in a nearby county vouched for H. as a good citizen, Mitcham changed his original offer from five years in prison to five months in a detention center plus ten years' probation. H. says he knew he had to pull some strings after Surrency never returned his phone calls: "I bet if [his clients] all lined up in a lineup he couldn't pick a person out."

Similarly, Mitcham was unaware of the circumstances of Tasha 15 McDonald's crime when he made his offer to her. McDonald is a single mother of three girls, the eldest of whom, Victoria, 10, is an honors student who suffers from muscular dystrophy. At the time of the crime McDonald was in school full time and working in the office of a local resort. There she stole a co-worker's credit card number to buy sheets, dishes, a microwave and a CD player from Sears. "Everything for the house," she says. "I was desperate at the time for me and my kids' sake." Since then she has repaid the money and started a new career as a phlebotomist, a specialist in drawing blood at a hospital. Mitcham, however, after consulting with the victim, offered three to four months in a detention center, which McDonald rejected for fear she'll lose her job and have her children taken away. "I'll lose my home," she says. "Give me fifty year's probation. I just can't be taken away from my kids." In a subsequent interview, Mitcham said he had no idea McDonald had a disabled child. "I am shocked," he said. "That would have made a difference in terms of her remaining in the home."

Surrency sees the problem as the defendant's misunderstanding of how the process works. "She didn't like me telling her what the state offered—as if I were working with the state because I was communicating with the client for the state," he said. The judge rescheduled McDonald's case to be heard in May. McDonald has since fired Surrency and hired private counsel.

One of the few people in Greene County who told me they were innocent was Julian Daniels, 21, a smallish man who works on a quail plantation hanging birds by their legs on a conveyer belt so they can be shocked and have their heads sawed off. He said he had physical proof that the drugs found in the back of his friend's car weren't his, but after calling Surrency three times and receiving no calls back, he resigned himself to paying a $925 fine during the two years he's on probation. "I don't got no choice," he said.

Indigent defense is again making the front pages, after George W. Bush's death penalty record in Texas became an issue in his presidential campaign. Studies proved inmates had been put to death in Texas despite representation by disbarred, suspended or incompetent attorneys. Still, Bush said he had no misgivings about the 145 people executed under his watch. This, together with new DNA technology that has freed eighty-seven inmates on death row, has raised widespread alarm. "I have yet to see a death case among the dozens coming to the Supreme Court on eve of execution petitions, in which the defendant was well represented at trial," Supreme Court Justice Ruth Bader Ginsburg said when she spoke at the University of the District of Columbia on April 9.

As a result of such scrutiny, Texas, with its former governor now ensconced in the Oval Office and its reputation for toughness secure, has lately conceded some ground. On April 10 the Texas State Senate passed the Texas Fair Defense Act, a bill that for the first time would provide state financing to hire lawyers for poor defendants and set standards for those lawyers. However, according to Bright, "there probably won't be a statewide public defender [system] in Texas in 2050." Experts say it's unlikely that Texas judges will give up control of their courtrooms. Now, each judge can maintain a fiefdom through the power to appoint lawyers. In a recent survey by the Texas State Bar, 30 percent of judges said they know colleagues who assigned counsel because they contributed to their judicial election campaigns. Others confessed to picking lawyers they knew would move dockets along and not give vigorous representation. In 1999 a coalition of judges pressured Governor Bush into vetoing another indigent defense bill, already passed by both houses. Says Bright: "I wish I could say that there is a political movement to change. Things get so bad in some places, like Texas, where so much attention was focused on lawyers sleeping during capital trials, etc., that it becomes enough of an embarrassment to the bar and the judges that they must do something."

Indeed, the outlook nationally is not encouraging. This April Bush 20 announced he would nominate Richard Nedelkoff for director of Bureau of Justice Assistance, an arm of the Justice Department that worked on indigent defense issues under Attorney General Janet Reno. Nedelkoff is currently executive director of the Texas governor's Criminal Justice Division, an agency that disburses more than $140 million annually in state and federal funds for criminal justice services. Under Nedelkoff, none of that money has gone to indigent defense. In addition, the American Council of Chief Defenders has sent word to Attorney General John Ashcroft that it would like to continue the periodic meetings it had with Reno, but it has heard nothing in return.

In Georgia, as elsewhere, entrenched interests resist any effort to raise or enforce minimum standards for legal assistance. Although in November the Georgia Supreme Court created a blue ribbon commission to study indigent defense, its investigations have been half-hearted, and it has yet to make a proposal to the legislature. In 1979 the state instituted the Georgia Indigent Defense Council, which recommends guidelines for countries receiving state funds. However, implementing the standards has been difficult. "When we try and suggest that the guidelines are real we get politicians saying they'll undo us," says Michael Shapiro, executive director of the council. Shapiro says that the $6.5 million the state provides to enforce guidelines is too meager to have any effect on counties already spending $40.6 million on counsel for the poor. By comparison, Indiana has reformed about half of its ninety-two counties by reimbursing them for 40 percent of costs for felony cases (and 50 percent in death penalty cases) as long as counties provide trained lawyers with adequate resources to mount a proper defense.

In some towns, defendants seem to have given up on the idea that a lawyer could help. Under Coweta County's contract system in Newnan, Georgia, 218 people—over one-third of indigent defendants—

represented themselves from January 1999 to May 2000, according to statistics from the Southern Center for Human Rights. Nationally, only 1 percent of felony defendants represented themselves in the nation's seventy-five largest counties in 1992.

In Georgia counties that employ court-appointed lawyers, things are sometimes not much better. At criminal court in East Point, a working-class suburb of Atlanta, judges can appoint lawyers, but they almost never do. During one recent afternoon to determine whether there is probable cause to keep a defendant in jail before indictment—a harried judge speed-read defendants their rights (including their right to an attorney): "eachofyouhavearightagainstselfincriminationtoconfrontawitnesstoberepresentedbyanattorneyandtherearesomeoffenses youcangetafreeattorney." One by one, African-American men and women, wearing orange prison garb for traffic violations, bad checks, assault, drug possession, robbery, driving under the influence and capital murder, agreed to proceed without a lawyer, thus waiving their Sixth Amendment rights. "You would have to be the most self-assured, savvy person on the planet to understand that after the judge reads that jumble of rights so quickly you need to say. 'Hey, I want a lawyer.'" said Marion Chartoff, a lawyer with the Southern Center for Human Rights. "Nobody knows that they have to do that."

Next, the judge would ask whether the defendant wanted a preliminary hearing without counsel or to be waived into a higher court. Most chose to be waived to a higher court, giving up their chance to have a preliminary hearing, and with it the chance to determine the prosecution's case against them, begin investigation, get a state's witnesses on the record before the prosecution can shape testimony or create the basis for motions to suppress evidence. "They are losing a critical opportunity that will prepare in getting an adequate defense," Chartoff says. When defendants ask for preliminary hearings, the judge immediately called police and witnesses to testify, and then asked the unrepresented defendant to do a cross-examination. Most defendants, poor and educated and almost certainly without law degrees, declined. The judge would then ask the defendant to make a statement. Inevitably, the defendant began to ramble about being guilty of some things, but not of others. "He basically asks them to incriminate themselves in open court," Chartoff says.

Why would a judge make a habit of not assigning counsel or in a 25 contract system, condone lawyering that is like nothing at all? Perhaps for the same reason that, in 1996, Congress decided to prohibit legal services lawyers from bringing class-action suits, even when using private funds (the Supreme Court found the law partly unconstitutional this February, in *Legal Services Corporation v. Velazquez*): It helps keep costs down and prevents poor people from clogging up the courts.

At the end of other day in Greene County, there are only three people left on the empty courtroom benches. One is Quentin Strong, a winsome 18-year-old charged with two sales of cocaine within 1,000 feet of a school to an undercover officer. He's sitting with his friend Deloise Jones, who is here to see her son's hearing in an unrelated drug charge. They have waited two days. This is Strong's fourth time in court for this case alone. A judge has already continued it three times for reasons he doesn't understand.

While a more impetuous teen might have given up coming to court and had a bench warrant issued for his arrest, Strong has an incentive to get his case over with. A high school graduate who has been taking the year off to make money, he wants to do this time before the fall, when he moves to Alabama to begin a full basketball scholarship at Tuskegee University. He is concerned about the evidence against him, and managed to talk with Surrency for fifteen minutes on the phone the previous week. The state has offered three months in county jail.

When his case is finally called, however, there is another snag. Mitcham, the assistant DA, isn't sure whether there are two or four counts against him. As Judge George is about to continue the case for the fourth time, Strong interrupts, explaining that he needs to do his time before he begins his scholarship in the fall. "If you have a basketball scholarship you don't want to enter a plea in something you didn't do," Judge George says, deciding to return to the case on a different day.

Afterwards, it is Surrency, not Strong, who is piqued. Following Strong out of court to the corridor, Surrency yells, "You want me to be your lawyer you can't talk! You gotta let me be your lawyer. You're jumping out there and disobeying me." Strong is astonished. Meanwhile, Deloise Jones sees an opportunity to get a chance to talk with Surrency. "What is going to happen to my son's case? Trial today?" Surrency doesn't answer her. Surrency shoots Strong an angry look and reaches for the courtroom door, which he shuts tightly.

For a moment they both stare at the door. But after a beat, Strong 30 realizes what has happened and begins to rant. "He got upset with me? He can't get upset with me because I want to tell the judge something about my case!" He curses. But Jones knows this is no time to reflect. She runs after Surrency. If she reaches him before the judge calls the next case, which could be her son's, she may get a minute.

What Did You Read?

1. What is a "contract lawyer"?

2. Why is it advantageous to the court that people accept plea agreements?

3. "The criminal justice system does a huge amount of sorting out once guilty . . . whether it's probation, death penalty, boot camp,

the punishment depends on the nature of the act." How does that apply to the low-budget contract system?

4. According to Bach, why is it judges condone lawyers who appear to do nothing at all?

What Do You Think?

1. How does everything you know about indigent defense affect your attitude toward the death penalty? Why?

2. Why is reform of the public defender system so difficult in Texas?

3. According to Bach, the justice system seems like a political, biased institution that favors white, wealthy, and influential people. Can anything be done to change that?

How Was It Done?

1. Around what deplorable situation is the article structured?

2. Could you argue that the term "contract defenders" best crystallizes the ideas in the article? How?

3. How do examples of authentic cases help to contribute to the substance of the explanations? Do the examples seem typical?

4. What corrupt values or priorities does the article seem to be structured around?

The Problem with the Chair

Carl M. Cannon

Carl M. Cannon presents a conservative's problem with the death penalty. In particular, Cannon points out that innocent people have been put to death, and the shockingly large number of people who have recently been removed from death row because DNA evidence has cleared them. Cannon suggests that a society that uses the death penalty, knowing there is a strong possibility at least some are innocent, must ask itself if it is participating in murder.

Key Words

erudite	learned
antagonized	acted in opposition to something
momentous	important
statutes	laws or rules set up by a governing body
portent	foreshadowing a coming event; omen
predator	one that preys, destroys, or devours

gallows	a frame of two upright posts and a transverse beam from which to hang criminals
exoneration	freed from blame, responsibility, or hardship
cockamamie	ridiculous; incredible
ubiquitous	being everywhere at the same time; widespread
posterity	all future generations
exculpatory	tending to clear from blame or guilt

At a dinner party in Georgetown during the Reagan years, I was seated next to a liberal journalist I didn't know too well—Sidney Blumenthal, then with *The New Republic*. No matter what has happened since, he was erudite and charming that night as we discussed the Washington scene. But my mind was largely elsewhere, for that week I had begun work on a story about a man convicted of murder who was possibly innocent. I was preoccupied, not with anything the administration might have been doing, but with the issue of capital punishment.

At some point, I asked my dinner companion his view of the death penalty.

"Oh, we're against it," he replied.

I recall being amused by that pronoun, "we"—Whom did he mean? The Democratic party? The elites?—but eventually I decided he meant the magazine he worked for. I asked him why.

"The moral issue," he said.   5

I remember also that this remark antagonized me. I do not support capital punishment either, but this was so inadequate an answer that I found myself arguing the other side of the question. I did so by invoking the specter of Steven Timothy Judy.

On April 28, 1979, Judy was cruising down the highway when he came across 23-year-old Terry Lee Chasteen, who was stranded with her kids by the side of the road in her disabled vehicle. Pretending to be a Good Samaritan, Steven Judy further disabled Chasteen's car by disconnecting the ignition wires, then drove her and her three children—Misty Ann, 5, Steve, 4, and Mark, 2—to a secluded location. He raped and strangled Chasteen and drowned the children, one by one, in a nearby creek.

Judy was quickly arrested and convicted of capital murder. At trial, he assured the jurors that if they didn't vote for the death penalty he'd kill again someday. "And it may be one of you next," he warned. "Or your family."

The jury obliged, and on March 9, 1981, the State of Indiana put Steven Judy to death in an electric chair nicknamed "Old Betsy." The "moral" aspect of allowing Judy to live eluded the grasp of not just me, but a majority of Americans. Except to the most ideological of criminal-justice liberals—and perhaps to Judy's fellow inmates at his Michigan City prison—his execution seemed a blow in behalf of civilization.

But if Judy's crimes were hideous even by the grisly standards of 10 Death Row, what makes his case notable almost 20 years later is that his execution—or rather, the lack of an outcry at his execution—was a signal that a momentous change was taking place in America. Until that night, there had been only three executions in the United States since the confusing 5-4 Supreme Court decision in 1976 invalidating all existing state death-penalty laws. But the states inclined to use this remedy had hurriedly rewritten their statutes to conform with the Court's requirements, and just five years later here was Steven Judy saying to the guards as he was strapped into Old Betsy, "I don't hold no grudges. This is my doing."

It was not generally apparent then that a flood of executions was about to begin. Judy's case seemed unproblematic in that he had not appealed his sentence. In so refusing, he had followed in the footsteps of Gary Mark Gilmore, executed by firing squad in Utah in 1977, and Jesse Bishop, who went to Nevada's gas chamber in 1979. John Spenkelink, electrocuted in Florida in 1979 after spurning a plea bargain that would have earned him a measly 20 years in prison—he argued self-defense—was the only one of the four to go to his death unwillingly. But it was the business-as-usual aspect of the Judy case that served as a portent.

The night he was executed, liberal activists descended on Michigan City in a familiar ritual: the candlelight vigil. A crowd of some 200 of them braved the wind and rain to be there, but they were not alone. Earlier, at a "Protect the Innocent" rally in a downtown park, Mark Chasteen, the slain woman's ex-husband, assured a pro-death penalty crowd that he'd "throw the switch" himself. As the hour approached, motorists passing the prison would slow down, honk their horns, and yell, "Burn, Judy!"

On that March night, the United States was heading briskly down a road it had not taken since the rough days of the Great Depression. Not much longer would executions be international news events. In a handful of states, most prominently Texas, they would actually become routine. In fact, within two years, crowds of several hundred Texans would be rallying outside the Huntsville prison on execution nights to celebrate. Battered by a violent-crime rate that threatened the very freedoms we are promised in our founding documents, and angered by repeated accounts of vicious predators who were paroled only to kill again, Americans were calling for a remedy prescribed long ago: "An eye for an eye!" demonstrators would chant.

And who can argue with this ancient wisdom? Well, I will. What if the issue is not an eye for an eye, but an eye for a finger? Or removing the eye of someone you thought put out your eye, but, in fact, only looks like the guy who did? This is not an academic question, and it never has been. And now, thanks to several high-profile cases in which condemned men were exonerated, and thanks to the added tool of DNA evidence, the true horror of the death penalty has made itself plain. The right question to ask is not whether capital punishment is an appropriate—or a moral—response to murders. It is whether the government should be in the business of executing people convicted of murder knowing to a certainty that some of them are innocent.

An Old Fight

Chicago, where Sid Blumenthal hails from, has long occupied center stage in the timeless debate over capital punishment. Seventy-five years ago, the liberal lawyer and activist Clarence Darrow convened weekly meetings in his Chicago home to discuss the social issues of the day. Paul Cline, my grandmother's husband, attended some of those meetings. I asked him once which discussions he remembered best. His answer: Those in which the great defense lawyer inveighed against capital punishment. Then, as now, the Left considered this remedy barbaric and capricious. It was, they said, applied too easily to the poor and the politically unpopular, especially to blacks, to whom the gallows were akin to lynching. Innocence was raised as an issue by liberals, but then, as now, it was not their primary objection.

Darrow was faced with a subtle dilemma, therefore, when he was retained as defense counsel in the Roaring Twenties' most sensational murder case, the Leopold and Loeb trial. These defendants were not poor or black or immigrants or involved in unpopular political causes. They were, in fact, white, rich, well educated, and not politically active—and their lawyer agreed that they were guilty as hell. In his impassioned closing argument, Darrow actually alluded to the internal conflict this presented for him, even as he labored to spare Nathan Leopold and Richard Loeb the noose.

"This case may not be as important as I think it is, and I am sure I do not need to tell this court, or to tell my friends, that I would fight just as hard for the poor as for the rich," said Darrow during his historic twelve-hour summation. "If I should succeed in saving these boys' lives and do nothing for the progress of the law, I should feel sad, indeed."

Darrow did save the "boys'" lives—at least one of them, anyway (Loeb was stabbed to death in the Joliet prison in 1936)—and he probably did much for the progress of the law as he saw it, too. His closing was taught in law schools for generations afterward, and it is still venerated by legal scholars who oppose capital punishment. "It left the presiding judge in tears," notes Douglas O. Linder of the University of

Missouri, Kansas City. "People still think of his summation in the Leopold-Loeb case as one of the most eloquent attacks on the death penalty ever made."

But a perusal of Darrow's argument today is not likely to reduce many conservatives to tears, or even sympathy. Although Darrow based much of his argument for mercy on the fact that neither defendant had yet reached his 20th birthday, the lawyer was also an avowed determinist who seemed to hold the defendants nearly blameless for their vicious crime. He also spent much of his time arguing that history was on a long, inexorable march away from capital punishment and that future generations would consider hanging as barbaric as crucifixion and burning at the stake. A modern conservative reading the trial transcript is more likely to identify with state's attorney Robert Crowe, a gifted Yale Law School graduate who was at the time a rising star in Illinois Republican politics.

In his closing argument, Crowe sarcastically characterized Darrow 20 as "the distinguished gentleman whose profession it is to protect murder in Cook County and whose health thieves inquire about before they go and commit a crime." The term "junk science" was not yet in vogue, but the prosecutor accused a defense psychiatrist of "prostituting his profession" and mocked Darrow's argument that the defendants weren't ultimately to blame for their actions: "My God, if one of them had a harelip I suppose Darrow would want me to apologize for having them indicted."

A Governor Doubts

And so it went for three-quarters of a century, during which the arguments for and against capital punishment barely changed at all—until this year, that is. The governor of Illinois—a conservative, Republican governor named George Ryan—read about one too many cases of Death Row inmates' being freed in his state because of new evidence that showed they were innocent of the crime. "Until I can be sure that everyone sentenced to death in Illinois is truly guilty; until I can be sure, with moral certainty, that no innocent man or woman is facing a lethal injection, no one will meet that fate," Ryan said. "I cannot support a system which, in its administration, has proven so fraught with error and has come so close to the ultimate nightmare, the state's taking of innocent life."

As many now know, 13 inmates condemned to death by the State of Illinois have been cleared of capital-murder charges in the 23 years since capital punishment was reinstated. During this time, the state has executed a dozen inmates convicted of murder, a ratio of governmental failure so alarming that it struck the man ultimately responsible for carrying out the death penalty in a very personal way. "There's going to be a lot of folks who are firm believers in the death penalty who may not agree with what I'm doing here today," Ryan explained. "But I am the fellow who has to make the ultimate decision whether someone is injected with a poison that's going to take their life."

The governor also cited a *Chicago Tribune* investigative series that examined each of the state's nearly 300 capital cases and found that these trials were routinely riddled with bias and error, including incompetent legal work by the defense lawyers, and that prosecutors relied on dubious jailhouse informants in about 50 of the cases. Two of the Illinois exonerations were brought about by Northwestern University professor Lawrence Marshall, who took on the cases without a fee. In one case, that of Rolando Cruz, Marshall's work resulted in 1) the freeing of an innocent man after twelve years on Death Row for the murder and rape of a ten-year-old girl, 2) criminal charges against the authorities who prosecuted Cruz, and 3) the identification of the actual killer.

The most famous reversals in Illinois came about because journalism students at Northwestern kept unearthing evidence that exonerated various convicts on Death Row. For example, four black men from Detroit had been convicted of abducting a white couple, raping the woman and killing both her and the man. Two of the four, Dennis Williams and Verneal Jimerson, were sentenced to death. Students under the direction of journalism professor David Protess investigated the case and discovered that the prosecution's star witness had an IQ of less than 75 and that prosecutors had fed her details of the crime and coached her into testifying about them.

Public pressure because of these revelations forced the district attorney's office to allow DNA tests—which promptly eliminated as suspects all four of the men convicted of the crime. The students, going through the records of the case, found something even more stunning in the state's files: the names of four other suspects who'd been identified to authorities, but never even questioned by the police. The students interviewed three of them (the fourth, the ringleader, had since died), and, incredibly, all three eventually confessed. They are now serving life sentences.

Then, a little over a year ago, Prof. Protess and five of his students, working with a private detective, wormed a confession out of a drug dealer for a 1982 double murder for which another man, Anthony Porter, had been convicted. Not just convicted, but sentenced to death. In September 1998, in fact, Porter had been two days away from execution when a state appeals court issued a stay to consider whether it was constitutional to execute someone with Porter's IQ (estimated at 51). It turns out his IQ is a bit higher than that, but the point is that the delay in the execution gave the Northwestern team time to dig through the records and finger the man who subsequently confessed to the crime.

"The judicial system commits errors," commented Prof. Protess, in a classic understatement, "because it's run by people."

This simple observation shouldn't come as a bolt from the blue—least of all to conservatives. It just shouldn't be a surprise that civil servants take shortcuts on the job, that juries drawn from the citizenry that gives Bill Clinton a 60 percent approval rating get swept up in the passions of the day, that political hacks appointed to the bench ratify those mistakes, and that bloated state-run bureaucracies are loath to correct them. "Criminal-justice system" is a high falutin phrase, but the courts are just a branch of government, and one that by design has less accountability than the other two.

In other words, if ideology and experience lead one to the conclusion that government is by nature inefficient and inept, then why should it be astonishing that the actions of one branch of government—the judicial branch—are so routinely wrong?

One Reporter's Experience

I will return to this point, but before I do, I want to explain why I am 30 absolutely certain that this is a universal problem, that there is nothing aberrant about the Illinois courts. Before I was 30 years old, I covered four cases in which defendants were charged with capital murder, but were, in fact, completely innocent. (In a fifth case, a man from Petersburg, Va.—George Roberts—was convicted of killing his wife, served seven years, and after being paroled, convinced the local cops that he'd been framed.)

In the first of these cases, police in Columbus, Ga., arrested a black man named Jerome Livas and charged him with strangling and raping two elderly white women. No physical evidence linked Livas to the crimes, he did not fit the psychological profile produced by the FBI, and he was borderline mentally retarded (the crimes had been meticulously planned and carried out). When the killings continued with the identical method of operation while Livas was locked up in jail, the cops blithely offered the cockamamie theory that a copycat killer must be on the loose. Livas, they said, had confessed and—this is a phrase that often comes up in these cases—possessed details "only the killer would know."

I covered the police beat in that town for the local paper, and a friendly cop called me at home one night to tell me that all those supposedly confidential details had, in fact, been fed to Livas by the detectives themselves, and that Livas was so unintelligent and so eager to please that he'd just parroted them back to the investigators. "This guy would admit to anything," said the cop. Subsequently I tested that theory in a session the *Washington Post* dubbed "a sensational jailhouse interview." It was sensational, all right, but sad. I succeeded in getting

Livas to sign a confession for killing Presidents John F. Kennedy and William McKinley and for kidnapping the Lindbergh baby. Red-faced authorities dropped the charges against Livas, and years later, long after I'd left Columbus, they got the right man—presumably—and he was executed. But it's pretty clear to me what would have happened to Jerome Livas if the real murderer had stopped killing when Livas was arrested.

I'm a Californian, so there was in those years a temptation to think that such miscarriages happen only in the Deep South or in jerkwater towns—but this proved not to be true. They can happen anywhere, in towns big and small, and they do. In my next job, at the *San Diego Union*, I was working the police beat when the Los Angeles Police Department publicly fingered a Massachusetts convict named George Francis Shamshak as a suspect in the so-called Hillside Stranglings. Daryl Gates, then the head of the Hillside Strangler Task Force, later to be famous (or infamous) as chief of the LAPD, even used that ubiquitous phrase "knowledge only the killer would have" to explain why they were sure they had the right guy. Except that Shamshak was in prison in Massachusetts when some of the killings took place, a fact I pointed out to Gates myself at an entertaining news conference. The details only the killer would know? Turns out that he'd read them in *Newsweek*.

In the early 1980s, a gifted investigative journalist named Jon Standefer and I wrote enough articles about an aged ex-con named Pete Pianezzi to shame Gov. Jerry Brown into giving him a pardon based on innocence, one of only seven such pardons in the state's history. Pianezzi had been framed for a sensational Los Angeles mob hit of the 1930s that was page-one news up and down the West Coast. There were no good suspects, but Pianezzi was Italian, he had a criminal record, and the district attorney needed a conviction to quell the public pressure on his office. The prosecutor sought the death penalty, but a lone woman juror spared Pianezzi's life by refusing to vote for execution. She reportedly explained her hesitation by saying that if it turned out the jury was making a mistake—the defendant insisted at trial that he was innocent—that error could be reversed if Pianezzi were in prison, but not if he had gone to the gas chamber. This was a prescient observation. Forty years later, at a victory party in San Francisco, Pete introduced Standefer and me to the North Beach crowd as his "saviors," a distinction that properly belonged to that holdout juror whose name has been lost to posterity. She is the person who prevented the state from killing an innocent man.

To me, the most disturbing aspect of the Pianezzi case is that it was such a high-profile murder trial. If it can happen there, what about the anonymous cases in, for example, East Texas, in which the defendant is lucky if a news reporter ever sits through a whole day of testimony? Moreover, the Pianezzi case is no isolated example. Doubt about the guilt of the condemned man is a common thread in some of the most celebrated murder trials in this nation's history. Bruno Richard Hauptmann's chances for a fair trial in the Lindbergh kidnapping—and the ability truly to ascertain his guilt or innocence—were compromised by perjured testimony, tampering with exhibits, and the suppression by the New Jersey state police of exculpatory evidence. People remember also that Cleveland doctor Sam Sheppard's guilty verdict was set aside because of the circus-like atmosphere of the courtroom and the shameful conduct of Cleveland's newspapers. But do they recall that he was acquitted at his second trial?

The Hardest Questions

Conservatives were rightly appalled when O. J. Simpson was acquitted after a screwy trial tainted by the defense's overtly racial appeals to the jury. But the moral of this story is not that black jurors will no longer convict black defendants (of the 3,652 people on Death Row, 43 percent are black), it's that juries make mistakes all the time. And sometimes—nobody knows how often—the mistakes they make are in the other direction: They convict innocent people.

In the years since Steven T. Judy was electrocuted, some 82 condemned people have had their capital-murder convictions set aside for one reason or another. A few, such as Steven Manning, a corrupt Chicago cop, didn't get a fair trial but may have been guilty and are serving time for other crimes in which their guilt is unquestioned. But many more are like poor Kirk Bloodsworth, an ex-Marine from the Eastern Shore of Maryland who had no previous criminal record—and no involvement whatsoever in the crime for which he was convicted and sentenced to death. These men are released after years on Death Row with a pardon or a halfhearted apology by the state and, if they are lucky, an inadequate monetary settlement.

"I was separated from my family and branded the worst thing possible—a child-killer and a rapist," said Bloodsworth on his release. "It can happen to anyone."

In eight of these cases, including Bloodsworth's, DNA evidence not previously available was used to free the condemned. Inevitably someone on the prosecution's side will mumble bromides about how this proves that the system "works." But that's not what it proves. These DNA cases underscore a few basic points that are far from reassuring: What about the majority of cases—the non-rape cases, mostly—in which DNA is irrelevant? Why do so many state prosecutors tout DNA as much stronger evidence than fingerprints when it points to guilt, but then put up roadblocks for defendants who want to use it to establish their innocence? Finally, how many innocent people were executed in the years before DNA tests became available?

This is the crux of the matter, and no one seems to have the an- 40
swer. Republican presidential candidate George W. Bush was asked directly how he could be certain that all 120-odd executions he has
presided over as governor of Texas were carried out against guilty defendants. He replied that he was, indeed, certain that nothing like
what had happened in Illinois had happened in Texas on his watch.
"Maybe they've had some problems in their courts," he said. "Maybe
they've had some faulty judgments. I've reviewed every case, and I'm
confident that every case that has come across my desk, I'm confident
of the guilt of the person who committed the crime."

Incidentally, Bush's brother Jeb, the governor of Florida, says the
same thing, even though Florida has set aside the capital-murder convictions of some 20 Death Row inmates since 1973—more than any
other state. Gerald Kogan, the former chief justice of Florida's
Supreme Court, entered the debate recently, saying he's convinced that
Florida has, in fact, put to death people who were not guilty. "Knowing as I do the imperfections in our system, I know that we have, on
occasions in the past, executed those people who are in fact innocent,"
Kogan said at a Capitol Hill press conference. This led, in turn, to a
challenge from Jeb Bush that Kogan name names. This is a fair point,
but present-day Florida officials hardly seem preoccupied with ensuring that only the guilty are put to death. When Gov. Ryan was imposing his moratorium, the legislature in Tallahassee was in special
session passing a law reducing the time convicted murderers have to
appeal their cases or bring new evidence to light.

If Republican governors are at odds with one another over the
issue, so too are conservatives generally. In recent weeks, Pat Robertson, George Will, and William F. Buckley Jr. have weighed in with op-
ed pieces that express reservations about the death penalty over this
matter of DNA and innocence.

Byron York, writing in *The American Spectator,* takes a different
tack, arguing that innocence is a Trojan horse being used by liberals to
advance a cause they have championed since the days of Darrow—
abolition of capital punishment on the typical grounds: barbarism,
racism, etc. The energetic Death Penalty Information Center in Washington, D.C., York points out, is virtually a wholly owned subsidiary
of John R. "Rick" MacArthur, a rich left-winger whose taste in causes
includes the Sandinistas and the Christic Institute.

York makes a valid point, and, as if to underscore it, all the usual
suspects on the left have weighed in against capital punishment by
simply topping their old arguments with a fresh concern about the
risk of executing the innocent. In Hollywood, the writers of *The Practice,* a TV show concerning the law, turn one of their episodes into an
anti-capital-punishment screed. From Chicago, Democratic representative Jesse Jackson Jr. authors a death-penalty-moratorium bill in the
House. In Washington, Jackson's father, wearing one of his many hats

as a CNN newsman—he hosts a show called *Both Sides,* a title Fidel Castro must love—interviews defense lawyer Barry Scheck, and no one else, about his book on condemned men who have been proven innocent by DNA. At one point in the decidedly one-sided program, Jackson invokes the memory of Supreme Court justice Harry Blackmun, who famously wrote in a 1994 dissent, "From this day forward, I no longer shall tinker with the machinery of death. I feel morally and intellectually obligated simply to concede that the death penalty has failed." Jackson and his lone guest keep using that word "moral" throughout the show, and the good reverend closes with the line "Let's choose life over death, but through it all, at least let's give life a chance."

In sum, it's enough to make any good conservative gag. Who 45 wants to be on the same side as the Hollywood Left, or the two Jesse Jacksons, or Blackmun, the champion of life who wrote the Roe decision, or, for that matter, Barry Scheck, who attempted to convince the O.J. jury that DNA testing was a bunch of white man's mumbo-jumbo? The answer is that conservatives need to ignore their impulse that anything the liberal establishment approves of, they must oppose. They should instead focus on this one issue: If a democratic society executes criminals with the foreknowledge that some percentage of them are innocent, are all members of that society implicitly guilty of murder themselves? And does it matter, from a moral and theological viewpoint, that we can't know which convicts, specifically, will go to their deaths for crimes they did not commit, if we admit that some will? I submit that it does not.

The Agony of Doubt

Interviewed for a comprehensive piece published last November in *The Atlantic Monthly,* Bill McCollum, a conservative Republican congressman from Florida, suggested that the possibility of executing an innocent person—he insists it's a remote likelihood—is the price the nation must pay if it wants to reduce violent crime. In that same article, Chicago prosecutor William Kunkle, who secured the death penalty for serial killer John Wayne Gacy and also charged the police officers for their conduct in the Rolando Cruz case, went even further. He argued that anyone who believes man can design and implement a system that catches only the guilty is kidding himself. "Sooner or later it's going to happen," Kunkle said. "It comes with the territory. It is not humanly possible to design a system that is perfect. And if people are not prepared for the eventuality that human institutions are going to make mistakes, then they shouldn't support the death penalty, and they shouldn't elect legislators who support it."

Amen, Mr. Kunkle. Murder is a terrible crime. And in the face of the awful truth presented to us by DNA testing, what name shall we call the state-sanctioned killing of an innocent man? That's why society must not be a party to it. As Benjamin Franklin once said, "They that give up essential liberty to obtain a little temporary safety deserve neither liberty nor safety."

In 1982, a small-time Mexican-American thug named Leonel Torres Herrera was convicted of murdering two South Texas police officers. Herrera was sentenced to death. Eight years later, on the verge of his execution, a lawyer signed an affidavit saying that Herrera's brother had confessed the killings. Texas courts refused to reopen the case because the new assertion had come long after their 30-day limit for additional evidence. Herrera's case went all the way to the U.S. Supreme Court, which ruled 6 to 3 that Texas's time limitations were not unconstitutional. The case sharply divided the high court. Justice Blackmun said caustically from the bench that "the execution of a person who can show that he is innocent comes perilously close to simple murder." Sandra Day O'Connor, looking at other evidence in the case, replied in her written opinion that Herrera was not innocent "in any sense of the word."

O'Connor's clear-eyed observation should not be forgotten. Most of the time, the condemned are guilty. I certainly hope she is right in the Herrera case. But I am haunted by the possibility, no matter how remote, that she isn't. In the two decades since Steven Judy went to his richly deserved death, 631 others have been executed. I do not share George W. Bush's easy confidence that all of them were guilty. In 1981, the same year that Judy died and Leonel Herrera was apprehended, Pete Pianezzi was pardoned. Pete, then a very old man, told me when he got the news that he never really despaired that he would someday be vindicated because innocence, like truth, exists as a power of its own in the world, independent of the machinations of men. Pete died a few years ago, but his faith was greater than mine. Only God—not any living man—knows, for instance, whether Leonel Herrera really did it. All we know for sure is what the condemned man himself said as he left this world.

"Something very wrong is taking place tonight," he cried. "I am 50 innocent, innocent, innocent."

What Did You Read?

1. Who is George Ryan and what did he do?

2. Why is what happened to Peter Pianezzi an excellent reason for why many object to capital punishment?

3. What is the author's greatest reason for objecting to capital punishment? Is it a typical reason? Explain.

What Do You Think?

1. What reasons might you use to support the death penalty? What reasons might you use to oppose it?

2. Why was it so immoral of Barry Scheck to tell the O.J. Simpson jury that DNA testing is "white man's mumbo-jumbo"?

3. Would you be more comfortable with the death penalty if laws required that DNA evidence confirm the identity of the killer?

How Was It Done?

1. The article revolves around what particular contradiction of values having to do with capital punishment?

2. Do the subtitles in the article help to streamline and organize the content? How so?

3. How is the opening anecdote an effective lead-in for the article?

4. What significant individuals does the article revolve around? How does this help the author substantiate his thesis?

Against Mandatory Minimums

John J. DiIulio, Jr.

John J. DiIulio, Jr., argues that an increasingly large percentage of the prison population is now made up of nonviolent drug offenders. These offenders are placed alongside the most violent criminals. This does not improve public safety since drug offenders are simply replaced on the streets by more drug offenders. Instead, the justice system is clogged with these offenders, taking resources away from dealing with violent criminals. The real culprits, DiIulio argues, are laws that tie judges' hands and force nonviolent drug offenders into prison stays. The solution is the repeal of mandatory minimum drug sentencing laws.

Key Words

libertarian	relating to the doctrine of absolute and unrestricted free will, especially of thought or action
inherently	of the essential character of something; intrinsically
repositories	places where something is stored
clemency	mercy; to moderate or release from punishment
incarcerated	jailed or imprisoned
gubernatorial	relating to a governor or the governorship of a state
suburbanization	to give a suburban character; to become a suburb, a residential area on the outskirts of a city
retrograde	moving backwards; tending toward a worse or previous state

There is a conservative crime-control case to be made for repealing mandatory-minimum drug laws now. That's a conservative crime-control case, as in a case for promoting public safety, respecting community mores, and reinstating the traditional sentencing prerogatives of criminal-court judges. This is not a libertarian drug-legalization case, as in, "The inherently unethical and hugely expensive Washington-led War on Drugs has failed." Nor is it a liberal criminal-liberation case: "Most drug offenders behind bars, like most prisoners generally, are helpless, hapless, harmless victims of poverty and racism." No, it is a conservative case, and I will tell you how I, one of the few academic analysts with a kind word for imprisonment, have come to embrace it.

Where were you on October 3, 1995, the day the O.J. verdict came in? I was in Albany, speaking before law-enforcement officials at a governor's forum. I concluded my address by arguing that New York, which in the 1970s led the nation in passing stern mandatory-minimum drug laws, should lead it again by repealing them.

New York, like most states, has a complex criminal code that includes several dozen specific laws prohibiting the possession or sale of various "dangerous drugs" and "controlled substances," and prescribing criminal penalties, including mandatory prison terms of a certain number of years. Most of these laws (including a few that germinated as "public health" laws) were enacted between 1973 and 1986. Over the years, many of them have been repealed or revised.

New York's two most resilient repositories of mandatory anti-drug laws are the Rockefeller Drug Law (RDL) and the Second Felony Offender Law (SFOL). Together, the two have earned New York its reputation as the state with the "toughest drug laws in the country."

Signed with gusto by Gov. Nelson Rockefeller in 1973, the RDL mandated terms of 15 years to life for numerous drug-trafficking crimes based largely on the weight of the drug sold. As criminal-justice historian Lawrence M. Friedman has noted, the RDL was controversial from the first, and "the legislature, in essence, got rid of it in 1979." But both the letter and the "essence" of the RDL's mandatory-sentencing regime survived in parts of the state's criminal code, including the SFOL.

5

A Rising Tide

Also enacted in 1973, the SFOL requires with some exceptions a mandatory state-prison term for persons convicted of a second felony offense. In 1993, 67 percent of those committed to prison for drug offenses in New York were sentenced under the SFOL. In their first 20 years, the SFOL, the RDL, and other anti-drug laws combined for a steep and steady rise in the portion of incoming prisoners whose last convicted crime was a drug felony. In 1980, a drug crime was the most serious conviction offense of 11 percent of the state's prisoners (886 people). By 1993, that fraction had risen to 44 percent (10,939 people).

On the day of the O.J. verdict, I strongly suspected something of which, owing to research I have recently completed with Harvard economist Anne Morrison Piehl and University of New Mexico sociologist Bert Useem, I now feel certain: Since the mid 1990s, a large fraction of New York's incoming prison population has consisted of offenders whose only past felony crimes, recorded and undetected, were genuinely low-level, nonviolent drug crimes. Many of these "drug-only offenders," as we term them, are themselves drug abusers or addicts who have never been in a well-structured, no-nonsense, community-anchored substance-abuse program.

New York is not alone. My first suspicions about drug-only prisoners were reported in a 1995 article co-authored with Piehl and published in the *Brookings Review*. As advisor to New Jersey's Sentencing Policy Commission in 1993 and '94, I and other Princeton researchers were able to survey the state's inmates, study its criminal and corrections data, and conduct interviews with key lawmakers, law-enforcement officials, judges, probation officers, and others. Based on that research, Piehl and I concluded that perhaps 15 percent or more of the state's incoming prisoners were drug-only offenders.

But our New Jersey study, like one we had previously done in Wisconsin, was not really designed to get cleanly at our questions about the incarceration of drug-only offenders. So with Useem we modified our design accordingly. During the first half of 1997, we surveyed some 1,500 incoming prisoners in three states—New York, New Mexico, and Arizona—and undertook other necessary research. (A report summarizing the main findings of our study will be released this month by the Manhattan Institute's Center for Civic Innovation.)

Even by our most conservative estimates, we find that all three 10 states are imprisoning large numbers of drug-only offenders: 28 percent of incoming male prisoners in New York, 15 percent in New Mexico, 18 percent in Arizona; and 49 percent of incoming female prisoners in New York, 14 percent in New Mexico, 20 percent in Arizona.

In 1997, 47 percent of New York's incoming prisoners (9,809 people) and 33 percent of all prisoners on any given day (22,670 people) were persons whose last and most serious conviction offense was a drug crime. If our aforementioned lower-bound estimates are in the ballpark, then at least half of the incoming drug offenders in the New York state-prison system are drug-only offenders.

Most of the relevant research literature—in addition to street lore coast to coast—indicates that when one drug-only offender is incarcerated, another one assumes his sales and effectively takes his place. Our three-state survey found that, at the time of the conviction offense, under a third of the prisoners now serving mandatory sentences for drugs either knew that the penalty was in effect or expected to go to jail if caught. So much for deterrence. Meanwhile, ever more incarcerated drug-only offenders are drug-dependent persons. In 1996, over half of all local-jail inmates reported having used drugs in the month before their offense, up from 44 percent in 1989. Likewise, in 1997, 57 percent of state prisoners reported having used drugs in the month before their offense, up from 50 percent in 1991. For federal prisoners, the fraction rose from 32 percent in 1991 to 45 percent in 1997. With mandatory minimums, there is no real suppression of the drug trade, only episodic substance-abuse treatment of incarcerated drug-only offenders, and hence only the most tenuous crime-control rationale for imposing prison terms—mandatory or otherwise—on any of them.

Back in Albany, I was being neither brave nor ungracious to Gov. George E. Pataki. For one thing, he was not present. For another, he was not then unsympathetic to the view that, as he himself stated publicly during his first days in office, "Rockefeller drug laws have filled New York's prisons and have not increased public safety."

Each subsequent December, Pataki has commuted the sentences of several drug-only offenders serving long mandatory prison terms. In December 1997, for example, he granted clemency to three such offenders, including one Angela Thompson, convicted at age 17 of trying to sell cocaine to an undercover cop at the behest of an uncle who was her legal guardian. Both she and her uncle got 15 years. She was granted gubernatorial grace and released after "only" eight years.

Earlier this year, however, Pataki appeared to back way off a move 15 in the legislature to radically reform or repeal the RDL. The political speculation has him fearing such a move at a moment when he might emerge as a viable law-and-order candidate for vice president, a fear heightened by his rocky relations with New York City mayor Rudolph Giuliani, himself a crime-busting GOP veep prospect and a vocal take-all-prisoners advocate of abolishing parole.

Here's hoping that Pataki shocks the cynics, captivates the press, and puts his tough-but-enlightened-statesmanship stamp on RDL repeal. His conservative crime-control case for repeal should acknowledge that the RDL and like drug laws have always netted some drug-only fish and fried them with mandatory prison terms. As one veteran prosecutor said to me following my Albany speech, early on these laws functioned "like Velcro" for drug kingpins and other "really bad asses," mainly plea-bargain-gorged streetwise felons who had not been adequately prosecuted or sentenced for previous non-drug crimes. Over the last several years, however, the mandatory drug laws, conceded another big-city prosecutor, have begun to function "like hell," with ever more drug-only offenders "going inside," while equally bad offenders (or worse ones) get low- or no-supervision probation or, as some now say, "O.J.," meaning they simply fail to appear in court on drug charges, plea-bargain their way home, or otherwise get off scot-free.

The New Prison Population

If you doubt such professional wisdom, just look at who's now on probation in most states. A report released by the U.S. Bureau of Justice Statistics in 1997 indicated that, in 1994, 29 percent of persons whose most serious conviction offense was a drug-trafficking felony got probation instead of incarceration; so did 31 percent of those whose most serious conviction offense was a weapons-crime felony. Weapons offenders were thus slightly more likely than drug merchants to escape incarceration and get probation. In Massachusetts and several other states, about half of probationers are under supervision for a violent crime, while half of those in prison for drug-law violations have no official record of violence. From a crime-control perspective, forcing drug-only offenders behind bars while violent offenders beat feet to the streets is just plain batty.

To continue to imprison drug-only offenders mandatorily is to hamstring further a justice system that controls crime in a daily war of inches, not miles, and that has among its main beneficiaries low-income urban dwellers. With massive private spending on personal security and massive suburbanization, most Americans do not rely heavily on government to keep themselves, their loved ones, and their possessions out of street crime's way. Through courts, cops, and corrections agencies, government combats but never comes close to conquering crime, least of all the violent crime that disproportionately afflicts inner-city minority households. Even on its most aggressive day, the justice system works like a sorting machine, incarcerating only a small fraction even of known, adjudicated, violent criminals.

In 1994, Americans experienced some 4.2 million murders, rapes, robberies, and aggravated assaults. That same year, states convicted about 146,000 persons for these violent crimes, but sent only about 95,000 of them to prison. Between 1980 and 1994, the nation's prison population increased by 213 percent; but the probation population increased by exactly the same percentage. By 1996, there were a million people in prison, and 3.3 million on probation.

From 1960 to 1980, the nation underwent a bout of prison bulimia 20 during which the ratio of prison admissions to arrests for serious crimes fell. From 1980 to the present, however, the nation has undergone a steady prison expansion targeted mainly on violent felons. Thus, between 1990 and 1997, violent offenders accounted for 50 percent of the increase in the nation's prison population, and all types of drug offenders for 25 percent. Truth-in-sentencing laws pushed the average time served by released prisoners convicted of murder, rape, robbery, or aggravated assault from 43 months in 1993 to 49 months in 1997. For all types of prisoners, the average time served increased from 22 months in 1990 to 25 months in 1996. The increase was neither huge nor particularly punitive, but it averted millions of street crimes and thousands of mortal wounds.

But where drug-only offenders are concerned, in the late 1990s we have gone from prison bulimia to a prison binge that is putting drug-only offenders behind bars with seemingly petty but dangerous "drug offenders" and repeat violent felons.

In a 1996 study I conducted with George Mitchell of the Wisconsin Policy Research Institute, we reconstructed almost the entire adult and juvenile criminal histories of a sample of prisoners from Milwaukee County. Take the case of the prisoner serving two years for "possession WITD" (with intent to distribute) a tenth of a gram of cocaine. He had five prior arrests, three prior incarcerations, and was a habitual parole and probation violator. He began building his diversified criminal portfolio with juvenile burglaries. He leavened it as an adult with occasional armed robberies. His pre-sentence investigation report stated that he "seems to rationalize his behavior and blames his drug usage as being the reason why he has engaged in new criminal behavior." The agent who wrote the report would have none of it, charging this "drug offender" with "a blatant disregard of the community."

Few citizens would shed a tear or withhold a dollar if mandatory-minimum drug laws ensured that such a career criminal could not con yet another judge or probation officer into brokering his release in the name of rehabilitation or community-based treatment.

But look at the flip side. Look, for example, at the estimated half of all "drug offenders" entering New York prisons who are much closer to being drug-only offenders than they are to being violent and chronic felons in petty drug possessor's clothing.

You be the judge. A career drug addict comes before you on his 25 second conviction for a drug sale. You read the pre-sentence investigation report. You learn that in Brooklyn and other parts of town, district attorneys and others have run remarkably effective "coerced abstinence" community-based programs. You know that these programs are not cheap, but generally do not cost as much, all told, as a year of incarceration. You entertain the probation officer's recommendation for a non-prison term featuring mandatory drug treatment.

On second thought, don't be the judge, because even real judges can't be. Don't bother imagining what the pre-sentence investigation report reveals about the offender, because a real report doesn't get consulted for purposes of sentencing anyway. And don't try to require community-supervised drug treatment as a condition of probation, because the law mandates that this pathetic two-time drug-only loser do 15 years to life in prison.

How did this happen? One last "don't": Don't join the critics in carping about how mandatory-minimum laws swallowed judicial discretion in favor of sentencing penalties set by the legislature, at least not until you suffer my little interpretive history of the rise and demise of their opposite numbers, the so-called indeterminate sentencing regimes.

After World War II, the broad sentencing discretion traditionally afforded to judges was progressively harnessed to psychobabble theories of criminal rehabilitation. By the 1960s, many criminal-court judges in New York and other states did the bidding of law professors and policy elites who were openly contemptuous of popular crime-control demands. Take the Model Criminal Code. Adopted by the American Law Institute in 1962, it explicitly rejected punishment as a purpose of the justice system. Henceforth adult criminals were to be "disposed" or "treated," not "punished." (The impact on the juvenile justice system was even worse, but that's another story.)

As indeterminate sentencing incarnate, right-thinking judges with virtually unlimited discretion were not simply to weigh a convicted criminal's mens rea as per the Anglo-American legal tradition. They were also to decide whether the criminal's willful, reckless, or malicious conduct was his fault or society's. When in doubt, they could split the difference and the sentence, then proceed to tailor from the bench whatever rehabilitation program and however many years— one to five, two to fifteen, whatever—they imagined the criminal's condition dictated. So between breakfast and lunch, courts all across the country were imposing radically different sentences on sane persons who, to the uninitiated eye, had committed virtually identical crimes under remarkably kindred life circumstances. The only uniform results were uniformly high prisoner recidivism rates and uniform growth in the discretionary power of parole boards.

By the late 1960s, some critics of indeterminate sentencing had come close to confessing that the system had defiled judicial discretion and become what they loathed: namely, not an applied legal science of rehabilitation, but a cesspool of arbitrary and disparate punishment. They consoled themselves that, if such was the price for rolling back Puritanical or otherwise intellectually retrograde views of crime and punishment, it was a price worth paying. They—or, rather, average Americans, especially those in the big cities—paid this price in the coin of unprecedented rates of criminal victimization.

In the end, the experts and their judges refused to concede that, while the justice system has a clear ethical and prudential stake in reforming criminals and returning them to their local communities as decent, law-abiding citizens, its two primary purposes lie elsewhere: first, to promote public safety by cost-effectively detecting, convicting, and, as necessary, restraining a small but significant fraction of persons who have criminally violated or threatened life, liberty, or property;

and second, to exact in the bargain not only a significant measure of criminal deterrence, but a just measure of criminal punishment for the transgression of the legal rights of others, with such punishment to be set and executed through the sovereign moral agency of the people's courts, and administered by appointed representatives of the offended commonwealth.

As political scientist William Mayer has documented, in the 1970s an increasingly frustrated, frightened, and conservative-minded public demanded that its elected leaders regain control of crime control. As Lawrence Friedman notes, their favorite tools included new laws mandating punishment, often in the form of imprisonment: "Use a gun, go to prison"; "sell a drug, go to jail"; and so on.

It was a net good while it lasted, but the pendulum has now swung too far away from traditional judicial discretion, not only in the states but most assuredly at the federal level as well, and especially where drug crimes are concerned. In their new book on sentencing guidelines in the federal courts, former federal prosecutor Kate Stith and federal judge Jose A. Cabranes detail how this "fear of judging" has packed federal prisons—largely, I would surmise, with drug-only offenders.

There is also a socially divisive racial rub to the RDL and all its mandatory-minimum kin. Over the years, I have written in defense of the proposition that there is little or no evidence of systematic racial disparities in post-1976 criminal sentencing. In its 1998 report, even the president's Initiative on Race conceded that "all or most of the differences in the likelihood of conviction and imprisonment can be explained" by factors other than racial discrimination, "such as severity of crime or prior record of the offender."

Still, in 1997, about 95 percent of all persons in New York prisons 35 whose last and most serious conviction was for a drug offense were black or Hispanic. Most people in the communities from which these prisoners tend to come strongly oppose drug legalization and want drug dealers routed from street corners. By the same token, most of them strongly favor drug treatment and do not support the long-term imprisonment of their drug-only-offending neighbors. Their preferences ought to register in new public anti-drug laws that mandate community-supervised sentences and treatment.

Will repeal happen? Legalization proponents, like the editors of this magazine (see "The War on Drugs Is Lost," February 12, 1996), do as much to burden as to brighten the prospects for repeal. Despite registering many sensible caveats and qualifications (for example, NR editor-at-large William F. Buckley Jr. favors stiff sentences for sales to minors and admits uncertainty about how far we really can and should go with legalization), they too often characterize all persons incarcerated for drug crimes as casualties of the War on Drugs. Likewise, they generally fail to acknowledge that, whether at an acceptable human and financial cost or not (therein dwelleth the real debate), law enforcement definitely adds to the potential risks, and limits the potential rewards, of illicit narcotics consumption and sales.

Get Real

Legalizers and their favorite free-market economists are entitled an occasional vacation from the rudimentary implications of price theory. They can be forgiven, too, for a lack of firsthand familiarity with open-air drug markets, which steal public spaces and disrupt daily life. They can even be suffered as they inveigh against the billions of dollars we spend each year on the enforcement part of the War on Drugs, though we spend barely 3 cents of every government dollar on all federal, state, and local justice-system functions combined. But gentlemen, please, get real.

My dear friend Ethan Nadelmann, director of New York's Lindesmith Center and the nation's foremost advocate of harm-reduction policies, once posed with admirable precision what to me remains the key unanswered drug-war query: What is the size and composition of the population for whom continued enforcement of the anti-drug laws represents the principal bulwark between an abstemious relationship with drugs and a self- or other-destructive relationship with them? Stated differently and with a drug warrior's twist, How many more persons would use or abuse drugs were they legal, and which socioeconomic and demographic strata of our society would be most adversely affected? Nobody—not Nadelmann, not me, not anyone—knows the answer.

The conservative crime-control case for repealing mandatory-minimum drug laws neither turns on such knowledge nor need await the dawn of legalization. I repeat here what James Q. Wilson and I wrote in *The New Republic* a decade ago this July: "Attempting to suppress drugs is very costly. Some people therefore conclude that we must eliminate all the costs of law enforcement by repealing the laws that are being enforced. The result (they suppose) would be less crime, fewer and weaker gangs, and an opportunity to address the public-health problems in a straightforward manner. But legalizing drugs would also entail costs. Those costs are hard to measure, in part because they are moral and in part because we have so little experience with legalized drugs."

Notice, violent crime is down 21 percent since 1993, and we are coping rather well by most accounts with AIDS and other public-health problems that intersect with the drug trade. We have not legalized drugs. And we need not repeal all drug laws—just the ones that are clearly missing every desirable mark.

Fittingly, the most serious case against repealing mandatory-minimum drug laws that I have encountered thus far has come with feeling from fellow crime-control conservatives, including law-enforcement folks. They would have me fret that decarcerating drug-only offenders would undermine so-called quality-of-life or "broken windows" policing in New York City and elsewhere. I have even been challenged by several whom I respect (including my own retired deputy sheriff father!) to imagine what message the criminal classes of the big cities would receive if the cops stopped making drug-law violators, even minor ones, an enforcement priority, and the prisons stopped warehousing them.

I accept the challenge. In 1998, the New York Police Department had nearly 31,000 drug-related felony warrants on file, unserved. Thirty-two percent of all persons arrested by the NYPD on drug charges simply fail to appear in court. Philadelphia has some 49,000 fugitives from justice, many of them wanted for drug crimes. Lots of credible research suggests that effectively managing and treating such offenders in the community could cut their recidivism rates, avert tens of thousands of crimes, and reduce the need for prison space.

Now: Repeal mandatory-minimum drug laws in New York and elsewhere. Find the fugitives. Serve the unserved warrants. Incarcerate the really bad guys. Mandate drug treatment for the drug-only addicts and abusers. The message on the street, I suspect, would be that life may sometimes feel like a lottery but the law is no joke—and no fool.

What Did You Read?

1. Do jail terms seem to be a deterrence to drug offenders? Explain.
2. Based on information in this article, are cities safer once a drug dealer is incarcerated? Why?
3. What does DiIulio mean when he refers to "psychobabble theories of criminal rehabilitation"?

What Do You Think?

1. Do you believe that the RDL and the SFOL were political weapons or effective strategies for combating crime?
2. What do you think the primary purpose of the justice system is?
3. How would you reform the existing drug laws? What changes would you make to the mandatory minimum sentencing laws? Why?

How Was It Done?

1. What laws does this article primarily focus on?
2. What pieces of fact and logic does DiIulio use to support his case that the drug laws in this country need to be revised?
3. Does the article revolve around facts and data concerning the ineffectuality of incarcerating those who are convicted only of drug-related offenses, or does it revolve around the values held by the authorities toward those drug offenders? Be specific in your explanation.

The Risks Juveniles Face

Jason Ziedenberg and Vincent Schiraldi

Jason Ziedenberg and Vincent Schiraldi present a case for how placing juvenile offenders into adult prisons puts them at extreme risk. These juveniles are victimized by other prisoners and prison guards, and when they leave the system, they leave as hardened criminals. The rates of rape, assault, and suicide for juveniles in adult facilities are high, and any chance of saving or rehabilitating these young criminals seems simply abandoned.

Key Words

atrocities	wicked, barbarous, or cruel acts
accentuates	intensifies; emphasizes
Spartan	marked by simplicity, frugality, and the avoidance of luxury and comfort
infraction	violation of rule or law
diminutive	small, tiny
victimization	to be made a victim; subject to deceit or fraud
incapacitation	disabled; unable to operate or function
allocated	distributed or designated; set apart

Nearly a century ago, the juvenile justice system was created because children were subjected to unspeakable atrocities in adult jails and returned to society as hardened criminals. As the system developed, it became clear that housing young offenders and adult inmates together was self-destructive and self-defeating.

Despite the lessons of history, Congress stands poised to reunite adults and juveniles in the same prison system. The "Violent and Repeat Juvenile Offender Act" (S-10) calls for housing juveniles with adult inmates, and would force states to transfer large numbers of young offenders to adult prisons in order to be eligible for federal funds. Child advocates, law enforcement officials and criminologists have urged Congress to consider the destructive effects of placing youths in adult jails and prisons—a substantial body of research shows that placing youths in adult institutions accentuates criminal behavior after release.

In a recent full-page advertisement in *The Washington Times*, sheriffs, district attorneys and legal professionals explained why they think the proposed legislation will make their jobs more difficult: "Lock up a 13-year-old with murderers, rapists and robbers, and guess what he'll want to be when he grows up?" the advertisement read. Even John Dilulio, head of the conservative Council on Crime in America, a group that has provided much of the statistical analytical support for the juvenile crime bill—doesn't think locking children up with adults is a good idea. Dilulio wrote in *The New York Times*, "[M]ost kids who get into serious trouble with the law need adult guidance. And they won't find suitable role models in prison. Jailing youths with adult felons under Spartan conditions will merely produce more street gladiators."

The most disturbing aspect of the new bill is the fear that the thousands of young people slated to be placed in adult prisons and jails are more likely to be raped or assaulted, or to commit suicide. Surveys have documented the higher risk juveniles face when placed in adult institutions, and people who work with youths know the all-too-familiar stories: In Ohio, a 15-year-old girl is sexually assaulted by a deputy jailer after she is placed in an adult jail for a minor infraction; in Kentucky, 30 minutes after a 15-year-old is put in a jail cell following an argument with his mother, the youth hangs himself; in one year, four children being held in Kentucky jails—for offenses ranging from disorderly conduct to status offenses, like running away from home—committed suicide.

While groups as diverse as the American Jail Association and the   5
American Civil Liberties Union have lobbied to keep youths out of the reach of adult inmates, the bills before Congress will result in substantially more children being imprisoned with adults. It is important to revisit the few statistics on how juveniles fare in adult institutions as Congress considers making these dramatic justice system changes.

Too Few Statistics

There is a dearth of data on rape, suicide and assault rates among the 4,000 juveniles who are sentenced to adult prisons, as well as the 65,000 children who pass through the adult jail system every year. Some states lump suicide deaths under the category "unspecified cause," making the problem invisible. Other states and jurisdictions list rape among "inmate assaults"—effectively masking the problem. Academics in this field warn that any statistics on rape are "very conservative at best, since discovery and documentation of this behavior are compromised by the nature of prison conditions, inmate codes and subcultures, and staff attitudes." There also are obvious incentives for prison officials to underreport incidents of rape and suicide because they are administratively embarrassing to the prison system, and could be used as evidence for lawsuits.

Even on the less politically charged measure of the number of "inmate-on-inmate" assaults, it is difficult to formulate a conclusive answer about whether offenders are more likely to be attacked in a juvenile institution or an adult prison. The Corrections Yearbook, an annual survey of the state of America's prisons compiled by the Criminal Justice Institute, suggests that assault rates vary from state to state. The yearbook's statistics show: Inmates are seven times more likely to be referred for medical attention due to an inmate assault in an adult prison in Connecticut than in one of the state's juvenile institutions; in Oklahoma, inmates are 10 times more likely to be referred; and in Kansas, they are 11 times more likely to see a medical professional due to an attack by another inmate. In other states, the difference seen here between reported assaults requiring medical attention in juvenile institutions and adult prisons is reversed.

Several academic surveys more clearly document what happens to youths who are placed in adult institutions.

Suicide

The most recent American study on juvenile suicide in adult institutions and youth facilities was conducted in 1980. Funded by the Office of Juvenile Justice and Delinquency Prevention, Michael G. Flaherty, a researcher with the Community Research Forum at the University of Illinois, surveyed the number of suicides in 1,000 jails and juvenile detention centers. The study found that the suicide rate of juveniles in adult jails is 7.7 times higher than it is in juvenile detention centers.

A more recent report on prison suicides completed by the British 10 Prison Reform Trust supports the findings of the Flaherty study. Analyzing data collected by Her Majesty's Prison Service, the Trust found that while people ages 15 to 21 made up only 13 percent of the prison population, they comprised 22 percent of all suicide deaths.

These studies confirm what law enforcement officials have been telling Congress—children are abused more regularly and driven to desperation more quickly in prison facilities. Adult prisons and jails are not equipped to protect young offenders from these risks. Therefore, these juveniles are more likely to fall through the cracks.

Rape

A 1989 study by a team of researchers, led by Professor Jeffrey Fagan of Columbia University's School of Public Health, compared how youths at a number of juvenile training schools and those serving time in adult prisons reported being treated. Five times as many youths held in adult prisons answered yes to the question, "Has anyone attempted to sexually attack or rape you?" than those held in juvenile institutions. Nearly 10 percent of the youths interviewed reported that another inmate had attempted to sexually attack or rape them in adult prisons, while closer to 1 percent reported the same in juvenile institutions.

Another set of studies concurs that sexual assault is more prevalent in adult than in juvenile institutions. A group of researchers in 1983 found that, among the residents of six juvenile institutions, 9.1 percent of youthful offenders reported being victims of sexual attacks. But a 1996 study of adult inmates in Kansas found that 15 percent reported being "forced to have sex against their will."

Surveys in other countries have found similarly higher rape rates for young offenders in adult institutions. An Australian survey shows that of 183 inmates, ages 18 to 25, surveyed in a New South Wales prison, one-quarter reported being raped or sexually assaulted, and more than half said they lived in fear of it. A recent Canadian survey showed that, among 117 inmates surveyed in a federal prison, 65 incidents involving sexual assault were reported. Among those, the odds of victimization were eight times higher for a 20-year-old inmate than for the oldest inmates in the system. Compared to "nonvictims," the study reports that, "victims tended to be younger, housed in higher security settings, and in the early part of their prison terms."

These statistics seem to fit with what some criminologists call the   15
"prototype" prison rape victim: a young, if not the youngest, inmate within a given institutional system. Fagan points out that "because they are physically diminutive, they [juveniles] are subject to attack . . . They will become somebody's 'girlfriend' very, very fast."

Fagan's study, which found such alarming statistics on youth rape in prisons, also found that children placed with adults were twice as likely to report being "beaten up" by staff. Nearly one in 10 juveniles reported being assaulted by staff. The juveniles in adult prisons also were 50 percent more likely to report being attacked with a weapon.

Conclusion

Whatever kind of threat you choose, be it rape, assault or suicide, prison is a most dangerous place for young offenders. But the frightening character of these statistics raises a larger issue in terms of how effective the new juvenile justice bill will be from a crime control perspective. As Fagan's study notes, "Victimization by violence has well-established consequences for subsequent violence and crime, and victims of rape or sexual assault are more likely to exhibit aggression toward women and children." The authors write "Although [juvenile] transfers decrease community risk through lengthy incapacitation of violent youngsters, the social costs of imprisoning young offenders in adult facilities may be paid in later crime and violence upon their release."

Each of the research areas represents crucial information currently being ignored by Congress. The present research bodes poorly for the large numbers of juveniles who will be transferred to adult prisons, as well as the children who will be jailed alongside adults under proposed legislation.

All 50 states have laws allowing juveniles to be tried as adults. During the past two years, 42 states have toughened those laws. Clearly, this is not an area that requires urgent federal intervention to spur the states into action.

The Justice Policy Institute recommends that Congress put much- 20 needed resources into a two-year, state-by-state evaluation of the changes in America's juvenile justice system. We further recommend that Congress hold off on sweeping and ill-advised legislation at this time. During that period, it is our recommendation that funds be specifically allocated to research:

- The different reoffense rates of similar groups of youthful offenders held in juvenile and adult institutions;
- The different rates of sexual and physical victimizations and suicides of juveniles in adult institutions, as compared to the rates in juvenile facilities; and
- A comparison of the different rates of juvenile crime in states with a large number of youthful offenders in adult jails, as compared to the rates of states with few or no juveniles in adult institutions.

No legislation that would reverse a century of juvenile justice reform and put thousands of young people into the adult prison system should be undertaken until this kind of research is conducted.

What Did You Read?

1. What is the Violent and Repeat Juvenile Offenders Act (S-10)?
2. What are some of the reasons the author presents for not locking up juveniles with adults?
3. Are statistics of rape of young offenders different in other countries?

4. What does the author hope to achieve by writing the article? In other words, what does he recommend?

What Do You Think?

1. In your opinion, should offenders under the age of 18 be treated differently than older offenders?
2. Do you think that the threat of physical violence is sufficient reason to keep younger offenders out of adult prisons?
3. What kinds of proposals would be helpful to young offenders so that they do not become hardened adult criminals?

How Was It Done?

1. What destructive effects of placing youths in adult prisons is the article centered on?
2. List some of the authorities or references that the authors use to give substance to their explanations.
3. How effective is the conclusion in offering the Justice Policy Institute's recommendation concerning America's juvenile court system?

Adult Consequences for Young Offenders

Adam Rich

Adam Rich reports on this nation's increasing practice of trying youths as adults. Rich takes a look at the history of the juvenile justice system, and he presents statistics that suggest that youths who are minorities are more likely to be tried as adults than white youths are. While the public perception is that youth crime is rampant, Rich notes the reality is youth crime is a relatively small portion of overall crime. He questions whether public support for trying youths as adults will continue as more information about its effects becomes available.

Key Words

cherubic	angelic; related to a beautiful, winged child
rehabilitation	restored to a good and useful state
homicide	murder
referendum	a public vote on a measure
egregious	conspicuous; flagrant; obviously bad
heinous	evil; abominable
enumerated	listed or numbered

recidivism   relapsing into criminal behavior
statutory   of or relating to laws
discretionary   exercised at one's own choosing

Kids in elementary school and teens not old enough to sign contracts, drive, marry, leave school or vote can be tried as adults in many states. States are moving more and more youthful offenders into adult court. Supporters say young criminals have to face tough sanctions.

When he was 11, Nathaniel Abraham fatally shot a stranger in the back of the head with a rifle. Last January, at the age of 13, he became the youngest American ever to be convicted, as an adult, of murder.

With his cherubic face and terrified eyes, Abraham quickly became the poster child for a 1997 Michigan law that is part of a sweeping and controversial trend. In the 1990s, every state but Nebraska either expanded the criteria that determines when a juvenile case can be transferred to the adult system, or expedited the process by which prosecutors make the transfers. Nationwide, the number of juvenile cases waived to the adult system leaped from 6,800 in 1987 to 10,000 in 1996.

Back to the Future?

Before Illinois established the first juvenile court in 1899, children as young as 7 could be tried by adult courts. But by the 1920s, all states had followed Illinois' lead in creating separate juvenile courts, where the focus was on rehabilitation rather than adult-sized punishment. Yet even as this new view toward juveniles took hold, there was a consensus that it might be appropriate to treat young offenders like adults in some cases.

Today, the age at which an offender is considered a juvenile varies   5 from state to state. In most states, there is no minimum age for transferring juveniles to the adult system in certain cases, while in others it is as young as 10. Between 1986 and 1997 states more than doubled the number of juvenile offenders they sent to adult prisons.

This trend comes at a time when the juvenile crime rate is actually declining. Though the rate peaked in 1994, after seven years of growth, it dropped 37 percent between 1993 and 1998. In that same period, juvenile homicide declined 56 percent. For youths under the age of 13, the homicide rate hit its lowest level since 1965.

Polls suggest there is a gap between public perception of juvenile crime and reality. Some attribute this to heavy media coverage of violent attacks such as school shootings. A Gallup poll found that Americans think juveniles commit 43 percent of violent crime, when in fact the real number is 12 percent. A poll by *The Wall Street Journal* found that 71 percent of respondents fear a shooting at their school, even though the odds of a fatal shooting in any given school are 1 in 2 million.

In light of this data, a University of California criminologist told *The Christian Science Monitor* that getting tough on juvenile crime now amounted to a "a solution in search of a problem."

States Get Tough on Juveniles

Nevertheless, states continue to move toward treating more young offenders like adults. The latest example is in California, where voters approved a juvenile crime referendum on March 7. One provision in the initiative, Proposition 21, requires that juveniles 14 or older be automatically sent to adult court if they are charged with murder or specified sex offenses. In Tennessee, a commission appointed by Gov. Don Sundquist has recommended a similar measure for those 15 and older.

Supporters of tougher measures say the current system is ill   10
equipped to deal with the changing nature of juvenile crime. "Our juvenile justice system is now over 50 years old," said California Sen. Chuck Poochigian, a major supporter of Proposition 21. "When it was crafted originally, we were dealing with a much different type of crime. Regrettably, we have seen, over the course of the decades, a dramatic increase in the number and scope of egregious and heinous crimes."

Poochigian said that Proposition 21 specifically targets gang-related crime, a particularly serious problem in California.

Tennessee Sen. David Fowler argues that juveniles who commit serious crimes should not be let off the hook simply because of their age "because the people who commit the enumerated heinous acts are not delinquents, they are criminals."

Proponents of the new laws insist that the system needs to protect society from violent and hardened juveniles—offenders for whom rehabilitation is unlikely. Critics, on the other hand, insist that treating kids like adults fails to take into account developmental and cognitive differences that make minors less able to form legal intent. Furthermore, critics say that adult treatment ignores the possibility of rehabilitation, increases recidivism rates and disproportionately affects minorities.

One interesting characteristic of the debate is that it blurs traditional political lines. For example, California Gov. Gray Davis, a Democrat, supported the strict provisions of Proposition 21, which had originally been proposed by his Republican predecessor, Pete Wilson.

In Texas, a state not known for being soft on crime, the Legislature   15
increased funding for the state agency that oversees the juvenile crime program, and the number of cases waived to adult court has dropped

from 596 in 1994 to 433 in 1998. "We had the resources to provide good education and rehabilitation programs," said Steve Robinson, the director of the Texas Youth Commission.

Three Types of Transfer

States use three methods to transfer juveniles to adult court. Judicial waiver gives a juvenile court judge the discretion to transfer a case to the adult system. Concurrent jurisdiction lets the prosecutor decide to try the offender as an adult or a juvenile. Statutory exclusion automatically transfers cases to the adult system based on statute-specified criteria like age and offense.

Most of the disagreement is over the criteria for and type of transfers.

In 1997, 46 states allowed for some type of judicial waiver to transfer juveniles into the adult system and most have a combination of transfer provisions.

Prior to the 1997 Michigan law, judges were able to waive juvenile cases into the adult system, but "it just never happened," said Sen. William Van Regenmorter, chair of the Senate Judiciary Committee. Van Regenmorter sponsored the successful bill to allow juveniles 16 and under to be tried as adults at the prosecutor's discretion.

Data is unclear on the effect of giving prosecutors, rather than 20 judges the right to approve transfers. In 1995, Florida prosecutors directly filed 7,000 juvenile offenders to the adult system, nearly as many as the 9,700 cases transferred by judges nationwide. A study by the Justice Policy Institute found that only 29 percent of the cases transferred by prosecutors in Florida involved juveniles charged with violent offenses. Fifty-five percent were property offenses, and 11 percent were drug offenses. In that same year, the national percentage of transferred cases that involved violent crime was 47 percent.

The results of direct filing are much different in Connecticut than in Florida. Rep. Michael Lawlor, who chairs the House Judiciary Committee, estimates that each year, "only 60 or 70 cases are being prosecuted in adult court, and only 5 or 10 actually result in lengthy prison sentences."

One difference is that in Connecticut, offenders 16 and older, and the most violent felons younger than 16 are transferred automatically to the adult system. But despite this difference, the Connecticut example still casts doubt on the notion that prosecutorial discretion leads to a flood of juvenile transfers.

Lawlor suggested that one reason for the difference between Florida and Connecticut is that Connecticut does not elect prosecutors, allowing them to be relatively insulated from political influence. Lawlor added that prosecutors often prefer young offenders to stay in juvenile court because adult courts are bogged down with many serious charges and might not have time to treat the juvenile offender as seriously or harshly as the juvenile courts.

Rather than leave transfer decisions to prosecutors or judges, the Tennessee proposal and California initiative automatically send certain juvenile offenders to the adult system. Legislators who seek consistent guidelines favor the option of statutory exclusion, but others contend taking discretionary power away from the court system is unfair.

"Each case is different," said Tennessee Rep. Keith Westmoreland, 25 a former deputy sheriff who is generally viewed as conservative on public safety issues. "If we make it all automatic, we don't need judges anymore. We can just put it all in a computer and let it spit it out."

Sanctions vs. Second Chances

Proponents of tougher sanctions point to declining crime rates and say that getting tough deters potentially violent kids.

"The goal is not to put as many juveniles into the adult system as possible," said Poochigian of California's Proposition 21. "It's to discourage violent behavior and to make sure [young offenders] know that the consequences will be swift, certain and tough."

Yet research suggests that among juveniles charged with the same offenses, those who go through the adult system may be more likely to commit a new offense than those who go through the juvenile system. A Florida study, published in the journal *Crime and Delinquency*, found that juveniles who were sent to the adult system were one-third more likely to be rearrested than their counterparts in the juvenile system. The study also found that juveniles coming out of the adult system committed new offenses almost twice as fast. Similar studies have found comparable results in Pennsylvania, New York and New Jersey.

However, these studies are not conclusive because they do not account for all differences between those sent to the adult system and those who stay in juvenile court. New studies are under way that seek to account for factors such as gang affiliation, drug use and criminal history.

Some argue that recidivism rates are higher for juveniles sent to 30 adult prison because they face harsher, more violent conditions than in juvenile facilities. "If we're turning out more hardened criminals, we're asking for trouble," said New Jersey Assemblywoman Mary Previte. "Yet, that's exactly the direction we're going in."

The Race Factor

Previte and others also cite data that shows there is a disproportionate effect of transfer provisions on minorities. In 1999, the U.S. Department of Justice's Office of Juvenile Justice and Delinquency Protection reported that blacks were more likely than whites to be waived from juvenile to adult court. The report shows that from 1990 to 1994, whites made up 31 percent of juvenile transfer felony defendants, while blacks and other races made up 69 percent. In 1998, 95 percent of juveniles serving time in adult prison for drug charges were minorities, and a Feb. 14 article in *Time* reported that in 1996, every juvenile serving time in adult prison in Texas and Connecticut was a minority.

"Let's face it: most of the children that get waived into adult court have dark faces," Previte said. "They are black, they are Latino. The white kid that sells a bag of cocaine at the high school maybe has a hotshot lawyer, who can get him into treatment. The black or Latino child goes into the criminal justice system."

Van Regenmorter argued that, at least in Michigan, the race issue is a red herring. "The law in Michigan is color blind," he said. "Race is simply a diversionary tactic used by the defense bar."

In California, a study conducted by the Justice Policy Institute found that minority juvenile offenders were 2.5 times more likely than whites to be tried as adults, and 8.3 times more likely to be incarcerated in the adult system. At press time, California Sen. John Vasconcellos, chair of the Senate Public Safety Committee, was planning to hold hearings on these findings.

One Proposition 21 supporter was disturbed by the possibility of 35 racial bias. "I'm a minority and it obviously bothers me that [Proposition 21 might disproportionately] effect those of the Latino race," said California Rep. Rod Pacheco.

Ultimately however, Pacheco and Poochigian agree that it is crucial to stay the course. "[The effect on minorities] is relevant and we ought to ascertain why it is so, if it is so. But that's not an argument against dealing in a very firm way with serious and violent felonies," Poochigian said.

A Popular Approach

One option that is increasingly popular with states is to give judges the option of combined juvenile and adult sentencing. OJJDP reports that by 1997, 20 states allowed "blended sentencing."

Under the 1997 Michigan law sponsored by Van Regenmorter, the judge in the Abraham case had the option of sending the defendant to a juvenile facility and reserving the right to decide on an adult sanction if he was not rehabilitated by age 21. Nevertheless, the judge rebuked the state Legislature's approach and sentenced Abraham to a strictly juvenile sentence, a decision Van Regenmorter called "a huge mistake."

Previte, who is also an administrator of a center for juvenile offenders in New Jersey, supports blended sentencing because it teaches juveniles to be responsible for their actions. "Over the last 26 years,

I've worked with the most dangerous children in New Jersey," Previte said. "I've looked thousands of children in the eyes and told them. 'You earn consequences. If you do a bad thing and commit another crime, you're gone.' Our kids need to be taught that there are choices."

An Upward Trend

The trend toward making it easier to transfer juvenile offenders to 40 adult court shows no sign of slowing down. In 1998, Congress made state eligibility for some block grants contingent on the implementation of certain transfer provisions. Legislation in conference committee as of February would make it easier to try juveniles in federal court. In the next couple of years, it seems likely that many more states will consider blended sentencing, based on interest expressed by officials across the country.

While the arguments against increased juvenile transfers have yet to make much of an impact, that could change if the data on recidivism and discrimination against minorities takes hold. The financial costs associated with more transfers also might become an issue. But for now, the public perception of an unchecked juvenile crime epidemic is echoed by elected officials.

"Opponents of juvenile justice reform think that our laws are tough enough already," Poochigian of California said. "I simply disagree."

What Did You Read?

1. According to Rich, why are we so adamant about trying juveniles as adults if they commit only 12 percent of the crime?

2. What is recidivism? How does it relate to minors and crime?

3. What are some of the reasons minority juveniles end up in the criminal justice system more than whites, according to Bach?

4. What is "blended sentencing"?

What Do You Think?

1. At what age do you think someone ought to be tried as an adult? Why?

2. Do you have a problem with the fact that the age at which an offender is considered a juvenile differs from state to state? Explain.

3. Do you agree or disagree with Van Regemorter when he argues that race plays no factor in the prosecution of juvenile offenders? Explain.

4. What problems can you see with the use of blended sentencing?

How Was It Done?

1. What "trend" concerning juvenile offenders is the article centered on?

2. What myth exists, according to Rich, concerning the perception of juvenile crime and the reality of it?

3. What primary appeal to values does Rich make for keeping children out of prison?

When the Evidence Lies

Belinda Luscombe et al.

Belinda Luscombe and others examine the actions of a forensic scientist whose errors in the analysis of DNA evidence led to convictions of two innocent men. The question of how scientific evidence can be mishandled, misinterpreted, and misunderstood goes to the heart of using DNA evidence in criminal investigations. Also, Luscomb et al. point out that the close relationship between police, district attorneys' offices, and forensic scientists could lead scientists to get the results the police and DA want. While the focus of the article is on the actions of a single scientist, the question is clear: How many more forensic scientists are making similar mistakes and getting innocent people convicted?

Key Words

forensic	of or relating to the application of scientific knowledge to legal problems, especially criminal investigations
compelling	forceful; convincing
meted	given out by measure
exonerated	freed from blame, responsibility, or hardship; declared innocent
blatant	obvious
reprimand	a severe or formal reproof; criticism for a fault or error
serology	the science that investigates serums, their reactions, and properties
retaliation	revenge; paid in kind

Jim Fowler has been struck twice by lightning. A retired house painter in Oklahoma City, Okla., Fowler lived through his 19-year-old son Mark's arrest in 1985 for murdering three people in a grocery-store holdup. Mark was sentenced to death. A year later Fowler's mother Anne Laura was raped and murdered, and a man named Robert Lee

Miller Jr. was sentenced to die for the crime. The same Oklahoma City police department forensic scientist, Joyce Gilchrist, testified at both trials. But DNA evidence later proved she was wrong about Miller. He was released after 10 years on death row, and a man previously cleared by Gilchrist was charged with the crime. Fowler can't help wondering if Gilchrist's testimony was equally inept at the trial of his son Mark, who was executed in January.

Last week gave Fowler even more reason to wonder. A state judge ordered a man named Jeffrey Pierce released after serving 15 years of a 65-year sentence for rape. Gilchrist placed him at the scene of the crime, but DNA evidence proved he was not the rapist. In response, Oklahoma Governor Frank Keating launched a review of every one of the thousands of cases Gilchrist touched between 1980 and 1993, starting with 12 in which death sentences were handed down. But in another 11 of her cases, the defendants have already been put to death. The state is giving the Oklahoma Indigent Defense System $725,000 to hire two attorneys and conduct DNA testing of any evidence analyzed by Gilchrist that led to a conviction. A preliminary FBI study of eight cases found that in at least five, she had made outright errors or overstepped "the acceptable limits of forensic science." Gilchrist got convictions by matching hair samples with a certainty other forensic scientists found impossible to achieve. She also appears to have withheld evidence from the defense and failed to perform tests that could have cleared defendants.

It's a bitter convolution of fate that Gilchrist should be based in Oklahoma City, the last place one would expect to find compelling arguments against the death penalty. Her story can't help but give Oklahomans pause about the quality of justice meted out by their courts. Says Gilchrist's lawyer, Melvin Hall: "The criticism of her around here is second only to that of Timothy McVeigh." But the allegations also underscore a national problem: the sometimes dangerously persuasive power of courtroom science. Juries tend to regard forensic evidence more highly than they regard witnesses because it is purportedly more objective. But forensic scientists work so closely with the police and district attorneys that their objectivity cannot be taken for granted.

Gilchrist told *Time* in an interview last week that she's bewildered by her predicament. "I'm just one entity within a number of people who testify," she says. "They're keying on the negative and not looking at the good work I did." In her 21-year career with the Oklahoma City police, she had an unbroken string of positive job evaluations and was Civilian Police Employee of the Year in 1985. Her ability to sway juries and win convictions earned her the nickname "Black Magic." In 1994 she was promoted from forensic chemist to supervisor. Until recently, Hall says, she did not have "a bad piece of paper in her file."

Now Gilchrist is on paid leave; in June she will face a two-day hearing to decide whether the police department should fire her. Meanwhile, her reputation has been shattered.

The hammer blow came when Pierce, a landscaper who was con- 5 victed of rape in 1986, was released last week after DNA testing exonerated him. He had been found guilty despite a clean record and plausible alibi largely because of Gilchrist's analysis of hair at the crime scene. "I'm just the one who opened the door," said Pierce. "There will be a lot more coming out behind me."

Pierce lost 15 years, his marriage and the chance to see his twin boys grow up. But some fear there were others who paid even more dearly: the 11 executed defendants. The Oklahoma attorney general has temporarily shut the gate on execution of the 12 still on death row in whose trials Gilchrist was involved. While the D.A.'s office believes that the convictions will stand, these cases will be the first to be reconsidered. Defense lawyers fear that the innocent who took plea bargains in the face of her expertise will never come to light.

Gilchrist told *Time*, "There may be a few differences because of DNA analysis," but she is confident most of her findings will be confirmed. "I worked hard, long and consistently on every case," she says. "I always based my opinion on scientific findings." She insists she didn't overstate those findings to please the D.A.'s office or secure convictions. "I feel comfortable with the conclusions I drew."

But defense lawyers say the Gilchrist investigation is long overdue. Her work has been making colleagues queasy for years. In January 1987, John Wilson, a forensic scientist with the Kansas City police crime lab, filed a complaint about her with the Southwestern Association of Forensic Scientists. (The association declined to take action.) Jack Dempsey Pointer, president of the Oklahoma Criminal Defense Lawyers Association, says his group has been fighting for an investigation "almost since the time she went to work" at the lab. "We have been screaming in the wind, and nobody has been listening."

Police Chief M.T. Berry says it wasn't until 1999 that the department had any reason to be suspicious about her work. That's when federal Judge Ralph Thompson lit into her for "untrue" testimony and the "blatant withholding of unquestionably exculpatory evidence" in the rape and murder trial of Alfred Brian Mitchell. (Thompson overturned the rape conviction but let the murder stand.) In March 2000 Gilchrist was put out to pasture at a police equine lab, where she says she had to do "demeaning tasks" like count test tubes.

Then this January, a devastating memo from Byron Boshell, cap- 10 tain of the police department's laboratory-services division, thudded onto Berry's desk. It filled four three-ring binders and noted reversals and reprimands the courts had handed Gilchrist, as well as the issues the professional journals had taken with her work.

Cases in Question

Mark Andrew Fowler

EXECUTED

CONVICTED Triple murder, robbery

THE CASE Fowler said he was a lookout and a co-defendant killed the victims. Gilchrist's evidence, questioned by defense experts, helped place Fowler at the scene.

Malcolm Rent Johnson

EXECUTED

CONVICTED First-degree murder

THE CASE Defense experts said Gilchrist's testimony was "wrong" and "misleading." An appeals court upheld the death penalty; the victim's property was at Johnson's house.

Loyd Winford LaFevers

EXECUTED

CONVICTED First-degree murder, third-degree arson

THE CASE Received a stay last year after DNA tests showed the victim's blood was not on his pants, as Gilchrist had testified, but executed Jan. 30.

Alfred Brain Mitchell

ON DEATH ROW

CONVICTED First-degree murder

THE CASE A U.S. district judge ruled Gilchrist's testimony "untrue" and overturned Mitchell's rape and sodomy convictions. The one for murder stands.

Curtis Edward McCarty

ON DEATH ROW

CONVICTED First-degree murder

THE CASE Conviction set aside in 1988, in part because Gilchrist gave an "improper opinion." McCarty was retried, found guilty and is appealing the death penalty.

Robert Lee Miller Jr.

RELEASED

EXONERATED First-degree murder

THE CASE Miller spent 10 years on death row for rape and murder, after Gilchrist testified hairs from a crime scene were consistent with his. DNA tests proved otherwise.

Under her supervision, it said, evidence was missing in cases in which new trials had been granted or were under review, and rape evidence had been destroyed after two years, long before the statute of limitations had expired. Gilchrist explained last week that she always followed established procedures with evidence and that the memo was simply the department's way of getting rid of her after she reported the sexual harassment of a colleague. "There is no doubt this [memo] is retaliation," says Gilchrist.

How did her career last this long? "She couldn't have got away with this if she weren't supported by prosecutors, ignored by judges and police who did nothing," says Wilson, who filed the original complaint against her 14 years ago. "The police department was asleep at the switch." The D.A.'s office simply says Gilchrist should not be tried in the media. But one prosecutor, who declined to be named, lays blame on the aggressive tactics of D.A. Bob Macy, who's proud to have sent more people to death row than any other active D.A. in the country.

Which raises a more troubling question. How many other Gilchrists are there? In Oklahoma City, Chief Berry has ordered a wholesale review of the serology/DNA lab. And while Governor Keating insists that no one has been executed who shouldn't have been, Pointer and the local defense-lawyers association plan to re-examine the cases of the 11 executed inmates. "Nobody cares about the dead," he says. "The state is not going to spend money to find out that they executed someone who might have been innocent."

What Did You Read?

1. Many people assume that scientists are objective in their findings. However, according to this essay, in what ways may forensic scientists face pressure to get results that lead to convictions in the courtroom?

2. How many already-executed defendants in Oklahoma might have had their cases affected by Gilchrist's errors?

3. Why was Gilchrist able to work for so long after problems with her testimonies became well known?

What Do You Think?

1. What effect does the discovery of errors in DNA analysis have on public support for the criminal justice system and the death penalty in particular?

2. What, if anything, can be done to make reparations to those who have been found guilty due to incompetent or false testimony by forensic scientists?

3. Why do you suppose prosecutors like Bob Macy are eager to send people to death row?

4. Can we justify continued use of the death penalty when cases of error and false testimony have led to convictions? How?

How Was It Done?

1. The article is structured around what individual? Explain the importance of that.

2. How does the list of cases at the end of the article help to dramatize and substantiate the authors' claim?

3. What kind of factual evidence gives primary weight to proving the authors' thesis?

12

Jobs in the 21st Century

What will you do when you leave college? For many students, this question is one of the most important they will need to answer. Part of the answer involves work. According to federal labor experts, there are over 20,000 official job titles. How is it possible to pick what you want from so many choices? Not only that, the workplace of today is drastically different from the workplace of a generation ago. No longer are people hired by a company that assumes an almost patriarchal power to provide lifelong employment and stability. Instead, in the fight to stay profitable, companies are no longer showing loyalty to their employees, cutting high-salaried workers for temporary workers, shipping jobs overseas, or using technology that allows them to cut their workforce.

In response, employees have begun to see that they must be competitive, too. They change employers frequently, change positions, and with new training and education, even change careers. The employees themselves are also changing: no longer is the WASP male the typical employee. Minorities and women are fully involved in the workforce, at all levels, and their presence in law school, medical school, and business school is attaining parity with white men. Also, many people continue to work at careers they love long after their 65th birthday, once the traditional retirement age.

The result may appear chaotic, and for those just starting out, a few guidelines may be helpful to sort out the challenges facing any new potential worker. In fact, a virtual cottage industry has developed of books, websites, and counselors that all purport to assist job seekers. Their promise is to help people find careers that will do more than provide money: they will find careers that provide fulfillment.

Part of this help is finding out where the jobs are. Job growth in the near future is expected to be largely in the areas of technology and health care. Other areas of growth include entertainment, education, and funeral services. However, as is often the case, people choose jobs based on individual desire, not national trends. How will you choose what to do? One comforting thought is that today's false step no longer means that you have ruined your opportunities for tomorrow. You do, though, need to take that first step.

In this final chapter, the Writing Lesson prepares you to write a research paper, a common end-of-the-semester assignment. The Writing Lesson presents the basics of doing research. The technique described is specifically designed to take you from larger, more generalized materials to more specific sources that cover a narrow range of the subject area. The idea is to conduct a search that is thorough yet manageable. Emphasis is placed on understanding and assessing the quality of research materials, which can be an overlooked aspect of research. The Writing Assignment then gives you an opportunity to investigate in depth this chapter's theme, the job market of today and tomorrow.

THE MAIN EVENT READING

Expanding Your Comfort Zone

Sandy Anderson

In her book, Women in Career & Life Transitions, *Anderson addresses how people hold themselves back from pursuing their dream jobs. In this section, she writes about how people can figure out just what exactly is holding them back. Included in this section are five barriers to change, and the internal obstacles that must be overcome.*

Key Words

autopilot	doing things without conscious decision making
subconscious	a level of understanding not immediately available to our conscious state
insight	knowledge; understanding
scenario	an imagined sequence of events
belittle	insult or degrade

"Avoiding danger is no safer in the long run than outright exposure. Life is either a daring adventure or nothing."

—Helen Keller

The comfort zone is that place where we perform well—practically on autopilot. When we move outside our comfort zone, we often feel anxious and stressed. These emotions result from the fear of doing something less than perfect or making a mistake. Our self-image feels threatened.

The reason we feel anxious and stressed outside our comfort zone is that our self-image works like a regulating mechanism. Just as a thermostat controls room temperature by sending electrical impulses to start or stop the heater whenever the room is below or above the temperature setting, we're controlled by tension when we move either above or below our comfort zone. Our self-image is the subconscious picture, or setting, of where we belong. It regulates our behavior by allowing us to move above or below our current comfort zone only slightly without experiencing stress and anxiety.

Hence, stepping out of our comfort zone to make a change involves risk, but with that risk comes opportunity—the opportunity for personal growth. During the process of change, it's normal to expect anxiety, stress, and old fears to be awakened. Unfortunately, the downside of living a "safe" life—resisting the scary emotions that come with change—is that it's like being in prison, and the boundaries get tighter and narrower as we get older. change means risk

In this chapter you'll be putting your top three career choices through the "barrier test" to find out how much you're willing to expand your comfort zone to make each choice a reality. We'll discuss how you can expand your comfort zone and take more risks to achieve your goals. The ultimate goal is to build increased self-belief and confidence so that you're ready and willing to take the first step.

The Barrier Test

You've done a lot of research on your top three career choices. You know what background and experience are required to do each job. Now comes the true test. Are you willing to do what it takes to achieve at least one of your career goals? 5
first test

In the following sections you'll find five barriers that commonly stand in the way of taking that first step in a new direction. Run each of your top career choices through the barrier test to see what you're willing to do (or not willing to do) to achieve it. Take notes in your journal for each career choice.

This screening device is a great way to shed light on what stands in the way of your dreams. By looking at each barrier one at a time for each career choice, you can break down your fears into digestible bites that you can easily deal with.

Time

Have you ever noticed how much busywork you do on a day-to-day basis? We often think we don't have enough time to change directions because we're so caught up in the routine of our everyday lives. A lot of our time is spent caring for others and pursuing the current chapter we're on. We all have certain roles, responsibilities, and commitments. The desire for change is knocking on your door—now. Do you tend to say, "No. Go away. I'm too busy. I don't have time to make a change"?

In Chapter 1, "Where Are You Now?" you did an exercise (Exercise 1.1, "Time Commitments") to see how you spend your time. You wrote down estimates of your current commitments. You also projected the amount of time you want to spend on each commitment. Take a look at your estimates to see where you're spending your time. What areas are you willing to cut back on to free up time to move in a new direction? The projections you made about the time you want to spend on each commitment will probably give you some insight.

If you're not willing to take a look at how you spend your time, then you might question how much you genuinely want to pursue a new direction. Maybe you're not ready at this time. There's usually a lot more time available than you think, because much time is wasted doing things you don't enjoy or appreciate. Wouldn't you be happier spending your time working toward something you desire instead of muddling along in your current routine, where you feel miserably safe?

How real is your desire for change?

10

Money

Do you allow money, or the lack thereof, to stand in your way? The most popular "excuse" goes something like this: "I can't change careers because I'm making a good income in my current line of work—income that I (or we) need to get by. If I change course and start over from square one, I'll have to forgo my salary and I (or my family) won't survive."

Maybe you want to pursue a new direction that will make little or no money at first—maybe it will even cost money, if you want to start a business or go back to school, for instance—and you feel pressured to take a job just for the income.

Look back again at another exercise in Chapter 1 (Exercise 1.2, "Financial Position") on itemizing your current monthly income and expenses as well as your goals for the areas you want to change. You might find that, as with your time, there are places where you can cut back (e.g., take fewer or less expensive vacations, eat out less often and microwave instead, shop for bargains instead of paying full price at a department store).

How doable is this?

If you have a partner who is earning income, can you forgo your income and live on your partner's for a year? I interviewed a number of home business owners—women and men—who did this in order to launch their business. They left well-paying jobs to start a business from home and be there to raise their children. They cut every corner possible to make their dream a reality. They made sacrifices and did without a lot of material things.

No matter what your situation—even if you're a divorced or sin-   15
gle parent—don't allow money to stand in your way. Open the door and investigate your options. If you're not willing to do this, and money continues to be your stopping block, then you might not be ready to pursue a new direction yet.

Education and Experience

You identified the education and experience required and preferred for each of your top three job choices in Chapter 4, "Evaluating Your Training and Educational Needs." Are you willing to complete the education and training that are lacking? Again, if your answer comes back around to doubting whether you have enough money or time to do these things, then you might want to pursue a career choice that's more in line with the education and experience you currently possess. Sometimes we fool ourselves into thinking that we want something, but in reality we're not willing to invest the time, energy, or money necessary to achieve it.

Expectations of Others

Are you living your life according to what others expect of you, or are you living the life you choose? If you pursue certain directions to please others and forgo your own desires, you're bound to end up angry and frustrated. You'll burn out in this situation. On the other hand, if you follow your dreams, you have so much energy to give   almost a
to others that you'll be amazed. You'll ooze with happiness and   cliché
enthusiasm.

Are you willing to deal with letdown, disapproval, or lack of support when you pursue a direction you choose that might not be favorable to others? Ask yourself whether it's more important for you to follow your instincts and do what makes you happy or to do what others advocate.

Values

In Chapter 1 (Exercise 1.4, "Career and Life Planning") you fantasized what your ideal scenario would be in all areas of your life. You visualized the kind of lifestyle that's desirable to you. This exercise put you in tune with your values—the things in life that really matter to you.

For each of your top career choices, check to see whether pursuing   20
each direction will conflict with any of your values—the ideal scenarios you visualized for everything from spending time with your children and the amount of leisure time you desire, to your diet, exercise,

and spiritual well-being. If you put little value on getting dressed up in professional clothes for work and your career choice requires that (or it's strongly preferred), then you might have a conflict. On the other hand, you might be able to overcome this conflict by working for yourself instead of for someone else.

The idea is to put on your critical thinking cap and see if you have any values that conflict with your top career choices. And with each conflict you find, ask yourself whether it is something that can be overcome or worked around or whether it is best to close the door on this particular career choice because it clearly conflicts with your values.

The Internal Obstacles to Change

how we hold ourselves back
Often the hardest part of a change process is getting started. Things stand in the way. Although we might not be able to reverse situations that are external to us—such as violence, aging parents, divorce, a dysfunctional family, or disease—we can change the internal obstacles inspired by others and by ourselves that keep us from being and doing our best.

When I speak of "internal" obstacles, I'm referring to obstacles of a psychological nature. Let's discuss the three most popular internal obstacles that keep us in our comfort zone: fear of change, negative self-beliefs, and procrastination. Then we'll look at a variety of ways to overcome them.

Fear of Change

The fear of change is more or less a generalized anxiety that keeps us from moving forward toward our dreams. When we stay immobile, our anxiety can turn into mild or severe depression. It's almost as if our dreams are a magnet, and the closer we move toward identifying the steps needed to realize them, the more our anxiety and discomfort build.

The important thing to understand is that these anxious feelings 25 are normal, and they pass when you begin to take action and get involved in the process of "becoming" your dream. The fear will dissipate, much as it does when you give a speech. At first you have anticipation anxiety, and the butterflies are running amok in your stomach. But as soon as you open your mouth and start talking, you feel a sense of relief. And as you really get into the speech and forget about yourself, the nervousness vanishes; the butterflies fly into formation, and you've got control.

If you confine yourself to a safe and familiar existence, you place overwhelming limitations on your chance for happiness. By breaking out of old routines and busting through obstacles as if there are no limitations, you have many opportunities to achieve your goals. This is all part of the process of stepping out of your comfort zone. In order to take advantage of opportunities, you must take a risk. As soon as you see progress, your fear will diminish.

Negative Self-Beliefs

Are you allowing situations and people from your past to hold you back? We all have emotional baggage from our upbringings. Our minds are like tape recorders that pick up on and remember everything we hear. As children, the significant people in our lives strongly influenced the image we created of ourselves. Our tape recorders worked overtime when we were exposed to comments such as "You're no good" and "You'll never amount to anything."

Hearing this abuse in our younger years takes its toll on our self-image if we grow to believe these belittling accusations. It stifles our

---

Connie, Age 43

specific,
developed
example

All her life, Connie's father made it clear that girls should grow up and find husbands to take care of them. When Connie wanted to go to college after high school, her father wasn't at all supportive. "I was determined to make my own way, with or without my dad's support," Connie says. "Because he practically shoved the idea of 'finding a husband' down my throat, that was the last thing I wanted to do. I wanted to be able to support myself first."

Connie bounced around from job to job, sometimes holding as many as three jobs at once. "I had no idea what I wanted to do," Connie says, "but in the back of my mind, the one thing I knew for certain was that I wanted to attend college and get my bachelor's degree." Connie allowed a lack of money and time to stand in her way, until she wound up feeling so depressed she sought counseling. She says, "I was tired of putting off my dream of going to school. It was eating away at me, but I had no one to really talk to about it. I finally found a great counselor, who I exchanged services with. I had started cleaning houses part time, and Mary Jo hired me to clean her house each week in exchange for a counseling session."

The counseling was just what Connie needed to work through her depression and take small steps toward going back to school. "I've always been self-sufficient and was embarrassed that I procrastinated and couldn't get going on my own," she says. "That's just not like me. But as far as I'm concerned, those counseling sessions were a major turning point that changed my attitude and changed my life."

Today Connie is a practicing attorney. She made it on her own without any emotional or financial assistance from her parents. Her biggest accomplishment yet? "I recently got married, and my husband and I adopted a son. Having a loving and supportive family of my own means everything to me!"

performance and makes us angry. When we're angry, we have a tendency to blame everything and everyone but ourselves—parents, teachers, bosses, the economy, the government—instead of working on what's going on inside. It's always easier and more convenient to assume that the blame lies elsewhere or with others than to hold ourselves accountable for our hurt feelings.

As adults, the anger and negative beliefs can continue to disrupt our lives. If the significant people we've acquired these beliefs from are no longer around to belittle us, our minds take over and do the pop psy-chology talking for them. This negative self-talk or chatter keeps us paralyzed. How can you make a move when you're telling yourself, "My family might abandon me" or "Everyone will hate me for doing this" or "I might go broke" or "I'll probably fail"? The good news is that we can use positive self-talk to combat negative self-talk, and I'll talk about that shortly.

Procrastination

Procrastination offers a great place to hide when you want to put 30 something off until tomorrow. It leaves you feeling fatigued and behind. We tell ourselves that we're simply "gathering energy" for our new direction, but in reality, taking action toward our goals increases our energy level, whereas procrastination drains our time and energy and leaves us with feelings of self-doubt. Usually fear is at the root of procrastination when it comes to making big life changes—fear of the unknown, fear of failure, fear of success, or fear of what others might think.

When you know you really want something and you keep putting it off, you risk losing your golden opportunity altogether. By following through with your dreams and desires, you might not always be successful, but you'll have fewer regrets.

What Did You Read?

1. What is "the comfort zone"?
2. What are the five barriers that commonly stand in the way of getting a new job?
3. According to the author, is it "normal" to fear change? Explain.

What Do You Think?

1. What do you think is your biggest internal obstacle to change?
2. Do you feel that your choices up to now for a career conflict with any of your personal values?
3. How important is money to you in considering a career?

How Was It Done?

1. Is the opening lead-in—the paradox that a comfort zone is anti-thetical to growth—an effective strategy to help people change their goals?

2. Are rhetorical questions used effectively in this article to help the audience move toward self-discovery?

3. How well does the example, "Connie, Age 43" crystallize the message about getting rid of obstacles and attaining one's goals?

THE MAIN EVENT WRITING ASSIGNMENT

Write a research-based paper in which you respond to one of the following assignments.

1. In what fields do you see the best job opportunities in the near future? Write a research paper in which you explore several fields and discuss the opportunities and challenges that each presents.

2. Explore careers for so-called handicapped or specially challenged individuals. Address the experiences of the disabled in the workplace.

3. Argue how job hunting and employment opportunities have been transformed by technology. Do research on traditional and nontraditional job-hunting strategies. Incorporate an understanding of the hiring processes of employers today.

4. What are the best fields in which an entrepreneur can start his or her own business? What special challenges do those fields present?

PREPARATION PUNCH LIST

Before you begin writing the essay, you need to prepare yourself to write. One way to prepare is to work through the following strategies.

1. Brainstorm about what you know about the job market today.

- Make a list of traditional jobs that you can think of, such as doctors, lawyers, and teachers. Write down as many of these as you can.
- Make a list of jobs related to technology
- Make a list of entrepreneurial jobs
- Make a list of jobs that seem to meet a specific demand in today's society

2. Find several job fields that interest you the most.

- What are your areas of interest? Health care? Technology? In being self-employed? In a traditional job? An alternative job? Are you interested in part-time work rather than full-time work?

- Consider where you would like to live. What jobs are needed most in that area?

- What jobs are connected to fields that you have studied in school? What academic field have you had the most success in, and what jobs are related to that?

3. Investigate in-depth three different job areas
that you have chosen.

- Find statistics on numbers employed, numbers that will be employed, specific job occupations and descriptions, related work, salaries, and areas of the country where that work will be needed most.

- Talk to someone who currently works in the job field you're interested in. Find out what they like about it, what special challenges they face, what education they need, and what special skills are needed.

- Go to the Internet and find listings of trade associations, unions, and other professional organizations that are connected to the job field. Names, addresses, phone numbers, and email addresses are available so you can directly contact these organizations regarding career guidance and internships. Go to Web-based bulletin boards to find job opportunities posted in your field of interest.

- Take a personality assessment test to find out what careers might best suit your interests, personality, and values.

THE MAIN EVENT WRITING LESSON: CONDUCTING RESEARCH

How often have you heard the phrase, "You could look it up!" This phrase implies that often important information is available—if you're willing to make the extra effort to go find it. Trying to find out what others have already learned is an intelligent, important step in writing essays. When you seek information in the works of others, you are conducting research.

Conducting research on any topic is done for a number of reasons. First, you need to educate yourself so that you can speak with knowledge on your topic. This involves reading about your topic enough so that you can essentially become an expert on it. While your expertise will obviously not match those who spend their professional careers investigating a certain field of study, you need to know more, a lot more, than is commonly understood by the average person.

Second, most readers will not merely accept you at your word. You will need facts, data, statistics, examples, and the opinions of recognized experts in order for your reader to be fully persuaded that what you present is true and valid. This can only be done with extensive research on your part.

Research allows you to better understand the areas of controversy and conflict within a given field. A casual outside observer may not know of many conflicts that are actually present. These conflicts, however, may be of interest to a larger audience. You can bring these conflicts, and their importance, to light for the reader.

After you decide to do research, the best place to physically start is likely to be at your local community or college library. Instead of wandering aimlessly through the stacks, or trying narrow subject searches that only give you limited results, begin with a broad search. The tendency to zero in like a laser beam on some narrow aspect of an issue is understandable; after all, a search of a large subject area might produce unmanageable results. However, while in-depth research is important, such a search can be misguided without knowledge of broader contexts. Try these steps, which are designed to take you from a broad search to a narrow search.

How to Begin

Look at general reference works first, especially if you are taking on a topic you know little about. General reference works include encyclopedias, dictionaries, atlases, and almanacs. Many instructors will not accept these types of sources within research papers because they are often too generalized and based on the research of others. However, these sources give students a quick overview of a subject area. So, while you may not quote or paraphrase from these sources in your research paper, you will benefit from having read the materials. If you do not know where the general reference works are in your library, ask a reference librarian for assistance.

Next, go to specialized reference works. These works, like general reference works, are often not considered as suitable primary sources for a research paper, but they give background information. Specialized texts focus on a particular field of inquiry, so they do not cover as broad a range as general reference works, but what they do cover is presented in greater detail. Again, ask a reference librarian for assistance if you do not know where these works are kept or which specialized reference works your library has.

The Next Step: Books

Books have several qualities that make them advantageous as a source of research: because of their length, books allow for depth of presentation and analysis. Books can fully examine a topic from many points of view. Books often come with indexes, which allow you to read only those parts of the book that you need. Books also may have bibliographies, which can be a treasure-trove of additional sources for you to investigate.

Of course, books do have a significant drawback: by their very nature, they cannot be completely up-to-date. There is always a time-lag between the writing of a book and the publishing of it, and even books that are frequently updated cannot keep up with current events and trends. Thus, the most valuable books are ones that include information that is not too time sensitive. Books can be wonderful sources for examples, theories, statistics, and opinions, but you should always be aware of how old the book is. Depending on the subject area, books that are even a few years old may be obsolete. If you do choose to use older books, you will need to supplement the older information with newer information as well.

Searching for Books

In the past, libraries used card catalogues to provide readers with a way to locate books. Now, most libraries store these catalogues on computers. The computers can make your searches quicker and more efficient.

Typically, you will want to begin your search with a subject search. All books in a library must be categorized into a subject, and then into certain subtopics within that subject area. Most public libraries, as well as primary and secondary school libraries, use the Dewey Decimal system as a way to organize their books. Most college and university libraries use the Library of Congress system. Find out which system your library is using.

Begin your search using the largest possible subject headings. This will likely give you many more books than you want, but it does have one advantage: it casts a very wide net. From this point, find a book that appears to meet your requirements, and then find out what subject headings the book is listed under. Typically, the computer will show you a subject heading that is narrower than the one you actually used. You may then use this narrower subject heading, and you will get a more manageable list of results.

Also, look at what additional subject headings the book appears under. Many books are listed under more than one subject heading. By using alternative subject headings, you can find books you would not have caught in more narrow subject searches.

One difficulty you may encounter occurs when your subject search results in few responses or wrong responses. For example, you might use the word "jobs" as a subject and wind up with books about Steven Jobs, co-founder of Apple Computers. Instead, the word "employment" may provide the responses you want. There are lists available that tell you what subject headings are used by libraries. You may consult *The Library of Congress Subject Headings* in your library to find the list of subject headings used in college and university libraries. Consult *Dewey Decimal Classification and Relative Index* to see how libraries using the Dewey Decimal system organize their subjects. By consulting these guides, you can save yourself the trouble of using improper subject headings.

Step Three: Periodicals

The term "periodicals" refers to anything published on a periodic basis. Typically, the term is applied to newspapers, magazines, and academic journals. Newspapers are daily or weekly publications that often serve a locality such as a city, town, or even neighborhood. Particularly when published daily, newspapers can serve as the source of the most current information available in text format. Magazines are usually published on a weekly, biweekly, monthly, or quarterly basis. Magazines can offer more in-depth and reflective reporting than many newspapers provide. Often, magazines present more context and perspective on an issue than is found in a daily newspaper. Magazines are published for profit, of course, and so they have an interest in accuracy lest they lose credibility. There are limits to magazines—they are written for entertainment more than information, and they are written for a general audience, so detailed information about a topic is often not given. For many researchers, instead of relying on magazines, they find that academic journals are the most reliable source of information available in a periodical. Therefore, it is important to understand what an academic journal is, and how it differs from a magazine.

Academic journals are the forums in which original research is published. Academic journals are written by experts for experts, meaning that those writing the articles are writing for an audience that is expected to already have a good grasp of the technical matters present in the article. Articles in journals are annotated and documented in the format appropriate for the academic field the journal covers. Most importantly, articles in academic journals have been peerreviewed, meaning that a panel of experts in the field has already looked at the article and has checked it for its accuracy, quality, relevance, and documentation. This means that articles in academic journals have the highest level of credibility you can expect.

Searching for Articles in Periodicals

In the past, library holdings of periodicals had to be found by using guides such as *The Reader's Guide to Periodical Literature*. A student would use the guide to perform a subject search, find a list of articles written about that subject, and the periodicals, issue dates, and page numbers on which those articles appeared. The student would then have to find each actual periodical with the article in it, or find it reproduced, usually on microfilm or microfiche. The student might have to go to a third location to get a physical paper copy made from the microfilm or microfiche, or photocopy from an actual physical copy of the periodical. Thus, a student might have to go to two or three locations within a library to get just one article.

While some libraries still operate this way, on many college and university campuses, microfilm and microfiche have been replaced by computerized databases. These databases have several advantages, not the least of which is that students can conduct their subject search and see the actual article text from the same computer terminal. The article can then be printed out. Many college and university libraries provide off-campus access to these databases through the Internet for their students. These computerized databases are called "subscription services."

Subscription services may be available through your college or university library, and you may have access to these services online if your library has a contract with the providers that allows for this. If so, this is a wonderful research asset. These services typically provide articles and essays that have been chosen from literally hundreds of different periodicals. Depending on the database, the articles may be just from newspapers, just from magazines, just from academic journals, or some combination. Sometimes these databases also provide abstracts, or short summaries of the article, which are good time-savers. You can read an abstract more quickly than the entire article, so you can quickly eliminate articles you have no interest in. Some of the more common subscription services include ProQuest, EbscoHOST, Ethnic Newswatch, Wilson Web, and NewsBank.

A key to effective research with computerized databases is to use good search terms. As you did with books, use broad search terms first—even though you will probably wind up with too many hits. Once you find an article that works for you, look up the exact subject headings under which that article was placed. With more precise subject headings, you can narrow your searches.

Another way to narrow your search is to use time limits. For example, if you are working on a topic that is time sensitive, you can usually use an Advanced Search function to look for articles published only in the last year or two.

Another limiting factor could be length of article. Many times extremely short pieces may not contain the kind of substance you need. Therefore, you can require that articles you look at must be a certain minimum number of pages or words. On the other hand, you might also put an upper-end limit on the length of articles, too.

Some databases allow the use of AND, NOT, and OR functions with the subject headings. The "AND" function allows you to add terms, which will narrow your search to only those articles containing *both* terms. For example, if you want to investigate problems of energy prices in the United States, you can use the terms "ENERGY *AND* UNITED STATES." The "NOT" function eliminates a certain subsection of the subject, so your search is narrowed. For example, if you want to examine laws governing the use of prescription drugs, you might put in a phrase like "DRUGS *NOT* ILLEGAL" so that you do not get articles concerning illegal narcotics. The "OR" function adds an additional term, which will broaden your search. If you want to research laws relating to the private ownership of guns, but you do not know what the correct term is, you could use "GUN CONTROL *OR* FIREARMS LAW."

Ultimately, the best sources for helping you to use your library are the librarians themselves. Do not hesitate to consult with the librarians to get help in conducting your research. After all, that is why they are there.

Step Four: The Internet

In the last decade, the advent of the Internet has had tremendous impact on education and research. A lot of information is available on the Internet, but not all of it is *good* information. The Internet is the "Wild West" of research—you never quite know what to expect every time you go to a website.

In order to use the Internet for research effectively, keep in mind an important difference between subscription services and websites that are available, either for free or for a charge, to virtually anyone. Subscription services, which are usually available to users only through a library, are collections of articles and essays that have appeared elsewhere in print. Material from these services has a high level of credibility—as high as the credibility of the original publisher of each article. However, websites can be put up by virtually anyone with a little money, a little programming knowledge, and computer access. Therefore, when you are investigating your subject, and you choose to look online for research, you need to be careful about the websites you find. Ask yourself the following questions:

1. Who is the organization, group, or individual that is sponsoring the website? What is their credibility or bias? If you don't know or

cannot determine the sponsoring organization, you should rethink using any material from the site.

2. Are links to other, similar organizations included? This may be a clue as to the bias or interests of the people who have put together the website.

3. Who are the authors of the material on the website? What credibility do they have? You may wish to double-check their credibility with an independent source and not take them at their word. For instance, run the author's name through your local or college library and see if the library has any books by that person, or check for his or her name in the *Library of Congress Books in Print* to see if the author has any books currently available in print.

4. Does the site include information about electronic publication dates? Does the site appear to be updated regularly?

5. Do the articles on the website include reference information? In other words, do they document what they say, or are they asking you to accept them at their word?

Use the same type of common sense for evaluating website sources that you bring to evaluating print sources. If you cannot identify the author, the organization, or the sources for the information, then do *not* use it.

Last: Personal Interviews

In Chapter 5, you learned about how to conduct an interview for the purpose of getting information and perspectives that might not be available anywhere else. For the purpose of gathering information for a research paper, personal interviews should not be conducted until after you have informed yourself thoroughly about the topic. That way, you can pose more intelligent questions and get more helpful responses from your interviewee.

The point of the research techniques detailed here is to provide you with the opportunity to "catch" all of the information available to you. Searches that are conducted in too narrow of a fashion can frustrate students and give them a false idea of what is actually out there, available on their topic. In a sense, this search strategy is similar to the paragraph discussion of Chapter 1—begin with a general idea and narrow your focus to the most specific ideas.

THE MAIN EVENT WRITING SAMPLE

The following is an essay written for this text in response to the Main Event Writing Assignment, Question #1.

Jobs for the Future

The cliché "the only thing constant is change" has probably never been more true than it is today. Baby boomers are starting to near retirement age, Generation Xers are not numerous enough to fill their jobs, and Generation Y is just starting to graduate from college. People are leaving the suburbs to live in cities or small, rural towns; immigration has changed the demographics of America; women are moving into positions of power and influence; and, there are more older, yet healthier, people than ever before in this country. All this significantly affects the job market in America. People are no longer willing to be in jobs that they do not like, that are environmentally unsafe, and that do not grow with their own goals and expectations. As one observer notes, ". . . the number of jobs is expected to rise by 15%—that's roughly 22 million— *Quotation* to a total of 168 million, according to the recent Bureau of Labor *from an article* Statistics (BLS) projections" (Cheng). Within that increase are jobs *from a* with a great potential for growth and career satisfaction. The econ- *website* omy will continue to generate opportunities for Americans, partic- *Thesis* ularly in the fields of health care, technology, and entrepreneurship. *statement*

Health care, particularly health care for the aged, will be a huge growth industry over the next generation. This is due in part because Baby Boomers are starting to near their sixties, and be- *Paraphrases* cause Americans as a whole are living longer lives than ever before. *from a* It used to be that when one thought of health care providers, one *book to* thought simply of doctors and nurses. This is no longer the case. *support* *the argu-* According to Louise Miller, although there are twenty-four areas *ment that* in which someone can be a board-certified physician, including al- *health* *care* lergy and immunology, dermatology, and plastic surgery, there are *workers* also now physician assistants who work with the physician or sur- *are in* *high* geon at odd hours of the day and night (50). Miller reports that in *demand*

1992, *Working Women* chose physician assistant as one of the top 25 hottest careers. Today, there are more than 22,000 working physician assistants in the United States (55). She points out that as well as traditional registered nurses, there are also now licensed practical/vocational nurses who work under the supervision of a physician or registered nurse; their training takes about eighteen months to complete (61). Other opportunities in the health care field include surgical technologists, medical technologists, and emergency medical technicians. Many of these jobs are known as night-owl jobs. They involve shift work and can conform to the changing lifestyles of people.

Because the aging population is growing, more people will be needed in the fields of health and medicine. Today's older people are healthier and more active than their predecessors, but they still need health care, and they are more apt to use it. "Among the jobs
More sup- with the best growth prospects in this field [health care], personal
port for and home-care positions are expected to soar 62%, to 672,000
health
care jobs from 414,000 in 2000, the BLS predicts" (Cheng). As noted in *100 Best Careers for the 21st Century,* health care for older Americans will increase as people specialize in areas, including care for those suffering from strokes or Alzheimer's. People will be working in "home care situations, senior citizen centers, retirement communities" among others (Field 94). Technology advances that make it possible to move people from hospitals into their own homes will fuel growth in these fields.

Technology has provided some of the largest growth in jobs over the last thirty years, and it will continue to provide new
Quotation growth in the future. According to the "U.S. Department of Com-
on tech-
nology merce, not only will the demand for higher-skilled Information
jobs Technology (IT) jobs jump from 874,000 in 1996 to 1.8 million in 2006, but an additional two million workers will be needed in the

industry" (Gurvis 89). A sampling of some of these jobs that can pay up to at least $50,000 includes computer scientists, hardware product developers, industrial engineers, information systems managers, and systems analysts. The industry is relatively young and unpredictable, and everything is brand new; the field is continuously changing and many of these jobs can be done at home. Working environments are flexible in terms of hours and venues. People can either work for a vendor or an end-user (one who uses computers), and the level of education varies, depending on the specialty they choose.

Whatever the profession, technology is likely to be a key component to jobs in the future. People need to be adept at technology. As Sally Field, author of *100 Best Careers for the 21st Century*, notes, "A high quality of work can be accomplished quicker and more efficiently with computers. Their extent of power continues to grow and shows no signs of leveling off" (112). This means that computer technology is going to play a part in virtually every field of work. This translates into more work in the computer industry itself. Billy Cheng, author of "Where the Job Machine Will Be Cranking," details some of this growth: "Software engineers should leap 95% by 2010, to some 1.36 million from 697,000 in 2000, says the BLS. Computer support specialists and system administrator positions will rise 92%, to 1.4 million from 734,000 two years ago." Job growth in the technology sector is extremely bullish.

Quotation on role of computers

Evidence of expected job growth

Then, there are those people who are uncomfortable in the cookie-cutter corporate world. These people wish to break out of the mold and find alternative careers. Many of these jobs involve self-employment. Although being self-employed can be high-risk and involve a multitude of financial and legal challenges, it can also be very rewarding (Anderson 48–49). Working for oneself can be good for those with special physical or psychological demands.

Paraphrase on self-employment

Many entrepreneurial opportunities will have to do with computers and the Internet. People with domestic abilities and a customer
service orientation can create careers to rival the rise of Martha
Stewart's empire. One common dream is to own a restaurant:
"With an estimated 9.5 million (estimated) employees in the

*Restau-
rant as a
common
business
to run*

restaurant industry alone, and with the projected 14% increase in
jobs by 2005, it is heartening to know that . . . food service and
hospitality are professions where you can still get ahead through
sheer drive, dedication, and hard work" (Gurvis 130). As Richard
N. Bolles, author of the best-selling job hunting book, *What Color
is Your Parachute?*, suggests, if a person can buy a fax machine, a
computer, and a few other technological wonders, he or she might
have enough right there to start a business (96).

Entrepreneurial opportunities arise to meet the new and
growing changes in society. Because more women with young
children work now than ever before, services dedicated to helping
these households function will continue to grow. Field points out

*Para-
phrase
about
home
businesses*

that the possibilities include child-care services, delivery services,
cleaning services, event planning services, and pet-sitting services.
Many of these services can, in fact, be run out of one's own home
(262–282). Consider pets. Dealing with animals is a lucrative,
growing industry. "With 120 million dogs and cats today, and 6 out
of 10 U.S. households having pets, this industry seems to be a cash
cow" (Gurvis 53). Not only do veterinarians make about $100,000
per year, but also there are kennel owners, animal handlers, pet
shop owners, and pet therapists (Gurvis 56–57). Other entrepreneurial opportunities arise as societal needs change. The one key is

*Motiva-
tional
statement
about
success*

to properly recognize and assess the presence of needs, and the
other is to take advantage of that. As Anthony Stith writes, "Success never happens by accident or luck, or because we are deserving or did good deeds. Success happens when an individual takes

reasonable risks. Risk takers don't wait for things to happen, they *make* things happen" (19). This serves as an excellent description for the successful entrepreneur.

Young people thinking about their futures and what careers to pursue have more opportunities than ever before. People no longer have to have a 9–5 job, and they do not have to have the job their parents had. Employees do not have to stay with an employer for thirty years. Employees will need some education, and they will need to be computer savvy. They will have to be willing to continue to learn long beyond college graduation, to upgrade skills as technology changes. The same kinds of qualities that have made people successful in the past will make people successful in the future: hard work, discipline, vision, creativity, and intelligent risk-taking. In addition to these characteristics, the new workers of the future must be adaptable, able to roll with change in the workplace, in the population, in lifestyle expectations, and the values Americans hold. The career paths of the 21st century will be varied, uncertain, and at times a little chaotic, but there is also the promise for greater career satisfaction for more people than ever before.

The job world of the future

Works Cited

Anderson, Sandy. *Women in Career & Life Transitions.* Indianapolis: Jist, 2000.

Bolles, Richard Nelson. *What Color is Your Parachute?* Berkeley: 10 Speed P, 2002.

Cheng, Billy. "Where the Job Machine will be Cranking." *Business Week Online.* July 15, 2002: n. pag. *MasterFILE Premier.* EBSCOHost. San Diego Mesa Coll. Lib. 24 Nov. 2002. <www.ebscohost.com>.

Field, Sally. *100 Best Careers for the 21st Century.* 2nd ed. Foster City, CA: IDG Books Worldwide, 1999.

Gurvis, Sandra. *Careers for Non-Comfortists.* New York: Marlowe, 2000.

Miller, Louise. *Careers for Night Owls & Other Insomniacs.* Lincolnwood, IL: VGM Career Horizons, 1995.

Stith, Anthony. *How to Build a Career in the New Economy: A Guide for Women and Minorities.* Toronto, ON: Warwick, 1999.

ADDITIONAL READINGS

Where the Job Machine Will Be Cranking

Bill Cheng

Cheng looks at the employment picture up to 2010, and examines where the main job growth will be. With baby boomers retiring, Generation Xers—those now in their thirties and early 40s—will be too few in number to replace them. Thus, younger, 20-somethings should see increased job opportunities. The job market may be best for geeks—those who are computer savvy, such as software engineers, computer support specialists, and system administrators. Health care will boom too; after all, someone has to take care of the aging boomers. Cheng's overall assessment is that today's college students may have the opportunity to enter into a job market every bit as promising as the one their parents did.

Key Word

moribund	in a death-like state
baby boomers	generally considered to refer to those born from 1946–1958, approximately
Generation Xers	generally considered to refer to those born from 1958–1977, approximately
CEO	Chief Executive Officer; the highest executive in a corporation
prestigious	of high value; honored
geeks	those who work easily with sophisticated computer technology
courier	a messenger

A new government report finds plenty of new positions are coming— just not evenly spread among industries and not right away.

If the moribund job market has you down, just wait a little. From now to 2010, the number of jobs in the U.S. is expected to rise by 15%—that's roughly 22 million—to a total of 168 million, according to recent Bureau of Labor Statistics (BLS) projections. The BLS report paints a picture of an economy that will continue to live up to its reputation as a generator of opportunity for Americans, especially in the technology and health-care fields.

"Barring any major wicked recession, there'll be a tremendous demand for people," says Harvey Bass, chief executive of Stascom Technologies, an executive search firm affiliated with Management Recruiters International that specializes in information-technology and medical placements. "The baby boomers will be retiring." Generation X-ers are a significantly smaller group than the boomers, Bass adds, which should lead to a serious shortage of talent as the number of jobs grows.

CEO Turnover?

One exception may be high-level executives, whose ranks should rise 15% by 2010, to about 3.46 million from about 2.99 million in 2000, predict the BLS economists who wrote the report, Roger Moncarz and Azure Reaser of the Office of Occupational Statistics & Employment Projections. They note that "competition for these prestigious jobs should remain keen because of the ample number of qualified applicants and relatively low turnover."

Of course, CEO turnover could spike in the short term, depending 5 on how many new corporate scandals erupt. Logically, though, given the latest accounting debacles, the number of jobs for accountants and auditors is expected to rise 19% over the next 10 years, to 1.16 million from 976,000 in 2000.

As might be expected, jobs for geeks will grow the most, the BLS projects. Software engineering jobs should leap 95% by 2010—to some 1.36 million from 697,000 in 2000, says the BLS. Computer support specialists and system administrator positions will rise 92%, to 1.4 million from 734,000 two years ago, according to the BLS.

Tech-Adept

How can that be, given the dot-com bust? One explanation could be a never-ending demand for people who know how to integrate new technologies into businesses and other organizations. Of course, another possibility is that the BLS could be wrong, as its projections have been at times in the past.

Whatever the profession, technology is likely to be a key component of jobs in the future, Bass says. "People are going to have to be fairly adept at technology," he adds. "The days of 'I don't know anything about a computer' are over."

Not all occupations are projected to expand. Jobs for farmers, ranchers, and agricultural managers will decline by about 22% because of farm consolidation, Moncarz and Reaser say. Automation, meanwhile, is expected to keep taking jobs away from humans in other fields, they add. Bank-teller jobs will drop by 12%, and meter-reader positions will fall 26%, according to their forecasts. Other positions where jobs will disappear include brokerage clerks, couriers, fishers, and repairers of home-entertainment electronics.

Helping the Aged

In other occupations, the percentage increase in job creation will be below the average for the overall economy, yet the number of new positions may be substantial. For example, secretary and administrative assistants jobs are expected to grow at a slower-than-average rate of 7%. Still, 265,000 of them are expected to be created by 2010, on top of the 4 million such positions that existed in 2000, the authors say.

Besides technology, the other top area for job creation will be health care—positions such as occupational therapists, registered nurses, dental hygienists, and pharmacists. That's because an aging population will require a lot more care. Among the jobs with the best growth prospects in this field, personal and home-care positions are expected to soar 62%, to 672,000 from 414,000 in 2000, the BLS predicts. Growth in these fields will be fueled by technology advances that make it possible to shift some types of care from hospitals to homes, the study's authors say.

To project employment growth over the next decade, the BLS looked at many factors, including economic performance, advances in technology, and historical industry trends, Moncarz and Reaser say. The authors caution that no guarantee can be made for how accurate their projections will be. "Unforeseen events or changes in consumer behavior, technology, or the balance of trade could radically alter future employment for individual occupations," they write. Their projections, for example, were completed before the terrorist attacks of September 11.

Revolving Doors

Here are projected increases for other select jobs: Financial analysts and personnel advisers (29%), funeral directors (2%), landscape architects (31%), biomedical engineers (31%), writers and editors (26%), social workers (30%), teachers (23%), lawyers (18%), psychologists (18%), physicians and surgeons (18%), pest-control workers (22%), correctional officers (32%), and hazardous-materials-removal workers (33%).

And don't knock film school. Jobs for actors, producers, and directors could rise 27%, the authors say. Here's one more thing to remember, the authors add. Jobs don't just come open when new positions are created. They become available, too, when existing workers move to other occupations or retire. The BLS projects that three of every five openings they expect from 2000 to 2010 will be for replacement workers.

If the BLS economists are right, once the economy recovers, the current generation of college students may enjoy the same level of prosperity their parents have.

What Did You Read?

1. From now until 2010, the number of jobs is expected to increase by how many?

2. Fill in the blank of this sentence from Cheng's article: "Whatever the profession, _____ is likely to be a key component of jobs in the future." Explain the statement.

3. Besides technology, what other areas will experience high job growth?

4. What occupations are expected to decline in the future?

What Do You Think?

1. Are you going to pick your career according to the job needs in the marketplace or according to your own passion?

2. Are you looking forward to the same level of prosperity that your parents have? Or better? Or worse? Explain why.

3. Of the three areas of large, future job growth that the author talks about—tech-adept, helping the aged, or revolving door—where might you see yourself?

How Was It Done?

1. How important are statistics to the development of this article?

2. What sources does the author employ? Are they credible?

3. Is it helpful that the author classifies the variety of jobs that are discussed in this article?

Creating a Successful Career

Anthony Stith

In his book, How to Build a Career in the New Economy, *Stith addresses particularly the needs of African Americans, other minorities, and women who are looking to start their careers. He tries to confront myths, such as the emphasis placed on starting pay. He follows with five points to finding a career path: knowing the difference between a job and a career; planning the career; not allowing money to be a determining factor; recognizing opportunities; and learning to take worthwhile risks.*

Key Words

principles	fundamental ideas
conditioned	learned, especially by experience

alienates	isolates
onerous	difficult; burdensome
gratification	satisfaction; happiness
foundation	a base or grounds for starting action; a moral center
passively	weakly; lack of asserting one's own will
visionary	marked by foresight and imagination

Before everything else, getting ready is the secret of success.

—Henry Ford

Before you can seek success in a career you must understand some important principles. They determine your level of success or failure long before your first day at work.

Unfortunately, most African Americans, other minorities and women fail to grasp these principles. They tend to base their career choices solely on how much money they will earn when they are hired. This kind of thinking is a holdover from the days when members of these groups had very few career options. At one time, the only employment they could expect to find was low paid and boring. As a result, their view of the working world tended to be negative. Their only measurement of a "good job" was how much it paid.

Today, minorities and women have many more career options. But they do not seem to have adjusted their attitudes toward paid work. This is one of the reasons why most minorities and women fail to find fulfillment, financial security, and happiness in their careers.

We need to become aware of these conditioned responses and replace them with new approaches. If you incorporate the five principles listed below into your life, you will find success and fulfillment. It requires a commitment to follow these principles, but their results far outweigh the effort it takes to apply them.

Five Principles That Make Careers Successful

1. Know the Difference between a Career and a Job

African Americans, minorities and women must stop seeking "jobs." 5
Instead of seeking jobs, they should be seeking careers.

There is a world of difference between having a job and having a career. A job is something we go to because we need money to pay bills. When we accept a job, it is for the sole purpose of obtaining money. The difference between jobs and careers becomes evident when we ask ourselves if the money provided by our jobs creates self-worth and happiness. How much money does it take to make us feel fulfilled? Without considering your income, does your job make you feel good? Are you proud of what you do to earn your income? Does it allow you to sleep comfortably at night?

The dictionary defines "job" as *an action requiring some exertion; a task, an undertaking. An activity performed in exchange for payment; especially, performed regularly as one's trade, occupation, or profession.*

The dictionary defines "career" as *a chosen pursuit; a profession or occupation. The general course or progression of one's life, especially one's profession. A path or course. A rapid course or swift progression, speed. The moment of highest pitch or peak activity. To move or run at full speed; go headlong; rush.*

As you can see, the definitions of the words "career" and "job" are different. The reasons why and the manner in which we perform them are based on different motives and objectives. The dictionary uses words and phrases such as, "exertion," "task," "undertaking" and "exchange for payment" to describe a job. None of these words show a job is pleasurable or something to look forward to doing.

The dictionary uses words and phrases such as "chosen pursuit," "progression of one's life," "moments of highest pitch or peak activity" to define a career. These words and phrases describe something we enjoy and look forward to every day. My definition of career is *something we desire to make a significant part of our lives. It provides feelings of satisfaction and enjoyment during the process of performing it. The activities in our careers give us something to look forward to each day. They provide feelings of self-worth, purpose, and a mission in life.* 10

A true career is something we would miss if we were unable to do it. It is something we willingly and freely devote one hundred and ten percent of our time and energy to. A career provides personal growth, opportunities, and financial rewards. It's something we are passionate about.

My definition of a job is *what we do out of necessity to earn a living to provide food, shelter and security. A job is anything you take to earn a living regardless of personal satisfaction. A job is what you do to earn money. Earning money is the only reason you work. A job is something you would leave in a flash if someone was willing to pay you a few dollars more.*

A job is something we resent doing. It makes us stressful, unhappy, and taxes our mental and physical health. It is something we spend our working and social hours complaining about. The constant whining about our jobs alienates us from friends and family. It often reaches the point where no one wants to associate with us for fear of having to listen to us talk about our horrible jobs.

We should not take this to mean that all jobs are difficult and all careers easy. We can have a job that is easy and a career that is demanding. The differences are the rewards we receive from them. When a job is demanding and difficult, it is perceived as a frustrating, nonenjoyable chore. When we have a job, staying motivated is difficult, and completing undesirable tasks is a strain. Our weekly paycheck or fears of being fired are our motivating factors. Since we are not getting paid or fired at the time we are doing these onerous tasks, our motivation is likely to be low or nonexistent.

People with jobs rely on a strong work ethic alone to complete the 15 difficult, undesirable tasks their work entails. When our work ethic is all that keeps us going, problems soon develop. We soon find ourselves in a constant state of turmoil. We perform our set tasks because we feel duty-bound to do so and are paid for doing them. At the same time, we dread work because we lack interest in it and the desire to perform it. There is a constant struggle between our emotions and values. The result is only stress, discomfort, and unhappiness.

It's a myth to believe a strong work ethic alone is enough to sustain us over long periods without love for what we do. Relying on a strong work ethic without a passion for what we do is often our greatest source of frustration.

The disparity between our wish to fulfill our duties and our desire to do them eventually makes our jobs unbearable, causing our performance to deteriorate. This results in our loss of self confidence and feelings of worthlessness. Only money binds us to our jobs. This happens to even the best employees who maintain jobs instead of building careers.

We develop a different attitude when we have careers. When we have a career, we view difficult tasks as challenges and barriers we will overcome. With a career, our objectives and desired results highly motivate us.

Successful people have passion for their careers. This passion sustains them during difficult times. It allows them to see negative situations as obstacles they are willing to overcome. Careers give us instant gratification as we perform our duties. Selecting the right career propels us toward success and happiness.

Understanding the difference between a job and career is the first 20 step toward achieving success.

2. Actively Plan Your Career

Too many of us begin our employment search with the newspaper classified section. We look for anything that is available. There are three problems with this:

First, it means we are just looking for a job instead of a career. For reasons explained above, this is a recipe for disaster.

The second problem is, using the newspaper classified section, or chance or luck as our primary sources for obtaining and developing a career are all ways of leaving it to outside circumstances to control our destiny. When we do this, we are rendering ourselves powerless.

Instead, we must take charge of our lives. As Benjamin Disraeli said, "Man is not the creature of circumstances, circumstances are the creatures of man." We must not see ourselves as victims of events that are out of our control. It is our responsibility and obligation to *create* the circumstances for our career success.

A third problem with the want-ad approach is that it doesn't allow 25 us to predetermine the career of our choice. When we fail to expend the time and energy to develop a career plan, we end up accepting any jobs that become available. Poor financial situations often mandate this. But when we do this, we create the foundation for our own failure. When we take any job we can find because we failed to plan our careers, we can end up locked into undesirable work for life. This is a frightening and dismal thought.

The first step in avoiding these problems is to make a conscious career choice. Unfortunately, our educational system does not provide proper career guidance for most students. Too many people finish high school or college with little or no idea of the career they will pursue. With proper career counselling they could have assessed their talents, skills and interests and then received a range of suitable career options to explore.

Instead, lacking proper guidance, many individuals select professions that are not suitable for them. They may base their decisions on what's available or convenient at the time they are looking for work. They may choose to follow what their relatives or friends do for a living. Either way, this is a hit and miss process. The likelihood of ending up doing work that enhances their lives is pretty slim.

Excellent career choices are ones that involve activities you love. I cannot overstate the importance of selecting a career you enjoy. Doing what you love to do is more than just a career. It's a joy. It creates a passion for living. It allows you to live life to the fullest. Even more important, when you near the end of your life, you can look back with few regrets. You won't feel life passed you by without doing the things you wished and dreamed you had done. Finding the right career is one of the greatest gifts life has to offer.

You are probably asking, how can I decide what career will make me happy before I experience it? The answer is not complicated. Just try to decide what you enjoy doing, what your abilities and talents are, and what gives you self-satisfaction.

The first step is to determine your interests. Many of us never dis- 30 cover what really interests us because we unconsciously impose limits on ourselves. By the time we reach adulthood, we've established certain habits and ways of thinking. We tend to move within a set social circle. We mock the unknown and discredit new ideas and experiences. We shy away from or ignore people who are different from us. We never explore the endless possibilities life offers. We stay within our comfort zone, among the things we are familiar with.

When we make our move into the working world, we emulate our family members and friends. We think if they like it, we should too. Even when we don't enjoy what these individuals do, they often influence our decisions. We become what they are and not who we are. We try to please others instead of ourselves.

We are bombarded with prejudices, frustrations and negative experiences from our families, friends and environment. We constantly hear how African Americans, minorities and women cannot find good careers, how unfairly they are treated in the working world. This negative thinking can set us up for failure even before we start our careers. It creates a fear of having a career. This fear paralyzes us. We never establish careers or we fail in our careers because we believed we would fail even before we started.

Many of us never find work that interests us because we allow all these outside influences to determine what we do, rather than discover what is best for us. Breaking out of this pattern requires a conscious effort. It can be frightening to move away from our comfort zone. We may worry about failing or making fools of ourselves if we try something new. We may fear being rejected if we try to approach people outside of our social class or ethnic background, Mastering such fears and worries is the first step in creating a more fulfilling life for yourself. Focus on all the positive aspects of this process, not on the negative things that might occur. In any case, if you are not happy in your present situation, what have you got to lose?

Remember that opportunities for women and minorities have greatly expanded—women can be mechanics; African Americans can be CEOs. Don't let the fears and prejudices of others keep you from exploring new avenues. Learn from others' negative experiences but don't let them hold you back.

Another reason you need to try new things is because there are so 35 many new things to try. The high technology revolution creates new positions and work titles all the time. How about becoming a webmaster or a multimedia content developer? Do you even know what these people do? If you don't, maybe you should find out—you may discover the career of your dreams!

There are many ways of finding out what kind of work might interest you. If you are still in school, visit your guidance counselor or career center. Ask to take aptitude tests. There are a number of them out there that will help you see where your skills lie. The results may surprise you. You may even learn about occupations you never knew existed. If your school doesn't offer these services, try a government employment office. You can also pay for professional career counseling, but it can be quite costly.

Of little or no cost and of perhaps greater benefit, is to devise your own program of discovery. It simply involves getting out there, trying new things and meeting new people. Ask positive and successful individuals about their professions, their likes and dislikes. Maintain an open mind about careers and occupations that are new and different. Read about people, what they do, where they go, and their experiences. Hobbies, school, volunteer work, social and business relationships and organizations, libraries, TV, radio and church contacts can reveal career possibilities. The key is to expose yourself to as many experiences as possible. See how these activities make you feel about yourself.

Selecting the right career requires that you take the time to know yourself. If you limit your experiences and exposure to what mere circumstance has presented to you during your lifetime, you will never know for sure what you are capable of. Once you know your interests and have explored career opportunities you can make an informed choice about what type of career to pursue.

In fact, you'll probably come up with a number of career options that interest you. You may see it as a problem to figure out which option in particular to focus on. This is not really a problem, for another important aspect of a successful working life is to always have multiple options.

You do have a real problem if you end up with only one option. 40 You need alternatives should your primary career plans fail to materialize. For instance, small numbers of blacks have successful and highly visible careers in entertainment and professional sports. This has caused the black population to express unrealistic interest in these careers. People tend to forget that only a small segment of the population will achieve success in the sports and entertainment fields. Therefore, it is unwise to single-mindedly pursue a career as a basketball player or professional musician. If the career never materializes or ends prematurely due to injury or changes in the public's tastes, there is nothing to fall back on. This is why we must have alternative career options.

Alternative career options can also sustain us until we are ready to return to our first career choice. In any area of endeavor, circumstances can end our careers. These circumstances can be beyond your control. New technological advances can make career and professions obsolete. Understanding that sometimes our first career choice may not be possible is important.

Having options provides security and confidence. They make it easier to succeed in our first career choice. Security and confidence overcome our fear of failure, the chief cause of disasters in our careers. We also may simply wish to change careers later on. A career change in later life can be invigorating, so it's good to have a number of options to explore.

Deciding which option to explore first may be a challenge. Your present financial situation may have a heavy influence on your decision, but never make the fatal mistake of thinking of payment solely in financial terms. Think of payment as gaining experience, contacts references, future career offers. Seek out knowledgeable people in the career you are pursuing. Use them as mentors and role models. Learn from their successes and failures. Contact organizations and businesses that relate to your career. Seek information to gain insight into your career, make contacts and friends. Volunteer your time to gain experience and exposure in your career. These activities open doors and create opportunities.

Once you select your career(s), immediately work toward establishing yourself in them. This means working out a career plan. Successful people planned their careers long before they started their first day of work. Unsuccessful people relied on newspaper classified ads, chance, luck, friends and families for jobs. Learn to create opportunities for yourself by making contacts, promoting yourself and gaining valuable experience in advance.

Grammar or high school is the ideal time to start developing career goals. Parents should encourage their children to have some idea of the career they want before they graduate from high school. This choice does not have to be locked in stone and can change later, but it helps students to start gearing themselves toward a career. We can also make new career plans when we are older. You may be working at a dead-end job or have just lost interest. It is never too late to start developing a career. The only limits in your career are the limits you place on yourself. 45

* * *

3. Never Allow Money to Determine What You Do and Become

Far too many of us become consumed by the desire to obtain money. We become slaves to it. We are willing to do anything to obtain it, regardless of whether it's right or wrong. We sacrifice our health, family and friends to obtain money. We abandon religious and moral beliefs for the opportunity to obtain it. We forfeit our values and who we are for the sake of money.

We destroy the most important aspect of ourselves when we allow our desire for money to turn us into someone we despise. Can you imagine living for 24 hours a day, day in, day out, year after year, with someone you despise? That's what happens when we allow our quest for money to turn us into someone we dislike. You are out of control when your desire to earn money does not allow you the time to relax and enjoy yourself and your family.

Too many people spend their lives creating fortunes, then die before they have a chance to enjoy it. They become so preoccupied with making money they neglect their personal well-being. They often betray their moral beliefs. The dollar becomes their religion and their god. They do not consider the consequences of their actions; they only consider the short-term benefits. These individuals have no problem stealing, swindling or taking advantage of others to make money. People who are solely guided by money are never willing to help others. They never volunteer their time unless they stand to profit by their actions.

There are many people out there with more money than they can spend in a hundred lifetimes and yet they are unhappy. You read about them in the papers every day—professional athletes, movie stars, singers, self-made millionaires, individuals who win lotteries, and so on. They have drug problems and emotional problems, commit suicide or murder, and get divorced. This shows that money itself does not solve life's problems.

When our actions are guided entirely by money, we live a selfish 50 and disappointing life. There is nothing wrong with making money. We should all strive to be wealthy. We must understand, though, that success and happiness cannot be created by what we own or how much money we have. These qualities are determined by the type of person we become during the process of earning our living. Have we enriched the lives of others? Did we help others without concern for pay? You have to live with yourself 24 hours a day for the rest of your life. Become a person you can be proud to love.

4. Seek, Recognize, and Utilize Opportunities

The reason for the failure of most careers is an inability to recognize and use opportunities. Most individuals incorrectly believe that opportunities present themselves as opportunities. We waste time looking for signs that read "Opportunities Here."

Opportunities are rarely so obvious. In fact, many career opportunities present themselves as problems or obstacles that must be overcome. When we see these situations, we dread them. Most of us don't want to be bothered with problems. We would rather walk away from them. Here is a typical example that you may have encountered yourself:

A young woman went for an interview at a large, prestigious company. At the close of their meeting, the interviewer said he would call her with his decision in a week's time. Two weeks came and went— and no phone call. After several weeks and still no response from the company, the young woman got angry. Obviously, they had chosen another candidate for the position, which was disappointing. But she was also annoyed by the interviewer's poor manners. His failure to call when he said he would was unprofessional, and just plain rude.

Many people encountering this situation would have just stewed in silence and tried to get over their disappointment. But this young woman decided to do something about it. She called up the person who had interviewed her. It took a few tries to get through to him. When she did, she took a deep breath and calmly asked why he had failed to call her as promised. Unsatisfied with the response from the interviewer, she wrote a professional letter explaining why she felt she had been treated improperly and why it reflected negatively on the company. She addressed it to the president of the company. As a result of her assertive action, this young woman ended up being offered another position elsewhere in the company.

This story shows how unhappy situations can turn out to be op- 55 portunities if we respond to them actively rather than passively. We must not see problems as obstacles but challenges and opportunities to advance our careers and lives.

5. Learn to Take Worthwhile Risks

Success does not happen by chance or by luck. Success will never come if you wait for it. Some of us believe we will achieve success because we are good people or because we deserve it. This is not only foolish but dangerous. Waiting for a miracle or a change of luck is a major factor in the failure of careers. It prevents us from taking action when it is most needed.

Success never happens by accident or luck, or because we are deserving or did good deeds. Success happens when an individual takes reasonable risks. Risk takers don't wait for things to happen, they *make* thing happen. When you create the conditions you want, you control your destiny and determine the success of your career.

It's unfortunate that most of us think of risks as something we should avoid. This could not be further from the truth. When we take risks, we distinguish ourselves from our peers. Remember, *you will not be noticed for doing the same things that everyone else does.*

It's important to distinguish worthwhile risks from foolish risks. Successful individuals do not take foolish risks, but realize there is a greater danger in not taking risks when the potential rewards outweigh potential losses. Instead of asking if they can afford to take the risk, they ask themselves if they can afford *not* to take the risk.

Risk takers are considered dynamic and visionary. They show per- 60 sonal power and a keen sense for making the right decisions. They don't wait for things to happen; they make them happen. They view options objectively from all points of view, putting aside their personal likes or dislikes. They determine which conditions will provide the best results. They know that what was the best approach yesterday may be inappropriate today. People with successful careers ask themselves four questions prior to taking risks:

1. What is the worst thing that could happen?
2. What is the best thing that could happen?
3. What probably *will* happen?
4. Can I afford not to take the risk?

By answering these four questions, you may realize that what at first appeared a great risk is actually not a risk at all. By using the answers to these questions you can examine your options. Your answers provide the wisdom and confidence to know which risks to take and which ones to avoid.

What Did You Read?

1. What is the difference between a job and a career?
2. What is wrong with searching for employment through the Classified section?
3. "Success happens when an individual takes _____ _____." What are the missing words? Explain what this sentence means.

What Do You Think?

1. What do you see as common traits in people who are very successful?
2. Do you agree with the author that grammar school or high school is a good time in your life to start a career goal? Why or why not?
3. The author believes people need to have alternative career options in case their first choice does not materialize. What are your alternative career options?

How Was It Done?

1. Is classifying the principles necessary to finding success and fulfillment an effective way of structuring the support?
2. Is the presentation of contrasting definitions of "job" and "career" an effective developmental strategy? Why?
3. Do you feel that the author's appeal to traditions concerning African Americans and women are logical and factual, or do they create bias?
4. What kinds of research are used as support in this work? Be specific.

Excellence: The Call to Greatness

Lawrence G. Boldt

In this passage from his book, How to Find the Work You Love, *Boldt encourages the reader to strive for excellence. Rather than simply accepting our own limitations, and perhaps letting those limitations dictate our lives, Boldt argues that we should aim high. After all, we'll never accomplish more than what we set out to do, so we should expect a lot from ourselves. Boldt says, "We are what we think."*

Key Words

aspirations	goals; desires
intractable	not moveable; unable to be removed or eliminated
destiny	fortune; a predetermined course of events; fate
abject	utter hopelessness
intervened	interfered; compelled or prevented an action
saturated	filled with something that pervades or permeates it

> In the long run you hit only what you aim at. Therefore, though you should fail immediately, you had better aim at something high.
>
> —Thoreau

There is something within all of us that aspires to greatness, something that calls us to be the best we can be, to do the highest quality work we are capable of. While the content of your life's work will be determined by your inspirations, sense of purpose, and talents, the quality of your work will depend on your expectations of yourself. Even more to the point, your expectations will determine the size of your dreams. Since we never rise higher than our aspirations, in choosing your aspirations you are choosing your life. To allow yourself to settle for less than your best is to decide to spend your life hounded and haunted by the ghost of might-have-been. It is to fail your conscience, your fellow man, and your talents. It is to fail your destiny.

The commitment to excellence requires that we put aside any false modesty. It is not a sign of arrogance to expect great things of ourselves. Some people take great pride in their limitations, in how intractable and stubborn their personal problems are. If we are to have pride, let it be in our accomplishments, not in our limitations.

Greatness is the birthright of every human being, available to all who will claim it. As Martin Luther King, Jr., put it, "Everybody can be great. Because anybody can serve. You don't have to have a college degree to serve. You don't have to make your subject and verb agree to serve. You don't have to know about Plato and Aristotle . . . Einstein's Theory of Relativity . . . [or] the Second Theory of Thermodynamics in physics to serve. You only need a heart full of grace. A soul generated by love."

If we are all capable of greatness, how, then, do we go about realizing it? Shakespeare said, "Some are born great; some achieve greatness, and some have greatness thrust upon them." Great or not, we have already been born, equipped at birth with all our natural abilities and talents. We could wait to have greatness thrust upon us, but we might spend our lives waiting for a thrust that never comes. For most of us, then, if we are ever to know greatness, it will be by the remaining course. It will be because we have consciously and deliberately determined to achieve it. As William Jennings Bryan said, "Destiny is not a matter of chance, it is a matter of choice; it is not a thing to be waited for, it is a thing to be achieved."

Excellence: A Matter of Expectation

> Hold yourself responsible for a higher standard than anyone else expects of you. Never excuse yourself.
>
> —Henry Ward Beecher

Expectation is the *context* in which we hold the events of our lives. It's 5 an intangible that sets one person apart from others. While we can't see the internal thought process of another, we can see its effects on his or her life. It's easy to spot those who expect a lot of themselves. Even in young people who have no track record to speak of, you can see it in their bearing and manner, in the way they do the little things. The sense of self-respect and belief in their destiny that they project gives them an aura of greatness. People who expect a lot of themselves are the ones you want on your team, whether you're playing basketball or business, whether you are looking for a marriage partner or a director for your nonprofit corporation.

Your talents indicate and, to a degree, limit what you *can* do. Your expectations determine what you *will* do. The whole effort of realizing the work you love is one of converting your "cans" into "wills." Expectation is the mental environment in which your talents will either be nurtured and developed or repressed and stunted. While you can no more change your innate talents than the color of your eyes, you can change your expectations.

Truly, we rise or fall with our expectations. Our expectations affect the way we view, approach, and do everything. Holding the expectation of greatness, having a sense of destiny about your life, is more important than having a crystal clear picture of the form your work will take. That will unfold as time goes along, and it may change.

We have repeatedly emphasized that to find anything, it helps to know what you are looking for. It also helps to expect that you will find it. Whether you are looking for a misplaced set of keys, a turn on a desolate, rural highway, or the work you love—expecting to find what you are looking for makes all the difference. It allows you to relax, stay focused on your objectives and moving toward them. It reduces the impatience and sense of frustration that might cause you to give up. While we all encounter difficulties and setbacks on the way to realizing our dreams, those who expect that they will ultimately succeed persist long after others have given up.

You Get What You Expect—So Expect the Best

Of course we want to realize our dreams and achieve our full potential, but when what we want conflicts with what we expect, we get what we expect, not what we want. Whether you expect yourself to do little, be "average," or make an outstanding contribution, expectation is the key to performance. Here, then, is another great key to finding and fulfilling your life's work: *Expect that you will. Believe in your destiny.*

> Always bear in mind that your own resolution to succeed is more important than any other one thing.
>
> —Abraham Lincoln

If you study the lives of the so-called greats of history, you will see   10
time and time again that these people had a sense of destiny about
them. They believed that they would ultimately be successful. That belief sustained them through dark periods when, by all appearance, they had no right or reason to believe that they would prevail.

It is low expectations, more than any lack of talent, character flaw, or external barrier, that keep us from realizing our full potential. Have you ever looked at a friend, relative, or loved one and thought to yourself: If he could only see what I see. . . . He has so much potential. . . . If only he believed in himself. It may not occur to you that people might be looking at you and thinking: If only she believed in herself . . . oh, what she could do! While we can't change the expectations of others, we can change our own.

Perhaps there is no greater example of the power of expectations than creativity itself. Studies were conducted to discover if there are any identifiable environmental or genetic characteristics that could be linked to creativity. Researchers looked at I.Q., social and economic background, education, and a number of other variables. The only variable that was found to in any way correlate with creativity, as measured by the researchers, was the individual's belief that he or she was creative. People who believe they are creative actually are more so. Even if you have doubts, claim your creativity and watch it grow.

Understanding Low Expectations

As a psychology student, I, like all college freshmen, was required to participate in psychological experiments. In one such study, the object was to measure the effects of positive and negative reinforcement on performance. Subjects were divided into two groups and were asked to learn and perform a simple task. In one group, the individual assigned to execute the task was provided with a partner who was to continually offer encouraging statements such as "I know you can do it," "You are doing very well," and so on. In the other group, the partner was to continually harass the subject by telling them how stupid they were, how they would never get it, how poorly they were performing, and so on.

Selected to play the part of a harassing partner, I refused to participate in the experiment. The effect it was designed to demonstrate seemed obvious on its face and not worth terrorizing an unwitting victim for. (Researchers had instructed us to continue with the harassment even if the individual broke down and began to cry or became angry.) We certainly don't need studies to tell us that people learn and perform better in the face of encouragement and the expectation of success than they do under constant belittlement.

No one can make you feel inferior without your consent.

—Eleanor Roosevelt

Yet, unfortunately, many of us carry around a harassing partner inside our own heads. It's constantly telling us that we will never amount to much, that we shouldn't risk disappointment by expecting too much of ourselves. Or it tells us that we are too stupid, too lazy, too undisciplined—too whatever—to expect that we will ever touch greatness. In the course of our upbringing, many of us became accustomed to settling for less, habituated to low expectations. Saddled with a negative self-image, we never got the idea that we could, should, or would accomplish anything great.

It is not difficult to understand why. In a research study conducted at Iowa University, graduate students followed two-year-olds around and recorded every time their parents said something positive to them and every time they said something negative. The results were startling. On average, the children heard fourteen negative statements for every positive one. This early indoctrination into negativity is internalized and carried over into later life.

A simple study conducted among college freshmen at UCLA demonstrates the pervasiveness of negative self-image. As one of the most prestigious universities in the California system, UCLA has relatively high admissions standards. Its college freshmen represent the "best and brightest" of their generation. Yet when these students were asked to list their strengths and weaknesses, their lists averaged six times more weaknesses than strengths. It is probably safe to say that *most* people are going through life carrying heavy burdens of negative beliefs that limit their expectations of and for themselves.

Raising Your Expectations: Nurturing Your Mind

If we could replace, once and for all, the inner voice of the harassing partner with that of an encouraging partner, we would see our capabilities soar. Fortunately, we can. Napoleon Hill, author of the classic success book *Think and Grow Rich,* grew up in abject poverty. He recognized that as a result of his upbringing, he had been programmed with a mindset of poverty. He knew that unless he deliberately intervened and changed his thought processes, his fate was sealed. Since he had already been conditioned to expect a life of poverty, he knew it was up to him to change his mind and give himself a higher standard to live up to. He understood that we cannot rise above our expectations.

> Nurture your minds with great thoughts. To believe in the heroic makes heroes.
>
> —Benjamin Disraeli

While we may not have grown up with the kind of poverty that Hill experienced, many of us are, in our own ways, limited by low expectations. For example, many expect that they will be materially comfortable, but don't expect to have much fun making their living. Others hold the belief that they can't both provide for themselves and serve others, that they must choose between doing something noble and doing something monetarily rewarding. Others expect that they will never have the opportunity to creatively express themselves in their work.

While our limiting beliefs are a result of our upbringing, it is futile 20 to waste time wishing that we had been raised differently. The better course is to raise yourself to a new level of expectation. Your parents (or parental surrogates) raised you for the first eighteen years or so. Yet with a normal life span, you will have another sixty years to raise yourself. Don't waste time crying over spilt milk. Begin at once to fill your mind with all the encouragement, confidence, and high expectations you can muster. Imagine that you are again an innocent and trusting child. What would you want to tell this child? What expectations would you want to hold for his or her life? William James said, "Human beings can alter their lives by altering their attitudes of mind." Alter your expectations and you alter what is possible for you to achieve.

> A man's dreams are an index to his greatness.
>
> —Zadok Rabinowitz

Since he wanted to be successful, Napoleon Hill made a point of studying the principles, or what he called "laws," of success. He saturated his mind with the thoughts he knew would bring success. He realized that thoughts show no respect of person, that great people are great *because* they think great thoughts. Take a person with the greatest talent and potential in the world, let him think low and miserable thoughts, and he will not amount to much. Take another with a quarter of his potential, let her mind be saturated with great thoughts, and she will shake the world. As someone once said, "You are as important as what you think about all day." More than what we eat, we are what we think.

Hill employed another useful technique, which he referred to as the "master mind" principle. This technique involves creating a kind of peer group of the mind. By reading the writings, biographies, and letters of the greats of history, you begin to identify with them as people like yourself. You break down the artificial barrier between yourself and greatness. As you "make friends with" great people, you begin to engage them in mental conversation, seeking insight, advice, and direction. You start to think the kinds of thoughts they thought, to expect of yourself the kinds of things they expected of themselves. You make common cause with those who have endeavored to hold up the light of human possibilities in every arena of human experience. You develop a deep sense of gratitude for their efforts.

As you appreciate the efforts of those who have gone before, you develop a sense of responsibility to those who will come after. Albert Einstein put it like this: "Many times a day I realize how much my own inner and outer life is built on the labors of other men, both living and dead, and how earnestly I must exert myself in order to give in return as much as I have received." This sense of responsibility is an essential characteristic of individuals who achieve excellence in any field. As Michael Korda put it: "Success on any major scale requires you to accept responsibility. . . . In the final analysis, the one quality that all successful people have . . . is the ability to take on responsibility."

What Did You Read?

1. What does the author mean by this statement: "Your talents indicate and, to a degree, limit what you *can* do. Your expectations determine what you *will* do."

2. What is one of the greatest deterrents to success?

3. How can you raise yourself to a new level of expectation?

4. What is the "master mind" principle?

What Do You Think?

1. Do your family and friends empower you or not? Explain.

2. Do you find that the pursuit of excellence comes at too high of a cost in other areas of your life?

3. If you were to list your strengths and weaknesses, would you have more weaknesses than strengths? Explain.

How Was It Done?

1. How effective are the inspirational quotations in the opening paragraphs? Are they clichés or do they appeal to your more noble values and ideology?
2. Is the distinction made between "expectations" and "talents" important to the overall support and clarity of the work?
3. What research went into the development of this work?

Suit Yourself:
The Secret of Career Satisfaction

Paul D. Tieger and Barbara Barron-Tieger

In Do What You Are, *the authors use the premise that people should assess their personalities according to four major categories: extraverted or introverted, sensing or intuitive, thinking or feeling, judging or perceiving. The different combinations result in sixteen potential personality types. In this passage, the authors are arguing that personality traits are largely ingrained, perhaps since before birth, and rather than fighting them, we should become aware of those traits and pick careers appropriate to our personalities.*

Key Words

nourishes	sustains; gives food for growth
innate	in-born
headhunter	someone who finds people to fill jobs, often high-level jobs that demand a certain degree of experience and training not commonly found
intrinsically	within the essential nature of something
intricacies	complicated parts or details of something
inane	boring
in utero	within the uterus; before birth

It's important to find the right job. Despite the universal fantasies of winning the lottery, buying expensive cars and homes, and doing fascinating work with interesting people in exotic places, the sober reality is that most of us have to work, hard, for a long time. If you spend forty to fifty years—not an unlikely scenario—working at jobs you'd rather not be doing, you are in truth throwing away a large part of your life. This is unnecessary and sad, especially since a career you can love is within your reach.

What Is the Ideal Job, Anyway?

The right job enhances your life. It is personally fulfilling because it nourishes the most important aspects of your personality. It suits the way you like to do things and reflects who you are. It lets you use your innate strengths in ways that come naturally to you, and it doesn't force you to do things you don't do well (at least, not often!).

How can you tell if you're in the right job? Here are some general guidelines. If you're not employed, keep them in mind as you search for your ideal job. If you are employed, see how your present job measures up.

If you're in the right job, you should:

- Look forward to going to work
- Feel energized (most of the time) by what you do
- Feel your contribution is respected and appreciated
- Feel proud when describing your work to others
- Enjoy and respect the people you work with
- Feel optimistic about your future

We'd like to make something clear right away. It's important to   5 recognize that there are as many different paths to career satisfaction as there are happily employed people. There is no one "ideal job" to which everyone should aspire. But there is an ideal job *for you.*

There are an infinite number of variables in the workplace. To achieve career satisfaction, you need to figure out what your preferences are and then find a job that accommodates them. Some jobs provide warmth and stability; some are risky and challenging. Some are structured, some aren't. One job may require a lot of socializing, while another may require quiet concentration. Do you know exactly what kind of job suits you best? Have you ever even stopped to think about it?

It's a good thing there are so many different kinds of jobs available, since people are so different in their abilities and priorities. Some people enjoy making high-level management decisions; others simply aren't suited to making these kinds of choices. For some people, money is a top priority. They want to make lots of it! Others, however, want most to make a contribution to society; the money is less important. Some people are perfectly comfortable with facts and details and statistics, while others get a headache just trying to read a profit-and-loss statement. And so on, and so on!

When we were hired to conduct a series of personal effectiveness training workshops for job placement professionals (also known as executive recruiters or headhunters), we came face-to-face with a dramatic example of how a job that is perfect for one person can be perfectly wrong for another.

We were training several headhunters who worked for the same recruiting firm. Their job was to find applicants to fill positions at a variety of companies by calling people who were already employed and convincing them to apply for these positions. If an applicant successfully switched jobs and stayed with the new company for at least three months, the placement counselor received a generous commission. It was a highly competitive, results-oriented job that required excellent communication skills and the ability to fill as many positions as possible as quickly as possible.

One of the placement counselors we trained, Arthur, couldn't have 10 been happier. He loved the fast pace of the job. Arthur was a high-energy person, a great talker who enjoyed meeting lots of people over the phone. He used his excellent reasoning skills to persuade other people to make a move to a new opportunity, and he got a lot of satisfaction out of meeting his goal and then some. Arthur knew and understood the formula: for every fifty calls he made, he'd get ten people who were interested, and out of these ten, he might make two or three placements. Arthur's "thick skin" helped him in the job because he often heard "no" during the day, but he never took the rejection personally. What Arthur found really energizing was closing the sale and moving on to the next challenge. He worked hard all day long and made a lot of money.

For Julie, it was a totally different story. Like Arthur, Julie enjoyed talking to lots of people all day and establishing relationships with them. However, unlike Arthur, Julie wanted to help each person find the job that would be really right for him or her. She liked to look for opportunities that would enable her applicants to grow and experience personal success and satisfaction. Julie had been cautioned repeatedly by her supervisor about spending too much time on the phone with each individual rather than quickly determining whether or not someone was interested in a position and then moving on to the next prospect. Rather than filling jobs, Julie was counseling clients. The fact that she could make a great deal of money did not motivate her. She found little reward in simply filling a job opening with a person who probably wasn't right for the position but whom she had successfully pressured into giving it a try.

When we returned six weeks later for a follow-up training session, we weren't surprised to learn that Julie had quit.

People are different in their needs, desires, interests, skills, values, and personalities. Unless you and I have similar personality types, work that you find intrinsically enjoyable is likely to have a different, even opposite, effect on me. Different jobs and even different aspects of jobs satisfy different types of people, a fundamental truth which has, in our view, not been fully appreciated by career advisers or career manuals—until now.

To Suit Yourself, You Must Know Yourself

As we said earlier, the secret of career satisfaction lies in doing what you enjoy most. A few lucky people discover this secret early in life, but most of us are caught in a kind of psychological wrestling match, torn between what we think we *can* do, what we (or others) feel we *ought* to do, and what we think we *want* to do. Our advice? Concentrate instead on *who you are,* and the rest will fall into place.

Not long ago, a friend called us. She calls all the time—there's a 15 phone in practically every room of her home—but this was more than a social call. Ellen was mad. A co-worker of hers whom she regarded as "more boring than a turnip" had been given a prime assignment designing a complex computer system for a growing retail chain. Ellen, who had been hired just six months before to do exactly this kind of work, was stunned. Obviously something was wrong—but what?

Ellen had evaluated her new job with the utmost care before accepting it. She had both the analytical ability and the background experience the job required. She was well liked and found the technical aspects of the job challenging. She'd had a series of unsatisfying jobs before, but this one was going to be different. So why was her golden opportunity turning to brass? Worse . . . why was the turnip doing better than she?

We thought we knew the answer. Ellen's co-worker, as she described him, was absolutely content to work long hours in relative isolation, quietly but steadily getting the job done. He wasn't a lot of fun around the office, but he was intelligent and dependable, and he never made waves. He was, in fact, the perfect person for the job—and he was happy doing it.

Ellen, on the other hand, loved the stimulation of rallying her staff for an urgent deadline and enjoyed talking to clients about their needs. She was terrific at explaining the intricacies of computer systems and could charm people into doing remarkable things. She liked going to industry conferences, and she didn't mind spending all day in meetings. Unfortunately, none of these activities were a significant part of her new position.

It was clear to us that even though Ellen could handle her responsibilities adequately, the job required more solitude, concentration, and what we call "task focus" than she liked. As she talked things through (and some people are like that—they like to think out loud), she began to recognize that in all her careful planning she had overlooked just one thing . . . her own personality!

At this point in our conversation, Ellen panicked. She was afraid 20 she had spent eight years in the wrong career. No wonder she'd found her previous jobs less than thrilling! However, she wasn't actually in the wrong field—she was just working in the wrong end of it. Ellen moved over into the sales division of the same company, and today she is thriving in her new position.

Perhaps a little experiment will clarify what we're talking about. On a piece of paper, or even in the margin, write your signature. Done? OK. Now do the same thing, using your opposite hand. (If you just groaned, you are not alone; most people have a similar reaction.) How did it feel when you used your preferred hand? Most people use words like "natural," "easy," "quick," "effortless." How did it feel when you used the opposite hand? Some typical responses: "slow," "awkward," "hard," "draining," "tiring," "it took much longer," "it required more energy and concentration."

We think that handedness is a good way to think about using your natural strengths in your work. The use of your preferred hand is comfortable and assured. If you were forced to use your other hand, you could no doubt develop your abilities—but using that hand would never be as effortless as using your preferred hand, and the finished product would never be as skillfully executed.

The Traditional Approach—and Why It Doesn't Work

Career professionals have long been aware that certain kinds of people are better at certain types of jobs, and that it's important to find as good a match as possible between the person you are and the kind of job you choose. The problem is that the traditional approach doesn't take enough considerations into account. The conventional analysis looks at only the "big three": your abilities, interests, and values.

As career counselors ourselves, we recognize the importance of these factors. Certainly you need the right skills to perform a job well. It also helps if you're interested in your work. And it's important to feel good about what you do. But this is far from the whole picture! Your personality has additional dimensions that also need to be recognized. As a general rule, the more aspects of your personality you match to your work, the more satisfied you'll be on the job.

As we saw with Ellen, a vital consideration—often overlooked—is 25 how much stimulation from other people you need in your work. Are you more energized by being around lots of people most of the time, or are you more comfortable in small groups, talking one-on-one, or maybe working alone? You can see what a profound impact this preference can have upon your choice of a job. Other important factors include the kind of information you naturally notice, the way you make decisions, and whether you prefer to live in a more structured or a more spontaneous way. These preferences reflect mental processes that are basic to every human being but that clearly differ from one personality type to another. Trying to find the best job for you without taking these preferences into account is like trying to find a tiny island in the vast ocean without a chart. With luck, you might get there—but you might not!

Joanne was a client of ours who came to us in a career crisis. At the age of thirty, she was at the end of her rope. After seven years of teaching math at the elementary school level she was completely burned out and was wondering if she was in the right career.

Being a teacher had seemed the most natural thing in the world for Joanne. The eldest of four, she had grown up taking care of children. She had excelled in math throughout school and was interested in education. Joanne had received some career counseling early on, and all the signs had seemed to point in the same direction. In high school, and again in college, Joanne had taken the standard career aptitude tests and assessment instruments to determine her skills, her interests, and her values. Each time, career counselors had encouraged her to obtain a teaching degree and to teach math to young kids. Everything seemed perfect.

After her first challenging year, Joanne became increasingly frustrated with the rigid structure of the public elementary school setting. She disliked the endless rules both she and the students had to live by as well as many of the rules she had to enforce. She hated having to prepare lesson plans six weeks in advance that left her unable to respond to the interests of the children and to her own creative inspirations. She found the standard workbooks inane, and the busywork that both she and her students were required to do left her drained and irritated. Joanne felt very isolated because her colleagues all seemed to have interests and values that were not like hers, and she began to discover that she missed the intellectual stimulation of working on challenging projects with her intellectual equals. She had tried switching grades and even changing schools, but nothing seemed to help.

After talking with us, Joanne was relieved to discover that she wasn't crazy; she was just in the wrong career. As her early counselors had determined, Joanne had many of the right qualifications for teaching. However, the things she found most stimulating—intellectual challenge, opportunities to raise her level of competence, and creative innovation—were totally lacking in her job. Moreover, the public school setting forced her to work in a highly structured and detailed way, which was not at all the way she liked to operate.

Luckily, the solution quickly became clear. We suggested that 30 Joanne return to school and obtain a master's degree in order to teach math—still a thriving interest of hers—in higher education. In a college setting, she would be able to enjoy much more flexibility in her work schedule and obligations, teach more complicated courses, and be part of an intellectual environment.

Joanne did get a master's degree, and shortly thereafter she accepted a position in the math department of a small college. Today she teaches graduate-level math courses while continuing her studies toward obtaining a Ph.D.

There's also another reason why the traditional approach to career counseling is inadequate. The "big three"—your abilities, interests, and values—all change with age. As you gain work experience, you gain new skills. As you live longer, you may pick up new interests and discard old ones. And often your goals are different later in life than they were earlier. You can keep changing your career according to where you find yourself at a particular point in time, or you can base your choice from the beginning on a deeper understanding of who you are (and who you'll always be!).

Alex is a thirty-nine-year-old internist with a successful practice in a Chicago suburb. While he was growing up it was always assumed that he would follow in the family tradition and become a doctor. Through twelve years of college, medical school, internship, and residency, he never allowed himself to question his decision. After practicing medicine for five years, he has come to a painful conclusion with far-reaching implications for himself and his family: he doesn't want to be a doctor any more. What's more, he realizes he probably never did.

Alex's predicament is not unusual. If you doubt this, pick any ten people you know and ask them, "If you could have any job you wanted, what would it be?" Our experience as career counselors suggests that at least *half* would rather be doing something else.

Most of us make our most important career decisions when we are 35 least prepared to do so. The decisions we make early in life set into motion a chain of events that will influence our entire lives. Yet when we're young we have little or no experience making job choices, and we tend to have an overabundance of idealistic enthusiasm, plus a reckless lack of concern for future consequences. We haven't lived long enough to see ourselves tested in a variety of situations, and we're highly susceptible to bad advice from well-intentioned parents, teachers, counselors, or friends. No wonder so many people get off to a poor start.

The solution? To achieve as great a degree of self-awareness as you can before making any decision with long-lasting career consequences. Happily, "finding yourself" does not require a guru, a lot of money, or any period of experimentation.

You Can't Help It—You Were Born That Way!

Since the right job flows directly out of all the elements of your personality type, you need to spend some time figuring out what makes you tick. By making a conscious effort to discover the "real you," you can learn how to focus your natural strengths and inclinations into a career you can love for as long as you choose to work. This is where Type is so helpful. It provides a systematic, effective way to evaluate both your strong points and your probable weaknesses or blind spots. Once you have these figured out, you'll know how to make sure you are always operating from a position of strength.

Each one of us has a distinct personality, like an innate blueprint that stays with us for life. We are born with a personality type, we go through life with that type, and when we are laid to rest (hopefully at the end of a long and fruitful life), it is with the same type.

Now you are probably wondering, "Wait a minute. I might be one way sometimes, but at other times I'm a very different person. Doesn't the situation influence my personality type?"

The answer is no, it doesn't. Do we change our behavior in certain 40 situations? Certainly! Most human beings have a tremendous repertoire of behaviors available to them. We couldn't function very successfully if we didn't. Sure, we act differently at work than we do at home, and it makes a difference whether we're with strangers, close friends, at a ball park, or at a funeral. But people don't change their basic personalities with every new door they walk through.

All this is not to say that environmental factors are not extremely important; they are. Parents, siblings, teachers, and economic, social, and political circumstances all can play a role in determining what directions our lives take. Some people are forced by circumstances to act in a certain way until they are literally "not themselves" (more about this later. But we all start off with a particular personality type that predisposes us to behave in certain ways for our entire lives.

If you are skeptical about the idea that personality type is inborn, take a look at different children from the same family. These could be your own children, your siblings, or even children from a family you know. Do they have different personalities? You bet they do, and often the differences are apparent from birth (or even in utero).

The concept of "personality type" is not new. People have always been aware of the similarities and differences between individuals, and over the centuries many systems and models for understanding or categorizing these differences have been developed. Today, our understanding of human behavior has been expanded to such a degree that we are now able to accurately identify sixteen distinctly different personality types.

Finding the right job for each of these distinct personalities may seem like an awesome task. However, all sixteen personality types do function in the world. As we will see, it is possible to identify your own personality type and the types of others, to understand why certain types flourish in certain kinds of jobs, and to clarify why people find career satisfaction in different ways.

What Did You Read?

1. What do the authors say are signs that you're in the right job?

2. What is the point of looking at the stories of Arthur, Julie, Ellen, and Joanne? What can we learn from these real-life examples?

3. What do the authors claim is the problem with the traditional approach to job hunting?

What Do You Think?

1. The authors base their text on the idea that certain jobs fit certain personality types best. The personality types are based on whether someone is an Introvert or Extravert, a Sensing Person or an Intuitive Person, a Thinking person or a Feeling person, and a Judging person or a Perceiving person. Which of these traits do you think describe you?

2. Does basing one's occupation on one's personality—as opposed to intellectual abilities, financial compensation, job availability, or other factors—make good sense to you? Why or why not?

3. Can you think of examples of people doing the same job with vastly different personalities? How might the authors account for this?

4. Are you convinced by the authors' argument that people should consider their personality types when choosing a career? Explain.

How Was It Done?

1. How do the subtitles help to structure the essay?

2. How do the case studies of Ellen, Joanne, and Alex support the authors' thesis?

3. Are bullets an effective way of highlighting material? Why or why not?

4. Does most of the support seem anecdotal and based on common sense, or is it factual and based on research? Explain.

Do You Fill the Bill?

Sandra Gurvis

This excerpt from Careers for Non-Conformists *speaks to the concerns of many people who do not want to work in a traditional office environment. The restrictions and daily routine of such environments may help business productivity, but for some, this surrounding can destroy their soul. Gurvis offers an alternative: a home-based job. She offers some pointers on who would do well starting their own business, and she offers some practical suggestions for those just starting out.*

Key Words

smarmy	sleazy; smug
camaraderie	friendship
obsolete	out of date; no longer useful
mores	morals or rules of behavior
pilfering	stealing
absconds	leaves secretly; sneaks away with something of value
maxim	a fundamental principle or truth
hone	to make more effective or accurate

From Darkness into the Light

Most of us have been there. In the movie *Office Space,* lead character Peter Gibbons sits in rush-hour traffic, changing lanes only to see the one he just exited move slowly forward. Meanwhile an elderly gentleman in a walker passes and disappears down the street, an irony not lost on most viewers. After that, things go from bad to worse, as Peter faces a typical workday: the staticky carpet that gives him a shock as he reaches for the metal doorknob; the temperamental copier that perpetually jams; the smarmy boss with his not-so-subtle innuendoes; the shrill receptionist, repeating the same greeting over and over.

Welcome to corporate hell, that 9-to-5 that just seems to get worse as the same faces and routines gradually grind away at your self-esteem and ambition. Some people deal with their frustration through devious rebellions, such as taping the underside of the boss's computer mouse. Technical support is called; the mouse is turned over and ha! ha! the manager looks like an idiot. Or they bend the metal tabs on floppy disks so they (the disks) get stuck in the drive, resulting in yet another panicked and seemingly foolish plea for help. Other would-be pranksters apply Vaseline to various pieces of equipment, wreaking havoc as the managerial unit tries to navigate his way around his office. Are we having fun yet? Still others get even more down and dirty, putting bodily fluids and other excretions in the "man's" (or "woman's") coffee, strewing porno magazines squirted with liquid soap on tables and chairs before a big meeting. Or they take it a step further by trying to steal money or supplies from the company, which can result in firing or jail time.

But rather than "sticking it" to the boss, why stick it out? Although there may be a certain amount of reassurance in coming into that cubicle every day and joining in camaraderie with the few friends who share your misery, the reality is that since the late 1980s, fluctuations in the economy along with increased health care, retirement, and operating costs have made job security obsolete. Due to downsizing and mergers, companies could no longer afford the expense and began laying off tenured workers, while hiring cheaper college or tech school grads, temps, or freelance consultants, a trend that continues today. This is true for all levels and types of jobs, from upper management to human resources to clericals. Americans beginning careers in the '90s can expect to work in more than ten jobs with at least five different employers.

The traditional office, with its pecking order of bosses, underlings, and rigid mores may be going the way of the dinosaur. The Organization Man—the WASP who devoted thirty years to a single company— is almost as defunct as the electric typewriter and the cute secretary who used to brew his coffee every morning and make sure his wife got flowers on her birthday (if both women were lucky). He's been replaced by a diverse workforce, consisting of females, African-Americans and other not-so-minorities. Nontraditional careers have also multiplied. Thanks to technology and the Internet, the world has shrunk into a "global village." Not only do online user's groups and professional associations provide important advice and support, but more and more folks are finding work and contacts outside the U.S. due to the Web and e-mail.

In the movie *Office Space,* the company burns down thanks to   5 Milton, an employee whose irritation reaches critical mass, due to, among many other things, his boss's constant pilfering of Milton's favorite red Swingline stapler and transfers to progressively worse work quarters. Afterwards, some characters locate similar positions at other firms, while another absconds with funds and ends up sipping coladas on a beach. Meanwhile Peter finds a totally different job that's fulfilling. It is in the spirit of the last that this book is written.

Are You Ready For This?

Although starting a home-based business or working on your own or in a "fun" job with no guaranteed income may sound exciting, reality can be quite intimidating. Along with paying your own taxes you may be responsible for billing, insurance, rental of space, managing employees, licensing, advertising, and other financial considerations all of which will be discussed in the next chapter. And many startups and even franchises fail within a year, due to overspending and other types of mismanagement. For example, a group of doctors and other business professionals started a deli in our neighborhood. They hired an excellent chef and the food was delicious. Everyone was excited about the enterprise, because there was really a need for this kind of cuisine and it was located close by. And although the restaurant was mobbed the first few weeks, soon people began to complain about poor or slow service and a menu that often didn't deliver what was promised. Clearly the investors were out of their element, although they and their families worked the business themselves, enlisting the help of friends. Nevertheless, the restaurant folded after a few months.

So, how can you avoid this kind of disaster when embarking upon a new career? Nothing holds a guarantee of success—and sometimes we learn more from our failures anyway. According to author Priscilla Huff, author of *101 Best Home-Based Business for Women* and *More 101 Best Home-Based Business for Women,* statistics show it may take as many as three attempts to make a go of an enterprise. "Failure in itself is not bad," she writes. "Entrepreneurs can learn from their mistakes, persisting until they succeed." The same can be said for anyone attempting to establish themselves in a nontraditional job.

Still, in order to avoid costly errors, you might want to consider the old Boy Scout maxim: Be prepared. The box below provides an overview of what it takes to be on your own.

Here are some very brief checklists that provide a basic overview of what being on your own requires:

Motivational needs

- Self-starter
- Organized
- Willing to spend time on the job
- Able to keep good records
- Disciplined, able to meet deadlines
- Like people, animals, or whatever you're working with
- Ability to follow through
- Can stick with a path, even if the initial payoff isn't great
- Belief in self, product, or service
- Willing to take chances

Financial and other challenges

- Evening, weekend hours
- Phone calls, interruptions at odd times
- Purchase of own equipment and/or franchise
- Overhead costs, such as rental of space, phone, electricity
- May have to hire, handle, and keep records on employees
- Ability to deal with rejection or skepticism
- May have to take an additional job to supplement income during startup

(continued)

Here are some very brief checklists that provide a basic overview of what being on your own requires: (continued)

Financial and legal questions

- What kind of insurance will be needed?
- What kind of permits and licenses are required by the state/city/county?
- Is there a need or market for the product or service?
- How do I set the price?
- Are there adequate capital and savings if things get tight?
- How will I handle tax records? Should I hire an accountant? What about deductibles?
- What kind of legal issues are involved? Is a lawyer needed?
- If applicable:
  - What about materials and supplies?
  - What about publicity and advertising?
  - If I decide to set up shop at home, what about zoning laws?

Further suggestions

- If at home:
  - Set up your own work space, including an answering machine with adult voice mail and not a child's
  - Arrange for child care; attempting to do the job right and meeting youngsters' constant needs don't mix
- Establish certain hours to be "on the job"
- Get everything in writing, particularly money matters
- Have a business plan, and evaluate periodically how well you're doing
- Maintain and keep in touch with a network of contacts
- Learn as much as possible about and keep up with the field, going to conventions, seminars, and interest group meetings
- Find out about the local economy, particularly your immediate competition
- Make sure this is what you *really* love. Only a select few find fame and fortune in their true vocation

---

And there is more to having staying power in your chosen field than making sure all bases are covered. A certain amount of emotional commitment is required. Although I've had twenty-some years as a freelance writer, I (as well as equally experienced colleagues) have gone through periods with minimal work and seemingly little progress. You feel as if the phone is never going to ring again or you'll never get another paycheck, a very scary concept when you're on your own. Following are some suggestions to help you through the inevitable tough times, which are bound to occur, particularly when you're first starting out:

- **Trust your instincts.** "Never listen to anyone else's advice on how to run your business unless they've successfully done it before," asserts Dallas-based Suzi Prokell, whose six-year-old public relations business boasts ten accounts and four employees. On the other hand, don't be afraid to ask for assitance; among other places, this book offers several resources. When I teach writing I tell students to listen to criticism with an open mind: use what they want or feel will help, and ignore the rest.

- **Find a mentor.** "Working on your own is entirely different from having an office job," observes Prokell. "You need someone to bounce ideas off of who can be objective about decisions." So surround yourself with one or two people who've been in the business for a while. Family support is important as well: Like Prokell, my husband's advice and guidance proved to be invaluable, and even when they were younger, my kids helped bolster my confidence when things got difficult. What you *don't* want to do is be around folks who are constantly negative.

- **Get some experience before venturing out on your own.** Prokell was employed by a big public-relations firm for a couple of years, and, in fact, her first client resulted from a last-minute referral. "You can only learn so much from college courses or even working at home. Nothing beats real-world experience, especially if you want to strike out on your own." Even seemingly unrelated tasks can help. For instance, my degree in sociology and years working in personnel for the U.S. Government helped hone my interviewing skills, and my brief stint as a textbook editor resulted in understanding of the elements of bookmaking and design which I was able to use in my own projects.

- **Plan ahead and save for a rainy day.** Assignments go away without notice—and these things seem to happen in spurts—and equipment breaks down unexpectedly, resulting in cash flow drains. Clients can pay late but your bills must always be met on time (creative ways to collect money and deal with credit issues will be discussed in the next chapter). But much of the terror of impending bankruptcy can be avoided. Along with putting a certain amount away for taxes, Prokell tries to save a minimum of ten percent of each month's billings. It's also important to devote a certain amount of time to cultivating new business, even when you're operating at full capacity. For example, I took a year and a half off to write my book *30 Great Cities to Start Out In*. By the time that project was done, my previous clients had found other writers, and I had to practically start from ground zero. It took a few months to build things back up, but I now make sure that other articles and books are at various stages of development, no matter how hectic my schedule. Also take time to periodically look at where your business is headed and set short and long-term goals. Where do you want your business to be in five years? In ten? Are you making enough of a profit, and if not, how can you increase your bottom line?

- **Utilize technology.** Learning a new operating system or application can be an overwhelming exercise in frustration, but the payoff is usually worth it. Prokell didn't know beans about computers when she first started. "But I read books, took classes. It's the only way to put yourself above the rest and remain competitive." Certain software applications save about fifteen hours a week of manual work, she says, and she gets at least fifty percent of her new business leads over the Internet. On the other hand, investing in each new gadget can result in overspending. When I find something that might be useful, I think about it for a while, do some comparison shopping, and see how the purchase will fit into the budget and the overall picture. Seeking "input" (so to speak) from colleagues and business contacts is also helpful. For example, would buying a newer, faster computer be more advantageous to selling/writing books and articles than a personalized Web page with an easy-to-remember "handle" like www.sgurvis.com? Since my four-year-old PC and software worked fine (although a bit slow) and I had a laptop for backup, I went with the Web space, increasing sales and exposure. The old adage: "If it ain't broke . . ." is good to consider before jumping into a new expenditure.

- **Employ experts and delegate.** None of us is an island, and doing it yourself, while seeming economical, can result in disaster. Both Prokell and I use an accountant (more on that in the next chapter); I also hire a "Webmaster" who for a reasonable fee maintains and updates my site and a researcher for certain book projects. The extra money spent is well worth it in time savings and avoiding costly mistakes.

- **Always be professional.** The importance of separating home and work life, even if both are in the same place, was touched upon in the previous box. Every morning I get up and get dressed, just as if I were going to a "real" job (OK, so it may be a jogging suit, but I always put on makeup!). The point is I feel like I'm ready for work. I always return phone calls, and check my answering machine and e-mail (if possible) when I'm on the road just in case something important happened. If I'm going to be out of town for a few days, my answering machine message will reflect this, telling callers when I'm going to be back in the office.

- **Plan for "down time."** Prokell confesses that when she began her business, she worked constantly and almost had a breakdown. "You have to take time away, even if you're just starting. Otherwise, you'll go crazy" and begin making mistakes, not to mention neglecting family relationships. Although the money and exposure can be tempting, avoid overcommitting yourself. Not only are you more likely to make errors, but you're adding undue stress to your life. After several years of being self-employed, I finally started playing tennis and do so one morning in the winter and twice in the summer, no matter how busy things get. Even when I'm preoccupied with work, by the end of the game, my troubles are forgotten. Adds Prokell: "I am so much more focused when I take time out for myself. At night, I close the office door and don't return until the morning." Not to worry, the work will be there.

What Did You Read?

1. What are some of the challenges for those who choose to go into business for themselves?
2. Why does the author say it is important to find a mentor when you are first starting out?
3. What sort of financial and legal concerns do you need to resolve when owning your own business?
4. What are some jobs that the author has had, other than being an author?

What Did You Read?

1. Do you see yourself as a 9-to-5er? Or do you think it would be more enjoyable to work in a more nontraditional format?
2. Would you like to own your own business? Why or why not?
3. What undesirable things can you foresee in working from your home?
4. Do you believe that you have to be more disciplined, more organized, and more hard-working when you work for yourself? Explain.

How Was It Done?

1. Do you find the opening paragraphs and reference to *Office Space* an amusing way to highlight the frustrations that revolve around 9-to-5 corporate America?
2. Are the checklists and bulleted suggestions effective organizational strategies in this work?
3. What research was utilized to develop this work?

Introduction: Advantages and Disadvantages of Night Owl Jobs

Louise Miller

Louise Miller's Careers for Night Owls and Other Insomniacs *is a guide to work opportunities for those who like to work swing shift or night shift hours. In her Introduction, Miller lists jobs in many fields that involve nonstandard work hours. Then, she lays out the problems, both in terms of social life and physical health, for those who work odd hours. However, despite these drawbacks, she encourages readers to pursue the career path they love because, if they love what they're doing, it won't matter what time it is. In this excerpt, Miller addresses the work and life of those who flourish after the sun goes down.*

Key Words

axis	a straight line about which the Earth rotates
paralegals	people with special legal skills who assist lawyers
taboo	a forbidden practice or behavior; banned on moral grounds
circadian	characterized as occurring in a 24-hour cycle
apprenticeship	a position in which one learns a skill or craft from another, more experienced person
internship	a position in which an advanced student, usually of medicine or law, gains supervised, practical experience
remedial	concerned with raising a student's general competence level

When most people are growing up and thinking about working for a living, they probably envision themselves in an office working from 9 to 5. It may never occur to them that their hours could be 5 to 9. Sometime after the invention of electricity, however, night became day and vice versa for many workers in the Industrial Age. Even though the Earth turns on its axis every 24 hours and we humans have adapted our lives to that cycle, the world suddenly was turned around and whole new work shifts became possible.

Many jobs have traditionally been conducted on a 24-hour basis. Medical personnel, factory workers, police officers, fire fighters, transportation workers, and emergency road crews have had to be available all day and all night. Today, however, more and more career possibilities are available that fool not only the clock on the wall but also our natural biological clocks.

These nonstandard work schedules, often called shift work, probably involve about 20 million Americans today. Some companies may have three shifts, running 24 hours a day, seven days a week. Others have split shifts; that is, employees work part of their shift in the morning, have an afternoon break, and finish their shift at night. Still others have rotating shifts. For a few days they work during the day and for a few days they work during the night. Those who work the night shift exclusively are said to work the "graveyard" shift. All these possibilities exist in the real work world, and we will explore how they might affect the work that you are considering.

For example, anyone who lives in a big city knows that some services are available all night long. Waiters, cashiers, and attendants are needed for all-night restaurants, laundromats, convenience stores, and gas stations. Police officers and fire fighters, as well as emergency snow crews, security guards, housekeepers, and cab and bus drivers, keep cities running smoothly at all hours. Doctors, nurses, and paramedics, along with ambulance drivers and veterinarians, make sure that humans and animals get the health care that they need at any time of day or night. Hotline operators, social workers, and psychologists may be on call 24 hours.

Without pilots, flight attendants, mechanics, baggage handlers,   5 and air traffic controllers working through the night, we would miss our early morning business meeting, our parents' anniversary, our daughter's wedding, or the morning mail. Truck drivers haul goods across country overnight so that we are fed and clothed; trains and buses run on an all-night schedule transporting goods and people. Drivers, engineers, porters, and waiters are needed for these jobs. Food-service personnel such as bakers work during the night so we can enjoy a fresh croissant with our morning coffee.

When we finally arrive at our destination after the late flight or train ride, we are happy that hotel managers, door people, bell persons, front desk clerks, housekeepers, and room service personnel are there to greet us, no matter how late it is. We may want to go out on the town, to a theater, nightclub, disco, bar, or concert. The actors, musicians, singers, dancers, bartenders, and waiters are there to entertain, feed, and serve us into the wee, small hours of the morning. Or maybe we'd rather go to an all-night movie house. There we'd find ticket agents, ushers, projectionists, night managers, and someone to sell us popcorn—at 5 A.M! Perhaps we're too tired to go out, and we decide to stay in the room and watch television or listen to the radio. Producers, directors, reporters, camera crews, deejays, and talk-show hosts are there to help us get to sleep or to make staying awake more enjoyable.

At breakfast, we will, of course, want to read the early edition of the local newspaper. How did it get there? Thanks to a group of reporters, photographers, writers, editors, word processors, printers, and delivery people who work all hours of the day and night, that's how.

Lawyers involved in a tough court case often work through the night in order to be prepared for the courtroom the next day. Working with them may be a team of paralegals, word processors, and proofreaders. They may send documents out to an all-night print shop where they are printed and bound for the next day. Teachers, especially in adult education programs, may work the morning and evening shifts. Military personnel work rotating shifts all over the world.

After that overview it may seem as if the whole world is doing shift work. That's not the case, but from now on when we see ourselves working for a living, we may not see exclusively the 9-to-5 shift. We know now that much of the work that is done during the day also has to be done during the night. Any one of us may be called upon to work different shifts during our working lives. It could be only temporary or we could decide that it's the only way we want to spend our work life. We may not be able to make up our minds until we actually try shift work, but there are some factors to consider, based on research and other people's experiences.

Advantages and Disadvantages of Night Owl Jobs

Those who work a graveyard, split, or rotating shift know the advantages and disadvantages of working nonstandard hours. Some of the advantages are that you don't have a lot of supervisors around at night, the phones are not constantly ringing to distract you from your work, the usual clients and vendors don't show up at night, and often you will enjoy a relaxed dress code (jeans, T-shirts, and gym shoes may be fine at night but taboo in daylight hours). Perhaps most significant, you may receive a pay differential for working graveyard. 10

People who work off hours also don't have to face rush-hour traffic. They can schedule doctor and dentist appointments during the day. Grocery shopping goes faster on weekdays than on Saturdays or Sundays because fewer people are shopping then. Department stores, cleaners, restaurants, car washes—all services are more accessible on weekdays.

However, unless you plan carefully, your social and family life may suffer, since the majority of people still work during the day and play at night. Your sleeping and eating habits may change radically—you could be eating breakfast in the evening and having a cocktail before dinner at 8 A.M. Sometimes sleeping during the day is not easy because of street noises and, of course, the sunlight streaming through the windows, even with the shades down and curtains drawn.

Some research also indicates that working nonstandard hours may have some adverse effects on health, and even safety, because our bodies have certain biological rhythms that are close to the 24-hour rotation of the Earth on its axis. These rhythms are referred to as circadian rhythms, and shift work can disrupt them. Your temperature, memory, and awareness can be affected, as well as your sleeping and eating habits.

More research has yet to be done, but some patterns have emerged in the limited research that has been conducted. For instance, there may be a tendency to have more gastrointestinal and cardiovascular disease, as well as reproductive problems—ranging from low birth weight, early births, and miscarriages due to hormonal disruptions—for shift workers. Shift workers may be more prone to accidents, too. Adverse health effects are, of course, highly individual. Some people suffer fatigue and, therefore, lower productivity, but others thrive on night work.

Some studies indicate that the use of bright lights in the workplace   15 and total darkness when sleeping or taking naps, and even some supervised use of drugs, can help night owls adjust their biological clocks. Also, if shifts are rotating, they should be rotated in a clockwise direction. That means that they should be shifted from day to evening to night rather than in the opposite, or counterclockwise, direction. Others recommend that shifts not be changed in less than 10-day increments and that shift workers be given at least 48 hours off between shift changes. It's also a good idea to be on the same shift for at least three weeks before another shift change takes place.

People who work rotating or night shift often feel lonely or isolated, at least in the beginning, because they realize that their family and friends are not available for socializing when they get off work. Special events must be planned carefully because shift workers are often scheduled for nights on holidays, graduation days, birthdays, and anniversaries. If they have schedules in advance, family and friends may adjust these celebrations to meet shift workers' special needs. For example, Christmas could be celebrated on the previous or following weekend rather than on the 25th. The graduation party could be scheduled for a date other than the actual graduation, and even birthday parties can be shifted to accommodate mom's or dad's schedule. Most people are willing to make these adjustments just to have the pleasure of loved ones' company at these special times.

Shift workers also might want to "practice" adjusting to a new shift by gradually going to sleep and getting up later than usual for a while before the change occurs. Before sleeping, it's a good idea to cut down on caffeine, alcohol, sugar, and heavy meals, thereby getting a night of uninterrupted sleep. If your job involves life-and-death situations, such as doctors, police officers, fire fighters, military personnel, or transportation workers, regulating your sleep patterns is essential for the safety of all concerned—you, the patient, victim, or passenger.

People who work at night have to be creative, independent, flexible, and have a sense of humor to get them through the night. They also have to love the work that they do. It also helps if their work involves some variety and they are allowed to take frequent breaks and even naps if possible. As more coordinated research is done about our circadian rhythms and how they affect our work life, including productivity and safety, as well as our emotional and social life, the more we will be prepared to do the work we love at any time of day or night.

And that is really the first step we all have to take in choosing a career—finding out what we love to do and how to do it. Since many jobs are now performed at night or at least in non-standard hours, we have to carefully analyze what we really like to do and where our capabilities lie. We can do that by reading, by talking to people who perform those jobs that appeal to us, by doing voluntary or part-time work in that field, or by taking aptitude tests through school placement centers or career counselors.

We should also contact professional organizations, colleges, and universities to see what their requirements are for admittance into the field we are pursuing.

Since we will be exploring a wide variety of career possibilities, you will see that, for some, very little or no previous training or education is necessary. On-the-job training and a few years' experience will give you the opportunity for advancement. For other careers, a great deal of formal education and experience will be necessary.

It's also a good idea to look into the possibilities of working for the military, the government, or private industry before you land on your final career goal. Each of these categories will have different requirements, some stricter than others. The earlier you check out these requirements, the more carefully you will be able to chart your educational course. If you're still in high school, you'll find out whether communication, math, science, or computer skills are more important for your chosen career. You'll see what testing and application procedures are necessary to get the job. You'll discover whether there are opportunities for volunteer work, summer jobs, or apprenticeships available in the field. You'll also see which of your personal qualities or characteristics is most desirable for this job: independence, flexibility, sense of humor, adaptability, or cooperation.

Some jobs will require you to take extensive oral and written examinations, adhere to strict physical requirements, pass psychological and drug tests, and submit to hands-on simulations of the real job. Some jobs require apprenticeships, licenses, certifications, and internships.

Other jobs require manual dexterity; still others require wit and problem-solving skills. Some will demand postgraduate work; others need only a high school diploma. For some, you will need to follow strict rules of applying for the job; for others, answering an ad in the newspaper will get you the job.

As you explore jobs that are available to you with shift work, take 25 a good look at your aptitudes. For example, you may decide that working the graveyard shift is for you. You also heard that many companies hire proofreaders to work through the night. It just so happens, though, that you never did well in English, don't know whether you should use a comma or a semi-colon, and have a terrible spelling problem. At this point, you either have to take some remedial courses—or decide to do something else!

Whichever career choice you make that may involve weird shifts and crazy hours, be prepared for an adventure in a topsyturvy world where 5 P.M. is starting time and 9 P.M. means quitting time. Your circadian rhythms will be turned upside down. The Earth may revolve counterclockwise, but if you're doing what you love, it doesn't matter what time it is.

What Did You Read?

1. What sorts of jobs does the author see as being needed around the clock?

2. What are the advantages that the author cites of working late shifts? What are the disadvantages?

3. According to the author, what personality types are best suited for working late nights?

4. What does the author mean by "circadian rhythms" and how are they affected by working late nights?

What Do You Think?

1. Are you a night person? Would you be interested in a job that had late-night hours?

2. The author speaks of the social isolation felt by people who work late nights. What suggestions do you have, besides those mentioned by the author, to combat such feelings?

3. One undercurrent in the author's passage is that working at night is in some ways a conflict with natural rhythms (i.e., the sun is down so we need electric lights, the human body naturally wants to go to sleep). Given this, does it seem unhealthy to establish a career that is based on working late at night?

How Was It Done?

1. The article is structured around what?

2. Is it an effective and credible strategy to present both advantages and disadvantages of night owl jobs?

3. Does the support lean toward the specific or the general? In other words, are there documented statistics concerning specific jobs and their health effects or more generalized information about generic night owl jobs?

Appendix I
MLA Documentation

Accurately documenting research materials is an important task for writers. One way to ensure consistent documentation is to use a well-known documentation standard. For students and scholars of English, literature, linguistics, humanities, and other related fields, one of the most frequently used standards is the one published by the Modern Language Association or MLA. This professional organization publishes the *MLA Handbook for Writers of Research Papers,* 6th edition, from which this discussion derives.

MLA documentation consists of two principal parts: the in-text documentation, which signals to the readers what material is derived from research and where that material comes from; and the list of Works Cited, which presents the bibliographic information for all the sources used in the text. The two parts create a clear line of documentation by using a point in common: the authorship of the text. This allows readers to identify the source for each quotation, paraphrase, or summary, and then consult the Works Cited page for more bibliographic information about the source.

IN-TEXT DOCUMENTATION

The MLA system uses parenthetical notes in the text to provide information needed to trace the source. The information is the authority and the page number from which the material comes.

Authority

The "authority" is usually the last name of the author of a work. The author's last name is given, followed by a space and the page number. No punctuation mark is placed between the author's name and page number, and no letters or punctuation precedes the page number. If the quotation ends in a period, the period from the quotation is deleted. A period is placed at the end of the entire sentence, after the parenthetical note.

Parenthetical in-text citation of a work with one author.

Example:

"One of the first things scientists learned about molecular manufacturing is how phenomenally difficult it was to carry out" (Crichton 133).

Parenthetical in-text citation of a work with two authors. Many works have more than one author. It is important to include that information. Do not name only the first author listed, but all authors listed.

Example:

"In measuring an individual's quality of life, we use yardsticks that accurately reflect how they assess their own lives" (Wallerstein and Blakeslee 28).

Parenthetical in-text citation of a work with three authors. List the authors in the order presented on the title page, with the word "and" before the last author.

Example:

"Hypoglycemia is always unpleasant. It can interfere with your thinking, making normal activities—such as driving a car, riding a bicycle, or operating machinery—dangerous or impossible" (Saudek, Rubin, and Shump 63).

Parenthetical in-text citation of a work with more than three authors. If a work has more than three authors, you may substitute the term "et al." (meaning "and others" in Latin) for all authors after the first one. Doing this makes the note easier to read as listing multiple names can become quite cumbersome. Note that this rule also applies to the work when listed in the Works Cited page. In other words, the authority must be presented in the same manner in both places: if you list all authors in the Works Cited page, you must list all their last names in the in-text note; if you use the "et al." in the text, use "et al." on the Works Cited page entry.

Example:

"We strove to get a representative sample, and in this we succeeded since no two individuals had the same background" (Bullough et al. 11).

Parenthetical in-text citation of a work with a corporate author. Sometimes works list no person as an author but a group. This could be a charity, religious organization, research foundation, college, governmental agency, or any other entity that publishes a work under a group name. Such works are not considered anonymous, but instead the authorship is to a "corporate author." This term is not limited to corporations or for-profit businesses, but for any group that authors a work under a group name.

Example:

"There is some evidence that local and regional heat therapy may stop cancers from growing and increase the effectiveness of radiation and chemotherapy in some cases" (American Cancer Society 131).

Parenthetical in-text citation of a work listed by the title (an anonymous work). Sometimes works have no stated author. When this occurs, the authority is the title of the work, whether it is a short work, such as an article or essay, or a longer work, such as a book. Be sure to preserve the punctuation that indicates that the words are part of a title. If the original title is an article or essay, use quotation marks. If the title is of a book, use underlining or italicizing. Only the first few words of a title are needed (other than "The," "A," or "An") for the purposes of identifying the title.

Example:

"Champagne corks popped and the sound of applause echoed down the street as the French Minister of Finance unveiled a bronze plaque to commemorate the building's inauguration" (*Le Cordon Bleu* x).

Parenthetical in-text citation of a work by an author who has two or more works in the Works Cited page. Indicate the exact work by giving the authority and the first significant word of the title after "A," "An," or "The."

Example:

"Buck would come down late in the evening, drink a pint of whiskey, and sit on the one claw-toed chair the pump cabin had and talk about the old man" (Ford, *A Piece* 48).

Parenthetical in-text citation of an indirect source. Many times one work will quote the words of someone else's work, either spoken or written. If you use those words, indicate that with the abbreviation "qtd. in" for "quoted in."

Example:

Some experts believe that "this recession could last until next year" (Robert Rowe qtd. in Mossant A1).

Incorporating Authority into the Text

The authority for a source can be given either within the parentheses following the borrowed material, or the authority can be introduced in the text leading into the quotation or paraphrase. This gives opportunity for the writer to embellish either upon the author or the source. When using an author's name in text for the first time, be sure to give the author's full name. After that, subsequent references are to the last name only.

Examples:

At the end of *The Great Gatsby*, F. Scott Fitzgerald writes, "So we beat on, boats against the current, borne back ceaselessly into the past" (182).

Researchers Judith S. Wallerstein, Ph.D., and Sandra Blakeslee, stated, "In measuring an individual's quality of life, we use yardsticks that accurately reflect how they assess their own lives" (28).

On other occasions, instead of introducing a quotation formally, you might integrate the quoted material into your own text. When you do so, you must make sure not to disrupt the grammar of the sentence. The sentence should read straight through, just as though there was no movement from your own words to someone else's.

Example:

Evidence gathered by Judith S. Wallerstein, Ph.D., and Sandra Blakeslee leads them to conclude that "in measuring an individual's quality of life, we use yardsticks that accurately reflect how they assess their own lives" (28).

Paraphrases

Another important advantage to presenting the authority in the text occurs when you have a paraphrase that is more than one sentence long. Since paraphrases are the ideas of someone else, they must be documented. However, because they are not the original words of the author or authors, paraphrases are not placed in quotation marks. A common problem in much student writing is the failure of students to distinguish between a student's own thoughts and ideas and those from a source. One way to ensure that this difference is clearly marked is by introducing an author's name in the text at the start of the borrowed material, and then placing the page number at the end of the paraphrase. Trouble can occur if a student only places a parenthetical note at the end of a long passage of paraphrase—the parenthetical note does not indicate how much of the material is from the original source, and how much is original to the student.

The following passage is taken from a text. What follows are two examples of documenting the paraphrase, one incorrect and one correct.

Original passage:

These biological propensities to act are shaped further by our life experiences and our culture. For instance, universally the loss of a loved one elicits sadness and grief. But how we show our grieving—how emotions are displayed or held back for private moments—is molded by culture, as are which particular people in our lives fall into the category of "loved ones" to be mourned.

Original source:

Goleman, Daniel. *Emotional Intelligence.* New York: Bantam, 1995.

Incorrect documentation of a paraphrase. The following passage is incorrectly documented because, by placing the parenthetical in-text documentation at the end of a series of sentences, the student has actually only documented the final sentence of the passage. In truth, the entire passage is based on Goleman's work.

Example:

We respond physically to life often based on culture. People respond to the death of a loved one, for example, based on their values which derive from culture. Even the choice of whose deaths should cause us the most grief is often culturally determined (Goleman 7).

Correct documentation of a paraphrase. In this passage, the student introduces the authority of the borrowed material at the beginning of the paraphrase, signaling to the reader that what follows is borrowed material. The borrowing ends with the parenthetical note that gives the page number.

Example:

Daniel Goleman points out that we respond physically to life often based on culture. People respond to the death of a loved one, for example, based on their values which derive from culture. Even the choice of whose deaths should cause us the most grief is often culturally determined (7).

Page Numbers

The page number of a text should be presented after the author. No additional letters or punctuation is included before the page number. If a quotation or paraphrase spans more than one page, use a hyphen to indicate the page range. Pages of prefatory material, such as a foreword, introduction, or preface, are often paginated in lowercase Roman numerals. In many newspapers, sections are indicated with a letter and individual pages with a number; sometimes the letter and number are joined with a hyphen and sometimes not. In all cases, present the page numbers exactly as the original text does.

A special circumstance occurs when materials are taken from electronic sources that do not have page numbers. Do *not* use pages of a printout as page numbers for the in-text citation. When you use an electronic source, often there are no page numbers to refer to, so no page number references are included. Instead, only the authority is given. However, if the paragraphs are numbered, you can refer to the paragraph number by using the abbreviation "par."

LIST OF WORKS CITED

The list of the works cited in your essay should be included at the end of your essay. It is considered part of the essay, so it should be paginated. All the sources that have been cited in your essay, whether they be quoted, paraphrased, or summarized, must appear in your list. Do not include any sources that are not cited in your essay.

Works in the Works Cited list should be arranged in alphabetical order, according to the first word of the entry. If there are two or more works by the same author, determine alphabetical order by the title of the works, disregarding the words "the," "a" and "an." If there is more than one work by the same author, after the first entry, use three hyphens and a period to signify that the author's name repeats. If there is no stated author, use the first word of the title, other than "the," "a," and "an." The entries on the Works Cited page should be double-spaced.

There are many types of sources, but the MLA documentation system consistently asks for the same types of information for all sources. This provides for consistency in the format. The following entries are examples of many different types of sources and how they are presented. However, if you come across a source that is different from what is here, you can consult the latest edition of the *MLA Handbook* for a precise example. The format for the MLA, however, is consistent, so you should be able to predict how many entries should look.

Book with one author. For a work with one author, present the entry with the last name first, then the first name, followed by a middle name or initial if given, and end with a period. Do not include any professional or educational abbreviations that may follow the name, such as "Ph.D." or "M.D."

Example:

Crichton, Michael. *Prey.* New York: Harper, 2002.

Book with two authors. For a work with two authors, invert only the first person's name, followed by a comma and the word "and."

Example:

Wallerstein, Judith S., and Sandra Blakeslee. *Second Chances: Men, Women, and Children a Decade After Divorce.* Boston: Houghton, 1996.

Book with three authors. For three authors, separate the first and second author with a comma.

Example:

Saudek, Christopher D., Richard R. Rubin, and Cynthia S. Shump. *The Johns Hopkins Guide to Diabetes: For Today and Tomorrow.* Baltimore: Johns Hopkins UP: 1997.

Book with more than three authors. If the work has more than three authors, you may cite only the first author and use the "et al." to indicate "and others" or you may list all the authors. Remember, if you include all the names in the Works Cited list, then all the names must be used in the in-text parenthetical references, too.

Example:

Bullough, Bonnie, et al. *How I Got Into Sex.* Amherst: Prometheus, 1997.

Or:

Bullough, Bonnie, Vern L. Bullough, Marilyn A. Fithian, William E. Hartman, and Randy Sue Klein. *How I Got Into Sex.* Amherst: Prometheus, 1997.

Book with a corporate author. A corporate author is a group that publishes under the group name, and the work should be listed by the full name of the group. Government publications are treated as a corporate author. List the governmental agency or body that published the book as the author.

Example:

American Cancer Society. *The American Cancer Society's Guide to Complementary and Alternative Cancer Methods.* Atlanta: American Cancer Society, 2000.

Book with no author. List the book according to the title.

Example:

Le Cordon Bleu at Home. New York: Hearst, 1991.

More than one book by the same author. For the second book, use three hyphens to indicate that the authorship is the same as for the prior work listed. Refer to the title to determine alphabetical order for works by the same author, ignoring the words "A," "An," and "The."

Example:

Ford, Richard. *Independence Day.* New York: Vintage-Random, 1995.

- - -. *A Piece of My Heart.* 1976. New York: Vintage-Random, 1985.

Book with an editor or editors. Some books have editors rather than authors, including books that are collections or anthologies. Present the editor or editors in the same way as authors' names, but place a comma after the last person's name. Then, use the abbreviation "ed."

for editor, or "eds." for editors, following the last name and before the period.

Example:

Kunz, Jeffrey R.M., and Asher J. Finkel, eds. *The American Medical Association Family Medical Guide.* Rev. ed. New York: Random, 1987.

Edited collection or anthology. Collections or anthologies are books that are made up of articles, essays, poems, excerpts, or other shorter works. If you are citing the entire collection (and not just one work from the collection), list the collection by the editor's name.

Example:

Colombo, Gary, ed. *Mind Readings: An Anthology for Writers.* Boston: Bedford-St. Martins, 2002.

Work (such as an article or essay) from a collection or anthology. Cite the author of the material whose work you are using, followed by the title of the work, followed by the title of the collection, the editor (preceded by the abbreviation "Ed." for "edited by"), and the publication information. Put the page numbers of the work at the end.

Example:

Kingston, Maxine Hong. "No-Name Woman." *Mind Readings: An Anthology for Writers.* Ed. Gary Colombo. Boston: Bedford-St. Martins, 2002. 206–17.

Edition after the first. Books may be revised or rewritten after initial publication. Indicate edition information after the title, but do not underline that information.

Example:

Harmon, William, and Hugh Holman. *A Handbook to Literature.* 9th ed. Upper Saddle River: Prentice Hall, 2003.

Reprint of a book. Some works are published again after their original publication date. Include the original publication date after the title and before the publication information.

Example:

Fitzgerald, F. Scott. *The Great Gatsby.* 1925. New York: Scribner's, 1959.

Book that has been translated. List the book by the author. Give the name of the translator before the publication information, using the abbreviation "Trans." Be aware that often books that have been translated are also reprinted works.

Example:

Marquez, Gabriel Garcia. *One Hundred Years of Solitude.* 1967. Trans. Gregory Rabassa. New York: Avon, 1970.

Book in a series. When a book is one in a series, list the name of the series after the title of the book, but not underlined. If the word "series" is in the name of the series, you may use the abbreviation "Ser."

Example:

Pitt, Barrie. *The Battle of the Atlantic.* World War II. Alexandria: Time-Life Books, 1980.

Work from an anthology or collection that is part of a series. Cite the name of the author, title of the short work, the editor of the collection, title of the collection, the name of the series, and the publication information.

Example:

Wyre, Ray. "Pornography Causes Sexual Violence." *Sexual Values* Ed. Charles P. Cozic. Opposing Viewpoints Ser. San Diego: Greenhaven, 1995. 145–52.

Multivolume work. For a work that extends over more than one volume, include the total number of volumes in the set.

Example:

Edwards, Paul, ed. *The Encyclopedia of Philosophy.* 8 vols. New York: MacMillan, 1967.

Single volume of a multivolume work. If you use only one volume of a multivolume work, give the single volume used after the title. The total number of volumes in the set may be given at the end of the entry.

Example:

Edwards, Paul, ed. The Encyclopedia of Philosophy. Vol. 2. New York: MacMillan, 1967. 8 vols.

Entry from a dictionary. List the entry by the word looked up. Do not include page numbers. Do not include editor information. If the dictionary is a well-known one, do not give full publication information but year of the edition.

Example:

"Justice." *The American Heritage Dictionary of the English Language.* 3rd ed. 1992.

Entry from an encyclopedia or other reference work. Cite by author if one is provided. If no author is provided, cite by the entry. For alphabetized works, no volume number is needed. For well-known reference works, do not give full publication information, but year of the edition.

Example:

Thompson, Howard. "Israel." *Encyclopedia Britannica.* 1989 ed.

Pamphlet. Treat a pamphlet as you would a book.

Example:

Carrier, Jim. *Ten Ways to Fight Hate: A Community Response Guide.* 3rd ed. Montgomery: Tolerance.org-Southern Poverty Law Center, 2001.

Article from a daily newspaper. List by author, title of article, name of newspaper (with no period after the title), date, colon, and page numbers. If the page numbers that an article appears on are not in sequential order, use a "+" after the first page number.

Example:

Tawaa, Renee. "Beloved 'Peanuts' Creator is Mourned Worldwide." *Los Angeles Times* 14 Feb. 2000: A1+

Article from a monthly magazine. Use the month and year on the cover of the magazine for the date. Abbreviate all months except for May, June, and July.

Example:

Talbot, Margaret. "Searching for Sacagawea." *National Geographic* Feb. 2003: 68–85.

Article from a weekly magazine. Present the date on the cover in the day–month–year format. Abbreviate all months except for May, June, and July.

Example:

Waller, Douglas. "The CIA's Secret Army." *Time* 3 Feb. 2003: 22–31.

Article with no author. As with a book with no author, list the article by the title.

Example:

"Copies Upon Copies: A Patent for Human Clones is Just the Next Step." *U.S. News and World Report* 7 Feb. 2000: 52.

Article from an academic journal. Instead of using a date, use volume and issue number after the title, followed by the issue year in parentheses. If the journal uses continuous pagination, in which the page numbers of all issues are sequential throughout the volume year, issue numbers are not needed. Journals that use noncontinuous pagination start each issue with page one, so the issue number for those periodicals is mandatory.

Example of continuous pagination:

Civin, Curt I. "Commitment to Biomedical Research . . . Clearing Unnecessary Impediments to Progress." *Stem Cells* 20 (2002): 482–84.

Example of noncontinuous pagination:

Love, Rebecca. "Stem Cell Transplantation Hope for Parkinson's Disease Treatment." *The Lancet* 359.9301 (2002): 138.

Personal or telephone interview. For interviews that you conduct yourself, cite the name of the person interviewed, the type of interview, and the date of the interview.

Examples:

Frakes, Robert M. Personal interview. 18 Dec. 2002.

Stallings, Carol. Telephone interview. 12 Jan. 2003.

Film. List by the name of the film, the director, the lead performers, the distributor, and the year the film was released.

Example:

American Beauty. Dir. Sam Mendes. Perf. Kevin Spacey, Annette Benning, Scott Bakula, Wes Bentley, and Mena Suvari. Dreamworks, 1999.

Videocassette or DVD of a film. List by the name of the movie, the director, the lead performers, and the year the movie was originally released. Then use the word "Videocassette" if your source was on videocassette, or "DVD" if the movie was on a DVD. Then present the name of the company that produced the videocassette or DVD and the year of its release.

Example:

Hairspray. Dir. John Waters. Perf. Sonny Bono, Ruth Brown, Divine, Debbie Harry, Ricki Lake, and Jerry Stiller. 1988. Videotape. Turner, 1995.

Website. When you wish to cite a website in its entirety, list the name of the website, the sponsoring organization, the access date, and the home page.

Example:

MLA. Modern Language Association. 30 Jan. 2003. <www.mla.org>

Document from a website. Cite the name of the author, the title, the name of the website, the electronic publication date, the sponsoring organization, the access date, and the complete URL. If the URL is too long to fit on one line, break the line at the point of a backslash (/) in the URL.

Example:

York, Anthony. "Three Strikes and You're In." *Salone.* 1 June 1999. Salone Media Group. 16 Dec. 2002. <http://www.salone.com/news/feature/1999/06/01/prisons/print.html>

Article from an online encyclopedia. List by the title of the entry or article found on the encyclopedia. Then give the name of the website, the year of electronic posting, the sponsoring organization, the date of access, and the URL of the exact source, or, if that is impractical, the site's search page.

Example:

"Spain." *Encyclopedia Britannica Online.* 2003. Encyclopedia Britannica. 29 Sept.
    2003. <http://search.eb.com/>.

Article from a magazine taken from the database of a subscription service.
List the article first with complete information for an article from a periodical. Then, include the name of the database underlined, the name
of the online service, the library from which the data was retrieved, the
access date, and the URL of the service's home page. Place the URL in
angle brackets.

Example:

Cavanagh, John, Carol Welch, and Simon Retallack. "Generating Poverty." *The
    Ecologist* Sept. 2000: 23–25. *MasterFile Premier.* EbscoHOST. San Diego
    Mesa Coll. Lib. 25 Nov. 2002. <http://ebscohost.com>

*Article from an academic journal taken from the database of a subscrip-
tion service.* Instead of using the date of publication, list by volume
and year in parenthesis. If the journal uses continuous pagination, no
issue number is needed. If the journal uses noncontinuous pagination,
include the issue number after the volume, separated by a period.

Example with continuous pagination:

McCullum, Christine. "Food Biotechnology in the New Millennium: Prom-
    ises, Realities, and Challenges." *Journal of the American Dietetic Associa-
    tion* 100 (2000): 5+ ProQuest. San Diego Mesa Coll. Lib. 13 Nov. 2003
    <http://www.umi.com/proquest>.

Example with noncontinuous pagination:

Elliott, Victoria Stagg. "Antibiotic Use May Help Slow Alzheimer's." *American
    Medical News* 46.40 (2003): 19+ ProQuest. San Diego Mesa Coll. Lib. 7
    Dec. 2003. <http://www.umi.com/proquest>.

*Article from a newspaper taken from the database of a subscription ser-
vice.* Underline the name of the database from the subscription service
if available. When the name of the city of publication is not included in
the name of the newspaper, include the city name in square brackets
after the newspaper name.

Example:

Reavy, Pat. "Utahns to Aid Californians." *Deseret News* [Salt Lake City] 31 Oct.
    2003: B01+ *Newsbank NewsFile.* Newsbank InfoWeb. San Diego Mesa
    Coll. Lib. 4 Nov. 2003 <http://infoweb.newsbank.com>.

Appendix II
APA Documentation

Accurately documenting research materials is an important task for writers. One way to ensure consistent documentation is to use a well-known documentation standard. For students and scholars in psychology and the behavioral sciences, sociology, business, economics, nursing, social work, criminology, and other related fields, one of the most frequently used standards is the one published by the American Psychological Association. This professional organization publishes the *Publication Manual of the American Psychological Association*, 5th edition, from which this discussion derives.

APA documentation consists of two parts: the in-text references, which signal to the reader what material is derived from research and where that material comes from; and the reference list, which presents the bibliographic information for all sources used in the text. The two parts create a clear line of documentation by using a point in common: the authorship of the text. This allows readers to identify the source for each quotation, paraphrase, or summary, and then consult the Reference List for more bibliographic information about the source.

REFERENCE CITATIONS IN TEXT

The APA system uses references in the text to the authorship of the work, followed by the year of publication in parentheses. At the end of a quotation, a page reference is given in parentheses, preceded by the abbreviation "p." Authorship, year, and page number can also be given together at the end of a quotation in the parenthetical note, separated by parentheses.

One author. Give the author's last name followed by the year of publication.

Example:

Crichton (2002) said, "One of the first things scientists learned about molecular manufacturing is how phenomenally difficult it was to carry out" (p. 133).

Or:

"One of the first things scientists learned about molecular manufacturing is how phenomenally difficult it was to carry out" (Crichton, 2002, p. 133).

Two authors. Cite both last names separated by "and" and followed by the year.

Example:

Wallerstein and Blakeslee (1996) noted, "In measuring an individual's quality of life, we use yardsticks that accurately reflect how they assess their own lives" (p. 28).

More than two authors. Cite the first six authors' names the first time the work is referred to in the text. For subsequent references to the work, use the last name of the first author and the phrase "et al." (meaning "and others" in Latin). For more than six authors, cite only the last name of the first author listed, followed by the phrase "et al." In the reference list, cite the first six authors and use the phrase "et al." for any additional authors.

Example:

Saudek, Rubin, and Shump (1997) wrote, "Hypoglycemia is always unpleasant. It can interfere with your thinking, making normal activities—such as driving a car, riding a bicycle, or operating machinery—dangerous or impossible" (p. 63).

Group author. Sometimes works list no person as an author but a group. This could be a charity, religious organization, research foundation, college, governmental agency, or any other entity that publishes a work under a group name. Such works are not considered anonymous, but instead the authorship is to a "group author." This term is not limited to corporations or for-profit businesses, but for any group that authors a work under a group name. Give the full name of the group author as given in the Reference List.

Example:

The American Cancer Society (2000) holds that "There is some evidence that local and regional heat therapy may stop cancers from growing and increase the effectiveness of radiation and chemotherapy in some cases" (p. 131).

Citation of a work listed by the title. Sometimes works have no stated author. When this occurs, the authority is the title of the work, whether it is a short work, such as an article or essay, or a longer work, such as a book. Be sure to preserve the punctuation that indicates that the words are part of a title. If the original title is an article or essay, use quotation marks. If the title is of a book, use italics. Only the first few words of a title are needed (other than "The," "A," or "An") for the purposes of identifying the title. Only if the authorship of a work is specifically designated as "Anonymous" should the term "Anonymous" be used as the author. Include enough of the title so as to allow easy identification in the Reference List.

Example:

"Champagne corks popped and the sound of applause echoed down the street as the French Minister of Finance unveiled a bronze plaque to commemorate the building's inauguration" (*Le Cordon Bleu*, 1991, p. x).

Citation of a secondary source. If the work you have refers to another work, which you do not have, indicate that with the phrase "as cited in" before presenting the author, year, and page number of the source you do have.

Example:

Rowe (2002) believes that "this recession could last until next year" (as cited in Mossant, 2003, p. 19).

Personal communications. Personal communications are considered nonrecoverable sources, so they are not included in the Reference List. Personal communications include personal interviews, telephone conversations, letters, memos, and some electronic communications, such as email and electronic bulletin boards. You may include personal communications in the text. Give the initials and last name of the communicator, the term "personal communication," and the exact date.

Examples:

R.M. Frakes (personal communication, December 18, 2002) said, "The perceived importance of learning history has hit an all-time low."

The real estate market is likely to see a 15% increase in sales (C. Stallings, personal communication, January 12, 2003).

In the APA system, authors are encouraged, although not required, to use page numbers to locate the source of paraphrases. Nevertheless, paraphrases are the ideas of someone else, so they must be documented. Because they are not the original words of the author or authors, paraphrases are not placed in quotation marks. A common problem in much student writing is the failure of students to distinguish between a student's own thoughts and ideas and those from a source. One way to ensure this difference is clearly marked is by introducing an author's name in the text, with the year in parentheses, at the start of the borrowed material, and then placing the page number at the end of the paraphrase. Trouble can occur if a student only places a parenthetical note at the end of a long passage of paraphrase—the parenthetical note does not indicate how much the material is from the original source, and how much is original to the student.

Original passage:

These biological propensities to act are shaped further by our life experiences and our culture. For instance, universally the loss of a loved one elicits sadness and grief. But how we show our grieving—how emotions are displayed or held back for private moments—is molded by culture, as are which particular people in our lives fall into the category of "loved ones" to be mourned. (Goleman, 1995, p. 7)

Original source:

Goleman, Daniel. (1995). *Emotional intelligence.* New York: Bantam Books.

Incorrect documentation of a paraphrase. The following passage is incorrectly documented because, by placing the documentation at the end of a series of sentences, the student has actually only documented the final sentence of the passage. In truth, the entire passage is based on Goleman's work.

Example:

We respond physically to life often based on culture. People respond to the death of a loved one, for example, based on their values which derive from culture. Even the choice of whose deaths should cause us the most grief is often culturally determined (Goleman, 1995, p. 7).

Correct documentation of a paraphrase. In this passage, the student introduces the author of the original text at the beginning of the paraphrase, signaling to the reader that what follows is borrowed material. The borrowing ends with the parenthetical note that gives the page number.

Example:

Goleman (1995) points out that we respond physically to life often based on culture. People respond to the death of a loved one, for example, based on their values which derive from culture. Even the choice of whose deaths should cause us the most grief is often culturally determined (p. 7).

Page Numbers

The page number of a text should be presented after the author. Use the abbreviation "p." before the page number. If a quotation or paraphrase spans more than one page, use a hyphen to indicate the page range. Pages of prefatory material, such as a foreword, introduction, or preface, are often paginated in lowercase Roman numerals. In many newspapers, sections are indicated with a letter and individual pages with a number; sometimes the letter and number are joined with a hyphen and sometimes not. In all cases, present the page numbers exactly as the original text does.

A special circumstance occurs when materials are taken from electronic sources that do not have page numbers. Do *not* use pages of a printout as page numbers for the citation. When you use an electronic source, often there are no page numbers to refer to, so no page number references are included. If the paragraphs are numbered in the source, then use the symbol "¶" followed by the paragraph number. If no page or paragraph number is presented, then no specific location reference is given.

REFERENCE LIST

The list of the works referred to in your essay should be included at the end of your essay. It is considered part of the essay, so it should be paginated. All the sources that have been cited in your essay, whether they be quoted, paraphrased, or summarized, must appear in your list. Do not include any sources that are not cited in your essay. The sources that appear on the reference list must be recoverable sources; this means that personal communications or nonarchived electronic sources should not be included in the list, even though they may appear in the text.

Works in the Reference List should be arranged in alphabetical order. If there are two or more works by the same author, determine alphabetical order by the year of publication, earliest first. The entries on the Reference List should be double-spaced. In APA style, only the first word of the title, proper nouns, and the first word after a colon are capitalized. The titles are italicized.

There are many types of sources, but the APA documentation system consistently asks for the same types of information for all sources. This provides for consistency in the format. The following entries are examples of many different types of sources and how they are presented. However, if you come across a source that is different from what is here, you can consult the latest edition of the *Publication Manual of the American Psychological Association* for a precise example. The format for the APA, however, is consistent, so you should be able to predict how many entries should look.

Book with one author. For a work with one author, present the entry with the last name first, then the first initial, followed by the middle initial if given, and end with a period. Do not include any professional or educational abbreviations that may follow the name, such as "Ph.D." or "M.D." Italicize the title of the book. (Only if you are using a typewriter should you use underlining instead of italics.)

Example:

Crichton, M. (2002). *Prey.* New York: Harper.

Two authors. For a work with two authors, invert both authors' names, separated by the symbol "&" for "and."

Example:

Wallerstein, J. S., & Blakeslee, S. (1996). *Second chances: Men, women, and children a decade after divorce.* Boston: Houghton.

More than two authors. Separate the authors with commas, and use the "&" symbol before the last one. If the work as more than six authors, list only the six authors and use the "et al." to indicate "and others."

Example:

Saudek, C. D., Rubin, R. R., & Shump, C. S. (1997). *The Johns Hopkins guide to diabetes: For today and tomorrow.* Baltimore: Johns Hopkins University Press.

Group author. A group author is any collection of people that publishes under the group name, and the work should be listed by the full name of the group. Government publications are treated as a corporate author. List the governmental agency or body that published the book as the author.

Example:

American Cancer Society. (2002). *The American Cancer Society's guide to complementary and alternative cancer methods.* Atlanta, GA: Author.

Book with no author. List the book according to the title.

Example:

Le Cordon Bleu at home. (1991). New York: Hearst Books.

More than one book by the same author. Refer to the year of publication to determine alphabetical order for works by the same author, earliest first.

Example:

Ford, R. (1985). *A piece of my heart.* New York: Vintage Contemporaries.

Ford, R. (1995). *Independence Day.* New York: Vintage Contemporaries.

Book with an editor or editors. Some books have editors rather than authors, including books that are collections or anthologies. Present the editor or editors in the same way as authors' names, but place a comma after the last person's name. Then, use the abbreviation "ed." for "editor" or "eds." for "editors" in parentheses before the period.

Example:

Kunz, J. R. M., & Finkel, A. J. (Eds.). (1987). *The American Medical Association family medical guide* (Rev. ed.). New York: Random House.

Edited collection or anthology. Collections or anthologies are books that are made up of articles, essays, poems, excerpts, or other shorter works. If you are citing the entire collection (and not just one work from the collection), list the collection by the editor's name.

Example:

Colombo, G. (Ed.). (2002). *Mind readings: An anthology for writers.* Boston: Bedford Books.

Work (such as an article or essay) from a collection or anthology. Cite the author of the material whose work you are using, followed by the title of the work, followed by the editor (preceded by the abbreviation "Ed." for "edited by"), the title of the collection, and the publication information. Put the page numbers of the work in parentheses after the title of the collection.

Example:

Kingston, M. H. (2002). No-name woman. In G. Colombo (Ed.), *Mind readings: An anthology for writers.* (pp. 206–217). Boston: Bedford Books.

Edition after the first. Books may be revised or rewritten after initial publication. Indicate edition information in parentheses after the title, followed by a period.

Example:

Harmon, W., & Holman, H. (2003). *A handbook to literature* (9th ed.). Upper Saddle River, NJ: Prentice Hall.

Reprint of a book. Some works are published again after their original publication date. Original publication date can be given in parentheses.

Example:

Fitzgerald, F. S. (1959). *The great Gatsby.* New York: Scribner's (Original work published 1925)

Book that has been translated. List the book by the author. Give the name of the translator before the publication information, using the abbreviation "Trans." Be aware that often books that have been translated are also reprinted works. For classical works and works from the Bible, original publication years are not given.

Examples:

> Marquez, G. G. (1970). *One hundred years of solitude* (G. Rabassa, Trans.). New York: Avon. (Original work published 1967)

> Sophocles. (1954). *Oedipus rex* (David Grene, Trans.). Chicago: University of Chicago Press.

Book in a series. When a book is one in a series, list the name of the series before the title of the book, separated by a colon. If the word "series" is in the name of the series, you may use the abbreviation "Ser."

Example:

> Pitt, B. (1980). *World War II: The battle of the Atlantic.* Alexandria, VA: Time-Life Books.

Work from an anthology or collection that is part of a series. Cite the name of the author, title of the short work, the editor of the collection, title of the collection, the name of the series, and the publication information. If the word "series" is in the name of the series, you may use the abbreviation "Ser."

Example:

> Wyre, R. (1995). Pornography causes sexual violence. In D. L. Bender (Ser. Ed.) & C. P. Cozic (Vol. Ed.), *Opposing viewpoints ser: Sexual values.* (pp. 145–152) San Diego, CA: Greenhaven Press.

Multivolume work. For a work that extends over more than one volume, include the total number of volumes in the set in parentheses after the title.

Example:

> Edwards, P. (Ed.). (1967). *The encyclopedia of philosophy* (Vols. 1–8). New York: MacMillan.

Single volume of a multivolume work. If you use only one volume of a multivolume work, give the single volume used after the title. The total number of volumes in the set may be given at the end of the entry.

Example:

> Edwards, P. (Ed.). (1967). *The encyclopedia of philosophy* (Vol. 2). New York: MacMillan.

Entry from a dictionary. List the entry by the word looked up. Do not include page numbers. Do not include editor information. If the dictionary is a well-known one, do not give full publication information, but year of the edition.

Example:

> Justice. (1992). In *The American Heritage dictionary of the English language* (3rd ed., p. 979). Boston: Houghton Mifflin.

Entry from an encyclopedia or other reference work. Cite by author if one is provided. If no author is provided, cite by the entry. For alphabetized works, no volume number is needed. For well-known reference works, do not give full publication information, but year of the edition.

Example:

> Thompson, H. (1989). Israel. In *The Encyclopedia Britannica* (Vol. 8, pp. 321–339). Chicago: Encyclopedia Britannica.

Brochure. Treat a brochure as you would a book. Indicate the source is a brochure in square brackets.

Example:

> Carrier, J. (2001). *Ten ways to fight hate: A community response guide* (3rd ed.) [Pamphlet]. Montgomery, AL: Tolerance.org-Southern Poverty Law Center.

Article from a daily newspaper. List by author. Follow with the year, a comma, then the specific date of publication in parentheses. Then, the title of article, name of newspaper (with a comma after the title), and page numbers.

Example:

> Tawaa, R. (2000, February 14). Beloved "Peanuts" creator is mourned worldwide. *Los Angeles Times,* pp. A1, A10.

Article from a monthly magazine. For the date, use year and then month from the cover of the magazine. Give the volume number after the title. For magazines and academic journals, with volume numbers do not put "p." or "pp." before the page numbers. For titles of periodicals, the capitalization follows the same conventions as in the MLA system. However, the titles of the articles are capitalized the same way as books, capitalizing only the first word, proper nouns, and the first word after a colon.

Example:

> Talbot, M. (2003, February). Searching for Sacagawea. *National Geographic, 203,* 68–85.

Article from a weekly magazine. For the date, use the year, then month and date from the cover.

Example:

> Waller, D. (2003, February 3). The CIA's secret army. *Time,* pp. 22–31.

Article with no author. As with a book with no author, list the article by the title.

Example:

Copies upon copies: A patent for human clones is just the next step. (2000, February 7). *U.S. News and World Report*, p. 52.

Article from an academic journal. Use volume and issue number after the title. If the journal uses continuous pagination, in which the page numbers of all issues are sequential throughout the volume year, issue numbers are not needed. Journals that use noncontinuous pagination start each issue with page one, so the issue number for those periodicals is mandatory. Issue numbers should be placed in parentheses after the volume number.

Example of continuous pagination:

Civin, C. I. (2002). Commitment to biomedical research . . . clearing unnecessary impediments to progress. *Stem Cells, 20,* 482–484.

Example of noncontinuous pagination:

Love, R. (2002). Stem cell transplantation hope for Parkinson's disease treatment. *The Lancet, 359*(9301), 138.

Personal or telephone interview. Interviews that you conduct yourself, because they are nonrecoverable sources, are not included in the reference list.

Motion picture. List by the name of the director or producer, and the year of release. The title is followed by the phrase "Motion picture" in square brackets. Then present the country of release and the movie studio.

Example:

Waters, J. (Director). (1988). *Hairspray* [Motion picture]. United States: New Line Cinema.

Document taken from a website. Cite the name of the author, the title, the name of the website, the electronic publication date, the sponsoring organization, the access date, and the complete URL. If the URL is too long to fit on one line, break the line at the point of a backslash (/) in the URL.

Example:

York, A. (1999, June 1). Three strikes and you're in. *Salone.* Retrieved December 16, 2002, from http://www.salone.com/news/feature/1999/06/01/ prisons/print.html

Article from a magazine taken from the database of a subscription service. List the article first with complete information for an article from a magazine. Then, give a retrieval statement indicating the date on which the material was retrieved and the database of the information.

Example:

Cavanagh, J., Welch, C., & Retallack, S. (2000, September). Generating poverty. *The Ecologist,* pp. 23–25. Retrieved November 25, 2002, from the *MasterFile Premier* database.

Article from an academic journal taken from the database of a subscription service. Instead of using the date of publication, list volume after the periodical title and year in parentheses after the author. If the journal uses continuous pagination, no issue number is needed. If the journal uses noncontinuous pagination, include the issue number after the volume, enclosed in parentheses.

Example with continuous pagination:

McCullum, C. (2000). Food biotechnology in the new millennium: Promises, realities, and challenges. *Journal of the American Dietetic Association, 100,* 5. Retrieved November 13, 2003, from *ProQuest.*

Example with noncontinuous pagination:

Elliott, V. S. (2003). Antibiotic use may help slow Alzheimer's. *American Medical News, 46*(40), 19–20. Retrieved December 7, 2003, from *ProQuest.*

Article from a newspaper taken from the database of a subscription service. When the name of the city of publication is not included in the name of the newspaper, include the city name in angle brackets after the newspaper name.

Example:

Reavy, P. (2003, October 31). Utahns to aid Californians. *Deseret News,* p. B01. Retrieved November 4, 2003, from the *Newsbank NewsFile* database.

Credits

CHAPTER 1

"The Stoned Screen" by Brian D. Johnson from *Maclean's*, April 16, 2001. Reprinted by permission of Maclean's Magazine.

"Fade to Black" by George Alexander from *Black Enterprise* by Matthew S. Scott. Copyright 2000 by Graves Ventures LLC. Reproduced with permission of Graves Ventures LLC in the format Textbook via Copyright Clearance Center.

"Go Ahead, Make Her Day" by Richard Corliss and Jeanne McDowell from *Time South Pacific*, April 16, 2001. © 2001 by TIME Inc. Reprinted by permission.

"You've Come Which Way, Baby?" by Elayne Rapping as appeared in *Women's Review of Books*, July 2000. Reprinted by permission of the author.

"Call It 'Kid-Fluence'" by Marianne Lavelle and Marci McDonald from *U.S. News & World Report*, July 30, 2001. Copyright © 2001 U.S. News & World Report, L.P. Reprinted with permission.

"The Market for Television Violence" by James T. Hamilton. Reprinted from *National Forum*, Volume 80, Number 4 (Summer 2001). Copyright by James T. Hamilton. By permission of the publishers.

"We Are Training Our Kids to Kill" by Dave Grossman as appeared in *Saturday Evening Post*, Sept/Oct 1999. Reprinted by permission of Lt. Col. Dave Grossman.

CHAPTER 2

"Crossing Boundaries" reprinted with the permission of The Free Press, a Division of Simon & Schuster Adult Publishing Group, from *Lives on the*

CHAPTER 3

CHAPTER 4

From *Relationship Rescue* by Phillip McGraw. Copyright © 2000 Phillip McGraw. Reprinted by permission of Hyperion.

"Love Lessons from a Divorce Lawyer" excerpted with permission of Atria Books, an imprint of Simon & Schuster Adult Publishing Group, from *Reconcilable Differences* by Robert Stephan Cohen, with Elina Furman. Copyright © 2002 by Robert Stephan Cohen.

"Marriage and Divorce American Style" by E. Mavis Hetherington, reprinted with permission from *The American Prospect*, Volume 13, Number 7: April 8, 2002. The American Prospect, 5 Broad Street, Boston, MA 02109. All rights reserved.

Muller Davis, "Is the Genie out of the Bottle?" in *Marriage, Health and the Professions*, eds. John Wall, Don Browning, William J. Doherty, and Stephen Post, © 2002 Wm. B. Eerdmans Publishing Co., Grand Rapids, MI. Used by permission.

"Warning: Living Together May Ruin Your Relationship" by Stephanie Staal as appeared in *Cosmopolitan*, September 2001. Copyright © 2001 by Stephanie Staal. Reprinted by permission of the author.

"Time, Sex and Money" by Gail S. Risch and Michael G. Lawler from *America*, May 14, 2001. Copyright © 2001. All rights reserved. Reprinted with permission of America Press. www.americamagazine.org

"The Marriage Rehearsal" by Peter Carter as appeared in *Chatelaine*, Sept. 2002. Reprinted by permission of the author.

CHAPTER 5

"Critical Mass or Incredible Mess?" by Bill Manson from *San Diego Home/Garden*, October 2002. Reprinted with permission from San Diego Home/ Garden Lifestyles magazine.

"Making Cities Civil" by Joseph Dolman from *New Leader*, January/February 2002. Reprinted with permission of The New Leader. Copyright © The American Labor Conference on International Affairs Inc.

"The Ecology of Hollywood" by Rory Spowers from *Geographical Magazine*, August 2000. Reprinted by permission of *Geographical*, the magazine of the Royal Geographical Society.

"The Future of New York" by Geoffrey Gagnon and Jonathan Alter from *Newsweek*, September 11, 2002. © 2002 Newsweek, Inc. All rights reserved. Reprinted by permission.

"In Detroit, A Crusade to Stop Child Killings" by Alexandra Marks, this article first appeared in *The Christian Science Monitor* on July 24, 2002 and is reproduced with permission. Copyright © 2002 The Christian Science Monitor (www.csmonitor.com). All rights reserved.

"Bitterness Taints a Sweet Victory" by David Lamb from *The Los Angeles Times*, September 19, 2002. Copyright, 2004, Los Angeles Times. Reprinted with permission.

"On the Playing Fields of Suburbia" by David Brooks from *The Atlantic Monthly*, January 2002. Reprinted by permission of The Atlantic Monthly.

CHAPTER 6

CHAPTER 7

Pages 9–16 from *The Zone* by Barry Sears with Bill Lawren. Copyright © 1995 by Barry Sears and William Lawren. Reprinted by permission of Harper-Collins Publishers Inc.

"Sports-Supplement Dangers." Copyright 2001 by Consumers Union of U.S., Inc., Yonkers, NY 10703-1057, a nonprofit organization. Reprinted with permission from the June 2001 issue of Consumer Reports® for educational purposes only. No commercial use or reproduction permitted. Log unto www.ConsumerReports.org®

CHAPTER 8

"Born in Fire: A Hip-Hop Odyssey" by Jeff Chang as appeared in *The Unesco Courier*, July/August 2000. Used with permission of Jeff Chang.

"Rave Fever" by Susan Oh and Ruth Atherley from *Maclean's*, April 24, 2000. Reprinted by permission of Maclean's Magazine.

"Get Ready for the Net Generation" by Mark L. Alch from *Training & Development*, February 2000. Reprinted by permission of American Society for Training & Development.

"Understanding Youth Popular Culture and the Hip Hop Influence" by Patricia Thandi Hicks Harper from *SIECUS Report*, June/July 2000. Reprinted with permission of the Sexuality Information and Education Council of The United States (SIECUS), 130 W. 42nd Street, Suite 350, New York, NY 10036.

"The Kids Are All Right", from *The Economist*, Dec, 2000–Jan 5, 2001. © 2000 The Economist Newspaper Ltd. All rights reserved. Reprinted with permission. Further reproduction prohibited. www.economist.com

"Going to Extremes" by Joan Raymond from *American Demographics*, June 2002. Reprinted with permission of the publisher. Copyright © 2002 Primedia Business Magazines & Media Inc. All rights reserved.

"Habla English?" by Rebecca Gardyn from *American Demographics*, April 2001. Reprinted with permission of the publisher. Copyright © 2001 Primedia Business Magazines & Media Inc. All rights reserved.

CHAPTER 9

Andrew Hoffman, *Inventing Mark Twain: The Lives of Samuel Langhorne Clemens*. New York: William Morrow and Company, Inc., 1997, pp. 72–74.

"It's Going To Happen" by Jim Erickson and James Wallace from *Hard Drive: Bill Gates and the Making of the Microsoft Empire*. Copyright © 1992 by John Wiley & Sons, Inc. This material is used by permission of John Wiley & Sons, Inc.

From "Prologue" from *The Rise of Theodore Roosevelt* by Edmund Morris, copyright © 1979 by Edmund Morris. Used by permission of Coward-McCann, Inc., a division of Penguin Group (USA) Inc.

"Prologue: Outside the Slaughterhouse" by Theodora Kroeber from *Ishi in Two Worlds: A Biography of the Last Wild Indian in North America*. Reprinted by permission Jed Riffe and Associates. © 1961 Regents of the University of

California, © 1989, renewed by John H. Quinn, © 2000, renewed by Jed Riffe and the Estate of John H. Quinn.

Excerpt from "Portraits of a Marriage" (pp. 360–364) from *Frida: A Biography of Frida Kahlo* by Hayden Herrera. Copyright © 1983 by Hayden Herrera. Reprinted by permission of HarperCollins Publishers Inc.

From *Shakey* by Neil Young and Jimmy McDonough, copyright © 2002 by James McDonough and Neil Young. Used by permission of Random House, Inc.

From *This Life* by Sidney Poitier, copyright © 1980 by Sidney Poitier. Used by permission of Alfred A. Knopf, a division of Random House, Inc.

Excerpt from "Then and Now" (pp. 3–7) from *Bare Blass* by Bill Blass. Copyright © 2002 by Bill Blass. Reprinted by permission of HarperCollins Publishers Inc.

CHAPTER 10

From *The Uses of Enchantment* by Bruno Bettelheim, copyright © 1975, 1976 by Bruno Bettelheim. Used by permission of Alfred A. Knopf, a division of Random House, Inc.

"The Fairy-Tale Lady" by Claire Whitcomb, as appeared in *Victoria Magazine,* 2001. Reprinted by permission of the author.

"From an Ounce of Sorrow" by Jan Knappert. This article appeared in August 2002 issue and is reprinted with permission from *The World & I*, a publication of The Washington Times Corporation, copyright © 2002.

CHAPTER 11

"Reasonable Doubts" by Stephen Pomper. Reprinted with permission from *The Washington Monthly.* Copyright by Washington Monthly Publishing, LLC, 733 15th St. NW, Suite 520, Washington, DC 20005. (202) 393-5155. Web site: www.washingtonmonthly.com.

"Death and Texas" by JoAnn Wipijewski. Reprinted with permission from the July 16, 2001 issue of *The Nation.* For subscription information, call 1-800-333-8536. Portions of each week's Nation magazine can be accessed at http://www.thenation.com.

"Justice on the Cheap" by Amy Bach. Reprinted with permission from the May 21, 2001 issue of *The Nation.* For subscription information, call 1-800-333-8536. Portions of each week's Nation magazine can be accessed at http://www.thenation.com.

"The Problem with the Chair" by Carl M. Cannon from *National Review,* June 19, 2000. © 2000 by National Review, Inc., 215 Lexington Avenue, New York, NY 10016. Reprinted by permission.

"Against Mandatory Minimums" by John J. Dilulio Jr. from *National Review,* May 17, 1999. © 1999 by National Review, Inc., 215 Lexington Avenue, New York, NY 10016. Reprinted by permission.

"The Risks Juveniles Face" by Jason Ziedenberg and Vincent Schiraldi from *Corrections Today*, August 1998. Reprinted with permission of the American Correctional Association, Lanham MD.

From "Adult Consequences for Young Offenders" by Adam Rich from *State Government News*, April 2000. Reprinted by permission of The Council of State Governments.

"When the Evidence Lies" by Belinda Luscombe, et al, from *Time South Pacific*, May 21, 2001. © 2001 TIME Inc. Reprinted by permission.

"Where the Job Machine Will Be Cranking" by Billy Cheng. Reprinted from the July 9, 2002 issue of *Business Week Online*, by special permission, copyright © 2002 by The McGraw-Hill Companies, Inc.

CHAPTER 12

"Expanding Your Comfort Zone" by Sandy Anderson from *Women in Career & Life Transitions*, 2000. Reprinted by permission of JIST Publishing.

Excerpt from the book *How to Build a Career in the New Economy: A Guide for Women and Minorities* by Anthony Stith—Worwick Publishing. Reprinted by permission of the author.

From "Excellence: The Call to Greatness" from *How to Find Work You Love* by Laurence G. Boldt, copyright © 1996 by Laurence G. Boldt. Used by permission of Viking Penguin, a division of Penguin Group (USA) Inc.

From *Do What You Are* by Paul D. and Barbara Barron-Tieger. Copyright © 1992, 1995 by Paul D. Tieger and Barbara Barron-Tieger. By permission of Little, Brown and Company, Inc.

"Do You Fill the Bill?" from the book *Careers for Nonconformists* by Sandra Gurvis. Copyright © 2000 by Sandra Gurvis. Appears by permission of the publisher, Marlowe & Company.

"Introduction" by Louise Miller from *Careers for Night Owls and Other Insomniacs*, by Andrew Hoffman and Catherine Hoffman. Reprinted with permission of The McGraw-Hill Companies.

Index